THIS IS YOUR
ACCESS CODE

nelson 4953 RBND

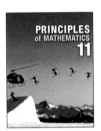

Enter your code
in myNelson to access:

Principles of Mathematics 11
Student eSource

Already a myNelson user?	New to myNelson?
ADD THIS PRODUCT TO YOUR DASHBOARD 1. Go to mynelson.com. 2. Log in using your email address and password. 3. Enter your code in the "Add new resource" field and click Submit. 4. Keep a record of your username and password.	**REGISTER** 1. Go to mynelson.com. 2. Follow the onscreen instructions to create an account. 3. Enter your code in the "Add new resource" field and click Submit. 4. Keep a record of your username and password.

For assistance, visit **mynelson.com** for tutorials and FAQs; contact Customer Support at **inquire@nelson.com**; or call Customer Support at 1-800-268-2222 from Monday to Friday, 8:00 a.m. to 6:00 p.m. EST.

NELSON

978-0-17-681342-0

PRINCIPLES
of MATHEMATICS
11

Authors and Consultants
Cathy Canavan-McGrath, Hay River, Northwest Territories
Serge Desrochers, Calgary, Alberta
Hugh MacDonald, Edmonton, Alberta
Carolyn Martin, Edmonton, Alberta
Michael Pruner, Vancouver, British Columbia
Hank Reinbold, St. Albert, Alberta
Rupi Samra-Gynane, Vancouver, British Columbia
Carol Shaw, Winnipeg, Manitoba
Roger Teshima, Calgary, Alberta
Darin Trufyn, Edmonton, Alberta

First Nations, Métis, and Inuit Cultural Reviewers
Joanna Landry, Regina, Saskatchewan
Darlene Olson-St. Pierre, Edmonton, Alberta
Sarah Wade, Arviat, Nunavut

Cultural Reviewer
Karen Iversen, Edmonton, Alberta

Assessment Reviewer
Gerry Varty, Wolf Creek, Alberta

NELSON

NELSON

Principles of Mathematics 11

Lead Educator
Chris Kirkpatrick

Authors
Cathy Canavan-McGrath
Michael Pruner
Carol Shaw
Darin Trufyn
Hank Reinbold

Editorial Director
Linda Allison

Publisher, Mathematics
Colin Garnham

Managing Editors, Development
Erynn Marcus
Alexandra Romic

Product Manager
Linda Krepinsky

Program Manager
Colin Bisset

Developmental Editors
Rachelle Boisjoli
Kathryn Chris
Shirley Barrett
Brenda McLoughlin
Bob Templeton, First Folio Resource
Group Inc.
Jacqueline Williams

Editorial Assistant
Jessica Reeve

**Director, Content and Media
Production**
Linh Vu

Content Production Editors
Debbie Davies
Montgomery Kersell
Susan Lee

Copyeditor
Paula Pettit-Townsend

Proofreader
Susan McNish

Indexers
Marilyn Augst
Noeline Bridge

Production Coordinator
Susan Ure

Design Director
Ken Phipps

Interior Design
Nesbitt Graphics, Inc.
Peter Papayanakis

Cover Design
Ken Phipps

Cover Image
Randy Lincks/Photolibrary

Asset Coordinator
Suzanne Peden

Illustrators
Nesbitt Graphics, Inc.

Compositor
Nesbitt Graphics, Inc.

Photo/Permissions Researcher
David Strand

Cover Research
Debbie Yea

Reviewers and Advisory Panel

Karen Buro
Instructor, Department of Mathematics and Statistics
MacEwan University
Edmonton, AB

Sean Chorney
Mathematics Department Head
Magee Secondary School
School District 39
Vancouver, BC

Serge Desrochers
Bishop McNally High School
Calgary Catholic School District
Calgary, AB

Steven Erickson
Mathematics Teacher
Sisler High School
Winnipeg School Division
Winnipeg, MB

Joanna Landry
Coordinator, First Nations, Inuit, and Métis Education
Services
Regina Catholic Schools (#81)
Regina, SK

George Lin
Mathematics Department Head
Pinetree Secondary School
School District 43
Coquitlam, BC

Hugh MacDonald
Principal
Austin O'Brien Catholic High School
Edmonton Catholic School District
Edmonton, AB

Carolyn Martin
Department Head of Mathematics
Archbishop MacDonald High School
Edmonton Catholic School Board
Edmonton, AB

Hank Reinbold
Retired Educator
Morinville, AB

Rupi Samra-Gynane
Vice-Principal
Magee Secondary School
Vancouver School Board (#39)
Vancouver, BC

Carol Shaw
Mathematics Department Head
Elmwood High School
Winnipeg School Division
Winnipeg, MB

Roger Teshima
Learning Leader of Mathematics
Bowness High School
Calgary Board of Education
Calgary, AB

Sarah Wade
Curriculum Developer
Nunavut Board of Education
Ottawa, ON

Table of Contents

Features of *Nelson Principles of Mathematics 11*

Getting Started

Chapters begin with two-page activities designed to activate concepts and skills you have already learned that will be useful in the coming chapter.

Lessons

Some lessons help to develop your understanding of mathematics through examples and questions. Most lessons give you a chance to explore or investigate a problem. Many of the problems are in a real-life context.

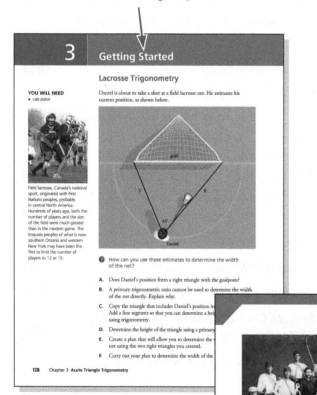

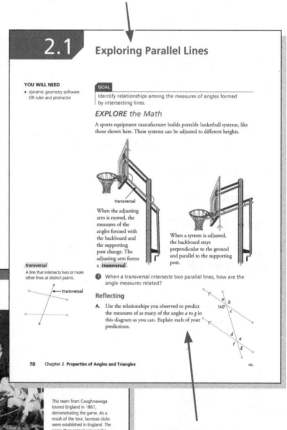

What Do You Think?

Statements about mathematical concepts are presented and you must decide whether you agree or disagree. Use your existing knowledge and speculations to justify your decisions. At the end of the chapter, revisit these statements to decide whether you still agree or disagree.

Reflecting

These questions give you a chance to reflect on the lesson so far and to summarize what you have learned.

You Will Need

Items you will need to carry out the lesson, such as a calculator or graph paper, will be listed here.

Explore

Try these at the beginning of each lesson. They may help you think in ways that will be useful in the lesson.

Definitions

New terms and ideas are highlighted in the text. In the margin nearby, you'll find a definition.

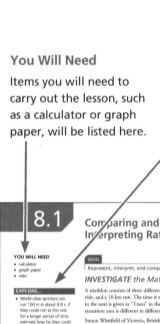

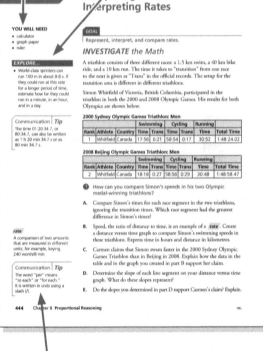

Communication Tips

These tips give explanations for why or when a specific mathematical convention or notation is used.

Your Turn

These questions appear after each Example. They may require you to think about the strategy presented in the example, or to solve a similar problem.

Examples

A complete solution to the example problem is given on the left. Explanations for steps in the solution are included in green boxes on the right. Use the examples to develop your understanding, and for reference while practising.

Features of *Nelson Principles of Mathematics 11*

In Summary

The In Summary box presents the Key Ideas for the lesson, and summarizes other useful information under Need to Know.

Practising

These problems and questions give you a chance to practise what you have just learned. There are a variety of types of questions, from simple practice questions that emphasize skill and knowledge development to problems that require you to make connections, visualize, and reason.

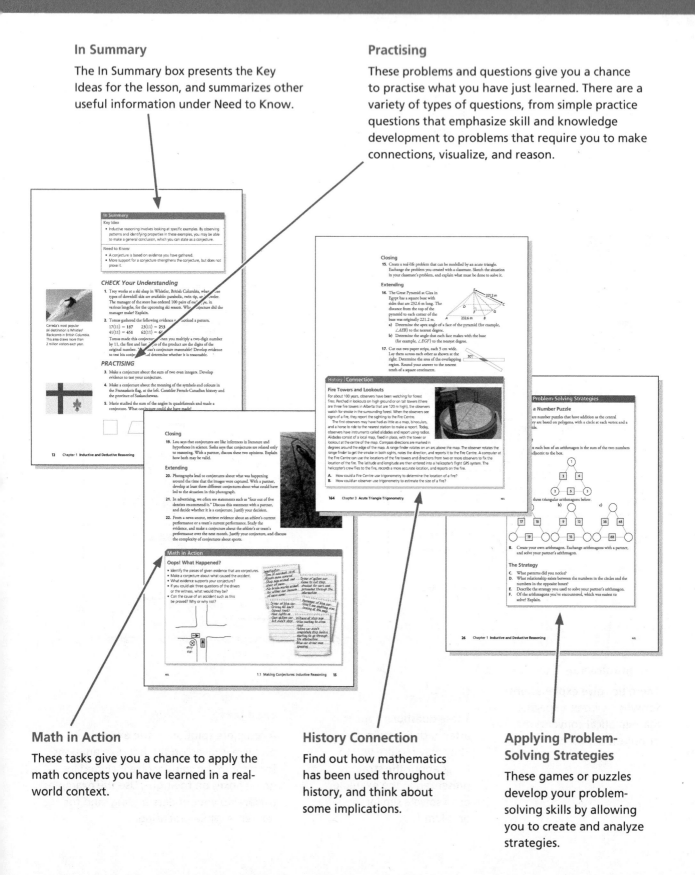

Math in Action

These tasks give you a chance to apply the math concepts you have learned in a real-world context.

History Connection

Find out how mathematics has been used throughout history, and think about some implications.

Applying Problem-Solving Strategies

These games or puzzles develop your problem-solving skills by allowing you to create and analyze strategies.

Mid-Chapter Review

See the Mid-Chapter Review for Frequently Asked Questions. Try the suggested Practising questions if you feel you need to test your understanding.

Chapter Self-Test

Try the Self-Test at the end of the chapter to discover if you have met the learning goals of the chapter. If you are uncertain about how to address any of the questions, look to the FAQs in the Mid-Chapter and Chapter Reviews for support.

Chapter Task

Have you developed a deep understanding of the mathematics presented in the chapter? Find out by trying this performance task.

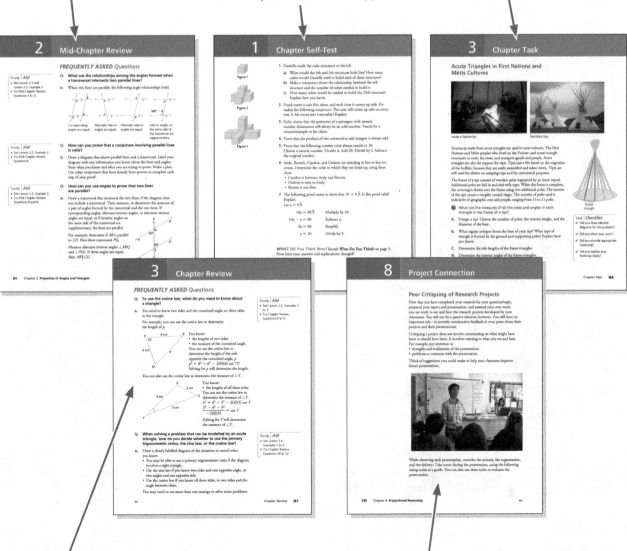

Chapter Review

Like the FAQ in the Mid-Chapter Review, the FAQ covers the immediately preceding lessons. Practising covers the whole chapter. There are also three Cumulative Reviews (not shown), which you can use to practise skills and use concepts you've learned in the preceding chapters.

Project Connection

You will be working on a project throughout the year. Project Connections support you as you decide on a topic, do your research, and develop your presentation.

NEL

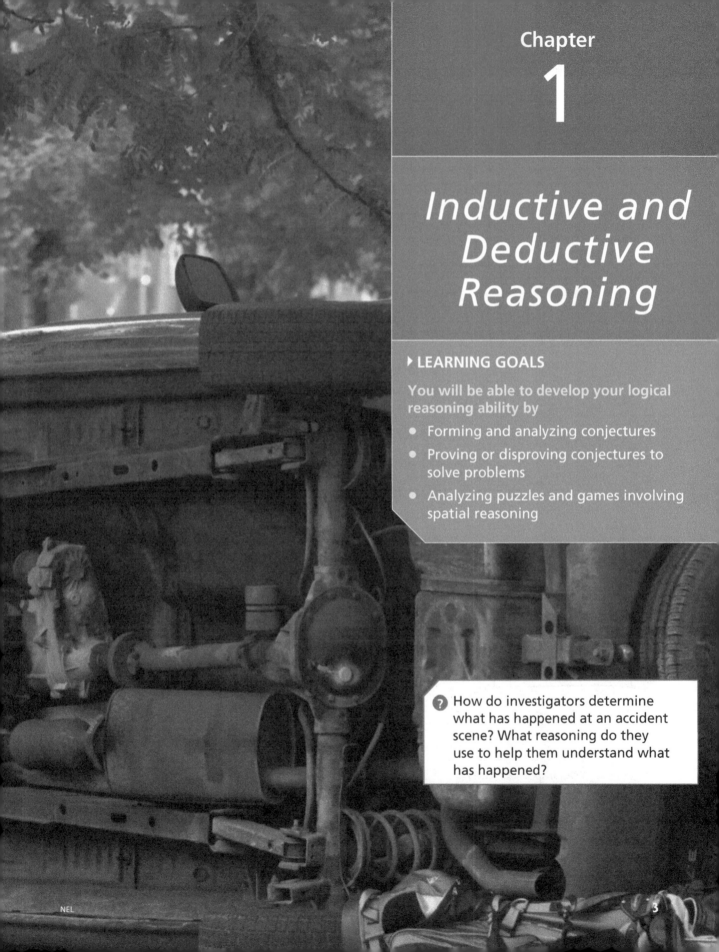

Inductive and Deductive Reasoning

▸ **LEARNING GOALS**

You will be able to develop your logical reasoning ability by

- Forming and analyzing conjectures
- Proving or disproving conjectures to solve problems
- Analyzing puzzles and games involving spatial reasoning

❓ How do investigators determine what has happened at an accident scene? What reasoning do they use to help them understand what has happened?

The Mystery of the *Mary Celeste*

The *Mary Celeste*, a Canadian-built 100-foot brigantine, set sail from New York on November 7, 1872, with Captain Briggs, his wife Sarah, his two-year old daughter Sophia, and a crew of seven. Five weeks later, on December 13, 1872, the *Mary Celeste* sailed into the Bay of Gibraltar with a completely different crew.

Timeline for the Voyage of the *Mary Celeste*

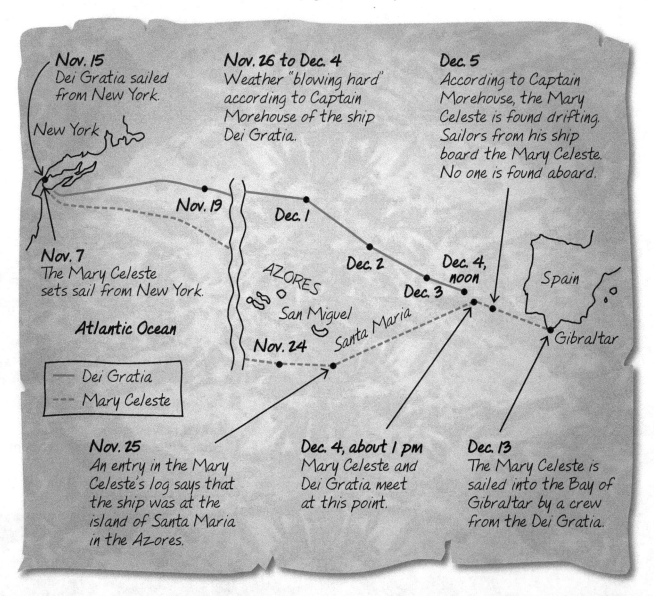

Nov. 15
Dei Gratia sailed from New York.

New York

Nov. 26 to Dec. 4
Weather "blowing hard" according to Captain Morehouse of the ship Dei Gratia.

Dec. 5
According to Captain Morehouse, the Mary Celeste is found drifting. Sailors from his ship board the Mary Celeste. No one is found aboard.

Nov. 19

Dec. 1

Nov. 7
The Mary Celeste sets sail from New York.

Dec. 2

Dec. 4, noon

Dec. 3

Spain

AZORES

Atlantic Ocean

San Miguel

Santa Maria

Gibraltar

Nov. 24

— Dei Gratia
- - - Mary Celeste

Nov. 25
An entry in the Mary Celeste's log says that the ship was at the island of Santa Maria in the Azores.

Dec. 4, about 1 pm
Mary Celeste and Dei Gratia meet at this point.

Dec. 13
The Mary Celeste is sailed into the Bay of Gibraltar by a crew from the Dei Gratia.

Condition of the *Mary Celeste*, as Reported to Captain Morehouse

- The ship's hull was not damaged.
- No crew or passengers were on board.
- No boats were on board.
- Ropes were dangling over the sides of the ship.
- Only one of two pumps was working.
- The forward and stern hatches were open.
- Water was found between the decks.
- The only dry clothing was found in a watertight chest.
- Kitchenware was scattered and loose in the galley.
- The galley stove was out of place.
- No chronometer or sextant was found on board. Both of these instruments are used for navigation.
- The ship's clock and compass were not working.
- The ship's register was missing. The ship's register is a document that notes home port and country of registration.
- The ship's papers were missing. These papers could have included a bill of sale, ownership information, crew manifest, and cargo information.
- The cargo, 1701 barrels of commercial alcohol, had not shifted. When unloaded in Genoa, 9 barrels were found to be empty.
- The alcohol was not safe to drink, but it could have been burned.

The ship shown here is the *Niagara*, which was built as a tribute to ships of the past, but it is of the same class as the *Mary Celeste*. Under full sail, the brigantine *Mary Celeste* would have looked a lot like this.

? How can you use this information to develop a plausible explanation about what happened to the crew?

A. With a partner, decide what pieces of evidence are most significant.

B. Discuss with your partner possible explanations for the evidence.

C. Choose one explanation, and develop an argument to support it.

D. Find a pair of students with a different explanation. Share your ideas.

E. Build a consensus for an explanation that your group of four could support.

F. What is one other piece of evidence, currently missing, that would further support your explanation?

WHAT DO *You Think?*

Decide whether you agree or disagree with each statement. Explain your decision.

1. When studying evidence or examples, the patterns you see will lead you to the correct conclusion.
2. Examining examples can help you discover patterns. A pattern can be useful for making predictions.
3. There is only one pattern that can be used to predict the next three terms after 1, 4, 9, 16, 25, ….

Making Conjectures: Inductive Reasoning

YOU WILL NEED

- calculator
- compass, protractor, and ruler, or dynamic geometry software

EXPLORE...

- If the first three colours in a sequence are red, orange, and yellow, what colours might be found in the rest of the sequence? Explain.

conjecture

A testable expression that is based on available evidence but is not yet proved.

GOAL

Use reasoning to make predictions.

INVESTIGATE the Math

Georgia, a fabric artist, has been patterning with equilateral triangles. Consider Georgia's **conjecture** about the following pattern.

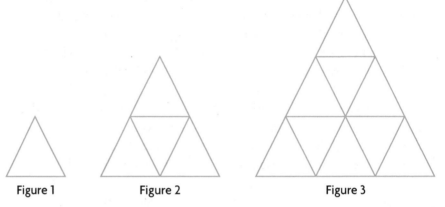

Figure 1   Figure 2   Figure 3

I think Figure 10 in this pattern will have 100 triangles, and all these triangles will be congruent to the triangle in Figure 1.

? How did Georgia arrive at this conjecture?

A. Organize the information about the pattern in a table like the one below.

Figure	1	2	3
Number of Triangles	1	4	

B. With a partner, discuss what you notice about the data in the table.

C. Extend the pattern for two more figures.

D. What numeric pattern do you see in the table?

Reflecting

E. Is Georgia's conjecture reasonable? Explain.

F. How did Georgia use **inductive reasoning** to develop her conjecture?

G. Is there a different conjecture you could make based upon the pattern you see? Explain.

inductive reasoning

Drawing a general conclusion by observing patterns and identifying properties in specific examples.

APPLY the Math

EXAMPLE 1 **Using inductive reasoning to make a conjecture about annual precipitation**

Lila studied the following five-year chart for total precipitation in Vancouver.

Precipitation in Vancouver (mm)												
	Jan.	Feb.	Mar.	Apr.	May	Jun.	Jul.	Aug.	Sep.	Oct.	Nov.	Dec.
2003	150.5	27.1	133.7	139.8	49.3	12.8	19.8	4.1	40.2	248.2	167.4	113.2
2004	249.6	45.8	132.8	90.2	68.6	49.6	43.6	28.6	53.6	155.4	136.6	160.8
2005	283.6	57.0	92.4	70.0	42.8	54.4	25.2	4.8	39.4	57.8	350.8	146.0
2006	181.4	116.0	214.8	76.2	37.0	80.0	53.0	8.4	73.6	155.2	116.2	210.6
2007	137.6	68.6	75.2	62.2	43.2	43.0	15.8	75.8	30.6	99.6	177.0	197.2

Environment Canada, National Climate Data and Information Archive

What conjecture could Lila make based on the data?

Lila's Solution

Jul.	Aug.	Sep.
19.8	4.1	40.2
43.6	28.6	53.6
25.2	4.8	39.4
53.0	8.4	73.6
15.8	75.8	30.6

Totals: 157.4   121.7   237.4

> I looked for patterns in the data. I noticed that the summer months seemed to have less precipitation than the other months. I checked the sum of the precipitation in July, August, and September over the five-year period.

Jan.	Feb.	Mar.
150.5	27.1	133.7
249.6	45.8	132.8
283.6	57.0	92.4
181.4	116.0	214.8
137.6	68.6	75.2

Totals: 1002.7   314.5   648.9

> Then I looked for the months with the greatest precipitation, anticipating that the winter months might have greater precipitation. I checked the sums for January, February, and March.

Nov.
167.4
136.6
350.8
116.2
177.0

Total: 948.0

> When I examined the information further, I saw that November had the highest value for precipitation: 350.8 mm. I checked the sum for November.

My conjecture is that fall and winter have more precipitation than spring and summer.

Apr.	May	Jun.	Jul.	Aug.	Sep.
438.4	240.9	239.8	157.4	121.7	237.4

Total: 1435.6 mm

Oct.	Nov.	Dec.	Jan.	Feb.	Mar.
716.2	948.0	827.8	1002.7	314.5	648.9

Total: 4458.1 mm

The data support my conjecture.

- - - - Since November is in the fall and January, February, and most of March are in the winter, I can make a conjecture about which seasons have the most precipitation.

I checked the totals for the five-year period. I found that spring and summer had a total of 1435.6 mm of precipitation, and fall and winter had a total of 4458.1 mm of precipitation.

Your Turn

Make a different conjecture based on patterns in the precipitation chart.

EXAMPLE 2   Using inductive reasoning to develop a conjecture about integers

Make a conjecture about the product of two odd integers.

Jay's Solution

$(+3)(+7) = (+21)$

- - - - Odd integers can be negative or positive. I tried two positive odd integers first. The product was positive and odd.

$(-5)(-3) = (+15)$

- - - - Next, I tried two negative odd integers. The product was again positive and odd.

$(+3)(-3) = (-9)$

- - - - Then I tried the other possible combination: one positive odd integer and one negative odd integer. This product was negative and odd.

My conjecture is that the product of two odd integers is an odd integer.

- - - - I noticed that each pair of integers I tried resulted in an odd product.

$(-211)(-17) = (+3587)$

- - - - I tried other integers to test my conjecture. The product was again odd.

Your Turn

Do you find Jay's conjecture convincing? Why or why not?

Make a conjecture about the difference between consecutive perfect squares.

Steffan's Solution: Comparing the squares geometrically

I represented the difference using unit tiles for each perfect square. First, I made a 3 × 3 square in orange and placed a yellow 2 × 2 square on top. When I subtracted the 2 × 2 square, I had 5 orange unit tiles left.

Next, I made 3 × 3 and 4 × 4 squares. When I subtracted the 3 × 3 square, I was left with 7 orange unit tiles. I decided to try greater squares.

My conjecture is that the difference between consecutive squares is always an odd number.

I saw the same pattern in all my examples: an even number of orange unit tiles bordering the yellow square, with one orange unit tile in the top right corner. So, there would always be an odd number of orange unit tiles left, since an even number plus one is always an odd number.

I tested my conjecture with the perfect squares 7 × 7 and 8 × 8. The difference was an odd number.

The example supports my conjecture.

Francesca's Solution: Describing the difference numerically

$2^2 - 1^2 = 4 - 1$
$2^2 - 1^2 = 3$

I started with the smallest possible perfect square and the next greater perfect square: 1^2 and 2^2. The difference was 3.

$4^2 - 3^2 = 7$
$9^2 - 8^2 = 17$

Then I used the perfect squares 3^2 and 4^2. The difference was 7. So, I decided to try even greater squares.

My conjecture is that the difference between consecutive perfect squares is always a prime number.

I thought about what all three differences—3, 7, and 17—had in common. They were all prime numbers.

$12^2 - 11^2 = 23$.

To test my conjecture, I tried the perfect squares 11^2 and 12^2. The difference was a prime number.

The example supports my conjecture.

Your Turn

How is it possible to have two different conjectures about the same situation? Explain.

Make a conjecture about the shape that is created by joining the midpoints of adjacent sides in any quadrilateral.

Marc's Solution: Using a protractor and ruler

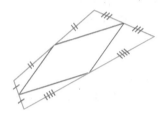

I drew an irregular quadrilateral on tracing paper. I used my ruler to determine the midpoints of each side. I joined the midpoints of adjacent sides to form a new quadrilateral. This quadrilateral looked like a parallelogram.

Next, I drew a trapezoid with sides that were four different lengths. I determined the midpoints of the sides. When the midpoints were joined, the new quadrilateral looked like a parallelogram.

I used my ruler to confirm that the opposite sides were equal.

My conjecture is that joining the adjacent midpoints of any quadrilateral will create a parallelogram.

Each time I joined the midpoints, a parallelogram was formed.

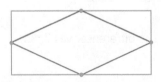

To check my conjecture one more time, I drew a rectangle. I determined its midpoints and joined them. This quadrilateral also looked like a parallelogram.

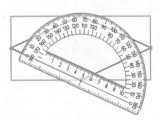

I checked the measures of the angles in the new quadrilateral. The opposite angles were equal. The new quadrilateral was a parallelogram, just like the others were.

The rectangle example supports my conjecture.

Tracey's Solution: Using dynamic geometry software

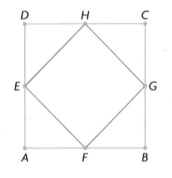

$\overline{HE}$ = 2.4 cm
$\overline{EF}$ = 2.4 cm
$\overline{FG}$ = 2.4 cm
$\overline{GH}$ = 2.4 cm

∠EFG = 90°
∠FGH = 90°
∠GHE = 90°
∠HEF = 90°

I constructed a square and the midpoints of the sides. Then I joined the adjacent midpoints. *EFGH* looked like a square. I checked its side lengths and angle measures to confirm that it was a square.

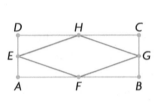

$\overline{HE}$ = 1.6 cm
$\overline{EF}$ = 1.6 cm
$\overline{FG}$ = 1.6 cm
$\overline{GH}$ = 1.6 cm

∠EFG = 143°
∠FGH = 37°
∠GHE = 143°
∠HEF = 37°

Next, I constructed a rectangle and joined the adjacent midpoints to create a new quadrilateral, *EFGH*. The side lengths and angle measures of *EFGH* showed that *EFGH* was a rhombus but not a square.

My conjecture is that the quadrilateral formed by joining the adjacent midpoints of any quadrilateral is a rhombus.

Since a square is a rhombus with right angles, both of my examples resulted in a rhombus.

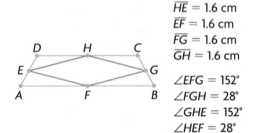

$\overline{HE}$ = 1.6 cm
$\overline{EF}$ = 1.6 cm
$\overline{FG}$ = 1.6 cm
$\overline{GH}$ = 1.6 cm

∠EFG = 152°
∠FGH = 28°
∠GHE = 152°
∠HEF = 28°

To check my conjecture, I tried an isosceles trapezoid. The new quadrilateral, *EFGH*, was a rhombus.

The isosceles trapezoid example supports my conjecture.

Your Turn

a) Why did the students draw different conjectures?

b) Do you think that both conjectures are valid? Explain.

CHECK Your Understanding

Canada's most popular ski destination is Whistler/ Blackcomb in British Columbia. This area draws more than 2 million visitors each year.

1. Troy works at a ski shop in Whistler, British Columbia, where three types of downhill skis are available: parabolic, twin tip, and powder. The manager of the store has ordered 100 pairs of each type, in various lengths, for the upcoming ski season. What conjecture did the manager make? Explain.

2. Tomas gathered the following evidence and noticed a pattern.

$$17(11) = \mathbf{187} \qquad 23(11) = \mathbf{253}$$
$$41(11) = \mathbf{451} \qquad 62(11) = \mathbf{682}$$

Tomas made this conjecture: When you multiply a two-digit number by 11, the first and last digits of the product are the digits of the original number. Is Tomas's conjecture reasonable? Develop evidence to test his conjecture and determine whether it is reasonable.

PRACTISING

3. Make a conjecture about the sum of two even integers. Develop evidence to test your conjecture.

4. Make a conjecture about the meaning of the symbols and colours in the Fransaskois flag, at the left. Consider French-Canadian history and the province of Saskatchewan.

5. Marie studied the sum of the angles in quadrilaterals and made a conjecture. What conjecture could she have made?

6. Use the evidence given in the chart below to make a conjecture. Provide more evidence to support your conjecture.

Polygon	quadrilateral	pentagon	hexagon
Fewest Number of Triangles	2	3	4

7. Sonia noticed a pattern when dividing the square of an odd number by 4. Determine the pattern and make a conjecture.

8. Dan noticed a pattern in the digits of the multiples of 3. He created the following table to show the pattern.

Multiples of 3	12	15	18	21	24	27	30
Sum of the Digits	3	6	9	3	6	9	3

   a) Make a conjecture based on the pattern in the table.
   b) Find a classmate who made a different conjecture. Discuss the reasonableness of both conjectures.
   c) Test one of the conjectures.

9. Make a conjecture about the sum of one odd integer and one even integer. Test your conjecture with at least three examples.

10. Make a conjecture about the temperature on November 1 in Hay River, Northwest Territories, based on the information in the chart below. Summarize the evidence that supports your conjecture.

Year	2000	2001	2002	2003	2004	2005	2006	2007	2008	2009
Maximum Temperature (°C)	+3.1	−2.2	−1.1	−10.1	−1.6	−3.9	−3.2	+2.9	+1.8	−3.0

11. Paula claims that whenever you square an odd integer, the result is an odd number. Is her conjecture reasonable? Justify your decision.

12. Ursula studied the diagonals of these rectangles to look for patterns. Make a conjecture about the diagonals of rectangles. What evidence supports your conjecture?

13. Text messages often include cryptic abbreviations, such as L2G (love to go), 2MI (too much information), LOL (laugh out loud), and MTF (more to follow). Make a conjecture about the cryptic abbreviations used in text messages, and provide evidence to support your conjecture.

14. Nick made a conjecture about the medians of a triangle. He used triangles of different sizes and types to gather evidence. The evidence always supported his conjecture. What might his conjecture have been? Provide additional evidence to support the conjecture.

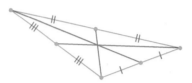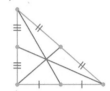

15. Farmers, travellers, and hunters depend on their observations of weather and storm systems to make quick decisions and to survive in different weather conditions. Weather predictions, passed on through oral tradition or cited in almanacs, are often based on long-term observations. Two predictive statements about weather are given below.
- If cows are lying down, then it is going to rain.
- Red sky at night; sailor's delight.

Find another such predictive statement from oral tradition, an Elder, a family member, an Internet source, or a text. Explain how and why this prediction may have been reached.

Red sky at sunset may predict calm weather. Based on the photo, how else could you predict that a storm isn't coming?

16. The map below does not have any roads or urban areas marked. However, there is a town of 7000 people somewhere in this area. Make a conjecture about where the town is. Justify your decision.

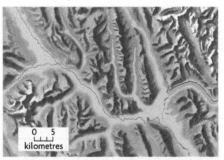

17. Suppose that social networking sites were the only method for passing information among people, and that everyone in Canada was a member of one of these sites. Make a conjecture about the amount of time it would take for the entire population of Canada to get information first shared at 8 a.m. Central Standard Time. With a partner, discuss the reasonableness of each of your conjectures and decide how you could gather evidence to support your conjectures.

18. Thérèse held up a piece of notebook paper in one hand and a pair of scissors in the other hand, and made the conjecture that she could walk through the piece of paper. With a partner, explore how Thérèse's conjecture could be possible.

Closing

19. Lou says that conjectures are like inferences in literature and hypotheses in science. Sasha says that conjectures are related only to reasoning. With a partner, discuss these two opinions. Explain how both may be valid.

Extending

20. Photographs lead to conjectures about what was happening around the time that the images were captured. With a partner, develop at least three different conjectures about what could have led to the situation in this photograph.

21. In advertising, we often see statements such as "four out of five dentists recommend it." Discuss this statement with a partner, and decide whether it is a conjecture. Justify your decision.

22. From a news source, retrieve evidence about an athlete's current performance or a team's current performance. Study the evidence, and make a conjecture about the athlete's or team's performance over the next month. Justify your conjecture, and discuss the complexity of conjectures about sports.

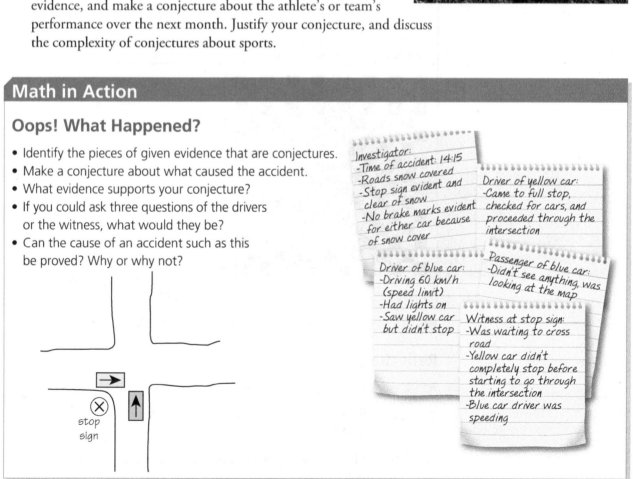

Math in Action

Oops! What Happened?

- Identify the pieces of given evidence that are conjectures.
- Make a conjecture about what caused the accident.
- What evidence supports your conjecture?
- If you could ask three questions of the drivers or the witness, what would they be?
- Can the cause of an accident such as this be proved? Why or why not?

Investigator:
- Time of accident: 14:15
- Roads snow covered
- Stop sign evident and clear of snow
- No brake marks evident for either car because of snow cover

Driver of yellow car:
- Came to full stop, checked for cars, and proceeded through the intersection

Driver of blue car:
- Driving 60 km/h (speed limit)
- Had lights on
- Saw yellow car but didn't stop

Passenger of blue car:
- Didn't see anything, was looking at the map

Witness at stop sign:
- Was waiting to cross road
- Yellow car didn't completely stop before starting to go through the intersection
- Blue car driver was speeding

Exploring the Validity of Conjectures

GOAL

Determine whether a conjecture is valid.

EXPLORE the Math

Your brain can be deceived.

Choose two of these four optical illusions.

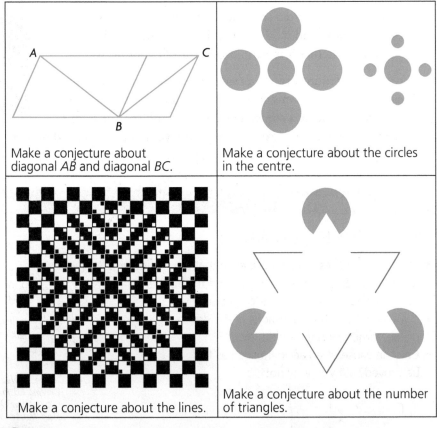

Make a conjecture about diagonal *AB* and diagonal *BC*.

Make a conjecture about the circles in the centre.

Make a conjecture about the lines.

Make a conjecture about the number of triangles.

? How can you check the validity of your conjectures?

Reflecting

A. Describe the steps you took to verify your conjectures.

B. After collecting evidence, did you decide to revise either of your conjectures? Explain.

C. Can you be certain that the evidence you collect leads to a correct conjecture? Explain.

In Summary

Key Idea

- Some conjectures initially seem to be valid, but are shown not to be valid after more evidence is gathered.

Need to Know

- The best we can say about a conjecture reached through inductive reasoning is that there is evidence either to support or deny it.
- A conjecture may be revised, based on new evidence.

FURTHER *Your Understanding*

1. Make a conjecture about the dimensions of the two tabletops. How can you determine if your conjecture is valid?

2. Examine the number pattern. Make a conjecture about this pattern. What steps can you take to determine if your conjecture is valid?

$$1^2 = 1$$
$$11^2 = 121$$
$$111^2 = 12321$$
$$1111^2 = 1234321$$

3. If two congruent regular heptagons are positioned so that they share a side, a dodecagon (12-sided polygon) is formed. If two congruent regular hexagons are positioned so that they share a side, a decagon is formed. If two congruent regular pentagons are positioned so that they share a side, an octagon is formed. Make a conjecture about positioning two congruent regular quadrilaterals so that they share a side. Determine whether your conjecture is valid. Record your evidence.

Using Reasoning to Find a Counterexample to a Conjecture

GOAL

Invalidate a conjecture by finding a contradiction.

LEARN ABOUT the Math

Kerry created a series of circles. Each circle had points marked on its circumference and joined by chords.

 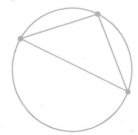 

As the number of points on the circumference increased, Kerry noticed a pattern for the number of regions created by the chords.

Number of Points	2	3	4
Number of Regions	2	4	8

She made the following conjecture: As the number of connected points on the circumference of a circle increases by 1, the number of regions created within the circle increases by a factor of 2.

? How can Kerry test the validity of her conjecture?

EXAMPLE 1   **Testing a conjecture**

Gather more evidence to test Kerry's conjecture.

Zohal's Solution

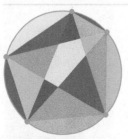

Number of Points	2	3	4	5
Number of Regions	2	4	8	16

I drew another circle and identified five points on its circumference. Then I joined the pairs of points with chords. I coloured the resulting regions to make them easier to count.

My diagram had 16 regions. This supported Kerry's conjecture because the pattern for the resulting regions was $2^1, 2^2, 2^3, 2^4$.

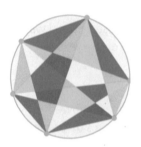

I drew another circle and identified six points on its circumference. Then I joined the pairs of points with chords and coloured the regions.

When I counted, I got only 31 regions, not 2^5 or 32 as Kerry's conjecture predicts.

Number of Points	2	3	4	5	6
Number of Regions	2	4	8	16	31

The number of regions did not increase by a factor of 2. This **counterexample** disproves Kerry's conjecture.

counterexample
An example that invalidates a conjecture.

Reflecting

A. Why do you think Zohal started her development of further evidence by using five points on the circumference of a circle?

B. Why is only one counterexample enough to disprove a conjecture?

APPLY the Math

EXAMPLE 2   Connecting to previous conjectures

In Lesson 1.1, page 9, Francesca and Steffan made conjectures about the difference between consecutive squares.

Steffan's conjecture: The difference between consecutive perfect squares is always an odd number.

Francesca's conjecture: The difference between consecutive perfect squares is always a prime number.

How can these conjectures be tested?

Luke's Solution: Communicating about Steffan's conjecture and more trials

Steffan's conjecture was true for the pairs of consecutive squares he chose: 2×2 and 3×3, 3×3 and 4×4, and 5×5 and 6×6.

First, I tried 1×1 and 2×2. I made the same tile squares as Steffan. When I took away the yellow square, I was left with a pair of tiles that shared an edge with the yellow square and a single tile in the top right corner.

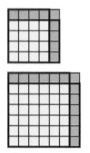

Next, I chose 4 × 4 and 5 × 5, since Steffan had skipped over these values. I was left with two groups of tiles, each with the same value as a side of the yellow square, plus one extra tile in the top right corner.

I tried consecutive squares of 6 × 6 and 7 × 7. The difference again showed the same pattern: two groups of tiles, each with the same value as a side of the yellow square, plus a single tile in the top right corner.

These three examples support Steffan's conjecture.

I visualized what the difference would look like for any pair of consecutive squares. There would always be two groups of orange tiles, each with the same value as a side of the smaller yellow square, plus one unpaired orange square in the corner. The total value of the two equal groups would always be an even number, since 2 times any number is even. The unpaired tile would make the difference odd.

All this evidence strengthens the validity of Steffan's conjecture. However, it doesn't prove the conjecture since I haven't tried all the possible cases.

Pierre's Solution: Connecting more evidence to Francesca's conjecture

Francesca used the consecutive squares of 1 and 2, 3 and 4, and 8 and 9.

I chose values so I could start to fill the gaps between the values that Francesca chose.

$3^2 - 2^2 = 5$

Five is a prime number.

$5^2 - 4^2 = 9$

The next gap was 4 and 5. Nine is not a prime number.

Francesca's conjecture, that the difference between consecutive squares is always a prime number, was disproved since a counterexample was found.

Your Turn

a) Find another counterexample to Francesca's conjecture.

b) Can you find a counterexample to Steffan's conjecture? Explain.

| EXAMPLE **3** | Using reasoning to find a counterexample to a conjecture |

Matt found an interesting numeric pattern:

$$1 \cdot 8 + 1 = \mathbf{9}$$
$$12 \cdot 8 + 2 = \mathbf{98}$$
$$123 \cdot 8 + 3 = \mathbf{987}$$
$$1234 \cdot 8 + 4 = \mathbf{9876}$$

Matt thinks that this pattern will continue.

Search for a counterexample to Matt's conjecture.

Kublu's Solution

$$\mathbf{1} \cdot 8 + \mathbf{1} = 9$$
$$\mathbf{12} \cdot 8 + \mathbf{2} = 98$$
$$\mathbf{123} \cdot 8 + \mathbf{3} = 987$$
$$\mathbf{1234} \cdot 8 + \mathbf{4} = 9876$$

> The pattern seemed to be related to the first factor (the factor that wasn't 8), the number that was added, and the product.

	A	B
1	$1 \cdot 8 + 1$	9
2	$12 \cdot 8 + 2$	98
3	$123 \cdot 8 + 3$	987
4	$1234 \cdot 8 + 4$	9876
5	$12345 \cdot 8 + 5$	98765
6	$123456 \cdot 8 + 6$	987654
7	$1234567 \cdot 8 + 7$	9876543
8	$12345678 \cdot 8 + 8$	98765432
9	$123456789 \cdot 8 + 9$	987654321

> I used a spreadsheet to see if the pattern continued.
>
> The spreadsheet showed that it did.

$$12345678\mathbf{10} \cdot 8 + \mathbf{10} = 98\ 765\ 431\ 290$$
$$1234567890 \cdot 8 + \mathbf{10} = 9\ 876\ 543\ 130$$
$$12345678\mathbf{10} \cdot 8 + \mathbf{0} = 98\ 765\ 431\ 280$$
$$1234567890 \cdot 8 + \mathbf{0} = 9\ 876\ 543\ 120$$

> When I came to the tenth step in the sequence, I had to decide whether to use 10 or 0 in the first factor and as the number to add. I decided to check each way that 10 and 0 could be represented.

The pattern holds true until 9 of the 10 digits are included. At the tenth step in the sequence, a counterexample is found.

> Since the pattern did not continue, Matt's conjecture is invalid.

Revised conjecture: When the value of the addend is 1 to 9, the pattern will continue.

> I decided to revise Matt's conjecture by limiting it.

Your Turn

If Kublu had not found a counterexample at the tenth step, should she have continued looking? When would it be reasonable to stop gathering evidence if all the examples supported the conjecture? Justify your decision.

CHECK *Your Understanding*

1. Show that each statement is false by finding a counterexample.
   a) A number that is not negative is positive.
   b) All prime numbers are odd.
   c) All basketball players are tall.
   d) The height of a triangle lies inside the triangle.
   e) On maps, the north arrow always points up.
   f) The square root of a number is always less than the number.
   g) The sum of two numbers is always greater than the greater of the two numbers.
   h) As you travel north, the climate gets colder.

2. Seth claims that all quadrilaterals with four equal sides are squares. Do you agree or disagree? Justify your decision.

PRACTISING

3. Jim claims that whenever you multiply two whole numbers, the product is greater than either of the two factors. Do you agree or disagree? Justify your decision.

4. Rachelle claims that the sum of a multiple of 3 and a multiple of 6 must be a multiple of 6. Do you agree or disagree? Justify your decision.

5. Hannah examined these multiples of 9: 18, 45, 63, 27, 81, 108, 216. She claimed that the sum of the digits in any multiple of 9 will add to 9. Do you agree or disagree? Justify your decision.

6. Colin made the following conjecture: If a quadrilateral has two opposite angles that are right angles, the quadrilateral is a rectangle. Do you agree or disagree? Justify your decision.

7. Claire noticed that the digits 4, 5, 6, and 7 could be used to express each value from 1 to 5 as shown to the right. She conjectured that these digits could be used to express each value from 1 to 20. Explain, with examples, whether Claire's conjecture is reasonable.

Number	Expression
1	$\dfrac{7-5}{6-4}$
2	$7-6+5-4$
3	$\dfrac{6(7-5)}{4}$
4	$7+6-5-4$
5	$5(\sqrt{64}-7)$

8. George noted a pattern that was similar to Matt's pattern in Example 3. George conjectured that the products would follow the pattern of ending with the digit 5 or 0. Gather evidence about George's conjecture. Does your evidence strengthen or disprove George's conjecture? Explain.

$$1 \cdot 4 + 1 = 5$$
$$12 \cdot 4 + 2 = 50$$
$$123 \cdot 4 + 3 = 495$$
$$1234 \cdot 4 + 4 = 4940$$

9. From questions 2 to 8, choose a conjecture that you have disproved. Based on your counterexample, revise the conjecture to make it valid.

10. Patrice studied the following table and made this conjecture: The sums of the squares of integers separated by a value of 2 will always be even.

$(-1)^2 + 1^2 = 2$	$2^2 + 4^2 = 20$	$(-3)^2 + (-5)^2 = 34$	$4^2 + 6^2 = 52$	$0^2 + 2^2 = 4$

Is Patrice's conjecture reasonable? Explain.

11. Geoff made the following conjecture: If the diagonals of a quadrilateral are perpendicular, then the quadrilateral is a square. Determine the validity of his conjecture. Explain your results.

12. Amy made the following conjecture: When any number is multiplied by itself, the product will be greater than this starting number. For example, in $2 \cdot 2 = 4$, the product 4 is greater than the starting number 2. Meagan disagreed with Amy's conjecture, however, because $\frac{1}{2} \cdot \frac{1}{2} = \frac{1}{4}$ and $\frac{1}{4}$ is less than $\frac{1}{2}$. How could Amy's conjecture be improved? Explain the change(s) you would make.

13. Create a general statement that is true in some cases but not in every case. Provide examples that support your statement. Provide a counterexample.

14. Tim conjectured that all natural numbers can be written as the sum of consecutive natural numbers, based on these examples:
$$10 = 1 + 2 + 3 + 4 \qquad 12 = 3 + 4 + 5$$
$$9 = 4 + 5 \qquad 94 = 22 + 23 + 24 + 25$$
Do you agree or disagree with Tim's conjecture? Justify your decision.

15. Blake claimed that all odd numbers can be expressed as the sum of three prime numbers. Explain, with evidence, the reasonableness of his claim.

16. German mathematician Christian Goldbach made the conjecture that every even number greater than 2 is the sum of two prime numbers. For example:

14 = 3 + 11
30 = 7 + 23

This conjecture has become known as Goldbach's conjecture. No one has ever been able to prove that it is true for all even numbers, but no one has ever found a counterexample.
   a) Find three other examples that support Goldbach's conjecture.
   b) If a counterexample exists, describe what it would look like.

17. Jarrod discovered a number trick in a book he was reading: Choose a number. Double it. Add 6. Double again. Subtract 4. Divide by 4. Subtract 2.
   a) Try the trick several times. Make a conjecture about the relation between the number picked and the final result.
   b) Can you find a counterexample to your conjecture? What does this imply?

Reasoning in Science

Scientific discoveries are often based on inductive reasoning. Scientists make conjectures after examining all the evidence they have. They test their conjectures by conducting experiments in which they compare how the universe actually behaves with how they predict it should behave. If the experiments have the predicted results, then the scientists' conjectures are strengthened. If the results contradict the conjectures, then the scientists use the results to revise their conjectures or to make new conjectures.

If Earth were a flat disc, it might look like this from space.

Many scientific conjectures have been changed over time as new information has come to light. One such conjecture relates to Earth itself. In ancient times, the world was believed to be flat. The flat world conjecture was held to be true until counterexamples required it to be changed. Aristotle, in about 330 BCE, was one of the first people to conjecture that the world was not a flat disc but a sphere. Pliny the Elder, in the 1st century CE, was able to suggest that the flat world conjecture was no longer valid because of the evidence that had been developed to contradict it. Pliny considered the possibility of an imperfect sphere. Modern evidence, from satellite images and spaceships, has provided no counterexamples to the spheroid theory, so this theory is generally accepted as fact today.

However, it actually looks like this.

A. What other conjectures about our universe have been revised after new evidence was gathered?
B. How does inductive reasoning play a part in our beliefs and understanding about our universe?

Closing

18. What relationship exists among inductive reasoning, evidence, and counterexamples?

Extending

19. Serge made the following conjecture: When 3 is subtracted from a perfect square that is greater than 4, the result is always a composite number. For example:

$15^2 - 3 = 222$

222 is a composite number because it is divisible by factors other than 1 and itself. Do you agree with Serge's conjecture? Justify your decision.

20. Environment Canada explains probability of precipitation forecasts as subjective estimates. These forecasts or estimates are actually conjectures based on numerical evidence and regional topography. They are important for people, such as building contractors, farmers, and surveyors, who work outside and for anyone else who is planning outdoor activities. As the time for precipitation comes closer, a forecaster's conjecture is revised to reflect newer data and increased accuracy.

   a) Environment Canada's chart below seems to be written for adults who live in a city or its suburbs. Revise the chart so that it is written for you, by including activities that you participate in.

   b) Explain your revisions. How did you decide which probabilities of precipitation could affect your activities?

A User's Guide to Probability of Precipitation

0%	No precipitation even though it may be cloudy.
10%	Little likelihood of rain or snow: only 1 chance in 10.
20%	No precipitation is expected.
30%	If you go ahead with your outdoor plans, keep an eye on the weather.
40%	An umbrella is recommended. Make alternate plans for outdoor activities that are susceptible to rain. Not a good day to pave the driveway. Keep your fingers crossed!
50%	It's 50–50 on whether you get precipitation or not.
60%	Want to water your lawn? The odds are favourable that Mother Nature might give you some help.
70%	Consider the effect of precipitation on your plans for outdoor activities. The chance for no precipitation is only 3 in 10!
80%	Rain or snow is likely.
90%	The occurrence of precipitation is a near certainty.
100%	Precipitation is a certainty.

Environment Canada, Probability of Precipitation brochure

21. Mohammed claims that the expression $n^2 + n + 2$ will never generate an odd number for a positive integer value of n. Do you agree or disagree? Justify your decision.

Analyzing a Number Puzzle

Arithmagons are number puzzles that have addition as the central operation. They are based on polygons, with a circle at each vertex and a box on each side.

The Puzzle

The number in each box of an arithmagon is the sum of the two numbers in the circles adjacent to the box.

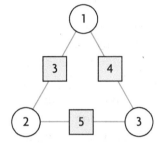

A. Solve the three triangular arithmagons below.

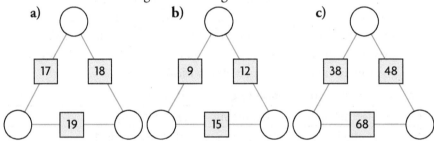

a)   b)   c)

B. Create your own arithmagon. Exchange arithmagons with a partner, and solve your partner's arithmagon.

The Strategy

C. What patterns did you notice?
D. What relationship exists between the numbers in the circles and the numbers in the opposite boxes?
E. Describe the strategy you used to solve your partner's arithmagon.
F. Of the arithmagons you've encountered, which was easiest to solve? Explain.

1.4 Proving Conjectures: Deductive Reasoning

YOU WILL NEED

- calculator
- ruler

GOAL

Prove mathematical statements using a logical argument.

LEARN ABOUT the Math

Jon discovered a pattern when adding integers:

$$1 + 2 + 3 + 4 + 5 = 15$$
$$(-15) + (-14) + (-13) + (-12) + (-11) = -65$$
$$(-3) + (-2) + (-1) + 0 + 1 = -5$$

He claims that whenever you add five consecutive integers, the sum is always 5 times the median of the numbers.

? How can you prove that Jon's conjecture is true for all integers?

EXPLORE...

- How can the conjecture "All teens like music" be supported inductively? Can this conjecture be proved? Explain.

proof

A mathematical argument showing that a statement is valid in all cases, or that no counterexample exists.

generalization

A principle, statement, or idea that has general application.

EXAMPLE 1   Connecting conjectures with reasoning

Prove that Jon's conjecture is true for all integers.

Pat's Solution

$$5(3) = 15$$
$$5(-13) = -65$$
$$5(-1) = -5$$

The median is the middle number in a set of integers when the integers are arranged in consecutive order. I observed that Jon's conjecture was true in each of his examples.

$$210 + 211 + 212 + 213 + 214 = 1060$$
$$5(212) = 1060$$

I tried a sample with greater integers, and the conjecture still worked.

Let x represent any integer.
Let S represent the sum of five consecutive integers.
$$S = (x - 2) + (x - 1) + x + (x + 1) + (x + 2)$$

I decided to start my **proof** by representing the sum of five consecutive integers. I chose x as the median and then wrote a **generalization** for the sum.

$$S = (x + x + x + x + x) + (-2 + (-1) + 0 + 1 + 2)$$
$$S = 5x + 0$$

I simplified by gathering like terms.

$$S = 5x$$
Jon's conjecture is true for all integers.

Since x represents the median of five consecutive integers, $5x$ will always represent the sum.

deductive reasoning

Drawing a specific conclusion through logical reasoning by starting with general assumptions that are known to be valid.

Reflecting

A. What type of reasoning did Jon use to make his conjecture?

B. Pat used **deductive reasoning** to prove Jon's conjecture. How does this differ from the type of reasoning that Jon used?

APPLY the Math

EXAMPLE 2   Using deductive reasoning to generalize a conjecture

In Lesson 1.3, page 19, Luke found more support for Steffan's conjecture from Lesson 1.1, page 9—that the difference between consecutive perfect squares is always an odd number.

Determine the general case to prove Steffan's conjecture.

Gord's Solution

The difference between consecutive perfect squares is always an odd number.

25 units	1 unit
25 units^2	25 units

> Steffan's conjecture has worked for consecutive perfect squares with sides of 1 to 7 units.

$$26^2 - 25^2 = 2(25) + 1$$
$$26^2 - 25^2 = 51$$

> I tried a sample using even greater squares: 26^2 and 25^2.
>
> The difference is the two sets of 25 unit tiles, plus a single unit tile.

Let x be any natural number.
Let D be the difference between consecutive perfect squares.
$$D = (x + 1)^2 - x^2$$

> Since the conjecture has been supported with specific examples, I decided to express the conjecture as a general statement. I chose x to be the length of the smaller square's sides. The larger square's sides would then be $x + 1$.

$$D = x^2 + x + x + 1 - x^2$$
$$D = x^2 + 2x + 1 - x^2$$
$$D = 2x + 1$$

> I expanded and simplified my expression. Since x represents any natural number, $2x$ is an even number, and $2x + 1$ is an odd number.

Steffan's conjecture, that the difference of consecutive perfect squares is always an odd number, has been proved for all natural numbers.

Your Turn

In Lesson 1.3, Luke visualized the generalization but did not develop the reasoning to support it. How did the visualization explained by Luke help Gord develop the general statement? Explain.

EXAMPLE **3**   Using deductive reasoning to make a valid conclusion

All dogs are mammals. All mammals are vertebrates. Shaggy is a dog.

What can be deduced about Shaggy?

Oscar's Solution

Shaggy is a dog.

All dogs are mammals.

> These statements are given. I represented them using a Venn diagram.

All mammals are vertebrates.

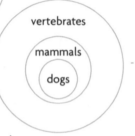

> This statement is given. I modified my diagram.

Therefore, through deductive reasoning,
Shaggy is a mammal and a vertebrate.

Your Turn

Weight-lifting builds muscle. Muscle makes you strong. Strength improves balance. Inez lifts weights. What can be deduced about Inez?

EXAMPLE **4**   Using deductive reasoning to prove a geometric conjecture

Prove that when two straight lines intersect, the vertically opposite angles are equal.

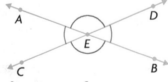

Jose's Solution: Reasoning in a two-column proof

Statement	Justification
$\angle AEC + \angle AED = 180°$	Supplementary angles
$\angle AEC = 180° - \angle AED$	Subtraction property
$\angle BED + \angle AED = 180°$	Supplementary angles
$\angle BED = 180° - \angle AED$	Subtraction property
$\angle AEC = \angle BED$	**Transitive property**

Your Turn

Use a **two-column proof** to prove that $\angle AED$ and $\angle CEB$ are equal.

transitive property

If two quantities are equal to the same quantity, then they are equal to each other.
If $a = b$ and $b = c$, then $a = c$.

two-column proof

A presentation of a logical argument involving deductive reasoning in which the statements of the argument are written in one column and the justifications for the statements are written in the other column.

EXAMPLE 5   Communicating reasoning about a divisibility rule

The following rule can be used to determine whether a number is divisible by 3:

Add the digits, and determine if the sum is divisible by 3. If the sum is divisible by 3, then the original number is divisible by 3.

Use deductive reasoning to prove that the divisibility rule for 3 is valid for two-digit numbers.

Lee's Solution

Expanded Number Forms		
Number	Expanded Form (Words)	Expanded Form (Numbers)
9	9 ones	9(1)
27	2 tens and 7 ones	2(10) + 7(1)
729	7 hundreds and 2 tens and 9 ones	7(100) + 2(10) + 9(1)
ab	a tens and b ones	$a(10) + b(1)$

Let ab represent any two-digit number.

> I let ab represent any two-digit number.

$ab = 10a + b$

> Since any number can be written in expanded form, I wrote ab in expanded form.

$ab = (9a + 1a) + b$
$ab = 9a + (a + b)$

> I decomposed $10a$ into an equivalent sum. I used $9a$ because I knew that $9a$ is divisible by 3, since 3 is a factor of 9.

The number ab is divisible by 3 only when $(a + b)$ is divisible by 3.

> From this equivalent expression, I concluded that ab is divisible by 3 only when both $9a$ and $(a + b)$ are divisible by 3. I knew that $9a$ is always divisible by 3, so I concluded that ab is divisible by 3 only when $(a + b)$ is divisible by 3.

The divisibility rule has been proved for two-digit numbers.

Your Turn

Use similar reasoning to prove that the divisibility rule for 3 is valid for three-digit numbers.

In Summary

Key Idea

- Deductive reasoning involves starting with general assumptions that are known to be true and, through logical reasoning, arriving at a specific conclusion.

Need to Know

- A conjecture has been proved only when it has been shown to be true for every possible case or example. This is accomplished by creating a proof that involves general cases.
- When you apply the principles of deductive reasoning correctly, you can be sure that the conclusion you draw is valid.
- The transitive property is often useful in deductive reasoning. It can be stated as follows: Things that are equal to the same thing are equal to each other. If $a = b$ and $b = c$, then $a = c$.
- A demonstration using an example is *not* a proof.

CHECK Your Understanding

1. Chuck made the conjecture that the sum of any seven consecutive integers is 7 times the median. Prove Chuck's conjecture.

2. Jim is a barber. Everyone whose hair is cut by Jim gets a good haircut. Austin's hair was cut by Jim. What can you deduce about Austin?

3. Lila drew a quadrilateral and its diagonals. What could Lila deduce about the angles formed at the intersection of the diagonals?

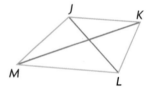

PRACTISING

4. Prove that the sum of two even integers is always even.

5. Prove that the product of an even integer and an odd integer is always even.

6. Prove that a, b, and c are equal.

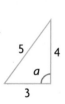
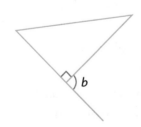
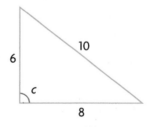

7. Drew created this step-by-step number trick:
   - Choose any number.
   - Multiply by 4.
   - Add 10.
   - Divide by 2.
   - Subtract 5.
   - Divide by 2.
   - Add 3.

   a) Show inductively, using three examples, that the result is always 3 more than the chosen number.

   b) Prove deductively that the result is always 3 more than the chosen number.

8. Examine the following example of deductive reasoning. Why is it faulty?

   Given: Khaki pants are comfortable. Comfortable pants are expensive. Adrian's pants are not khaki pants.
   Deduction: Adrian's pants are not expensive.

9. Recall Jarrod's number trick from Lesson 1.3, page 24:
   - Choose a number.
   - Double it.
   - Add 6.
   - Double again.
   - Subtract 4.
   - Divide by 4.
   - Subtract 2.

   Prove that any number you choose will be the final result.

10. Prove that whenever you square an odd integer, the result is odd.

11. Cleo noticed that whenever she determined the difference between the squares of consecutive even numbers or the difference between the squares of consecutive odd numbers, the result was a multiple of 4. Show inductively that this pattern exists. Then prove deductively that it exists.

12. Create a number trick with five or more steps, similar to the number trick in question 9. Your number trick must always result in a final answer of 6. Prove that your number trick will always work.

13. Prove that any four-digit number is divisible by 2 when the last digit in the number is divisible by 2.

14. Prove that any two-digit or three-digit number is divisible by 5 when the last digit in the number is divisible by 5.

15. To determine if a number is divisible by 9, add all the digits of the number and determine if the sum is divisible by 9. If it is, then the number is divisible by 9. Prove that the divisibility rule for 9 works for all two-digit and three-digit numbers.

16. Look for a pattern when any odd number is squared and then divided by 4. Make a conjecture, and then prove your conjecture.

Closing

17. Simon made the following conjecture: When you add three consecutive numbers, your answer is always a multiple of 3. Joan, Garnet, and Jamie took turns presenting their work to prove Simon's conjecture. Which student had the strongest proof? Explain.

Joan's Work	Garnet's Work	Jamie's Work
$1 + 2 + 3 = 6$　$3 \cdot 2 = 6$ $2 + 3 + 4 = 9$　$3 \cdot 3 = 9$ $3 + 4 + 5 = 12$　$3 \cdot 4 = 12$ $4 + 5 + 6 = 15$　$3 \cdot 5 = 15$ $5 + 6 + 7 = 18$　$3 \cdot 6 = 18$ and so on … Simon's conjecture is valid.	$3 + 4 + 5$ The two outside numbers (3 and 5) add to give twice the middle number (4). All three numbers add to give 3 times the middle number. Simon's conjecture is valid.	Let the numbers be $n, n + 1,$ and $n + 2$. $n + n + 1 + n + 2 = 3n + 3$ $n + n + 1 + n + 2 = 3(n + 1)$ Simon's conjecture is valid.

Extending

18. The table below outlines one possible personal strategy for calculating the square of a number.

Step	Method	Example
1	Round the number down to the nearest multiple of 10.	37 is the number to be squared. Round down to 30.
2	Determine the difference between the original number and the rounded number. Add the difference to the original number.	$37 - 30 = 7$ $7 + 37 = 44$
3	Multiply the rounded number by the number from step 2.	$(30)(44) = 1320$
4	Add the square of the difference between the original number and the rounded number.	$1320 + 7^2 = 1369$

From the given example, determine deductively the general rule for x^2.

19. Prove that the expression $n^2 + n + 2$ will always generate an even number for every natural number, n.

20. Make a conjecture about the product of two consecutive natural numbers. Prove your conjecture.

FREQUENTLY ASKED *Questions*

Study | *Aid*

- See Lesson 1.1, Examples 1 to 4, and Lesson 1.4, Examples 1 to 5.
- Try Mid-Chapter Review Questions 1 to 3 and 9 to 12.

Q: What is the difference between inductive reasoning and deductive reasoning?

A: Inductive reasoning involves identifying patterns through examples to develop a conjecture, or a general statement. A set of examples, however, is not a proof. The examples can only support the conjecture. In comparison, deductive reasoning proves a general rule, which can then be applied to any specific case.

Inductive Reasoning	Deductive Reasoning
$1 + 2 = 3$ $4 + 5 = 9$ $-7 + (-6) = -13$ $128 + 129 = 257$ From the pattern shown in the examples, I think that the sum of two consecutive integers is always an odd number. But I can't be sure that my conjecture is valid in every case based on only this evidence.	I can represent two consecutive integers as x and $x + 1$. The sum of two consecutive integers can be expressed as $(x) + (x + 1)$. This expression can be simplified to $2x + 1$. Since $2x$ is an even number, then $2x + 1$ is an odd number. Since the conjecture has been proved, I know that it is valid for any two consecutive integers.

Study | *Aid*

- See Lesson 1.3, Examples 1 to 3.
- Try Mid-Chapter Review Questions 5 to 8.

Q: What is the purpose of finding counterexamples?

A: Counterexamples are examples that disprove a conjecture. Counterexamples may be used to revise the conjecture.

For example,
Conjecture: In November, daily temperatures in Hay River, Northwest Territories, do not exceed 10 °C.
Counterexample: On November 19, 2005, the maximum daily temperature was 11.8 °C.
Revised conjecture: In November, daily temperatures in Hay River, Northwest Territories, do not exceed 10 °C more than once every five years.

PRACTISING

Lesson 1.1

1. A medicine wheel consists of a cairn of stones surrounded by a circle of rocks, with lines of rocks extending from the centre to the circle. The Moose Mountain Medicine Wheel is a sacred site, created by First Nations peoples more than 2000 years ago. Its exact purpose is not known. Make a conjecture about the purpose or usage of the Medicine Wheel.

2. Evaluate the following squares.

67^2 667^2 6667^2 66667^2

What pattern do you notice? Make a conjecture about the 25th term in the pattern.

3. Part of Pascal's triangle is shown below. The column on the right represents the sums of the numbers in the rows of Pascal's triangle.

$$
\begin{array}{ccc}
1 & & 1 \\
1\ 1 & & 2 \\
1\ 2\ 1 & & 4 \\
1\ 3\ 3\ 1 & & 8 \\
1\ 4\ 6\ 4\ 1 & & 16 \\
1\ 5\ 10\ 10\ 5\ 1 & & 32 \\
1\ 6\ 15\ 20\ 15\ 6\ 1 & & 64 \\
\end{array}
$$

a) Based on the evidence in the column on the right, make a conjecture about the sum of the numbers in the 10th row.

b) Make a conjecture about the sum of any row.

Lesson 1.2

4. Glenda found a website that had a list of all the countries in the world. As she scanned the list, she made the conjecture that more of the names end with a vowel than a consonant. Gather evidence about Glenda's conjecture. How reasonable is her conjecture?

Lesson 1.3

5. Tony claims that the best hockey players in the world are from Canada. Find a counterexample to his claim.

6. Leanne says that if the diagonals of a quadrilateral bisect each other, then the quadrilateral is a rectangle. Do you agree or disagree? Explain.

7. Ned says that if you can find 10 or more examples that support a mathematical statement, then you can conclude that the statement is always true. Do you agree or disagree? Explain.

Lesson 1.4

8. Use inductive reasoning to make a conjecture about each number trick below. Then use deductive reasoning to prove your conjecture.
   a) Choose a number. Add 3. Multiply by 2. Add 4. Divide by 2. Subtract the number you started with. What is the result?
   b) Choose a number. Double it. Add 9. Add the number you started with. Divide by 3. Add 4. Subtract the number you started with. What is the result?

9. Prove that the sum of four consecutive natural numbers is always even.

10. Consider the following statement: The square of the sum of two positive integers is greater than the sum of the squares of the same two integers. Test this statement inductively with three examples, and then prove it deductively.

11. Prove that the difference between the square of any odd integer and the integer itself is always an even integer.

Proofs That Are Not Valid

YOU WILL NEED
- grid paper
- ruler
- scissors

EXPLORE...

- Consider the following statement: There are tthree errorss in this sentence. Is the statement valid?

GOAL

Identify errors in proofs.

INVESTIGATE *the Math*

Moh was working with tiles on grid paper. He used right triangles and right trapezoids.

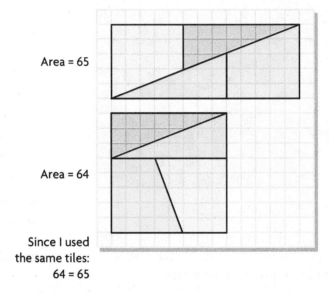

Area = 65

Area = 64

Since I used the same tiles:
64 = 65

❓ **How was it possible for 64 to equal 65?**

A. Construct, as precisely as possible, the square figure on grid paper.

B. Separate the square into its right triangles and right trapezoids.

C. Cut out the shapes. Then reconfigure the shapes to make the rectangle.

D. Determine the accuracy of the positions of the shapes by looking for overlap or empty space.

E. Does Moh's rearrangement of tiles prove that 64 equals 65? Explain.

Reflecting

F. What does any overlap or empty space suggest about the areas of the figures?

G. How do the colours make the rectangle and the square appear to have the same area?

H. Explain how you can check for errors in your constructions.

APPLY the Math

> **EXAMPLE 1**   Using reasoning to determine the validity of an argument

Athletes do not compete in both the Summer and Winter Olympics. Hayley Wickenheiser has represented Canada four times at the Winter Olympics. Therefore, Hayley Wickenheiser has not participated in the Summer Olympics.

Tia read these statements and knew that there was an error. Identify the error in the reasoning.

Hayley Wickenheiser has represented Canada four times at the Winter Olympics.

Tia's Solution

Athletes do not compete in both the Summer and Winter Olympics.

> I did some research and found that 18 athletes have competed in both Games. This statement is not valid.

Hayley Wickenheiser has represented Canada four times at the Winter Olympics.

> This statement is true. She has played on the national hockey team.

Therefore, Hayley Wickenheiser has not participated in the Summer Olympics.

> The conclusion was false because the first statement was false. Hayley played for Canada in the softball competition in the 2000 Summer Olympics.

Your Turn

Zack is a high school student. All high school students dislike cooking. Therefore, Zack dislikes cooking. Where is the error in the reasoning?

> **EXAMPLE 2**   Using reasoning to determine the validity of a proof

Bev claims he can prove that $3 = 4$.

Bev's Proof

Suppose that: $a + b = c$

This statement can be written as: $4a - 3a + 4b - 3b = 4c - 3c$

After reorganizing, it becomes: $4a + 4b - 4c = 3a + 3b - 3c$

Using the distributive property, $4(a + b - c) = 3(a + b - c)$

Dividing both sides by $(a + b - c)$, $4 = 3$

Show that Bev has written an   **invalid proof** .

Communication | Tip

Stereotypes are generalizations based on culture, gender, religion, or race. There are always counterexamples to stereotypes, so conclusions based on stereotypes are not valid.

---

invalid proof

A proof that contains an error in reasoning or that contains invalid assumptions.

Pru's Solution

Suppose that:
$$a + b = c$$ ✔

premise

A statement assumed to be true.

> Bev's **premise** was made at the beginning of the proof. Since variables can be used to represent any numbers, this part of the proof is valid.

$$4a - 3a + 4b - 3b = 4c - 3c$$ ✔

> Bev substituted $4a - 3a$ for a since $4a - 3a = a$.
> Bev substituted $4b - 3b$ for b since $4b - 3b = b$.
> Bev substituted $4c - 3c$ for c since $4c - 3c = c$.

$$4a + 4b - 4c = 3a + 3b - 3c$$ ✔

> I reorganized the equation and I came up with the same result that Bev did when he reorganized. Simplifying would take me back to the premise. This part of the proof is valid.

$$4(a + b - c) = 3(a + b - c)$$ ✔

> Since each side of the equation has the same coefficient for all the terms, factoring both sides is a valid step.

$$\frac{4(a + b - c)}{(a + b - c)} = \frac{3(a + b - c)}{(a + b - c)}$$

> This step appears to be valid, but when I looked at the divisor, I identified the flaw.

$$a + b = c$$
$$a + b - c = c - c$$
$$a + b - c = 0$$

> When I rearranged the premise, I determined that the divisor equalled zero.

Dividing both sides of the equation by $a + b - c$ is not valid. Division by zero is undefined.

Your Turn

How could this type of false proof be used to suggest that $65 = 64$?

EXAMPLE **3**

Using reasoning to determine the validity of a proof

Liz claims she has proved that $-5 = 5$.

Liz's Proof

I assumed that $-5 = 5$.

Then I squared both sides: $(-5)^2 = 5^2$

I got a true statement: $25 = 25$

This means that my assumption, $-5 = 5$, must be correct.

Where is the error in Liz's proof?

Simon's Solution

I assumed that $-5 = 5$. -----

> Liz started off with the false assumption that the two numbers were equal.

Then I squared both sides: $(-5)^2 = 5^2$
I got a true statement: $25 = 25$ -----

> Everything that comes after the false assumption doesn't matter because the reasoning is built on the false assumption.

> Even though $25 = 25$, the underlying premise is not true.

$-5 \neq 5$ -----

> Liz's conclusion is built on a false assumption, and the conclusion she reaches is the same as her assumption.

If an assumption is not true, ----- then any argument that was built on the assumption is not valid.

> **Circular reasoning** has resulted from these steps. Starting with an error and then ending by saying that the error has been proved is arguing in a circle.

circular reasoning
An argument that is incorrect because it makes use of the conclusion to be proved.

Your Turn

How is an error in a premise like a counterexample?

EXAMPLE **4**   Using reasoning to determine the validity of a proof

Hossai is trying to prove the following number trick:
Choose any number. Add 3. Double it. Add 4. Divide by 2. Take away the number you started with.

Each time Hossai tries the trick, she ends up with 5. Her proof, however, does not give the same result.

Hossai's Proof

n	Choose any number.
$n + 3$	Add 3.
$2n + 6$	Double it.
$2n + 10$	Add 4.
$2n + 5$	Divide by 2.
$n + 5$	Take away the number you started with.

Where is the error in Hossai's proof?

Sheri's Solution

$1 \longrightarrow 5$
$10 \longrightarrow 5$ .... I tried the number trick twice, for the number 1 and the number 10. Both times, I ended up with 5. The math trick worked for Hossai and for me, so the error must be in Hossai's proof.

n ✔ .... The variable n can represent any number. This step is valid.

$n + 3$ ✔ .... Adding 3 to n is correctly represented.

$2n + 6$ ✔ .... Doubling a quantity is multiplying by 2. This step is valid. Its simplification is correct as well.

$2n + 10$ ✔ .... Adding 4 to the expression is correctly represented, and the simplification is correct.

$2n + 5$ ✘ .... The entire expression should be divided by 2, not just the constant. This step is where the mistake occurred.

I corrected the mistake:

$$\frac{2n + 10}{2} = n + 5$$

$n + 5 - n = 5$ .... I completed Hossai's proof by subtracting n. I showed that the answer will be 5 for any number.

Your Turn

Is there a number that will not work in Hossai's number trick? Explain.

EXAMPLE **5**   Using reasoning to determine the validity of a proof

Jean says she can prove that $\$1 = 1¢$.

Jean's Proof

$\$1$ can be converted to 100¢.

100 can be expressed as $(10)^2$.

10 cents is one-tenth of a dollar.

$(0.1)^2 = 0.01$

One hundredth of a dollar is one cent, so $\$1 = 1¢$.

How can Jean's friend Grant show the error in her reasoning?

Grant's Solution

$\$1$ can be converted to 100¢. ✔ ┄┄┄┄┄┄┄┄┄ It is true that 100 cents is the same as $\$1$.

100 can be expressed as $(10)^2$. ✔ ┄┄┄┄┄┄┄┄┄ It is true that $(10)^2$ is $10 \cdot 10$, which is 100.

10 cents is one-tenth of a dollar. ✔ ┄┄┄┄┄┄┄┄┄ It is true that 10 dimes make up a dollar.

$(0.1)^2 = 0.01$ ✔ ┄┄┄┄┄┄┄┄┄ Arithmetically, I could see that this step was true. But Jean was ignoring the units. It doesn't make sense to square a dime. The units $¢^2$ and $\$^2$ have no meaning.

A dollar is equivalent to $(10)(\$0.10)$ or $10(10¢)$, not to $(10¢)(10¢)$ or $(\$0.10)(\$0.10)$.

$$\$1 \neq 1¢$$

Your Turn

Does Grant's explanation fully show the error in Jean's reasoning? Explain.

In Summary

Key Idea

- A single error in reasoning will break down the logical argument of a deductive proof. This will result in an invalid conclusion, or a conclusion that is not supported by the proof.

Need to Know

- Division by zero always creates an error in a proof, leading to an invalid conclusion.
- Circular reasoning must be avoided. Be careful not to assume a result that follows from what you are trying to prove.
- The reason you are writing a proof is so that others can read and understand it. After you write a proof, have someone else who has not seen your proof read it. If this person gets confused, your proof may need to be clarified.

Calories burned while running depend on mass, distance, and time. A runner of mass 70 kg who runs 15 km in 1 h will burn about 1000 Calories.

CHECK *Your Understanding*

1. Determine the error in each example of deductive reasoning.
   a) All runners train on a daily basis. Gabriel is a runner. Therefore, Gabriel trains daily.
   b) All squares have four right angles. Quadrilateral $PQRS$ has four right angles. Therefore, $PQRS$ is a square.

2. According to this proof, $5 = 7$. Identify the error.

   Proof
   $$1 = 1 + 1$$
   $$2(1) = 2(1 + 1)$$
   $$2(1) + 3 = 2(1 + 1) + 3$$
   $$2 + 3 = 4 + 3$$
   $$5 = 7$$

PRACTISING

3. Mickey says he can prove that $2 = 0$. Here is his proof.
   Let both a and b be equal to 1.

$a = b$	Transitive property
$a^2 = b^2$	Squaring both sides
$a^2 - b^2 = 0$	Subtracting b^2 from both sides
$(a - b)(a + b) = 0$	Factoring a difference of squares
$\dfrac{(a - b)(a + b)}{(a - b)} = \dfrac{0}{(a - b)}$	Dividing both sides by $a - b$
$1(a + b) = 0$	Simplifying
$a + b = 0$	
$1 + 1 = 0$	Substitution
$2 = 0$	

   Explain whether each statement in Mickey's proof is valid.

4. Noreen claims she has proved that $32.5 = 31.5$.

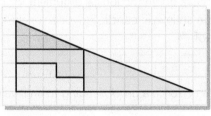

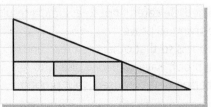

   Is Noreen's proof valid? Explain.

5. Ali created a math trick in which she always ended with 4. When Ali tried to prove her trick, however, it did not work.

Ali's Proof

n	I used n to represent any number.
$2n$	Multiply by 2.
$2n + 8$	Add 8.
$2n + 4$	Divide by 2.
$n + 4$	Subtract your starting number.

Identify the error in Ali's proof, and explain why her reasoning is incorrect.

6. Connie tried this number trick:
- Write down the number of your street address.
- Multiply by 2.
- Add the number of days in a week.
- Multiply by 50.
- Add your age.
- Subtract the number of days in a year.
- Add 15.

Connie's result was a number in which the tens and ones digits were her age and the rest of the digits were the number from her street address. She tried to prove why this works, but her final expression did not make sense.

Let n represent any house number.	
$2n$	Multiply by 2.
$2n + 7$	Add the number of days in a week.
$100n + 350$	Multiply by 50.
Let a represent any age.	
$100n + 350 + a$	Add your age.
$100n + 350 + a - 360$	Subtract the number of days in a year.
$100n + a + 5$	Add 15.

a) Try this number trick to see if you get the same result as Connie.
b) Determine the errors in her proof, and then correct them.
c) Explain why your final algebraic expression describes the result of this number trick.

7. According to this proof, $2 = 1$. Determine the error in reasoning.
Let $a = b$.

$$a^2 = ab \qquad \text{Multiply by } a.$$
$$a^2 + a^2 = a^2 + ab \qquad \text{Add } a^2.$$
$$2a^2 = a^2 + ab \qquad \text{Simplify.}$$
$$2a^2 - 2ab = a^2 + ab - 2ab \qquad \text{Subtract } 2ab.$$
$$2a^2 - 2ab = a^2 - ab \qquad \text{Simplify.}$$
$$2(a^2 - ab) = 1(a^2 - ab) \qquad \text{Factor.}$$
$$2 = 1 \qquad \text{Divide by } (a^2 - ab).$$

Closing

8. Discuss with a partner how false proofs can appear to be both reasonable and unreasonable at the same time. Summarize your discussion.

Extending

9. Brittney said she could prove that a strip of paper has only one side. She took a strip of paper, twisted it once, and taped the ends together. Then she handed her friend Amber a pencil, and asked Amber to start at any point and draw a line along the centre of the paper without lifting the pencil. Does a strip of paper have only one side? Why or why not?

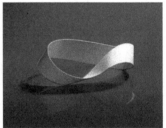

10. Brenda was asked to solve this problem:

Three people enjoyed a meal at a Thai restaurant. The waiter brought a bill for $30. Each person at the table paid $10.

Later the manager realized that the bill should have been for only $25, so she sent the waiter back to the table with $5.

The waiter could not figure out how to divide $5 three ways, so he gave each person $1 and kept $2 for himself.

Each of the three people paid $9 for the meal.

$9 \cdot 3 = 27$

The waiter kept $2.

$27 + 2 = 29$

What happened to the other dollar?

Does the question make sense? How should Brenda answer it?

Solve problems using inductive or deductive reasoning.

INVESTIGATE the Math

Emma was given this math trick:
• Choose a number.
• Multiply by 6.
• Add 4.
• Divide by 2.
• Subtract 2.

Emma was asked to use inductive reasoning to make a conjecture about the relationship between the starting and ending numbers, and then use deductive reasoning to prove that her conjecture is always true. Here is her response to the problem:

Inductive reasoning:

#	×6	+4	÷2	−2
5	30	34	17	15
−3	−18	−14	−7	−9
0	0	4	2	0
24	144	148	74	72

I followed the steps to work through four examples.

Conjecture: It is 3 times.

Deductive reasoning:
I chose d.
Then I multiplied, added, divided, and subtracted to get an expression.

$$\left(\frac{6d + 4}{2}\right) - 2$$

It worked.

It simplified to $3d$.

? How can Emma's communication about her reasoning be improved?

A. With a partner, explain why Emma might have chosen the values she did.

B. What details are missing from the deductive reasoning Emma used to arrive at the expression $3d$?

C. Improve Emma's conjecture, justifications, and explanations.

Reflecting

D. How does it help to understand the mathematics when both symbols and words are used in an explanation?

E. Why is it important to explain your reasoning clearly?

APPLY the Math

EXAMPLE 1   Using reasoning to solve a problem

The members of a recently selected varsity basketball team met each other at their first team meeting. Each person shook the hand of every other person. The team had 12 players and 2 coaches. How many handshakes were exchanged?

Kim's Solution

> I decided to think about how many times each person shook hands. There were 14 people in total, so person 1 shook hands with each of the other 13 people.

13 handshakes

> Person 2 had already shaken hands with person 1. Person 2 shook hands with each of the remaining 12 people.

13 + 12 handshakes

$$13 + 12 + 11 + 10 + 9 + 8 + 7 + 6 + 5 + 4 + 3 + 2 + 1$$
$$= 91 \text{ handshakes}$$

> This pattern of handshakes continued until there were two people left when the last handshake happened.

Your Turn

Discuss, with a partner, whether Kim used inductive or deductive thinking in her solution. How do you know?

EXAMPLE **2**   Using reasoning to solve a problem

Sue signed up for games at her school's fun night. Seven other people were assigned to her group, making up four pairs of partners. The other members of her group were Dave, Angie, Josh, Tanya, Joy, Stu, and Linus. When the games started, Dave and his partner were to the left of Stu. Across from Dave was Sue, who was to the right of Josh. Dave's brother's partner, Tanya, was across from Stu. Joy was not on Stu's right.

Name the four pairs of partners.

Vicky's Solution

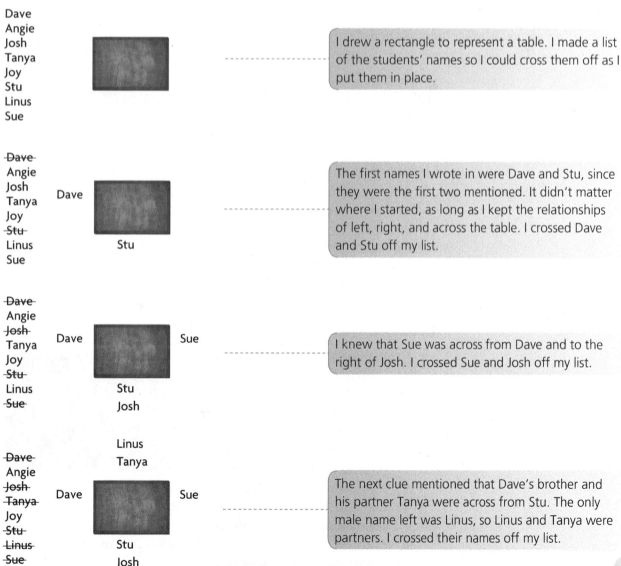

Dave
Angie
Josh
Tanya
Joy
Stu
Linus
Sue

I drew a rectangle to represent a table. I made a list of the students' names so I could cross them off as I put them in place.

~~Dave~~
Angie
Josh   Dave
Tanya
Joy
~~Stu~~
Linus   Stu
Sue

The first names I wrote in were Dave and Stu, since they were the first two mentioned. It didn't matter where I started, as long as I kept the relationships of left, right, and across the table. I crossed Dave and Stu off my list.

~~Dave~~
Angie
~~Josh~~   Dave   Sue
Tanya
Joy
~~Stu~~
Linus   Stu
~~Sue~~   Josh

I knew that Sue was across from Dave and to the right of Josh. I crossed Sue and Josh off my list.

                    Linus
                    Tanya
~~Dave~~
Angie
~~Josh~~   Dave   Sue
~~Tanya~~
Joy
~~Stu~~
~~Linus~~   Stu
~~Sue~~   Josh

The next clue mentioned that Dave's brother and his partner Tanya were across from Stu. The only male name left was Linus, so Linus and Tanya were partners. I crossed their names off my list.

Linus
Tanya

~~Dave~~
~~Angie~~
~~Josh~~
~~Tanya~~
~~Joy~~
~~Stu~~
~~Linus~~
~~Sue~~

Dave
Joy

Sue
Angie

> If Joy was not on Stu's right, then she must have been on his left. Therefore, she must have been Dave's partner. So, the last person to match was Angie with Sue.

Stu
Josh

The four pairs of partners were Linus and Tanya, Dave and Joy, Sue and Angie, and Stu and Josh.

> The partners sat together, on the same side of the table.

Your Turn

Discuss with a partner whether inductive or deductive reasoning was used for this solution. How do you know?

In Summary

Key Idea

- Inductive and deductive reasoning are useful in problem solving.

Need to Know

- Inductive reasoning involves solving a simpler problem, observing patterns, and drawing a logical conclusion from your observations to solve the original problem.
- Deductive reasoning involves using known facts or assumptions to develop an argument, which is then used to draw a logical conclusion and solve the problem.

CHECK Your Understanding

1. Explain which type of reasoning is demonstrated by each statement.
   a) Over the past 12 years, a tree has produced plums every other year. Last year, the tree did not produce plums. Therefore, the tree will produce plums this year.
   b) Mammals have hair. Dogs are mammals. Therefore, dogs have hair.
   c) Every Thursday, a train arrives at 2:30 p.m. Today is Thursday, so the train will arrive at 2:30 p.m.
   d) Every even number has a factor of 2. 24 is an even number. Therefore, 24 has a factor of 2.
   e) For the pattern 3, 12, 21, 30, 39, the next term is 48.

2. Copy this diagram. Place the digits 1 through 9 in the circles so that the sum of the numbers on the outside triangle is double the sum of the numbers on the inside triangle. Explain whether more than one solution is possible.

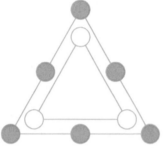

PRACTISING

3. Draw the next figure in this sequence.

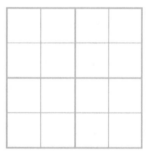

Figure 1   Figure 2   Figure 3

4. a) Substitute numbers for the letters to create an addition problem with a correct answer.
b) How many solutions are possible?

$$\begin{array}{r} y \\ xxx \\ xxx \\ xxx \\ + \; xxx \\ \hline yxxx \end{array}$$

5. a) Choose four different colours. Fill in the cells in a copy of this chart, so that each row and column has four different colours and each quadrant also has four different colours.

b) Compare your strategy with a classmate's strategy. How are your strategies the same? How are they different?

6. A farmer wants to get a goat, a wolf, and a bale of hay to the other side of a river. His boat is not very big, so it can only carry him and one other thing. If the farmer leaves the goat alone with the bale of hay, the goat will eat the hay. If he leaves the wolf alone with the goat, the wolf will eat the goat. When the farmer is present, the goat and the hay are safe from being eaten. How does the farmer manage to get everything safely to the other side of the river?

7. Determine the unknown term in this pattern: 17, 22, ___, 35, 43. Explain your reasoning.

8. Suppose that you are marooned on an island where there are only liars and truth-tellers. Liars always tell lies, and truth-tellers always tell the truth. You meet two siblings. The brother says, "My sister told me that she is a liar." Is he a liar or a truth-teller? Explain how you know.

Goats have the reputation that they will eat almost anything. In fact, they will taste just about anything, but they are picky about what they eat. They do eat hay.

9. Bob, Kurt, and Morty are football players. One is a quarterback, one is a receiver, and one is a kicker. The kicker, who is the shortest of the three, is not married. Bob, who is Kurt's father-in-law, is taller than the receiver. Who plays which position?

10. A set of 10 cards, each showing one of the digits from 0 to 9, is divided between five envelopes so that there are two cards in each envelope. The sum of the cards inside each envelope is written on the envelope:

   A sum of 8 could be made by these pairs of cards: (8, 0), (7, 1), (6, 2), and (5, 3).
   a) Explain which of these pairs of cards cannot possibly be in the envelope marked 8.
   b) Describe the reasoning you used to solve this problem.

11. Solve the multiplication problem below. Each letter represents a different digit, and the product is correct.
   $abcd \cdot 4 = dcba$

12. At lunchtime, a soccer team meets in the school cafeteria to help organize a tournament. There are 18 players and 2 coaches at the meeting. The tables in the cafeteria are rectangular. Two people can sit on each of the long sides, and one person can sit at each end.
   a) What arrangement of tables would enable the team members to sit as close to each other as possible, so that everyone can be heard?
   b) Compare your solution with other students' solutions. As a group, decide which is the best solution for the team.

13. Early in a bicycle race, Tamara led Kateri by 3 km, while Justine was behind Shreya by 2 km. Shreya was ahead of Kateri by 1 km. By the halfway point, Tamara and Shreya had exchanged places, but they were still the same distance apart. Justine had pulled even with Tamara. Over the last part of the race, Justine dropped 1 km behind Tamara, and Kateri passed Shreya; there were no other changes of position. Who finished third?

14. Use inductive reasoning to determine the number of diagonals that can be drawn in a decagon (a polygon with 10 sides).

Competitors in the Eco-Challenge race 500 km through the mountains of British Columbia.

15. Max, Karl, Terri, and Suganthy live on the first floor of an apartment building. One is a manager, one is a computer programmer, one is a singer, and one is a teacher.

    a) Use the statements below to determine which person is the manager.

- Suganthy and Terri eat lunch with the singer.
- Karl and Max carpool with the manager.
- Terri watches football on television with the manager and the singer.

    b) Describe the reasoning you used to solve this problem.

16. There are six pails in a row. The first three pails are filled with water. How can you move only one pail to make the following pattern: full pail, empty pail, full pail, empty pail, full pail, empty pail?

Closing

17. How do you recognize a problem that can be solved using inductive reasoning? How do you recognize a problem that can be solved using deductive reasoning? Is it always possible to tell which kind of reasoning is needed to solve a problem? Explain.

Extending

18. During Sid's vacation, it rained on five days. However, when it rained in the morning, the afternoon was sunny, and every rainy afternoon was preceded by a sunny morning. There were six sunny mornings and nine sunny afternoons. How long was Sid's vacation?

19. Two girls, Arlene and Cathy, and two boys, Leander and Dean, are athletes. One is a long distance runner, one is a softball player, one is a hockey player, and one is a golfer. At lunchtime, they sit around a square table, usually in the same places.

- The runner sits on Arlene's left.
- The hockey player sits across from Leander.
- Cathy and Dean sit next to each other.
- A girl sits on the softball player's left.

Who is the golfer?

20. The labels have been placed on the wrong boxes. You may select one fruit from one box, but you may not look in the box. Based on the fruit you have selected, how can you immediately label all the boxes correctly?

Analyzing Puzzles and Games

YOU WILL NEED
- counters or coins

GOAL

Determine, explain, and verify a reasoning strategy to solve a puzzle or to win a game.

INVESTIGATE the Math

EXPLORE...

- Three students are playing a game. Two of the students flip a coin, and the third student records their scores. Student 1 gets a point if the result is two heads, student 2 gets a point if the result is two tails, and student 3 gets a point if the result is a head and a tail. The first student to get 10 points wins. Explain whether you would prefer to be student 1, student 2, or student 3.

To solve a leapfrog puzzle, coloured counters are moved along a space on a board. The goal is to move each set of coloured counters to the opposite side of the board.

Board at start

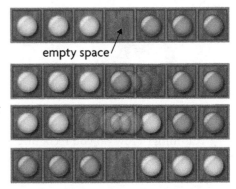

empty space

A counter can move into the empty space.

A counter can leapfrog over another counter into the empty space.

Board at end

? What is the minimum number of moves needed to switch five counters of each colour?

A. Develop a group strategy to switch the blue and red counters using as few moves as possible.

B. Execute your strategy, counting each move you make.

C. How many moves did you need to complete the switch?

Reflecting

D. How did you know that you had completed the switch in the fewest number of moves?

E. Did you use inductive or deductive reasoning to solve the puzzle? Explain.

F. Predict the minimum number of moves needed to solve the puzzle if you had six counters of each colour. Explain how you made your prediction.

G. Did you use inductive or deductive reasoning in step F? Explain.

APPLY the Math

EXAMPLE 1 **Using reasoning to determine possible winning plays**

Frank and Tara are playing darts, using the given rules. Their scores are shown in the table below. To win, Frank must reduce his score to exactly zero and have his last counting dart be a double.

Rules
- Each player's score starts at 501.
- The goal is to reduce your score to zero.
- Players alternate turns.
- Each player throws three darts per turn.

Frank		Tara	
Turn Score	Total Score	Turn Score	Total Score
	501		501
100	401	85	416
95	306	85	331
140	166	140	191
130	36	91	100

dart in this ring scores triple points
dart in this ring scores double points
dart in outer bull scores 25 points
dart in inner bull scores 50 points (the inner bull also counts as a double)

double score 40 points
score 20 points
triple score 15 points
Total score for turn: 75 points

What strategies for plays would give Frank a winning turn?

Frank's Solution

$2(18) = 36$ ⎯⎯⎯⎯⎯⎯⎯ I could win with a single dart in double 18.

$18 + 2(9) = 36$ ⎯⎯⎯⎯⎯⎯⎯ If I hit 18 instead of double 18, then I could use my second dart to try for double 9.

$18 + 9 = 27$ ⎯⎯⎯⎯⎯⎯⎯ If I hit 9 instead of double 9 with my second dart,
9 would be left. then I couldn't win this turn. That's because I can't score 9 with a double.

Your Turn

a) Describe two other ways that Frank could win the game on his turn.

b) If Frank does not win on his turn, describe a strategy that Tara could use to win on her next turn.

Nadine and Alice are playing a toothpick game. They place a pile of 20 toothpicks on a desk and alternate turns. On each turn, the player can take one or two toothpicks from the pile. The player to remove the last toothpick is the winner. Nadine and Alice flip a coin to determine the starting player.

Is there a strategy Alice can use to ensure that she wins the game?

Alice's Solution

I need to make sure that there are one or two toothpicks left after Nadine's last turn.

> I will win the game if I can take the last toothpick. If I work backward, I might see a pattern I can use to win.

To make sure this happens, I have to leave three toothpicks on the desk for Nadine.

> If I leave three toothpicks, Nadine has to take either one or two toothpicks. If she takes only one, I can take the two that are left and win. If she takes two, I can take the last one and win.

To make sure this happens, I have to leave six toothpicks on the desk for Nadine.

> If I leave six toothpicks, Nadine has to take either one or two toothpicks. If she takes only one, I can take two, which would leave three. If she takes two, I can take one and leave her with three.

To make sure this happens, I have to leave nine toothpicks on the desk for Nadine.

> If I leave nine toothpicks, Nadine has to take either one or two toothpicks. If she takes only one, then I can take two, which would leave six. If she takes two, I can take one and leave her with six.

I can see that I need to leave 12, 15, and 18 toothpicks for Nadine.

> There is a pattern to the number of toothpicks I must leave for Nadine: 3, 6, 9, 12, 15, 18.

I will win if I go first and take two toothpicks. Each turn after that, I need to pick one or two so that I leave Nadine with a number of toothpicks that is a multiple of 3.

> If Nadine goes first and knows this strategy, I can't win. If she goes first and doesn't know this strategy, however, I can win by arranging to leave her a number of toothpicks that is a multiple of 3.

Your Turn

a) Which part of Alice's strategy involved deductive reasoning? Explain.

b) Which part of Alice's strategy involved inductive reasoning? Explain.

Key Idea

- Both inductive reasoning and deductive reasoning are useful for determining a strategy to solve a puzzle or win a game.

Need to Know

- Inductive reasoning is useful when analyzing games and puzzles that require recognizing patterns or creating a particular order.
- Deductive reasoning is useful when analyzing games and puzzles that require inquiry and discovery to complete.

CHECK Your Understanding

1. In the leapfrog puzzle, what would be the minimum number of moves needed to exchange 10 red counters with 10 blue counters? Explain how you know.

2. Frank and Tara are playing another game of darts. Tara's game score is 66. List three different strategies she could use to win on her turn.

3. In the toothpick game, suppose that players are allowed to take one, two, or three toothpicks. Determine a strategy you could use to ensure that you win if you do not have the first turn.

PRACTISING

4. Rearrange three golf balls so that the arrowhead points down instead of up.

5. a) Draw a diagram like the one to the right. Place the numbers 1 through 9 in the circles so that the sum of the numbers on each side of the triangle is 17.
   b) Explain the strategy you used.

6. Examine this square. It has a magic sum.
   a) Describe the patterns you see.
   b) Selva noticed that when he added three numbers that were not in the same row or column, the sum was 36 (the magic sum). This number is 3 times the number in the middle square. Create your own magic square using the patterns you identified. Do Selva's observations hold in your square?
   c) Prove algebraically that Selva's observations hold in any square that is created using these patterns.

5	9	13
8	12	16
11	15	19

7. Place the numbers 1 to 5 in a V shape, as shown, so that the two arms of the V have the same total.

   a) How many different solutions are there?

   b) What do you notice about all the solutions you found?

   c) How could you convince someone that you have identified all the possible solutions?

8. Draw a 4-by-4 grid that is large enough to place a coin in any square. Your opponent in this game has seven paper clips. Each paper clip is large enough to cover two squares when placed horizontally or vertically. You need to place a coin on each of any two squares so that your opponent is unable to cover the remaining squares with the seven paper clips. Determine a strategy to ensure that you will always win.

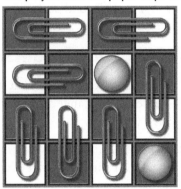

The player with the paper clips wins.

9. Who started this game of tic-tac-toe: player X or player O? Explain. Assume that both players are experienced at playing tic-tac-toe.

10. Sudoku requires both inductive and deductive reasoning skills. The numbers that are used to complete a Sudoku puzzle relate to the size of the grid. For a 6-by-6 grid, the numbers 1 to 6 are used. For a 9-by-9 grid, the numbers 1 to 9 are used. The grid must be filled so that each column, row, or block contains all the numbers. No number can be repeated within any column, row, or block. Solve each of the Sudoku puzzles below.

a)

5			2	6	
		4			
1					6
			1	5	
	3			2	1
			6		

b)

6			4	8	2			
						1	4	
					6		3	5
					1		4	
8	9	2						1
		1	3	2	9			
4				5				6
5						9	3	

11. Fill in the missing numbers, from 1 to 9, so that the sum of the numbers in each row, column, and diagonal is 15.

a)

		6
		1
4	3	8

b)

		4
	5	3
		8

12. How many ways can the mouse navigate the maze to reach the trail mix, if the mouse can only travel down?

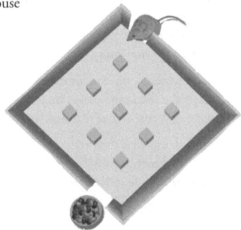

13. KenKen, like Sudoku, requires both inductive and deductive reasoning skills. Solve this 6 × 6 KenKen puzzle using only the numbers 1 to 6. Do not repeat a number in any row or column. The darkly outlined sets of squares are cages. The numbers in each cage must combine in any order to produce the target number, using the operation shown. For example, the target in the top left cage is 30 ×, which means 30 by multiplication. The two numbers in the cage must be 5 and 6, because no other combination of two factors (from 1 to 6) gives a product of 30. A number may be repeated in a cage as long as it is not in the same row or column.

30 ×		36 ×	2 ÷		18 +
3 +			7 +		
	20 ×		5 −		
1 −	2 −			13 +	
	7 +		2 −		
2 ÷			3 −		

Closing

14. Explain how inductive and deductive reasoning can help you develop a strategy to play a game or to solve a puzzle.

Extending

15. a) Suppose that the goal for tic-tac-toe is changed, so that you have to force your opponent to place three markers in a row, column, or diagonal in order to win. How would your strategy change?

b) What role does inductive and deductive reasoning play in helping you develop your new strategy?

Figure 1

Figure 2

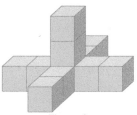

Figure 3

1. Danielle made the cube structures to the left.

  a) What would the 4th and 5th structures look like? How many cubes would Danielle need to build each of these structures?

  b) Make a conjecture about the relationship between the *n*th structure and the number of cubes needed to build it.

  c) How many cubes would be needed to build the 25th structure? Explain how you know.

2. Frank tosses a coin five times, and each time it comes up tails. He makes the following conjecture: The coin will come up tails on every toss. Is his conjecture reasonable? Explain.

3. Koby claims that the perimeter of a pentagon with natural number dimensions will always be an odd number. Search for a counterexample to his claim.

4. Prove that the product of two consecutive odd integers is always odd.

5. Prove that the following number trick always results in 10: Choose a natural number. Double it. Add 20. Divide by 2. Subtract the original number.

6. Andy, Bonnie, Candice, and Darlene are standing in line to buy ice cream. Determine the order in which they are lined up, using these clues:
- Candice is between Andy and Bonnie.
- Darlene is next to Andy.
- Bonnie is not first.

7. The following proof seems to show that $10 = 9.\overline{9}$. Is this proof valid? Explain.

Let $a = 9.\overline{9}$.

$$10a = 99.\overline{9} \qquad \text{Multiply by 10.}$$

$$10a - a = 90 \qquad \text{Subtract } a.$$

$$9a = 90 \qquad \text{Simplify.}$$

$$a = 10 \qquad \text{Divide by 9.}$$

WHAT DO You Think Now? Revisit **What Do You Think?** on page 5. How have your answers and explanations changed?

FREQUENTLY ASKED *Questions*

Q: **Why is it important to check carefully any proof you develop and the associated reasoning you used?**

A: If you have made a statement using flawed reasoning, you can end up with a conclusion that does not make sense. For example:
All pitbulls are ferocious dogs.
Jake is a pitbull.
Jake is a ferocious dog.

In this example, the premise is faulty. Pitbulls are known to be a ferocious breed, but we cannot be certain that every pitbull in the world is a ferocious dog. This leads to the invalid conclusion that Jake is ferocious.

Q: **What can deductive reasoning and inductive reasoning be used for?**

A1: Inductive reasoning can help you make conjectures. You can look for patterns in several examples or cases. The patterns you observe in specific cases can be generalized to a statement that includes all cases. This forms the basis for a conjecture. Deductive reasoning gives you the ability to prove that your conjecture is valid for every possible case.

For example, when you examine the sum of three consecutive natural numbers, you can see a pattern.
$1 + 2 + 3 = 6$
$2 + 3 + 4 = 9$
$3 + 4 + 5 = 12$
$4 + 5 + 6 = 15$

Each sum is a multiple of 3. Based on this pattern, you can make the following conjecture: The sum of three consecutive natural numbers is divisible by 3. You can then use deductive reasoning to prove your conjecture.

$x, x + 1, x + 2$	Let x, $x + 1$, and $x + 2$ represent three consecutive natural numbers.
$x + x + 1 + x + 2$	Write an expression for the sum.
$3x + 3$	Collect like terms.
$3(x + 1)$	Factor.
$3(x + 1)$ is divisible by 3.	Since 3 is a factor of the expression, the expression will always be divisible by 3.

> **Study** *Aid*
> • See Lesson 1.5, Examples 1 and 2.
> • Try Chapter Review Questions 11 and 12.

Study **Aid**
- See Lesson 1.6, Examples 1 and 2, and Lesson 1.7, Examples 1 and 2.
- Try Chapter Review, Questions 12 to 15.

A2: Inductive and deductive reasoning are useful strategies for solving problems, some types of puzzles, and some types of games.

Word puzzle: Identify a five-letter word correctly in five or fewer attempts. After each attempt, the person who knows the word will show you the correct letters in the correct positions in yellow, the correct letters in the wrong positions in red, and the incorrect letters with no colour.

	Response
My first guess is RENTS, since it has letters that are often used in English words.	**R**ENTS
I know that S is in the correct position. R is in the word but in a different position. E, N, and T are not in the word. The letter R is often used after the letters C, D, F, G, and P, so that could put R in the second position. I chose DRAWS as my next guess, because A is the next most common vowel.	DRAWS
I know that the vowel has to be I, O, or U. I also know that the consonants D, R, and W are in the word, but in the wrong positions in DRAWS. From my guesses, I think that R goes in the third position since I can't think of a word that would have either _WDRS or _DWRS. Also, from the patterns of letters, I think the R and D go together. That would make the unknown word to be W_RDS. The only vowel that would fit is O. My guess is WORDS.	WORDS

Problem: Make five lines of counters, with four counters in each line, using only 10 counters.

Since an array of (5)(4) counters would require 20 counters, I deduce that most counters must be part of more than one line. This means that the lines must overlap.

I can also deduce that the lines need to overlap more than once since there are only 10 counters available. Lines of four counters could overlap at any counter.

PRACTISING

Lesson 1.1

1. Charles studied the diagonals of the parallelograms below to look for patterns. Make a conjecture about the diagonals of parallelograms. What evidence supports your conjecture?

2. Consider the following sequence of triangular numbers:

1   3   6   10

   a) Describe the pattern, and use it to determine the next four triangular numbers.
   b) Consider the products $1 \cdot 2$, $2 \cdot 3$, $3 \cdot 4$, $4 \cdot 5$. Explain how these products are related to each triangular number.
   c) Make a conjecture about a formula you could use to determine the nth triangular number.

3. Examine the following number pattern:

   $1^3 = 1$ and $1 = 1^2$
   $1^3 + 2^3 = 9$ and $9 = 3^2$
   $1^3 + 2^3 + 3^3 = 36$ and $36 = 6^2$
   $1^3 + 2^3 + 3^3 + 4^3 = 100$ and $100 = 10^2$
   a) Describe the pattern you see.
   b) Use your observations to predict the next equation in the pattern.
   c) Make a conjecture about the sum of the first n cubes.

Lesson 1.2

4. a) Examine this pattern to determine the next equation:
   $37 \times 3 = 111$
   $37 \times 6 = 222$
   $37 \times 9 = 333$
   $37 \times 12 = 444$

   b) Is your conjecture correct? Explain how you know.
   c) This pattern eventually breaks down. Determine when the breakdown occurs.

Lesson 1.3

5. a) What is a counterexample?
   b) Explain why counterexamples are useful.

6. Harry claims that if opposite sides of a quadrilateral are the same length, the quadrilateral is a rectangle. Do you agree or disagree? Justify your decision.

7. Sadie claims that the difference between any two positive integers is always a positive integer. Do you agree or disagree? Justify your decision.

Lesson 1.4

8. Complete the conclusion for the following deductive argument: If an integer is an even number, then its square is also even. Six is an even number, therefore, ….

9. Prove that the product of two odd integers is always odd.

10. Linda came across this number trick on the Internet and tried it:
   - Think about the date of your birthday.
   - Multiply the number for the month of your birthday by 5. (For example, the number for November is 11.)
   - Add 7.
   - Multiply by 4.
   - Add 13.
   - Multiply by 5.
   - Add the day of your birthday.
   - Subtract 205.
   - Write your answer.
   a) Try the trick. What did you discover?
   b) Prove how this trick works. Let m represent the number for the month of your birthday and d represent the day.

11. Examine the relationships below.
$$2(3^2 + 5^2) = 2^2 + 8^2$$
$$2(2^2 + 3^2) = 1^2 + 5^2$$
$$2(7^2 + 4^2) = 3^2 + 11^2$$
a) Describe the patterns you see.
b) Jen makes the following conjecture: If you double the sum of two squares, the product is always the sum of two squares. Prove Jen's conjecture.

Lesson 1.5

12. The following proof seems to show that $2 = 1$. Examine this proof, and determine where the error in reasoning occurred.

Let $a = b$.

$a^2 = ab$	Multiply by a.
$a^2 - b^2 = ab - b^2$	Subtract b^2.
$(a - b)(a + b) = b(a - b)$	Factor.
$a + b = b$	Divide by $(a - b)$.
$b + b = b$	$a = b$
$2b = b$	Simplify.
$2 = 1$	Divide by b.

13. Julie was trying to prove that a number trick always results in 5:

Julie's Proof

n	Choose a number.
$n + 10$	Add 10.
$5n + 10$	Multiply the total by 5.
$5n - 40$	Subtract 50.
$\dfrac{5n - 40}{n}$	Divide by the number you started with.

Identify the error in Julie's proof, and correct it.

Lesson 1.6

14. Two mothers and two daughters got off a city bus, reducing the number of passengers by three. Explain how this is possible.

15. The three little pigs built three houses: one of straw, one of sticks, and one of bricks. By reading the six clues, deduce which pig built each house, the size of each house, and the town in which each house was located.

Clues
- Penny Pig did not build a brick house.
- The straw house was not medium in size.
- Peter Pig's house was made of sticks, and it was neither medium nor small in size.
- Patricia Pig built her house in Pleasantville.
- The house in Hillsdale was large.
- One house was in a town called Riverview.

Lesson 1.7

16. If you are playing next in this game of tic-tac-toe, you can use a strategy that guarantees you will win the game. Explain what this strategy is.

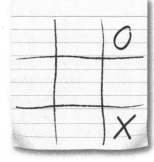

17. The rules for the game of 15 are given below:

- The cards are placed on a table between two players.
- Players take turns choosing a card (any card they like).
- The winner is the first player to have three cards that add to 15.
  For example, if you drew 1, 5, 6 and 8, then you would win, because $1 + 6 + 8 = 15$.
a) Is it possible to win the game in three moves?
b) Devise a winning strategy. Explain your strategy.

How Many Sisters and Brothers?

Rob, Yu, and Wynn challenged each other to create a number trick that ended with the number of siblings they have. Their number tricks are given below.

Rob's Number Trick

- Choose a number.
- Add 3.
- Multiply by 2.
- Subtract 2.
- Multiply by 5.
- Divide by 10.
- Add 3.
- Subtract the starting number.

Wynn's Number Trick

- Choose a number.
- Multiply by 4.
- Add 8.
- Divide by 4.
- Subtract the starting number.

Yu's Number Trick

- Choose a number.
- Subtract 2.
- Multiply by 0.
- Divide by 5.

?   What would your number trick be?

A. Create a number trick that always ends with the number of siblings you have. Use at least three different operations and at least four steps. Test your number trick to make sure that it works.

B. Trade number tricks with a classmate, and test your classmate's trick at least three times.

C. Make a conjecture about the number of siblings your classmate has.

D. Use deductive reasoning to develop a proof of your conjecture.

E. Is there a number that will not work in your number trick? Explain.

Task | *Checklist*

✔ Are the steps in your number trick clear?

✔ Did your conjecture correctly predict the result of your classmate's trick?

✔ Are the statements in your proof valid and clear?

✔ Did you provide your reasoning?

Creating an Action Plan

Deadlines are part of life. Completing projects on time is just as important in the workplace as it is in school. So, how can you avoid having to rush through all the stages of your research project at the last minute? One way is to use a strategy called backward planning: develop a formal action plan, and create a timeline based on this action plan.

A major research project must successfully pass through several stages. On the next page is an outline for an action plan, with a list of these stages. Completing this action plan will help you organize your time and give you goals and deadlines you can manage. The times that are suggested for each stage are only a guide, with one day equivalent to any regular day in your life. Adjust the time you will spend on each stage to match the scope of your project. For example, a project based on primary data (data that you collect) will usually require more time than a project based on secondary data (data that other people have collected and published). You will also need to consider your personal situation—the issues that are affecting you and may interfere with completion of the project.

Issues Affecting Project Completion

Consider the issues that may interfere with completion of the project in a time-efficient manner. For example:

- part-time job
- after-school sports and activities
- regular homework
- assignments for other courses
- tests in other courses
- driving school
- time you spend with friends
- school dances and parties
- family commitments
- access to research sources and technology

What other issues can you add to this list?

Your Turn

A. Take some time to complete an action plan for your project. Start by deciding on the probable length of time for each stage. Do not forget to include buffer space in your action plan. Buffer space is not a stage, but it is important. If something goes wrong (for example, if you are unable to gather appropriate data for your topic and must select a new topic), having that buffer space in your action plan may allow you to finish your project on time, without making extraordinary efforts.

1. Select the topic you would like to explore.
Suggested time: 1 to 3 days
Your probable time:
Finish date:

2. Create the research question that you would like to answer.
Suggested time: 1 to 3 days
Your probable time:
Finish date:

3. Collect the data.
Suggested time: 5 to 10 days
Your probable time:
Finish date:

Buffer space
Suggested time: 3 to 7 days
Your probable time:
Finish date:

4. Analyze the data.
Suggested time: 5 to 10 days
Your probable time:
Finish date:

5. Create an outline for your presentation.
Suggested time: 2 to 4 days
Your probable time:
Finish date:

6. Prepare a first draft.
Suggested time: 3 to 10 days
Your probable time:
Finish date:

7. Revise, edit, and proofread.
Suggested time: 3 to 5 days
Your probable time:
Finish date:

8. Prepare and practise your presentation.
Suggested time: 3 to 5 days
Your probable time:
Finish date:

B. Use a calendar and your probable times for each stage to work backwards from the presentation date to create a schedule you can follow. This will ensure that you will be able to complete all the stages of your project in the time available. In your schedule, include regular conferences with your teacher—5 to 10 min to discuss your progress.

Properties of Angles and Triangles

▶ LEARNING GOALS

You will be able to develop your spatial sense by

- Proving properties of angles formed by intersecting lines
- Proving properties of angles in triangles and other polygons
- Proving pairs of triangles congruent
- Using proven properties to solve geometric problems

❓ The Museum of Anthropology at the University of British Columbia houses approximately 6000 archaeological objects from British Columbia's First Nations. Arthur Erickson, a Vancouver-born architect, designed this world-renowned museum. How did he use geometry to enhance his design?

Getting Started

Geometric Art

Fawntana used polygons to represent a dog as a mosaic for her art class.

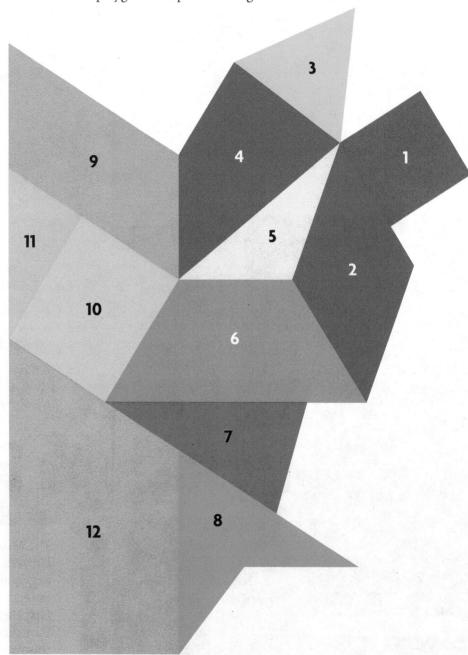

? What rules can you use to sort these polygons?

A. With a partner, sort the polygons in Fawntana's art.

B. Compare your sorting with the sortings of other students, and discuss the rules used for each.

C. Record your sorting in a table like the one below, including the following polygons: quadrilateral, trapezoid, parallelogram, rhombus, rectangle, square, triangle, scalene triangle, isosceles triangle, equilateral triangle, acute triangle, obtuse triangle, and right triangle.

Polygon	Properties	Polygon in Mosaic
quadrilateral	has four sides	1, 2, 4, 6, 8, 9, 10, 12
trapezoid	has one pair of parallel sides	

D. Create your own mosaic, using at least four different polygons. Classify the polygons you used, and explain your classification.

WHAT DO You Think?

Decide whether you agree or disagree with each statement. Explain your decision.

1. There is a specific relationship between parallel lines and the angles formed by these lines and other lines that intersect them.

2. The sum of the measures of the interior angles of a triangle is 180°, so the sum of the measures of the **exterior angles** around a triangle is also 180°.

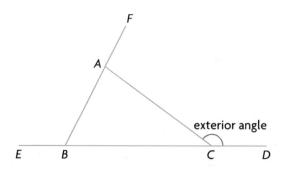

exterior angle of a polygon

The angle that is formed by a side of a polygon and the extension of an adjacent side.

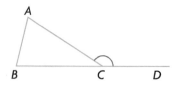

∠ACD is an exterior angle of △ABC.

Exploring Parallel Lines

GOAL

Identify relationships among the measures of angles formed
by intersecting lines.

EXPLORE *the Math*

A sports equipment manufacturer builds portable basketball systems, like
those shown here. These systems can be adjusted to different heights.

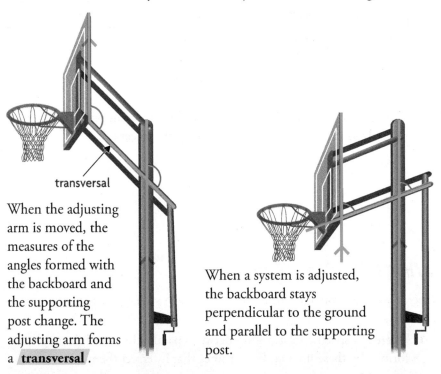

transversal

When the adjusting
arm is moved, the
measures of the
angles formed with
the backboard and
the supporting
post change. The
adjusting arm forms
a **transversal**.

When a system is adjusted,
the backboard stays
perpendicular to the ground
and parallel to the supporting
post.

transversal

A line that intersects two or more
other lines at distinct points.

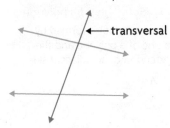

transversal

❓ When a transversal intersects two parallel lines, how are the
angle measures related?

Reflecting

A. Use the relationships you observed to predict
the measures of as many of the angles *a* to *g* in
this diagram as you can. Explain each of your
predictions.

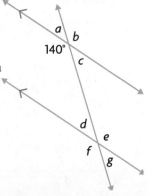

B. Jonathan made the following conjecture: "When a transversal intersects two parallel lines, the **corresponding angles** are always equal." Do you agree or disagree? Explain, using examples.

C. Did you discover any counterexamples for Jonathan's conjecture? What does this imply?

D. Sarah says that the **converse** of Jonathan's conjecture is also true: "When a transversal intersects two lines and creates corresponding angles that are equal, the two lines are parallel." Do you agree or disagree? Explain.

E. Do your conjectures about angle measures hold when a transversal intersects a pair of non-parallel lines? Use diagrams to justify your decision.

interior angles

Any angles formed by a transversal and two parallel lines that lie inside the parallel lines.

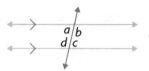

a, b, c, and *d* are interior angles.

exterior angles

Any angles formed by a transversal and two parallel lines that lie outside the parallel lines.

e, f, g, and *h* are exterior angles.

corresponding angles

One interior angle and one exterior angle that are non-adjacent and on the same side of a transversal.

converse

A statement that is formed by switching the premise and the conclusion of another statement.

In Summary

Key Ideas

- When a transversal intersects a pair of parallel lines, the corresponding angles that are formed by each parallel line and the transversal are equal.

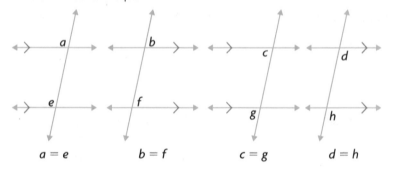

$a = e$ $b = f$ $c = g$ $d = h$

- When a transversal intersects a pair of lines creating equal corresponding angles, the pair of lines is parallel.

Need to Know

- When a transversal intersects a pair of non-parallel lines, the corresponding angles are not equal.
- There are also other relationships among the measures of the eight angles formed when a transversal intersects two parallel lines.

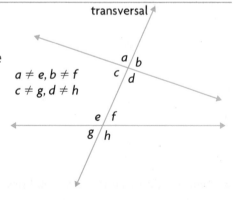

$a \neq e, b \neq f$
$c \neq g, d \neq h$

FURTHER Your Understanding

Edmonton's High Level Bridge was designed to carry trains, streetcars, autos, and pedestrians over the North Saskatchewan River. The railway has since been closed, but streetcars still cross, mainly as a tourist attraction.

1. a) Identify examples of parallel lines and transversals in this photograph of the High Level Bridge in Edmonton.
   b) Can you show that the lines in your examples really are parallel by measuring angles in a tracing of the photograph? Explain.

2. Which pairs of angles are equal in this diagram? Is there a relationship between the measures of the pairs of angles that are not equal?

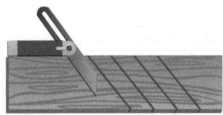

3. Explain how you could construct parallel lines using only a protractor and a ruler.

4. An adjustable T-bevel is used to draw parallel lines on wood to indicate where cuts should be made. Explain where the transversal is located in the diagram and how a T-bevel works.

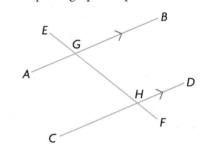

5. In each diagram, is *AB* parallel to *CD*? Explain how you know.

a)

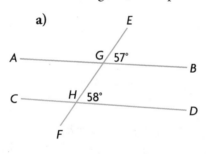

c)

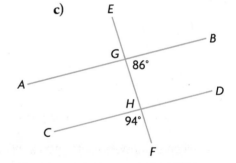

b)

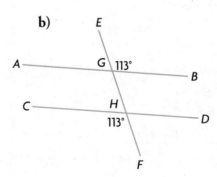

d)

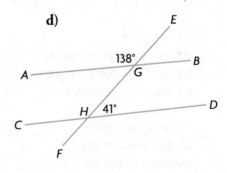

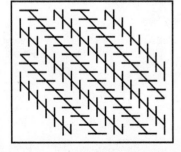

6. Nancy claims that the diagonal lines in the diagram to the left are not parallel. Do you agree or disagree? Justify your decision.

2.2 Angles Formed by Parallel Lines

Prove properties of angles formed by parallel lines and a transversal, and use these properties to solve problems.

YOU WILL NEED
- compass
- protractor
- ruler

INVESTIGATE the Math

Briony likes to use parallel lines in her art. To ensure that she draws the parallel lines accurately, she uses a straight edge and a compass.

? How can Briony use a straight edge and a compass to ensure that the lines she draws really are parallel?

A. Draw the first line. Place a point, labelled *P*, above the line. *P* will be a point in a parallel line.

P.

B. Draw a line through *P*, intersecting the first line at *Q*.

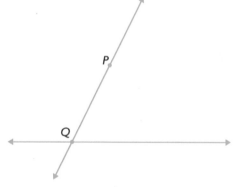

EXPLORE...

- Parallel bars are used in therapy to help people recover from injuries to their legs or spine. How could the manufacturer ensure that the bars are actually parallel?

C. Using a compass, construct an arc that is centred at *Q* and passes through both lines. Label the intersection points *R* and *S*.

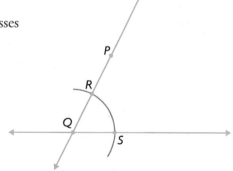

D. Draw another arc, centred at P, with the same radius as arc RS. Label the intersection point T.

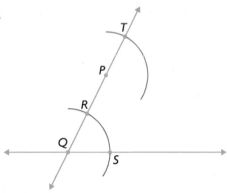

E. Draw a third arc, with centre T and radius RS, that intersects the arc you drew in step D. Label the point of intersection W.

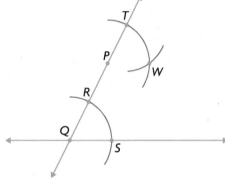

F. Draw the line that passes through P and W. Show that $PW \parallel QS$.

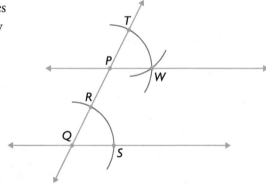

Reflecting

G. How is $\angle SQR$ related to $\angle WPT$?

H. Explain why the compass technique you used ensures that the two lines you drew are parallel.

I. Are there any other pairs of equal angles in your construction? Explain.

APPLY the Math

EXAMPLE 1 | Reasoning about conjectures involving angles formed by transversals

Make a conjecture that involves the interior angles formed by parallel lines and a transversal. Prove your conjecture.

Tuyet's Solution

My conjecture: When a transversal intersects a pair of parallel lines, the **alternate interior angles** are equal.

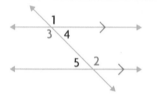

> I drew two parallel lines and a transversal as shown, and I numbered the angles. I need to show that $\angle 3 = \angle 2$.

Statement	Justification
$\angle 1 = \angle 2$	Corresponding angles
$\angle 1 = \angle 3$	Vertically opposite angles
$\angle 3 = \angle 2$	Transitive property

> Since I know that the lines are parallel, the corresponding angles are equal.

> When two lines intersect, the opposite angles are equal.

> $\angle 2$ and $\angle 3$ are both equal to $\angle 1$, so $\angle 2$ and $\angle 3$ are equal to each other.

My conjecture is proved.

alternate interior angles
Two non-adjacent interior angles on opposite sides of a transversal.

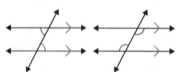

Ali's Solution

My conjecture: When a transversal intersects a pair of parallel lines, the interior angles on the same side of the transversal are supplementary.

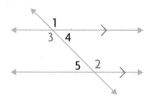

> I need to show that $\angle 3$ and $\angle 5$ are supplementary.

> Since the lines are parallel, the corresponding angles are equal.

$$\angle 1 = \angle 2$$

$$\angle 2 + \angle 5 = 180°$$

> These angles form a straight line, so they are supplementary.

$$\angle 1 + \angle 5 = 180°$$

Since $\angle 2 = \angle 1$, I could substitute $\angle 1$ for $\angle 2$ in the equation.

$$\angle 1 = \angle 3$$

Vertically opposite angles are equal. Since $\angle 1 = \angle 3$, I could substitute $\angle 3$ for $\angle 1$ in the equation.

$$\angle 3 + \angle 5 = 180°$$

alternate exterior angles

Two exterior angles formed between two lines and a transversal, on opposite sides of the transversal.

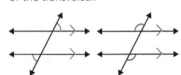

My conjecture is proved.

Your Turn

Naveen made the following conjecture: " **Alternate exterior angles** are equal." Prove Naveen's conjecture.

EXAMPLE 2   Using reasoning to determine unknown angles

Determine the measures of a, b, c, and d.

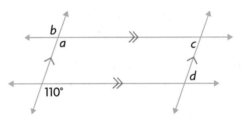

Kebeh's Solution

$\angle a = 110°$

The 110° angle and $\angle a$ are corresponding. Since the lines are parallel, the 110° angle and $\angle a$ are equal.

$\angle a = \angle b$
$\angle b = 110°$

Vertically opposite angles are equal.

$\angle c + \angle a = 180°$
$\angle c + 110° = 180°$
$\angle c = 70°$

$\angle c$ and $\angle a$ are interior angles on the same side of a transversal. Since the lines are parallel, $\angle c$ and $\angle a$ are supplementary.

I updated the diagram.

$\angle c = \angle d$
$\angle d = 70°$

$\angle c$ and $\angle d$ are alternate interior angles. Since the lines are parallel, $\angle c$ and $\angle d$ are equal.

The measures of the angles are:
$\angle a = 110°$; $\angle b = 110°$;
$\angle c = 70°$; $\angle d = 70°$.

Your Turn

a) Describe a different strategy you could use to determine the measure of $\angle b$.

b) Describe a different strategy you could use to determine the measure of $\angle d$.

EXAMPLE 3   Using angle properties to prove that lines are parallel

One side of a cellphone tower will be built as shown. Use the angle measures to prove that braces *CG*, *BF*, and *AE* are parallel.

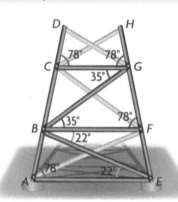

Morteza's Solution: Using corresponding angles

∠*BAE* = 78° and ∠*DCG* = 78° ---------------------- Given

AE ∥ *CG* -------------------------- When corresponding angles are equal, the lines are parallel.

∠*CGH* = 78° and ∠*BFG* = 78° -------------------- Given

CG ∥ *BF* ------------------------- When corresponding angles are equal, the lines are parallel.

AE ∥ *CG* and *CG* ∥ *BF* ----------------------- Since *AE* and *BF* are both parallel to *CG*, all three lines are parallel to each other.

The three braces are parallel.

Jennifer's Solution: Using alternate interior angles

Statement	Justification	
∠*CGB* = 35° and ∠*GBF* = 35°	Given	
CG ∥ *BF*	Alternate interior angles	When alternate interior angles are equal, the lines are parallel.
∠*FBE* = 22° and ∠*BEA* = 22°	Given	
BF ∥ *AE*	Alternate interior angles	When alternate interior angles are equal, the lines are parallel.
CG ∥ *BF* and *BF* ∥ *AE*	Transitive property	Since *CG* and *AE* are both parallel to *BF*, they must also be parallel to each other.

The three braces are parallel.

Your Turn

Use a different strategy to prove that *CG*, *BF*, and *AE* are parallel.

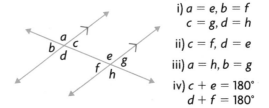
CHECK Your Understanding

1. Determine the measures of $\angle WYD$, $\angle YDA$, $\angle DEB$, and $\angle EFS$. Give your reasoning for each measure.

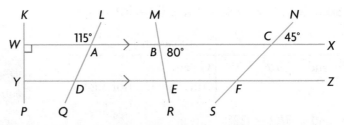

2. For each diagram, decide if the given angle measures prove that the blue lines are parallel. Justify your decisions.

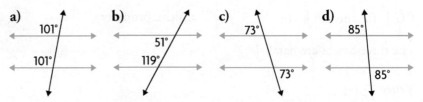

a) 101° 101°

b) 51° 119°

c) 73° 73°

d) 85° 85°

PRACTISING

3. A shelving unit is built with two pairs of parallel planks. Explain why each of the following statements is true.

a) $\angle k = \angle p$

b) $\angle a = \angle j$

c) $\angle j = \angle q$

d) $\angle g = \angle d$

e) $\angle b = \angle m$

f) $\angle e = \angle p$

g) $\angle n = \angle d$

h) $\angle f + \angle k = 180°$

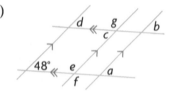

4. Determine the measures of the indicated angles.

a)

b)

c)

5. Construct an isosceles trapezoid. Explain your method of construction.

6. a) Construct parallelogram *SHOE*, where $\angle S = 50°$.

b) Show that the opposite angles of parallelogram *SHOE* are equal.

7. a) Identify pairs of parallel lines and transversals in the embroidery pattern.

b) How could a pattern maker use the properties of the angles created by parallel lines and a transversal to draw an embroidery pattern accurately?

8. a) Joshua made the following conjecture: "If $AB \perp BC$ and $BC \perp CD$, then $AB \perp CD$." Identify the error in his reasoning.

Joshua's Proof

Statement	Justification
$AB \perp BC$	Given
$BC \perp CD$	Given
$AB \perp CD$	Transitive property

b) Make a correct conjecture about perpendicular lines.

Embroidery has a rich history in the Ukrainian culture. In one style of embroidery, called *nabiruvannia*, the stitches are made parallel to the horizontal threads of the fabric.

The Bank of China tower has a distinctive 3-D shape. The base of the lower part of the building is a quadrilateral. The base of the top is a triangle, making it stable and wind-resistant.

9. The Bank of China tower in Hong Kong was the tallest building in Asia at the time of its completion in 1990. Explain how someone in Hong Kong could use angle measures to determine if the diagonal trusses are parallel.

10. Jason wrote the following proof. Identify his errors, and correct his proof.

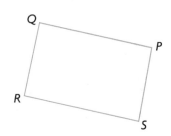

Given: $QP \perp QR$

$QR \perp RS$

$QR \parallel PS$

Prove: $QPSR$ is a parallelogram.

Jason's Proof

Statement	Justification
$\angle PQR = 90°$ and $\angle QRS = 90°$	Lines that are perpendicular meet at right angles.
$QP \parallel RS$	Since the interior angles on the same side of a transversal are equal, QP and RS are parallel.
$QR \parallel PS$	Given
$QPSR$ is a parallelogram	$QPSR$ has two pairs of parallel sides.

11. The roof of St. Ann's Academy in Victoria, British Columbia, has dormer windows as shown. Explain how knowledge of parallel lines and transversals helped the builders ensure that the frames for the windows are parallel.

12. Given: $\triangle FOX$ is isosceles.

$\angle FOX = \angle FRS$
$\angle FXO = \angle FPQ$

Prove: $PQ \parallel SR$ and $SR \parallel XO$

13. a)   Draw a triangle. Construct a line segment that joins two sides of your triangle and is parallel to the third side.

b)   Prove that the two triangles in your construction are similar.

14. The top surface of this lap
harp is an isosceles trapezoid.
   a) Determine the measures
   of the unknown angles.
   b) Make a conjecture about
   the angles in an isosceles
   trapezoid.

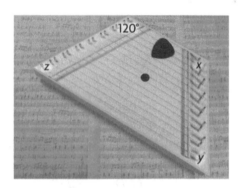

15. Determine the measures of all the
unknown angles in this diagram,
given $PQ \parallel RS$.

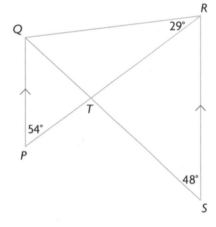

16. Given $AB \parallel DE$ and $DE \parallel FG$, show that
$\angle ACD = \angle BAC + \angle CDE$.

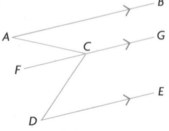

17. When a ball is shot into the side or end of a pool table, it will rebound
off the side or end at the same angle that it hit (assuming that there is
no spin on the ball).
   a) Predict how the straight paths of the ball will compare with each
   other.
   b) Draw a scale diagram of the top of a pool
   table that measures 4 ft by 8 ft. Construct the
   trajectory of a ball that is hit from point A on
   one end toward point B on a side, then C, D,
   and so on.
   c) How does path AB compare with path CD?
   How does path BC compare with path DE? Was
   your prediction correct?
   d) Will this pattern continue? Explain.

18. Given: $QP \parallel SR$
   RT bisects $\angle QRS$.
   QU bisects $\angle PQR$.
   Prove: $QU \parallel RT$

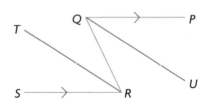

Closing

19. a) Ashley wants to prove that $LM \parallel QR$. To do this, she claims that she must show all of the following statements to be true:
   i) $\angle LCD = \angle CDR$
   ii) $\angle XCM = \angle CDR$
   iii) $\angle MCD + \angle CDR = 180°$
   Do you agree or disagree? Explain.
   b) Can Ashley show that the lines are parallel in other ways? If so, list these ways.

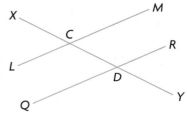

Extending

20. Solve for x.

a)

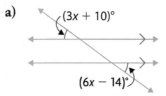

$(3x + 10)°$
$(6x - 14)°$

b)

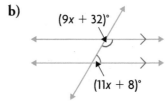

$(9x + 32)°$
$(11x + 8)°$

21. The window surface of the large pyramid at Edmonton City Hall is composed of congruent rhombuses.
   a) Describe how you could determine the angle at the peak of the pyramid using a single measurement without climbing the pyramid.
   b) Prove that your strategy is valid.

The Edmonton City Hall pyramids are a city landmark.

Checkerboard Quadrilaterals

One strategy for solving a puzzle is to use inductive reasoning. Solve similar but simpler puzzles first, then look for patterns in your solutions that may help you solve the original, more difficult puzzle.

The Puzzle

How many quadrilaterals can you count on an 8-by-8 checkerboard?

The Strategy

A. How many squares or rectangles can you count on a 1-by-1 checkerboard?

B. Draw a 2-by-2 checkerboard. Count the quadrilaterals.

C. Draw a 3-by-3 checkerboard, and count the quadrilaterals.

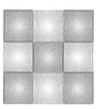

D. Develop a strategy you could use to determine the number of quadrilaterals on any checkerboard. Test your strategy on a 4-by-4 checkerboard.

E. Was your strategy effective? Modify your strategy if necessary.

F. Determine the number of quadrilaterals on an 8-by-8 checkerboard. Describe your strategy.

G. Compare your results and strategy with the results and strategies of your classmates. Did all the strategies result in the same solution? How many different strategies were used?

H. Which strategy do you like the best? Explain.

FREQUENTLY ASKED Questions

Q: **What are the relationships among the angles formed when a transversal intersects two parallel lines?**

A: When two lines are parallel, the following angle relationships hold:

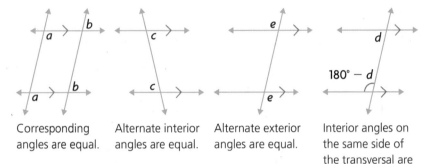

Corresponding angles are equal.

Alternate interior angles are equal.

Alternate exterior angles are equal.

Interior angles on the same side of the transversal are supplementary.

Q: **How can you prove that a conjecture involving parallel lines is valid?**

A: Draw a diagram that shows parallel lines and a transversal. Label your diagram with any information you know about the lines and angles. State what you know and what you are trying to prove. Make a plan. Use other conjectures that have already been proven to complete each step of your proof.

Q: **How can you use angles to prove that two lines are parallel?**

A: Draw a transversal that intersects the two lines, if the diagram does not include a transversal. Then measure, or determine the measure of, a pair of angles formed by the transversal and the two lines. If corresponding angles, alternate interior angles, or alternate exterior angles are equal, or if interior angles on the same side of the transversal are supplementary, the lines are parallel.

For example, determine if AB is parallel to CD. First draw transversal PQ.

Measure alternate interior angles $\angle ARQ$ and $\angle PSD$. If these angles are equal, then $AB \parallel CD$.

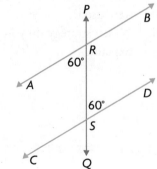

PRACTISING

1. In each diagram, determine whether $AB \parallel CD$. Explain how you know.

a)

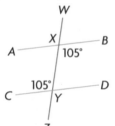

c)

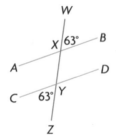

b)

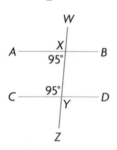

d)

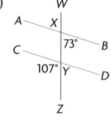

2. Classify quadrilateral *PQRS*. Explain how you know.

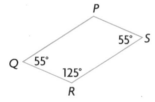

3. Are the red lines in the artwork parallel? Explain.

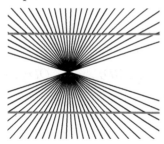

Lesson 2.2

4. Draw a parallelogram by constructing two sets of parallel lines. Explain your method.

5. a) Determine the measures of all the unknown angles in the diagram.

   b) Is *BD* parallel to *EF*? Explain how you know.

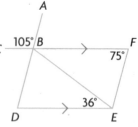

6. Given: $\triangle BFG \sim \triangle BED$

   Prove: a) $AC \parallel ED$
            b) $FG \parallel ED$
            c) $AC \parallel FG$

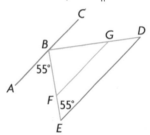

7. Explain how knowledge of parallel lines and transversals could be used to determine where to paint the lines for these parking spots.

8. The Franco-Yukonnais flag is shown. Are the long sides of the white shapes parallel to the long sides of the yellow shape? Explain how you know.

Angle Properties in Triangles

YOU WILL NEED

- dynamic geometry software OR compass, protractor, and ruler
- scissors

EXPLORE...

On a rectangular piece of paper, draw lines from two vertices to a point on the opposite side. Cut along the lines to create two right triangles and an acute triangle.

- What do you notice about the three triangles?
- Can you use angle relationships to show that the sum of the measures of the angles in any acute triangle formed this way is 180°?

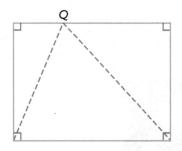

GOAL

Prove properties of angles in triangles, and use these properties to solve problems.

INVESTIGATE the Math

Diko placed three congruent triangular tiles so that a different angle from each triangle met at the same point. She noticed the angles seemed to form a straight line.

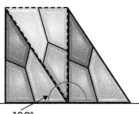

180°

> **?** Can you prove that the sum of the measures of the interior angles of any triangle is 180°?

A. Draw an acute triangle, $\triangle RED$. Construct line PQ through vertex D, parallel to RE.

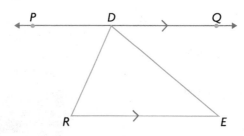

B. Identify pairs of equal angles in your diagram. Explain how you know that the measures of the angles in each pair are equal.

C. What is the sum of the measures of $\angle PDR$, $\angle RDE$, and $\angle QDE$? Explain how you know.

D. Explain why:
$\angle DRE + \angle RDE + \angle RED = 180°$

E. In part A, does it matter which vertex you drew the parallel line through? Explain, using examples.

F. Repeat parts A to E, first for an obtuse triangle and then for a right triangle. Are your results the same as they were for the acute triangle?

Reflecting

G. Why is Diko's approach not considered to be a proof?

H. Are your results sufficient to prove that the sum of the measures of the angles in any triangle is 180°? Explain.

APPLY the Math

EXAMPLE 1	Using angle sums to determine angle measures

In the diagram, $\angle MTH$ is an **exterior angle** of $\triangle MAT$. Determine the measures of the unknown angles in $\triangle MAT$.

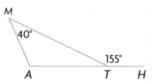

Serge's Solution

$\angle MTA + \angle MTH = 180°$ ············ $\angle MTA$ and $\angle MTH$ are
$\angle MTA + (155°) = 180°$ supplementary since they form a
$\angle MTA = 25°$ straight line.

$\angle MAT + \angle AMT + \angle MTA = 180°$ ---- The sum of the measures of the
$\angle MAT + (40°) + (25°) = 180°$ interior angles of any triangle
$\angle MAT = 115°$ is 180°.

The measures of the unknown angles are:
$\angle MTA = 25°$; $\angle MAT = 115°$.

Your Turn

If you are given one interior angle and one exterior angle of a triangle, can you always determine the other interior angles of the triangle? Explain, using diagrams.

EXAMPLE **2**	**Using reasoning to determine the relationship between the exterior and interior angles of a triangle**

Determine the relationship between an exterior angle of a triangle and its **non-adjacent interior angles** .

non-adjacent interior angles

The two angles of a triangle that do not have the same vertex as an exterior angle.

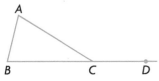

$\angle A$ and $\angle B$ are non-adjacent interior angles to exterior $\angle ACD$.

Joanna's Solution

I drew a diagram of a triangle with one exterior angle. I labelled the angle measures a, b, c, and d.

$$\angle d + \angle c = 180°$$
$$\angle d = 180° - \angle c$$

$\angle d$ and $\angle c$ are supplementary. I rearranged these angles to isolate $\angle d$.

$$\angle a + \angle b + \angle c = 180°$$
$$\angle a + \angle b = 180° - \angle c$$

The sum of the measures of the angles in any triangle is 180°.

$$\angle d = \angle a + \angle b$$

Since $\angle d$ and ($\angle a + \angle b$) are both equal to $180° - \angle c$, by the transitive property, they must be equal to each other.

The measure of an exterior angle of a triangle is equal to the sum of the measures of the two non-adjacent interior angles.

Your Turn

Prove: $\angle e = \angle a + \angle b$

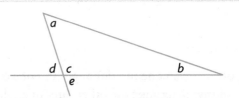

EXAMPLE **3**	**Using reasoning to solve problems**

Determine the measures of $\angle NMO$, $\angle MNO$, and $\angle QMO$.

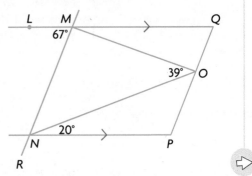

88   Chapter 2 **Properties of Angles and Triangles**

NEL

Tyler's Solution

MN is a transversal of parallel lines LQ and NP. ┄┄┄┄┄┄┄ *MN intersects parallel lines LQ and NP.*

$\angle MNO + 20° = 67°$ ┄┄┄┄┄┄┄┄┄┄┄
$\qquad \angle MNO = 47°$

> Since $\angle LMN$ and $\angle MNP$ are alternate interior angles between parallel lines, they are equal.

$\angle NMO + \angle MNO + 39° = 180°$ ┄┄┄┄┄┄┄┄
$\quad \angle NMO + (47°) + 39° = 180°$
$\qquad\quad \angle NMO + 86° = 180°$
$\qquad\qquad\quad \angle NMO = 94°$

> The measures of the angles in a triangle add to 180°.

$\angle NMO + \angle QMO + 67° = 180°$ ┄┄┄┄┄┄┄
$\quad (94°) + \angle QMO + 67° = 180°$
$\qquad\quad 161° + \angle QMO = 180°$
$\qquad\qquad\quad \angle QMO = 19°$

> $\angle LMN$, $\angle NMO$, and $\angle QMO$ form a straight line, so their measures must add to 180°.

The measures of the angles are:
$\angle MNO = 47°$; $\angle NMO = 94°$; $\angle QMO = 19°$.

Dominique's Solution

$\angle NMO + \angle MNO + 39° = 180°$ ┄┄┄┄┄┄┄
$\qquad \angle NMO + \angle MNO = 141°$

> The sum of the measures of the angles in a triangle is 180°.

$(\angle NMO + \angle QMO) + (\angle MNO + 20°) = 180°$ ┄┄┄
$\qquad\quad \angle NMO + \angle MNO + \angle QMO = 160°$

> The angles that are formed by $(\angle NMO + \angle QMO)$ and $(\angle MNO + 20°)$ are interior angles on the same side of transversal *MN*. Since $LQ \parallel NP$, these angles are supplementary.

$(141°) + \angle QMO = 160°$ ┄┄┄┄┄┄┄┄
$\qquad\quad \angle QMO = 19°$

> I substituted the value of $\angle NMO + \angle MNO$ into the equation.

$\angle NMO + \angle QMO + 67° = 180°$ ┄┄┄┄┄┄┄
$\quad \angle NMO + (19°) + 67° = 180°$
$\qquad\qquad\quad \angle NMO = 94°$

$\angle NMO + \angle MNO = 141°$
$\quad (94°) + \angle MNO = 141°$
$\qquad\qquad \angle MNO = 47°$

> $\angle LMN$, $\angle NMO$, and $\angle QMO$ form a straight line, so the sum of their measures is 180°.

The measures of the angles are:
$\angle QMO = 19°$; $\angle NMO = 94°$; $\angle MNO = 47°$.

Your Turn

In the diagram for Example 3, $QP \parallel MR$. Determine the measures of $\angle MQO$, $\angle MOQ$, $\angle NOP$, $\angle OPN$, and $\angle RNP$.

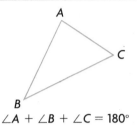
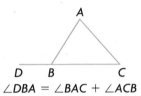
CHECK *Your Understanding*

1. Harrison drew a triangle and then measured the three interior angles. When he added the measures of these angles, the sum was 180°. Does this prove that the sum of the measures of the angles in any triangle is 180°? Explain.

2. Marcel says that it is possible to draw a triangle with two right angles. Do you agree? Explain why or why not.

3. Determine the following unknown angles.

   a) $\angle YXZ, \angle Z$

   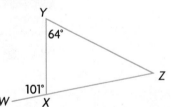

   b) $\angle A, \angle DCE$

   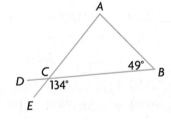

PRACTISING

4. If $\angle Q$ is known, write an expression for the measure of one of the other two angles.

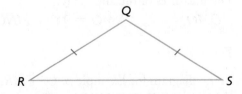

5. Prove: $\angle A = 30°$

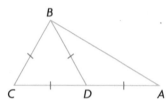

6. Determine the measures of the exterior angles of an equilateral triangle.

7. Prove: $SY \parallel AD$

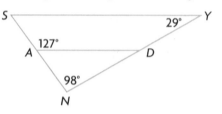

8. Each vertex of a triangle has two exterior angles, as shown.

a) Make a conjecture about the sum of the measures of $\angle a$, $\angle c$, and $\angle e$.

b) Does your conjecture also apply to the sum of the measures of $\angle b$, $\angle d$, and $\angle f$? Explain.

c) Prove or disprove your conjecture.

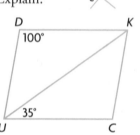

9. *DUCK* is a parallelogram. Benji determined the measures of the unknown angles in *DUCK*. Paula says he has made an error.

Benji's Solution

Statement	Justification
$\angle DKU = \angle KUC$	$\angle DKU$ and $\angle KUC$ are alternate interior angles.
$\angle DKU = 35°$	
$\angle UDK = \angle DUC$	$\angle UDK$ and $\angle DUC$ are corresponding angles.
$\angle DUK + \angle KUC = 100°$	$\angle DUK$ and $\angle UKC$ are alternate interior angles.
$\qquad \angle DUK = 65°$	
$\qquad \angle UKC = 65°$	
$\angle UCK = 180° - (\angle KUC + \angle UKC)$	The sum of the measures of the angles in a
$\angle UCK = 180° - (35° + 65°)$	triangle is 180°.
$\angle UCK = 80°$	
	I redrew the diagram, including the angle measures I determined.

a) Explain how you know that Benji made an error.

b) Correct Benji's solution.

10. Prove that quadrilateral *MATH* is a parallelogram.

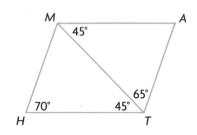

11. A manufacturer is designing a reclining lawn chair, as shown. Determine the measures of ∠*a*, ∠*b*, ∠*c*, and ∠*d*.

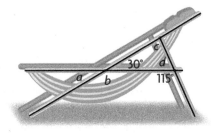

12. a) Tim claims that *FG* is not parallel to *HI* because ∠*FGH* ≠ ∠*IHJ*. Do you agree or disagree? Justify your decision.

b) How else could you justify your decision? Explain.

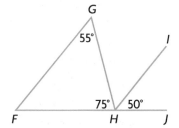

13. Use the given information to determine the measures of ∠*J*, ∠*JKO*, ∠*JOK*, ∠*KLM*, ∠*KLN*, ∠*M*, ∠*LNO*, ∠*LNM*, ∠*MLN*, ∠*NOK*, and ∠*JON*.

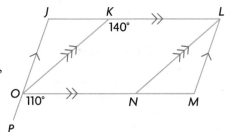

14. Determine the measures of the interior angles of △*FUN*.

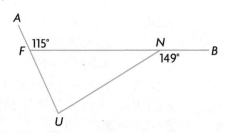

15. a) Determine the measures of ∠*AXZ*, ∠*XYC*, and ∠*EZY*.

b) Determine the sum of these three exterior angles.

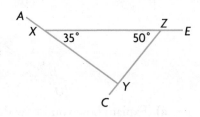

16. MO and NO are angle bisectors.
Prove: $\angle L = 2\angle O$

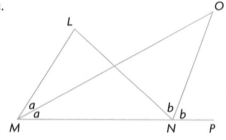

Closing

17. Explain how drawing a line that is parallel to one side of any triangle can help you prove that the sum of the angles in the triangle is 180°.

Extending

18. Given: AE bisects $\angle BAC$.

$\triangle BCD$ is isosceles.

Prove: $\angle AEB = 45°$

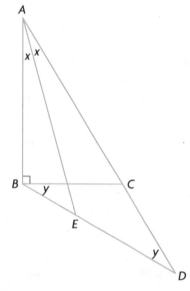

19. $\triangle LMN$ is an isosceles triangle in which $LM = LN$. ML is extended to point D, forming an exterior angle, $\angle DLN$. If $LR \parallel MN$, where N and R are on the same side of MD, prove that $\angle DLR = \angle RLN$.

Angle Properties in Polygons

YOU WILL NEED
- dynamic geometry software OR protractor and ruler

EXPLORE...
- A pentagon has three right angles and four sides of equal length, as shown. What is the sum of the measures of the angles in the pentagon?

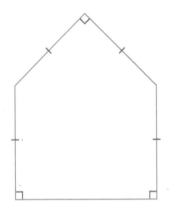

GOAL

Determine properties of angles in polygons, and use these properties to solve problems.

INVESTIGATE the Math

In Lesson 2.3, you proved properties involving the interior and exterior angles of triangles. You can use these properties to develop general relationships involving the interior and exterior angles of polygons.

? How is the number of sides in a polygon related to the sum of its interior angles and the sum of its exterior angles?

Part 1 Interior Angles

A. Giuseppe says that he can determine the sum of the measures of the interior angles of this quadrilateral by including the diagonals in the diagram. Is he correct? Explain.

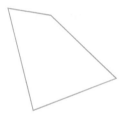

B. Determine the sum of the measures of the interior angles of any quadrilateral.

C. Draw the polygons listed in the table below. Create triangles to help you determine the sum of the measures of their interior angles. Record your results in a table like the one below.

Polygon	Number of Sides	Number of Triangles	Sum of Angle Measures
triangle	3	1	180°
quadrilateral	4		
pentagon	5		
hexagon	6		
heptagon	7		
octagon	8		

D. Make a conjecture about the relationship between the sum of the measures of the interior angles of a polygon, S, and the number of sides of the polygon, n.

E. Use your conjecture to predict the sum of the measures of the interior angles of a dodecagon (12 sides). Verify your prediction using triangles.

Part 2 Exterior Angles

F. Draw a rectangle. Extend each side of the rectangle so that the rectangle has one exterior angle for each interior angle. Determine the sum of the measures of the exterior angles.

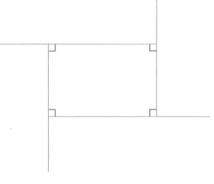

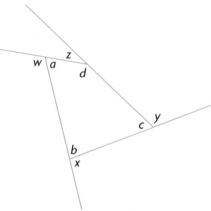

G. What do you notice about the sum of the measures of each exterior angle of your rectangle and its adjacent interior angle? Would this relationship also hold for the exterior and interior angles of the irregular quadrilateral shown? Explain.

H. Make a conjecture about the sum of the measures of the exterior angles of any quadrilateral. Test your conjecture.

I. Draw a pentagon. Extend each side of the pentagon so that the pentagon has one exterior angle for each interior angle. Based on your diagram, revise your conjecture to include pentagons. Test your revised conjecture.

J. Do you think your revised conjecture will hold for polygons that have more than five sides? Explain and verify by testing.

Reflecting

K. Compare your results for the sums of the measures of the interior angles of polygons with your classmates' results. Do you think your conjecture from part *D* will be true for any polygon? Explain.

L. Compare your results for the sums of the measures of the exterior angles of polygons with your classmates' results. Do you think your conjecture from part I will apply to any polygon? Explain.

APPLY the Math

Prove that the sum of the measures of the interior angles of any n-sided **convex polygon** can be expressed as $180°(n - 2)$.

convex polygon

A polygon in which each interior angle measures less than 180°.

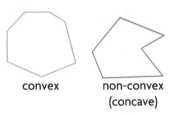

convex   non-convex (concave)

Viktor's Solution

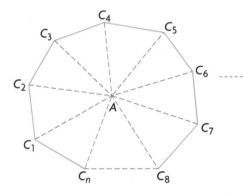

I drew an n-sided polygon. I represented the nth side using a broken line. I selected a point in the interior of the polygon and then drew line segments from this point to each vertex of the polygon. The polygon is now separated into n triangles.

The sum of the measures of the angles in each triangle is 180°.

The sum of the measures of the angles in n triangles is $n(180°)$.

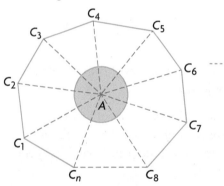

Two angles in each triangle combine with angles in the adjacent triangles to form two interior angles of the polygon.

Each triangle also has an angle at vertex A. The sum of the measures of the angles at A is 360° because these angles make up a complete rotation. These angles do not contribute to the sum of the interior angles of the polygon.

The sum of the measures of the interior angles of the polygon, $S(n)$, where n is the number of sides of the polygon, can be expressed as:

$S(n) = 180°n - 360°$

$S(n) = 180°(n - 2)$

The sum of the measures of the interior angles of a convex polygon can be expressed as $180°(n - 2)$.

Your Turn

Explain why Viktor's solution cannot be used to show whether the expression $180°(n - 2)$ applies to non-convex polygons.

EXAMPLE **2**
Reasoning about angles in a regular polygon

Outdoor furniture and structures like gazebos sometimes use a regular hexagon in their building plan. Determine the measure of each interior angle of a regular hexagon.

Nazra's Solution

Let $S(n)$ represent the sum of the measures of the interior angles of the polygon, where n is the number of sides of the polygon.

$$S(n) = 180°(n - 2)$$ ·················· A hexagon has six sides, so $n = 6$.
$$S(6) = 180°[(6) - 2]$$
$$S(6) = 720°$$
$$\frac{720°}{6} = 120°$$ ·················· Since the measures of the angles in a regular hexagon are equal, each angle must measure $\frac{1}{6}$ of the sum of the angles.

The measure of each interior angle of a regular hexagon is 120°.

Your Turn

Determine the measure of each interior angle of a regular 15-sided polygon (a pentadecagon).

2.4 Angle Properties in Polygons

EXAMPLE **3**　　Visualizing tessellations

A floor tiler designs custom floors using tiles in the shape of regular polygons. Can the tiler use congruent regular octagons and congruent squares to tile a floor, if they have the same side length?

Vanessa's Solution

$S(n) = 180°(n - 2)$

$S(8) = 180°[(8) - 2]$

$S(8) = 1080°$

$\dfrac{1080°}{8} = 135°$

The measure of each interior angle in a regular octagon is 135°.

The measure of each internal angle in a square is 90°.

> Since an octagon has eight sides, $n = 8$.

> First, I determined the sum of the measures of the interior angles of an octagon. Then I determined the measure of each interior angle in a regular octagon.

Two octagons fit together, forming an angle that measures:

$2(135°) = 270°$.

This leaves a gap of 90°.

$2(135°) + 90° = 360°$

A square can fit in this gap if the sides of the square are the same length as the sides of the octagon.

> I knew that three octagons would not fit together, as the sum of the angles would be greater than 360°.

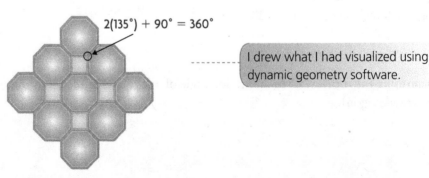

$2(135°) + 90° = 360°$

> I drew what I had visualized using dynamic geometry software.

The tiler can tile a floor using regular octagons and squares when the polygons have the same side length.

Your Turn

Can a tiling pattern be created using regular hexagons and equilateral triangles that have the same side length? Explain.

CHECK Your Understanding

1. **a)** Determine the sum of the measures of the interior angles of a regular dodecagon.

   b) Determine the measure of each interior angle of a regular dodecagon.

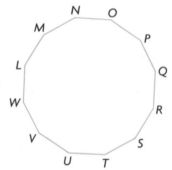

2. Determine the sum of the measures of the angles in a 20-sided convex polygon.

3. The sum of the measures of the interior angles of an unknown polygon is 3060°. Determine the number of sides that the polygon has.

PRACTISING

4. Honeybees make honeycombs to store their honey. The base of each honeycomb is roughly a regular hexagon. Explain why a regular hexagon can be used to tile a surface.

5. Is it possible to create a tiling pattern with parallelograms? Explain.

6. Determine the measure of each interior angle of a loonie.

7. Each interior angle of a regular convex polygon measures 140°.
   a) Prove that the polygon has nine sides.
   b) Verify that the sum of the measures of the exterior angles is 360°.

8. a) Determine the measure of each exterior angle of a regular octagon.
   b) Use your answer for part a) to determine the measure of each interior angle of a regular octagon.
   c) Use your answer for part b) to determine the sum of the interior angles of a regular octagon.
   d) Use the function

   $$S(n) = 180°(n - 2)$$

   to determine the sum of the interior angles of a regular octagon. Compare your answer with the sum you determined in part c).

9. a) Wallace claims that the opposite sides in any regular hexagon are parallel. Do you agree or disagree? Justify your decision.
   b) Make a conjecture about parallel sides in regular polygons.

Math in Action

"Circular" Homes

A building based on a circular floor plan has about 11% less outdoor wall surface area than one based on a square floor plan of the same area. This means less heat is lost through the walls in winter, lowering utility bills.

Most "circular" buildings actually use regular polygons for their floor plans.

- Determine the exterior angle measures of a floor plan that is a regular polygon with each of the following number of sides: 12, 18, 24. Explain why a building would be closer to circular as the number of sides increases.

- List some practical limitations on the number of sides a building could have.

- Based on the practical limitations, suggest an optimal number of sides for a home. Sketch a floor plan for a home with this number of sides.

10. *LMNOP* is a regular pentagon.

    a) Determine the measure of $\angle OLN$.

    b) What kind of triangle is $\triangle LON$? Explain how you know.

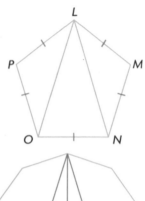

11. Sandy designed this logo for the jerseys worn by her softball team. She told the graphic artist that each interior angle of the regular decagon should measure $162°$, based on this calculation:

$$S(10) = \frac{180°(10 - 1)}{10}$$

$$S(10) = \frac{1620°}{10}$$

$$S(10) = 162°$$

Identify the error she made and determine the correct angle.

12. Astrid claims that drawing lines through a polygon can be used as a test to determine whether the polygon is convex or non-convex (concave).

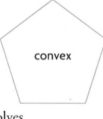

convex

non-convex

    a) Describe a test that involves drawing a single line.

    b) Describe a test that involves drawing diagonals.

13. Martin is planning to build a hexagonal picnic table, as shown.

    a) Determine the angles at the ends of each piece of wood that Martin needs to cut for the seats.

    b) How would these angles change if Martin decided to make an octagonal table instead?

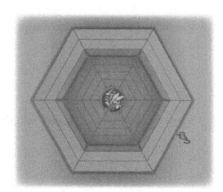

14. Three exterior angles of a convex pentagon measure 70°, 60°, and 90°. The other two exterior angles are congruent. Determine the measures of the interior angles of the pentagon.

15. Determine the sum of the measures of the indicated angles.

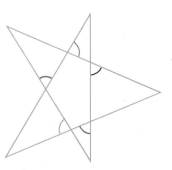

16. In each figure, the congruent sides form a regular polygon. Determine the values of *a*, *b*, *c*, and *d*.

a)

b)

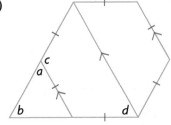

17. Determine the sum of the measures of the indicated angles.

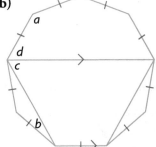

18. Given: *ABCDE* is a regular pentagon with centre *O*.
△*EOD* is isosceles, with *EO* = *DO*.
DO = *CO*
Prove: △*EFD* is a right triangle.

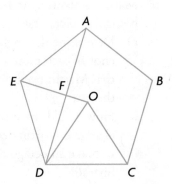

Closing

19. The function representing the sum of the measures of the interior angles of a polygon with n sides is:

$$S(n) = 180°(n - 2)$$

Explain how the expression on the right can be deduced by considering a polygon with n sides.

Extending

20. A pentagon tile has two 90° angles. The other three angles are equal. Is it possible to create a tiling pattern using only this tile? Justify your answer.

21. Each interior angle of a regular polygon is five times as large as its corresponding exterior angle. What is the common name of this polygon?

History | Connection

Buckyballs—Polygons in 3-D

Richard Buckminster "Bucky" Fuller (1895–1983) was an American architect and inventor who spent time working in Canada. He developed the geodesic dome and built a famous example, now called the Montréal Biosphere, for Expo 1967. A spin-off from Fuller's dome design was the buckyball, which became the official design for the soccer ball used in the 1970 World Cup.

In 1985, scientists discovered carbon molecules that resembled Fuller's geodesic sphere. These molecules were named fullerenes, after Fuller.

The Montréal Biosphere and its architect

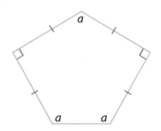

FIFA soccer ball, 1970

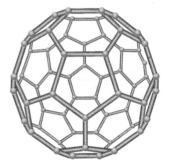

Carbon molecule, C_{60}

A. Identify the polygons that were used to create the buckyball.
B. Predict the sum of the three interior angles at each vertex of the buckyball. Check your prediction.
C. Explain why the value you found in part B makes sense.

YOU WILL NEED

- dynamic geometry software OR protractor and ruler

GOAL

Determine the minimum amount of information needed to prove that two triangles are congruent.

EXPLORE the Math

A tenting company is designing a new line of outdoor shades in a triangular shape.

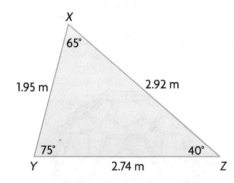

The designer produced a scale diagram of the shade. If the shade had been a rectangle, the designer would have had to provide only two measurements—length and width—to the company's manufacturing department. For the triangular shade, however, the designer has six measurements that could be provided: three side lengths and three angle measures. Only three of these measurements are needed.

? Which three pieces of information could be provided to the manufacturing department to ensure that all the triangular shades produced are identical?

Reflecting

A. Which combinations of given side and angle measurements do not ensure that only one size and shape of shade can be produced?

B. Which combinations of given side and angle measurements ensure that all the shades produced are congruent?

In Summary

Key Idea

- There are minimum sets of angle and side measurements that, if known, allow you to conclude that two triangles are congruent.

Need to Know

- If three pairs of corresponding sides are equal, then the triangles are congruent. This is known as side-side-side congruence, or *SSS*.

  For example:

  $AB = XY$

  $BC = YZ$

  $AC = XZ$

  $\therefore \triangle ABC \cong \triangle XYZ$

- If two pairs of corresponding sides and the contained angles are equal, then the triangles are congruent. This is known as side-angle-side congruence, or *SAS*.

  For example:

  $AB = XY$

  $\angle B = \angle Y$

  $BC = YZ$

  $\therefore \triangle ABC \cong \triangle XYZ$

- If two pairs of corresponding angles and the contained sides are equal, then the triangles are congruent. This is known as angle-side-angle congruence, or *ASA*.

  For example:

  $\angle B = \angle Y$

  $BC = YZ$

  $\angle C = \angle Z$

  $\therefore \triangle ABC \cong \triangle XYZ$

Communication | *Tip*

The symbol $\therefore$ represents the word "therefore." In geometry, this symbol is generally used when stating a conclusion drawn from preceding facts or deductions.

FURTHER Your Understanding

1. For each pair of triangles, state why it is possible to conclude that
   △ABC is congruent to △XYZ.

a)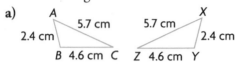

c)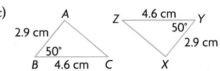

b)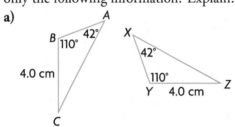

d)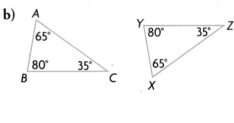

2. Is it possible to conclude that △ABC is congruent to △XYZ, given
   only the following information? Explain.

a)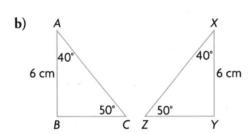

b)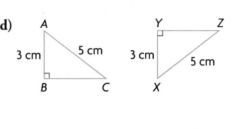

3. For each pair of congruent triangles, state the corresponding angles
   and sides, and explain how you know that they are equal. Then write
   the congruence statement.

a)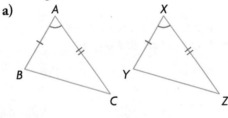

c)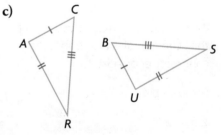

b)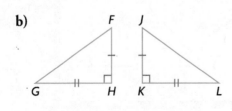

d)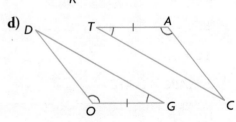

4. Is it possible to draw more than one triangle for △XYZ if you know
   the measures of ∠Z, XY, and YZ?

GOAL

Use deductive reasoning to prove that triangles are congruent.

LEARN ABOUT the Math

Scaffolding is frequently used by tradespeople to reach high places. Each end of the scaffolding consists of a ladder with the rungs equally spaced. It is important for the scaffolding to be braced for strength. In this photograph, braces *AB* and *CD* are parallel. Braces *CB* and *ED* are also parallel. *AC* and *CE* are both four ladder rungs high.

? How can you prove that the triangles formed by these braces are congruent?

YOU WILL NEED
- dynamic geometry software OR ruler and compass

EXPLORE...

The Sierpinski triangle pattern is an example of a fractal.
- Explain how each figure is created from the previous one.
- Will the blue triangles within each figure always be congruent? Explain.

Figure 1

Figure 2

Figure 3

EXAMPLE 1   Using reasoning in a two-column proof

Prove: $\triangle ABC \cong \triangle CDE$

Elan's Solution

$AB \parallel CD$	Given
$\angle BAC = \angle DCE$	Corresponding angles are equal.

AB is parallel to *CD*, so the corresponding angles are equal.

I drew a diagram, and then I updated my diagram as I proved parts equal.

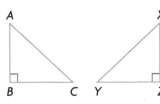

Communication | *Tip*

When describing two triangles by their vertices, make sure that the corresponding vertices are in the same order in both descriptions. For example, when stating that these two triangles are congruent, you could write

$\triangle ABC \cong \triangle XZY$

or

$\triangle ACB \cong \triangle XYZ$

$CB \parallel ED$	Given
$\angle BCA = \angle DEC$	Corresponding angles are equal.

> CB is parallel to ED, so the corresponding angles are equal.

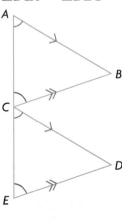

$AC = CE$	AC and CE are both four ladder rungs high, and the ladder rungs are equally spaced.

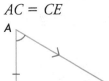

$\therefore \triangle ABC \cong \triangle CDE$	ASA

Reflecting

A. What other congruent triangles do you see in the photograph of the scaffolding?

B. Explain how you could prove that those triangles are congruent.

APPLY the Math

EXAMPLE 2   Reasoning about congruency to prove that sides are equal

Given: $TP \perp AC$
        $AP = CP$

Prove: $\triangle TAC$ is isosceles.

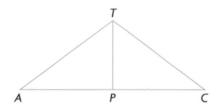

Jamaica's Solution

$\angle TPA$ and $\angle TPC$ are right angles.	$TP \perp AC$ ----	Angles formed by perpendicular lines are right angles.
$\angle TPA = \angle TPC$	Right angles are equal.	
$AP = CP$	Given	

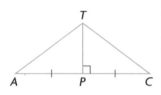

---- I marked a diagram with the known information.

$TP = TP$	Common side ----	TP is shared by both triangles.
$\therefore \triangle TAP \cong \triangle TCP$	SAS	
$TA = TC$	If two triangles are congruent, then their corresponding sides are equal.	
$\therefore \triangle TAC$ is isosceles.	An isosceles triangle has two equal sides.	

Your Turn

Explain how you could use the Pythagorean theorem to prove that $\triangle TAC$ is isosceles.

EXAMPLE 3   Reasoning about congruency to prove that angles are equal

Given: AE and BD bisect each other at C.
        $AB = ED$

Prove: $\angle A = \angle E$

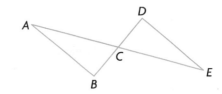

Monique's Solution

$AC = EC$ and $BC = DC$	AE and BD bisect each other at C. - - - - - - -	"Bisect" means cut in half. Here, two line segments that bisect each other create equal corresponding sides in $\triangle ABC$ and $\triangle EDC$.
$AB = ED$	Given	

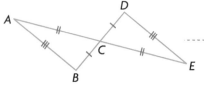

- - - - - - - - - - - - - - - - - - I drew a diagram to record the equal sides.

$\therefore \triangle ABC \cong \triangle EDC$ $\angle A = \angle E$	SSS - - - - - - - - - If two triangles are congruent, then their corresponding angles are equal.	I had shown that all three pairs of corresponding sides are equal in length.

Your Turn

Add line segments AD and BE to the diagram above. Prove that $AD \parallel BE$.

EXAMPLE 4   Reasoning about congruency to prove an angle relationship

The main entrance to the Louvre in France is through a large pyramid. The base of each face is 35.42 m long. The other two edges of each face are equal length.

Prove: The two base angles on each face are equal.

The Louvre pyramid was designed by Ieoh Ming Pei in 1984. He also designed the Bank of China tower shown in Lesson 2.2.

Grant's Solution: Using an angle bisector strategy

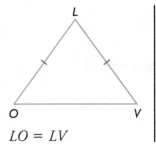

- - - - - - - - - - - - - - - - I drew a face of the pyramid. I knew that the face is an isosceles triangle because two of the edges are equal length.

$LO = LV$ | $\triangle LOV$ is isosceles.

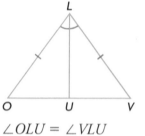

I bisected the vertical angle by drawing line segment *LU*.

$\angle OLU = \angle VLU$	*LU* bisects $\angle OLV$.
$LU = LU$	Common
$\triangle LOU \cong \triangle LVU$	SAS
$\angle LOV = \angle LVO$	If two triangles are congruent, then their corresponding angles are equal.

I had proved that two corresponding sides and the corresponding contained angles are equal.

The two angles at the base of each face are equal.

Yale's Solution: Using a reflecting strategy

$\triangle A'B'C'$ is the reflection of $\triangle ABC$.

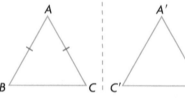

I drew a triangle with two equal sides to represent a face of the pyramid. Then I reflected the triangle across a vertical line to form a second triangle that was its image.

$BC = B'C'$	$B'C'$ is a reflection of *BC*.
$AC = AB$	Given
$AB = A'B'$	$A'B'$ is a reflection of *AB*.
$AC = A'C'$	$A'C'$ is a reflection of *AC*.
$AC = A'B'$	Transitive property
$AB = A'C'$	Transitive property
$\therefore \triangle ABC \cong \triangle A'B'C'$	SSS
$\angle B = \angle C'$	If two triangles are congruent, then their corresponding angles are equal.
$\angle C = \angle C'$	C' is the reflection of *C*, so the angles are equal.
$\angle B = \angle C$	Transitive property

I had proved that all three pairs of corresponding sides are equal.

Your Turn

Which strategy do you prefer? Explain why.

CHECK Your Understanding

1. For each of the following, determine whether the two triangles are congruent. Explain your reasoning.

a)

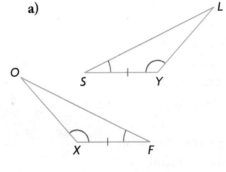

c)

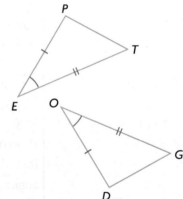

b)

d)

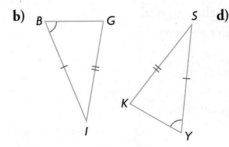

2. For each pair of triangles, write the pairs of equal angles or sides. Then state the triangle congruence, if there is one.

a)

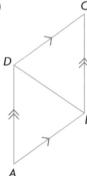

b)

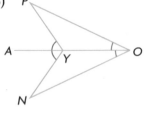

c)

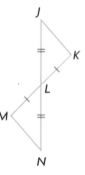

PRACTISING

3. a) Do the triangles on the sides of the Twin Towers in Regina, Saskatchewan, appear to be congruent? Explain.
   b) What measurements could you take to determine if these triangles are congruent?

4. Prove: $IN = AN$

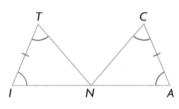

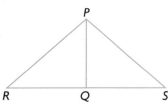

Perhaps the most recognizable architecture in Regina is that displayed in the McCallum Hill Centre Towers.

5. Given: $TQ = PQ$
           $RQ = SQ$
   Prove: $TR = PS$

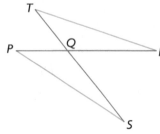

6. Given: WY bisects $\angle XWZ$
           and $\angle XYZ$.
   Prove: $XY = ZY$

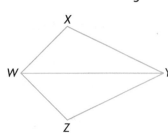

7. Given: $\angle PRQ = \angle PSQ$
           Q is the midpoint of RS.
   Prove: $PQ \perp RS$

2.6 Proving Congruent Triangles **113**

8. Given: $QP \perp PR$
$SR \perp RP$
$QR = SP$
Prove: $\angle PQR = \angle RSP$
a) by using the Pythagorean theorem
b) by using trigonometry

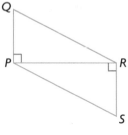

9. Given: $AB = DE$
$\angle ABC = \angle DEC$
Prove: $\triangle BCE$ is isosceles.

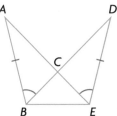

10. Given: MT is the diameter of the circle.
$TA = TH$
Prove: $\angle AMT = \angle HMT$

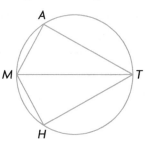

11. Duncan completed the following proof, but he made errors. Identify his errors, and write a corrected proof.

Given: $AB \parallel CD$
$BF \parallel CE$
$AE = DF$
Prove: $BF = CE$

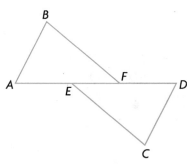

Duncan's Proof

$AB \parallel CD$	Given
$\angle BAF = \angle CDE$	Alternate interior angles
$BF \parallel CE$	Given
$\angle ABF = \angle DCE$	Alternate interior angles
$\angle BFA = \angle CED$	If there are two pairs of equal angles, the third pair must be equal.
$AE = DF$	Given
$\triangle BAF \cong \triangle CDE$	ASA

12. Prove: $\triangle ABC \cong \triangle AED$

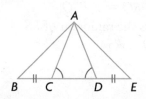

13. Given: $TA = ME$
$\angle MEA = \angle TAE$
Prove: $\angle TEM = \angle MAT$

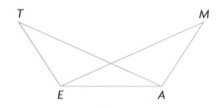

14. Given: $GH \perp HL$
$ML \perp HL$
$HJ = LK$
$GH = ML$
Prove: $\triangle NJK$ is isosceles.

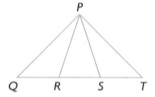

15. Given: $PQ = PT$
$QS = TR$
Prove: $\triangle PRS$ is isosceles.

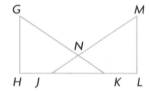

16. The horizontal steel pieces of the arm of a crane are parallel. The diagonal support trusses of the arm are of equal length. Prove that the triangle shapes in the arm are congruent.

17. Given: $QA = QB$
$AR = BS$
Prove: $RB = SA$

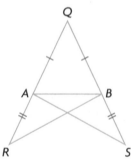

Tower cranes like this one are anchored to the ground. Due to the combination of height and lifting capacity, they are often used in the construction of tall buildings.

Closing

18. Create a problem that involves proving the congruency of two triangles. State the given information, as well as what needs to be proven. Exchange problems with a classmate, and write a two-column proof to solve each other's problems. Exchange proofs and discuss. Use your classmate's proof and the discussion to improve your problem.

Extending

19. Prove that the diagonals of a parallelogram bisect each other.

20. Prove that the diagonals of a rhombus are perpendicular bisectors of each other.

2.6 Proving Congruent Triangles

1. Determine the values of *a*, *b*, and *c*.

a)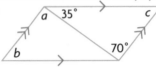

b)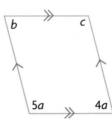

2. Determine the value of *x* in the following diagrams.

a)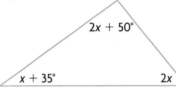

b)

3. a) Construct a pair of parallel lines and a transversal using a protractor and a straight edge.

b) Label your sketch, and then show by measuring that the alternate interior angles in your sketch are equal.

c) Name all the pairs of equal angles in your sketch.

4. Joyce is an artist who uses stained glass to create sun catchers, which are hung in windows. Joyce designed this sun catcher using triangles and regular hexagons. Determine the measure of the interior angles of each different polygon in her design.

5. *ABCDEFGH* is a regular octagon.

a) Draw an exterior angle at vertex *C*.

b) Determine the measure of the exterior angle you created.

c) Prove: $AF \parallel BE$

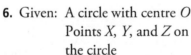

6. Given: A circle with centre *O*
Points *X*, *Y*, and *Z* on the circle
$YX = ZX$
Prove: $\angle OXY = \angle OXZ$

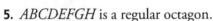

7. Given: $LM = NO$
$\angle LMO = \angle NOM$
Prove: *LMNO* is a parallelogram.

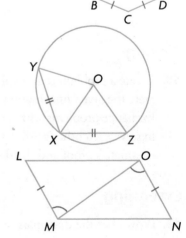

WHAT DO You Think Now?

Revisit **What Do You Think?** on page 69. How have your answers and explanations changed?

FREQUENTLY ASKED *Questions*

Q: **How are angle properties in convex polygons developed using other angle properties?**

A1: If you draw a line through one of the vertices of a triangle parallel to one of the sides, you will create two transversals between two parallel lines. You can use the angle property that alternate interior angles are equal to show that the sum of the measures of the three interior angles of a triangle is 180°.

> **Study | *Aid***
> - See Lesson 2.3.
> - Try Chapter Review Questions 7 and 8.

A2: The sum of the measures of the angles in any triangle is 180°. You can use this property to develop a relationship between the number of sides in a convex polygon and the sum of the measures of the interior angles of the polygon.

> **Study | *Aid***
> - See Lesson 2.4, Example 1.
> - Try Chapter Review Questions 9 and 10.

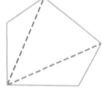

$n = 3$, triangle	$n = 4$, quadrilateral	$n = 5$, pentagon
Sum of Interior Angles = (180°) 1	Sum of Interior Angles = (180°) 2	Sum of Interior Angles = (180°) 3

Using inductive reasoning, you can show that for any polygon with n sides, the sum of the measures of the interior angles, $S(n)$, can be determined using the relationship:

$$S(n) = 180°(n - 2)$$

A3: When two angles share a vertex on a straight line, the angles are supplementary. You can use this angle property, along with the angle measure sum property for convex polygons, to develop a property about the exterior angles of a convex polygon. If you extend each side of a convex polygon, you will create a series of exterior angles.

> **Study | *Aid***
> - See Lesson 2.4.
> - Try Chapter Review Question 10.

$n = 3$, triangle	$n = 4$, quadrilateral	$n = 5$, pentagon
Sum of Interior Angles = (180°) 1	Sum of Interior Angles = (180°) 2	Sum of Interior Angles = (180°) 3
Sum of Exterior Angles:	Sum of Exterior Angles:	Sum of Exterior Angles:
3(180°) − (180°) 1 = 360°	4(180°) − 2(180°) = 360°	5(180°) − 3(180°) = 360°

Using inductive reasoning, you can show that for any polygon with n sides, the sum of the exterior angles, $A(n)$, is determined using the relationship:

$$A(n) = n(180°) - (n - 2)180°$$
$$A(n) = 360°$$

Q: **What is the minimum side and angle information you must show equal before you can conclude that a pair of triangles is congruent?**

Study | **Aid**

- See Lessons 2.5 and 2.6.
- Try Chapter Review Questions 12 to 19.

A: If you can show one of the following combinations of sides and angles equal in a pair of triangles, you can conclude that the triangles are congruent:

- three pairs of corresponding sides (*SSS*)
- two pairs of corresponding sides and the contained angles (*SAS*)
- two pairs of corresponding angles and the contained sides (*ASA*)

Q: **Can you prove that two triangles are congruent by *ASA* if the equal sides are not contained between the known pairs of equal angles?**

A: Yes. If there are two pairs of equal corresponding angles, then the remaining pair of corresponding angles must also be equal, since the sum of the measures of the angles in any triangle is 180°. Thus the pair of equal sides must be contained between two pairs of equal corresponding angles.

For example, in $\triangle PQR$ and $\triangle XYZ$,

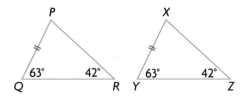

$\angle P = 180° - (\angle Q + \angle R)$	$\angle X = 180° - (\angle Y + \angle Z)$
$\angle P = 180° - (63° + 42°)$	$\angle X = 180° - (63° + 42°)$
$\angle P = 75°$	$\angle X = 75°$
$\angle P = \angle X$	Proven above
$PQ = XY$	Given
$\angle Q = \angle Y$	Given
$\triangle PQR \cong \triangle XYZ$	*ASA*

PRACTISING

Lesson 2.1

1. Kamotiqs are sleds that are dragged behind vehicles, such as snowmobiles, over snow and sea ice. Identify a set of parallel lines and a transversal in the photograph of a kamotiq.

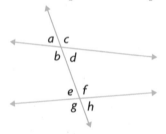

2. **a)** Name the pairs of corresponding angles.

   b) Are any of the pairs you indentified in part a) equal? Explain.
   c) How many pairs of supplementary angles can you see in the diagram? Name one pair.
   d) Are there any other pairs of equal angles? If so, name them.

3. Determine the values of a and b.

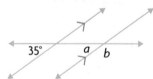

4. Is AB parallel to CD? Explain how you know.

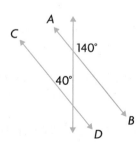

Lesson 2.2

5. Determine the values of a, b, and c.

   a)   **b)**

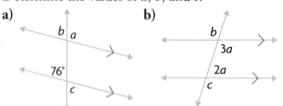

6. **a)** Construct a pair of parallel lines using a straight edge and a compass.
   b) Explain two different ways you could verify that your lines are parallel using a protractor.

7. Given: $QR \parallel ST$
            $\angle QRS = \angle TRS$
   Prove: $ST = TR$

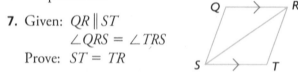

Lesson 2.3

8. Determine the values of x, y, and z.

   a)   **b)**

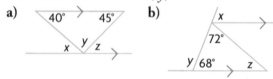

9. Given: $LM \perp MN$
            $LP = LO$
            $NO = NQ$
   Prove: $\angle POQ = 45°$

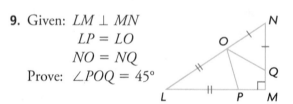

Lesson 2.4

10. **a)** Determine the sum of the measures of the interior angles of a 15-sided regular polygon.
    b) Show that each exterior angle measures 24°.

11. Given: $ABCDE$ is a regular pentagon.
    Prove: $AC \parallel ED$

12. Write the congruence relations for the pairs of congruent triangles shown below. Explain your decisions.

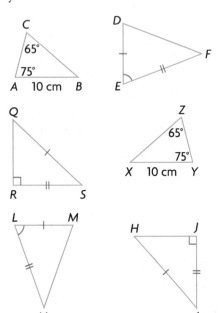

13. For each of the following, what additional piece of information would allow you to conclude that the two triangles are congruent?

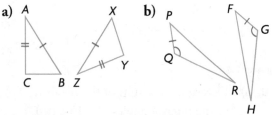

a)   b)

14. Given: *XY* and *WZ* are chords of a circle centred at *O*.
        $XY = WZ$
Prove: $\triangle XYO \cong \triangle WZO$

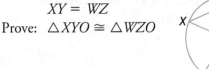

15. Given: $\angle QTR = \angle SRT$
        $QT = SR$
Prove: $QR = ST$

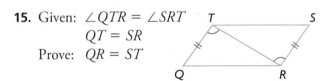

16. Given: $DA \perp AB$
        $CB \perp AB$
        $\angle DBA = \angle CAB$
Prove: $\angle ADB = \angle BCA$

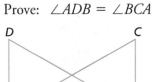
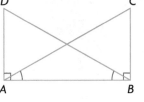

17. Given: $LO = NM$
        $ON = ML$
Prove: $LO \parallel NM$

18. Mark was given this diagram and asked to prove that *BF* and *CF* are the same length. He made an error in his proof.

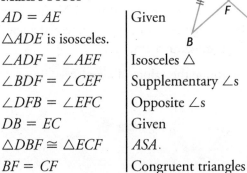

Mark's Proof

$AD = AE$	Given
$\triangle ADE$ is isosceles.	
$\angle ADF = \angle AEF$	Isosceles $\triangle$
$\angle BDF = \angle CEF$	Supplementary $\angle$s
$\angle DFB = \angle EFC$	Opposite $\angle$s
$DB = EC$	Given
$\triangle DBF \cong \triangle ECF$	ASA.
$BF = CF$	Congruent triangles

a) Identify and describe Mark's error.
b) Correct Mark's proof.

19. Given: *H* is a point on *DF*.
        $DE = DG$
        $EF = GF$
Prove: $EH = GH$

Designing Logos

A logo is often used to represent an organization and its products or services. The combination of shapes, colours, and fonts that are used in a logo is unique, making the logo stand out from the logos of other organizations. Logos transmit a message about the nature of an organization and its special qualities.

Logos appeal to our most powerful sense—the visual. After seeing a logo a few times, consumers can often identify the organization instantaneously and without confusion when they see the logo again.

? How can you design a logo that incorporates parallel lines and polygons?

A. What kind of organization do you want to design a logo for? What message do you want to convey with your logo?

B. How can you use shapes and lines to convey the message?

C. Draw a sketch of your logo. Mark parallel lines, equal sides, and angle measures. Explain how you know that each of your markings is correct.

D. Use your sketch to draw the actual logo you would present to the board of directors of the organization.

Task | *Checklist*

✔ Did you clearly explain your message?

✔ Did you provide a labelled sketch and a finished design?

✔ Did you provide appropriate reasoning?

Selecting Your Research Topic

To decide what to research, you can start by thinking about subjects and then consider specific topics. Some examples of subjects and topics are shown in the table below.

Subject	Topic
entertainment	• effects of new devices • file sharing
health care	• doctor and/or nurse shortages • funding
post-secondary education	• entry requirements • graduate success
history of the West and North	• relations between First Nations • immigration

It is important to take the time to consider several topics carefully before selecting a topic for your research project. Below is a list of criteria that will help you to determine if a topic you are considering is suitable.

Criteria for Selecting Your Research Topic

- **Does the topic interest you?**
  You will be more successful if you choose a topic that interests you. You will be more motivated to do the research, and you will be more attentive while doing the research. As well, you will care more about the conclusions you draw.

- **Is the topic practical to research?**
  If you decide to use first-hand data, can you generate the data in the time available, with the resources you have? If you decide to use second-hand data, are there multiple sources of data? Are these sources reliable, and can you access them in a timely manner?

- **Is there an important issue related to the topic?**
  Think about the issues related to the topic. If there are many viewpoints on an issue, you may be able to gather data that support some viewpoints but not others. The data you collect should enable you to come to a reasoned conclusion.

- **Will your audience appreciate your presentation?**
  Your topic should be interesting to others in your class, so they will be attentive during your presentation. Avoid a topic that may offend anyone in your class.

Sarah identified some subjects that interest her. Below she describes how she went from subjects to topics and then to one research topic.

Sarah's Research Topic

I identified five subjects that interested me and seemed to be worth exploring: health care, entertainment, post-secondary education, peoples of the West and North, and the environment. I used a mind map to organize my thoughts about each subject into topics. (Part of my mind map is shown here.) This gave me a list of possible topics to choose from.

I needed to narrow down my list by evaluating each topic. I wanted a topic that would be fun to research and might interest others in my class. I also wanted a topic that had lots of available data. Finally, I wanted a topic that involved an issue for a chance to come to a useful conclusion. I circled the two topics that seemed most likely to work. Then I did an initial search for information about these topics.

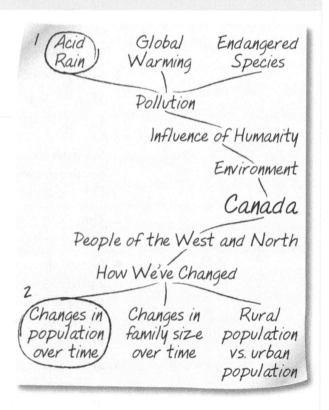

1. I spent some time researching the history of acid rain in Canada. I discovered that the problem was identified in the 1960s, but it has been a problem mostly in Eastern Canada. However, I did come across some newspaper articles and journal reports warning that acid rain may become a problem in the West. As I searched for data to support this claim, I found little historical data. I concluded that this topic would be too difficult to research.

2. I knew that the federal government conducts a census every four years to collect information about the people who live in Canada, so I was confident that I would be able to find lots of historical data. When I searched the Internet, I found several data sources for Canada's population. I feel that changes in the population of the West and North would make a good topic for my project.

Your Turn

A. Choose several subjects that interest you. Then make a list of topics that are related to each subject. A graphic organizer, such as a concept web or mind map, is useful for organizing your thoughts.

B. Once you have chosen several topics, do some research to see which topic would best support a project. Of these, choose the one that you think is the best. Refer to "Criteria for Selecting Your Research Topic."

1. **a)** What is a conjecture?
   b) Explain how inductive reasoning can be used to make a conjecture.
   c) How can inductive reasoning lead to a false conjecture? Explain using an example.

2. Maja gathered the following evidence and noticed a pattern.

   $$1^3 + 2^3 + 3^3 = 36 \qquad 7^3 + 8^3 + 9^3 = 1584$$
   $$3^3 + 4^3 + 5^3 = 216 \qquad 10^3 + 11^3 + 12^3 = 4059$$

   She made a conjecture: The sum of the cubes of any three consecutive positive integers is a multiple of 9. Is her conjecture reasonable? Develop evidence to test her conjecture.

3. How many counterexamples are needed to disprove a conjecture? Explain using an example.

4. Noreen claims that a quadrilateral is a parallelogram if the diagonals of the quadrilateral bisect each other. Do you agree or disagree? Justify your decision.

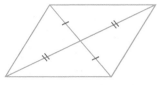

5. **a)** Use inductive reasoning to make a conjecture about the sum of two odd numbers.
   b) Use deductive reasoning to prove your conjecture.

6. Sung Lee says that this number trick always ends with the number 8: Choose a number. Double it. Add 9. Add the number you started with. Divide by 3. Add 5. Subtract the number you started with. Prove that Sung Lee is correct.

7. **a)** Determine the rule for the number of circles in the nth figure. Use your rule to determine the number of circles in the 15th figure.

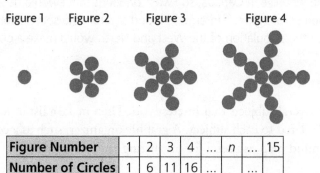

Figure 1   Figure 2   Figure 3   Figure 4

Figure Number	1	2	3	4	...	n	...	15
Number of Circles	1	6	11	16	...		...	

   b) Did you use inductive or deductive reasoning to answer part a)? Explain.

8. Prove the following conjecture for all three-digit numbers: If the digit in the ones place of a three-digit number is 0, the number is divisible by 10.

9. There are three switches in a hallway, all in the off position. Each switch corresponds to one of three light bulbs in a room with a closed door. You can turn the switches on and off, and you can leave them in any position. You can enter the room only once. Describe how you would identify which switch corresponds to which light bulb.

10. Determine the measure of each indicated angle.

a)

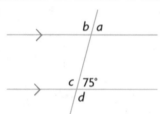

b)

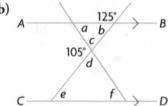

c)

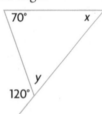

d)

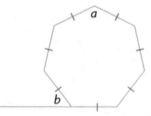

11. What information would you need to prove that *AB* is parallel to *CD*?

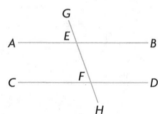

12. This photograph is an aerial view of the Pentagon in Washington, D.C.
   a) Determine the sum of the interior angles of the courtyard.
   b) Determine the measure of each interior angle of the courtyard.
   c) Determine the sum of the exterior angles of the building.

13. Given: $LO \parallel MN$

   $LO = MN$

   Prove: $\triangle LOP \cong \triangle NMP$

14. Given: $\triangle ABC$ is isosceles.

   $AB = CB$

   Prove: $AE = CD$

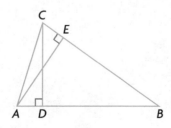

Yellowknife

1566 km

67.3°

Vancouver

1870 km

Acute Triangle Trigonometry

▶ **LEARNING GOALS**

You will be able to develop your spatial sense by

- Using the sine law to determine side lengths and angle measures in acute triangles
- Using the cosine law to determine side lengths and angle measures in acute triangles
- Solving problems that can be modelled using acute triangles

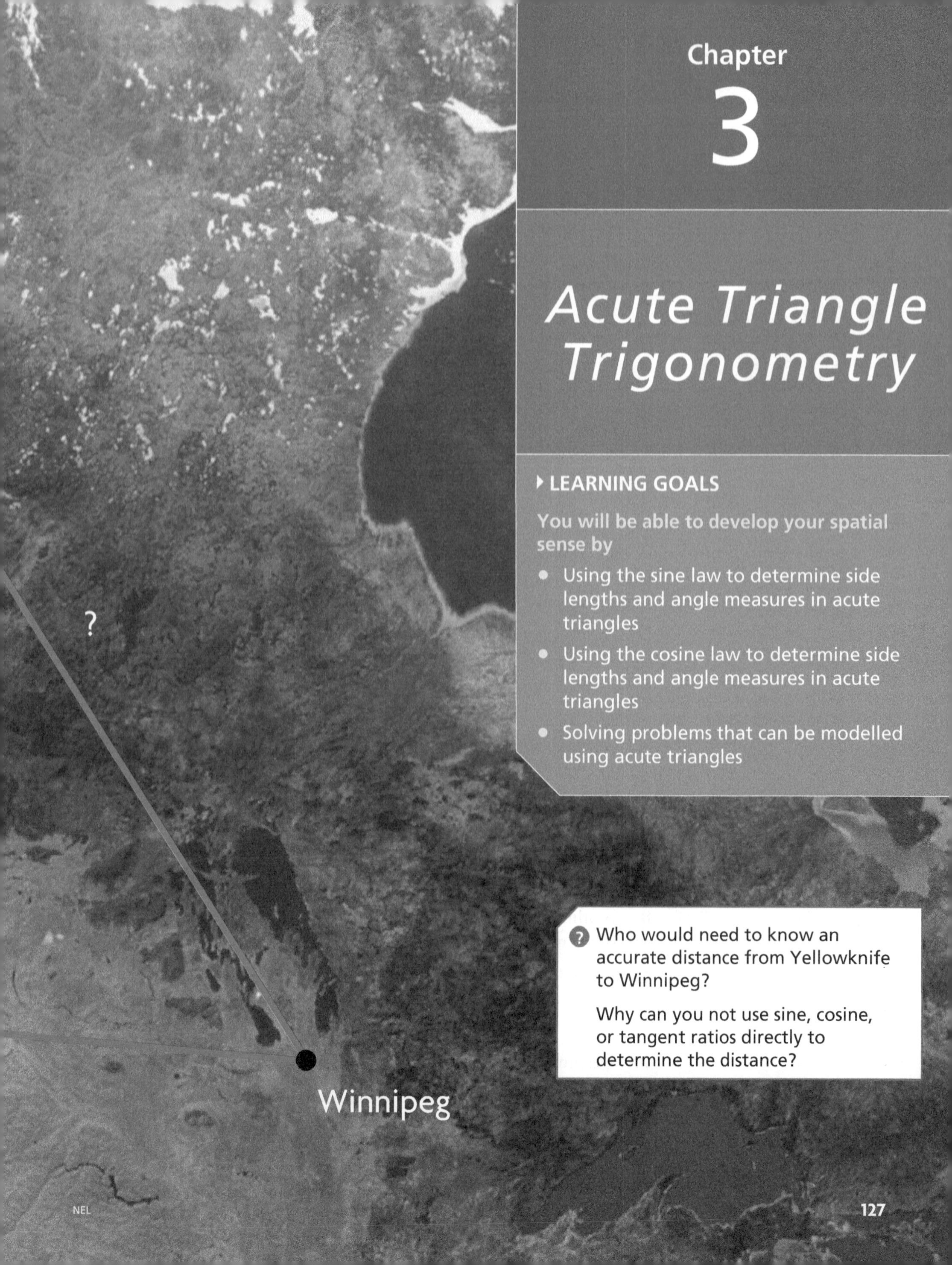

?

Winnipeg

? Who would need to know an accurate distance from Yellowknife to Winnipeg?

Why can you not use sine, cosine, or tangent ratios directly to determine the distance?

Lacrosse Trigonometry

Field lacrosse, Canada's national sport, originated with First Nations peoples, probably in central North America. Hundreds of years ago, both the number of players and the size of the field were much greater than in the modern game. The Iroquois peoples of what is now southern Ontario and western New York may have been the first to limit the number of players to 12 or 15.

Daniel is about to take a shot at a field lacrosse net. He estimates his current position, as shown below.

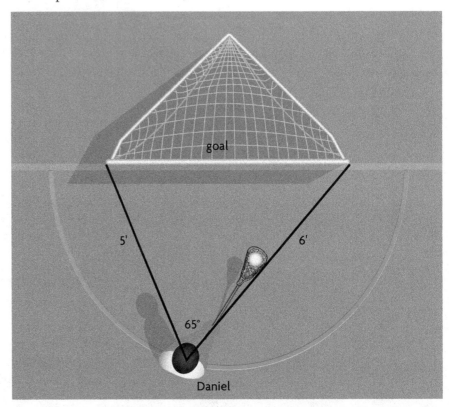

? How can you use these estimates to determine the width of the net?

A. Does Daniel's position form a right triangle with the goalposts?

B. A primary trigonometric ratio cannot be used to determine the width of the net directly. Explain why.

C. Copy the triangle that includes Daniel's position in the diagram above. Add a line segment so that you can determine a height of the triangle using trigonometry.

D. Determine the height of the triangle using a primary trigonometric ratio.

E. Create a plan that will allow you to determine the width of the lacrosse net using the two right triangles you created.

F. Carry out your plan to determine the width of the net.

This team from Caughnawaga toured England in 1867, demonstrating the game. As a result of the tour, lacrosse clubs were established in England. The game then spread around the world.

The Canadian team won the bronze medal at the 2009 Women's Lacrosse World Cup in Prague, Czech Republic.

WHAT DO You Think?

Decide whether you agree or disagree with each statement. Explain your decision.

1. When using proportional reasoning, if you apply the same operation, using the same number, to all the terms, the ratios remain equivalent.

2. If you know the measures of two angles and the length of any side in an acute triangle, you can determine all the other measurements.

Exploring Side–Angle Relationships in Acute Triangles

YOU WILL NEED

- dynamic geometry software OR ruler and protractor

Inukshuks can have many meanings. Some inukshuks direct travel, some indicate rich fishing or hunting areas, and some warn of danger.

GOAL

Explore the relationship between each side in an acute triangle and the sine of its opposite angle.

EXPLORE the Math

As they explore the North, the Inuit leave stone cairns, called inukshuks, as markers for those who follow in their path.

You have used the primary trigonometric ratios to determine side lengths and angle measures in right triangles. Can you use primary trigonometric ratios to determine unknown sides and angles in all acute triangles?

Choose one of the triangles below. The first triangle is a scale diagram of the side of the inukshuk shown. The second triangle represents a general acute triangle.

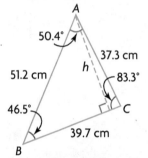

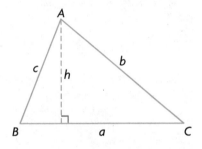

? **What are two equivalent expressions that represent the height of △ABC?**

Reflecting

A. Find a classmate who chose a different triangle than you did. Compare each set of expressions. How are they the same and how are they different?

B. If you drew the height of △ABC from a different vertex, how would the expressions for that height be different? Explain.

C. Create an equation using the expressions you created in part A. Show how your equation can be written so that each ratio in the equation involves a side and an angle. Repeat for the expressions you described in part B.

D. Explain how you could determine the measure of ∠E in this acute triangle.

In Summary

Key Idea

- The ratios of $\dfrac{\text{length of opposite side}}{\sin (\text{angle})}$ are equivalent for all three side–angle pairs in an acute triangle.

Need to Know

- In an acute triangle, $\triangle ABC$,

$$\frac{a}{\sin A} = \frac{b}{\sin B} = \frac{c}{\sin C}$$

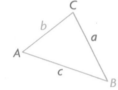

FURTHER Your Understanding

1. For each acute triangle,
   i) copy the triangle and label the sides.
   ii) write two expressions for the height of each triangle, and use your expressions to create equivalent ratios.

   a)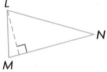

   b)

2. i) Sketch a triangle that corresponds to each equation below.
   ii) Solve for the unknown side length or angle measure. Round your answer to one decimal place.

   a) $\dfrac{w}{\sin 50°} = \dfrac{8.0}{\sin 60°}$

   c) $\dfrac{6.0}{\sin M} = \dfrac{10.0}{\sin 72°}$

   b) $\dfrac{k}{\sin 43°} = \dfrac{9.5}{\sin 85°}$

   d) $\dfrac{12.5}{\sin Y} = \dfrac{14.0}{\sin 88°}$

3. Michel claims that if x and y are sides in an acute triangle, then:

   $$x \sin Y = y \sin X$$

   Do you agree or disagree? Justify your decision.

4. If you want to determine an unknown side length or angle measure in an acute triangle, what is the minimum information that you must have?

5. Do you think the ratios of $\dfrac{\text{opposite side}}{\sin (\text{angle})}$ are equivalent for all three side–angle pairs in a right triangle? Construct two right triangles, and measure their sides and angles. Use your measurements to test your conjecture.

> **Communication | Tip**
>
> The expression $x \sin Y$ is a product. It is equivalent to $x(\sin Y)$.

Proving and Applying the Sine Law

YOU WILL NEED

- ruler
- protractor
- calculator

GOAL

Explain the steps used to prove the sine law. Use the law to solve triangles.

EXPLORE...

- The angles in an acute triangle measure 40°, 55°, and 85°. Could two of the side lengths be 5 cm and 4 cm? Explain.

INVESTIGATE the Math

In Lesson 3.1, you discovered a side–angle relationship in acute triangles. Before this relationship can be used to solve problems, it must be proven to work in all acute triangles. Consider Ben's **proof**:

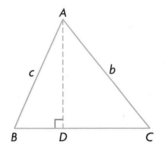

Step 1
I drew an acute triangle with height *AD*.

In △*ABD*,

$$\sin B = \frac{\text{opposite}}{\text{hypotenuse}}$$

$$\sin B = \frac{AD}{c}$$

$$c \sin B = AD$$

In △*ACD*,

$$\sin C = \frac{\text{opposite}}{\text{hypotenuse}}$$

$$\sin C = \frac{AD}{b}$$

$$b \sin C = AD$$

Step 2
I wrote equations for the sine of ∠*B* and the sine of ∠*C* in the two right triangles.

$$c \sin B = b \sin C$$

$$\frac{c \sin B}{\sin C} = b$$

$$\frac{c}{\sin C} = \frac{b}{\sin B}$$

Step 3
I set the expressions for *AD* equal to each other.

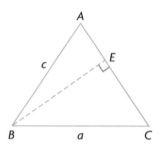

In $\triangle ABE$,

$$\sin A = \frac{BE}{c}$$

$$c \sin A = BE$$

In $\triangle CBE$,

$$\sin C = \frac{BE}{a}$$

$$a \sin C = BE$$

Step 4

I had expressions that involved sides b and c and $\angle B$ and $\angle C$, but I also needed an expression that involved a and $\angle A$. I drew a height from B to AC and developed two expressions for BE.

$$c \sin A = a \sin C$$

$$c = \frac{a \sin C}{\sin A}$$

$$\frac{c}{\sin C} = \frac{a}{\sin A}$$

Step 5

I set the expressions for BE equal to each other.

$$\frac{a}{\sin A} = \frac{b}{\sin B} = \frac{c}{\sin C}$$

Step 6

I set all three ratios equal to each other.

? How can you improve Ben's explanation of his proof?

A. Work with a partner to explain why Ben drew height AD in step 1.

B. In step 2, he created two different expressions that involved AD. Explain why.

C. Explain why he was able to set the expressions for AD equal in step 3.

D. Explain what Ben did to rewrite the equation in step 3.

E. In steps 4 and 5, Ben drew a different height BE and repeated steps 2 and 3 for the right triangles this created. Explain why.

F. Explain why he was able to equate all three ratios in step 6 to create the **sine law**.

Reflecting

G. Why did Ben not use the cosine ratio or tangent ratio to describe the heights of his acute triangle?

H. If Ben drew a perpendicular line segment from vertex C to side AB, which pair of ratios in the sine law do you think he could show to be equal?

I. Why does it make sense that the sine law can also be written in the form $\frac{\sin A}{a} = \frac{\sin B}{b} = \frac{\sin C}{c}$?

sine law

In any acute triangle,

$$\frac{a}{\sin A} = \frac{b}{\sin B} = \frac{c}{\sin C}$$

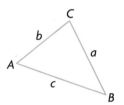

3.2 Proving and Applying the Sine Law   **133**

APPLY the Math

EXAMPLE 1   Using reasoning to determine the length of a side

A triangle has angles measuring 80° and 55°. The side opposite the
80° angle is 12.0 m in length. Determine the length of the side opposite the
55° angle to the nearest tenth of a metre.

Elizabeth's Solution

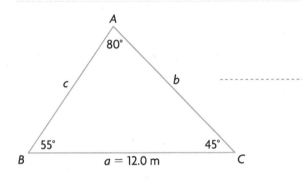

I named the triangle *ABC* and decided that the 80°
angle was ∠A. Then I sketched the triangle,
including all of the information available.

I knew that the third angle, ∠C, had to measure
45°, because the angles of a triangle add to 180°.
I needed to determine *b*.

Since the triangle does not contain a right angle,
I couldn't use the primary trigonometric ratios.

$$\frac{a}{\sin A} = \frac{b}{\sin B}$$

$$\frac{12.0}{\sin 80°} = \frac{b}{\sin 55°}$$

$$\sin 55°\left(\frac{12.0}{\sin 80°}\right) = \sin 55°\left(\frac{b}{\sin 55°}\right)$$

$$\sin 55°\left(\frac{12.0}{\sin 80°}\right) = b$$

$$9.981... = b$$

I could use the sine law if I knew an opposite
side–angle pair, plus one more side or angle in
the triangle. I knew *a* and ∠A and I wanted to
know *b*, so I related *a*, *b*, sin *A*, and sin *B* using
$\frac{a}{\sin A} = \frac{b}{\sin B}$. Since *b* was in the numerator,
I could multiply both sides by sin 55° to solve
for *b*.

The length of *AC* is 10.0 m.

I rounded to the nearest tenth. It made sense that
the length of *AC* is shorter than the length of *BC*,
since the measure of ∠B is less than the measure
of ∠A.

Your Turn

Using △*ABC* above, determine the length of *AB* to the nearest tenth of a metre.

EXAMPLE **2**   Solving a problem using the sine law

Toby uses chains attached to
hooks on the ceiling and a winch
to lift engines at his father's garage.
The chains, the winch, and the
ceiling are arranged as shown.
Toby solved the triangle using the
sine law to determine the angle
that each chain makes with the
ceiling to the nearest degree. He
claims that $\theta = 40°$ and $\alpha = 54°$. Is
he correct? Explain, and make any
necessary corrections.

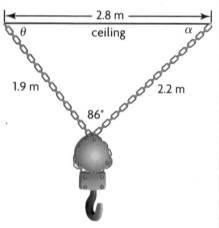

> **Communication | Tip**
>
> Greek letters are often used as
> variables to represent the
> measures of unknown angles.
> The most commonly used
> letters are θ (theta), α (alpha),
> β (beta), and γ (gamma).

Sanjay's Solution

I know Toby's calculations
are incorrect, since α must
be the smallest angle in the
triangle.

> In any triangle, the shortest side
> is across from the smallest angle.
> Since 1.9 m is the shortest side,
> $\alpha < \theta$. Toby's values do not
> meet this condition.

$$\frac{\sin \alpha}{1.9} = \frac{\sin 86°}{2.8}$$

> To correct the error, I used the
> sine law to determine α.

$$1.9\left(\frac{\sin \alpha}{1.9}\right) = 1.9\left(\frac{\sin 86°}{2.8}\right)$$

$$\sin \alpha = 1.9\left(\frac{\sin 86°}{2.8}\right)$$

> I multiplied both sides by 1.9 to
> solve for $\sin \alpha$. Then I evaluated
> the right side of the equation.

$$\sin \alpha = 0.6769...$$
$$\alpha = \sin^{-1}(0.6769...)$$
$$\alpha = 42.603...°$$

$$\theta = 180° - 86° - 42.603...°$$
$$\theta = 51.396...°$$

> I used the fact that angles
> in a triangle add to 180° to
> determine θ.

Toby was incorrect. The correct
measures of the angles are:

$$\alpha \doteq 43°$$
and
$$\theta \doteq 51°$$

> My determinations are
> reasonable, because the shortest
> side is opposite the smallest angle.

Communication | *Tip*

Directions are often stated in terms of north and south on a compass. For example, N30°E means travelling in a direction 30° east of north. S45°W means travelling in a direction 45° west of south.

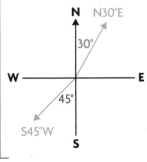

EXAMPLE 3 Using reasoning to determine the measure of an angle

The captain of a small boat is delivering supplies to two lighthouses, as shown. His compass indicates that the lighthouse to his left is located at N30°W and the lighthouse to his right is located at N50°E. Determine the compass direction he must follow when he leaves lighthouse *B* for lighthouse *A*.

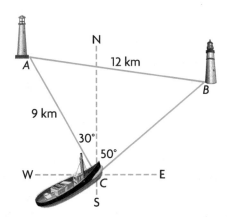

Anthony's Solution

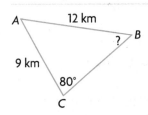

I drew a diagram. I labelled the sides of the triangle I knew and the angle I wanted to determine.

$$\frac{\sin B}{AC} = \frac{\sin C}{AB}$$

I knew *AC*, *AB*, and ∠*C*, and I wanted to determine ∠*B*. So I used the sine law that includes these four quantities.

I used the proportion with sin *B* and sin *C* in the numerators so the unknown would be in the numerator.

$$\frac{\sin B}{9} = \frac{\sin 80°}{12}$$

$$9\left(\frac{\sin B}{9}\right) = 9\left(\frac{\sin 80°}{12}\right)$$

$$\sin B = 9\left(\frac{\sin 80°}{12}\right)$$

$$\sin B = 0.7386...$$

$$\angle B = \sin^{-1}(0.7386...)$$
$$\angle B = 47.612...°$$

I substituted the given information and then solved for $\sin B$.

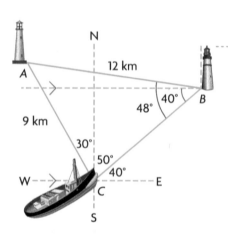

The Fisgard Lighthouse in Victoria, British Columbia, was the first lighthouse built on Canada's west coast and is still in operation today.

The measure of $\angle B$ is 48°.

The answer seems reasonable. $\angle B$ must be less than 80°, because 9 km is less than 12 km.

I drew a diagram and marked the angles I knew. I knew east-west lines are all parallel, so the alternate interior angle at B must be 40°.

The captain must head N82°W from lighthouse B.

The line segment from lighthouse B to lighthouse A makes an 8° angle with west-east. I subtracted this from 90° to determine the direction west of north.

Your Turn

In $\triangle ABC$ above, CB is about 9.6 km. Use the sine law to determine $\angle A$. Verify your answer by determining the sum of the angles.

In Summary

Key Idea

- The sine law can be used to determine unknown side lengths or angle measures in acute triangles.

Need to Know

- You can use the sine law to solve a problem modelled by an acute triangle when you know:
  - two sides and the angle opposite a known side.

  - two angles and any side.

 or

- If you know the measures of two angles in a triangle, you can determine the third angle because the angles must add to 180°.

- When determining side lengths, it is more convenient to use:

$$\frac{a}{\sin A} = \frac{b}{\sin B} = \frac{c}{\sin C}$$

- When determining angles, it is more convenient to use:

$$\frac{\sin A}{a} = \frac{\sin B}{b} = \frac{\sin C}{c}$$

CHECK *Your Understanding*

1. Write three equivalent ratios using the sides and angles in the triangle at the right.

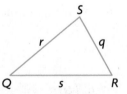

2. **a)** Determine length b to the nearest tenth of a centimetre.

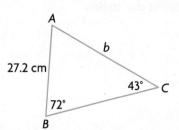

   b) Determine the measure of θ to the nearest degree.

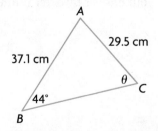

138 Chapter 3 **Acute Triangle Trigonometry**   NEL

PRACTISING

3. Determine the indicated side lengths to the nearest tenth of a unit and the indicated angle measures to the nearest degree.

a)

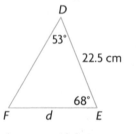

d)

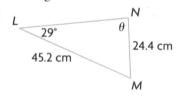

b)

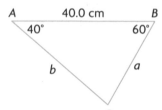

e)

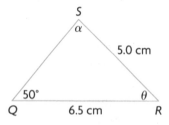

c)

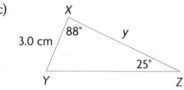

f)

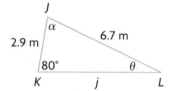

4. Scott is studying the effects of environmental changes on fish populations in his summer job. As part of his research, he needs to know the distance between two points on Lake Laberge, Yukon. Scott makes the measurements shown and uses the sine law to determine the lake's length as 36.0 km.

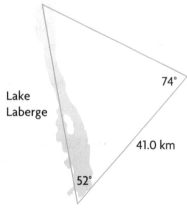

The acidity of northern lakes may be affected by acid rain and snow caused by development.

a) Agathe, Scott's research partner, says that his answer is incorrect. Explain how she knows.

b) Determine the distance between the two points to the nearest tenth of a kilometre.

5. An architect designed a house and must give more instructions to the builders. The rafters that hold up the roof are equal in length. The rafters extend beyond the supporting wall as shown. How long are the rafters? Express your answer to the nearest inch.

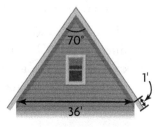

6. Draw a labelled diagram for each triangle. Then determine the required side length or angle measure.
   a) In $\triangle SUN$, $n = 58$ cm, $\angle N = 38°$, and $\angle U = 72°$.
      Determine the length of side u to the nearest centimetre.
   b) In $\triangle PQR$, $\angle R = 73°$, $\angle Q = 32°$, and $r = 23$ cm.
      Determine the length of side q to the nearest centimetre.
   c) In $\triangle TAM$, $t = 8$ cm, $m = 6$ cm, and $\angle T = 65°$.
      Determine the measure of $\angle M$ to the nearest degree.
   d) In $\triangle WXY$, $w = 12.0$ cm, $y = 10.5$ cm, and $\angle W = 60°$.
      Determine the measure of $\angle Y$ to the nearest degree.

7. In $\triangle CAT$, $\angle C = 32°$, $\angle T = 81°$, and $c = 24.1$ m.
   Solve the triangle. Round sides to the nearest tenth of a metre.

8. a) Determine the value of n to the nearest tenth using
      i) a primary trigonometric ratio.
      ii) the sine law.
   b) Explain why your answers for part a) are the same. Do others in your class agree with your explanation?

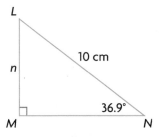

9. Janice is sailing from Gimli on Lake Winnipeg to Grand Beach. She had planned to sail 26.0 km in the direction S71°E; however, the wind and current pushed her off course. After several hours, she discovered that she had actually been sailing S79°E. She checked her map and saw that she must sail S18°W to reach Grand Beach. Determine, to the nearest tenth of a kilometre, the distance remaining to Grand Beach.
   a) Draw a diagram of this situation, then compare it with a classmate's. Make any adjustments needed in your diagrams.
   b) Solve the problem.

Gimli, Manitoba, is a fishing village with a rich Icelandic heritage.

10. A telephone pole is supported by two wires on opposite sides. At the top of the pole, the wires form an angle of 60°. On the ground, the ends of the wires are 15.0 m apart. One wire makes a 45° angle with the ground.
   a) Draw a diagram of this situation, then compare it with a classmate's.
   b) How long are the wires, and how tall is the pole? Express your answers to the nearest tenth of a metre.

11. In $\triangle PQR$, $\angle Q = 90°$, $r = 6$, and $p = 8$. Explain two different ways to determine the measure of $\angle P$. Share your explanation with a partner. How might you improve your explanation?

12. Stella decided to ski to a friend's cabin. She skied 10.0 km in the direction N40°E. She rested, then skied S45°E and arrived at the cabin. The cabin is 14.5 km from her home, as the crow flies. Determine, to the nearest tenth of a kilometre, the distance she travelled on the second leg of her trip.

13. A bridge has been built across a gorge. Jordan wants to bungee jump from the bridge. One of the things she must know, to make the jump safely, is the depth of the gorge. She measured the gorge as shown. Determine the depth of the gorge to the nearest tenth of a metre.

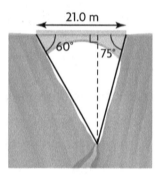

14. Sketch an acute triangle.
   a) List three pieces of information about the triangle's sides and angles that would allow you to solve for all the other side lengths and angle measures of the triangle.
   b) List three pieces of information about the triangle's sides and angles that would not allow you to solve the triangle.

15. Jim says that the sine law cannot be used to determine the length of side c in $\triangle ABC$. Do you agree or disagree? Explain.

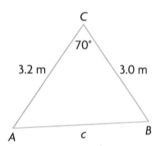

Closing

16. Suppose that you know the length of side p in $\triangle PQR$, as well as the measures of $\angle P$ and $\angle Q$. What other sides and angles could you determine? Explain to a classmate how you would determine these measurements.

Extending

17. In $\triangle ABC$, $\angle A = 58°$, $\angle C = 74°$, and $b = 6$. Determine the area of $\triangle ABC$ to one decimal place.

18. An isosceles triangle has two sides that are 10.0 cm long and two angles that measure 50°. A line segment bisects one of the 50° angles and ends at the opposite side. Determine the length of the line segment to the nearest tenth of a centimetre.

19. Use the sine law to write a ratio that is equivalent to each expression for $\triangle ABC$.
   a) $\dfrac{\sin A}{\sin B}$
   b) $\dfrac{a}{c}$
   c) $\dfrac{a \sin C}{c \sin A}$

FREQUENTLY ASKED Questions

Q: **What is the sine law, and what is it used for?**

A: The sine law describes the relationship between the sides and their opposite angles in a triangle.

In $\triangle ABC$,

$$\frac{a}{\sin A} = \frac{b}{\sin B} = \frac{c}{\sin C}$$

or

$$\frac{\sin A}{a} = \frac{\sin B}{b} = \frac{\sin C}{c}$$

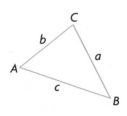

The sine law can be used to determine unknown side lengths and angle measures in acute and right triangles.

Q: **When can you use the sine law?**

A: Use the sine law if you know any three of these four measurements: two sides and their opposite angles. The sine law allows you to determine the unknown length or angle measure. If you know any two angles in a triangle, you can determine the third angle.

For example, the sine law can be used to determine the length of AB in the triangle at the right.

Side AB is opposite $\angle C$, which measures $72°$.

Side AC is of length 500 m and is opposite $\angle B$.

$\angle B = 180° - 52° - 72°$

$\angle B = 56°$

Use the sine law to write an equation and solve for AB.

$$\frac{AB}{\sin 72°} = \frac{500}{\sin 56°}$$

$$AB = \sin 72°\left(\frac{500}{\sin 56°}\right)$$

$$AB = 573.590...$$

The length of AB is about 574 m.

PRACTISING

Lesson 3.1

1. Write the equivalent sine law ratios for acute triangle *XYZ*.

2. a) Sketch an acute triangle that illustrates the relationship described in the equation below.

$$\frac{x}{\sin 60°} = \frac{10}{\sin 80°}$$

    b) Determine the value of *x* to the nearest tenth.

3. $\triangle DEF$ is an acute triangle. Nazir claims that

$$\frac{d}{\sin F} = \frac{f}{\sin D}$$

Do you agree or disagree? Explain.

Lesson 3.2

4. Determine the values indicated with variables to the nearest tenth of a unit.

a)

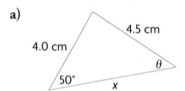

b)

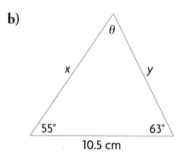

5. Solve each triangle. Where necessary, round answers to the nearest tenth of a unit.

a)

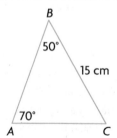

b)

6. In $\triangle XYZ$, the values of *x* and *z* are known. What additional information do you need to know if you want to use the sine law to solve the triangle?

7. Two Jasper National Park rangers in their fire towers spot a fire.

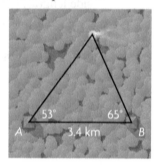

    a) Which tower is closer to the fire? Explain.
    b) Determine the distance, to the nearest tenth of a kilometre, from this tower to the fire.

8. As Chloe and Ivan are paddling north on Lac La Ronge in Saskatchewan, they notice a campsite ahead, at N52°W. They continue paddling north for 800 m, which takes them past the campsite. The campsite is then at S40°W. How far away, to the nearest metre, is the campsite from their position at the second sighting?

9. Determine, to the nearest tenth of a centimetre, the perimeter of each isosceles triangle.

a)   **b)**

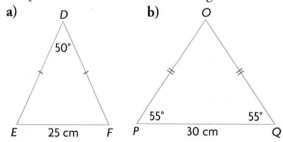

Proving and Applying the Cosine Law

- ruler
- protractor
- calculator

GOAL

Explain the steps used to prove the cosine law. Use the cosine law to solve triangles.

EXPLORE...

- One side of a right triangle is 8 cm. One angle is 50°. What could the other side lengths be?

INVESTIGATE the Math

The sine law cannot always help you determine unknown angle measures or side lengths. Consider these triangles:

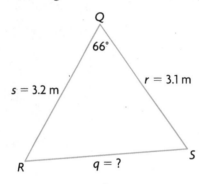

where $\dfrac{3.1}{\sin R} = \dfrac{3.2}{\sin S} = \dfrac{q}{\sin 66°}$

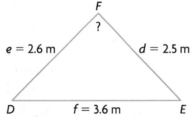

where $\dfrac{\sin E}{2.6} = \dfrac{\sin D}{2.5} = \dfrac{\sin F}{3.6}$

cosine law

In any acute triangle,

$a^2 = b^2 + c^2 - 2bc \cos A$
$b^2 = a^2 + c^2 - 2ac \cos B$
$c^2 = a^2 + b^2 - 2ab \cos C$

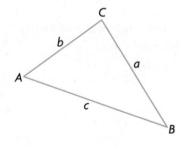

There are two unknowns in each pair of equivalent ratios, so the pairs cannot be used to solve for the unknowns. Another relationship is needed. This relationship is called the **cosine law**, and it is derived from the Pythagorean theorem.

Before this relationship can be used to solve problems, it must be proven to work in all acute triangles. Consider Heather's proof of the cosine law:

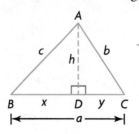

Step 1
I drew an acute triangle *ABC*. Then I drew the height from *A* to *BC* and labelled the intersection point as point *D*. I labelled this line segment *h*. I labelled *BD* as *x* and *DC* as *y*.

$$b^2 = c^2 - x^2$$
$$b^2 = b^2 - y^2$$

Step 2
I wrote two different expressions for h^2.

$$c^2 - x^2 = b^2 - y^2$$
$$c^2 = x^2 + b^2 - y^2$$

Step 3
I set the two expressions equal to each other and solved for c^2.

$x = a - y$, so
$$c^2 = (a - y)^2 + b^2 - y^2$$
$$c^2 = a^2 - 2ay + y^2 + b^2 - y^2$$
$$c^2 = a^2 + b^2 - 2ay$$

Step 4
I wrote an equivalent equation that only used the variable y and simplified.

$$\cos C = \frac{y}{b}, \text{ so}$$
$$b \cos C = y$$

Step 5
I determined an equivalent expression for y.

$$c^2 = a^2 + b^2 - 2ay$$
$$c^2 = a^2 + b^2 - 2ab \cos C$$

Step 6
I substituted the expression $b \cos C$ for y in my equation.

? How can you improve Heather's explanations in her proof of the cosine law?

A. Work with a partner to explain why she drew height AD in step 1.

B. In step 2, Heather created two different expressions that involved h^2. Explain how she did this.

C. Explain why she was able to set the expressions for h^2 equal in step 3.

D. In step 4, Heather eliminated the variable x. Explain how and why.

E. Explain how she determined an equivalent expression for y in step 5.

F. Explain why the final equation in step 6 is the most useful form of the cosine law.

Reflecting

G. Les wrote a similar proof, but he substituted $a - x$ for y instead of $a - y$ for x in the equation in step 3. How would his result differ from Heather's?

H. François started his proof by drawing a height from B to AC. How would this affect his final result?

I. **i)** Explain why you can use the cosine law to determine the unknown side q in $\triangle QRS$ on the previous page.

   ii) Explain why you can use the cosine law to determine the unknown $\angle F$ in $\triangle DEF$ on the previous page.

APPLY the Math

EXAMPLE **1**   Using reasoning to determine the length of a side

Determine the length of *CB* to the nearest metre.

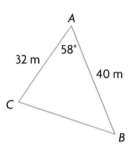

Justin's Solution

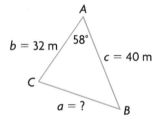

I labelled the sides with letters.
I couldn't use the sine law, because I didn't know a side length and the measure of its opposite angle.

$a^2 = b^2 + c^2 - 2bc \cos A$
$a^2 = 32^2 + 40^2 - 2(32)(40) \cos 58°$

I knew the lengths of two sides (*b* and *c*) and the measure of the contained angle between these sides ($\angle A$). I had to determine side *a*, which is opposite $\angle A$. I chose the form of the cosine law that includes these four values. Then I substituted the values I knew into the cosine law.

$a^2 = 1024 + 1600 - 2560 \cos 58°$
$a^2 = 2624 - 2560 \cos 58°$
$a^2 = 1267.406...$

$a = \sqrt{1267.406...}$
$a = 35.600...$

CB is 36 m.

Your Turn

After determining the length of *CB* in $\triangle ABC$ above, Justin used the sine law to determine that the measure of $\angle B$ is 50°, then concluded that the measure of $\angle C$ must be 72°. Use the cosine law to verify his solution for $\triangle ABC$.

EXAMPLE **2**   Using reasoning to determine the measure of an angle

The diagram at the right shows the plan for a roof, with support beam *DE* parallel to *AB*. The local building code requires the angle formed at the peak of a roof to fall within a range of 70° to 80° so that snow and ice will not build up. Will this plan pass the local building code?

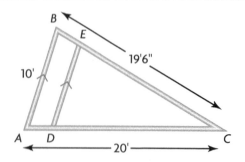

Luanne's Solution: Substituting into the cosine law, then rearranging

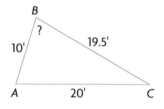

I drew a sketch, removing the support beam since it isn't needed to solve this problem.

The peak of the roof is represented by ∠B.

I labelled the sides I knew in the triangle.

I wrote all the lengths using the same unit, feet.

$a = 19.5,\ b = 20,$ and $c = 10$

Since I only knew the lengths of the sides in the triangle, I couldn't use the sine law.

$$b^2 = a^2 + c^2 - 2ac\cos B$$

I had to determine ∠B, so I decided to use the form of the cosine law that contained ∠B.

$$20^2 = 19.5^2 + 10^2 - 2(19.5)(10)\cos B$$
$$400 - 380.25 - 100 = -390\,(\cos B)$$
$$-80.25 = -390\,(\cos B)$$

I substituted the side lengths into the formula and simplified.

I had to isolate cos B before I could determine ∠B.

$$\frac{-80.25}{-390} = \cos B$$

$$\cos^{-1}\left(\frac{80.25}{390}\right) = \angle B$$
$$78.125...° = \angle B$$

The angle formed at the peak of the roof is 78°. This plan will pass the local building code.

My answer is reasonable because ∠B should be the angle with the largest measure in the triangle.

78° lies within the acceptable range of 70° to 80°.

Emilie's Solution: Rearranging the cosine law before substituting

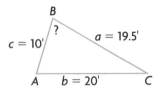

I drew a diagram, labelling the sides and angles.
I wrote all the side lengths in terms of feet.

$$b^2 = a^2 + c^2 - 2ac \cos B$$

Since I wanted to determine $\angle B$ and I knew the length of all three sides, I wrote the form of the cosine law that contains $\angle B$.

$$b^2 + 2ac \cos B = a^2 + c^2 - 2ac \cos B + 2ac \cos B$$
$$b^2 + 2ac \cos B = a^2 + c^2$$
$$b^2 + 2ac \cos B - b^2 = a^2 + c^2 - b^2$$
$$2ac \cos B = a^2 + c^2 - b^2$$
$$\frac{2ac \cos B}{2ac} = \frac{a^2 + c^2 - b^2}{2ac}$$
$$\cos B = \frac{a^2 + c^2 - b^2}{2ac}$$

I decided to rearrange the formula to solve for cos B by adding $2ac \cos B$ to both sides of the equation. Then I subtracted b^2 from both sides. Finally I divided both sides by $2ac$.

$$\cos B = \frac{19.5^2 + 10^2 - 20^2}{2(19.5)(10)}$$

I substituted the information that I knew into the rearranged formula and evaluated the right side.

$$\cos B = \frac{80.25}{390}$$
$$\cos B = 0.2057...$$

$$\angle B = \cos^{-1}(0.2057...)$$
$$\angle B = 78.125...°$$

The angle formed at the peak of the roof is 78°.
This plan passes the local building code.

I rounded to the nearest degree. The value of this angle is within the acceptable range.

Your Turn

a) Compare Luanne's Solution and Emilie's Solution. What are the advantages of each strategy?

b) Which strategy do you prefer for this problem? Explain.

c) Use your strategy and the cosine law to determine $\angle A$ in $\triangle ABC$ above.

EXAMPLE **3** Solving a problem using the cosine law

A three-pointed star is made up of an equilateral triangle and three congruent isosceles triangles. Determine the length of each side of the equilateral triangle in this three-pointed star. Round the length to the nearest centimetre.

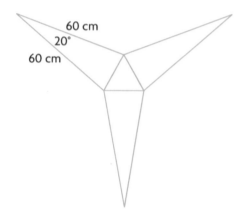

The world's largest Ukrainian Easter egg (called a pysanka) is located in Vegreville, Alberta. It is decorated with 2208 equilateral triangles and 524 three-pointed stars.

Dakoda's Solution

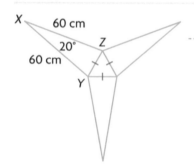

I named the vertices of one of the isosceles triangles.

$(YZ)^2 = (XY)^2 + (XZ)^2 - 2(XY)(XZ) \cos (\angle YXZ)$
$(YZ)^2 = 60^2 + 60^2 - 2(60)(60) \cos 20°$
$(YZ)^2 = 3600 + 3600 - 6765.786...$

I knew two sides and the contained angle in each isosceles triangle, so I used the cosine law to write an equation that involved YZ. Then I substituted the information that I knew.

$(YZ)^2 = 434.213...$
$YZ = \sqrt{434.213...}$
$YZ = 20.837...$

Each side of the equilateral triangle has a length of 21 cm.

Key Idea

- The cosine law can be used to determine an unknown side length or angle measure in an acute triangle.

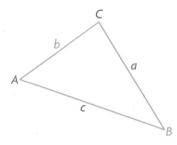

$$a^2 = b^2 + c^2 - 2bc \cos A$$
$$b^2 = a^2 + c^2 - 2ac \cos B$$
$$c^2 = a^2 + b^2 - 2ab \cos C$$

Need to Know

- You can use the cosine law to solve a problem that can be modelled by an acute triangle when you know:
  - two sides and the contained angle.
  - all three sides.

 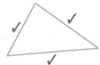

- The contained angle is the angle between two known sides.
- When using the cosine law to determine an angle, you can:
  - substitute the known values first, then solve for the unknown angle.
  - rearrange the formula to solve for the cosine of the unknown angle, then substitute and evaluate.

CHECK Your Understanding

1. Suppose that you are given each set of data for △ABC. Can you use the cosine law to determine c? Explain.
   a) $a = 5$ cm, $\angle A = 52°$, $\angle C = 43°$
   b) $a = 7$ cm, $b = 5$ cm, $\angle C = 43°$

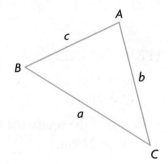

2. Determine the length of side x to the nearest centimetre.

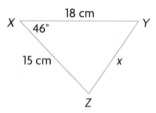

3. Determine the measure of $\angle P$ to the nearest degree.

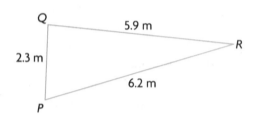

PRACTISING

4. Determine each unknown side length to the nearest tenth of a centimetre.

a)

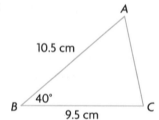

b)

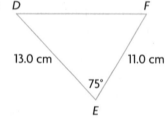

5. Determine the measure of each indicated angle to the nearest degree.

a)

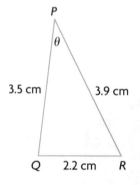

b)

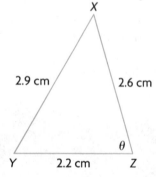

6. Sketch each triangle, based on the given equation. Then solve for the unknown side length or angle measure. Round all answers to the nearest tenth of a unit.

a) $w^2 = 15^2 + 16^2 - 2(15)(16) \cos 75°$

b) $k^2 = 32^2 + 35^2 - 2(32)(35) \cos 50°$

c) $48^2 = 46^2 + 45^2 - 2(46)(45) \cos Y$

d) $13^2 = 17^2 + 15^2 - 2(17)(15) \cos G$

7. Solve each triangle. Round all answers to the nearest tenth of a unit.
   a) In $\triangle DEF$, $d = 5.0$ cm, $e = 6.5$ cm, and $\angle F = 65°$.
   b) In $\triangle PQR$, $p = 6.4$ m, $q = 9.0$ m, and $\angle R = 80°$.
   c) In $\triangle LMN$, $l = 5.5$ cm, $m = 4.6$ cm, and $n = 3.3$ cm.
   d) In $\triangle XYZ$, $x = 5.2$ mm, $y = 4.0$ mm, and $z = 4.5$ mm.

8. The pendulum of a grandfather clock is 100.0 cm long. When the pendulum swings from one side to the other side, the horizontal distance it travels is 9.6 cm.
   a) Draw a diagram of the situation.
   b) Determine the angle through which the pendulum swings. Round your answer to the nearest tenth of a degree.

9. Determine the perimeter of $\triangle SRT$, if $\angle S = 60°$, $r = 15$ cm, and $t = 20$ cm. Round your answer to the nearest tenth of a centimetre.

10. A parallelogram has sides that are 8 cm and 15 cm long. One of the angles in the parallelogram measures 70°. Explain how you could determine the length of the shorter diagonal.

11. a) A clock has a minute hand that is 20 cm long and an hour hand that is 12 cm long. Determine the distance between the tips of the hands at
      i) 2:00.   ii) 10:00.
    b) Discuss your results for part a).

12. Emilie makes stained glass windows to sell at the Festival du Bois in Maillardville, British Columbia. Each piece of glass is surrounded by lead edging. Emilie claims that she can create an acute triangle in part of a window using pieces of lead that are 15 cm, 36 cm, and 60 cm. Is she correct? Justify your decision.

The Festival du Bois, one of British Columbia's greatest celebrations of French-Canadian culture, is held in March.

13. Two drivers leave their school at the same time and travel on straight roads that diverge by 70°. One driver travels at an average speed of 33.0 km/h. The other driver travels at an average speed of 45.0 km/h. How far apart will the two drivers be after 45 min, to the nearest tenth of a kilometre?

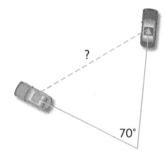

Closing

14. Use the triangle at the right to create a problem that involves side lengths and interior angles. Then describe how to determine the length of side d. Exchange your problem with a classmate.

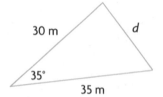

30 m d 35° 35 m

Extending

15. The distance from the centre, O, of a regular decagon to each vertex is 12 cm. Determine the area of the decagon. Round your answer to the nearest square centimetre.

12 cm O

16. The centre, O, of a regular pentagon is a perpendicular distance of 1.5 cm from each side. Determine the perimeter, to the nearest tenth of a centimetre, and area, to the nearest tenth of a square centimetre, of the pentagon.

17. An ulu is an Inuit all-purpose knife, traditionally used by women. The metal blade of one type of ulu is roughly triangular in shape, with the cutting edge opposite the vertex where the handle is attached. The other sides of the ulu are roughly equal. Describe a functional ulu that has a 14 cm blade, measured point to point. Include the vertex angle at the handle and the side lengths in your description.

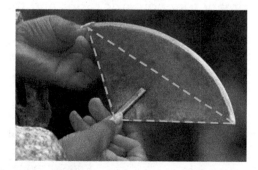

Solving Problems Using Acute Triangles

- ruler
- calculator

GOAL

Solve problems using the primary trigonometric ratios and the sine and cosine laws.

EXPLORE...

- Two planes leave an airport on different runways at the same time. One heads S40°W and the other heads S60°E. Create a problem about the planes that can be solved only by using the cosine law. Solve the problem.

LEARN ABOUT the Math

Two security cameras in a museum must be adjusted to monitor a new display of fossils. The cameras are mounted 6 m above the floor, directly across from each other on opposite walls. The walls are 12 m apart. The fossils are displayed in cases made of wood and glass. The top of the display is 1.5 m above the floor. The distance from the camera on the left to the centre of the top of the display is 4.8 m. Both cameras must aim at the centre of the top of the display.

? What is the angle of depression for each camera?

EXAMPLE 1 | Connecting an acute triangle model to a situation

Determine the **angles of depression**, to the nearest degree, for each camera.

Vlad's Solution: Using primary trigonometric ratios and the cosine law

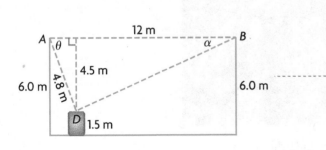

I drew a diagram. I placed the cameras 6 m from the floor, 12 m away from each other on opposite walls at points A and B. I wasn't sure where to place the display or its centre, D. The display had to be closer to camera A since the distance from camera A to the display was only 4.8 m. Subtracting the display height from 6 m gave me the distance from the display to the horizontal between the cameras. I labelled the angles of depression using θ and α.

$$\sin \theta = \frac{4.5}{4.8}$$

$$\theta = \sin^{-1}\left(\frac{4.5}{4.8}\right)$$

$$\theta = 69.635...°$$

> In the right triangle containing angle θ, the side of length 4.5 m is opposite angle θ, and the side of length 4.8 m is the hypotenuse. I could use the sine ratio to determine the measure of θ.

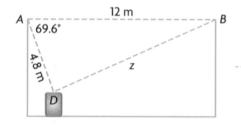

> I knew the lengths of two sides in $\triangle ABD$ and the angle between them. So, I was able to use the cosine law to determine the length of the side opposite camera A, which I labelled z.

$$z^2 = 12^2 + 4.8^2 - 2(12)(4.8) \cos 69.635...°$$

$$z^2 = 126.952...$$

$$z = \sqrt{126.952...}$$

$$z = 11.267...$$

$$\sin \alpha = \frac{4.5}{11.267...}$$

> Based on the sides I knew in the right triangle containing angle α, I wrote an equation using the sine ratio.

$$\alpha = \sin^{-1}\left(\frac{4.5}{11.267...}\right)$$

$$\alpha = 23.539...°$$

To monitor the display effectively, camera A must be adjusted to an angle of depression of 70° and camera B must be adjusted to an angle of depression of 24°.

Michel's Solution: Using only primary trigonometric ratios

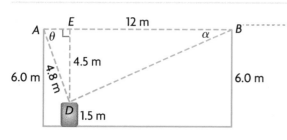

> I drew a diagram by placing the cameras at points A and B and the centre of the display at point D. I knew point D had to be closer to camera A because the distance between it and camera B had to be greater than 4.8 m. Subtracting the display height from the camera height gave me the length of DE, the height of $\triangle ABD$. I labelled the angles of depression θ and α.

$$\sin \theta = \frac{4.5}{4.8}$$

$$\theta = \sin^{-1}\left(\frac{4.5}{4.8}\right)$$

$$\theta = 69.635...°$$

In right triangle *ADE*, *DE* is opposite angle θ and *AD* is the hypotenuse. Since I knew the lengths of both sides, I used the sine ratio to determine angle θ.

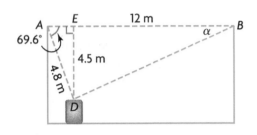

In right triangle *ADE*, *AE* is adjacent to angle θ and *AD* is the hypotenuse. Since I knew the length of *AD* and the measure of angle θ, I used the cosine ratio to determine the length of *AE*.

$$\cos 69.635...° = \frac{AE}{4.8}$$

$$4.8\left(\cos 69.635...°\right) = AE$$

$$1.670... = AE$$

$$EB = 12 - 1.670...$$

$$EB = 10.329...$$

To determine the length of *EB*, I subtracted the length of *AE* from 12.

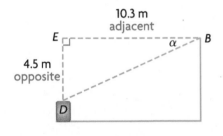

Based on the sides I knew in right triangle *DEB*, I wrote an equation using the tangent ratio to determine angle α.

$$\tan \alpha = \frac{4.5}{10.329...}$$

$$\alpha = \tan^{-1}\left(\frac{4.5}{10.329...}\right)$$

$$\alpha = 23.539...°$$

Camera A must be adjusted to an angle of depression of 70° and camera B must be adjusted to an angle of depression of 24° to ensure that they both point to the centre of the display.

Reflecting

A. Why do you think Vlad started his solution by using the right triangle that contained angle θ instead of the right triangle that contained angle α?

B. Could Vlad have determined the value of α using the sine law? Explain.

C. Which solution do you prefer? Justify your choice.

APPLY *the Math*

> **EXAMPLE 2**   Connecting acute triangle models to indirect measurement

The world's tallest free-standing totem pole is located in Beacon Hill Park in Victoria, British Columbia. It was carved from a single cedar log by noted carver Chief Mungo Martin of the Kwakiutl (Kwakwaka'wakw), with a team that included his son David and Henry Hunt. It was erected in 1956.

While visiting the park, Manuel wanted to determine the height of the totem pole, so he drew a sketch and made some measurements:

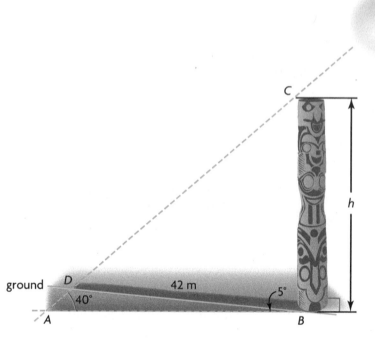

- I walked along the shadow of the totem pole and counted 42 paces, estimating each pace was about 1 m.
- I estimated that the **angle of elevation** of the Sun was about 40°.
- I observed that the shadow ran uphill, and I estimated that the angle the hill made with the horizontal was about 5°.

How can Manuel determine the height of the totem pole to the nearest metre?

Manuel's Solution

h is the height of $\triangle ABC$, but it is also a side in acute triangle DCB.

> I needed to determine the angles in this triangle to be able to determine h using the sine law.

$\angle ADB = 180° - 40° - 5°$
$\angle ADB = 135°$

> I used the two angles I knew in $\triangle ADB$ to determine the third angle in this triangle, since the angles in a triangle add to 180°.

$\angle CDB = 180° - 135°$
$\angle CDB = 45°$

> I subtracted $\angle ADB$ from 180° to determine $\angle CDB$, since these are supplementary angles.

$\angle CBD = 90° - 5°$
$\angle CBD = 85°$

> I subtracted $\angle DBA$ from 90° to determine $\angle CBD$, since these are complementary angles.

$\angle DCB = 180° - 45° - 85°$
$\angle DCB = 50°$

> I used the two angles I determined in $\triangle DCB$ to determine the third angle in this triangle.

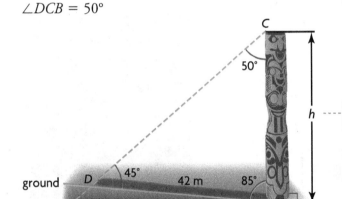

> I added all the information I determined about $\triangle DCB$ to my sketch.

$$\frac{h}{\sin 45°} = \frac{42}{\sin 50°}$$

> I used the sine law to write an equation that contained h. Then I solved for h.

$$\sin 45°\left(\frac{h}{\sin 45°}\right) = \sin 45°\left(\frac{42}{\sin 50°}\right)$$

$$h = \sin 45°\left(\frac{42}{\sin 50°}\right)$$

$$h = 38.768\ldots$$

The totem pole is 39 m tall.

Your Turn

List some sources of error that may have occurred in Manuel's strategy that would affect the accuracy of his determination.

EXAMPLE **3**   Solving a three-dimensional problem

Brendan and Diana plan to climb the cliff at Dry Island Buffalo Jump, Alberta. They need to know the height of the climb before they start. Brendan stands at point B, as shown in the diagram. He uses a clinometer to determine $\angle ABC$, the angle of elevation to the top of the cliff. Then he estimates $\angle CBD$, the angle between the base of the cliff, himself, and Diana, who is standing at point D. Diana estimates $\angle CDB$, the angle between the base of the cliff, herself, and Brendan.

Determine the height of the cliff to the nearest metre.

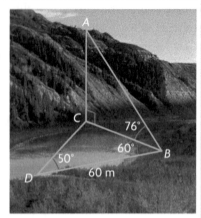

Diana's Solution

	I didn't have enough information about $\triangle ABC$ to determine the height, AC. I needed the length of BC. BC is in $\triangle ABC$, but it is also in $\triangle DBC$.
In $\triangle DBC$, $\angle BCD = 180° - 60° - 50°$ $\angle BCD = 70°$	I knew two angles and a side length in $\triangle DBC$. Before I could determine BC, I had to determine $\angle BCD$. I used the fact that the sum of all three interior angles is 180°.
$\dfrac{BC}{\sin D} = \dfrac{BD}{\sin C}$ $\dfrac{BC}{\sin 50°} = \dfrac{60}{\sin 70°}$	I used the sine law to write an equation that involved BC in $\triangle DBC$.
$\sin 50°\left(\dfrac{BC}{\sin 50°}\right) = \sin 50°\left(\dfrac{60}{\sin 70°}\right)$	To solve for BC, I multiplied both sides of the equation by $\sin 50°$.
$BC = \sin 50°\left(\dfrac{60}{\sin 70°}\right)$ $BC = 48.912...$	
$\tan 76° = \dfrac{AC}{BC}$ $\tan 76° = \dfrac{AC}{48.912...}$	I knew that $\triangle ABC$ is a right triangle. I also knew that AC is opposite the 76° angle and BC is adjacent to it. So, I used the tangent ratio to write an equation that involved AC.

$48.912...(\tan 76°) = 48.912...\left(\dfrac{AC}{48.912...}\right)$

$\qquad 196.177... = AC$

The height of the cliff is 196 m.

Your Turn

Create a three-dimensional problem that can be solved using Diana's strategy. What features of your problem make it necessary to use two triangles to solve the problem?

In Summary

Key Idea

- The sine law, the cosine law, the primary trigonometric ratios, and the sum of angles in a triangle may all be useful when solving problems that can be modelled using acute triangles.

Need to Know

- To decide whether you need to use the sine law or the cosine law, consider the information given about the triangle and the measurement to be determined.

Information Given	Measurement to be Determined	Use
two sides and the angle opposite one of the sides 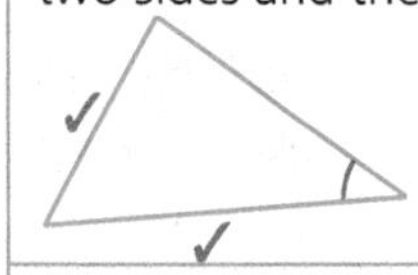	angle	sine law
two angles and a side 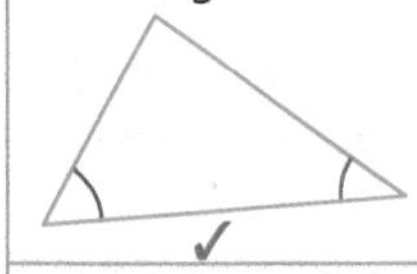 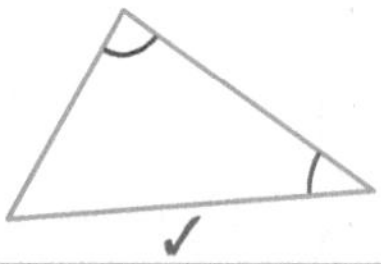	side	sine law
two sides and the contained angle 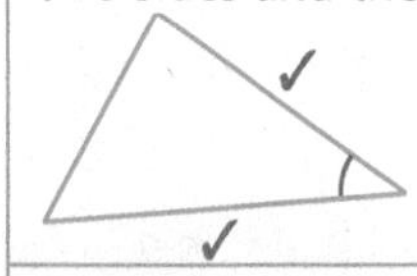	side	cosine law
three sides 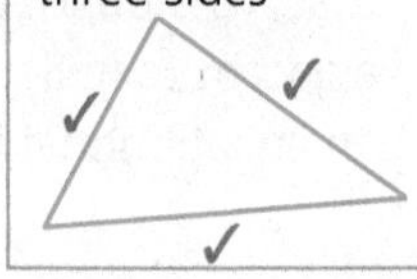	angle	cosine law

- Drawing a clearly labelled diagram makes it easier to select a strategy for solving a problem.

CHECK Your Understanding

1. Explain how you would determine the indicated angle measure or side length in each triangle.

a)
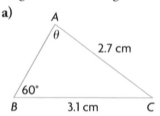

b)
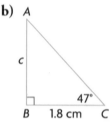

c)
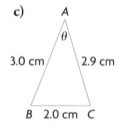

2. **a)** Use the strategies you described to determine the measurements indicated in question 1. Round your answers to the nearest tenth of a unit.

   b) Compare your answers for questions 1 and 2a) with a classmate's answers. Which strategy seems to be most efficient for each?

PRACTISING

3. A kayak leaves Rankin Inlet, Nunavut, and heads due east for 5.0 km, as shown in the diagram. At the same time, a second kayak travels in a direction S60°E from the inlet for 4.0 km. How far apart, to the nearest tenth of a kilometre, are the kayaks?
   a) Describe how you can solve the problem.
   b) Determine the distance between the kayaks.

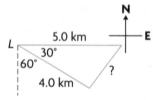

4. How long, to the nearest inch, is each rafter in the roof shown?

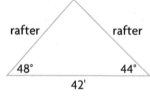

5. A crane stands on top of a building, as shown.
   a) How far is the point on the ground from the base of the building, to the nearest tenth of a metre?
   b) How tall is the crane?

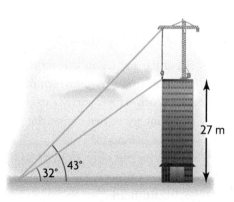

6. A tree is growing on a hillside, as shown. The hillside is inclined at an angle of 15° to the horizontal. The tree casts a shadow uphill. How tall is the tree, to the nearest metre?

   a) Describe how you can solve the problem.

   b) Determine the height of the tree.

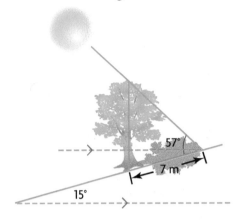

7. A radar operator on a ship discovers a large sunken vessel lying parallel to the ocean surface, 200 m directly below the ship. The length of the vessel is a clue to which wreck has been found. The radar operator measures the angles of depression to the front and back of the sunken vessel to be 56° and 62°. How long, to the nearest tenth of a metre, is the sunken vessel?

8. Fred and Agnes are 520 m apart. As Brendan flies overhead in an airplane, they estimate the angle of elevation of the airplane. Fred, looking south, estimates the angle of elevation to be 60°. Agnes, looking north, estimates it to be 40°. What is the altitude of the airplane, to the nearest tenth of a metre?

9. Two support wires are fastened to the top of a communications tower from points A and B on the ground. The points are on opposite sides of the tower and in line. One wire is 18 m long, and the other wire is 12 m long. The angle of elevation of the longer wire to the top of the tower is 38°.

   a) How tall is the tower, to the nearest tenth of a metre?

   b) How far apart are points A and B, to the nearest tenth of a metre?

10. A regular pentagon is inscribed in a circle with centre O, as shown in the diagram.

   a) Work with a partner to develop a strategy to determine the perimeter of the pentagon.

   b) Carry out your strategy to determine the perimeter to the nearest tenth of a centimetre.

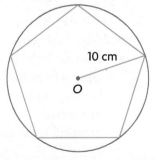

Ships are sometimes deliberately sunk (scuttled) to form breakwaters and artificial reefs.

11. Ryan is in a police helicopter, 400 m directly above the Sea to Sky highway near Whistler, British Columbia. When he looks north, the angle of depression to a car accident is 65°. When he looks south, the angle of depression to the approaching ambulance is 30°.
    a) How far away is the ambulance from the scene of the accident, to the nearest tenth of a metre?
    b) The ambulance is travelling at 80 km/h. How long will it take the ambulance to reach the scene of the accident?

12. The radar screen in the air-traffic control tower at the Edmonton International Airport shows that two airplanes are at the same altitude. According to the range finder, one airplane is 100 km away, in the direction N60°E. The other airplane is 160 km away, in the direction S50°E.
    a) How far apart are the airplanes, to the nearest tenth of a kilometre?
    b) If the airplanes are approaching the airport at the same speed, which airplane will arrive first?

13. In a parallelogram, two adjacent sides measure 10 cm and 12 cm. The shorter diagonal is 15 cm. Determine, to the nearest degree, the measures of all four angles in the parallelogram.

14. Two students decided to determine the altitude, h, of a promotional blimp flying over McMahon Stadium in Calgary. The students' measurements are shown in the diagram. Determine h to the nearest tenth of a metre. Explain each of your steps.

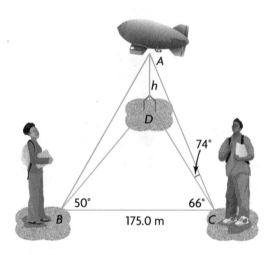

Math in Action

How Good Is Your Peripheral Vision?

When you stare straight ahead, you can still see objects to either side. This is called peripheral vision. It can be measured using an angle. For example, the angle for your right eye would be swept out from a point directly in front of your nose to the point where you can no longer see objects on the far right. This angle is about 60° for those with normal peripheral vision.

- Work with a partner or in a small group.
- Make a plan to measure the peripheral vision of your eyes. The only materials you can use are a pencil, a metre stick, and string.
- Test your plan. What is your peripheral vision?
- Evaluate your plan. What adjustments did you need to make during the test? Are you satisfied that your plan worked well? Explain.

Closing

15. Create a real-life problem that can be modelled by an acute triangle. Exchange the problem you created with a classmate. Sketch the situation in your classmate's problem, and explain what must be done to solve it.

Extending

16. The Great Pyramid at Giza in Egypt has a square base with sides that are 232.6 m long. The distance from the top of the pyramid to each corner of the base was originally 221.2 m.

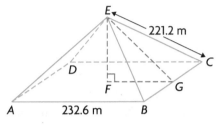

a) Determine the apex angle of a face of the pyramid (for example, ∠*AEB*) to the nearest degree.

b) Determine the angle that each face makes with the base (for example, ∠*EGF*) to the nearest degree.

17. Cut out two paper strips, each 5 cm wide. Lay them across each other as shown at the right. Determine the area of the overlapping region. Round your answer to the nearest tenth of a square centimetre.

Fire Towers and Lookouts

For about 100 years, observers have been watching for forest fires. Perched in lookouts on high ground or on tall towers (there are three fire towers in Alberta that are 120 m high), the observers watch for smoke in the surrounding forest. When the observers see signs of a fire, they report the sighting to the Fire Centre.

The first observers may have had as little as a map, binoculars, and a horse to ride to the nearest station to make a report. Today, observers have instruments called alidades and report using radios. Alidades consist of a local map, fixed in place, with the tower or lookout at the centre of the map. Compass directions are marked in degrees around the edge of the map. A range finder rotates on an arc above the map. The observer rotates the range finder to get the smoke in both sights, notes the direction, and reports it to the Fire Centre. A computer at the Fire Centre can use the locations of the fire towers and directions from two or more observers to fix the location of the fire. The latitude and longitude are then entered into a helicopter's flight GPS system. The helicopter's crew flies to the fire, records a more accurate location, and reports on the fire.

A. How could a Fire Centre use trigonometry to determine the location of a fire?

B. How could an observer use trigonometry to estimate the size of a fire?

Analyzing a Trigonometry Puzzle

Puzzles do not always have precise solutions. They cannot always be solved purely by deduction, although logic helps.

YOU WILL NEED
- ruler
- scissors

The Puzzle

A. Below are seven similar right triangles. Trace the triangles, and cut them out.

B. Use all seven triangles to form a single square, with no overlapping.

C. If the hypotenuse of the greatest triangle is 10 units long, what is the area of the square?

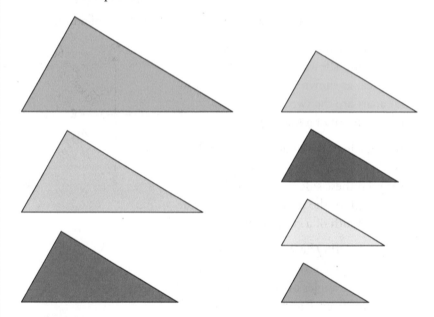

The Strategy

D. Describe the strategy you used to form the square.

E. Describe the strategy you used to determine the area of the square.

1. Determine the indicated side length or angle measure in each triangle. Round answers to the nearest tenth of a unit.

a)

A

82° 4.1 cm

C

θ   6.0 cm

B

b)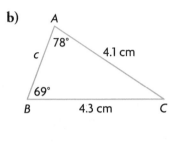

A

78° 4.1 cm

c

69°

B   4.3 cm   C

2. In $\triangle PQR$, $\angle P = 80°$, $\angle Q = 48°$, and $r = 20$ cm. Solve $\triangle PQR$. Where necessary, round answers to the nearest tenth of a unit.

3. The radar screen of a Coast Guard rescue ship shows that two boats are in the area, as shown in the diagram. How far apart are the two boats, to the nearest tenth of a kilometre?

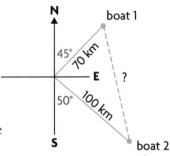

4. A parallelogram has adjacent sides that are 11.0 cm and 15.0 cm long. The angle between these sides is 50°. Determine the length of the shorter diagonal to the nearest tenth of a centimetre.

5. Points P and Q lie 240 m apart in line with and on opposite sides of a communications tower. The angles of elevation to the top of the tower from P and Q are 50° and 45°, respectively. Determine the height of the tower to the nearest tenth of a metre.

6. Terry is designing a triangular patio, as shown. Determine the area of the patio to the nearest tenth of a square metre.

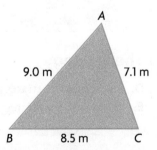

7. In an acute triangle, two sides are 2.4 cm and 3.6 cm. One of the angles is 37°. How can you determine the third side in the triangle? Explain.

8. Why do you need both the sine law and the cosine law to determine side lengths in an acute triangle?

WHAT DO You Think Now? Revisit **What Do You Think?** on page 129. How have your answers and explanations changed?

FREQUENTLY ASKED Questions

Q: **To use the cosine law, what do you need to know about a triangle?**

A: You need to know two sides and the contained angle, or three sides in the triangle.

For example, you can use the cosine law to determine the length of p.

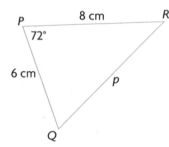

You know:
- the lengths of two sides.
- the measure of the contained angle.

You can use the cosine law to determine the length of the side opposite the contained angle, p.

$$p^2 = 8^2 + 6^2 - 2(8)(6) \cos 72°$$

Solving for p will determine the length.

You can also use the cosine law to determine the measure of $\angle Y$.

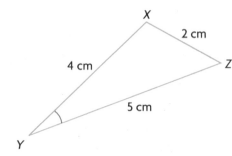

You know:
- the lengths of all three sides.

You can use the cosine law to determine the measure of $\angle Y$.

$$2^2 = 4^2 + 5^2 - 2(4)(5) \cos Y$$

$$\frac{2^2 - 4^2 - 5^2}{-2(4)(5)} = \cos Y$$

Solving for Y will determine the measure of $\angle Y$.

Study | **Aid**
- See Lesson 3.3, Examples 1 to 3.
- Try Chapter Review Questions 6 to 9.

Q: **When solving a problem that can be modelled by an acute triangle, how do you decide whether to use the primary trigonometric ratios, the sine law, or the cosine law?**

A: Draw a clearly labelled diagram of the situation to record what you know.
- You may be able to use a primary trigonometric ratio if the diagram involves a right triangle.
- Use the sine law if you know two sides and one opposite angle, or two angles and one opposite side.
- Use the cosine law if you know all three sides, or two sides and the angle between them.

You may need to use more than one strategy to solve some problems.

Study | **Aid**
- See Lesson 3.4, Examples 1 to 3.
- Try Chapter Review Questions 10 to 12.

PRACTISING

Lesson 3.1

1. Jane claims that she can draw an acute triangle using the following information: $a = 6$ cm, $b = 8$ cm, $c = 10$ cm, $\angle A = 30°$, and $\angle B = 60°$. Is she correct? Explain.

2. Which of the following are not correct for acute triangle DEF?

   a) $\dfrac{d}{\sin D} = \dfrac{f}{\sin F}$ c) $f \sin E = e \sin F$

   b) $\dfrac{\sin E}{e} = \dfrac{\sin D}{d}$ d) $\dfrac{d}{\sin D} = \dfrac{\sin F}{f}$

Lesson 3.2

3. Determine the indicated side or angle in each triangle to the nearest tenth of a unit.

   a)   b)

   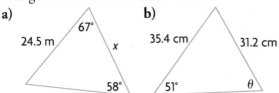

4. Solve $\triangle ABC$, if $\angle A = 75°$, $\angle B = 50°$, and the side between these angles is 8.0 cm. Round answers to the nearest tenth of a unit.

5. Allison is flying a kite. She has released the entire 150 m ball of kite string. She notices that the string forms a 70° angle with the ground. Marc is on the other side of the kite and sees the kite at an angle of elevation of 30°. How far is Marc from Allison, to the nearest tenth of a metre?

   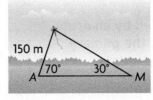

Lesson 3.3

6. Which of these is not a form of the cosine law for $\triangle ABC$? Explain.

   a) $a^2 = b^2 + c^2 - 2bc \cos B$
   b) $c^2 = a^2 + b^2 - 2ab \cos C$
   c) $b^2 = a^2 + c^2 - 2ac \cos B$

7. Determine the indicated side or angle. Round answers to the nearest tenth of a unit.

   a)   b)

   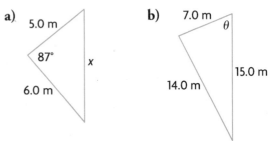

8. Solve $\triangle ABC$, if $\angle A = 58°$, $b = 10.0$ cm, and $c = 14.0$ cm. Round answers to the nearest tenth of a unit.

9. Two airplanes leave the Hay River airport in the Northwest Territories at the same time. One airplane travels at 355 km/h. The other airplane travels at 450 km/h. About 2 h later, they are 800 km apart. Determine the angle between their paths, to the nearest degree.

Lesson 3.4

10. From a window in an apartment building, the angle of elevation to the top of a flagpole across the street is 9°. The angle of depression is 22° to the base of the flagpole. How tall is the flagpole, to the nearest tenth of a metre?

11. A bush pilot delivers supplies to a remote camp by flying 255 km in the direction N52°E. While at the camp, the pilot receives a radio message to pick up a passenger at a village. The village is 85 km S21°E from the camp. What is the total distance, to the nearest kilometre, that the pilot will have flown by the time he returns to his starting point?

12. A canoeist starts from a dock and paddles 2.8 km N34°E. Then she paddles 5.2 km N65°W. What distance, and in which direction, should a second canoeist paddle to reach the same location directly, starting from the same dock? Round all answers to the nearest tenth of a unit.

Acute Triangles in First Nations and Métis Cultures

Inside a Dakota tipi

Blackfoot tipis

Structures made from acute triangles are used in most cultures. The First Nations and Métis peoples who lived on the Prairies used acute-triangle structures to cook, dry meat, and transport goods and people. Acute triangles are also the support for tipis. Tipis suit a life based on the migration of the buffalo, because they are easily assembled and taken down. Tipis are still used for shelter on camping trips and for ceremonial purposes.

The frame of a tipi consists of wooden poles supported by an inner tripod. Additional poles are laid in and tied with rope. When the frame is complete, the covering is drawn over the frame using two additional poles. The interior of the tipi creates a roughly conical shape. The number of poles used is indicative of geographic area and people, ranging from 13 to 21 poles.

frame triangle

❓ What are the measures of all the sides and angles in each triangle in the frame of a tipi?

A. Design a tipi. Choose the number of poles, the interior height, and the diameter of the base.

B. What regular polygon forms the base of your tipi? What type of triangle is formed by the ground and supporting poles? Explain how you know.

C. Determine the side lengths of the frame triangles.

D. Determine the interior angles of the frame triangles.

E. Explain why your design is functional.

Task | *Checklist*
- ✔ Did you draw labelled diagrams for the problem?
- ✔ Did you show your work?
- ✔ Did you provide appropriate reasoning?
- ✔ Did you explain your thinking clearly?

Creating Your Research Question or Statement

A well-written research question or statement clarifies exactly what your project is designed to do. It should have the following characteristics:
• The research *topic* is easily identifiable.
• The *purpose* of the research is clear.
• The question/statement is *focused*. The people who are listening to or reading the question/statement will know what you are going to be researching.

A good question requires thought and planning. Below are three examples of initial questions or statements and how they were improved.

Unacceptable Question/Statement	Why?	Acceptable Question/Statement
Is mathematics used in computer technology?	too general	What role has mathematics played in the development of computer animation?
Water is a shared resource.	too general	Homes, farms, ranches, and businesses east of the Rockies all use runoff water. When there is a shortage, that water must be shared.
Do driver's education programs help teenagers parallel park?	too specific, unless you are going to generate your own data	Do driver's education programs reduce the incidence of parking accidents?

Evaluating Your Research Question or Statement

You can use the following checklist to determine if your research question/statement is effective.

1. Does the question/statement clearly identify the main objective of the research? After you read the question/statement to a few classmates, can they tell you what you will be researching?
2. Are you confident that the question/statement will lead you to sufficient data to reach a conclusion?
3. Is the question/statement interesting? Does it make you want to learn more?
4. Is the topic you chose purely factual, or are you likely to encounter an issue, with different points of view?

Sarah chose the changes in population of the Western provinces and the territories over the last century as her topic. Below, she describes how she determined that her research question for this topic is effective.

Sarah's Question

My question is, "Which Western province or territory grew the fastest over the last century and why?" I will use 1900 to 2000 as the time period.

Chinese immigrants and workers arrive at William Head Quarantine Station, British Columbia, in 1917. What factors affected where they chose to settle?

I evaluated my question using the research question checklist, and I feel that it is a good one. Here is why:

1. My question tells what I plan to do: I read my question to three friends, and they all described what I had in mind.

2. I am confident that there is a lot of data available on populations, and that there is a lot of historical information available on why the populations changed.

3. I'm really interested in history, but I don't know enough about how the West and North grew and why. I'll find out lots of new things. Whatever I find out should also interest some of my classmates, as it's about where we live.

4. I expect that I will find several different points of view on why populations grew, and I hope that I will be able to conclude which factors were most important.

This photograph shows a potash mine in Saskatchewan. How do resources affect population growth?

Your Turn

A.   Write a research question for your topic.

B.   Use the checklist to evaluate your question. Adjust your question as needed.

C.   Make an appointment to discuss the pros and cons of your research question with your teacher. Be prepared to discuss your plan for collecting the data you will need to come to a conclusion. Adjust your question as needed.

NEL

Radicals

▶ **LEARNING GOALS**

You will be able to develop your number sense and logical reasoning ability by

- Simplifying radical expressions
- Solving problems that involve operations on radicals with numerical and variable radicands
- Solving problems that involve radical equations

❓ The rocket launch of the New Horizons probe was so powerful that the probe escaped Earth's gravity. It will reach Pluto in 2015. Escape velocity, V_e, is the speed an object needs to break free from the gravitational pull of another object. At the surface of Earth, the escape velocity for an object is about 11 172 m/s. Escape velocity can be calculated using the formula

$$V_e = \sqrt{\frac{2GM}{r}}$$

where G, the gravitational constant, is $6.67 \cdot 10^{-11} \frac{Nm^2}{kg^2}$, and r, the radius of Earth, is $6.38 \cdot 10^6$ m. How can this formula be used to determine M, the mass of Earth, in kilograms?

Photography

Carla is taking a photography course. She started using the f-stop ring on her camera lens knowing that the f-stop ring controls the aperture.

f-stop settings:
1.4, 2, 2.8, 4, 5.6, 8, 11, 16

Aperture is a physical measure of how "open" a lens is. A lens opens and closes to allow more or less light to enter the camera as shown in the diagram on the next page. The aperture functions in the same way the irises of our eyes adjust to bright and dark light conditions. The f-stop number represents the ratio of the focal length of the lens, which is fixed, to the diameter of the opening, which is variable. As the diameter of the opening increases, the f-stop number decreases.

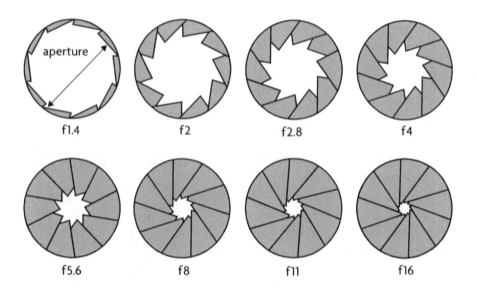

f1.4   f2   f2.8   f4

f5.6   f8   f11   f16

❓ How are the f-stop numbers on a camera determined?

A. Start with the number $\sqrt{2}$ and multiply it by $\sqrt{2}$. What **entire radical** do you get?

B. Take your answer from part A and multiply it by $\sqrt{2}$. What entire radical do you get?

C. Repeat step B five more times.

D. Write the list of entire radicals you get as a sequence of numbers in increasing order.

E. Express each entire radical in your sequence in simplest form. Which radicals were **perfect squares**? Which radicals resulted in **mixed radicals**?

F. Evaluate each number in your sequence from part D to one decimal place using a calculator.

G. Explain how the f-stop numbers are related to the values you found in part F.

WHAT DO You Think?

Decide whether you agree or disagree with each statement. Explain your decision.

1. Every real number has only one square root.

2. The radicand of a mixed or entire radical can never be a negative number.

3. Any solution to an equation obtained using inverse operations will be valid.

Mixed and Entire Radicals

GOAL

Compare and express numerical radicals in equivalent forms.

LEARN ABOUT *the Math*

EXPLORE...
• Draw a number line from −10 to 10 and choose any two opposite numbers. Square these numbers. What do you notice? Will you always get the same result when you square two opposite numbers? What does this imply about the square root of a number?

Sandy is designing a mainsail for a new catamaran with the dimensions shown. He needs to estimate the area of the sail, to know how much material to buy. On the Internet, Sandy found Heron's formula, which can be used to determine the area of a triangle, A:

$$A = \sqrt{p(p - a)(p - b)(p - c)}$$

where a, b, and c are the triangle's side lengths and p is half of the triangle's perimeter.

? How can Sandy estimate the area of the sail?

EXAMPLE 1   **Estimating an area**

Estimate the area of the mainsail using Heron's formula.

Tim's Solution

principal square root
The positive square root of a real number, x, denoted as $\sqrt{x}$; for example, the principal square root of 16 is $\sqrt{16}$, or 4.

secondary square root
The negative square root of a real number, x, denoted as $-\sqrt{x}$; for example, the secondary square root of 16 is $-\sqrt{16}$, or −4.

Half of the triangular sail's perimeter, p, is:

$$p = \frac{40 + 38 + 30}{2}$$

$$p = \frac{108}{2}$$

$$p = 54$$

> First I determined p, the value of half the perimeter.

> The square root of a positive number provides two answers; the **principal square root**, and the **secondary square root**. As area cannot be negative, I know I want to determine only the principal square root.

The area of the triangular sail, A, is:

$$A = \sqrt{p(p - a)(p - b)(p - c)}$$

$$A = \sqrt{(54)(54 - 40)(54 - 38)(54 - 30)}$$

$$A = \sqrt{(54)(14)(16)(24)}$$

> I substituted the value of p and the lengths of the three sides into Heron's formula and simplified.

$$A = \sqrt{(2 \cdot 3^3)(2 \cdot 7)(2^4)(2^3 \cdot 3)}$$

> I wrote each factor in terms of its prime factors to try to write the entire radical as a mixed radical with the smallest radicand. This would make estimation easier.

$$A = \sqrt{2^9 \cdot 3^4 \cdot 7}$$

> I used the exponent laws to combine like bases.

$$A = \sqrt{2^8 \cdot 3^4} \cdot \sqrt{2 \cdot 7}$$

> Any power squared results in a power whose exponent doubles, $(a^n)^2 = a^{2n}$. So, to determine the square root of a power, the exponents must be divisible by 2 or be even. I rearranged the factors into two products, one of which had the largest even exponents possible.

$$A = 2^4 \cdot 3^2 \sqrt{14}$$
$$A = 16 \cdot 9 \sqrt{14}$$
$$A = 144 \sqrt{14}$$

> I determined the square root of the first factor by dividing each exponent by 2, the index of the radical. Then I simplified the expression.

$$140 \cdot 4 = 560$$

> I know $\sqrt{16} = 4$, so $\sqrt{14}$ must be a little less than 4. I rounded 144 to 140. The product must be less than 560.

The surface area of the mainsail is a little less than 560 ft².

Reflecting

A. Why does it make sense to use only the principal square root in this situation?

B. Why do you think Tim wrote the radicand as a product of prime factors?

C. Did Tim express this entire radical as a mixed radical in simplest form? Explain how you know.

APPLY the Math

EXAMPLE 2   Expressing a radical in simplest form

Express each entire radical in simplest form.

a) $\sqrt{3600}$ **b)** $\sqrt{288}$ **c)** $\sqrt[3]{432}$

Calvin's Solution

a) $\sqrt{3600} = \sqrt{2 \cdot 2 \cdot 2 \cdot 2 \cdot 3 \cdot 3 \cdot 5 \cdot 5}$ ·········· I factored 3600 into prime factors.

$\quad\quad\quad = \sqrt{2^4 \cdot 3^2 \cdot 5^2}$ ·········· I wrote the factors as powers.

$\quad\quad\quad = 2^2 \cdot 3 \cdot 5$ ·········· Each power had an even exponent. So, I divided each exponent by 2 to determine the square root of each power.

$\quad\quad\quad = 4 \cdot 3 \cdot 5$

$\quad\quad\quad = 60$ ·········· I multiplied the products to express $\sqrt{3600}$ in simplest form, which in this case is an integer with no radical.

b) $\sqrt{288} = \sqrt{2 \cdot 2 \cdot 2 \cdot 2 \cdot 2 \cdot 3 \cdot 3}$ ·········· I factored 288 into prime factors.

$\quad\quad\quad = \sqrt{2^5 \cdot 3^2}$ ·········· I wrote the factors as powers.

$\quad\quad\quad = \sqrt{2^4 \cdot 2^1 \cdot 3^2}$ ·········· The index of this radical is 2. I wrote 2^5 as a product with an even exponent, so I could determine square roots.

$\quad\quad\quad = \sqrt{2^4 \cdot 3^2 \cdot 2^1}$ ·········· I put the factors with even exponents together.

$\quad\quad\quad = \sqrt{2^4 \cdot 3^2} \cdot \sqrt{2^1}$ ·········· I wrote the expression as the product of two radicals, one with the highest even exponents possible.

$\quad\quad\quad = 2^2 \cdot 3^1 \cdot \sqrt{2}$ ·········· I wrote the radical with even exponents as the product of integers, by dividing the exponents by 2.

$\quad\quad\quad = 4 \cdot 3 \cdot \sqrt{2}$ ·········· I expressed each power as an integer.

$\quad\quad\quad = 12\sqrt{2}$ ·········· I multiplied the integers. I cannot simplify $\sqrt{2}$, since 2 is prime.

c) $\sqrt[3]{432} = \sqrt[3]{2 \cdot 2 \cdot 2 \cdot 2 \cdot 3 \cdot 3 \cdot 3}$ .... I factored 432 into prime factors.

$= \sqrt[3]{2^4 \cdot 3^3}$ .... I wrote the factors as powers.

$= \sqrt[3]{2^3 \cdot 2^1 \cdot 3^3}$ .... The index of this radical is 3. I wrote 2^4 as a product with one exponent that is a multiple of 3, so I could determine cube roots.

$= \sqrt[3]{2^3 \cdot 3^3 \cdot 2^1}$ .... I put the factors with exponents of 3 together.

$= \sqrt[3]{2^3 \cdot 3^3} \cdot \sqrt[3]{2^1}$ .... I wrote the expression as the product of two radicals, one with exponents of 3.

$= 2 \cdot 3 \cdot \sqrt[3]{2}$ .... I divided the exponents of the first radical by 3 to determine the cube root of each power.

$= 6\sqrt[3]{2}$ .... I multiplied the integers. I cannot simplify $\sqrt[3]{2}$, since 2 is prime.

Your Turn

Write $\sqrt{88\ 200}$ in simplest form.

EXAMPLE 3 | **Expressing a mixed radical as an entire radical**

Express each mixed radical as an entire radical.

a) $4\sqrt{5}$ **b)** $-5\sqrt{2}$ **c)** $-2\sqrt[3]{5}$

Sebastian's Solution

a) $4\sqrt{5} = \sqrt{4^2} \cdot \sqrt{5}$ .... I wrote 4 as the principal square root of 4^2.

$= \sqrt{4^2 \cdot 5}$ .... I expressed the product of the two radicals as the radical of the product, which I could do since both radicals had the same index, 2.

$= \sqrt{16 \cdot 5}$ .... I wrote 4^2 as a natural number.

$= \sqrt{80}$ .... I multiplied to obtain the entire radical.

$\Rightarrow$

b) $-5\sqrt{2} = -1 \cdot 5\sqrt{2}$

The index of the radical is 2, so the radicand cannot be negative. I wrote the expression as the product of -1 and a mixed radical.

$= -1 \cdot \sqrt{25} \cdot \sqrt{2}$

I wrote 5 as the square root of 5^2, or $\sqrt{25}$.

$= -1 \cdot \sqrt{25 \cdot 2}$

I expressed the product of the two radicals as the radical of the product, which I could do since both radicals had the same index, 2.

$= -1\sqrt{50}$

$= -\sqrt{50}$

I multiplied the numbers under the radical. Since the original radical expression is a negative mixed radical, the entire radical must also be negative.

c) $-2\sqrt[3]{5} = \sqrt[3]{(-2)^3} \cdot \sqrt[3]{5}$

The index of the radical is 3, so the radicand can be negative. I wrote -2 as the cube root of $(-2)^3$.

$= \sqrt[3]{-8} \cdot \sqrt[3]{5}$

I wrote $(-2)^3$ as -8.

$= \sqrt[3]{-8 \cdot 5}$

I expressed the product of the two radicals as the radical of the product, which I could do since both radicals had the same index, 3.

$= \sqrt[3]{-40}$

I multiplied the values under the radical.

Your Turn

Express $7\sqrt{10}$ as an entire radical.

Key Ideas

- You can express a radical in simplest form by using prime factors.
  For example:

  $$\sqrt{75} = \sqrt{5^2 \cdot 3} \qquad \sqrt[3]{375} = \sqrt[3]{5^3 \cdot 3}$$
  $$= 5\sqrt{3} \qquad\qquad\qquad = 5\sqrt[3]{3}$$

  When expressing square roots in simplest form, try to combine prime factors to create powers with even exponents. When working with cube roots, try to create powers with exponents that are multiples of 3.

- You can express a mixed radical as an entire radical, by writing the leading number as a radical, then multiplying the radicands.
  For example:

  $$4\sqrt{2} = \sqrt{16} \cdot \sqrt{2}$$
  $$= \sqrt{16 \cdot 2}$$
  $$= \sqrt{32}$$

Need to Know

- A radical is in simplest form when each exponent of the fully factored radicand is less than the index of the radical. For example, $12\sqrt{3^1}$ and $13\sqrt[3]{2^2}$ are in simplest form, while $12\sqrt{2^2}$ is not.

- A square has a principal square root, which is positive, and a secondary square root, which is negative. For example, the principal square root of 16 is $\sqrt{16}$ or 4, and the secondary square root of 16 is $-\sqrt{16}$ or -4. The radical of a square root may be negative, but the radicand of a square root must be positive.

- If you express an answer as a radical, the answer will be exact. If you write a radical in decimal form, the answer will be an approximation, except when the radicand is a perfect square. For example, $\sqrt{12}$ expressed as $2\sqrt{3}$ remains an exact value, while $\sqrt{12}$ expressed as 3.464... is an approximation. Both $\sqrt{9}$ and 3 are exact values.

CHECK Your Understanding

1. True or false? Explain why.

   a) The principal square root of 25 is -5.

   b) $\sqrt{16} = \pm 4$

   c) $\sqrt[3]{(-4)^3} = \pm 4$

   d) $\sqrt{-4} = -2$

   e) $-\sqrt{4} = -2$

   f) $\sqrt{36} = -6$

2. Match each radical on the left with its equivalent value on the right.

   a) $2\sqrt{31}$

   b) $\sqrt{112}$

   c) $8\sqrt{3}$

   d) $\sqrt[3]{120}$

   i) $4\sqrt{7}$

   ii) $2\sqrt[3]{15}$

   iii) $2\sqrt{48}$

   iv) 11.1

3. Given: $\sqrt{432}$ and $5\sqrt[3]{2}$

   a) Which is expressed as an entire radical and which is a mixed radical?

   b) Write each radical in its alternative form.

PRACTISING

4. Express each radical as a mixed radical in simplest form.

   a) $\sqrt{72}$ b) $\sqrt{600}$ c) $\sqrt[3]{40}$ d) $\sqrt[3]{250}$

5. Express each radical as a mixed radical in simplest form.

   a) $\sqrt{4000}$ b) $-\sqrt{2835}$ c) $\sqrt[3]{-72}$ d) $\sqrt[3]{648}$

6. Express each radicand as a product of primes with the greatest possible exponents.

   a) $\sqrt{3888}$ b) $\sqrt{100\ 000}$ c) $\sqrt{16\ 000}$ d) $\sqrt{16\ 875}$

7. Express each radical as a product of two radicals.

   a) $\sqrt{196}$ b) $\sqrt{3600}$ c) $\sqrt[3]{64}$ d) $\sqrt[3]{3375}$

8. Express each radical as an integer using two different groups of exponents.

   a) $\sqrt{64}$ b) $\sqrt{3600}$ c) $\sqrt[3]{8000}$

9. Kenny states that he has demonstrated that $-\sqrt{16} = 4$. What error did Kenny make?

$$(-4) = -4$$
$$\sqrt{(-4)(-4)} = -4$$
$$\sqrt{16} = -4$$
$$-\sqrt{16} = 4$$

10. Estimate the value of each radical. Then evaluate it to the nearest hundredth.

   a) $\sqrt{47}$ b) $\sqrt{41\ 000}$ c) $\sqrt{790}$ d) $\sqrt[3]{900}$

11. Express each mixed radical as an entire radical.
    a) $6\sqrt{5}$
    b) $12\sqrt{7}$
    c) $4\sqrt[3]{14}$
    d) $-3\sqrt[3]{4}$

12. Given: $4, 4\sqrt{3}, \sqrt{14}, 3\sqrt{2}, 4\sqrt{5}$
    a) Write each number as an entire radical.
    b) Arrange the numbers in increasing order.

13. Manuel insists that he can add $2\sqrt{4}$ and $5\sqrt[3]{4}$ in radical form because both values are positive. Do you agree or disagree? Justify your answer.

14. The number 1 is a natural number whose principal square root and cube root are also natural numbers: $\sqrt{1} = 1$ and $\sqrt[3]{1} = 1$. Determine two other natural numbers with this property.

15. Write all the mixed radicals that are equivalent to $\sqrt{800}$. Which is written in simplest form? Explain how you know.

16. The speed of an airplane is given by $S = 0.1\sqrt{L}$, where S represents the speed in metres per second and L represents the lift, in newtons (N).
    a) Suppose the lift for a particular airplane is 810 000 N. Determine the speed of the plane to the nearest metre per second.
    b) Express your answer for part a) in kilometres per hour. Is this a reasonable speed for a plane? Explain.

17. Highway engineers design on-ramps and off-ramps to be safe and efficient. The relation describing the maximum speed at which a car can safely travel around a flat curve without skidding is

$$S = \sqrt{6.86\,R}$$

where S represents the maximum speed, in metres per second, and R represents the radius of the curve, in metres. What is the maximum speed, in kilometres per hour, at which a car can safely travel on a ramp with a radius of 50 m? Round to the nearest unit.

Closing

18. A school playground covers an area of $\sqrt{14\,000}$ m².
    a) Express this radical as a mixed radical in simplest form. For your first step, express the radicand as the product of prime factors.
    b) Could this playground be square? Explain.

Extending

19. A Pythagorean triple is a set of three natural numbers that satisfy the Pythagorean theorem; for example, 3, 4, and 5 since $3^2 + 4^2 = 5^2$. Another way to write this would be $9 + 16 = 25$. List two other sets of Pythagorean triples. Explain how you used radicals to locate these numbers.

20. Is each statement true or false? Justify your answer.
    a) $\left(\sqrt{x}\right)^4 = x^2$
    b) $\left(\sqrt{x}\right)^3 = x\sqrt{x}$

Adding and Subtracting Radicals

YOU WILL NEED
• square piece of paper

EXPLORE...

• Fold a square piece of paper in half to produce a rectangle. Tear apart the two halves. Fold one rectangle in half to produce a square. Fold the square along its diagonal to produce a triangle. Fold the triangle in half. Unfold your paper and determine the dimensions of the smallest triangle.

GOAL

Select a strategy to add two radicals.

LEARN ABOUT the Math

Karen's uncle is planning to replace the fascia on one side of the roof of his house and gardening shed. Fascia is the flat surface immediately below the edge of a roof. He has determined the measurements of the sides of the roofs using the Pythagorean theorem.

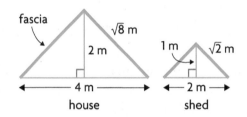

? What length of fascia is needed?

EXAMPLE 1   Adding radicals

Determine the length of fascia needed.

Quinton's Solution: Adding radicals by reducing them to simplest form

The length of fascia needed, L, is:
$$L = \sqrt{8} + \sqrt{8} + \sqrt{2} + \sqrt{2}$$

> The sides of the house roof are each $\sqrt{8}$ m and those of the shed are each $\sqrt{2}$ m, so I needed to add the lengths. The $\sqrt{8}$ and $\sqrt{2}$ are not in the form of like radicals, so I could not add them at this point.

$$L = \sqrt{4} \cdot \sqrt{2} + \sqrt{4} \cdot \sqrt{2} + \sqrt{2} + \sqrt{2}$$
$$L = 2\sqrt{2} + 2\sqrt{2} + 1\sqrt{2} + 1\sqrt{2}$$

> I wrote the $\sqrt{8}$ radicals in simplest form. $\sqrt{2}$ is in simplest form already.

$$L = 6\sqrt{2}$$

> I know that $2x + 2x + x + x = 6x$ when I combine like terms. So, I can add the $\sqrt{2}$ radical terms in the same way to get my answer of $6\sqrt{2}$.

$$L \doteq 6 \cdot 1.5$$
$$L \doteq 9 \text{ m}$$

> I need to estimate because the exact answer won't help Karen's uncle at the hardware store. $\sqrt{2}$ is a little less than 1.5.

Karen's uncle should buy 9 m of fascia.

> This will be a little more than he needs.

Tyron's Solution: Adding radicals using a calculator

The length of fascia needed, L, is:

$$L = \sqrt{8} + \sqrt{8} + \sqrt{2} + \sqrt{2}$$

$$L \doteq 8.485\ldots$$

> I entered each term in the radical expression on my calculator and added.

Karen's uncle needs about 8.5 m of fascia.

> I rounded to the nearest tenth to ensure he has enough material.

Reflecting

A. How would calculating $\sqrt{8} - \sqrt{2}$ be the same as adding $\sqrt{8} + \sqrt{2}$? How would it be different?

B. Todd claims that Tyron could have arrived at his answer two different ways. Do you agree or disagree? Explain.

C. In the third line of Quinton's Solution, why do you think he wrote each $\sqrt{2}$ as $1\sqrt{2}$?

APPLY the Math

EXAMPLE 2 Subtracting radicals

Determine the difference in length between each pair of sides.

a) *PS* and *SR*

b) *RQ* and *PQ*

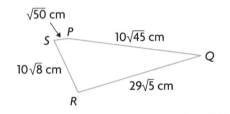

Paula's Solution

a) Let D represent the difference between *PS* and *SR*.

$D = PS - SR$

$D = \sqrt{50} - 10\sqrt{8}$

$D = 5\sqrt{2} - 20\sqrt{2}$ ┈┈┈┈┈┈┈ I expressed the side lengths in simplest form.

$D = -15\sqrt{2}$ ┈┈┈┈┈┈ I subtracted the like radicals.

The difference between *PS* and *SR* is $15\sqrt{2}$ cm. ┈┈┈┈ My answer is negative, because I subtracted a greater number from a smaller one, however, I know length can only be positive.

b) Let E represent the difference between *RQ* and *PQ*.

$E = RQ - PQ$

$E = 29\sqrt{5} - 10\sqrt{45}$

$E = 29\sqrt{5} - 30\sqrt{5}$ ┈┈┈┈┈┈ I expressed the side lengths in simplest form.

$E = -\sqrt{5}$ ┈┈┈┈┈┈ I subtracted the like radicals. Again, I know length can't be negative, so my answer is positive.

The difference between *RQ* and *PQ* is $\sqrt{5}$ cm.

Your Turn

Determine the difference between a side of length $\sqrt{243}$ cm and one of length $15\sqrt{3}$ cm.

EXAMPLE 3   Simplifying radical expressions

Simplify each expression.

a) $2\sqrt{27} - 4\sqrt{3} - \sqrt{12}$ b) $2\sqrt{24} - 3\sqrt{96} + \sqrt{432}$

Vanessa's Solution

a) $2\sqrt{27} - 4\sqrt{3} - \sqrt{12}$

$= 2\sqrt{9} \cdot \sqrt{3} - 4\sqrt{3} - \sqrt{4} \cdot \sqrt{3}$ I determined the simplest form of each term.

$= 2 \cdot 3\sqrt{3} - 4\sqrt{3} - 2\sqrt{3}$

$= 6\sqrt{3} - 4\sqrt{3} - 2\sqrt{3}$ The terms were all like radicals, so I was able to subtract.

$= 0\sqrt{3}$ I subtracted from left to right, as with any calculation.

$= 0$

b) $2\sqrt{24} - 3\sqrt{96} + \sqrt{432}$

$= (2\sqrt{2^2} \cdot \sqrt{2 \cdot 3}) - (3\sqrt{2^4} \cdot \sqrt{2 \cdot 3}) + (\sqrt{2^4 \cdot 3^2} \cdot \sqrt{3})$ I determined the simplest form of each term in the expression.

$= 2 \cdot 2\sqrt{6} - 3 \cdot 2^2\sqrt{6} + 2^2 \cdot 3\sqrt{3}$

$= 4\sqrt{6} - 12\sqrt{6} + 12\sqrt{3}$ I subtracted the like radicals, but I couldn't add the unlike radical.

$= -8\sqrt{6} + 12\sqrt{3}$

Your Turn

Create a negative mixed radical using one addition sign, one subtraction sign, and the radicals $\sqrt{32}$, $3\sqrt{8}$, and $\sqrt{18}$.

In Summary

Key Ideas

- Radicals with the same radicand and index are considered like radicals.
- You can add or subtract like radicals. For example:

$6\sqrt{3} + 2\sqrt{3} = (6 + 2)\sqrt{3}$, or $8\sqrt{3}$

$6\sqrt{3} - 2\sqrt{3} = (6 - 2)\sqrt{3}$, or $4\sqrt{3}$

- You cannot add or subtract unlike radicals, such as $6\sqrt{2}$ and $4\sqrt{5}$.

Need to Know

- When you add or subtract radicals, it helps to express each one in its simplest form first.
- When calculating, keep numbers in radical form until the end of the solution, so you can determine the exact value instead of an approximation.

CHECK Your Understanding

1. When simplified, are the radicals in each set like or unlike radicals?
   a) $4\sqrt{2}, 5\sqrt{2}, 12\sqrt{2}, -3\sqrt{2}$
   b) $4\sqrt[3]{2}, 7\sqrt[3]{3}, 6\sqrt{2}, -6\sqrt{2}$
   c) $6\sqrt{5}, -5\sqrt{5}, 4\sqrt{5}, 4\sqrt{125}$
   d) $\sqrt[3]{-8}, -\sqrt{16}, 2\sqrt{4}, 4\sqrt{4}$

2. Simplify.
   a) $4\sqrt{6} + 3\sqrt{6} + 2\sqrt{6}$
   b) $15\sqrt{3} - 3\sqrt{3} - 8\sqrt{3}$
   c) $5\sqrt{2} - 9\sqrt{2} - \sqrt{2} + 11\sqrt{2}$
   d) $-7\sqrt{10} - 4\sqrt{10} - 3\sqrt{10} + 12\sqrt{10}$

3. Simplify $\sqrt{12} + 2\sqrt{27}$. Explain each step.

4. Write in mixed radical form, then simplify.
   a) $\sqrt{8} - \sqrt{32} + \sqrt{512}$
   b) $-\sqrt{27} + \sqrt{75} - \sqrt{12}$

PRACTISING

5. Simplify.
   a) $\sqrt{72} + \sqrt{50}$
   b) $7\sqrt{3} + 2\sqrt{45} + \sqrt{108}$
   c) $\sqrt{32} + 5\sqrt{2} + \sqrt{400}$
   d) $3\sqrt{20} + 4\sqrt{60} + \sqrt{125}$

6. Simplify.
   a) $\sqrt{40} - \sqrt{360}$
   b) $6\sqrt{27} - \sqrt{75} - 4\sqrt{48}$
   c) $5\sqrt{32} - 7\sqrt{2} - \sqrt{484}$
   d) $3\sqrt{18} - 6\sqrt{45} - 5\sqrt{108}$

7. Kimmi wants to sew a ribbon border around a small triangular cushion with sides of $\sqrt{63}$ cm, $\sqrt{50}$ cm, and $\sqrt{72}$ cm.
   a) Determine the exact length of ribbon Kimmi needs.
   b) Determine the length Kimmi needs to a tenth of a centimetre.

8. The sum of any two sides of a triangle must be greater than the third side. Can you create a triangle with side lengths of $\sqrt{28}$ cm, $\sqrt{63}$ cm, and $\sqrt{147}$ cm? Explain your answer.

9. Express the perimeter of each figure in simplest form.

   a)

   b)

   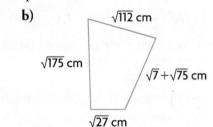

10. John has two small square cushions, one 400 cm² in area and the other 578 cm² in area. Determine, in two different ways, the combined perimeter of the two cushions. Provide an exact answer.

11. A design for an overpass is shown. Determine the total length of steel needed to form the angled support section of the bridge. Express your answer as a radical in simplest form.

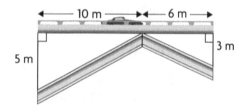

12. This house covers a square with an area of 90 m², and the garage covers a square with an area of 40 m². Determine the combined length of the front of the house and garage as a radical in simplest form.

13. An architect is designing the floor plan of a car dealership, as shown, with the sales office between the square showroom and the square car lot. The front of the entire dealership is exactly $17\sqrt{5}$ m long. Determine the exact width of the sales office.

14. Express $3\sqrt{32} - \sqrt{8} + 2\sqrt{50} - \sqrt{18}$ in simplest form.

15. Express $3\sqrt{80} - 5\sqrt{150} + 4\sqrt{384} - 3\sqrt{45}$ in simplest form.

16. James was asked to express $12\sqrt{24} + 12\sqrt{3}$ in simplest form. He wrote the following:

$$12\sqrt{24} + 12\sqrt{3} = 12\sqrt{2 \cdot 2 \cdot 2 \cdot 3} + 12\sqrt{3}$$
$$= 12 \cdot \sqrt{2^2} \cdot \sqrt{2 \cdot 3} + 12\sqrt{3}$$
$$= 12 \cdot 2 \cdot \sqrt{6} + 12\sqrt{3}$$
$$= 24\sqrt{6} + 12\sqrt{3}$$
$$= 36\sqrt{9}$$

What error did James make? What should the answer be?

17. Explain how to determine how many different terms a radical expression will have in its simplest form. Support your explanation with an example.

18. Express $\sqrt{600} - \sqrt{486} + \sqrt{150}$ in simplest form.

19. Write each expression in simplest form.

    a) $\sqrt{50} - 6\sqrt{2}$ **b)** $-3\sqrt{3} + \sqrt{192}$ **c)** $\sqrt{3125} - 2\sqrt{5} - 3\sqrt{20}$

Closing

20. How is adding and subtracting radicals, such as $3\sqrt{42} + 4\sqrt{36}$, the same as adding and subtracting algebraic terms, such as $3x + 4x$? How is it different? Explain.

Extending

21. Jasmine drew two squares on graph paper. Square A had an area of 2 square units and Square B had an area of 8 square units. How many times longer are the sides of Square B than the sides of Square A? Determine your answer using your knowledge of adding radicals. Confirm your answer using graph paper.

History | Connection

It's Radical

Radical numbers, such as $\sqrt{2}$, have been known since at least the time of Pythagoras, more than 2000 years ago. But it was "only" about 800 years ago, in the 1200s, that mathematicians started to use symbols to indicate radicals. Originally, mathematicians used the Latin word *radix*, which means "root," to indicate that a number was a radical. Then they shortened that, just using the letter "R" with a line crossing its right leg, much like the symbol used in today's medical prescriptions.

   The radical sign as we know it today first appeared in print in the 1500s, in a German book on algebra by Christoff Rudolff. (This book also introduced the signs "+" and "−" to the world.)

A. Suppose Jackie is asked to solve this problem:

$$\sqrt{4x + 12x} - \sqrt{2x + 2x} = 4$$

Suppose Jim is asked to solve this problem:

> The difference between the radix of the sum of four equal measures and twelve equal measures and the radix of the sum of two equal measures and two equal measures is equal to four units. Determine the number of units in one equal measure.

Who do you think would solve their problem more quickly? Explain.

B. How did other mathematical symbols develop over the centuries? Pick two and present the results of your research.

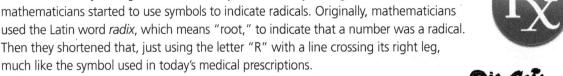

Die Coss
Christoffs Rudolffs
Die schönen Exempeln der Coss
Durch
Michael Stifel
Gebessert vnd sehr gemehret.

Den Junhalt des gantzen Buchs
such nach der Vorred.

Zu Königsperg in Preussen
Gedruckt / durch Alexandrum
Lutomyslensem im jar
1 5 5 3.

The title page of *Die Coss*, Christoff Rudolff's algebra text

Multiplying and Dividing Radicals

GOAL

Multiply and divide numerical radicals.

INVESTIGATE the Math

For a school logo, Hugo will paint the north wall of the gym with yellow, green, and blue right triangles, as shown. The height of the yellow triangle and the length of its base will be in a 3 : 2 ratio. A 4 L can of paint covers about 32.5 m². Hugo plans to apply two coats of paint.

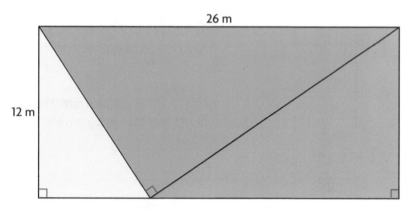

EXPLORE...

• A bowl contains 36 cubes of sugar. Each sugar cube is 1 cm on a side. Cathy stacks the cubes in a rectangular prism with the smallest possible surface area. What is the length of the longest diagonal measure in her prism?

? How much green paint should Hugo buy?

A. Determine the dimensions of each triangle in radical form.

B. Express the area of the green triangle in simplest form.

C. Find a classmate who used the formula for area of a triangle using a different method from yours. How are your solutions alike? How are they different? Explain.

D. How many cans of green paint does Hugo need to buy?

Reflecting

E. Why was it useful to keep the dimensions of the green triangle in the form of radicals?

F. How can you verify your answer without using radicals?

APPLY the Math

EXAMPLE 1	Multiplying radicals with the same index

Show that the following equations are true.

a) $\sqrt{3} \cdot \sqrt{5} = \sqrt{15}$ b) $\dfrac{\sqrt{3}}{\sqrt{5}} = \sqrt{\dfrac{3}{5}}$

Marcus's Solution

LS	RS
a) $\sqrt{3} \cdot \sqrt{5}$	$\sqrt{15}$
$3^{\frac{1}{2}} \cdot 5^{\frac{1}{2}}$	
$(3 \cdot 5)^{\frac{1}{2}}$	
$15^{\frac{1}{2}}$	
$\sqrt{15}$	

I know that the square root of a number is the same as the radicand having an exponent of $\dfrac{1}{2}$.

By the laws of exponents, I can apply the same exponent to the product.

I wrote $15^{\frac{1}{2}}$ as a square root. This proves that the expressions are equal.

$$\sqrt{3} \cdot \sqrt{5} = \sqrt{15}$$

LS	RS
b) $\dfrac{\sqrt{3}}{\sqrt{5}}$	$\sqrt{\dfrac{3}{5}}$
$\dfrac{3^{\frac{1}{2}}}{5^{\frac{1}{2}}}$	
$\left(\dfrac{3}{5}\right)^{\frac{1}{2}}$	
$\dfrac{\sqrt{3}}{\sqrt{5}}$	
$\sqrt{\dfrac{3}{5}}$	

I can use a similar proof to that in part a).

By the laws of exponents, I can apply the same exponent to the quotient.

I wrote $\left(\dfrac{3}{5}\right)^{\frac{1}{2}}$ as a square root. This proves that the expressions are equal.

Your Turn

Bryce makes this claim:

$$\sqrt{9} \cdot \sqrt{8} = 6\sqrt{2}$$

Is he correct? Explain.

EXAMPLE **2**   Multiplying radicals using the distributive property

Express in simplest form.

a) $4\sqrt{2}(7\sqrt{5} + \sqrt{3})$ **b)** $(5\sqrt{3} + 2\sqrt{6})^2$

Luba's Solution

a) $4\sqrt{2}(7\sqrt{5} + \sqrt{3})$

$= 4\sqrt{2} \cdot 7\sqrt{5} + 4\sqrt{2} \cdot \sqrt{3}$

> I cannot add the radicals in the brackets because they are not alike. I expanded by distributing $4\sqrt{2}$ to each term in the brackets.

$= 28\sqrt{10} + 4\sqrt{6}$

> I multiplied the integers and the radicals of each term. I could not reduce the radicals any further, so this is the expression in simplest form.

b) $(5\sqrt{3} + 2\sqrt{6})^2$

$= (5\sqrt{3} + 2\sqrt{6}) \cdot (5\sqrt{3} + 2\sqrt{6})$

> I wrote the expression as a product.

$= 5\sqrt{3} \cdot 5\sqrt{3} + 5\sqrt{3} \cdot 2\sqrt{6} + 2\sqrt{6} \cdot 5\sqrt{3} + 2\sqrt{6} \cdot 2\sqrt{6}$

> I expanded the binomial.

$= 25\sqrt{9} + 10\sqrt{18} + 10\sqrt{18} + 4\sqrt{36}$

$= 25 \cdot 3 + 20\sqrt{18} + 4 \cdot 6$

> I evaluated the perfect squares and added the like radicals.

$= 75 + 24 + 20\sqrt{18}$

$= 99 + 20\sqrt{18}$

$= 99 + 20\sqrt{9} \cdot \sqrt{2}$

$= 99 + 20 \cdot 3\sqrt{2}$

$= 99 + 60\sqrt{2}$

> I simplified.

Your Turn

Express $2\sqrt{3}(\sqrt{12} - \sqrt{7})$ in simplest form.

EXAMPLE **3**   Dividing radicals by a monomial

Express each of the following in simplest form.

a) $\dfrac{6\sqrt{48}}{3\sqrt{6}}$

b) $\dfrac{4\sqrt{12} - 10\sqrt{6}}{2\sqrt{3}}$

Benito's Solution: Calculating rational numbers and radicals separately

a) $\dfrac{6\sqrt{48}}{3\sqrt{6}}$

	The mixed radicals in the numerator and the denominator are products.
$= \dfrac{6}{3} \cdot \sqrt{\dfrac{48}{6}}$	I wrote the expression as a product of an integer quotient and a single radical quotient.
$= 2 \cdot \sqrt{8}$	I simplified by dividing.
$= 2 \cdot \sqrt{2^2 \cdot 2}$ $= 2 \cdot 2\sqrt{2}$ $= 4\sqrt{2}$	I expressed $\sqrt{8}$ as a mixed radical using prime factorization and then multiplied the two rational numbers.

b) $\dfrac{4\sqrt{12} - 10\sqrt{6}}{2\sqrt{3}}$

$= \dfrac{4\sqrt{12}}{2\sqrt{3}} - \dfrac{10\sqrt{6}}{2\sqrt{3}}$	I wrote the expression as a subtraction statement involving two terms so I could work with each term separately.
$= \left(\dfrac{4}{2} \cdot \sqrt{\dfrac{12}{3}}\right) - \left(\dfrac{10}{2} \cdot \sqrt{\dfrac{6}{3}}\right)$	I wrote each term as the product of an integer quotient and a single radical quotient.
$= 2 \cdot \sqrt{4} - 5 \cdot \sqrt{2}$	I simplified the terms by dividing.
$= 2 \cdot 2 - 5\sqrt{2}$	I wrote $\sqrt{4}$ as 2. I couldn't reduce $\sqrt{2}$ any further, since 2 is a prime number.
$= 4 - 5\sqrt{2}$	I multiplied the two rational numbers to obtain the simplest form.

Yvette's Solution: Rationalizing the denominator

a) $\dfrac{6\sqrt{48}}{3\sqrt{6}}$

$= \dfrac{2\sqrt{48}}{\sqrt{6}}$

I divided the numerator and denominator by the common factor 3 to eliminate the coefficient in the denominator.

Communication | Tip

By convention, a radical expression is in simplest form only when the denominator of the expression is a rational number.

$= \dfrac{2\sqrt{48}}{\sqrt{6}} \cdot \dfrac{\sqrt{6}}{\sqrt{6}}$

$= \dfrac{2\sqrt{48} \cdot \sqrt{6}}{6}$

I wanted to **rationalize the denominator,** so I multiplied the expression by $\dfrac{\sqrt{6}}{\sqrt{6}}$. Since this is equal to 1, the value of the expression did not change.

rationalize the denominator

The process used to write a radical expression that contains a radical denominator as an equivalent expression with a rational denominator.

$= \dfrac{2\sqrt{8} \cdot \sqrt{6} \cdot \sqrt{6}}{6}$

$= \dfrac{2\sqrt{8} \cdot 6}{6}$

$= 2\sqrt{8}$

I expressed $\sqrt{48}$ as a product of two radicals, $\sqrt{8}$ and $\sqrt{6}$, because $\sqrt{6^2}$ eliminates the radical sign. I simplified using the fact that $\dfrac{6}{6} = 1$.

$= 2 \cdot 2\sqrt{2}$

I wrote $\sqrt{8}$ in simplest form.

$= 4\sqrt{2}$

I multiplied to obtain the simplest form.

b) $\dfrac{4\sqrt{12} - 10\sqrt{6}}{2\sqrt{3}}$

$= \dfrac{2\sqrt{12} - 5\sqrt{6}}{\sqrt{3}}$

I divided each term in the numerator and denominator by the common factor 2 to eliminate the integer in the denominator.

$= \dfrac{(2\sqrt{12} - 5\sqrt{6})}{\sqrt{3}} \cdot \dfrac{\sqrt{3}}{\sqrt{3}}$

I multiplied the expression by 1, in the form $\dfrac{\sqrt{3}}{\sqrt{3}}$, so I could express the radical in the denominator as a rational number.

$= \dfrac{2\sqrt{36} - 5\sqrt{18}}{3}$

I multiplied both terms in the numerator and the term in the denominator by $\sqrt{3}$.

$$= \frac{2 \cdot 6 - 5 \cdot 3\sqrt{2}}{3}$$

I simplified the radicals.

$$= \frac{12 - 15\sqrt{2}}{3}$$

I multiplied to produce a new numerator.

$$= 4 - 5\sqrt{2}$$

I divided each term by the common factor of 3 to eliminate the denominator and obtain the simplest form.

Maria's Solution: Eliminating common factors

a) $\dfrac{6\sqrt{48}}{3\sqrt{6}}$

$$= \frac{2 \cdot 3 \cdot \sqrt{6} \cdot \sqrt{8}}{3 \cdot \sqrt{6}}$$

I factored the numerator. I noticed that it and the denominator had the common factor of $3\sqrt{6}$.

$$= 2\sqrt{8}$$

I eliminated the denominator by dividing by $3\sqrt{6}$.

$$= 2 \cdot \sqrt{2^3}$$
$$= 2 \cdot \sqrt{2^2} \cdot \sqrt{2}$$

I wrote $\sqrt{8}$ as a mixed radical.

$$= 2 \cdot 2\sqrt{2}$$
$$= 4\sqrt{2}$$

I multiplied the rational numbers to write the expression in simplest form.

b) $\dfrac{4\sqrt{12} - 10\sqrt{6}}{2\sqrt{3}}$

$$= \frac{2\sqrt{3} \cdot (2\sqrt{4} - 5\sqrt{2})}{2\sqrt{3}}$$

I factored the numerator. I noticed that it and the denominator had the common factor of $2\sqrt{3}$.

$$= 2\sqrt{4} - 5\sqrt{2}$$

I eliminated the denominator by dividing by $2\sqrt{3}$.

$$= 2 \cdot 2 - 5\sqrt{2}$$

I wrote $\sqrt{4}$ as 2.

$$= 4 - 5\sqrt{2}$$

I multiplied the rational numbers to obtain the simplest form.

Your Turn

Compare Yvette's Solution, Benito's Solution, and Maria's Solution. What are the advantages and disadvantages of each strategy?

In Summary

Key Idea

- You can use the same properties you use with rational numbers to multiply and divide radical numbers:
  - the commutative property; for example:
  $$5\sqrt{2} = \sqrt{2} \cdot 5$$
  - the associative property; for example:
  $$\sqrt{3}(5\sqrt{2}) = 5(\sqrt{3} \cdot \sqrt{2}) \text{ or } \sqrt{2}(5\sqrt{3})$$
  - the distributive property; for example:
  $$\sqrt{4}(\sqrt{2} + 1) = \sqrt{4} \cdot \sqrt{2} + \sqrt{4} \cdot 1$$
  - the multiplicative identity property; for example:
  $$\sqrt{5} \cdot 1 = \sqrt{5} \cdot \frac{\sqrt{5}}{\sqrt{5}}$$

Need to Know

- The product of two square roots is equal to the square root of the product.

$$\sqrt{a} \cdot \sqrt{b} = \sqrt{a \cdot b}$$ For example: $\sqrt{3} \cdot \sqrt{2} = \sqrt{3 \cdot 2}$ or $\sqrt{6}$

  when $a \geq 0, b \geq 0$

- The product of two mixed radicals is equal to the product of the rational numbers times the product of the radicals.

$$c\sqrt{a} \cdot d\sqrt{b} = c \cdot d\sqrt{ab}$$ For example: $3\sqrt{2} \cdot 5\sqrt{7} = 3 \cdot 5 \cdot \sqrt{2} \cdot \sqrt{7}$ or $15\sqrt{14}$

  when $a \geq 0, b \geq 0$

- The quotient of two square roots is equal to the square root of the quotient.

$$\frac{\sqrt{a}}{\sqrt{b}} = \sqrt{\frac{a}{b}}$$ For example: $\dfrac{\sqrt{6}}{\sqrt{2}} = \sqrt{\dfrac{6}{2}}$ or $\sqrt{3}$

  when $a \geq 0, b > 0$

- The quotient of two mixed radicals is equal to the product of the quotient of the coefficients and the quotient of the radicals.

$$\frac{c\sqrt{a}}{d\sqrt{b}} = \frac{c}{d}\sqrt{\frac{a}{b}}$$ For example: $\dfrac{15\sqrt{14}}{5\sqrt{7}} = \dfrac{15}{5} \cdot \sqrt{\dfrac{14}{7}}$ or $3\sqrt{2}$

  when $a \geq 0, b > 0, d \neq 0$

- One way to simplify an expression with a radical in the denominator is called rationalizing the denominator. To do this, multiply by 1 in a form that will change the denominator to a rational number.

  For example: $\dfrac{3\sqrt{7}}{4\sqrt{5}} = \dfrac{3\sqrt{7}}{4\sqrt{5}} \cdot \dfrac{\sqrt{5}}{\sqrt{5}}$ or $\dfrac{3\sqrt{35}}{20}$

CHECK Your Understanding

1. Write each expression in simplest form.

   a) $\sqrt{5} \cdot \sqrt{6}$

   b) $\sqrt{12} \cdot \sqrt{20}$

   c) $2\sqrt{3} \cdot \sqrt{24}$

   d) $7\sqrt{32} \cdot 2\sqrt{48}$

2. a) Write $\dfrac{1}{\sqrt{5}}$ in its rationalized form.

   b) Explain why you can multiply $\dfrac{1}{\sqrt{5}}$ by $\dfrac{\sqrt{5}}{\sqrt{5}}$ without changing its value.

3. Simplify $\dfrac{\sqrt{64}}{\sqrt{4}}$ using three different methods. Explain what you did in each method.

PRACTISING

4. Express each product in mixed radical form and entire form.

   a) $\sqrt{12} \cdot \sqrt{24}$

   b) $3\sqrt{15} \cdot 2\sqrt{10}$

   c) $-1\sqrt{30} \cdot \sqrt{54}$

   d) $-2\sqrt{14} \cdot -1\sqrt{21}$

5. Expand each expression and simplify.

   a) $7(3 + \sqrt{12})$

   b) $\sqrt{5}(4 - \sqrt{10})$

   c) $\sqrt{6}(\sqrt{10} - 8\sqrt{3})$

   d) $2\sqrt{3}(\sqrt{18} + 5\sqrt{2})$

   e) $(6 + \sqrt{6})(5 + \sqrt{10})$

   f) $(2\sqrt{3} - 5\sqrt{8})^2$

6. a) Simplify $2\sqrt{12} \cdot \sqrt{18} \cdot 5\sqrt{6}$ in two different ways.

   b) Which property (associative, commutative, or distributive) allowed you to do this? Explain.

7. Given: $\sqrt{192}$ and $\sqrt{4800}$

   a) Express each radical as a product of smaller radicals, each with a different radicand.

   b) Write each radical in simplest form. How did rewriting each radical first make this step easier?

8. Determine which figure covers the greater area. Do not use a calculator.

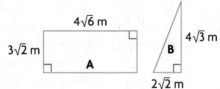

9. a) Determine which figure covers the greater area.

   b) Did you need to express the areas in decimal form to answer part a)? Explain.

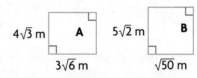

10. Clare was asked to write $\sqrt{8}$ in simplest form. She wrote:

$$\sqrt{8} = \sqrt{2 + 2 + 2 + 2}$$
$$= \sqrt{2} + \sqrt{2} + \sqrt{2} + \sqrt{2}$$
$$= 4\sqrt{2}$$

Identify the error in Clare's reasoning and write the correct answer.

11. Steve and Danny were asked to evaluate $(\sqrt{2} - 1)^2$.

a) Who is incorrect? Justify your answer.

b) Complete the correct solution.

Steve's Solution	**Danny's Solution**
$(\sqrt{2} - 1)^2$	$(\sqrt{2} - 1)^2$
$(\sqrt{2})^2 - 1^2$	$(\sqrt{2} - 1)(\sqrt{2} - 1)$

12. The time it takes for a spring with a mass attached to move up and down until reaching its original position (one complete cycle) can be approximated by

$$T = 2\pi\sqrt{\frac{M}{K}}$$

where T represents the time in seconds, M represents the object's mass in kilograms, and K represents the spring's constant in newtons per metre (N/m).

Consider a spring holding a mass of 4 kg with a spring constant of 2 N/m.

a) Determine T in simplest form.

b) Determine T to the nearest hundredth of a second.

spring

mass

13. Rationalize the denominator in each expression.

a) $\dfrac{\sqrt{7}}{\sqrt{2}}$

b) $\dfrac{-1}{4\sqrt{5}}$

c) $\dfrac{-3\sqrt{8}}{\sqrt{6}}$

d) $\dfrac{\sqrt{72}}{2\sqrt{8}}$

14. Write each expression in simplest form.

a) $\dfrac{\sqrt{12}}{\sqrt{3}}$

b) $\dfrac{4\sqrt{15}}{-1\sqrt{5}}$

c) $\dfrac{-3\sqrt{30}}{\sqrt{6}}$

d) $\dfrac{-2\sqrt{98}}{\sqrt{8}}$

15. Sasha claims that she can simplify $\sqrt{0.16}$ by first representing the radicand as a division of whole numbers. Do you agree or disagree? Explain.

16. Write each expression in simplest form by rationalizing the denominator.

a) $\dfrac{5\sqrt{10}}{\sqrt{3}}$

c) $\dfrac{\sqrt{6} + \sqrt{2}}{\sqrt{6}}$

b) $\dfrac{2\sqrt{2} - \sqrt{5}}{\sqrt{5}}$

d) $\dfrac{\sqrt{80} + 2\sqrt{3}}{3\sqrt{5}}$

17. Sound travels through different materials at different speeds. The speed of sound is modelled by

$$S = \sqrt{\frac{E}{d}}$$

where S represents the speed in metres per second, E represents the elasticity of the material in newtons per square metre (N/m^2), and d represents the density of the material in kilograms per cubic metre (kg/m^3). Determine the speed of sound through each material as a radical in simplest form.
   a) a material with $E = 4000$ N/m^2 and $d = 0.25$ kg/m^3
   b) a material with $E = 320$ N/m^2 and $d = 0.20$ kg/m^3

18. Buildings in snowy areas often have steep roofs. The steepness, or pitch, is expressed as the height of a roof divided by its width. Determine the pitch, in simplest form, for a building whose roof is $4\sqrt{3}$ m high and $2\sqrt{14}$ m wide.

19. Determine the width, w, of each rectangle.

   a)

   $w = ?$ $A = 24\sqrt{3}$ m²

   $l = 4\sqrt{6}$ m

   b)

   $w = ?$ $A = 140\sqrt{3}$ m²

   $l = 4\sqrt{15}$ m

20. Which expression has the lesser value? Explain how you know.

   A. $2\sqrt{2}(9\sqrt{3} - \sqrt{12})$ **B.** $\dfrac{\sqrt{288} + 30\sqrt{2}}{2\sqrt{3}}$

21. a) Explain why you should keep numbers as radicals when calculating. Justify your response with an example.

   b) Simplify $\dfrac{3\sqrt{8}}{\sqrt{6}} \cdot \dfrac{\sqrt{24}}{\sqrt{2}}$. Show your work, and explain what properties you used.

Closing

22. How is multiplying and dividing radicals like multiplying and dividing algebraic expressions? Explain using an example.

Extending

23. Morana rewrote $\dfrac{1}{\sqrt[3]{3}}$ with a rational denominator in the form $\dfrac{\sqrt[3]{9}}{3}$. Are these equivalent expressions? Explain.

Defining a Fractal

A Pythagorean fractal tree starts at stage 1 with a square of side length 1 unit. At every consecutive stage, two squares are attached to the last square(s) drawn.

YOU WILL NEED
- graph paper
- ruler

The Puzzle

A. The first three stages of a Pythagorean fractal tree are shown. Determine the lengths of the sides of the smallest square at each stage.

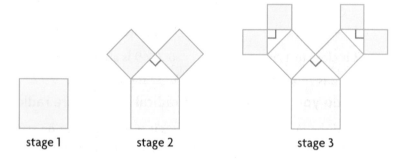

stage 1   stage 2   stage 3

B. What pattern exists between the measurements? Explain.

C. Draw two more stages and determine the side lengths of the added squares.

D. Determine the exact area of each of the first five stages of this Pythagorean fractal tree.

The Strategy

E. Explain the strategy you used to determine the measurements of the sides.

F. Explain the strategy you used to determine the area of each stage.

G. What pattern exists in the area measurements? Explain.

H. Describe how you would calculate the area of the 10th stage of the fractal tree.

FREQUENTLY ASKED Questions

Study | **Aid**
- See Lesson 4.1.
- Try Mid-Chapter Review Questions 1, 2, 4, and 5.

Q: **How do you compare numerical radicals?**

A: To compare radicals, express them in their simplest form by expressing the radicand in terms of powers of its prime factors. Then estimate using the values of perfect squares.

For example: Which numerical radical is greater?

$$\sqrt{32} = \sqrt{2^5}$$
$$= \sqrt{2^4} \cdot \sqrt{2}$$
$$= 2^2\sqrt{2}$$
$$= 4\sqrt{2}$$

$\sqrt{2}$ is close to 1.5, so $4\sqrt{2}$ is about 6.

$$\sqrt[3]{72} = \sqrt[3]{2 \cdot 2 \cdot 2 \cdot 3 \cdot 3}$$
$$= \sqrt[3]{2^3} \cdot \sqrt[3]{3 \cdot 3}$$
$$= 2\sqrt[3]{9}$$

9 is greater than 8 but close to it, so $2\sqrt[3]{9}$ is about $2 \cdot 2$ or 4. $\sqrt{32}$ is greater than $\sqrt[3]{72}$.

Study | **Aid**
- See Lesson 4.1.
- Try Mid-Chapter Review Questions 2, 4, and 5.

Q: **How do you express a mixed radical as an entire radical?**

A: Expand the mixed radical and express it as a multiplication statement of its factors, then determine the product of those factors.

For example:

$$-6\sqrt{5} = -1 \cdot \sqrt{6 \cdot 6 \cdot 5}$$
$$= -\sqrt{180}$$

$$7\sqrt[3]{2} = \sqrt[3]{7 \cdot 7 \cdot 7 \cdot 2}$$
$$= \sqrt[3]{686}$$

Study | **Aid**
- See Lesson 4.2.
- Try Mid-Chapter Review Questions 6 to 9.

Q: **How do you add and subtract radicals?**

A: To add and subtract radicals, the radicals must have the same index and radicand.

For example:
$$12\sqrt{5} - \sqrt{180} = 12\sqrt{5} - \sqrt{2^2 \cdot 3^2} \cdot \sqrt{5}$$
$$= 12\sqrt{5} - 2 \cdot 3 \cdot \sqrt{5}$$
$$= 12\sqrt{5} - 6\sqrt{5}$$
$$= 6\sqrt{5}$$

Study | **Aid**
- See Lesson 4.3.
- Try Mid-Chapter Review Questions 10 to 13.

Q: **How do you multiply and divide radicals?**

A: To multiply radicals, multiply the radicands. To divide radicals, divide the radicands and simplify. You can also rationalize the denominator and simplify.

For example:
$$\frac{12\sqrt{5}}{\sqrt{45}} = \frac{12}{1}\sqrt{\frac{5}{45}}$$
$$= 12\sqrt{\frac{1}{9}}$$
$$= 12 \cdot \frac{1}{3}$$
$$= 4$$

PRACTISING

1. Estimate. Write your answers to the nearest tenth, if necessary.
   a) $\sqrt{81}$
   b) $\sqrt{249}$
   c) $-\sqrt[3]{64}$
   d) $-\sqrt{102}$
   e) $\sqrt[3]{27}$
   f) $\sqrt[3]{-125}$

2. Express as a mixed radical.
   a) $\sqrt{32}$
   b) $\sqrt{128}$
   c) $-\sqrt[3]{532}$
   d) $-\sqrt{54}$
   e) $\sqrt[3]{108}$
   f) $\sqrt[3]{-1024}$

3. Express as an entire radical.
   a) $5\sqrt{3}$
   b) $11\sqrt{4}$
   c) $-4\sqrt[3]{216}$
   d) $-4\sqrt{2}$
   e) $2\sqrt[3]{81}$
   f) $6\sqrt[3]{-8}$

4. Order from least to greatest:
   $$-\sqrt{101}, \ -2\sqrt[3]{8}, \ 4\sqrt[3]{-27}, \ -\sqrt{121}, \ -2\sqrt{25}$$

5. Jackson is creating a triangular window for his cottage out of stained glass. One design has side lengths of 130 cm, 130 cm, and 200 cm. A second design has side lengths of 140 cm, 140 cm, and 140 cm. Which design will use more stained glass?

Lesson 4.2

6. Simplify.
   a) $2\sqrt{3} + 4\sqrt{3} + \sqrt{3}$
   b) $7\sqrt{2} + 9\sqrt{2} + 2\sqrt{2}$
   c) $-2\sqrt{5} + 7\sqrt{5} + 3\sqrt{5}$
   d) $-2\sqrt{7} + \sqrt{7} + 8\sqrt{7}$
   e) $\sqrt{8} + 6\sqrt{8} + 5\sqrt{8}$

7. Simplify.
   a) $\sqrt{6} - 2\sqrt{6} - \sqrt{6}$
   b) $-\sqrt{4} - 5\sqrt{4} - 3\sqrt{4}$
   c) $-2\sqrt{3} - 8\sqrt{3} - \sqrt{3}$
   d) $\sqrt{10} - 2\sqrt{10} - 7\sqrt{10}$
   e) $-2\sqrt{12} - \sqrt{12} - 4\sqrt{12}$

8. Simplify.
   a) $\sqrt{75} + \sqrt{150}$
   b) $\sqrt{81} + \sqrt{27} - \sqrt{49}$
   c) $2\sqrt{7} + \sqrt{28} - \sqrt{63}$
   d) $2\sqrt{98} - \sqrt{50}$
   e) $2\sqrt{3} + \sqrt{108} - 5\sqrt{2}$

9. Tamlyn covered the top of a rectangular cake with 1200 cm^2 of chocolate fondant (a sheet of pliable icing). The length of the cake is twice the width of the cake. What are the dimensions of the top of the cake in radical form?

Lesson 4.3

10. Simplify. Express your answer in simplest form.
    a) $\sqrt{7} \cdot \sqrt{8}$
    b) $\sqrt{12} \cdot \sqrt{10}$
    c) $3\sqrt{5} \cdot \sqrt{15}$
    d) $-\sqrt{26} \cdot \sqrt{14} \cdot \sqrt{2}$
    e) $-2\sqrt{25} \cdot -3\sqrt{10} \cdot -\sqrt{3}$

11. Simplify. Express your answer in simplest form.
    a) $\dfrac{2\sqrt{10}}{\sqrt{5}}$
    b) $\dfrac{12\sqrt{7}}{-2\sqrt{7}}$
    c) $\dfrac{-13\sqrt{12}}{26\sqrt{6}}$
    d) $\dfrac{28\sqrt{10}}{2\sqrt{2}}$
    e) $\dfrac{27\sqrt{15}}{-9\sqrt{3}}$

12. Expand and simplify.
    a) $\sqrt{2}(4 + 5\sqrt{3})$
    b) $-7\sqrt{6}(6\sqrt{8} - 2)$
    c) $(\sqrt{3} + \sqrt{7})(5 + 8\sqrt{10})$
    d) $(2\sqrt{3} + 3\sqrt{5})(2\sqrt{3} - 3\sqrt{5})$

13. Raj used 14.5 m^3 of cement for his square patio. The height of the patio is 0.25 m. Determine the exact length and exact width of the patio.

Simplifying Algebraic Expressions Involving Radicals

Simplify radical expressions that contain variable radicands.

- Choose two numbers that are opposites. Plot both numbers on a number line. How far is each of these numbers from zero? Is distance a positive or negative quantity? Repeat for several other pairs of opposite numbers. Compare results with other students and discuss what you found.

LEARN ABOUT the Math

Algebraic expressions contain variables. Some algebraic expressions contain radicals, such as $\sqrt{x}$, $\sqrt{x^2}$, $\sqrt{x^3}$, and $\sqrt{x^4}$.

? Are radical expressions that involve variables defined for all real numbers, and is it possible to express them in simplest form?

restrictions

The values of the variable in an expression that ensure the expression is defined.

EXAMPLE 1   Working with radicals that contain variables

For each expression above, explain any **restrictions** on the variable, then write the expression in its simplest form.

Melinda's Solution

a) $\sqrt{x}$ is defined when $x \geq 0$, where $x \in R$.

All the radical expressions above involve the principal square root, because the square root sign indicates the positive square root. You cannot determine the square root of a negative number, so the expression $\sqrt{x}$ is defined only for real numbers greater than or equal to zero.

$\sqrt{x}$ cannot be simplified further.

I cannot express x as a power with an even exponent, so I cannot write this expression in simpler terms. x is the smallest possible radicand.

b) $\sqrt{x^2}$ is defined when $x \in R$.

Since the variable is squared, the result will always be positive regardless of whether x is positive or negative. So, the square root can always be determined.

$$\sqrt{x^2} = |x|$$

The square root of x^2 must equal the **absolute value** of x.

Since I am determining the principal square root, the result is always positive, which is what the absolute value symbol ensures.

For example, if $x = -3$ and I want to determine $\sqrt{x^2}$, then by substitution I know that $\sqrt{(-3)^2} = \sqrt{9}$ and $\sqrt{9} = 3$. So, $\sqrt{(-3)^2} = 3$. If I had written $\sqrt{x^2} = x$, my answer could be -3, which would be incorrect.

absolute value

The distance of a number from 0 on a number line; the absolute value of x is denoted as

$$|x| = \begin{cases} x, & \text{If } x \geq 0 \\ -x, & \text{If } x < 0 \end{cases}$$

e.g., $|-5| = 5$

Both 5 and -5 are 5 units from 0.

c) $\sqrt{x^3}$ is defined when $x \geq 0$, where $x \in \mathbb{R}$.

When a positive number is cubed, the result is positive; but when a negative number is cubed, the result is negative. Since you cannot determine the square root of a negative number, the expression $\sqrt{x^3}$ is defined only for real numbers 0 or greater.

$$\sqrt{x^3} = \sqrt{x^2} \cdot \sqrt{x}$$
$$\sqrt{x^3} = |x| \cdot \sqrt{x}$$

I wrote x^3 as the product of two powers, one of which has an even exponent. When a power has even exponents it is a perfect square, so its square root can be determined by dividing the exponent by 2. I used the fact that $\sqrt{x^2} = |x|$ to simplify.

Communication | Tip

When working with radicands that contain a variable, the use of absolute value notation ensures that the principal square root is always represented. To simplify things, from this point forward in this resource, assume that x is the principal square root of x^2. In other words, $\sqrt{x^2} = x$.

d) $\sqrt{x^4}$ is defined when $x \in \mathbb{R}$.

Since the variable is raised to an even exponent, the result will always be positive regardless whether x is positive or negative. So, this square root can always be determined.

$$\sqrt{x^4} = \sqrt{x^2} \cdot \sqrt{x^2}$$
$$\sqrt{x^4} = |x| \cdot |x|$$
$$\sqrt{x^4} = x^2$$

I wrote x^4 as the product of two powers, both of which have even exponents. I used the fact that $\sqrt{x^2} = |x|$ to simplify.

x^2 will always be positive, regardless of whether x is positive or negative.

Reflecting

A. Consider $\sqrt{x^n}$, where $n \in N$. For what values of x is this expression defined? Explain.

B. Mark claims that $\sqrt{x^{2n}} = x^n$, where $n \in N$. Is he correct? Explain.

C. José claims that $\sqrt[3]{x^3} = x$. Do you agree or disagree? Justify your decision.

APPLY the Math

EXAMPLE 2   Adding and subtracting algebraic expression involving radicals

State any restrictions on the variable, then simplify each expression.

a) $\sqrt{x} + 5\sqrt{x}$ **b)** $2\sqrt{4x^4} - \sqrt{8x^4}$

Bert's Solution

a) $\sqrt{x} + 5\sqrt{x}$ is defined
when $x \geq 0$,
where $x \in R$.

$\sqrt{x}$ is defined only when x is either zero or positive.

$1\sqrt{x} + 5\sqrt{x} = 6\sqrt{x}$

These are like radicals. I simplified by adding the coefficients.

b) $2\sqrt{4x^4} - \sqrt{8x^4}$ is defined
when $x \in R$.

Both radicands will be greater than or equal to zero for any real number value of the variable.

$2\sqrt{4x^4} - \sqrt{8x^4} = 2 \cdot \sqrt{2^2 \cdot x^4} - \sqrt{2^2 \cdot x^4} \cdot \sqrt{2}$

To simplify, I factored each expression under the radicand using prime factors that had the highest even exponents possible.

$= 2 \cdot 2x^2 - 2 \cdot x^2\sqrt{2}$

$= 4x^2 - 2x^2\sqrt{2}$

I can't simplify further.

EXAMPLE 3   Simplifying algebraic expressions involving radicals

State any restrictions on the variable, then simplify each expression.

a) $4\sqrt{18x^3}$ **b)** $-7y^2\sqrt{8y^5}$ **c)** $\sqrt{x-5}$

Meg's Solution

a) $4\sqrt{18x^3}$ is defined
when $x \geq 0$,
where $x \in R$.

> When a positive number is raised to an odd power, the result is positive; but when a negative number is raised to an odd power, the result is negative. Since you cannot determine the square root of a negative number, the expression is defined only for real numbers greater than or equal to zero.

$$4\sqrt{18x^3} = 4\sqrt{3^2 \cdot x^2} \cdot \sqrt{2x}$$

> I wrote $18x^3$ as the product of two radicals. In the first radical, I chose factors that had the largest even exponents possible to create a perfect square.

$$= 4 \cdot 3 \cdot x \cdot \sqrt{2x}$$

$$= 12 \cdot x \cdot \sqrt{2x}$$

> I multiplied the integers to simplify.

b) $-7y^2\sqrt{8y^5}$ is defined
when $y \geq 0$, where $y \in R$.

> If y is negative, then the expression under the radical sign will be negative and undefined. The expression is defined only for real numbers greater than or equal to 0.

$$-7y^2\sqrt{8y^5} = -7y^2\sqrt{2^2 \cdot y^4} \cdot \sqrt{2y}$$

> I wrote $8y^5$ as the product of two radicals. In the first radical, I chose factors that had the largest even exponents possible to create a perfect square.

$$= -7y^2 \cdot 2y^2 \cdot \sqrt{2y}$$

> I used the fact that $\sqrt{y^4} = y^2$ to simplify.

$$= -14y^4\sqrt{2y}$$

> I multiplied the integer coefficients and added the exponents on the variable to simplify.

c) $\sqrt{x-5}$ is defined when $x - 5 \geq 0$.
The expression is defined
when $x \geq 5$, where $x \in R$.

> The square root sign tells me that $x - 5$ must be positive. This will occur when x is 5 or greater.

$\sqrt{x-5}$ cannot be simplified.

> $x - 5$ cannot be expressed using prime factors that involve even exponents.

Your Turn

Explain how you can manipulate a radical that contains both numbers and variables in its radicand to create a perfect square that can be used to simplify the expression. Use an example in your explanation.

EXAMPLE **4**   Multiplying algebraic expressions involving radicals

State any restrictions on the variable, then simplify each expression.

a) $(5\sqrt{6x^2})(-2x\sqrt{2x})$ **b)** $-3\sqrt{x}(2\sqrt{2} - 3x)$ **c)** $(2\sqrt{x} + 3)(5 - 3\sqrt{x})$

Chantelle's Solution

a) $(5\sqrt{6x^2})(-2x\sqrt{2x})$ is defined

when $x \geq 0$, where $x \in \mathbb{R}$.

> $6x^2$ will always be positive, since x is squared, so $\sqrt{6x^2}$ is defined for any value of x. But $\sqrt{2x}$ is defined only when $2x$ is positive. Therefore, x must be greater than or equal to zero to ensure both radicands will never be negative.

$(5\sqrt{6x^2})(-2x\sqrt{2x}) = (5)(-2x) \cdot (\sqrt{6x^2})(\sqrt{2x})$

> I rearranged the terms so the radicals were beside each other, and multiplied.

$$= -10x \cdot \sqrt{12x^3}$$
$$= -10x \cdot \sqrt{2^2 \cdot x^2} \cdot \sqrt{3x}$$

> I simplified the radical.

$$= -10x \cdot 2 \cdot x \cdot \sqrt{3x}$$

> I multiplied again to simplify further.

$$= -20x^2\sqrt{3x}$$

b) $-3\sqrt{x}(2\sqrt{2} - 3x)$ is defined

when $x \geq 0$, where $x \in \mathbb{R}$.

> $\sqrt{x}$ is defined only when x is either 0 or positive. This means x must be greater than or equal to zero.

$-3\sqrt{x}(2\sqrt{2} - 3x) = (-3\sqrt{x})(2\sqrt{2}) - (-3\sqrt{x})(3x)$

> I used the distributive property to expand. I multiplied the products in each term.

$$= -6\sqrt{2x} + 9x\sqrt{x}$$

> I couldn't simplify any further because the expression didn't contain like radicals.

c) $(2\sqrt{x} + 3)(5 - 3\sqrt{x})$ is defined

when $x \geq 0$, where $x \in \mathbb{R}$.

> $\sqrt{x}$ is defined only when x is either 0 or positive. This means x must be greater than or equal to zero.

$(2\sqrt{x} + 3)(5 - 3\sqrt{x})$

> I used the distributive property to expand.

$$= (2\sqrt{x})(5) + (2\sqrt{x})(-3\sqrt{x}) + (3)(5) + (3)(-3\sqrt{x})$$

$$= 10\sqrt{x} - 6\sqrt{x^2} + 15 - 9\sqrt{x}$$

$$= 10\sqrt{x} - 6x + 15 - 9\sqrt{x}$$ --------- I simplified by subtracting like radicals.

$$= -6x + \sqrt{x} + 15$$

Your Turn

When do you need to use the distributive property to multiply expressions that contain radicals? Use examples in your explanation.

EXAMPLE 5   Simplifying algebraic expressions involving radicals and division

State any restrictions on the variable, then simplify each expression.

a) $\dfrac{15\sqrt{x^3}}{-3\sqrt{x^2}}$ b) $\dfrac{6\sqrt{5} - 2\sqrt{24x^3}}{2\sqrt{x}}$

Dwayne's Solution

a) $\dfrac{15\sqrt{x^3}}{-3\sqrt{x^2}}$ is defined for $x > 0$,

where $x \in R$.

> $-3\sqrt{x^2}$ is defined for any value of x, because x^2 is always positive.
>
> $15\sqrt{x^3}$ is defined for any positive value of x.
>
> The entire expression is undefined when $x = 0$, because division by zero is undefined.

$$= -5\sqrt{\dfrac{x^3}{x^2}}$$

> I divided the integers. The radicals in the numerator and denominator had the same index, so I combined them into one radical.

$$= -5\sqrt{x}$$

> I divided the terms in the radicand by subtracting the exponents to write the expression in simplest form.

b) $\dfrac{6\sqrt{5} - 2\sqrt{24x^3}}{2\sqrt{x}}$ is defined

for $x > 0$, where $x \in R$.

$2\sqrt{x}$ is defined for any positive value of x.

$-2\sqrt{24x^3}$ is defined for any positive value of x.

The entire expression is undefined when $x = 0$, because division by zero is undefined.

$$= \dfrac{3\sqrt{5} - \sqrt{24x^3}}{\sqrt{x}}$$

I divided each integer in each radical by 2 in the numerator and the denominator.

$$= \dfrac{(3\sqrt{5} - \sqrt{24x^3})}{\sqrt{x}} \cdot \dfrac{\sqrt{x}}{\sqrt{x}}$$

I rationalized the denominator by multiplying by $\sqrt{x}$ in both the numerator and denominator.

$$= \dfrac{3\sqrt{5x} - \sqrt{24x^4}}{\sqrt{x^2}}$$

I used the distributive property to expand the numerator and multiplied the radicals in the denominator.

$$= \dfrac{3\sqrt{5x} - \sqrt{4x^4} \cdot \sqrt{6}}{x}$$

$$= \dfrac{3\sqrt{5x} - 2x^2\sqrt{6}}{x}$$

I simplified.

Your Turn

Create a rational algebraic expression that contains radicals that cannot be simplified by dividing. State the restrictions on the variables of your expression, then simplify it.

Key Ideas

- When working with an algebraic expression involving radicals, it is important to state any restrictions on the variable; otherwise, the expression does not have meaning. For example, $\sqrt{x-2}$ is defined only when $x \geq 2$, $x \in R$.
- The square root of all powers with an even exponent, such as $\sqrt{x^2}$, $\sqrt{x^4}$, and $\sqrt{x^6}$, is defined for all values of x; the square root of powers with an odd exponent, such as $\sqrt{x}$, $\sqrt{x^3}$, and $\sqrt{x^5}$, is defined for $x \geq 0$, $x \in R$.
- The symbol $\sqrt{}$ indicates the principal square root, which is always positive.
- The square root of x^2 must equal the absolute value of x, denoted $|x|$, to ensure that the principal square root is represented.
- You simplify, add, subtract, multiply, and divide algebraic expressions with radicals using the same principles used for numerical expressions with radicals.

Need to Know

- You can add or subtract like radicals when they have the same index and radicand:
$$6\sqrt{x} + 2\sqrt{x} = 8\sqrt{x}$$
- You can use the following properties to help simplify algebraic radical expressions:
  - the commutative property: $5\sqrt{x} = \sqrt{x} \cdot 5$
  - the associative property: $\sqrt{x}(5\sqrt{2}) = 5(\sqrt{x} \cdot \sqrt{2})$ or $\sqrt{2}(5\sqrt{x})$
  - the distributive property: $2(\sqrt{x} + 1) = 2\sqrt{x} + 2 \cdot 1$
  - the multiplicative identity property: $\dfrac{2}{\sqrt{x}} = \dfrac{2}{\sqrt{x}} \cdot \dfrac{\sqrt{x}}{\sqrt{x}}$

CHECK *Your Understanding*

1. State any restrictions on the variable in each expression. Explain how you decided.

   a) $4\sqrt{x^6}$

   b) $2\sqrt{x^3}$

   c) $\sqrt{x+3}$

   d) $\dfrac{\sqrt{x}}{x}$

2. State any restrictions on the variable, then simplify.

   a) $2\sqrt{45x^4}$

   b) $\sqrt{9x^2}$

   c) $2\sqrt{12x^3}$

   d) $-3x\sqrt{8x^5}$

3. State any restrictions on the variable(s), then simplify.

a) $15\sqrt{2x} - 7\sqrt{2x} - \sqrt{2x}$

b) $36\sqrt{3x^3} - 10\sqrt{3x^3} + 28\sqrt{3x^3}$

c) $(5\sqrt{x})(2\sqrt{x})$

d) $\dfrac{9\sqrt{x^5}}{-3\sqrt{x}}$

PRACTISING

4. Simplify.

a) $(5x^3\sqrt{x})(\sqrt{2x^3})$

c) $\dfrac{-36\sqrt{x^3}}{12\sqrt{x}}$

b) $(-5\sqrt{x})(2\sqrt{8x^3})$

d) $\dfrac{(3\sqrt{x})(4\sqrt{x^3})}{6\sqrt{x^4}}$

Communication | Tip

When no restrictions on the variables are stated in a problem, assume that the variables are of the set of real numbers, R.

5. Charlene simplified $7x\sqrt{x} + 3\sqrt{x^3}$ as shown, but some of her writing was smudged.

a) Determine the missing elements in each step.

b) Explain what Charlene did in each step.

$$7x\sqrt{x} + 3\sqrt{x^3}$$

Step 1: $\quad 7x\sqrt{x} + 3 \cdot \sqrt{\blacksquare} \cdot \sqrt{x}$

Step 2: $\quad 7x\sqrt{x} + 3 \cdot \blacksquare \cdot \sqrt{x}$

Step 3: $\quad \sqrt{x}\,(\blacksquare + \blacksquare)$

6. Simplify.

a) $\sqrt{12x} - 5\sqrt{3x} + \sqrt{27x}$

c) $\dfrac{3 - x}{\sqrt{x}}$

b) $(2x\sqrt{x})(\sqrt{x} + 4\sqrt{x^5})$

d) $\dfrac{4\sqrt{x^3}}{\sqrt{8x}}$

7. Explain how dividing radicals and rationalizing radical expressions are the same and how they are different. Provide an example that supports your reasoning.

8. Simplify.

a) $(5\sqrt{x})(2\sqrt{2x})$

c) $(-3\sqrt{x})(\sqrt{x^3} - 4x)$

b) $\sqrt{2x}\,(\sqrt{2x} + 4x)$

d) $(\sqrt{x} + 2)(\sqrt{x} + 5)$

9. Simplify.

a) $\sqrt{4x} + 2\sqrt{16x}$

c) $3\sqrt{y}(4 - 2\sqrt{y^3})$

b) $4\sqrt{x^4} - 2\sqrt{x^4}$

d) $(5 - \sqrt{y})^2$

10. Simplify.

a) $\dfrac{\sqrt{x^7}}{\sqrt{x}}$
b) $\dfrac{\sqrt{8x^3}}{\sqrt{2x}}$
c) $\dfrac{\sqrt{50x^4}}{\sqrt{2x^2}}$
d) $\dfrac{6\sqrt{x^4}}{3x^2}$

11. State the restrictions on the variable in each expression.

a) $\sqrt{x-9}$
b) $\sqrt{x+4}$
c) $\sqrt{3x+6}$
d) $\sqrt{3x-2}$

12. What would you multiply each quotient by in order to rationalize the denominator of each expression?

a) $\dfrac{\sqrt{x}}{\sqrt{5}}$
b) $\dfrac{-3}{\sqrt{x}}$
c) $\dfrac{12}{\sqrt{7x}}$
d) $\dfrac{5}{2\sqrt{x}}$

13. Explain how to rationalize the denominator of $\dfrac{3+2\sqrt{x}}{4\sqrt{x}}$.

14. At Trent's local mall, a circular water fountain is set inside a triangular prism, as shown. Trent has learned that this inscribed circle is related to the sides of this supporting triangle by the formula

$$r = \sqrt{\dfrac{(s-a)(s-b)(s-c)}{s}}$$

where r represents the radius of the inscribed circle in metres, s is half the perimeter of the triangle, and a, b, and c represent the lengths of the sides of the triangle.

He would like to determine the radius of the fountain.

a) Trent feels that he can divide each s in the numerator with the s in the denominator. Is he correct? Explain.

b) What should Trent do first to simplify this expression?

c) What are the restrictions on s in this context? Explain.

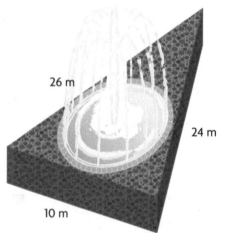

26 m

24 m

10 m

15. State the restrictions on the variable, then simplify the expression:

$$\dfrac{(3\sqrt{2}-2x)(3\sqrt{2}+2x)}{2\sqrt{x}}$$

Closing

16. How is multiplying and dividing algebraic expressions with radicals like multiplying and dividing numerical expressions with radical values? Explain, using an example.

Extending

17. The lateral surface area for a paper cup, S, is defined by

$$S = \pi r \cdot \sqrt{r^2 + h^2}$$

where r represents the radius and h represents the height. Melanie simplified this as shown to the right. Is she correct? Justify your answer.

Melanie's Solution

$S = \pi r \sqrt{r^2 + h^2}$

$S = \pi r \left(\sqrt{r^2} + \sqrt{h^2}\right)$

$S = \pi r \left(r + h\right)$

$S = \pi r^2 + \pi r h$

4.5 Exploring Radical Equations

YOU WILL NEED

- variety of different-sized balls
- string, rulers, tape measure
- calculator

GOAL

Develop a strategy for solving radical equations.

EXPLORE the Math

Alex is in charge of organizing a table tennis tournament. During a break in the tournament, he began to wonder about the surface area and volume of the table tennis balls. He determined both values using a ruler, a piece of string, and these formulas for the radius of a ball, r:

$$r = \sqrt{\frac{A}{4\pi}}$$

where A represents the surface area of the ball

$$r = \sqrt[3]{\frac{3V}{4\pi}}$$

where V represents the volume of the ball

? How can you use these materials and formulas to determine the volume and surface area of any spherical ball?

Reflecting

Communication | Tip

Use the π key on your calculator. Round your answer only at the end of your calculations.

A. How did you determine the radius of your ball? What difficulties did you have, if any?

B. How did you determine the surface area and volume of your ball using the given formulas? How was the strategy you used the same and how was it different for each situation?

C. Sam says you can determine the surface area of a sphere using $A = 4\pi r^2$ and its volume using $V = \frac{4}{3}\pi r^3$. Calculate the surface area and volume of your ball using these formulas. What do you notice?

D. How are the formulas in part C related to those Alex used? Explain.

FURTHER *Your Understanding*

1. Solve each equation.

   a) $5\sqrt{x} = 35$

   c) $\sqrt[3]{\dfrac{4x}{5}} = 2$

   b) $\sqrt{\dfrac{x + 3}{2}} = 4$

   d) $\sqrt[3]{x - 1} = 3$

2. Ella installs lawn watering systems. The radius of sprayed water, r, in metres, can be expressed as

$$r = \sqrt{0.64\,A}$$

   where A represents the area watered, in square metres.

   Ella has set each sprayer to spray at a radius of 1.2 m. Determine the area of grass watered by one sprayer, to the nearest tenth of a square metre.

3. The speed of a tsunami, S, in kilometres per hour, can be modelled by

$$S = 356\sqrt{d}$$

   where d represents the average depth of the water, in kilometres. Determine the average depth of the water, to the nearest hundredth of a kilometre, for a tsunami travelling at 100 km/h.

4. The radius of a cylindrical tank, r, in metres, is given by

$$r = \sqrt{\dfrac{V}{1.5\pi}}$$

   where V represents the volume of water the tank holds, in cubic metres. Determine the volume of water in a tank with a radius of 0.9 m, to the nearest hundredth of a cubic metre.

5. The square root of the sum of twice a number and 5 is 7.
   a) Create the radical equation defined by the above statement.
   b) Solve your radical equation.
   c) Repeat parts a) and b) if "square root" in the statement is changed to "cube root."

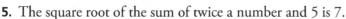

Solving Radical Equations

YOU WILL NEED
- calculator

EXPLORE...

- Marnie claims that the equation
$$\sqrt{(2x - 1)^2} = x$$
has two solutions:

$x = 1$ and $x = \dfrac{1}{3}$.

Do you agree or disagree? Justify your decision.

GOAL

Solve and verify radical equations that contain a single radical.

LEARN ABOUT the Math

In the previous lesson, you solved radical equations by using inverse operations. The equations you used all had a single solution. Consider these equations:

A. $\sqrt{3x} = 6$

B. $\sqrt{x + 2} = -3$

C. $\sqrt{x - 1} + 3 = 4$

D. $\sqrt[3]{2x} = 4$

? Does a radical equation always have a solution?

| EXAMPLE **1** | Using inverse operations to solve radical equations |

Solve each of the radical equations above. Explain your solution.

Melvin's Solution

Equation A: $3x \geq 0$
$$x \geq 0$$
$\sqrt{3x} = 6$ is defined for $x \geq 0$, where $x \in R$.

> The radicand in this equation must be greater than or equal to zero, since its index is 2, indicating a square root. I solved the inequality to determine the restrictions on x.

$$\sqrt{3x} = 6$$
$$(\sqrt{3x})^2 = (6)^2$$
$$3x = 36$$
$$x = 12$$

> The radical is isolated, so I squared both sides of the equation to eliminate the radical. This resulted in a linear equation I could solve.

Verify:

$$\sqrt{3x} = 6$$
$$x = 12$$

LS	RS
$\sqrt{3(12)}$	6
$\sqrt{36}$	
6	

This equation has one solution, $x = 12$.

> I verified my solution by substituting 12 for x in the original equation. Since the left side and right side are equal, $x = 12$ is the solution.

Equation B: $x + 2 \geq 0$
$$x \geq -2$$

$\sqrt{x + 2} = -3$ is defined for $x \geq -2$, where $x \in \mathbb{R}$.

> The radicand in this equation must be greater than or equal to zero, since its index is 2, indicating a square root. I solved the inequality to determine the restrictions on x.

$$\sqrt{x + 2} = -3$$
$$(\sqrt{x + 2})^2 = (-3)^2$$
$$x + 2 = 9$$
$$x = 7$$

> The radical is isolated, so I squared both sides of the equation to eliminate the radical then solved the resulting equation.

Verify:

$$\sqrt{x + 2} = -3$$
$$x = 7$$

LS	RS
$\sqrt{7 + 2}$	-3
$\sqrt{9}$	
3	

> I verified my solution by substituting 7 for x in the original equation. Since the left side and right side are not equal, $x = 7$ is not a solution. In this situation, 7 is an **extraneous root**.

This equation has no solution.
When $\sqrt{x + 2}$ was squared, -3 was also squared, resulting in the equation
$$(\sqrt{x + 2})^2 = (-3)^2$$

But you get the same equation when you square both sides when solving
$$\sqrt{x + 2} = 3$$
$$(\sqrt{x + 2})^2 = 3^2$$

$x = 7$ is the solution to this equation, but not the given equation.

extraneous root
A root that does not satisfy the initial conditions that were introduced while solving an equation. Root is another word for solution.

Equation C: $x - 1 \geq 0$

$$x \geq 1$$

$\sqrt{x - 1} + 3 = 4$ is defined for $x \geq 1$, where $x \in R$.

> The radicand in this equation must be greater than or equal to 0, since its index is 2, indicating a square root. I solved the inequality to determine the restriction on x.

$$\sqrt{x - 1} + 3 = 4$$
$$\sqrt{x - 1} = 1$$

> I isolated the radical by subtracting 3 from both sides of the equation.

$$(\sqrt{x - 1})^2 = 1^2$$
$$x - 1 = 1$$
$$x = 2$$

> I squared both sides to eliminate the radical.

Verify:
$$\sqrt{x - 1} + 3 = 4$$
$$x = 2$$

LS	RS
$\sqrt{2 - 1} + 3$	4
$\sqrt{1} + 3$	
$1 + 3$	
4	

> I verified the solution by substituting 2 for x in the original equation.

This equation has one solution, $x = 2$.

Equation D: $\sqrt[3]{2x} = 4$ is defined for $x \in R$.

> The radicand in this equation can be either negative, zero, or positive, since its index is 3, indicating a cube root. This means that the equation is defined for all real numbers.

$$\sqrt[3]{2x} = 4$$
$$(\sqrt[3]{2x})^3 = (4)^3$$
$$2x = 64$$
$$x = 32$$

> The radical is isolated, so I cubed both sides to eliminate the radical.

Verify:
$$\sqrt[3]{2x} = 4$$
$$x = 32$$

LS	RS
$\sqrt[3]{2(32)}$	4
$\sqrt[3]{64}$	
4	

> I checked my solution by substituting 32 for x in the original equation. Since the left side and right side are equal, $x = 32$ is the solution.

This equation has one solution, $x = 32$.

Reflecting

A. Jim says he could tell that equation B had no solution by inspection. Do you agree? Explain.

B. How do you eliminate a radical while solving an equation?

C. Explain why you should always verify the solutions of a radical equation.

APPLY the Math

EXAMPLE 2   Modelling a situation with a radical equation

The forward and backward motion of a swing can be modelled using the formula

$$T = 2\pi\sqrt{\frac{L}{9.8}}$$

where T represents the time in seconds for a swing to return to its original position, and L represents the length of the chain supporting the swing, in metres. When Cara was swinging, it took 2.5 s for the swing to return to its original position. Determine the length of the chain supporting her swing to the nearest centimetre.

Ramesh's Solution: Isolating the variable then substituting

The expression on the right of the formula is defined for $L \geq 0$, where $L \in \mathbb{R}$.

$$T = 2\pi\sqrt{\frac{L}{9.8}}$$

I needed to isolate L. However, I needed to start by isolating the radical. To do so, I divided both sides of the equation by 2π.

$$\frac{T}{2\pi} = \sqrt{\frac{L}{9.8}}$$

$$\left(\frac{T}{2\pi}\right)^2 = \left(\sqrt{\frac{L}{9.8}}\right)^2$$

I squared both sides of the equation to eliminate the radical.

$$\left(\frac{T}{2\pi}\right)^2 = \frac{L}{9.8}$$

$$9.8\left(\frac{T}{2\pi}\right)^2 = L$$

I multiplied both sides by 9.8 to isolate L.

$$9.8\left(\frac{2.5}{2\pi}\right)^2 = L$$

I substituted the given information into the equation.

$$9.8(0.397...)^2 = L$$

$$9.8(0.158...) = L$$

$$1.551... = L$$

The length of the swing's chain is 1.55 m, which is 155 cm.

Nicola's Solution: Substituting then isolating the variable

The expression on the right of the formula is defined for $L \geq 0$, where $L \in R$.

$$T = 2\pi\sqrt{\frac{L}{9.8}}$$

I substituted the given information into the formula.

$$\frac{2.5}{2\pi} = \sqrt{\frac{L}{9.8}}$$

$$\left(\frac{2.5}{2\pi}\right)^2 = \left(\sqrt{\frac{L}{9.8}}\right)^2$$

I squared both sides of the equation to eliminate the radical.

$$\left(\frac{2.5}{2\pi}\right)^2 = \frac{L}{9.8}$$

$$9.8\left(\frac{2.5}{2\pi}\right)^2 = L$$

I multiplied both sides by 9.8 to isolate L.

$$9.8\left(\frac{2.5}{2\pi}\right)^2 = L$$

$$9.8(0.397...)^2 = L$$

$$9.8(0.158...) = L$$

$$1.551... = L$$

I evaluated the numerical expression on the left side of the equation.

The length of the swing's chain is 1.55 m or 155 cm.

Your Turn

Verify the solution.

In Summary

Key Idea

- When you solve an equation with a variable in the radical, first isolate the radical on one side of the equation. Then square both sides of the equation if the radical is a square root. Cube both sides if the radical is a cube root. Then solve for the variable as you would normally.

Need to Know

- When you solve an equation with a variable in the radical,
  - you need to restrict the variable to ensure that the radicand of a square root is not negative; however, the radicand of a cube root may be negative
  - squaring a radical may introduce an invalid solution, called an extraneous root; for this reason, you need to verify each solution by substituting into the original equation

CHECK Your Understanding

1. State any restrictions on x, then solve each equation.

a) $\sqrt{x} = 4$

b) $\sqrt{x} = 6$

c) $\sqrt{x+1} = 2$

d) $\sqrt{x+3} = 4$

2. State any restrictions on x, then solve each equation.

a) $\sqrt[3]{x} = -3$

b) $\sqrt{2x} = 5$

c) $\sqrt[3]{x+4} = -2$

d) $\sqrt{2x+4} = 6$

3. Wendy said that there are no solutions for the equation

$$\sqrt{2x} = -4$$

Is she correct? Explain how you know.

PRACTISING

4. State any restrictions on x, then solve each equation.

a) $\sqrt{4x} = 4$

b) $\sqrt[3]{8x} = 2$

5. Describe the first step you would take to solve each equation. Justify your decision.

a) $\sqrt{x} = 7$

b) $\sqrt{x+5} = 12$

c) $\sqrt[3]{x-3} = 4$

d) $8 = \sqrt{2x+7} - 1$

6. State any restrictions on x, then solve each equation.

a) $\sqrt{x-3} = 5$

b) $\sqrt[3]{4x+7} = 3$

c) $2\sqrt{5x+3} = 11$

d) $\frac{1}{2}\sqrt{3x-2} = 4$

7. There are many equations related to electrical engineering. For instance, the voltage of an electrical device, V, is related to the power used, P, in watts (W), and resistance, R, in ohms (Ω), by the equation

$$V = \sqrt{P \cdot R}$$

Determine the amount of power needed to run a device that requires a voltage of 120 V and that contains a 2 Ω resistor.

8. State any restrictions on x, then solve each equation.

a) $\sqrt{2x+17} = 5$

b) $\sqrt[3]{6-2x} + 1 = -1$

c) $\sqrt{2(5x+3)} = -4$

d) $\sqrt{33-6x} + 4 = 13$

9. Create a radical equation that results in an extraneous root. Verify that your equation has no solution.

10. Bob claims that $-\sqrt{4x + 1} = -5$ and $\sqrt{4x + 1} = 5$ have the same solution, but $\sqrt{4x + 1} = -5$ has no solution. Do you agree or disagree? Explain.

11. A space station needs to rotate to create the illusion of gravity. A formula for determining the rotation rate to reproduce Earth's gravity is

$$N = \frac{42}{\pi}\sqrt{\frac{5}{r}}$$

where N represents the number of revolutions per minute and r represents the radius of the station in metres.

A station rotates 6.7 times per minute, producing an effect on the interior wall equivalent to Earth's gravity. Determine the radius of the space station.

12. Some collectors view comics as an investment. The effective rate of interest, r, earned by an investment can be defined by the formula

$$r = \sqrt[n]{\frac{A}{P}} - 1$$

where P represents the initial investment, in dollars, that grows to a value of A dollars after n years.

Determine the initial price of a rare comic book that resold for $1139 after two years, earning its owner 18% interest.

13. The amount of energy, P, in watts (W), that a wind turbine with vanes 40 m long generates, is related to the wind speed, S, by the formula

$$S = \sqrt[3]{\frac{2P}{5026.5D}}$$

where D represents the density of the air where the turbine operates. If a wind turbine is built in an area in which the air density is 0.9 kg/m^3 and the average wind speed is 8 m/s, determine how much power this turbine can generate.

wind vane

40 m

14. Melinda bought a circular table for her deck. When she placed it on the deck, she concluded that its area was about a quarter of the area of her 5 m by 5 m square deck. Determine the radius of the table to two decimal places. Justify your response.

15. Solve $\sqrt{20x + 50} + 3 = 11$. State the restrictions on x.

Closing

16. Create a radical equation and explain what steps are needed to solve it.

Extending

17. Solve $\sqrt[4]{x + 5} + 1 = 4$. Explain each step and state any restrictions on the variable.

Math in Action

How Far Is the Horizon?

If you have ever seen a ship appear on the horizon, you saw the top of the ship first, then the rest of the ship. This gradual appearance of the ship is owing to Earth's curvature. You can determine the sightline distance, D, using the radius of Earth, r, the height of the eyes of the observer above the surface, H, and the Pythagorean theorem.

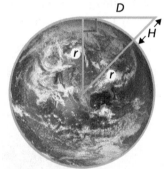

- Use a basketball as a model of Earth.
- Tape to the basketball a small object, such as a pencil sharpener, to represent you.
- Use a ruler to determine the measures of D and H as these relate to your object.
- Use these measures to estimate the radius of the basketball.
- Compare your results with those of other groups.

1. Express each radical as a mixed radical in simplest form.

   a) $\sqrt{1176}$ **b)** $-\sqrt{896}$ **c)** $\sqrt[3]{1296}$ **d)** $\sqrt[3]{-2560}$

2. Order the numbers $12\sqrt{2}$, $3\sqrt{12}$, $\sqrt{121}$, $4\sqrt{5}$, $\sqrt[3]{1000}$ from least to greatest without using a calculator. Explain what you did.

3. Simplify each expression. Explain each step.

   a) $5\sqrt{3} + 4\sqrt{2} - \sqrt{3} - 2\sqrt{2}$

   b) $\sqrt{275} + \sqrt{27} - \sqrt{363} - \sqrt{176}$

4. Express in simplest form.

   a) $(2\sqrt{10})(-3\sqrt{5})$

   b) $-3\sqrt{6}(\sqrt{18} - 2\sqrt{5})$

   c) $(2 + 3\sqrt{x})^2$

5. Simplify.

   a) $\dfrac{3\sqrt{80}}{2\sqrt{4}}$ **b)** $\dfrac{3\sqrt{7}}{\sqrt{5}}$ **c)** $\dfrac{9\sqrt{x^5}}{3\sqrt{x}}$

6. State the restrictions on the variables, then simplify.

   a) $x\sqrt{72x^4}$ **b)** $(2x\sqrt{x^2})(-3x\sqrt{x^3})$

7. Kshawn has been contracted to water lawns for the summer using circular sprayers. The radius of the sprayed water, r, in metres, is modelled by

   $$r = \sqrt{1.6A}$$

   where A represents the area of grass watered in square metres. Kshawn has set a sprayer to spray a radius of 1.5 m. Determine the area of grass watered by the sprayer, to the nearest tenth of a square metre.

8. Explain why you need to consider restrictions when working with radical expressions. Provide an example of a monomial radicand and a binomial radicand and state the restrictions for both examples.

9. **a)** State the restrictions on x, then solve:

   $$\sqrt{16x + 20} - 3 = -1$$

   b) Is the root extraneous? Explain.

WHAT DO You Think Now? Revisit **What Do You Think?** on page 175. How have your answers and explanations changed?

FREQUENTLY ASKED Questions

Study | Aid
- See Lesson 4.4, Examples 1, 2, 3, 4, and 5.
- Try Chapter Review Question 7.

Q: **How can you simplify a radical expression with variable radicands?**

A1: You can factor the radicand and express the factors as powers, just as you would a numerical radicand.

For example:

$6\sqrt{80x^3}$ Since the radical sign indicates a square root, the expression is defined for $x \geq 0$, where $x \in R$.

$$= 6\sqrt{2^4 \cdot 5 \cdot x^2 \cdot x}$$
$$= 6 \cdot 2^2 \cdot x\sqrt{5x}$$
$$= 24x\sqrt{5x}$$

A2: You can multiply or divide radicals with the same index.

For example:

$\dfrac{18\sqrt{x^3}}{-6\sqrt{x^2}}$ Since division by zero is not allowed, then $x \neq 0$. Since the radical sign over x^3 indicates a square root, then the expression is defined for $x > 0$, where $x \in R$.

$$= \frac{18}{-6}\sqrt{\frac{x^3}{x^2}}$$
$$= -3\sqrt{x}$$

A3: You can rationalize an expression with a radical in the denominator by multiplying the numerator and denominator by the same radical expression.

For example:

$\dfrac{2\sqrt{14}}{3\sqrt{x}}$ Since division by zero is not allowed, then $x \neq 0$. Since the radical sign indicates a square root, the expression is defined for $x > 0$, where $x \in R$.

It is not possible to divide, because there are no common factors. So,

$$= \frac{2\sqrt{14}}{3\sqrt{x}} \cdot \frac{3\sqrt{x}}{3\sqrt{x}}$$

multiplying by 1, in the form $\dfrac{\sqrt{x}}{\sqrt{x}}$,

$$= \frac{2\sqrt{14} \cdot \sqrt{x}}{3\sqrt{x} \cdot \sqrt{x}}$$

allows the expression to be simplified.

$$= \frac{2\sqrt{14x}}{3x}$$

Q: **How can you solve an equation with a variable in the radical?**

A: First state the restrictions on the variable. Then isolate the radical and either square both sides of the equation (if the radical is a square root) or cube both sides (if the radical is a cube root). Then solve for the variable as you would normally. Lastly, substitute each solution into the original equation to ensure it is not extraneous.

Study **Aid**

- See Lesson 4.6, Examples 1 and 2.
- Try Chapter Review Questions 8 to 11.

For example:

a) $\sqrt{2x + 5} - 1 = 4$

Since $\sqrt{2x + 5}$ cannot be negative, then $2x + 5 \geq 0$, or $x \geq -2.5$.

The restrictions are $x \geq -2.5$, where $x \in R$.

$$\sqrt{2x + 5} = 4 + 1$$

Isolate the radical by adding 1 to both sides.

$$(\sqrt{2x + 5})^2 = (5)^2$$

Square both sides.

$$2x + 5 = 25$$
$$2x = 20$$
$$x = 10$$

Verify:

$$\sqrt{2x + 5} - 1 = 4$$
$$x = 10$$

LS	RS
$\sqrt{2(10) + 5} - 1$	4
$\sqrt{25} - 1$	
4	

The solution $x = 10$ is valid.

b) $\sqrt{4x} = -6$

Since $4x$ cannot be negative, then $4x \geq 0$, or $x \geq 0$.

This equation has no solution. Squaring both sides and solving for x will lead to an extraneous root.

The left side of the equation indicates the principal square root, which is positive. This means the left side can never equal the right side, since the right side is negative.

PRACTISING

1. Express each radical as a mixed radical in simplest form.

   a) $\sqrt{72}$ **c)** $\sqrt{40}$

   b) $\sqrt{600}$ **d)** $\sqrt[3]{250}$

2. Express each mixed radical as an entire radical.

   a) $6\sqrt{5}$ **c)** $4\sqrt{14}$

   b) $12\sqrt{7}$ **d)** $-3\sqrt[3]{4}$

Lesson 4.2

3. Simplify.

   a) $\sqrt{36} + \sqrt{42}$

   b) $6\sqrt{2} + 3\sqrt{48} + \sqrt{96}$

   c) $4\sqrt{104} - 6\sqrt{2} - \sqrt{242}$

   d) $6\sqrt{36} - 6\sqrt{48} - 5\sqrt{216}$

Lesson 4.3

4. Simplify.

   a) $\sqrt{24} \cdot \sqrt{42}$

   b) $3\sqrt{25} \cdot 5\sqrt{10}$

   c) $-2\sqrt{30} \cdot 2\sqrt{40}$

   d) $-2\sqrt{14} \cdot -2\sqrt{42}$

5. Simplify.

   a) $6(4 + \sqrt{12})$

   b) $\sqrt{5}(2 - \sqrt{15})$

   c) $\sqrt{6}(\sqrt{20} - 8\sqrt{6})$

   d) $(5\sqrt{2} - \sqrt{3})(2\sqrt{2} + 4\sqrt{3})$

6. Tom was asked to write $\sqrt{12}$ in simplest form. He wrote:

   $$\sqrt{12} = \sqrt{2 + 2 + 2 + 2 + 2 + 2}$$
   $$= \sqrt{2} + \sqrt{2} + \sqrt{2} + \sqrt{2} + \sqrt{2} + \sqrt{2}$$
   $$= 6\sqrt{2}$$

   What was Tom's error?

Lesson 4.4

7. State any restrictions on the variable(s), then simplify.

   a) $(4x^3\sqrt{x})(\sqrt{2x^3})$ **c)** $\dfrac{-128\sqrt{x^3}}{6\sqrt{x}}$

   b) $\dfrac{-18\sqrt{8x^3}}{9\sqrt{2x}}$ **d)** $\dfrac{2\sqrt{5x}}{3\sqrt{6x}}$

Lesson 4.5

8. Police can use skid marks to determine how fast a vehicle was travelling. The speed, s, in kilometres per hour, is related to the length of the skid mark, d, in metres, and the coefficient of friction of the road, f, by this formula:

   $$s = \sqrt{252df}$$

   Determine the length of a skid mark made by a car travelling at 80 km/h on a concrete road with a coefficient of friction measuring 0.76.

Lesson 4.6

9. State the restrictions on x, then solve each equation.

   a) $\sqrt{x} = 11$ **c)** $3\sqrt{7x} + 3 = 12$

   b) $\sqrt{x + 3} = 14$ **d)** $\dfrac{1}{4}\sqrt{5x - 2} = 6$

10. State the restrictions on x, then solve each equation.

    a) $\sqrt{3x + 16} = -5$

    b) $\sqrt[3]{7 - 2x} + 1 = -3$

    c) $\sqrt{4(3x + 12)} = 6$

    d) $\sqrt{22 - 6x} + 4 = 2$

11. Jenny solved $\sqrt{x - 4} - 1 = 2$ as follows:

    Step 1: $\sqrt{x - 4} = 2 - 1$

    Step 2: $x - 4 = 1^2$

    Step 3: $x = 1 + 4$

    Step 4: $x = 5$

    a) What are the restrictions on the variable? Justify your decision.

    b) Where did Jenny make her first error? Explain.

Designing a Radical Math Game

To celebrate Numeracy Week, the math club at Sonora's school has decided to hold a series of competitive math games during lunch hour. Groups of club members each chose a topic and created a game.

? What game can you create that demands skill in working with numerical and algebraic radicals?

A. Create a game for two or four players in which the players must answer questions. Players must demonstrate their ability to
- express entire radicals as mixed radicals in simplest form
- express mixed radicals as entire radicals
- simplify radical expressions that involve the operations addition, subtraction, multiplication, and division
- solve radical equations
- state restrictions on variables

B. Exchange games with another group and play each other's game. The creators should observe while their game is being played. After you have played both games, discuss what worked well and what needed improvement. Revise your game, based on the feedback.

C. Write a report that describes how the game is played and its rules. Include in your report all the questions and answers needed for the game. Discuss how you revised your game.

> ### Task | *Checklist*
> ✔ Are the rules of your game written clearly?
>
> ✔ Did you include answers to all the questions?
>
> ✔ Is your explanation of how and why you revised your game clear?

Carrying Out Your Research

As you continue with your project, you will need to conduct research and collect data. The strategies that follow will help you collect data.

Considering the Type of Data You Need

There are two different types of data that you need to consider: primary and secondary. Primary data is data that you collect yourself using surveys, interviews, and direct observations. Secondary data is data you obtain through other sources, such as online publications, journals, magazines, and newspapers.

Both primary data and secondary data have their pros and cons. Primary data provides specific information about your research question or statement, but may take time to collect and process. Secondary data is usually easier to obtain and can be analyzed in less time. However, because the data was gathered for other purposes, you may need to sift through it to find what you are looking for.

The type of data you choose can depend on many factors, including the research question, your skills, and available time and resources. Based on these and other factors, you may choose to use primary data, secondary data, or both.

Assessing the Reliability of Sources

When collecting primary data, you must ensure the following:
- For surveys, the sample size must be reasonably large and the random sampling technique must be well designed.
- For surveys or interviews, the questionnaires must be designed to avoid bias.
- For experiments or studies, the data must be free from measurement bias.
- The data must be compiled accurately.

When obtaining secondary data, you must ensure that the source of your data is reliable:

- If the data is from a report, determine what the author's credentials are, how up-to-date the data is, and whether other researchers have cited the same data.
- Be aware that data collection is often funded by an organization with an interest in the outcome or with an agenda that it is trying to further. When presenting the data, the authors may give higher priority to the interests of the organization than to the public interest. Knowing which organization has funded the data collection may help you decide how reliable the data is, or what type of bias may have influenced the collection or presentation of the data.
- If the data is from the Internet, check it against the following criteria:
  - Authority: The credentials of the author are provided and can be checked. Ideally, there should be a way to contact the author with questions.
  - Accuracy: The domain of the web address may help you determine the accuracy of the data. For example, web documents from academic sources (domain .edu), non-profit organizations and associations (domains .org and .net) and government departments (domains such as .gov and .ca) may have undergone vetting for accuracy before being published on the Internet.
  - Currency: When pages on a site are updated regularly and links are valid, the information is probably being actively managed. This could mean that the data is being checked and revised appropriately.

Accessing Resources

To gather secondary data, explore a variety of resources:

- textbooks
- scientific and historical journals and other expert publications
- newsgroups and discussion groups
- library databases, such as Electric Library Canada, which is a database of books, newspapers, magazines, and television and radio transcripts

People may be willing to help you with your research, perhaps by providing information they have or by pointing you to sources of information. Your school or community librarian can help you locate relevant sources, as can the librarians of local community colleges or universities. Other people, such as teachers, your parents or guardians, local professionals, and Elders and Knowledge Keepers may have valuable input. (Be sure to respect local community protocols when approaching Elders or Knowledge Keepers.) The only way to find out if someone can and will help is to ask. Make a list of people who might be able to help you obtain the information you need, and then identify how you might contact each person on your list.

PROJECT EXAMPLE   Carrying out your research

Sarah chose, "Which Western province or territory grew the fastest over the last century, and why?" as her research question. She has decided to use 1900 to 2000 as the time period. How can she find relevant data?

Sarah's Search

Since my question involves a historical event over a wide area, I decided to rely on secondary data. I started my search using the Internet. I did a search for "provincial populations Canada 1900 to 2000" and found many websites. I had to look at quite a few until I found the following link:

[PDF] History resources from Statistics **Canada**
File Format: PDF/Adobe Acrobat - Quick View
Population of Canada, by **province**, census dates, 1851 to 1976. A125-163. ... series reviews conditions in **Canada** from **1900 to 2000**. Articles include: ...
www.cshc.ubc.ca/TC_Smith.pdf - Similar

This led me to a document from the University of British Columbia that cited a document from Statistics Canada, based on census data, that showed the provincial populations from 1851 to 1976. I went to the Statistics Canada website and searched for the census data, but I couldn't find it. So I tried another general search, "historical statistics Canada population," and found the link below:

Historical statistics of Canada: Section A: Population and Migration
Oct 22, 2008 ... Table A1 **Estimated population of Canada**, 1867 to 1977. ..... and **Migration**", in the **Historical Statistics of Canada**, first edition, p. ...
www.statcan.gc.ca › Home › Sections - Cached - Similar

This led me to data I was looking for:

Table A2-14
Population of Canada, by province, census dates, 1851 to 1976

Source: for 1851 to 1951, Statistics Canada (formerly Dominion Bureau of Statistics), *Census of Canada, 1951*, vol. X, table 1; for 1956, *Census of Canada, 1956*, vol. I, table 1; for 1961 *Census of Canada, 1961*, Vol. I, part 1, table 12, (Catalogue 92-536); for 1966, *Census of Canada, 1966*, vol. I, table 14, (Catalogue 92-608); for 1971, *Census of Canada, 1971*, vol. I, part 2, table 14, (Catalogue 92-716); for 1976, *Census of Canada, 1976*, vol. II, table 11, (Catalogue 92-824).

For a brief discussion of possible under-enumeration in earlier censuses, 1851, 1861 and 1871, see first edition of this volume, pp. 3-4. For completeness of enumeration in censuses of 1961 to 1976, see series A15-53 below.

I now have some data I can use. I feel confident that the data is authoritative and accurate, because I believe that the source is reliable. I will continue looking for more current data, from 1976 to 2000. I will also need to search for information about reasons for population changes during this time period. I will ask the school librarian to help me look for other sources.

Your Turn

A. Decide if you will use primary data, secondary data, or both. Explain how you made your decision.

B. Make a plan you can follow to collect your data.

C. Carry out your plan to collect your data. Make sure that you record your successful searches, so you can easily access these sources at a later time. You should also record detailed information about your sources, so you can cite them in your report. See your teacher for the preferred format for endnotes, footnotes, or in-text citations.

Statistical Reasoning

▶ **LEARNING GOALS**

You will be able to develop your statistical reasoning ability by

- Calculating and interpreting standard deviation for given sets of data
- Understanding the properties of normally distributed data
- Determining and using the properties of the normal curve to compare sets of data that approximate normal distributions
- Solving problems that involve normal distributions using z-scores
- Interpreting data using confidence intervals, confidence levels, and margin of error

? Research shows that the polar bear population is declining and the species is at risk of becoming endangered. How can statistics help to monitor the polar bear population, to determine whether it stabilizes or whether polar bears become an endangered species?

5 Getting Started

YOU WILL NEED
- calculator
- grid paper

Comparing Salaries

The payrolls for three small companies are shown in the table. Figures include year-end bonuses. Each company has 15 employees. Sanela wonders if the companies have similar "average" salaries.

Employee Payrolls ($)		
Media Focus Advertising	**Computer Rescue**	**Auto Value Sales**
245 000	362 000	97 500
162 000	112 000	66 900
86 000	96 500	64 400
71 000	96 500	63 800
65 000	63 000	62 800
61 000	62 500	62 300
61 000	59 200	61 500
57 500	59 000	58 900
47 400	56 500	58 300
42 500	55 900	58 200
39 500	55 200	57 900
36 200	53 800	57 300
33 400	53 100	56 900
28 500	52 700	55 250
27 300	52 300	55 250

? What is the best indicator of an "average" salary for each company?

A. What is the **range** of salaries for each company?

B. Examine the data. Which companies have data that would be considered **outliers**? Tell how you know.

C. Determine the measures of central tendency (**mean**, **median**, and **mode**) for the salaries for each company.

D. Which measure of central tendency is most affected by outliers? Explain.

E. Create a **line plot** for each of the three companies. Look for outliers, measures of central tendency, and the range on your line plots. Which of these features are easily visible?

F. Which measure of central tendency best illustrates the "average" salary for each company? Why?

outlier
A value in a data set that is very different from other values in the set.

line plot
A graph that records each data value in a data set as a point above a number line.

WHAT DO You Think?

Decide whether you agree or disagree with each statement. Explain your decision.

1. To compare two sets of data, you need only the mean, the median, and the mode.

2. Most sets of data are evenly distributed about their mean.

3. By looking at the data for a survey, you can decide if the results for the sample that was surveyed closely match the results you would get if you surveyed the whole population.

Exploring Data

GOAL

Explore the similarities and differences between two sets of data.

EXPLORE the Math

Paulo needs a new battery for his car. He is trying to decide between two different brands. Both brands are the same price. He obtains data for the lifespan, in years, of 30 batteries of each brand, as shown below.

Measured Lifespans of 30 Car Batteries (years)									
Brand X					Brand Y				
5.1	7.3	6.9	4.7	5.0	5.4	6.3	4.8	5.9	5.5
6.2	6.4	5.5	5.7	6.8	4.7	6.0	4.5	6.6	6.0
6.0	4.8	4.1	5.2	8.1	5.0	6.5	5.8	5.4	5.1
6.3	7.5	5.0	5.7	8.2	5.7	6.8	5.6	4.9	6.1
3.3	3.1	4.3	5.9	6.6	4.9	5.7	6.2	7.0	5.8
5.8	6.4	6.1	4.6	5.7	6.8	5.9	5.3	5.6	5.9

> **?** How can you compare the data to help Paulo decide which brand of battery to buy?

Reflecting

A. Describe how the data in each set is distributed. Describe any similarities and differences between the two sets of data.

B. Explain why the mean and median do not fully describe the difference between these two brands of batteries. Consider the range, which is one measure of **dispersion** for data. Explain what additional information can be learned from the range of the data.

C. Is the mode useful to compare in this situation? Explain.

D. Suppose that one battery included in the set of data for brand Y is defective, and its lifespan is 0.5 years instead of 5.9 years. Discuss how this would or would not affect Paulo's decision.

dispersion

A measure that varies by the spread among the data in a set; dispersion has a value of zero if all the data in a set is identical, and it increases in value as the data becomes more spread out.

In Summary

Key Ideas

- Measures of central tendency (mean, median, mode) are not always sufficient to represent or compare sets of data.
- You can draw inferences from numerical data by examining how the data is distributed around the mean or the median.

Need to Know

- To compare sets of data, the data must be organized in a systematic way.
- When analyzing two sets of data, it is important to look at both similarities and differences in the data.

FURTHER *Your Understanding*

1. a) Construct a graph to illustrate the average daily temperatures in Langley, British Columbia, and Windsor, Ontario.

Average Daily Temperatures in Langley, BC												
Month	**Jan.**	**Feb.**	**Mar.**	**Apr.**	**May**	**Jun.**	**Jul.**	**Aug.**	**Sep.**	**Oct.**	**Nov.**	**Dec.**
average daily temperature (°C)	2.2	4.4	6.3	8.6	11.8	14.2	16.7	17.0	14.2	9.8	5.1	2.7

Average Daily Temperatures in Windsor, ON												
Month	**Jan.**	**Feb.**	**Mar.**	**Apr.**	**May**	**Jun.**	**Jul.**	**Aug.**	**Sep.**	**Oct.**	**Nov.**	**Dec.**
average daily temperature (°C)	−4.5	−3.2	2.0	8.2	14.9	20.1	22.7	21.6	17.4	11.0	4.6	−1.5

Environment Canada

b) Determine the range, mean, and median for the average daily temperatures in the two cities.

c) Use your graph and your results from part b) to compare the temperatures in the two cities.

d) Why might a comparison of the two sets of data be useful?

2. a) Use the range and measures of central tendency (mean, median, and mode) to compare the results for two geography tests given by the same teacher to the same class in the same semester.

Unit 1 Test				
81	76	73	71	64
80	75	73	71	63
79	75	73	68	61
79	74	73	67	58
78	73	72	66	57

Unit 2 Test				
98	84	73	71	57
95	81	73	69	53
93	79	73	64	44
89	79	73	59	41
87	76	73	59	37

b) Did the class perform better on the Unit 1 test or Unit 2 test? Justify your decision.

c) Were the modes useful to compare in this situation? Explain.

3. a) Describe the distribution of data for average housing prices in 11 major Canadian cities in 1996, 1998, and 2000. Then compare the three sets of data.

Average Housing Prices ($)			
City	1996	1998	2000
St. John's	116 443	118 519	137 665
Halifax	117 990	141 353	156 988
Toronto	206 738	220 049	224 246
Winnipeg	144 858	161 337	166 761
Regina	147 889	152 784	152 114
Calgary	157 768	180 258	193 275
Edmonton	146 280	164 808	172 503
Vancouver	212 010	218 025	236 617
Victoria	208 400	246 135	228 983
Whitehorse	157 677	167 396	170 986
Yellowknife	181 790	175 646	221 632

Statistics Canada

b) Why might a comparison of the three sets of data be useful?

5.2

Frequency Tables, Histograms, and Frequency Polygons

YOU WILL NEED
- calculator
- grid paper

GOAL

Create frequency tables and graphs from a set of data.

LEARN ABOUT the Math

EXPLORE...
- Margaret inherited her grandfather's coin collection. How can she organize a catalogue of the coins to see how many of each type of coin she has?

Flooding is a regular occurrence in the Red River basin. During the second half of the 20th century, there have been nine notable floods, four of which have been severe, occurring in 1950, 1979, 1996, and 1997. The flood that occurred in 1997 is known as the "flood of the century" in Manitoba and North Dakota.

The following data represents the flow rates of the Red River from 1950 to 1999, as recorded at the Redwood Bridge in Winnipeg, Manitoba.

Maximum Water Flow Rates for the Red River, from 1950 to 1999, Measured at Redwood Bridge*									
Year	Flow Rate (m³/s)	Year	Flow Rate (m³/s)	Year	Flow Rate (m³/s)	Year	Flow Rate (m³/s)	Year	Flow Rate (m³/s)
1950	3058	1960	1965	1970	2280	1980	881	1990	396
1951	1065	1961	481	1971	1526	1981	159	1991	280
1952	1008	1962	1688	1972	1589	1982	1458	1992	1399
1953	357	1963	660	1973	530	1983	1393	1993	946
1954	524	1964	1002	1974	2718	1984	1048	1994	1121
1955	1521	1965	1809	1975	1671	1985	991	1995	1877
1956	1974	1966	2498	1976	1807	1986	1812	1996	3058
1957	654	1967	1727	1977	187	1987	2339	1997	4587
1958	524	1968	510	1978	1750	1988	564	1998	1557
1959	991	1969	2209	1979	3030	1989	1390	1999	2180

National Research Council Canada

(*assumes NO flood protection works in place, for data after 1969 when the floodway was in use)

? How can you approximate the water flow rate that is associated with serious flooding in Winnipeg?

EXAMPLE **1**   Creating a frequency distribution

Determine the water flow rate that is associated with serious flooding
by creating a **frequency distribution**.

> **frequency distribution**
> A set of intervals (table or
> graph), usually of equal
> width, into which raw data
> is organized; each interval is
> associated with a frequency
> that indicates the number of
> measurements in this interval.

Francine's Solution: Creating a frequency distribution table

Highest water flow rate: 4587 m^3/s, in 1997
Lowest water flow rate: 159 m^3/s, in 1981

> I decided to organize the data from the table
> on page 241 into a frequency distribution table
> because there are too many numbers to order
> easily. A table would allow me to see, at a glance,
> the frequency of various flow rates.

Range: 4587 − 159, or 4428

> I determined the range of the data so that I could
> choose a suitable interval.

$$\frac{4428}{10} = 442.8$$

If the interval width is 500, the intervals will
end at 500, 1000, 1500, 2000, 2500,
3000, 3500, 4000, 4500, and 5000.

> Most tables have between 5 and 12 intervals, so I
> decided to use 10 equally sized intervals to sort the
> data. Since the range is 4428, I needed an interval
> width of at least 442.8. I decided to round this
> value to 500, since 500 will be easier to work with.

Flow Rate (m³/s)	Tally	Frequency (number of years)
0–500	ⅣⅢ I	6
500–1000	ⅣⅢ ⅣⅢ I	11
1000–1500	ⅣⅢ IIII	9
1500–2000	ⅣⅢ ⅣⅢ IIII	14
2000–2500	ⅣⅢ	5
2500–3000	I	1
3000–3500	III	3
3500–4000		0
4000–4500		0
4500–5000	I	1

> Each interval begins just after the first value in
> the row and includes all the numbers up to and
> including the last number. The first interval begins
> at 0.01 and goes up to 500. This ensures that a
> number like 500 is counted in only one row.

Communication | *Tip*

In frequency tables in this resource, the upper limit of
each interval includes that number. For example, in
the Flow Rate table to the left, 2000 is included in the
interval 1500–2000 and not in the interval 2000–2500.

Flow Rate (m³/s)	Tally	Frequency (number of years)
0–500	卌 I	6
500–1000	卌 卌 I	11
1000–1500	卌 IIII	9
1500–2000	卌 卌 IIII	14
2000–2500	卌	5
2500–3000	I	1
3000–3500	III	3 floods
3500–4000		0
4000–4500		0
4500–5000	I	1 flood

I could see that 17 of the 50 years had a water flow less than or equal to 1000 m³/s. There would have been no flooding in those years.

From the data, I knew that the "flood of the century" had a flow rate of 4587 m³/s. Looking at the last row in my frequency table, I noticed that this was significantly higher than all the other flow rates.

I knew that there were nine floods, and four were severe. Since there were floods in the four years when flow rates were greater than 3000 m³/s, flow rate and flooding are likely connected. Four of the six flow rates in the 2000–3000 interval would probably have caused floods. The minimum flow rate that results in a flood should be in the 2000–2500 interval.

I predict that water flow rates that result in serious flooding are greater than 2000 m³/s.

I can check my prediction by comparing the years that had flow rates from 2000 to 3000 m³/s with the historical records of flooding.

Tasha's Solution: Creating a histogram

Flow Rate (m³/s)	Tally	Frequency (number of years)
150–600	卌 卌 I	11
600–1050	卌 IIII	9
1050–1500	卌 I	6
1500–1950	卌 卌 II	12
1950–2400	卌 I	6
2400–2850	II	2
2850–3300	III	3
3300–3750		0
3750–4200		0
4200–4650	I	1

I created a frequency table using an interval width of 450 for the Red River water flow data from page 241.

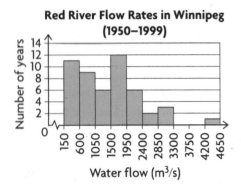

Red River Flow Rates in Winnipeg (1950–1999)

Number of years (vertical axis: 0, 2, 4, 6, 8, 10, 12, 14)

Water flow (m³/s) (horizontal axis: 150, 600, 1050, 1500, 1950, 2400, 2850, 3300, 3750, 4200, 4650)

I drew a **histogram** to represent the data in the frequency distribution, since the data is grouped into intervals.

The interval width for my histogram is 450. I labelled the intervals on the horizontal axis. I labelled the frequency on the vertical axis "Number of years."

histogram

The graph of a frequency distribution, in which equal intervals of values are marked on a horizontal axis and the frequencies associated with these intervals are indicated by the areas of the rectangles drawn for these intervals.

In general, with the exception of the interval 1500–1950, as the maximum flow rate increases, the number of data points in each interval decreases. Low maximum flow rates have been more common than high maximum flow rates.

There were nine floods. Based on my histogram, the flow rate was greater than 1950 m³/s in only 12 years. These 12 years must include the flood years. I predict that floods occur when the flow rate is greater than 1950 m³/s.

Monique's Solution: Creating a frequency polygon

Flow Rate (m³/s)	Midpoint	Frequency (number of years)
150–600	375	11
600–1050	825	9
1050–1500	1275	6
1500–1950	1725	12
1950–2400	2175	6
2400–2850	2625	2
2850–3300	3075	3
3300–3750	3525	0
3750–4200	3975	0
4200–4650	4425	1

I created a frequency table using an interval width of 450 for the Red River water flow data from page 241. I determined the midpoint of each interval by adding the boundaries of each interval and dividing by 2.

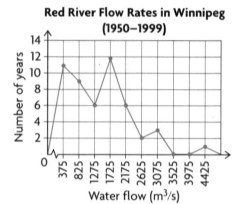

Red River Flow Rates in Winnipeg (1950–1999)

Most of the data is in the first four intervals, and the most common water flow is between 1500 and 2000 m³/s. After this, the frequencies drop off dramatically.

There were six years where the flow rate was around 2625, 3075, or 4425 m³/s. These must have been flood years. The other three floods should have occurred when the flow rate was around 2175 m³/s. According to my frequency polygon, there were flows around that midpoint in six years. Assuming that the flow rate in three of those years was 2175 m³/s or greater, floods should occur when the flow rate is 2175 m³/s or greater.

Next, I labelled the axes on my graph.

Finally, I plotted the midpoints and joined them to form a **frequency polygon**. I included one interval above the highest value, with a frequency of 0, and connected the first midpoint to 0 to close the polygon.

The graph made it easy to see that the flow rate of 4425 m³/s was unusual.

frequency polygon
The graph of a frequency distribution, produced by joining the midpoints of the intervals using straight lines.

Reflecting

A. Identify similarities and differences in the frequency distributions created by Francine, Tasha, and Monique.

B. Francine used a different interval width than Tasha and Monique. How did this affect the distribution of the data? Explain.

C. Suppose that Francine created a frequency distribution using an interval width of 200. Do you think this interval would make it easier to see which water flow rates result in flooding? Why or why not?

D. Would 2000 be a good interval width for determining critical water flow rates? Explain.

APPLY the Math

EXAMPLE 2   Comparing data using histograms

The magnitude of an earthquake is measured using the Richter scale.
Examine the histograms for the frequency of earthquake magnitudes in
Canada from 2005 to 2009. Which of these years could have had the most
damage from earthquakes?

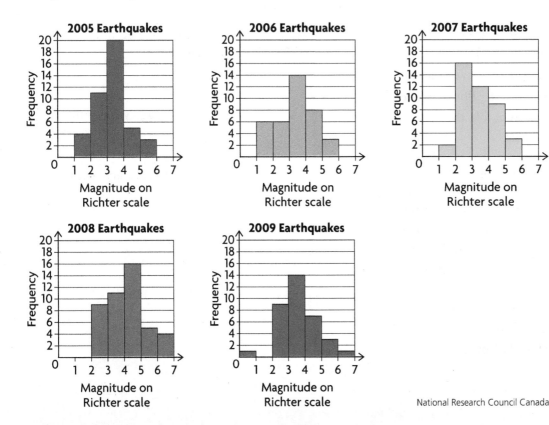

National Research Council Canada

Understanding the Richter Scale*	
Magnitude	**Effects**
less than 3.0	recorded by seismographs; not felt
3.0–3.9	feels like a passing truck; no damage
4.0–4.9	felt by nearly everyone; movement of unstable objects
5.0–5.9	felt by all; considerable damage to weak buildings
6.0–6.9	difficult to stand; partial collapse of ordinary buildings
7.0–7.9	loss of life; destruction of ordinary buildings
more than 7.9	widespread loss of life and destruction

*Every unit increase on the Richter scale represents an earthquake 10 times more
powerful. For example, an earthquake measuring 5.6 is 10 times more powerful than
an earthquake measuring 4.6.

Bilyana's Solution: Using a frequency table

2005 had the most earthquakes in any one category: 20 earthquakes with a magnitude from 3.0 to 3.9.

Year	2005	2006	2007	2008	2009
Frequency of Earthquakes from 4.0 to 4.9	5	8	9	16	7

2008 had the greatest number of earthquakes with the potential for minor damage.

Four of the years had three earthquakes with magnitudes from 5.0 to 5.9, while 2008 had five earthquakes with these magnitudes.

Year	Magnitude on Richter Scale			Total
	4.0–4.9	5.0–5.9	6.0–6.9	
2008	16	5	4	25
2009	7	3	1	11

Therefore, 2008 could have had the most damage from earthquakes.

> At first glance, it seemed that 2005 was the worst year, because it had the highest bar. However, an earthquake of magnitude 3 on the Richter scale does not cause much damage.

> I knew that some minor damage will occur if the magnitude of an earthquake is from 4.0 to 4.9 on the Richter scale. I decided to examine the frequency of these earthquakes for 2005 to 2009.

> Only 2008 and 2009 had earthquakes with magnitudes from 6.0 to 6.9, with the potential to cause moderate damage. I decided to examine these years more carefully.

> I created a table for earthquakes from 4.0 to 6.9 on the Richter scale for these years.

Miguel's Solution: Comparing frequency polygons

Both 2008 and 2009 had the strongest earthquakes, registering from 6.0 to 6.9 on the Richter scale.

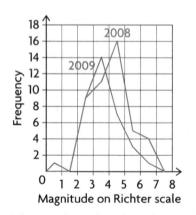

The number of earthquakes in the three highest intervals was greater in 2008 than in 2009, so 2008 could have had the most damage from earthquakes.

> I examined the histograms. There were only two histograms with earthquakes that registered more than 6 on the Richter scale. These years could have had the most damage, because an earthquake registering from 6.0 to 6.9 will result in moderate damage.

> I decided to draw frequency polygons, instead of histograms, for these two years. I drew both polygons on the same graph to compare them.

> I compared the shapes of the frequency polygons.

Your Turn

a) Compare Bilyana's solution with Miguel's solution.

b) What other factors should be considered when determining which year could have had the most damage from earthquakes?

In Summary

Key Ideas

- Large sets of data can be difficult to interpret. Organizing the data into intervals and tabulating the frequency of the data in each interval can make it easier to interpret the data and draw conclusions about how the data is distributed.
- A frequency distribution is a set of intervals and can be displayed as a table, a histogram, or a frequency polygon.

Need to Know

- A frequency distribution should have a minimum of 5 intervals and a maximum of 12 intervals, although any number of intervals is possible. Too many or too few intervals will result in a table or a graph that may not effectively show how the data is distributed.
- The interval width can be determined by dividing the range of the data by the desired number of intervals and then rounding to a suitable interval width.
- The height of each bar in a histogram corresponds to the frequency of the interval it represents.
- Because the individual pieces of data are not visible in a frequency distribution, the minimum and maximum values and the median cannot be determined directly.
- Frequency polygons serve the same purpose as histograms. However, they are especially helpful for comparing multiple sets of data because they can be graphed on top of each other.

CHECK Your Understanding

1. The numbers of earthquakes in the world during two five-year periods are shown in the frequency table.

	Years	
Magnitude	2000–04	2005–09
0.1–0.9	253	5
1.0–1.9	6 957	133
2.0–2.9	28 391	19 120
3.0–3.9	33 717	43 701
4.0–4.9	43 890	58 100
5.0–5.9	6 487	8 948
6.0–6.9	675	770
7.0–7.9	70	61
8.0–9.9	5	8

a) Draw a frequency polygon for the numbers of earthquakes during each five-year period on the same graph.

b) Use your graph to compare the earthquakes in the world during the two five-year periods.

2. Emmanuella walks her golden retriever regularly. She kept track of the lengths of her walks for one month and grouped the data in a frequency table.

a) The first walk was 15 min long. In which interval did she place this piece of data?

b) Draw a frequency polygon to represent the data in the table. Describe how the data is distributed.

Length of Walk (min)	Frequency
5–10	1
10–15	3
15–20	7
20–25	10
25–30	6
30–35	11
35–40	8
40–45	5
45–50	4
50–55	2
55–60	3

PRACTISING

3. A cherry orchard has 30 trees with these heights, given in inches.

78	70	83	79	74	81	80	65	66	76
85	82	74	63	75	76	86	80	72	72
80	69	71	80	77	81	75	75	64	87

  a) Make a frequency table with six intervals to organize the heights.
  b) Construct a histogram of the data.
  c) Which range of heights occurs most frequently? Which occurs least frequently?

4. The amounts withdrawn from an ATM, in dollars, are recorded for a single Wednesday.

20	120	50	70	60	80	140	120	80	160
80	60	110	100	100	80	180	160	40	100
50	80	200	140	160	60	40	80	60	140
100	140	160	200	140	20	80	20	100	70
40	20	120	40	140	100	40	50	180	60

  a) What interval width will give a good representation of how the data is distributed?
  b) Sort the amounts in a frequency distribution table.
  c) Construct a histogram to represent the table in part b).
  d) Describe how the data is distributed.

5. The final scores for the 30 women who competed in the women's figure skating competition at the Vancouver 2010 Olympics are shown. Canadian Joannie Rochette captured the bronze medal.

78.50	63.76	61.02	53.16	50.74	43.84
73.78	63.02	59.22	52.96	49.74	43.80
71.36	62.14	57.46	52.16	49.04	41.94
64.76	61.92	57.16	51.74	49.02	40.64
64.64	61.36	56.70	50.80	46.10	36.10

  a) Make a frequency table to organize the scores.
  b) Draw a histogram of the data.
  c) Does your histogram help you see the range of scores that corresponded to a top-five placement? Explain.

Joannie Rochette trains in St-Leonard, Quebec.

6. a) On the same graph, draw frequency polygons to show the populations of males and females in Canada for the year 2009.

b) Examine your graph. Describe any differences you notice in the populations of the two sexes.

Population by Gender and Age Group in 2009		
Age Group	Male (%)	Female (%)
0–4	5.6	5.3
5–9	5.5	5.1
10–14	6.0	5.7
15–19	6.9	6.5
20–24	7.1	6.6
25–29	7.1	6.8
30–34	6.8	6.6
35–39	6.9	6.7
40–44	7.5	7.2
45–49	8.4	8.2
50–54	7.7	7.6
55–59	6.5	6.6
60–64	5.5	5.7
65–69	4.1	4.3
70–74	3.0	3.4
75–79	2.4	2.9
80–84	1.6	2.4
85–89	0.9	1.6
90+	0.3	0.9
Total	99.8%	100.1%

Statistics Canada

7. The following frequency table shows the number of production errors in vehicles coming off an assembly line during the first, second, third, and fourth hour of the day shift.

Number of Errors		1	2	3	4	5	6	7	8
Frequency	**1st Hour**	17	13	8	5	4	3	1	1
	2nd Hour	26	10	6	5	4	2	0	0
	3rd Hour	30	10	5	3	1	1	0	0
	4th Hour	35	8	3	2	1	0	0	0

a) Draw all the frequency polygons for the data on the same graph.

b) What conclusions can you make, based on your graph?

8. Holly and Jason have 14-week training programs to prepare them to run a marathon. On different days during their programs, they run different distances. Holly plans to run the half marathon (21.1 km). Jason plans to run the full marathon (42.2 km). The distances that they run on various training days are shown below.

a) Construct a frequency distribution table for each training program. Explain the size of interval that you choose.

b) Use your frequency distribution table to graph a frequency polygon for each runner on the same graph.

c) Compare the two training programs.

	Holly's Program (km)					Jason's Program (km)					
Week	Tues.	Wed.	Thurs.	Fri.	Sun.	Mon.	Tues.	Wed.	Thurs.	Fri.	Sun.
1	8	5	8	5	10	off	13	5	13	6	16
2	8	5	10	5	10	off	13	6	13	6	19
3	10	5	13	5	13	off	13	6	16	6	22
4	10	5	13	6	13	5	13	6	16	6	26
5	10	6	13	6	13	6	16	6	16	6	19
6	13	6	13	6	16	6	16	6	16	6	29
7	13	6	13	6	16	6	16	6	19	6	29
8	13	6	13	6	13	6	16	8	19	8	29
9	13	6	16	6	16	6	16	8	19	10	32
10	13	8	13	8	13	8	16	8	16	13	35
11	13	8	16	8	19	6	16	8	16	8	22
12	16	6	16	6	22	10	16	10	19	6	35
13	10	5	13	5	10	5	13	5	10	5	16
14	8	off	8	3	race day	5	10	5	8	3	race day

Serious Injuries in Car Accidents		
Age Group	Driver (%)	Passenger (%)
0 – 4	0	5.2
5 – 14	0.4	10.8
15 – 24	24.6	33.5
25 – 34	20.6	12.5
35 – 44	18.9	9.7
45 – 54	15.7	8.1
55 – 64	9.5	6.7
65+	9.9	9.5
not stated	0.4	3.9
Total	100	99.9

9. Examine the given data for injuries, taken from the Canadian Motor Vehicle Traffic Collision Statistics. On the same graph, draw two frequency polygons to illustrate the percent of serious injuries for drivers and for passengers, by age group. Compare the data distributions. What conclusions can you make?

10. For a histogram to display the distribution of data accurately, intervals of equal width must be used. Explain why, using examples.

Closing

11. a) What are the advantages of grouping raw data into intervals?

  b) How does a histogram differ from a frequency polygon? When would using frequency polygons be better than using histograms?

Extending

12. This table gives the Aboriginal population in 151 metropolitan areas across Canada, based on statistics from the 2006 census. In 2006, the total Aboriginal population was 1 172 785.

  a) Use this table to estimate the mean population. Explain what you did.

  b) Use this table to estimate the median population. Explain what you did.

  c) Using the actual data, the value for the median population is 1700 and the value for the mean is 4275. How do your estimates compare with these values? Explain any discrepancies.

Aboriginal Populations in Cities, 2006	
Population	**Frequency**
0–5 000	122
5 000–10 000	16
10 000–15 000	4
15 000–20 000	2
20 000–25 000	2
25 000–30 000	2
30 000–35 000	0
35 000–40 000	0
40 000–45 000	1
45 000–50 000	0
50 000–55 000	1
55 000–60 000	0
60 000–65 000	0
65 000–70 000	1

Statistics Canada

History | Connection

Duff's Ditch

Winnipeg's Red River Floodway was constructed between 1962 and 1968 to protect the city from severe flooding. Affectionately known as Duff's Ditch (after Premier Duff Roblin, who insisted that the project go forward), the floodway is a 47 km channel that diverts water around the city to allow river levels in Winnipeg to remain below flood level. The gates to the floodway are opened whenever the city is threatened by flooding.

A. Flooding starts to happen in Winnipeg when the water level is 5.5 m. This is equivalent to a flow rate of about 1470 m³/s. When the level gets close to 4.6 m, sandbagging is needed in low-lying areas and the floodway is opened. How many times between its first use in 1969 and 1999 was the floodway opened? (Use the data tables on page 241.)

B. Do you think that high flow rates are becoming the norm rather than the exception? Refer to the data tables on page 241, and do research to find more recent data. Justify your answer.

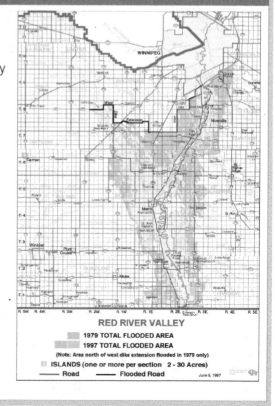

RED RIVER VALLEY

1979 TOTAL FLOODED AREA
1997 TOTAL FLOODED AREA
(Note: Area north of west dike extension flooded in 1979 only)
ISLANDS (one or more per section 2 - 30 Acres)
Road   Flooded Road   June 9, 1997

Standard Deviation

- calculator OR computer with spreadsheet software

GOAL

Determine the standard deviation for sets of data, and use it to solve problems and make decisions.

EXPLORE...

- A teacher has two chemistry classes. She gives the same tests to both classes. Examine the mean mark for each of the first five tests given to both classes. Compare the results for the two classes.

Test	Class A (%)	Class B (%)
1	94	84
2	56	77
3	89	76
4	67	81
5	84	74

INVESTIGATE the Math

The coach of a varsity girls' basketball team keeps statistics on all the players. Near the end of one game, the score is tied and the best starting guard has fouled out. The coach needs to make a substitution. The coach examines the field goal stats for five guards on the bench in the last 10 games.

Player	Field Goal Percent in Last 10 Basketball Games									
Anna	36	41	43	39	45	27	40	37	31	28
Patrice	36	39	36	38	35	37	35	36	38	34
Morgan	34	41	38	37	48	19	33	43	21	44
Paige	34	35	33	35	33	34	33	35	34	33
Star	41	33	39	36	38	36	29	34	38	39

? How can the coach use the data to determine which player should be substituted into the game?

A. Which player seems to be the most consistent shooter? Explain.

B. Analyze the data for Paige using a table like the one shown on the next page. Determine the mean of the data, $\bar{x}$, for Paige, and record this value in the first column.

C. Complete the second column for the **deviation** of each field goal percent: $(x - \bar{x})$

D. Complete the third column for the squares of the deviations.

Communication | Tip

The symbol $\bar{x}$ (read as "x bar") represents the mean of the data.

deviation

The difference between a data value and the mean for the same set of data.

Paige's Field Goal (%)	Deviation $(x - \bar{x})$	Square of Deviation $(x - \bar{x})^2$
34	0.1	0.01
35	1.1	1.21
33		

E. Determine the **standard deviation** of Paige's data by following these steps:

Step 1: Determine the mean of the squares of the deviations.
Step 2: Determine the square root of the mean from Step 1. This number is the standard deviation.

F. Analyze all the data using a spreadsheet like the one below. Enter the field goal percent for Anna in row 2, and for Patrice, Morgan, Paige, and Star in rows 3, 4, 5, and 6, as shown.

standard deviation
A measure of the dispersion or scatter of data values in relation to the mean; a low standard deviation indicates that most data values are close to the mean, and a high standard deviation indicates that most data values are scattered farther from the mean.

	A	B	C	D	E	F	G	H	I	J	K	L	M
1	Game Player	1	2	3	4	5	6	7	8	9	10	Mean	Standard Deviation
2	Anna	36	41	43	39	45	27	40	37	31	28		
3	Patrice	36	39	36	38	35	37	35	36	38	34		
4	Morgan	34	41	38	37	48	19	33	43	21	44		
5	Paige	34	35	33	35	33	34	33	35	34	33		
6	Star	41	33	39	36	38	36	29	34	38	39		

G. Using the features of the spreadsheet software, determine the mean and standard deviation for each set of data.

H. Compare your result from part E with your results for Paige from part G. What do you notice?

I. Examine the means of the players. Would you use the most consistent player identified in part A as a substitute? Explain.

J. Which player has the greatest percent range? Which player has the least? How do the standard deviations of these players compare?

K. Compare the means and standard deviations of the data sets for all the players. Which player's data has the lowest standard deviation? What does this imply about her shooting consistency?

L. Based on past performance, which player has the potential to shoot most poorly? Which player has the potential to shoot most successfully?

M. If you were the coach, which player would you substitute into the game? Explain why.

Reflecting

N. The mean, $\bar{x}$, can be expressed using symbols:

$$\bar{x} = \frac{\Sigma x}{n}$$

Based on your understanding of the mean, what does the symbol Σ represent?

O. The standard deviation, σ, can also be expressed using symbols:

$$\sigma = \sqrt{\frac{\Sigma(x - \bar{x})^2}{n}}$$

Interpret this expression verbally.

> **Communication | Tip**
>
> The symbol σ (read as "sigma") represents the standard deviation of the data.

P. Standard deviation is a measure of dispersion, of how the data in a set is distributed. How would a set of data with a low standard deviation differ from a set of data with a high standard deviation?

APPLY the Math

EXAMPLE 1   Using standard deviation to compare sets of data

Brendan works part-time in the canteen at his local community centre. One of his tasks is to unload delivery trucks. He wondered about the accuracy of the mass measurements given on two cartons that contained sunflower seeds. He decided to measure the masses of the 20 bags in the two cartons. One carton contained 227 g bags, and the other carton contained 454 g bags.

Masses of 227 g Bags (g)			
228	220	233	227
230	227	221	229
224	235	224	231
226	232	218	218
229	232	236	223

Masses of 454 g Bags (g)			
458	445	457	458
452	457	445	452
463	455	451	460
455	453	456	459
451	455	456	450

How can measures of dispersion be used to determine if the accuracy of measurement is the same for both bag sizes?

Brendan's Solution

227 g bags:
Range = 236 g − 218 g
Range = 18 g

454 g bags:
Range = 463 g − 445 g
Range = 18 g

> I examined each set of data and found the greatest mass and least mass. Then I determined the range. The range was the same for both cartons.

227 g bags:
$\bar{x} = 227.15$ g
$\sigma = 5.227...$ g

454 g bags:
$\bar{x} = 454.4$ g
$\sigma = 4.498...$ g

> I used my graphing calculator to determine the mean and standard deviation for each set of data.
>
> Both means were above the mass measurements given on the two cartons.

The accuracy of measurement is not the same for both sizes of bag.

The standard deviation for the 454 g bags is less than the standard deviation for the 227 g bags.

> The difference in the standard deviations indicates that the masses of the larger bags were closer to their mean mass.

Therefore, the 454 g bags of sunflower seeds have a more consistent mass.

Your Turn

a) Explain why the standard deviations for the masses of the two sizes of bag are different, even though the ranges of the masses are the same.
b) How might standard deviation be used by the company that sells the sunflower seeds for quality control in the packaging process?

EXAMPLE 2   Determining the mean and standard deviation of grouped data

Angèle conducted a survey to determine the number of hours per week that Grade 11 males in her school play video games. She determined that the mean was 12.84 h, with a standard deviation of 2.16 h.

Janessa conducted a similar survey of Grade 11 females in her school. She organized her results in this frequency table. Compare the results of the two surveys.

Gaming Hours per Week for Grade 11 Females	
Hours	Frequency
3–5	7
5–7	11
7–9	16
9–11	19
11–13	12
13–15	5

Cole's Solution: Determining $\bar{x}$ and σ manually

Note: The purpose of Cole's Solution is to provide an understanding of what technology does to calculate the mean and standard deviation when working with grouped data. Students are not expected to determine mean and standard deviation manually.

An estimate for the mean of the gaming hours for Grade 11 females is 9.

I predicted that the mean is about 9 h because most of the data is in the 7 to 11 intervals. However, I need to verify my estimate.

A	B	C	D
Hours	Frequency (f)	Midpoint of Interval (x)	f · x
3–5	7	4	28
5–7	11	6	66
7–9	16	8	128
9–11	19	10	190
11–13	12	12	144
13–15	5	14	70
	70		626

I didn't know the actual values in each interval, so I determined the midpoint of each interval. I knew that some values would be greater than the midpoint and some values would be less, but I thought that the midpoint could represent all the values in each interval.

I multiplied the frequency by the midpoint for each interval to determine the number of hours in each interval.

$$\bar{x} = \frac{\Sigma(f)(x)}{n}$$

$$\bar{x} = \frac{626}{70}$$

$$\bar{x} = 8.942... \text{ h}$$

Next, I determined the mean for the data set. I divided the total number of hours by the total number of data values.

C	D	E	F
Midpoint of Interval (x)	f · x	(x − x̄)²	f · (x − x̄)²
4	28	24.431...	171.022...
6	66	8.660...	95.264...
8	128	0.888...	14.223...
10	190	1.117...	21.233...
12	144	9.346...	112.153...
14	70	25.574...	127.873...
	626		541.771...
$\bar{x} = 8.942...$ h			

In column E, I squared the deviation from the midpoint for each interval.

In column F, I multiplied each squared value by the frequency, and I added these products to estimate the total square deviations for all the data.

$$\sigma = \sqrt{\frac{\Sigma f (x - \bar{x})^2}{n}}$$

$$\sigma = \sqrt{\frac{541.771...}{70}}$$

$\sigma = 2.782...$ h

I determined the standard deviation by dividing the sum of the squares of the deviations by the number of data values and then taking the square root.

Males: Females:

$\bar{x} = 12.84$ h $\bar{x} = 8.942...$ h

$\sigma = 2.16$ h $\sigma = 2.782...$ h

I compared the results for the two groups.

The males played nearly 4 h more per week than the females, on average.

The standard deviation for males is lower than the standard deviation for females. Therefore, the males' playing times are closer to their mean (almost 13 h) and don't vary as much.

The mean playing time for males is higher than the mean playing time for females.

The data for the females is more dispersed than the data for the males.

Danica's Solution: Using technology to determine $\bar{x}$ and σ

First, I determined the midpoints of the intervals for Janessa's data and entered these values in one list on my calculator. Then I entered the frequency in a second list.

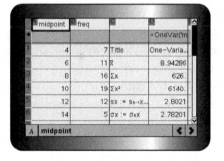

I determined the mean and the standard deviation.

Gaming hours per week for Grade 11 females:

$\bar{x} = 8.942...$ h $\sigma = 2.782...$ h

Gaming hours per week for Grade 11 males:

$\bar{x} = 12.84$ h $\sigma = 2.16$ h

I compared the results for the two groups.

The standard deviation for the females is higher than the standard deviation for the males.

Therefore, the females' times vary more from their mean of about 9 h.

The standard deviation for the males is lower. Therefore, their data is more consistent, even though their mean is higher.

> The females, on average, spent less time playing video games per week. However, some females played a lot more or a lot less than the mean.
>
> The males played more hours per week, and their times were fairly close to their mean.

Your Turn

Could the mean and standard deviation for the female data differ from those determined by Danica and Cole, if the actual data is used? Explain.

In Summary

Key Ideas

- To determine how scattered or clustered the data in a set is, determine the mean of the data and compare each data value to the mean.
- The standard deviation, σ, is a measure of the dispersion of data about the mean.
- The mean and standard deviation can be determined using technology for any set of numerical data, whether or not the data is grouped.

Need to Know

- When data is concentrated close to the mean, the standard deviation, σ, is low. When data is spread far from the mean, the standard deviation is high. As a result, standard deviation is a useful statistic to compare the dispersion of two or more sets of data.
- When determining the standard deviation, σ, for a set of data using technology, this is the process that is followed:
  1. The square of the deviation of each data value (or the midpoint of the interval) from the mean is determined: $(x - \bar{x})^2$
  2. The mean of the squared deviations of all the data values is determined.
  3. The square root of the mean from step 2 is determined. This value is the standard deviation.
- Standard deviation is often used as a measure of consistency. When data is closely clustered around the mean, the process that was used to generate the data can be interpreted as being more consistent than a process that generated data scattered far from the mean.

CHECK Your Understanding

Test	Class A (%)	Class B (%)
1	94	84
2	56	77
3	89	76
4	67	81
5	84	74

1. **a)** Determine, by hand, the standard deviation of test marks for the two chemistry classes shown.
   b) Verify your results from part a) using technology.
   c) Which class had the more consistent marks over the first five tests? Explain.

Use technology to determine the mean and standard deviation, as needed, in questions 2 to 14.

2. Ali bowls in a peewee league. Determine the mean and standard deviation of Ali's bowling scores, rounded to two decimal places.

135	156	118	133
141	127	124	139
109	131	129	123

Bowling Scores	Frequency
101–105	1
106–110	3
111–115	4
116–120	7
121–125	9
126–130	14
131–135	11
136–140	8
141–145	6
146–150	5
151–155	3
156–160	1

3. The bowling scores for the six players on Ali's team are shown at the right.
   a) Determine the mean and standard deviation of the bowling scores for Ali's team, rounded to two decimal places.
   b) Using the mean and standard deviation, compare Ali's data from question 2 to the team's data.

4. Marie, a Métis beadwork artist, ordered packages of beads from two online companies. She is weighing the packages because the sizes seem inconsistent. The standard deviation of the masses of the packages from company A is 11.7 g. The standard deviation of the masses of the packages from company B is 18.2 g.
   a) What does this information tell you about the dispersion of the masses of the packages from each company?
   b) Marie is working on an important project. She needs to make sure that her next order will contain enough beads to complete the project. Should she order from company A or company B?

PRACTISING

5. Four groups of students recorded their pulse rates, as given below.

Group 1	63	78	79	75	73	72	62	75	63	77	77	65	70	69	80
Group 2	72	66	73	80	74	75	64	68	67	70	70	69	69	74	74
Group 3	68	75	78	73	75	68	71	78	65	67	63	69	59	68	79
Group 4	78	75	76	76	79	78	78	76	74	81	78	76	79	74	76

Determine the mean and standard deviation for each group, to one decimal place. Which group has the lowest mean pulse rate? Which group has the most consistent pulse rate?

The Métis are known for floral beadwork. The symmetrical traditional beadwork is illustrated here on the deerskin coat of Louis Riel. Seeds were used to create the beads.

6. Nazra and Diko are laying patio stones. Their supervisor records how many stones they lay each hour.

Hour	1	2	3	4	5	6
Nazra	34	41	40	38	38	45
Diko	51	28	36	44	41	46

a) Which worker lays more stones during the day?

b) Which worker is more consistent?

7. Former Winnipeg Blue Bomber Milt Stegall broke several Canadian Football League (CFL) records, including the most touchdowns (TDs) in a season and the most TDs in a career.

Year	'95	'96	'97	'98	'99	'00	'01	'02	'03	'04	'05	'06	'07	'08
TDs	4	6	14	7	7	15	14	23	15	7	17	7	8	3

Milt Stegall

a) Determine the mean and standard deviation of the TDs that Milt scored in the years he played, to one decimal place.

b) Why do you think that his first and last years had the lowest number of TDs?

c) Determine the mean and standard deviation, to one decimal place, for the years 1996 to 2007.

d) Compare your results from parts a) and c). What do you notice?

8. Milt Stegall also broke the CFL record for most yards receiving.

a) Determine the mean and standard deviation of his statistics, to one decimal place.

Year	'95	'96	'97	'98	'99	'00	'01	'02	'03	'04	'05	'06	'07	'08
Yards	469	613	1616	403	1193	1499	1214	1862	1144	1121	1184	1252	1108	470

b) Allen Pitts, who played for the Calgary Stampeders, held the CFL record for most yards receiving until Milt Stegall surpassed him. Pitts had the following statistics for yards gained per year: mean 1353.7 and standard deviation 357.1. Which player was more consistent in terms of yards gained per year?

9. Two health clubs monitor the number of hours per month that a random sample of their members spend working out.

Fitness Express	
Hours	Frequency
8–10	9
10–12	18
12–14	23
14–16	32
16–18	39
18–20	42
20–22	31
22–24	22
24–26	16
26–28	11
28–30	7

Fit for Life	
Hours	Frequency
6–9	8
9–12	13
12–15	32
15–18	47
18–21	52
21–24	42
24–27	27
27–30	19

a) Determine the mean and standard deviation of the hours per month for members of each club, to one decimal place.

b) The health clubs believe that workout consistency is more important than workout length. Which club is more successful at encouraging its members to work out consistently?

10. Jaime has 20 min to get to her after-school job. Despite her best efforts, she is frequently late. Her employer says that unless she arrives to work on time consistently, she will lose her job. She has recorded her travel times (in minutes) for the last two weeks: 18, 20, 22, 27, 16, 23, 25, 26, 19, 28. Over the next two weeks, she continues to record her travel times: 22, 20, 19, 16, 20, 23, 25, 18, 19, 17. Do you think Jaime will lose her job? Use statistics to justify your answer.

11. The manager of a customer support line currently has 200 unionized employees. Their contract states that the mean number of calls that an employee should handle per day is 45, with a maximum standard deviation of 6 calls. The manager tracked the number of calls that each employees handles. Does the manager need to hire more employees if the calls continue in this pattern?

Daily Calls	Frequency
26–30	2
31–35	13
36–40	42
41–45	53
46–50	42
51–55	36
56–60	8
61–65	4

Jordin Tootoo, from Rankin Inlet, Nunavut, played for the Brandon Wheat Kings of the WHL from 1999 to 2003. In 2003, he became the first player of Inuit descent to play in a regular-season NHL game.

12. The following table shows Jordin Tootoo's regular season statistics while playing in the Western Hockey League (WHL) and the NHL from 1999 to 2010.

Season	Games Played	Goals	Assists	Points
1999–2000	45	6	10	16
2000–2001	60	20	28	48
2001–2002	64	32	39	71
2002–2003	51	35	39	74
2003–2004	70	4	4	8
2005–2006	34	4	6	10
2006–2007	65	3	6	9
2007–2008	63	11	7	18
2008–2009	72	4	12	16
2009–2010	51	6	10	16

a) Determine the mean and standard deviation for each column of data.

b) In the 2005–2006 season, Jordin played only 34 games. As a result, he had fewer opportunities to score points. Predict the effect on the standard deviation of each column if this season is omitted.

c) Determine the mean and standard deviation for each column, excluding the 2005 – 2006 season.

d) How do your results for part c) compare with your results for part a)?

e) Justify the following statement: "Goals + assists = points, whether you are looking at the data for each season or you are looking at the means and standard deviations for many seasons."

Closing

13. Twins Jordana and Jane wrote a total of 10 tests in math class. They have the same mean test score, but different standard deviations. Explain how this is possible.

Extending

14. If you glance at a random dot stereogram (also called a "Magic Eye image"), it looks like a collection of dots or shapes. If you look at it properly, however, it resolves into a 3-D image.

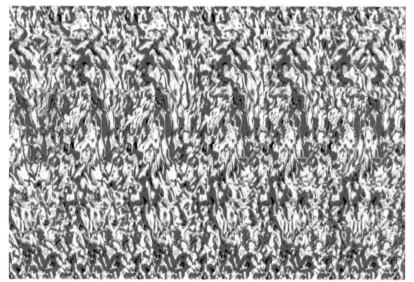

©2010 Magic Eye Inc.

An experiment was done to determine whether people could "fuse" the image faster if they knew what shape they were looking for. The results of the experiment are shown in the table to the right. The people in group A were given no information about the image. The people in group B were given visual information about the image. The number of seconds that the people needed to recognize the 3-D image are listed in the table.

a) Determine the mean and standard deviation for each group, rounded to the nearest hundredth of a second.

b) Were the people who were given visual information able to recognize the image more quickly? Which group was more consistent?

Times for Group A (s)		Times for Group B (s)	
47.2	5.6	19.7	3.6
22.0	4.7	16.2	3.5
20.4	4.7	15.9	3.3
19.7	4.3	15.4	3.3
17.4	4.2	9.7	2.9
14.7	3.9	8.9	2.8
13.4	3.4	8.6	2.7
13.0	3.1	8.6	2.4
12.3	3.1	7.4	2.3
12.2	2.7	6.3	2.0
10.3	2.4	6.1	1.8
9.7	2.3	6.0	1.7
9.7	2.3	6.0	1.7
9.5	2.1	5.9	1.6
9.1	2.1	4.9	1.4
8.9	2.0	4.6	1.2
8.9	1.9	1.0	1.1
8.4	1.7	3.8	
8.1	1.7		
7.9	6.9		
7.8	6.3		
6.1			

FREQUENTLY ASKED Questions

Study | *Aid*

• See Lesson 5.1 and Lesson 5.2, Examples 1 and 2.
• Try Mid-Chapter Review Questions 1 to 3.

Q: How can you make a large set of data more manageable to work with and analyze?

A: Create a frequency distribution by organizing the data into equal-sized intervals. This simplifies the data into a manageable number of intervals, which show how the data is distributed. To visualize the data in the frequency table more easily, draw a histogram or a frequency polygon.

For example, consider the weight, in pounds, of the members of the Edmonton Eskimos CFL team.

165	185	188	195	205	210	225	235	250	270	300	320
170	185	189	196	210	215	225	235	255	300	302	335
175	185	191	197	210	215	229	240	255	300	310	
183	188	195	205	210	216	230	248	265	300	315	

First, determine the lowest weight and highest weight, and the range.

Range = 335 − 165 or 170 lb

Next, decide on the number of intervals and the interval width. Generally, the number of intervals is from 5 to 12. Since the range is 170, an interval width of 15 would require 12 intervals.

The first interval should start slightly below the lowest weight. The last interval should end slightly above the highest weight. Use a tally to count the number of players in each interval.

Draw the graph. To plot each vertex for the frequency polygon, determine the midpoint of the interval. Join the vertices with line segments, and then connect the endpoints to the horizontal axis.

Weight	Frequency
160–175	3
175–190	7
190–205	7
205–220	7
220–235	6
235–250	3
250–265	3
265–280	1
280–295	0
295–310	6
310–325	2
325–340	1

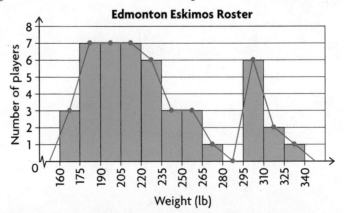

Edmonton Eskimos Roster

Q: How can you determine standard deviation using technology?

A1: For ungrouped data, enter the data into a list. Use the appropriate statistics formula to determine the standard deviation.

A2: For grouped data, determine the midpoint of each interval using a graphing calculator or spreadsheet. Enter the midpoints into column 1 and the frequencies into column 2. Use the appropriate functions to determine the standard deviation.

Study *Aid*
• See Lesson 5.3, Examples 1 and 2.
• Try Mid-Chapter Review Questions 4 to 6.

Q: What does standard deviation measure, and how do you interpret it?

A: Standard deviation measures the dispersion of a data set. It is an indication of how far away most of the data is from the mean. It is useful for comparing two or more sets of data.

Study *Aid*
• See Lesson 5.3.
• Try Mid-Chapter Review Questions 1 to 3.

For example, consider two different health clubs.

Health Club	Mean Age of Members (years)	Standard Deviation of Ages (years)
A	37	5.3
B	43	11.4

The standard deviation for Health Club B is more than double the standard deviation for Health Club A. This means that there is a much wider range of ages in Health Club B, and the ages are less clustered around the mean.

PRACTISING

Lesson 5.1

1. Compare the mean monthly temperatures, in degrees Celsius, for Paris, France, and Sydney, Australia.

	Jan.	Feb.	Mar.	Apr.	May	Jun.	Jul.	Aug.	Sept.	Oct.	Nov.	Dec.
Paris	6	7	12	16	20	23	25	24	21	16	10	7
Sydney	23	23	21	19	15	13	12	13	15	18	20	22

2. Construct a graph for Wayne Gretzky's goals per NHL season. Describe the data distribution.

Goals	Number of Seasons
0 to 10	2
10 to 20	3
20 to 30	3
30 to 40	2
40 to 50	3
50 to 60	4
60 to 70	1
70 to 80	2
80 to 90	1
90 to 100	1

3. Jackson and Jillian are trying to control the number of text messages they send. They record the number they send every day in April.

Jackson: 2, 7, 20, 4, 11, 25, 6, 27, 3, 6, 18, 5, 13, 4, 10, 16, 23, 22, 5, 8, 3, 12, 6, 13, 12, 7, 8, 26, 9, 17

Jillian: 2, 9, 11, 15, 8, 8, 0, 21, 16, 12, 14, 14, 15, 20, 11, 12, 10, 9, 8, 0, 7, 24, 19, 18, 19, 15, 12, 8, 1, 13

a) Choose an interval width.
b) Create a frequency table for the data.
c) Compare the two sets of data using a frequency polygon.

Lesson 5.3

4. Compare the two sets of data in question 3 by determining the means and standard deviations, to the nearest tenth.

5. Liam keeps track of the amount he spends, in dollars, on weekly lunches during one semester:

19	15	6	24	27	26	48
19	23	18	29	17	14	22
19	26	20	17	28		

a) Determine the range, mean, and standard deviation, correct to two decimal places.

b) Remove the greatest and the least weekly amounts. Then determine the mean, standard deviation, and range for the remaining amounts.

c) What effect does removing the greatest and least amounts have on the standard deviation?

6. Tiffany researched the annual salaries of males versus females for her project on gender issues. She obtained the following data about 441 full-time employees who work in laboratories. Determine the mean and standard deviation for each set of data, and compare the data.

Females	
Salary Range ($)	Frequency
20 000–25 000	92
25 000–30 000	52
30 000–35 000	19
35 000–40 000	10
40 000–45 000	4
45 000–50 000	1
50 000–55 000	3
55 000–60 000	3

Males	
Salary Range ($)	Frequency
20 000–30 000	86
30 000–40 000	78
40 000–50 000	28
50 000–60 000	20
60 000–70 000	22
70 000–80 000	10
80 000–90 000	4
90 000–100 000	5
100 000–110 000	2
110 000–120 000	1
120 000–130 000	0
130 000–140 000	1

The Normal Distribution

GOAL

Determine the properties of a normal distribution, and compare
normally distributed data.

INVESTIGATE *the Math*

Many games require dice. For example, the game
of Yacht requires five dice.

? What shape is the data distribution for
the sum of the numbers rolled with
dice, using various numbers of dice?

A. If you rolled a single die 50 000 times, what do you think the graph
would look like?

B. Predict what the graph would look like if you rolled two dice 50 000 times.

C. With a partner, roll two dice 50 times. Record the sum for each roll
in a frequency distribution table. Then draw a graph to represent the
distribution of the data. Comment on the distribution of the data.

D. Combine the data for the entire class, and draw a graph. Comment on
the distribution of the combined data.

E. Using a dice simulator, roll two dice 50 000 times. Compare the graph
for this set of data with the graph you drew in part D.

F. Make a conjecture about what the graph would look like if you rolled
three dice 50 000 times.

G. Using a dice simulator, roll three dice 50 000 times. What do you
notice about the shape of the graph as the number of rolls increases?
Draw a frequency polygon to represent the distribution of the data.
Was your conjecture correct?

H. Make a conjecture about what the graph would look like if you rolled
four dice 50 000 times. What would the graph look like for five dice
rolled 50 000 times?

I. Using a dice simulator, roll four dice and then five dice 50 000 times.
What do you notice about the shape of the graph as the number of
rolls increases? Draw a frequency polygon to represent the distribution
of the data for both four dice and five dice. Describe the shape of each
polygon. Was your conjecture correct?

YOU WILL NEED

- calculator
- grid paper
- dice
- dice simulator

EXPLORE...

- Sometimes the distribution
  of data has a special shape.
  For example, the first graph
  below has one peak, so the
  shape has one mode. Describe
  the shape of each graph, and
  suggest a context that the
  graph could represent.

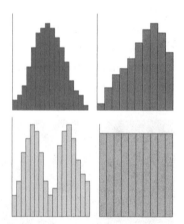

Reflecting

J. How does increasing the number of dice rolled each time affect the distribution of the data?

K. How does increasing the sample size affect the distribution of the data for three dice, four dice, and five dice?

L. What do you think a graph that represents 100 000 rolls of 10 dice would look like? Why do you think this shape is called a **normal curve**?

M. As the number of dice increases, the graph approaches a **normal distribution**. What does the line of symmetry in the graph represent?

APPLY the Math

EXAMPLE 1   Examining the properties of a normal distribution

Heidi is opening a new snowboard shop near a local ski resort. She knows that the recommended length of a snowboard is related to a person's height. Her research shows that most of the snowboarders who visit this resort are males, 20 to 39 years old. To ensure that she stocks the most popular snowboard lengths, she collects height data for 1000 Canadian men, 20 to 39 years old. How can she use the data to help her stock her store with boards that are the appropriate lengths?

Height (in.)	Frequency
61 or shorter	3
61–62	4
62–63	10
63–64	18
64–65	30
65–66	52
66–67	64
67–68	116
68–69	128
69–70	147
70–71	129
71–72	115
72–73	63
73–74	53
74–75	29
75–76	20
76–77	12
77–78	5
taller than 78	2

Heidi's Solution

$\bar{x} = 69.521$ in.

$\sigma = 2.987...$ in.

I decided to use 60.5 as the midpoint of the first interval and 78.5 as the midpoint of the last interval. I calculated the mean and standard deviation using a graphing calculator.

I examined the table. The median is the average of the 500th and the 501st height.

There are 147 heights in the 69–70 in. interval. The 73rd person is about midway through this interval, so the median height is approximately 69.5 in.

There are 425 heights less than or equal to 69 in. The median height is the height of the 73rd person in the 69 – 70 in. interval.

I don't know where the mode is, but it is more likely to be in the interval that contains the greatest number of data values, which is the 69–70 in. interval. I can assume that all three measures of central tendency have about the same value.

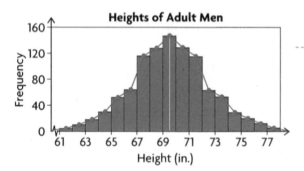

Heights of Adult Men

I drew a histogram to show the height distribution.

I drew a vertical line on my histogram to represent the mean.

Then I drew a frequency polygon by connecting the midpoints at the top of each bar of the graph.

The data is almost symmetrical about the mean and tapers off in a gradual way on both sides. The frequency polygon resembles a bell shape.

The data has a normal distribution.

Heights within one standard deviation of the mean:

$69.521 - 2.987...$ or 66.5 in.

$69.521 + 2.987...$ or 72.5 in.

I determined the range of heights within one standard deviation of the mean by adding and subtracting the standard deviation from the mean.

I also determined the range of heights within two standard deviations of the mean.

Heights within two standard deviations of the mean:

$69.521 - 2(2.987...)$ or 63.5 in.

$69.521 + 2(2.987...)$ or 75.5 in.

I summarized my results in a table and compared them to my histogram. The range for one standard deviation appears to include most of the data. The range for two standard deviations appears to include almost all of the data.

Range	Height Range
$\bar{x} - 1\sigma$ to $\bar{x} + 1\sigma$	about 66.5 in. to 72.5 in.
$\bar{x} - 2\sigma$ to $\bar{x} + 2\sigma$	about 63.5 in. to 75.5 in.

Number of males within one standard deviation of the mean from 67 in. to 73 in.:
$116 + 128 + 147 + 129 + 115 + 63$, or 698

Number of males within two standard deviations of the mean from 64 in. to 76 in.:
$30 + 52 + 64 + 116 + 128 + 147 + 129 +$
$115 + 63 + 53 + 29 + 20$, or 944

I estimated the percent of the heights that were within one and two standard deviations of the mean.

To determine the number of heights in each range, I rounded up to find the lower and upper boundaries in each range. Then I summed the number of people from the table that were in these ranges.

Range	Height Range	Percent of Data
$\bar{x} - 1\sigma$ to $\bar{x} + 1\sigma$	66.5 in. to 72.5 in.	$\frac{698}{1000}$ or 69.8%
$\bar{x} - 2\sigma$ to $\bar{x} + 2\sigma$	63.5 in. to 75.5 in.	$\frac{946}{1000}$ or 94.6%

About 70% of the heights are within one standard deviation of the mean.

Heights within one standard deviation of the mean are most common.

A high percent of heights are within two standard deviations of the mean.

About 95% of the heights are within two standard deviations of the mean.

I predict that about 70% of my male customers will need snowboards for heights from 66.5 to 72.5 in.

Your Turn

What percent of all the heights is within three standard deviations of the mean?

EXAMPLE **2**   Analyzing a normal distribution

Jim raises Siberian husky sled dogs at his kennel.
He knows, from the data he has collected over
the years, that the weights of adult male dogs
are normally distributed, with a mean of 52.5 lb
and a standard deviation of 2.4 lb. Jim used this
information to sketch a normal curve, with

- 68% of the data within one standard deviation
  of the mean

- 95% of the data within two standard deviations
  of the mean

- 99.7% of the data within three standard
  deviations of the mean

The Canadian Championship Dog Derby, held in
Yellowknife, Northwest Territories, is one of the oldest
sled-dog races in North America. Top mushers gather to
challenge their dogs in the fast-paced, three-day event.

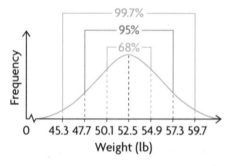

What percent of adult male dogs at Jim's kennel would you expect to have
a weight between 47.7 lb and 54.9 lb?

> **Communication** | *Tip*
>
> In statistics, when an entire
> population is involved,
> use the symbol μ (read as
> "mu") for the mean of the
> population.

Ian's Solution

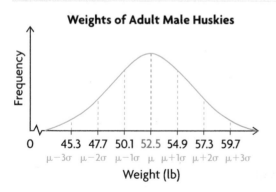

> I sketched the graph and labelled the mean, μ,
> below the horizontal axis. Since the standard
> deviation is 2.4 lb, I can label the scale to the right
> of the mean as $\mu + 1\sigma$, $\mu + 2\sigma$, and $\mu + 3\sigma$.
>
> I labelled the scale to the left of the mean as
> $\mu - 1\sigma$, $\mu - 2\sigma$, and $\mu - 3\sigma$.

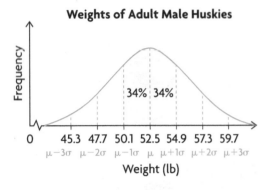

Weights of Adult Male Huskies

I reasoned that the area under the curve is symmetrical around μ, so if 68% of the dogs have weights within one standard deviation, then 34% must have weights between μ − 1σ and μ, and 34% must have weights between μ and μ + 1σ.

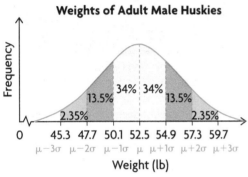

Weights of Adult Male Huskies

I knew that 95% of the weights lie within two standard deviations of the mean. Since 68% of the weights lie within one standard deviation of the mean, 27% of the weights must lie between one and two standard deviations, or 13.5% for each side of the graph.

Using the same reasoning, I figured out the percent of data that would lie between two and three standard deviations from the mean for each side of the graph:

$$\frac{99.7\% - 95\%}{2} = 2.35\%$$

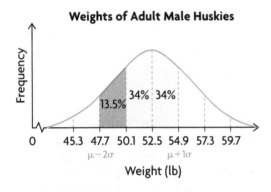

Weights of Adult Male Huskies

For the percent that fits between 47.7 lb and 54.9 lb, I determined the location of each weight.

$$\mu + 1\sigma = 54.9$$
$$\mu - 2\sigma = 47.7$$

I used my diagram to determine the sum of the percent of data between these locations.

The percent of dogs with weights between 47.7 lb and 54.9 lb, x, can be represented as

$$x = 13.5\% + 34\% + 34\%$$
$$x = 81.5\%$$

Approximately 81.5% of adult male dogs should have a weight between 47.7 lb and 54.9 lb.

Your Turn

a) What percent of adult male dogs at Jim's kennel would you expect to have a weight between 50.1 lb and 59.7 lb?

b) What percent of adult male dogs at Jim's kennel would you expect to have a weight less than 45.3 lb?

EXAMPLE **3**   Comparing normally distributed data

Two baseball teams flew to the North American Indigenous Games.
The members of each team had carry-on luggage for their sports
equipment. The masses of the carry-on luggage were normally
distributed, with the characteristics shown to the right.

Team	μ (kg)	σ (kg)
Men	6.35	1.04
Women	6.35	0.59

a) Sketch a graph to show the distribution of the masses of the luggage
for each team.

b) The women's team won the championship. Each member received a
medal and a souvenir baseball, with a combined mass of 1.18 kg, which
they packed in their carry-on luggage. Sketch a graph that shows how
the distribution of the masses of their carry-on luggage changed for the
flight home.

Samara's Solution

a)

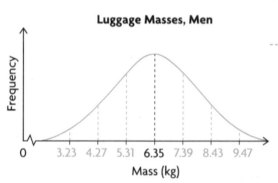

I sketched the normal distribution of the masses
of the luggage for the men's team. I marked the
values for μ, $\mu + 1\sigma$, $\mu + 2\sigma$, $\mu + 3\sigma$, $\mu - 1\sigma$,
$\mu - 2\sigma$, and $\mu - 3\sigma$.

I knew that the area under the normal curve
represents 100% of the data, so I could think of
the area as equal to 1 unit.

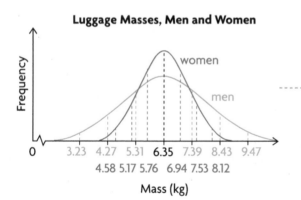

On the same graph, I sketched the normal curve
for masses of the luggage for the women's team.
I knew that this curve must be narrower than
the curve for the men's team, since the standard
deviation is lower.

I also knew that the area under this curve
represents 100% of the data for the women's
luggage, so the area under the red curve is also
equal to 1 unit. For the area under both curves to
be the same, the normal curve for the women's
team must be taller.

b) Data for masses of luggage for women's team on flight home:

$$\mu = 6.35 + 1.18 \text{ or } 7.53 \text{ kg}$$
$$\sigma = 0.59 \text{ kg}$$

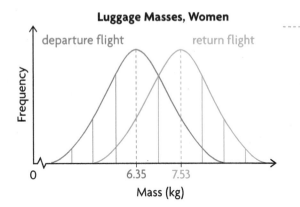

Luggage Masses, Women

departure flight   return flight

Frequency

Mass (kg)

0   6.35   7.53

Since each member of the women's team will add 1.18 kg to the mass of her carry-on luggage, the mean mass will increase by 1.18 kg. Although the mass of each piece of luggage will change, the distribution of the masses will stay the same, and the standard deviation will still be 0.59 kg.

I sketched a graph to show the new masses of the luggage for the women's team. It made sense that the new graph would simply move 1.18 to the right of the old graph. The shape stayed the same because the standard deviations of the two graphs are the same.

Your Turn

Suppose that the women had gone shopping and had also added their purchases to their carry-on luggage. How would you sketch a graph to show the distribution of the masses of their luggage for the trip home? Explain.

EXAMPLE 4   Analyzing data to solve a problem

Shirley wants to buy a new cellphone. She researches the cellphone she is considering and finds the following data on its longevity, in years.

2.0	2.4	3.3	1.7	2.5	3.7	2.0	2.3	2.9	2.2
2.3	2.7	2.5	2.7	1.9	2.4	2.6	2.7	2.8	2.5
1.7	1.1	3.1	3.2	3.1	2.9	2.9	3.0	2.1	2.6
2.6	2.2	2.7	1.8	2.4	2.5	2.4	2.3	2.5	2.6
3.2	2.1	3.4	2.2	2.7	1.9	2.9	2.6	2.7	2.8

a) Does the data approximate a normal distribution?
b) If Shirley purchases this cellphone, what is the likelihood that it will last for more than three years?

Shirley's Solution

a) $\mu = 2.526$
$\sigma = 0.482$
median $= 2.55$

Using my calculator, I determined the mean, the standard deviation, and the median. The median is close to the mean, which indicates that the data may be normally distributed.

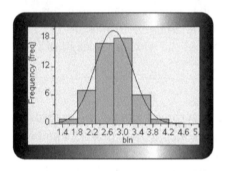

I created a frequency table to generate a histogram.

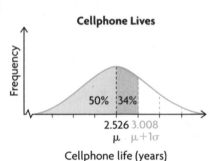

I created a histogram of the data, with an interval width of σ. My histogram looked almost symmetrical, so I decided to check the data to see how closely it approximates a normal distribution.

I generated a normal distribution curve on top of the histogram.

-1σ to 1σ	-2σ to 2σ	-3σ to 3σ
$\dfrac{35}{50} = 70\%$	$\dfrac{48}{50} = 96\%$	100%

I determined the percent of the data within one, two, and three standard deviations of the mean. I think the percents are reasonably close to those for a normal distribution (68%, 95%, and 99.7%).

The data approximates a normal distribution.

b)

Cellphone Lives

50% 34%

2.526 3.008
μ   μ+1σ

Cellphone life (years)

I sketched a normal curve with the mean at 2.526 and the mean + 1 standard deviation at 3.008. I could use this location on the graph to determine the percent of values greater than three years.

I knew that the left-half area of the curve contains 50% of the data, and the area between 2.526 and 3.008 contains approximately 34% of the data.

$\mu + 1\sigma = 2.526 + 0.482$, or 3.008

$100\% - (50\% + 34\%) = 16\%$

About 16% of the cellphones lasted more than three years.

The area under the curve to the right of 3.008 is the white section. I subtracted the area of the coloured sections from 100%.

Your Turn

If Shirley purchases this cellphone, what is the likelihood that it will last at least 18 months?

In Summary

Key Ideas

- Graphing a set of grouped data can help you determine whether the shape of the frequency polygon can be approximated by a normal curve.
- You can make reasonable estimates about data that approximates a normal distribution, because data that is normally distributed has special characteristics.
- Normal curves can vary in two main ways: the mean determines the location of the centre of the curve on the horizontal axis, and the standard deviation determines the width and height of the curve.

Need to Know

- The properties of a normal distribution can be summarized as follows:
  - The graph is symmetrical. The mean, median, and mode are equal (or close) and fall at the line of symmetry.
  - The normal curve is shaped like a bell, peaking in the middle, sloping down toward the sides, and approaching zero at the extremes.
  - About 68% of the data is within one standard deviation of the mean.
  - About 95% of the data is within two standard deviations of the mean.
  - About 99.7% of the data is within three standard deviations of the mean.
  - The area under the curve can be considered as 1 unit, since it represents 100% of the data.

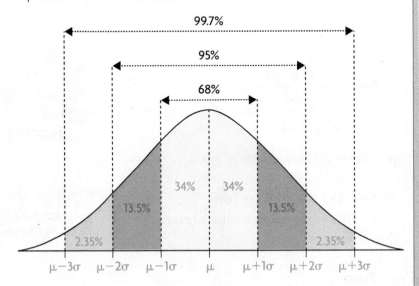

- Generally, measurements of living things (such as mass, height, and length) have a normal distribution.

CHECK Your Understanding

1. The ages of members of a seniors curling club are normally distributed, with a mean of 63 years and a standard deviation of 4 years. What percent of the curlers is in each of the following age groups?
   a) between 55 and 63 years old
   b) between 67 and 75 years old
   c) older than 75 years old

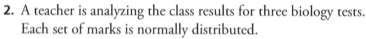

2. A teacher is analyzing the class results for three biology tests. Each set of marks is normally distributed.

Test	Mean (μ)	Standard Deviation (σ)
1	77	3.9
2	83	3.9
3	77	7.4

   a) Sketch normal curves for tests 1 and 2 on one graph. Sketch normal curves for tests 1 and 3 on a different graph.
   b) Examine your graphs. How do tests 1 and 3 compare? How do tests 1 and 2 compare?
   c) Determine Oliver's marks on each test, given the information shown at the right.

Test	Oliver's Mark
1	$\mu + 2\sigma$
2	$\mu - 1\sigma$
3	$\mu + 3\sigma$

3. Is the data in each set normally distributed? Explain.

   a)
Interval	10–19	20–29	30–39	40–49	50–59	60–69
Frequency	3	5	17	20	11	4

   b)
Interval	2–5	6–9	10–13	14–17	18–21	22–25
Frequency	2	8	8	3	4	5

   c)
Interval	10–24	25–39	40–54	55–69	70–84	85–99
Frequency	2	7	16	10	4	1

PRACTISING

4. Tiegan is organizing her movie collection. She decides to record the length of each movie, in minutes.

91	129	95	96	96	90	101	87	100	90
86	78	105	99	81	106	101	122	91	102
89	125	162	155	89	89	180	94	84	99
73	100	99	100	117	135	100	89	87	110
125	103	94	99	98	102	96	88	154	144

   a) Determine the mean and standard deviation for the set of data.
   b) Create a frequency table, using σ as the interval width.
   c) Are the lengths of Tiegan's movies normally distributed? Explain.

The Indian monsoon, or rainy season, usually begins in June or July, depending on location, and ends late in September.

5. The data in each of the following sets has been ordered from least to greatest. For each set,
   i) calculate the mean, median, and standard deviation;
   ii) create a frequency polygon; and
   iii) explain why the distribution is or is not approximately normal.
   a) daily maximum temperatures (°C) in monsoon season in India:
      41.5, 42.4, 42.6, 42.7, 42.9, 43.0, 43.6, 44.0, 44.5, 44.6, 44.6, 44.8, 45.0, 45.3, 45.5, 45.5, 45.6, 45.7, 45.8, 46.1, 46.3, 46.4, 46.5, 46.6, 46.8, 47.0, 47.2, 47.6, 47.6, 47.9
   b) class marks on a pop quiz out of 15:
      2, 4, 5, 6, 6, 6, 7, 7, 7, 7, 8, 8, 8, 8, 8, 8, 9, 9, 9, 10, 10, 11, 11, 11, 12, 12, 13, 13, 15

6. A manufacturer offers a warranty on its coffee makers. The coffee makers have a mean lifespan of 4.5 years, with a standard deviation of 0.7 years. For how long should the coffee makers be covered by the warranty, if the manufacturer wants to repair no more than 2.5% of the coffee makers sold?

7. Hila found the data at the left that shows the number of ways that each sum can be obtained when rolling three dice.
   a) Determine the mean and the standard deviation.
   b) Draw a frequency polygon to show the data.
   c) Does the data have a normal distribution? Explain.

8. The company payroll of Sweetwater Communications has a mean monthly salary of $5400, with a standard deviation of $800.
   a) Sketch a normal curve to represent the salaries for the company.
   b) Sketch a curve to show the effects of Proposal 1: Each employee receives a raise of $270 per month.
   c) Sketch a curve to show the effects of Proposal 2: Each employee receives a 5% raise on the original salary.

9. The results for the first round of the 2009 Masters golf tournament are given below.

Rolling 3 Dice	
Sum	Frequency
3	1
4	3
5	6
6	10
7	15
8	21
9	25
10	27
11	27
12	25
13	21
14	15
15	10
16	6
17	3
18	1

65	68	70	71	72	73	74	76
66	69	70	71	72	73	74	76
66	69	70	72	73	73	75	77
67	69	71	72	73	73	75	77
67	69	71	72	73	73	75	77
68	69	71	72	73	73	75	78
68	69	71	72	73	73	75	78
68	70	71	72	73	73	75	78
68	70	71	72	73	73	75	79
68	70	71	72	73	74	75	79
68	70	71	72	73	74	75	79
68	70	71	72	73	74	76	80

a) Are the golf scores normally distributed?

b) Explain how the measures of central tendency support your decision in part a).

10. A school of 130 bottlenose dolphins is living in a protected environment. The life expectancy of the dolphins is normally distributed, with a mean of 39 years and a standard deviation of 3.5 years. How many of these dolphins can be expected to live more than 46 years?

11. Julie is an engineer who designs roller coasters. She wants to design a roller coaster that 95% of the population can ride. The average adult in North America has a mass of 71.8 kg, with a standard deviation of 13.6 kg.

a) What range of masses should Julie consider in her design?

b) If Julie wanted to design a roller coaster that 99.7% of the population could ride, what range of masses should she consider?

c) What assumption is being made, which could cause problems if it is not valid?

12. A new video game is being tested with a sample of students. The scores on the first attempt for each player are recorded in the table.

a) Graph the data. Does the data appear to have a normal distribution?

b) Determine the mean and standard deviation of the data. Do these values validate your answer to part a)?

13. In a dog obedience class, the masses of the 60 dogs enrolled were normally distributed, with a mean of 11.2 kg and a standard deviation of 2.8 kg. How many dogs would you expect to fall within each range of masses?

a) between 8.4 kg and 14.0 kg

b) between 5.6 kg and 16.8 kg

c) between 2.8 kg and 19.6 kg

d) less than 11.2 kg

Scores	Freq.
less than 18 000	2
18 000–27 000	5
27 000–36 000	14
36 000–45 000	36
45 000–54 000	77
54 000–63 000	128
63 000–72 000	163
72 000–81 000	163
81 000–90 000	127
90 000–99 000	80
99 000–108 000	33
108 000–117 000	14
117 000–126 000	6
greater than 126 000	2

14. The mass of an Appaloosa horse is generally in the range of 431 kg to 533 kg. Assuming that the data is normally distributed, determine the mean and standard deviation for the mass of an Appaloosa. Justify your answers.

Closing

15. Explain why a selection of 10 students from a class can have marks that are not normally distributed, even when the marks of the whole class are normally distributed.

The Appaloosa Horse Club of Canada Museum is located in Claresholm, Alberta.

Extending

16. Newfoundland dogs have masses that are normally distributed. The mean mass of a male dog is 63.5 kg, with a standard deviation of 1.51 kg. The mean mass of a female dog is 49.9 kg, with a standard deviation of 1.51 kg. Esteban claims that he used to have two adult Newfoundland dogs: a male that was 78.9 kg and a female that was 29.9 kg. Using your knowledge of normal distribution, do you think he is being truthful? Explain.

Applying Problem-Solving Strategies

Predicting Possible Pathways

A Galton board is a triangular array of pegs that is used for statistical experiments. Balls are dropped, one at a time, onto the top peg and fall either right or left. Then, as they hit a peg in the next row, they fall either right or left again, until they finally pass through a slot at the bottom, where they can be counted. Each ball is equally likely to fall either way.

The Puzzle

A. For an array with 2 rows and 3 pegs, there is one way for a ball to fall into each end slot, and two ways for a ball to fall into the middle slot. For an array with 3 rows and 6 pegs, there is one way for a ball to fall into each end slot, and three ways for a ball to fall into the two middle slots.

Determine the number of ways for a ball to fall through an array with 4 rows and 10 pegs.

B. Examine each array in step A. Look for a pattern to determine how many pegs there would be in a 5-row array and a 6-row array.

C. Look for a pattern in the number of ways for a ball to fall into each slot in the arrays in part A. Use this pattern to determine the number of ways for a ball to fall into each slot in a 5-row array and a 6-row array.

The Strategy

D. Describe a strategy you could use to determine the number of ways for a ball to fall into each slot in an array of any size.

E. Use your strategy to determine the number of ways for a ball to fall into each slot in an array with 10 rows.

F. Draw a histogram or a frequency polygon to illustrate the results for a 10-row array. Comment on the distribution.

GOAL

Use z-scores to compare data, make predictions, and solve problems.

LEARN ABOUT the Math

Hailey and Serge belong to a running club in Vancouver. Part of their training involves a 200 m sprint. Below are normally distributed times for the 200 m sprint in Vancouver and on a recent trip to Lake Louise. At higher altitudes, run times improve.

Location	Altitude (m)	Club Mean Time: μ for 200 m (s)	Club Standard Deviation: σ (s)	Hailey's Run Time (s)	Serge's Run Time (s)
Vancouver	4	25.75	0.62	24.95	25.45
Lake Louise	1661	25.57	0.60	24.77	26.24

? At which location was Hailey's run time better, when compared with the club results?

EXPLORE...

- Alexis plays in her school jazz band. Band members practise an average of 16.5 h per week, with a standard deviation of 4.2 h. Alexis practises an average of 22 h per week. As a class, discuss how you might estimate the percent of the band that, on average, practises a greater number of hours than Alexis.

EXAMPLE 1   Comparing z-scores

Determine at which location Hailey's run time was better, when compared with the club results.

Marcel's Solution

For any given score, x, from a normal distribution,

$x = \mu + z\sigma$,

where z represents the number of standard deviations of the score from the mean.

Solving for z results in a formula for a **z-score** :

$$z = \frac{x - \mu}{\sigma}$$

Hailey's run time is less at Lake Louise, but so is the club's mean run time. I can't compare these times directly, because the means and standard deviations are different for the two locations. To make the comparison, I have to standardize Hailey's times to fit a common normal distribution.

A z-score indicates the position of a data value on a **standard normal distribution** . ⇨

z-score

A standardized value that indicates the number of standard deviations of a data value above or below the mean.

standard normal distribution

A normal distribution that has a mean of zero and a standard deviation of one.

Vancouver:

$$z = \frac{x - \mu}{\sigma}$$

$$z = \frac{24.95 - 25.75}{0.62}$$

$$z = -1.290 \ldots$$

Lake Louise:

$$z = \frac{x - \mu}{\sigma}$$

$$z = \frac{24.77 - 25.57}{0.60}$$

$$z = -1.333 \ldots$$

I know that z-scores can be used to compare data values from different normal distributions. I calculated the z-score for Hailey's run times at each location.

Hailey's run time is about 1.29 standard deviations below the mean in Vancouver, and 1.33 standard deviations below the mean in Lake Louise.

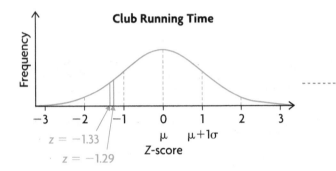

I sketched the standard normal curve, which has a mean of zero and a standard deviation of 1. Then I drew a line on the graph for each z-score.

The z-score for Hailey's Lake Louise run is farther to the left than the z-score for her Vancouver run.

Hailey's time for 200 m was better than the club's mean in both locations. However, Hailey's z-score for Lake Louise was lower than her z-score for Vancouver, so her time was better in Lake Louise.

I can make this comparison because both times have been translated to a normal distribution that has the same mean and standard deviation.

Reflecting

A. Use z-scores to determine which of Serge's runs was better.

B. Explain why the lower z-score represents a relatively faster run.

C. What can you say about a data value if you know that its z-score is negative? positive? zero?

APPLY *the Math*

EXAMPLE 2

Using *z*-scores to determine the percent of data less than a given value

IQ tests are sometimes used to measure a person's intellectual capacity at a particular time. IQ scores are normally distributed, with a mean of 100 and a standard deviation of 15. If a person scores 119 on an IQ test, how does this score compare with the scores of the general population?

Malia's Solution: Using a *z*-score table

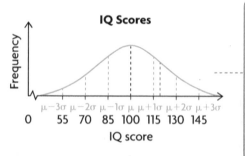

IQ Scores

First, I sketched a normal curve and determined the IQ scores for one, two, and three standard deviations from the mean.

Then I drew a line that represented an IQ score of 119.

I noticed that my line was between one and two standard deviations above the mean.

$$z = \frac{x - \mu}{\sigma}$$

$$z = \frac{119 - 100}{15}$$

$$z = 1.2666...$$

I determined the *z*-score for an IQ of 119.

An IQ score of 119 is about 1.27 standard deviations above the mean. I sketched this on a standard normal curve.

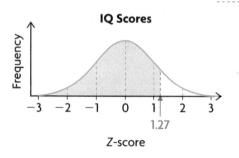

IQ Scores

I knew that I needed to determine the percent of people with IQ scores less than 119. This is equivalent to the area under the curve to the left of 1.27 on the standard normal curve.

A table that displays the fraction of data with a z-score that is less than any given data value in a standard normal distribution.
(There is a z-score table on pages 580 to 581.)

z	0.0	0.01	0.06	0.07
0.0	0.5000	0.5040	0.5239	0.5279
0.1	0.5398	0.5438	0.5636	0.5675
1.1	0.8643	0.8665	0.8770	0.8790
1.2	0.8849	0.8869	0.8962	**0.8980**
1.3	0.9032	0.9049	0.9131	0.9147

The value in the z-score table is 0.8980. This means that an IQ score of 119 is greater than 89.80% of IQ scores in the general population.

I used a **z-score table** .

$1.27 = 1.2 + 0.07$

I used the 1.2 row and the 0.07 column.

The value in the table, 0.8980, is the fraction of the area under the curve to the left of the z-score.

Desiree's Solution: Using a graphing calculator

I used the statistics function for normal distributions on my calculator to determine the percent of the population that has an IQ score between 0 and 119.

I entered the lower bound of 0, the upper bound of 119, the mean of 100, and the standard deviation of 15.

An IQ score of 119 is greater than 89.74% of all the scores.

My solution is slightly different from Malia's because this method does not use a rounded z-score.

Your Turn

Megan determined the area under the normal curve using slightly different reasoning: "I know that the total area under a normal curve is 100%, so the area under the curve to the left of the mean is 50%. I used my graphing calculator to calculate the area between a z-score of 0 and a z-score of 1.27, by entering these as the lower and upper bounds. My calculator gave a result of 0.397... ."

How could Megan use this result to complete her solution?

EXAMPLE **3** Using *z*-scores to determine data values

Athletes should replace their running shoes before the shoes lose their ability to absorb shock.

Running shoes lose their shock-absorption after a mean distance of 640 km, with a standard deviation of 160 km. Zack is an elite runner and wants to replace his shoes at a distance when only 25% of people would replace their shoes. At what distance should he replace his shoes?

Rachelle's Solution: Using a *z*-score table

I sketched the standard normal curve. I needed the *z*-score for 25% of the area under the curve, or 0.25.

z	0.09	0.08	0.07	0.06	0.05
−0.7	0.2148	0.2177	0.2206	0.2236	0.2266
−0.6	0.2451	0.2483	0.2514	0.2546	0.2578
−0.5	0.2776	0.2810	0.2843	0.2877	0.2912

I searched the *z*-score table for a value that is close to 0.25.

The *z*-score that represents an area of 0.25 is about halfway between −0.67 and −0.68, or about −0.675.

$$z = \frac{x - \mu}{\sigma}$$

$$(-0.675) = \frac{x - (640)}{(160)}$$

$$-108 = x - 640$$

$$532 = x$$

I substituted the values I knew into the *z*-score formula and solved for *x*.

Zack should replace his running shoes after 532 km.

Renalda's Solution: Using a graphing calculator

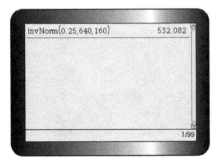

invNorm(0.25,640,160)   532.082

1/99

I used the statistics function on my calculator.

I entered the decimal value for the percent of data to the left of the z-score I needed. Then I entered the mean and standard deviation of the data.

Zack should replace his running shoes after 532 km.

Therefore, 25% of people would replace their shoes after 532 km.

Your Turn

Quinn is a recreational runner. He plans to replace his running shoes when 70% of people would replace their shoes. After how many kilometres should he replace his running shoes?

EXAMPLE 4   Solving a quality control problem

The ABC Company produces bungee cords. When the manufacturing process is running well, the lengths of the bungee cords produced are normally distributed, with a mean of 45.2 cm and a standard deviation of 1.3 cm. Bungee cords that are shorter than 42.0 cm or longer than 48.0 cm are rejected by the quality control workers.

a) If 20 000 bungee cords are manufactured each day, how many bungee cords would you expect the quality control workers to reject?
b) What action might the company take as a result of these findings?

Logan's Solution: Using a z-score table

a) Minimum length = 42 cm   Maximum length = 48 cm

$$z_{min} = \frac{x - \mu}{\sigma}$$

$$z_{max} = \frac{x - \mu}{\sigma}$$

$$z_{min} = \frac{42.0 - 45.2}{1.3}$$

$$z_{max} = \frac{48.0 - 45.2}{1.3}$$

$$z_{min} = -2.461...$$

$$z_{max} = 2.153...$$

I determined the z-scores for the minimum and maximum acceptable lengths.

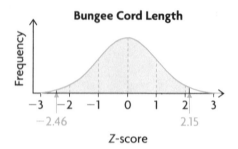

Bungee Cord Length

Frequency

−3 −2 −1 0 1 2 3

−2.46   2.15

Z-score

I sketched the standard normal curve. The area under the curve to the left of −2.46 represents the percent of rejected bungee cords less than 42 cm. The area under the curve to the right of 2.15 represents the percent of rejected bungee cords greater than 48 cm.

Area to left of −2.46 = 0.0069

Area to right of 2.15 = 1 − 0.9842
Area to right of 2.15 = 0.0158

I looked up each z-score in the z-score table. The z-score table gives the area to the left of the z-score, which I want for 42 cm.

Since I wanted the area to the right of the z-score for 48 cm, I had to subtract the corresponding area from 1.

Percent rejected = Area to the left of −2.46
                            + Area to the right of 2.15
Percent rejected = 0.0069 + 0.0158
Percent rejected = 0.0227 or 2.27%

I added the two areas to determine the percent of bungee cords that are rejected.

Total rejected = (0.0227)(20 000) or 454

I determined the number of bungee cords that are rejected.

b) ABC needs a more consistent process, because 454 seems like a large number of bungee cords to reject. The company should adjust its equipment so that the standard deviation is lowered.

Lowering the standard deviation will reduce the percent of rejected bungee cords.

Nathan's Solution: Using a graphing calculator

a)

normCdf(42, 48, 45.2, 1.3)   0.9774568

1/99

I used the statistics function on my calculator to determine the percent of bungee cords that are an acceptable length. I entered the minimum and maximum acceptable lengths and then the mean and standard deviation.

Number accepted = 20 000 × 0.977...
Number accepted = 19 549.135...
About 19 549 bungee cords meet the standard every day, so 451 bungee cords are rejected every day.

I determined the number of bungee cords that meet the standard. Then I subtracted to determine the number rejected.

My solution is slightly different from Logan's solution because this method does not use a rounded z-score value.

b) I think the company should adjust its
equipment to get a lower standard deviation,
so fewer bungee cords are discarded.

Your Turn

a) What percent of all the bungee cords are accepted?
b) A client has placed an order for 12 000 bungee cords, but will only
accept bungee cords that are between 44.0 cm and 46.0 cm in length.
Can this client's order be filled by one day's production, with the
equipment operating as is? Explain.

EXAMPLE 5   Determining warranty periods

A manufacturer of personal music players has determined that the mean
life of the players is 32.4 months, with a standard deviation of 6.3 months.
What length of warranty should be offered if the manufacturer wants to
restrict repairs to less than 1.5% of all the players sold?

Sacha's Solution

1.5% = 0.015

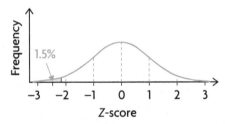

I used my graphing calculator to determine
the z-score that corresponds to an area under
the normal curve of 0.015.

$z = -2.17$

$$z = \frac{x - \mu}{\sigma}$$

$$(-2.17) = \frac{x - (32.4)}{(6.3)}$$

$$-13.671 = x - 32.4$$

$$18.729 = x$$

I substituted the known values into the z-score
formula and solved for x.

The manufacturer should offer an
18-month warranty.

Since the manufacturer wants to repair less than
1.5% of the music players, I rounded down to
18 months.

Your Turn

a) If 10 000 personal music players are sold, how many could the manufacturer expect to receive for repairs under warranty?

b) The manufacturer wants to offer the option of purchasing an extended warranty. If the manufacturer wants to repair, at most, 20% of the players under the extended warranty, what length of extended warranty should be offered?

In Summary

Key Ideas

- The standard normal distribution is a normal distribution with mean, μ, of 0 and a standard deviation, σ, of 1. The area under the curve of a normal distribution is 1.
- Z-scores can be used to compare data from different normally distributed sets by converting their distributions to the standard normal distribution.

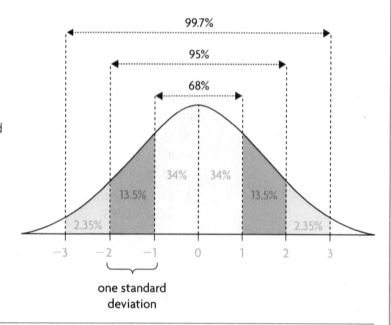

Need to Know

- A z-score indicates the number of standard deviations that a data value lies from the mean. It is calculated using this formula:

$$z = \frac{x - \mu}{\sigma}$$

- A positive z-score indicates that the data value lies above the mean. A negative z-score indicates that the data value lies below the mean.
- The area under the standard normal curve, to the left of a particular z-score, can be found in a z-score table or determined using a graphing calculator.

CHECK Your Understanding

1. Determine the z-score for each value of x.
   a) $\mu = 112, \sigma = 15.5, x = 174$
   c) $\mu = 82, \sigma = 12.5, x = 58$
   b) $\mu = 53.46, \sigma = 8.24, x = 47.28$
   d) $\mu = 245, \sigma = 22.4, x = 300$

2. Using a z-score table (such as the table on pages 580 to 581), determine the percent of the data to the left of each z-score.
   a) $z = 1.24$
   b) $z = -2.35$
   c) $z = 2.17$
   d) $z = -0.64$

3. Determine the percent of the data between each pair of z-scores.
   a) $z = -2.88$ and $z = -1.47$
   b) $z = -0.85$ and $z = 1.64$

4. What z-score is required for each situation?
   a) 10% of the data is to the left of the z-score.
   b) 10% of the data is to the right of the z-score.
   c) 60% of the data is below the z-score.
   d) 60% of the data is above the z-score.

PRACTISING

In the following questions, assume that the data approximates a normal distribution.

5. Calculate the z-score for each value of x.
   a) $\mu = 24, \sigma = 2.8, x = 29.3$
   c) $\mu = 784, \sigma = 65.3, x = 817$
   b) $\mu = 165, \sigma = 48, x = 36$
   d) $\mu = 2.9, \sigma = 0.3, x = 3.4$

6. Determine the percent of the data to the left of each z-score.
   a) $z = 0.56$
   b) $z = -1.76$
   c) $z = -2.98$
   d) $z = 2.39$

7. Determine the percent of the data to the right of each z-score.
   a) $z = -1.35$
   b) $z = 2.63$
   c) $z = 0.68$
   d) $z = -3.14$

8. Determine the percent of the data between each pair of z-scores.
   a) $z = 0.24$ and $z = 2.53$
   b) $z = -1.64$ and $z = 1.64$

9. Determine the z-score for each situation.
   a) 33% of the data is to the left of the z-score.
   b) 20% of the data is to the right of the z-score.

10. Meg wonders if she should consider a career in the sciences, because she does well in mathematics. However, she also does well in English and has thought about becoming a journalist.
    a) Determine the z-score for each of Meg's marks.
    b) Which subject is Meg better in, relative to her peers?
    c) What other factors should Meg consider?

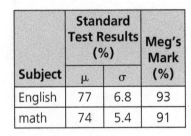

Subject	Standard Test Results (%)		Meg's Mark (%)
	μ	σ	
English	77	6.8	93
math	74	5.4	91

11. A hardwood flooring company produces flooring that has an average thickness of 175 mm, with a standard deviation of 0.4 mm. For premium-quality floors, the flooring must have a thickness between 174 mm and 175.6 mm. What percent, to the nearest whole number, of the total production can be sold for premium-quality floors?

12. Violeta took part in a study that compared the heart-rate responses of water walking versus treadmill walking for healthy college females. Violeta's heart rate was 68 on the treadmill for the 2.55 km/h walk and 145 in the water for the 3.02 km/h walk. For which event was her heart rate lower, compared with the others who took part in the study?

Speed	Treadmill (beats/min)		Water (beats/min)	
	μ	σ	μ	σ
Resting	68	8.43	71	6.15
2.55 km/h	76	9.15	130	13.50
2.77 km/h	79	11.66	146	11.96
3.02 km/h	81	11.33	160	13.50
3.31 km/h	81	10.27	167	12.58

13. In 2006, the ages of mothers who had children aged 4 and under were approximately normally distributed, with a mean age of 32 years and a standard deviation of 5.9 years. The data is shown in the table at the right.
   a) Determine the percent of mothers who were less than 40 years old.
   b) Determine the percent of mothers who were less than 21 years old.
   c) Determine the percent of mothers who were 18 years old or less. Why might someone want to know this?

Age of Mother (years)	2006 Census (%)
15 – 19	1.1
20 – 24	8.8
25 – 29	23.2
30 – 34	33.7
35 – 39	23.8
40 – 44	8.2
45 – 49	1.2
Total	100

14. In a population, 50% of the adults are taller than 180 cm and 10% are taller than 200 cm. Determine the mean height and standard deviation for this population.

15. A medical diagnostic test counts the number of blood cells in a sample. The red blood cell count (in millions per cubic microlitre) is normally distributed, with a mean of 4.8 and a standard deviation of 0.3.
   a) What percent of people have a red blood cell count that is less than 4?
   b) What percent of people have a count between 4.7 and 5.0?
   c) What red blood cell count would someone have if 95% of people have a lower count?

16. An MP3 player has a one-year warranty. The mean lifespan of the player is 2.6 years, with a standard deviation of 0.48 years.
   a) A store sells 4000 players. How many of these players will fail before the warranty expires?
   b) Tyler is offered an extended warranty, for one extra year, when he buys a player. What is the likelihood that he will make a claim on this warranty if he takes it?

17. A manufacturer of plasma televisions has determined that the televisions require servicing after a mean of 67 months, with a standard deviation of 7.2 months. What length of warranty should be offered, if the manufacturer wants to repair less than 1% of the televisions under the warranty?

18. A tutor guarantees that 10% of her students will obtain an A on every test they write. For the last test, the mean mark is 68 and the standard deviation is 6. What mark is required to receive an A on the test?

19. In the insurance industry, standard deviation is used to quantify risk—the greater the risk, the higher the standard deviation. For example, consider the cost of a car accident for two different cars: a high-priced luxury car and a mid-priced car. The expected cost of repairs for both cars is $2500. However, the standard deviation for the high-priced car is $1000, and the standard deviation for the mid-priced car is $400. Explain why the probability that the repairs will cost more than $3000 is 31% for the high-priced car but only 11% for the mid-priced car.

20. **a)** A club accepts members only if they have an IQ score that is greater than the scores for 98% of the population. What IQ score would you need to be accepted into this club? (Recall that $\mu = 100$ and $\sigma = 15$ for the general population.)

   b) Only 0.38% of the population are considered to be geniuses, as measured by IQ scores. What is the minimum IQ score that is required to be considered a genius?

   c) Jarrod was told that his IQ score is in the top 30% of the population. What is his IQ score?

Closing

21. What is a z-score, how do you determine it, and what is it used for?

Extending

22. A company packages sugar into 5 kg bags. The filling machine can be calibrated to fill to any specified mean, with a standard deviation of 0.065 kg. Any bags with masses that are less than 4.9 kg cannot be sold and must be repackaged.

   a) If the company wants to repackage no more than 3% of the bags, at what mean should they set the machine?

   b) Assuming that the company sets the machine at the mean you determined in part a), what percent of the bags will have more than 5 kg of sugar? Do you think the company will be satisfied with this percent?

23. Approximately 40% of those who take the LSAT, or Law School Admission Test, score from 145 to 155. About 70% score from 140 to 160.

   a) Determine the mean score and standard deviation for the LSAT.

   b) Harvard University also uses other methods to choose students for its law school, but the minimum LSAT score that is required is about 172. What percent of people who take the LSAT would be considered by Harvard for admission?

24. Create your own problem involving z-score analysis, using any of the normally distributed data from Lesson 5.4. Exchange problems with classmates, and solve the problems. Provide suggestions for improving the problems.

The LSAT must be taken by people who want to gain admission to a law school. The test focuses on logical and verbal reasoning skills.

Confidence Intervals

GOAL

Use the normal distribution to solve problems that involve confidence intervals.

YOU WILL NEED

- calculator
- z-score tables (pages 580 to 581)

LEARN ABOUT the Math

A telephone survey of 600 randomly selected people was conducted in an urban area. The survey determined that 76% of people, from 18 to 34 years of age, have a social networking account.

The results are accurate within plus or minus 4 percent points, 19 times out of 20.

? How can this result be interpreted, if the total population of 18- to 34-year-olds is 92 500?

EXAMPLE 1   Analyzing and applying survey results

Calculate the range of people that have a social networking account, and determine the certainty of the results.

Danica's Solution

The **margin of error** for the data is ± 4%, so the **confidence interval** is 76% ± 4%, which is from (76 − 4)% or 72% to (76 + 4)% or 80%.

> I interpreted the survey statement.

The **confidence level** of the survey is 95%. The probability of error for this result is 5%. If the survey were conducted 100 times, then 95 times out of 100, the percent of people in the population with a social networking account would be from 72% to 80%.

> The results are accurate 19 times out of 20, which is 95% of the time.

EXPLORE...

- Often it is impractical to survey an entire population. For example, if a light bulb company wants to test the number of hours that a light bulb will burn before failing, it cannot test every bulb. Propose a method that the company could use to determine the longevity of its light bulbs.

margin of error

The possible difference between the estimate of the value you're trying to determine, as determined from a random sample, and the true value for the population; the margin of error is generally expressed as a plus or minus percent, such as ±5%.

confidence interval

The interval in which the true value you're trying to determine is estimated to lie, with a stated degree of probability; the confidence interval may be expressed using ± notation, such as 54.0% ± 3.5%, or ranging from 50.5% to 57.5%.

confidence level

The likelihood that the result for the "true" population lies within the range of the confidence interval; surveys and other studies usually use a confidence level of 95%, although 90% or 99% is sometimes used.

92 500 × 76% = 70 300
92 500 × 4% = 3700
The confidence interval for the
population is 70 300 ± 3700.

> I used the confidence interval,
> 76% ± 4%, and the population,
> 92 500, to calculate the range
> of the number of people in the
> population who have a social
> networking account.

70 300 − 3700 = 66 600
70 300 + 3700 = 74 000
It can be said, with 95% confidence,
that 66 600 to 74 000 people, in a
population of 92 500 people from
ages 18 to 34, have a social networking account.

Reflecting

A. Based on this survey, what is the range for 18- to 34-year-olds who do not have a social networking account?

B. The same telephone survey was conducted by a different company, using a sample of 600 randomly selected people in both urban and rural areas. According to this survey, 76% of people, from 18 to 34 years of age, have a social networking account. (The results are accurate within plus or minus 5.3 percent points, 99 times out of 100.) How are the results of this survey different from those of the first survey? How are they the same?

APPLY the Math

| EXAMPLE 2 | Analyzing the effect of sample size on margin of error and confidence intervals |

Polling organizations in Canada frequently survey samples of the population to gauge voter preference prior to elections. People are asked:

1. "If an election were held today, which party would you vote for?"

If they say they don't know, then they are asked:

2. "Which party are you leaning toward voting for?"

The results of three different polls taken during the first week of November, 2010, are shown on the next page. The results of each poll are considered accurate 19 times out of 20.

Polling Organization & Data	Conservative (%)	Liberal (%)	NDP (%)	Bloc Quebecois (%)	Green Party (%)	Other (%)
Ekos	29	29	19	9	11	3
sample size, 1815 margin of error, ±2.3%						
Nanos	37	32	15	11	5	n.a.
sample size, 844 margin of error, ±3.4%						
Ipsos	35	29	12	11	12	n.a.
sample size, 1000 margin of error, ±3.1%						

source: http://www.sfu.ca/~aheard/elections/polls.html

How does the sample size used in a poll affect:
a) the margin of error in the reported results?
b) the confidence interval in the reported results?

Martin's Solution

a) $\dfrac{19}{20} = 95\%$

In this case, the confidence level used by each polling organization is the same. This enables me to compare the effect that sample size has on the margin of error.

The confidence level of each poll is 95%.

	Nanos	Ipsos	Ekos
sample size	844	1000	1815
margin of error	±3.4%	±3.1%	±2.3%

I created a table to compare the polls. I arranged the polls in increasing order of sample size, then looked for a trend in the margin of error.

If polls are assessed using the same confidence level, when the sample size increases, the margin of error decreases.

A larger sample size results in the possibility of a poll that more accurately represents the population.

My observation makes sense because a larger sample should be a better indicator of how the population might vote.

b) Let n represent the number of people polled.

Nanos

$n = 844$

37% ± 3.4% or 33.6% to 40.4%

> I decided to compare the confidence interval for the Conservative Party for each of the 3 different polls. I wrote the confidence interval for each poll in increasing order of sample size.

Ipsos

$n = 1000$

35% ± 3.1% or 31.9% to 38.1%

Ekos

$n = 1815$

29% ± 2.3% or 26.7% to 31.3%

The Nanos poll predicts that 33.6% to 40.4% of the population will vote for a Conservative. That is a range of 6.8%.

> I interpreted each of the confidence intervals for these polls.

The Ipsos poll predicts that 31.9 % to 38.1% of the population will vote for a Conservative. That is a range of 6.2%.

The Ekos poll predicts that 26.7% to 31.3% of the population will vote for a Conservative. That is a range of 4.6%.

If polls are conducted using the same confidence level, when the sample size increases, the range in the confidence interval decreases.

> My observation makes sense because the confidence interval is determined by the margin of error. So, as the sample size increases, the margin of error decreases and in turn the range of the confidence interval decreases.

Your Turn

Compare the confidence intervals for the Liberal Party for each of the three polls. Do your results reflect Martin's results above? Explain.

EXAMPLE 3   Analyzing the effect of confidence levels on sample size

To meet regulation standards, baseballs must have a mass from 142.0 g to 149.0 g. A manufacturing company has set its production equipment to create baseballs that have a mean mass of 145.0 g.

To ensure that the production equipment continues to operate as expected, the quality control engineer takes a random sample of baseballs each day and measures their mass to determine the mean mass. If the mean mass of the random sample is 144.7 g to 145.3 g, then the production equipment is running correctly. If the mean mass of the sample is outside the acceptable level, the production equipment is shut down and adjusted. The quality control engineer refers to the chart shown on the next page when conducting random sampling.

Confidence Level	Sample Size Needed
99%	110
95%	65
90%	45

a) What is the confidence interval and margin of error the engineer is using for quality control tests?
b) Interpret the table.
c) What is the relationship between confidence level and sample size?

Geoffrey's Solution

a) The confidence interval is 144.7 g to 145.3 g.

> The confidence interval is the range that the mean mass of the random sample can fall in and be acceptable.

Margin of error:
145.3 − 145.0 or 0.3
144.7 − 145.0 or −0.3
The margin of error is ±0.3 g.

> I subtracted the mean from the upper and lower limits of the confidence interval to determine the margin of error.

b) • In order to be confident that, 99 out of 100 times, the mean mass of the sample measures from 144.7 g to 145.3 g, the engineer needs to take a random sample of 110 baseballs from the production line.
• In order to be confident that, 95 out of 100 times, the mean mass of the sample measures from 144.7 g to 145.3 g, the engineer needs to take a random sample of 65 baseballs from the production line.
• In order to be confident that, 90 out of 100 times, the mean mass of the sample measures from 144.7 g to 145.3 g, the engineer needs to take a random sample of 55 baseballs from the production line.

> I interpreted each entry in the table.

c) For a constant margin of error, as the confidence level increases, the size of the sample needed to attain that confidence level increases. To have greater confidence that the baseballs meet quality standards, the engineer must use a larger sample.

> I observed the trend in the table.

Your Turn

After making adjustments in equipment, the quality control engineer decided that the mean mass of baseballs must lie in the range 144.2 g to 146.4 g.
a) What margin of error is being used in the new sampling process?
b) What is the mean mass of a baseball that the engineer is trying to achieve?
c) Will the new baseballs meet regulation standards?

EXAMPLE **4**   Analyzing statistical data to support a position

A poll was conducted to ask voters the following question: If an election were held today, whom would you vote for? The results indicated that 53% would vote for Smith and 47% would vote for Jones. The results were stated as being accurate within 3.8 percent points, 19 times out of 20. Who will win the election?

Kylie's Solution

Smith would have 53% of the votes, and Jones would have only 47% of the votes. Based on these numbers, Smith should win.

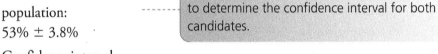
I examined the mean percent of votes that each candidate would receive, based on the poll.

Percent of votes for Jones in the population: 47% ± 3.8%	Percent of votes for Smith in the population: 53% ± 3.8%
Confidence interval: 43.2% to 50.8%	Confidence interval: 49.2% to 56.8%

The margin of error is 3.8%. I used this value to determine the confidence interval for both candidates.

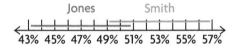

The two confidence intervals overlap from 49.2% to 50.8%.

I graphed the confidence intervals on a number line.

If the poll is accurate, Smith is more likely to win. However, there also is a chance that Jones will win, since the confidence intervals overlap by 1.6% of the votes.

If voters' opinions are the same on election day, Smith may receive only 49.5% of the votes and Jones could receive 50.5% of the votes.

Your Turn

Is it possible that Smith could receive more than 56.8% of the votes, according to this survey? Explain why or why not.

In Summary

Key Ideas

- It is often impractical, if not impossible, to obtain data for a complete population. Instead, random samples of the population are taken, and the mean and standard deviation of the data are determined. This information is then used to make predictions about the population.
- When data approximates a normal distribution, a confidence interval indicates the range in which the mean of any sample of data of a given size would be expected to lie, with a stated level of confidence. This confidence interval can then be used to estimate the range of the mean for the population.
- Sample size, confidence level, and population size determine the size of the confidence interval for a given confidence level.

Need to Know

- A confidence interval is expressed as the survey or poll result, plus or minus the margin of error.
- The margin of error increases as the confidence level increases (with a constant sample size). The sample size that is needed also increases as the confidence level increases (with a constant margin of error).
- The sample size affects the margin of error. A larger sample results in a smaller margin of error, assuming that the same confidence level is required.

  For example:
  - A sample of 1000 is considered to be accurate to within $\pm 3.1\%$, 19 times out of 20.
  - A sample of 2000 is considered to be accurate to within $\pm 2.2\%$, 19 times out of 20.
  - A sample of 3000 is considered to be accurate to within $\pm 1.8\%$, 19 times out of 20.

CHECK *Your Understanding*

In the following questions, assume that the data approximates a normal distribution.

1. A poll determined that 81% of people who live in Canada know that climate change is affecting Inuit more than the rest of Canadians. The results of the survey are considered accurate within ±3.1 percent points, 19 times out of 20.

   a) State the confidence level.
   b) Determine the confidence interval.
   c) The population of Canada was 33.5 million at the time of the survey. State the range of the number of people who knew that climate change is affecting Inuit more than the rest of Canadians.

2. A cereal company takes a random sample to check the masses of boxes of cereal. For a sample of 200 boxes, the mean mass is 542 g, with a margin of error of ±1.9 g. The result is considered accurate 95% of the time.

   a) State the confidence interval for the mean mass of the cereal boxes.
   b) Three other samples of different sizes were taken using the same confidence level, as shown at left, but the margin of error for each sample was mixed up. Match the correct margin of error with each sample size.

Sample Size	Margin of Error (g)
50	1.2
100	3.9
500	2.7

PRACTISING

3. An advertisement for a new toothpaste states that 64% of users reported better dental checkups. The results of the poll are accurate within 3.4 percent points, 9 times out of 10.

   a) State the confidence level.
   b) Determine the confidence interval.
   c) If all 32 students in a mathematics class used this toothpaste, determine the range of the mean number of classmates who could expect better dental checkups.

4. In a 2006 Centre de recherche sur l'opinion publique (CROP) poll, 81% of Canadians indicated that they support bilingualism in Canada and that they want Canada to remain a bilingual country. This poll was reported accurate ±2.2%, 19 times out of 20.

   a) Interpret the poll.
   b) Mark claims that this poll must be flawed because if the majority of Canadians felt this way, then most people would speak both French and English, but they don't. Do you agree with Mark? Justify your decision.

5. The responses to another question in the poll from question 1 were summarized as follows: 58% of people living in Canada know that the cost of living for the average Inuit is 50% higher than the cost of living for other Canadians.

a) Determine the confidence interval for this question.
b) Predict the range of the mean number of people in your city or town who could have answered this question correctly.

6. Toxic materials, such as arsenic, lead, and mercury, can be released into the air if a discarded cellphone is incinerated. Toxins can be released into groundwater if a discarded cellphone ends up in a landfill. In a recent survey, 89% of those surveyed answered yes to the following question: Would you recycle your cellphone if it were convenient? The survey is considered accurate to within 4.3 percent points, 99 times out of 100.

a) Determine the confidence level and the confidence interval.
b) If 23 500 000 people in Canada own cellphones, state the range of the number of people who would indicate that they would recycle their cellphone if it were convenient.

7. a) Look in print or electronic media to find an example of a poll or survey that used a confidence level to report the results.
b) Determine the confidence interval.
c) Do you agree or disagree with any concluding statements that were made about the data from the poll or survey? Explain.

8. A company produces regulation ultimate discs. The discs have a mean mass of 175.0 g, with a standard deviation of 0.9 g. To ensure that few discs are rejected, the quality control manager must ensure that the mean mass of the discs lies in the acceptable range of 174.8 g to 175.2 g. During each shift, a random sample of discs is selected and the mass of each disc in the sample is measured. The table shown helps guide the sampling process.

a) What is the confidence interval and margin of error this company is using for its quality control tests?
b) Approximately how many discs should be measured to ensure the mean mass is within ±0.2 g, 99% of the time?
c) The manager wants to save on labour costs by using a smaller sample. She knows that any discs that do not meet the regulation standards can be sold as recreational discs. Approximately how many discs should be measured to ensure that the mean mass is within ±0.2 g, 90% of the time?
d) Estimate the number of discs the company should measure to be confident that the mean mass of the ultimate discs lies in the acceptable range 19 times out of 20.

Confidence Level	Sample Size Needed
90%	55
95%	78
99%	135

Finding and Interpreting Data in the Media

Research and polling firms regularly conduct surveys of samples of specific populations in areas such as agribusiness, food and animal health, energy, financial services, health care, higher education, lotteries and gaming, media and entertainment, retail, technology and communications, travel and tourism, and public opinion on political issues. Many companies and organizations rely on the data that is collected to make business and marketing decisions.

- With a partner or in a small group, look in print or electronic media for examples that cite confidence intervals or confidence levels. List the important statistical information that is given.
- Do you agree or disagree with the statements about the survey results in your examples? Use your knowledge of statistics to support your reasoning.
- What could be done to change the outcome of a future survey about one of these subjects? (For example, many different approaches have been taken to curb smoking addictions in Canada.)
- How much of a change would there have to be in the survey responses to make the outcome noticeably different?

9. Use confidence intervals to interpret each of the following statements.

a) In a recent survey, 54% of post-secondary graduates indicated that they expected to earn at least $100 000/year by the time they retire. The survey is considered accurate within $\pm 4.5\%$, 9 times in 10.

b) A market research firm found that among online shoppers, 63% search for online coupons or deals when they purchase something on the Internet. The survey is considered accurate within ± 2.1 percent points, 99% of the time.

c) A recent report indicated that Canadians spend an average of 18.1 h per week online, compared with 16.9 h per week watching television. The results are considered accurate with a margin of error of $\pm 3.38\%$, 19 times out of 20.

d) A survey conducted at the expense of the political party that holds office indicated that 39% of decided voters said they would not vote for candidates of that party in the next election. The result is considered accurate within $\pm 3\%$, 95% of the time.

Closing

10. Explain why, for a given confidence level,

a) the margin of error decreases as the sample size increases

b) the margin of error increases as the confidence level increases

Extending

11. As sample size increases, the margin of error, expressed as a percent, decreases. Consider the table below.

Sample Size	Margin of Error (%)
100	9.80
400	4.90
900	3.27
1600	2.45
2500	1.96
3600	1.63

a) What mathematical relationship exists between increased sample size and the margin of error?

b) What would be the margin of error for a sample size of
i) 4900
ii) 2000

c) Use your results from parts a) and b) to explain why a relatively small sample will give a fairly accurate indication of the trend for an entire population.

1. Students recorded their heights, in inches, when they graduated from kindergarten in 1999 and again when they graduated from high school in 2011.

   1999: 39 41 41 43 45 46 47 46 48 47 44 38 41 39 43 46 44

   2011: 60 74 76 62 64 61 66 68 71 76 74 73 72 69 64 63 60

   a) Determine the mean and standard deviation for each year.
   b) Compare the heights for the two years. Which set of heights has a greater standard deviation? Describe some of the possible reasons for this greater deviation.

2. The chest circumferences of Scottish militiamen in the 19th century are given in the frequency table to the right.

   a) Are the chest circumferences normally distributed? Explain.
   b) Determine the z-score for a Scottish militiaman with a 42 in. chest circumference.

Chest Circumference (in.)	Frequency
33	3
34	18
35	81
36	185
37	420
38	749
39	1073
40	1079
41	934
42	658
43	370
44	92
45	50
46	21
47	4
48	1

3. Brenda searched the Environment Canada website and found that the mean daily temperature in Edmonton in March is $-2.6\ °C$, with a standard deviation of $3.2\ °C$. The mean daily temperature in Calgary in March is $-1.9\ °C$, with a standard deviation of $2.8\ °C$. Compare the temperatures at these two locations in March.

4. In a Canada Day poll, 1009 Canadians were asked "What are things about Canada that make you proud?" 88% of respondents said the flag, 80% said hockey, and 44% said the Canadian justice system. The poll was reported accurate to within $\pm3.1\%$, 19 times out of 20.

   a) Use confidence intervals to interpret the poll results.
   b) At the time of the poll, Statistics Canada estimated Canada's population at 34 019 000. Determine the range of people in Canada, based on this poll, who would answer hockey makes them proud of Canada.
   c) If the polling company conducted this same survey using the same sample size, but used a confidence level of 99%, what would happen to the margin of error? Explain.

WHAT DO You Think Now? Revisit **What Do You Think?** on page 237. How have your answers and explanations changed?

FREQUENTLY ASKED Questions

Study Aid
- See Lesson 5.4, Examples 1 and 2.
- Try Chapter Review Questions 7 and 8.

Q: **What is a normal distribution, and what are its properties?**

A: When data is normally distributed, 50% of the data is above the mean and 50% is below the mean. This makes the distribution symmetrical. The measures of central tendency are equal or close to each other. The graph of a normal distribution (data

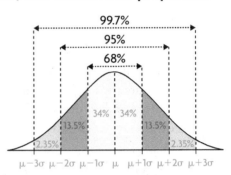

values versus frequency) is a bell curve. For a normal distribution, approximately 68% of the data is within one standard deviation of the mean, 95% is within two standard deviations of the mean, and 99.7% is within three standard deviations of the mean.

Study Aid
- See Lesson 5.5, Examples 1, 2, and 3.
- Try Chapter Review Questions 9 and 10.

Q: **What is a z-score, and how do I calculate it?**

A: A z-score indicates the distance of a data value from the mean of the set, measured in standard deviations. If the z-score is positive, the data value is greater than the mean. If the z-score is negative, the data value is less than the mean.

For example, a z-score of 2.00 means that the data value is 2.00 standard deviations above the mean.

To calculate a z-score, use the following formula:

$$z = \frac{x - \mu}{\sigma}$$

To determine the z-score, given $x = 23.5$, $\mu = 18.6$, and $\sigma = 3.2$, substitute each value into the z-score formula.

$$z = \frac{23.5 - 18.6}{3.2}$$

$$z = 1.531...$$

The value is about 1.53 standard deviations above the mean.

Q: **How do I compare two values from two normally distributed sets of data?**

A: Determine the z-score of each piece of data. The value with the higher z-score is the greater relative value.

City	μ ($)	σ ($)
Edmonton	375 000	75 000
Calgary	415 000	80 000

Study **Aid**
• See Lesson 5.5, Example 1.
• Try Chapter Review Question 10.

For example, Max sells his house in Edmonton for $392 000 and purchases a house in Calgary for $417 000. The mean and standard deviations for houses in each city are shown in the table above.

Edmonton:	Calgary:
$z = \dfrac{392\ 000 - 375\ 000}{75\ 000}$	$z = \dfrac{417\ 000 - 415\ 000}{80\ 000}$
$z = 0.226...$	$z = 0.025$

The house in Edmonton has the greater relative value because the z-score is higher.

Q: **What is the difference between margin of error, confidence interval, and confidence level?**

A: The purpose of a poll or survey is to gather information that can be used to make predictions about a population.

Study **Aid**
• See Lesson 5.6, Examples 1 and 4.
• Try Chapter Review Questions 11 and 12.

For example, in a recent telephone poll, 33% of Canadians, 18 years of age and older, thought that Olympic athletes who were caught using performance-enhancing drugs should be banned from competition for life (Nanos National Poll, Dec. 2009). The results were accurate to within 3.1 percent points, 19 times out of 20.

The margin of error is $\pm$ 3.1%, which indicates the sampling error in the poll. The margin of error can be combined with the result of the poll to generate a confidence interval. For this poll, we expect that if the entire population of Canadians, 18 years of age and older, were asked the same question, between 29.9% and 36.1% would indicate that they want drug-using athletes banned.

The confidence level of the poll is stated as 19 times out of 20, which is equivalent to 95%. If this poll were conducted over and over again, 95% of the time the result would fall within the confidence interval, 29.9% to 36.1%.

PRACTISING

Lesson 5.1

1. Twila and Amber keep a log of the amount of time, in minutes, they spend on homework each school day for two weeks. Determine the mean and range for each girl's data, and compare the two sets of data.

   Twila: 45   55   50   40   55   40   60   45   40   35

   Amber: 80   10   65   15   75   30   40   85   20   35

Lesson 5.2

2. Melody is comparing education levels of her generation with education levels of her parents' generation. She obtained the data in the table. Draw two frequency polygons on the same graph to compare the education levels. Comment on the results.

Level of Education	People 25 to 34 Years Old (%)	People 55 to 64 Years Old (%)
less than high school	11	23
high school diploma	23	24
trades certificate	10	13
college diploma	23	16
university certificate or diploma	5	6
university degree	29	18

Lesson 5.3

3. **a)** Predict which girl's data in question 1 will have the lowest standard deviation. Justify your answer.

   b) Determine the standard deviation for each girl's data. Was your prediction correct?

4. The following data was taken from a 2000 federal government survey on the mean salary in each province for three categories.

Education	Salary (thousands of dollars)												
Province	NL	PE	NS	NB	QC	ON	MB	SK	AB	BC	YT	NT	NU
no diploma	16	15	18	17	21	23	19	18	22	22	19	20	15
high school	17	18	21	20	24	28	23	22	26	26	26	32	27
post-secondary	31	29	33	32	35	44	34	33	41	38	38	48	43

   a) Determine the mean and standard deviation for each level of education.

   b) Which level of education yields the highest mean salary?

   c) Which level of education has the greatest variability in salary?

5. Marc usually puts a bag of either sunflower seeds or raisins in his lunch. The first table shows the number of sunflower seeds in the last 30 bags of sunflower seeds that Marc has had in his lunch. The second table shows the number of raisins in the last 30 bags of raisins that Marc has had in his lunch. Is Marc more likely to get the mean number of items in a bag of sunflower seeds or a bag of raisins? Justify your thinking.

Sunflower Seeds per Bag	28	29	30	31	32	33
Frequency	2	4	11	9	3	1

Raisins per Bag	27	28	29	30	31
Frequency	1	12	7	3	7

6. Scientists monitor the masses of polar bears. In 2010, the following data was obtained:

Adult Female	$\bar{x} = 247$ kg	$\sigma = 33$ kg
Adult Male	$\bar{x} = 461$ kg	$\sigma = 51$ kg

The masses of two polar bears were measured. The female had a mass of 277 kg, and the male had a mass of 499 kg. Use z-scores to determine which bear had the greater mass compared with other bears of the same sex.

Polar bears go ashore when the sea ice melts. If the sea ice melts too early in the year, the polar bears must go ashore before they are ready. This forces them into a prolonged fast. Global warming may result in polar bears becoming too thin to reproduce.

Lesson 5.4

7. Judy always waits until her gas tank is nearly empty before refuelling. She keeps track of the distance she drives on each tank of gas. The distance varies depending on the weather and the amount she drives on the highway. The distance has a mean of 824 km and a standard deviation of 28 km.

   a) Sketch a normal curve to show the distribution of the driving distances for a tank of gas. Mark the kilometres driven for values that are 1, 2, and 3 standard deviations from the mean.

   b) What percent of the time does Judy drive between 796 km and 852 km on a tank of gas?

   c) What percent of the time does she drive between 740 km and 796 km on a tank of gas?

   d) Between what two values will she drive 95% of the time?

8. The body temperatures of 130 adults are recorded in the frequency table to the right.

   a) Determine the mean and standard deviation of the data.

   b) Are the temperatures normally distributed? Explain.

Temperature (°C)	Frequency
35.8	2
36.0	3
36.2	5
36.4	11
36.6	14
36.8	29
37.0	27
37.2	20
37.4	13
37.6	3
37.8	2
38.0	0
38.2	0
38.4	1

9. TJ is a Congo African Grey parrot. This species of parrot has a life expectancy of 50 years, with a standard deviation of 8 years. What is the likelihood that TJ will live over 60 years?

10. *Computers For All* offers an extended 3-year replacement warranty on its computers. The mean lifespan of its computers is 3.8 years, with a standard deviation of 0.45. *Everything Electronic* offers a 2-year replacement warranty on its computers. The mean lifespan of an *Everything Electronic* computer is 2.6 years, with a standard deviation of 0.31. Which computer is more likely to fail before its warranty period is over?

Lesson 5.6

11. A poll was conducted to determine where Canadians obtain health-related information. 61.9% said they research information on the Internet, 68.9% said they ask friends or family, and 17.9% said they call a health line. The results of this survey are considered accurate within ±1.4 percent points, 99 times out of 100.

   a) Determine the confidence interval for each information source.
   b) In a city with an adult population of 345 000, predict the range of the number of adults who will say they use each source.

12. Two different market research companies conducted a survey on the same issue. Company A used a 99% confidence level and company B used a 95% confidence level.

   a) If both companies used a sample size of 1000, what does this imply about the margin of error for each survey?
   b) If both companies used the same margin of error of ±2%, what does this imply about the sample size for each survey?

True-False Tests

Sometimes you may have to make a decision based on limited or no knowledge.

Have you ever wondered what would happen if you guessed all the answers on a true-false test? Would it matter how many questions were on the test?

❓ How can you determine the likelihood of passing a true-false test if you guessed all the answers?

Part 1: Generate the Data

A. Write a short true-false question about yourself. Make sure that none of your classmates would know the answer to your question. Example: "The name of my first pet was Fido" or "I had spaghetti for dinner last Sunday." Give your question, along with the correct answer, to your teacher.

B. As a class, take the "test." Your teacher will read each question, and you will write "true" or "false" on a sheet of paper. Leave the answer to the question that you created blank. Your teacher will add one question at the end of the test.

C. Mark the tests as a class, and convert each test score to a percent. Record each person's score on the board, both with and without your teacher's question included.

Part 2: Analyze the Data

D. Determine the mean and standard deviation of the data that does not include your teacher's question. Is the data normally distributed? Explain.

E. Repeat step D for the data that includes your teacher's question.

F. Compare the results for the two sets of data. What do you notice?

G. Is it likely that you would pass a true-false test if you guessed all the answers?

Task | *Checklist*

✔ Did you present the data effectively?

✔ Did you use appropriate mathematical language?

✔ Were your conclusions presented clearly and concisely?

Analyzing Your Data

Statistical tools can help you analyze and interpret the data you collect. You need to think carefully about which statistical tool to use and when, because other people will be scrutinizing your data. A summary of relevant tools is given below.

Measures of Central Tendency

Selecting which measure of central tendency (mean, median, or mode) to use depends on the distribution of your data. As the researcher, you must decide which measure most accurately describes the tendencies of the population. Consider the following criteria when you are deciding which measure of central tendency best describes your set of data.

- Outliers affect the mean the most. If the data includes outliers, use the median to avoid misrepresenting the data. If you want to use the mean, remove the outliers before calculating the mean.
- If the distribution of the data is not symmetrical, but instead strongly skewed, the median may best represent the set of data.
- If the distribution of the data is roughly symmetrical, the mean and median will be close, so either may be appropriate to use.
- If the data is not numeric (for example, colour), or if the frequency of the data is more important than the values, use the mode.

Measures of Dispersion

Both the range and the standard deviation give you information about the distribution of the data in a set.

The range of a set of data changes considerably because of outliers. The disadvantage of using range is that it does not show where most of the data in a set lies—it only shows the spread between the highest and lowest values. The range is an informative tool that can be used to supplement other measures, such as standard deviation, but it is rarely used as the only measure of dispersion.

Standard deviation is the measure of dispersion that is most commonly used in statistical analysis when the mean is used to calculate central tendency. It measures the spread relative to the mean for most of the data in the set.

Outliers can affect standard deviation significantly. Standard deviation is a very useful measure of spread for symmetrical distributions with no outliers.

Standard deviation helps with comparing the spread of two sets of data that have approximately the same mean. The set of data with the smaller standard deviation has a narrower spread of measurements around the mean, and therefore usually has comparatively fewer high or low values.

Normal Distribution and Z-Scores

When working with several sets of data that approximate normal distributions, you can use z-scores to compare the data values. A z-score table enables you to find the area under a normal distribution curve with a mean of zero and a standard deviation of one. To determine the z-score for any data value in a set that is normally distributed, you can use the formula

$$z = \frac{x - \mu}{\sigma}$$

where x is any observed data value, μ is the mean of the set, and σ is the standard deviation of the set.

Margin of Error and Confidence Level

When analyzing the results of a survey, you may need to interpret and explain the significance of some additional statistics. Most surveys and polls draw their conclusions from a sample of a larger group. The margin of error and the confidence level indicate how well the sample represents the larger group. For example, a survey may have a margin of error of plus or minus 3% at a 95% level of confidence. This means that if the survey were conducted 100 times, the data would be within three percent points above or below the reported results in 95 of the 100 surveys.

The size of the sample that is used for a poll affects the margin of error. If you are collecting data, consider the size of the sample you need for a desired margin of error.

Sarah chose the changes in population of the Western provinces and the territories over the last century as her topic. Below, she describes how she determined which statistical tools to use.

Sarah's Analysis

I obtained my data from a government census. Since a census surveys the entire population and not a sample, I do not need to consider margin of error or confidence level. I am using time series data, which shows trends from 1900 to 2000. The data is not normally distributed, so I do not need to use z-scores.

I could use a measure of central tendency to represent the "average" population of each province or territory over this period. I am not interested in frequency, so the mode is not appropriate. I think the mean would be the best measure to use in this situation. I could also look at the spread in population for each province or territory over this period using range and standard deviation. These values may allow me to compare the populations of the provinces and territories.

Your Turn

A. Which statistical tools are appropriate for your data? Explain why.

B. Use the tools you selected, and calculate the statistics.

C. Use these statistics to analyze your data.

1. Determine the measure of all indicated sides to the nearest tenth of a unit.

a)

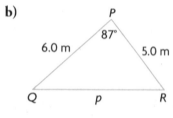

b)

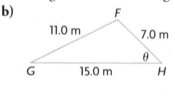

2. Determine the measure of each indicated angle to the nearest degree.

a)

b)

3. In $\triangle DEF$, $\angle D$ is $58°$, e is 10.0 cm, and f is 14.0 cm. Solve $\triangle DEF$. Round your answers to the nearest tenth of a unit.

4. Mohammed has been driving his ATV on the Vedder Mountain Trail System, near Chilliwack, British Columbia, for 3.2 km. He has been travelling in a compass direction of N54°E. He uses his compass to change direction to a new course of S5°W and continues for 4.6 km. If Mohammed wants to return directly to his starting point, how far must he travel, to the nearest tenth of a kilometre? In which direction should he travel, to the nearest tenth of a degree?

5. A cellphone tower is located on the side of a hill. The hill rises steadily at an angle of 8° to the horizon. The tower is 63 m tall and is supported by two guy wires that are attached to the top of the tower. One guy wire is anchored 60 m downhill from the tower. The other guy wire is anchored 60 m uphill from the tower. The two anchor points and the base of the tower are in line. What is the length of each guy wire?

6. Three circles touch at two points on their circumference. The first circle has a radius of 3 cm, the second circle has a radius of 4 cm, and the third circle has a radius of 5 cm. A triangle is formed by connecting the centres of the three circles. Determine the measures of the angles in the triangle.

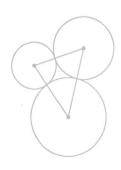

7. Caitlin wants to determine the height of a tree on the opposite bank of a river. She starts by laying out a baseline that is 100 m long. Then she estimates the angles from the ends of the baseline to the base of the tree as $80°$ and $30°$. From the end of the baseline with the $80°$ angle, she estimates the angle of elevation to the top of the tree as $20°$.

a) Sketch a diagram to model this situation.

b) Determine the height of the tree, to the nearest tenth of a metre.

8. a) Express each expression as an entire radical.

i) $-8\sqrt{5}$ ii) $2x^2\sqrt{3x}$

b) State the restrictions on the variables in part ii).

9. Simplify each expression.

a) $-3\sqrt{8} - 2\sqrt{18} + 5\sqrt{72}$

b) $4(2\sqrt{2} - 1)(3\sqrt{2} + 2) - 3(\sqrt{2} - 1)$

c) $\dfrac{12\sqrt{22}}{-4\sqrt{11}}$

d) $\dfrac{\sqrt{20} - 2\sqrt{10}}{4\sqrt{5}}$

10. Simplify each expression, and state the restrictions on the variables when necessary.

a) $4a\sqrt{12} - 2a\sqrt{27} + a\sqrt{75}$ c) $3\sqrt{a}(4 - 5\sqrt{a})$

b) $3\sqrt{x^2} - 2\sqrt{x^4}$ d) $(4\sqrt{2x} - 3)^2$

11. Solve each equation.

a) $\sqrt{2x - 1} = 5$ b) $3\sqrt{b} - 2 = 2\sqrt{b} + 4$

12. The distance d, in feet, that an object will fall in t seconds is given by the following formula:

$$t = \sqrt{\dfrac{d}{16}}$$

The designers of a ride for an amusement park want the riders to experience 4 s of vertical free fall. What distance does the ride need to fall?

13. In a study of the longevity of a particular breed of dog, veterinarians recorded the lifespans of 30 dogs.
  a) Create a frequency table and histogram for the data.
  b) Does the data approximate a normal distribution? Explain.
  c) Determine the range and standard deviation of the data. Describe what these measures tell you about the data.

Lifespans of Dogs (years)				
12.9	13.2	14.1	13.9	12.8
13.1	13.2	13.6	13.0	13.4
12.9	13.3	11.8	12.8	14.6
10.4	14.8	11.5	13.5	13.6
9.6	14.5	13.5	13.8	14.4
13.1	13.6	12.8	12.9	13.3

14. The average daily temperature in Winnipeg, Manitoba, during the month of January is $-17.8\ °C$, with a standard deviation of $3.9\ °C$. The average daily temperature in Whitehorse, Yukon, during the month of January is $-17.7\ °C$, with a standard deviation of $7.3\ °C$. Compare the temperatures at these two locations in January.

15. Zac is 195 cm tall. In a recent survey of students at his school, it was determined that the heights of the students are normally distributed, with a mean of 170 cm and a standard deviation of 12.5 cm.
  a) What percent of the students at Zac's school are shorter than Zac?
  b) What percent of the students are taller than Zac?

16. A manufacturer of smart phones has created a new model. The mean life of this new model is 48 months, with a standard deviation of 12 months. The manufacturer has offered a 24-month warranty on this model.
  a) Determine the percent of phones that are expected to malfunction during the warranty period.
  b) What percent of phones is expected to malfunction during the second and third year of use?

17. From May 29 to June 3, 2010, Nanos Research conducted a random telephone survey of 1008 Canadians, 18 years of age and older, to ask the following question: What are the most important issues facing Canadians today? The responses are shown in the table.
  a) State the margin of error and the confidence level for this survey.
  b) Determine the confidence interval for each of the following responses.
    i) health care
    ii) environment

Responses	(%)*
health care	23.1
jobs/economy	19.2
environment	12.6
high taxes	5.3
education	2.5
unsure	13.3

*Percent values may not add to 100 due to rounding.

This survey is accurate, plus or minus 3.1 percent points, 19 times out of 20.

18. Explain why the confidence level for a poll or survey is decreased when
  a) the margin of error decreases for a specific sample size
  b) the sample size that is needed for a specific margin of error decreases

Chapter
6

Quadratic Functions

▸ **LEARNING GOALS**

You will be able to develop your algebraic and graphical reasoning by

- Determining the characteristics of quadratic functions
- Sketching graphs of quadratic functions
- Solving problems that can be modelled with quadratic functions

? If you drew a graph of height versus time for a javelin throw, what would it look like? How could you use your graph to determine how long the javelin was in the air?

String Art

Robert's grandmother is teaching him how to make string art. In string art, nails are spaced evenly on a board and connected to each other by lines of string or yarn. The board that Robert is using has an array of 38 nails: 19 placed horizontally and 19 placed vertically as shown. The nails are 1 cm apart. Robert started to make the artwork and noticed that the lines of yarn were different lengths.

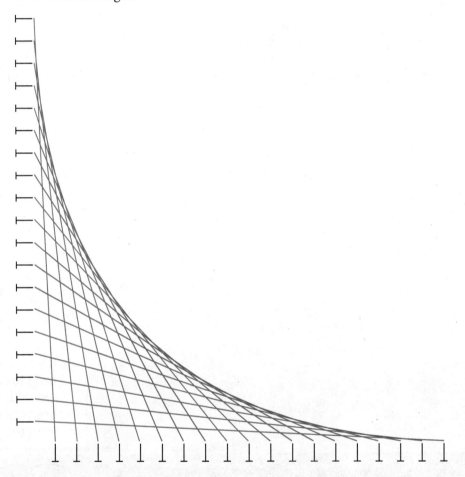

? Use a model to describe the relation between the position of each nail and the length of the yarn that connects it to another nail.

A. Model Robert's art on a coordinate grid, using line segments to represent the pieces of string.

B. Determine the length of each line segment.

C. Create a table of values like the one shown to compare nail position with string length.

Nail Position, x	String Length, y
1	
2	
3	

D. Describe any patterns you see in your table of values.

E. Is the relation linear? Explain.

F. Determine the domain and range for the relation.

G. Graph the relation.

H. What conclusions about string length can you make from your models?

WHAT DO You Think?

Decide whether you agree or disagree with each statement. Explain your decision.

1. Graphs of functions are straight lines.

2. Functions are not symmetrical.

3. If the domain of a function is the set of real numbers, then its range will also be the set of real numbers.

Exploring Quadratic Relations

GOAL

Determine the characteristics of quadratic relations.

EXPLORE *the Math*

quadratic relation

A relation that can be written in the standard form $y = ax^2 + bx + c$, where $a \neq 0$; for example, $y = 4x^2 + 2x + 1$

A moving object that is influenced by the force of gravity can often be modelled by a **quadratic relation** (assuming that there is no friction). For example, on one hole of a mini-golf course, the ball rolls up an incline after it is hit, slowing all the way due to gravity. If the ball misses the hole, it rolls back down the incline, accelerating all the way. If the initial speed of the ball is 6 m/s, the distance of the ball from its starting point in metres, y, can be modelled by the quadratic relation

$$y = -2.5x^2 + 6x$$

where x is the time in seconds after the ball leaves the putter.

? How does changing the coefficients and constant in a relation that is written in the form $y = ax^2 + bx + c$ affect the graph of the relation?

Reflecting

parabola

The shape of the graph of any quadratic relation.

A. Describe the common characteristics of each of the **parabolas** you graphed.

B. Describe any symmetry in your graphs.

C. Are the quadratic relations that you graphed functions? Justify your decision.

D. What effects do the following changes have on a graph of a quadratic relation?
   i) The value of a is changed, but b and c are left constant.
   ii) The value of b is changed, but a and c are left constant.
   iii) The value of c is changed, but a and b are left constant.

E. The graphs of three quadratic relations are shown. Predict possible values of *a*, *b*, and *c* in the equation for each graph.

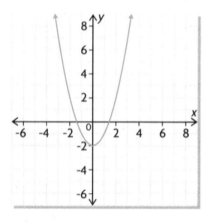 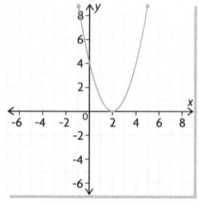 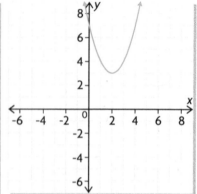

In Summary

Key Ideas

- The degree of all quadratic functions is 2.
- The standard form of a quadratic function is

$$y = ax^2 + bx + c$$

where $a \neq 0$.
- The graph of any quadratic function is a parabola with a single vertical line of symmetry.

Need to Know

- A quadratic function that is written in standard form, $y = ax^2 + bx + c$, has the following characteristics:
  - The highest or lowest point on the graph of the quadratic function lies on its vertical line of symmetry.
  - If *a* is positive, the parabola opens up. If *a* is negative, the parabola opens down.

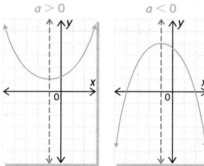

  - Changing the value of *b* changes the location of the parabola's line of symmetry.
  - The constant term, *c*, is the value of the parabola's *y*-intercept.

FURTHER Your Understanding

1. Which graphs appear to represent quadratic relations? Explain.

a)

c)

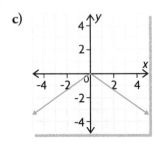

e)

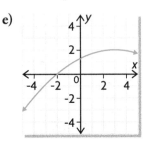

b)

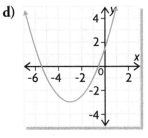

d)

f)

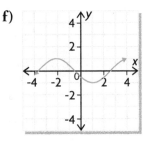

2. Which of the following relations are quadratic? Explain.
   - a) $y = 2x - 7$
   - b) $y = 2x(x + 3)$
   - c) $y = (x + 4)^2 + 1$
   - d) $y = x^2 - 5x - 6$
   - e) $y = 4x^3 + x^2 - x$
   - f) $y = x(x + 1)^2 - 7$

3. State the y-intercept for each quadratic relation in question 2.

4. Explain why the condition $a \neq 0$ must be stated when defining the standard form, $y = ax^2 + bx + c$.

5. Each of the following quadratic functions can be represented by a parabola. Does the parabola open up or down? Explain how you know.
   - a) $y = x^2 - 4$
   - b) $y = -2x^2 + 6x$
   - c) $y = 9 - x + 3x^2$
   - d) $y = -\dfrac{2}{3}x^2 - 6x + 1$

6. Each table of values lists points in a quadratic relation. Decide, without graphing, the direction in which the parabola opens.

a)

x	−4	−3	−2	−1	0	1
y	12	5	0	−3	−4	−3

b)

x	0	1	2	3	4	5
y	−13	−3	3	5	3	−3

c)

x	−5	−4	−3	−2	−1	0
y	3.0	−0.5	−3.0	−4.5	−5.0	−4.5

d)

x	0	1	2	3	4	5
y	−4	19	40	59	76	91

Properties of Graphs of Quadratic Functions

GOAL

Identify the characteristics of graphs of quadratic functions, and use the graphs to solve problems.

LEARN ABOUT the Math

Nicolina plays on her school's volleyball team. At a recent match, her Nonno, Marko, took some time-lapse photographs while she warmed up. He set his camera to take pictures every 0.25 s. He started his camera at the moment the ball left her arms during a bump and stopped the camera at the moment that the ball hit the floor. Marko wanted to capture a photo of the ball at its greatest height. However, after looking at the photographs, he could not be sure that he had done so. He decided to place the information from his photographs in a table of values.

From his photographs, Marko observed that Nicolina struck the ball at a height of 2 ft above the ground. He also observed that it took about 1.25 s for the ball to reach the same height on the way down.

Time (s)	Height (ft)
0.00	2
0.25	6
0.50	8
0.75	8
1.00	6
1.25	2

EXPLORE...

- Parabolic skis are marketed as performing better than traditional straight-edge skis. Parabolic skis are narrower in the middle than on the ends. Design one side of a parabolic ski on a coordinate grid. In groups, discuss where any lines of symmetry occur and how the parabolic shape works in your design.

? When did the volleyball reach its greatest height?

EXAMPLE 1	Using symmetry to estimate the coordinates of the vertex

Marko's Solution

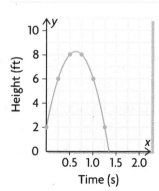

I plotted the points from my table, and then I sketched a graph that passed through all the points.

The graph looked like a parabola, so I concluded that the relation is probably quadratic.

vertex

The point at which the quadratic function reaches its maximum or minimum value.

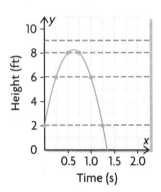

I knew that I could draw horizontal lines that would intersect the parabola at two points, except at the **vertex**, where a horizontal line would intersect the parabola at only one point.

Using a ruler, I drew horizontal lines and estimated that the coordinates of the vertex are around (0.6, 8.2).

This means that the ball reached maximum height at just over 8 ft, about 0.6 s after it was launched.

Equation of the axis of symmetry:

$$x = \frac{0 + 1.25}{2}$$

$$x = 0.625$$

axis of symmetry

A line that separates a 2-D figure into two identical parts.

For example, a parabola has a vertical axis of symmetry passing through its vertex.

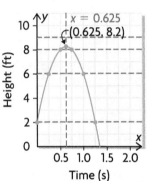

I used points that have the same y-value, (0, 2) and (1.25, 2), to determine the equation of the **axis of symmetry**. I knew that the axis of symmetry must be the same distance from each of these points.

From the equation, the x-coordinate of the vertex is 0.625. From the graph, the y-coordinate of the vertex is close to 8.2.

Therefore, 0.625 s after the volleyball was struck, it reached its maximum height of approximately 8 ft 2 in.

I revised my estimate of the coordinates of the vertex.

Reflecting

A. How could Marko conclude that the graph was a quadratic function?

B. If a horizontal line intersects a parabola at two points, can one of the points be the vertex? Explain.

C. Explain how Marko was able to use symmetry to determine the time at which the volleyball reached its maximum height.

APPLY the Math

EXAMPLE 2   Reasoning about the maximum value of a quadratic function

Some children are playing at the local splash pad. The water jets spray water from ground level. The path of water from one of these jets forms an arch that can be defined by the function

$$f(x) = -0.12x^2 + 3x$$

where x represents the horizontal distance from the opening in the ground in feet and $f(x)$ is the height of the sprayed water, also measured in feet. What is the maximum height of the arch of water, and how far from the opening in the ground can the water reach?

Manuel's Solution

$$f(x) = -0.12x^2 + 3x$$

> I knew that the degree of the function is 2, so the function is quadratic. The arch must be a parabola.
>
> I also knew that the coefficient of x^2, a, is negative, so the parabola opens down. This means that the function has a **maximum value,** associated with the y-coordinate of the vertex.

$$f(0) = 0$$

> I started to create a table of values by determining the y-intercept. I knew that the constant, zero, is the y-intercept. This confirms that the stream of water shoots from ground level.

$$f(1) = -0.12(1)^2 + 3(1)$$
$$f(1) = -0.12 + 3$$
$$f(1) = 2.88$$

> I continued to increase x by intervals of 1 until I noticed a repeat in my values. A height of 18.72 ft occurs at horizontal distances of 12 ft and 13 ft.

x	0	1	2	⟩⟩	12	13
f(x)	0	2.88	5.52	⟩⟩	18.72	18.72

Based on symmetry and the table of values, the maximum value of $f(x)$ will occur halfway between (12, 18.72) and (13, 18.72).

> The arch of water will reach a maximum height between 12 ft and 13 ft from the opening in the ground.

maximum value
The greatest value of the dependent variable in a relation.

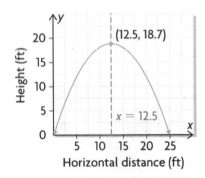

I used my table of values to sketch the graph. I extended the graph to the x-axis. I knew that my sketch represented only part of the function, since I am only looking at the water when it is above the ground.

$$x = \frac{12 + 13}{2}$$

$$x = 12.5$$

I used two points with the same y-value, (12, 18.72) and (13, 18.72), to determine the equation of the axis of symmetry.

Equation of the axis of symmetry:
$x = 12.5$

Height at the vertex:
$$f(x) = -0.12x^2 + 3x$$
$$f(12.5) = -0.12(12.5)^2 + 3(12.5)$$
$$f(12.5) = -0.12(156.25) + 37.5$$
$$f(12.5) = -18.75 + 37.5$$
$$f(12.5) = 18.75$$

I knew that the x-coordinate of the vertex is 12.5, so I substituted 12.5 into the equation to determine the height of the water at this horizontal distance.

The water reaches a maximum height of 18.75 ft when it is 12.5 ft from the opening in the ground.

Due to symmetry, the opening in the ground must be the same horizontal distance from the axis of symmetry as the point on the ground where the water lands. I simply multiplied the horizontal distance to the axis of symmetry by 2.

The water can reach a maximum horizontal distance of 25 ft from the opening in the ground.

The domain of this function is $0 \leq x \leq 25$, where $x \in \mathbb{R}$.

Your Turn

Another water arch at the splash pad is defined by the following quadratic function:

$$f(x) = -0.15x^2 + 3x$$

a) Graph the function, and state its domain for this context.
b) State the range for this context.
c) Explain why the original function describes the path of the water being sprayed, whereas the function in *Example 1* does not describe the path of the volleyball.

EXAMPLE **3**   Graphing a quadratic function using a table of values

Sketch the graph of the function:
$$y = x^2 + x - 2$$
Determine the y-intercept, any x-intercepts, the equation of the axis of symmetry, the coordinates of the vertex, and the domain and range of the function.

Anthony's Solution

$y = x^2 + x - 2$

The function is a quadratic function in the form
$y = ax^2 + bx + c$
$a = 1$
$b = 1$
$c = -2$

The degree of the given equation is 2, so the graph will be a parabola.

Since the coefficient of x^2 is positive, the parabola opens up.

Since the y-intercept is less than zero and the parabola opens up, there must be two x-intercepts and a **minimum value**.

x	−3	−2	−1	0	1
y	4	0	−2	−2	0

I made a table of values. I included the y-intercept, (0, −2), and determined some other points by substituting values of x into the equation.

I stopped determining points after I had identified both x-intercepts, because I knew that I had enough information to sketch an accurate graph.

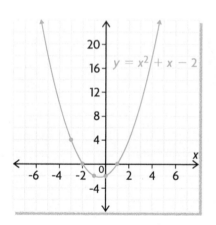

I graphed each coordinate pair and then drew a parabola that passed through all the points.

Equation of the axis of symmetry:
$$x = \frac{-2 + 1}{2}$$
$$x = \frac{-1}{2}$$
$$x = -0.5$$

I used the x-intercepts to determine the equation of the axis of symmetry.

minimum value

The least value of the dependent variable in a relation.

y-coordinate of the vertex:

$y = (-0.5)^2 + (-0.5) - 2$

$y = 0.25 - 0.5 - 2$

$y = -2.25$

The vertex is $(-0.5, -2.25)$.

> I knew that the vertex is a point on the axis of symmetry. The *x*-coordinate of the vertex must be -0.5. To determine the *y*-coordinate of the vertex, I substituted -0.5 for *x* in the given equation.

The *y*-intercept is -2.

The *x*-intercepts are -2 and 1.

The equation of the axis of symmetry is

$x = -0.5$.

The vertex is $(-0.5, -2.25)$.

> The vertex, $(-0.5, -2.25)$, defines the minimum value of *y*.

Domain and range:

$\{(x, y) \mid x \in \mathbb{R}, y \geq -2.25, y \in \mathbb{R}\}$

> No restrictions were given for *x*, so the domain is all real numbers.

Your Turn

Explain how you could decide if the graph of the function $y = -x^2 + x + 2$ has *x*-intercepts.

EXAMPLE 4   Locating a vertex using technology

A skier's jump was recorded in frame-by-frame analysis and placed in one picture, as shown.

The skier's coach used the picture to determine the quadratic function that relates the skier's height above the ground, *y*, measured in metres, to the time, *x*, in seconds that the skier was in the air:

$$y = -4.9x^2 + 15x + 1$$

Graph the function. Then determine the skier's maximum height, to the nearest tenth of a metre, and state the range of the function for this context.

Isidro's Solution

$$y = -4.9x^2 + 15x + 1$$

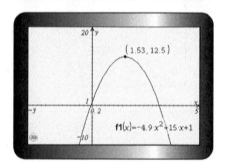

x	f1(x):=
	-4.9*x^2+15*x+1
0.	1.
0.5	7.275
1.	11.1
1.5	12.475
2.	11.4
0.	

x	f1(x):=
	-4.9*x^2+15*x+1
1.5	12.475
2.	11.4
2.5	7.875
3.	1.9
3.5	-6.525
3.5	

> I entered the equation into my calculator.

> To make sure that the graph models the situation, I set up a table of values. The skier's jump will start being timed at 0 s, and the skier will be in the air for only a few seconds, so I set the table to start at an x-value of zero and to increase in increments of 0.5.

> I decided to set the minimum height at 0 m—it doesn't make sense to extend the function below the x-axis, because the skier cannot go below the ground. I checked the table and noticed that the greatest y-value is only 12.475... m, and that y is negative at 3.5 s. I used these values to set an appropriate viewing window for the graph.

(1.53, 12.5)

$f1(x) = -4.9 x^2 + 15 x + 1$

> I graphed the function and used the calculator to locate the maximum value of the function.

The skier achieved a maximum height of 12.5 m above the ground 1.5 s into the jump.

The range of the function is
$\{y \mid 0 \le y \le 12.5, y \in R\}$.

> In this situation, the height of the skier varies between 0 m and 12.5 m.

Your Turn

On the next day of training, the coach asked the skier to increase his speed before taking the same jump. At the end of the day, the coach analyzed the results and determined the equation that models the skier's best jump:

$$y = -4.9x^2 + 20x + 1$$

How much higher did the skier go on this jump?

Key Idea

- A parabola that is defined by the equation $y = ax^2 + bx + c$ has the following characteristics:
  - If the parabola opens down ($a < 0$), the vertex of the parabola is the point with the greatest y-coordinate. The y-coordinate of the vertex is the maximum value of the function.
  - If the parabola opens up ($a > 0$), the vertex of the parabola is the point with the least y-coordinate. The y-coordinate of the vertex is the minimum value of the function.
  - The parabola is symmetrical about a vertical line, the axis of symmetry, through its vertex.

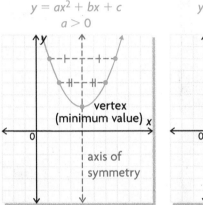

$y = ax^2 + bx + c$
$a > 0$

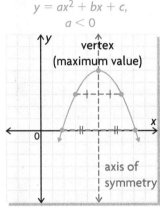

$y = ax^2 + bx + c,$
$a < 0$

Need to Know

- For all quadratic functions, the domain is the set of real numbers, and the range is a subset of real numbers.
- When a problem can be modelled by a quadratic function, the domain and range of the function may need to be restricted to values that have meaning in the context of the problem.

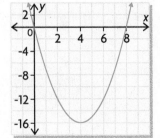

CHECK *Your Understanding*

1. **a)** Determine the equation of the axis of symmetry for the parabola.
   b) Determine the coordinates of the vertex of the parabola.
   c) State the domain and range of the function.

2. State the coordinates of the *y*-intercept and two additional ordered pairs for each function.

a) $f(x) = 2x^2 + 8x + 8$ b) $f(x) = 4x - x^2$

3. For each function, identify the *x*- and *y*-intercepts, determine the equation of the axis of symmetry and the coordinates of the vertex, and state the domain and range.

a)

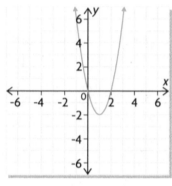

b)

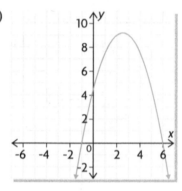

PRACTISING

4. For each function, identify the equation of the axis of symmetry, determine the coordinates of the vertex, and state the domain and range.

a)

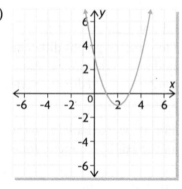

c)

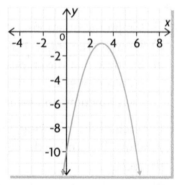

b)

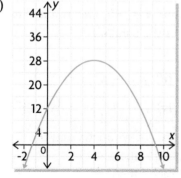

d)

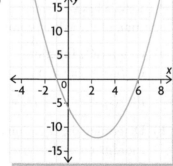

6.2 Properties of Graphs of Quadratic Functions

5. Each parabola in question 4 is defined by one of the functions below.
   a) $f(x) = x^2 - 5x - 6$
   c) $f(x) = -x^2 + 6x - 10$
   b) $f(x) = -x^2 + 8x + 12$
   d) $f(x) = x^2 - 4x + 3$

   Identify the function that defines each graph. Then verify the coordinates of the vertex that you determined in question 4.

6. State whether each parabola has a minimum or maximum value, and then determine this value.

a)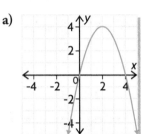

b)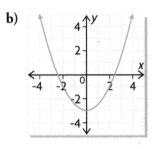

c)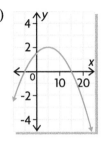

x	−4	−2	0	2	4
y					

7. a) Complete the table of values shown for each of the following functions.

   i) $y = -\dfrac{1}{2}x^2 + 5$
   ii) $y = \dfrac{3}{2}x^2 - 2$

   b) Graph the points in your table of values.
   c) State the domain and range of the function.

8. a) Graph the functions $y = 2x^2$ and $y = -2x^2$.
   b) How are the graphs the same? How are the graphs different?
   c) Suppose that the graphs were modified so that they became the graphs of $y = 2x^2 + 4$ and $y = -2x^2 + 4$. Predict the vertex of each function, and explain your prediction.

9. For each of the following, both points, (x, y), are located on the same parabola. Determine the equation of the axis of symmetry for each parabola.
   a) $(0, 2)$ and $(6, 2)$
   c) $(-6, 0)$ and $(2, 0)$
   b) $(1, -3)$ and $(9, -3)$
   d) $(-5, -1)$ and $(3, -1)$

10. A parabola has x-intercepts $x = 3$ and $x = -9$. Determine the equation of the axis of symmetry for the parabola.

11. a) Graph each function.
    i) $f(x) = 2x^2 + 3$
    iii) $f(x) = x^2 - 6x + 9$
    ii) $f(x) = -x^2 - 7x + 4$
    iv) $f(x) = \dfrac{1}{2}x^2 - 4x + 3$

    b) Determine the equation of the axis of symmetry and the coordinates of the vertex for each parabola.
    c) State the domain and range of each function.

12. In southern Alberta, near Fort Macleod, you will find the famous Head-Smashed-In Buffalo Jump. In a form of hunting, Blackfoot once herded buffalo and then stampeded the buffalo over the cliffs. If the height of a buffalo above the base of the cliff, $f(x)$, in metres, can be modelled by the function

$$f(x) = -4.9x^2 + 12$$

where x is the time in seconds after the buffalo jumped, how long was the buffalo in the air, to the nearest hundredth of a second?

13. In the game of football, a team can score by kicking the ball over a bar and between two uprights. For a kick in a particular game, the height of the ball above the ground, y, in metres, can be modelled by the function

$$y = -4.9x^2 + 25x$$

where x is the time in seconds after the ball left the foot of the player.
a) Determine the maximum height that this kick reached, to the nearest tenth of a metre.
b) State any restrictions that the context imposes on the domain and range of the function.
c) How long was the ball in the air?

14. An annual fireworks festival, held near the seawall in downtown Vancouver, choreographs rocket launches to music. The height of one rocket, $h(t)$, in metres over time, t, in seconds, is modelled by the function

$$h(t) = -4.9t^2 + 80t$$

Determine the domain and range of the function that defines the height of this rocket, to the nearest tenth of a metre.

15. Melinda and Genevieve live in houses that are next to each other. Melinda lives in a two-storey house, and Genevieve lives in a bungalow. They like to throw a tennis ball to each other through their open windows. The height of a tennis ball thrown from Melinda to Genevieve, $f(x)$, in feet, over time, x, measured in seconds is modelled by the function

$$f(x) = -5x^2 + 6x + 12$$

What are the domain and range of this function if Genevieve catches the ball 4 ft above the ground? Draw a diagram to support your answer.

16. Sid knows that the points $(-1, 41)$ and $(5, 41)$ lie on a parabola defined by the function

$$f(x) = 4x^2 - 16x + 21$$

a) Does $f(x)$ have a maximum value or a minimum value? Explain.

b) Determine, in two different ways, the coordinates of the vertex of the parabola.

Closing

17. a) Explain the relationship that must exist between two points on a parabola if the x-coordinates of the points can be used to determine the equation of the axis of symmetry for the parabola.

b) How can the equation of the axis of symmetry be used to determine the coordinates of the vertex of the parabola?

Extending

18. Gamez Inc. makes handheld video game players. Last year, accountants modelled the company's profit using the equation

$$P = -5x^2 + 60x - 135$$

This year, accountants used the equation

$$P = -7x^2 + 70x - 63$$

In both equations, P represents the profit, in hundreds of thousands of dollars, and x represents the number of game players sold, in hundreds of thousands. If the same number of game players were sold in these years, did Gamez Inc.'s profit increase? Justify your answer.

19. A parabola has a range of $\{y \,|\, y \le 14.5, y \in R\}$ and a y-intercept of 10. The axis of symmetry of the parabola includes point $(-3, 5)$. Write the function that defines the parabola in standard form if $a = \dfrac{-1}{2}$.

6.3 Factored Form of a Quadratic Function

GOAL

Relate the factors of a quadratic function to the characteristics of its graph.

YOU WILL NEED

- graph paper and ruler OR graphing technology

INVESTIGATE the Math

Ataneq takes tourists on dogsled rides. He needs to build a kennel to separate some of his dogs from the other dogs in his team. He has budgeted for 40 m of fence. He plans to place the kennel against part of his home, to save on materials.

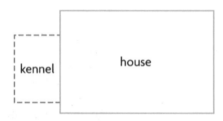

EXPLORE...

- John has made a catapult to launch baseballs. John positions the catapult and then launches a ball. The height of the ball, $h(t)$, in metres, over time, t, in seconds, can be modelled by the function $h(t) = -4.9t^2 + 14.7t$ From what height did John launch the ball? How long was the ball in the air?

? What dimensions should Ataneq use to maximize the area of the kennel?

A. Using x to represent the width of the kennel, create an expression for the length of the kennel.

B. Write a function, in terms of x, that defines the area of the kennel. Identify the factors in your function.

C. Create a table of values for the function, and then graph it.

D. Does the function contain a maximum or a minimum value? Explain.

E. Determine the x-intercepts of the parabola.

F. Determine the equation of the axis of symmetry of the parabola and the coordinates of the vertex.

G. What are the dimensions that maximize the area of the kennel?

Reflecting

H. How are the x-intercepts of the parabola related to the factors of your function?

I. Explain why having a quadratic function in factored form is useful when graphing the parabola.

Communication | Tip

A quadratic function is in factored form when it is written in the form $y = a(x - r)(x - s)$

APPLY *the Math*

| EXAMPLE **1** | Graphing a quadratic function given in standard form |

Sketch the graph of the quadratic function:
$$f(x) = 2x^2 + 14x + 12$$
State the domain and range of the function.

Arvin's Solution

$f(x) = 2x^2 + 14x + 12$
The coefficient of x^2 is $+2$,
so the parabola opens upward.

> The parabola opens upward when a is positive in the standard form of the function.

$f(x) = 2(x^2 + 7x + 6)$
$f(x) = 2(x + 1)(x + 6)$

> I factored the expression on the right side so that I could determine the **zeros** of the function.

zero

In a function, a value of the variable that makes the value of the function equal to zero.

Zeros:
$0 = 2(x + 1)(x + 6)$
$x + 1 = 0 \qquad$ or $\qquad x + 6 = 0$
$\qquad x = -1 \qquad\qquad\qquad x = -6$
The x-intercepts are $x = -1$
and $x = -6$.

> To determine the zeros, I set $f(x)$ equal to zero. I knew that a product is zero only when one or more of its factors are zero, so I set each factor equal to zero and solved each equation.
>
> The values of x at the zeros of the function are also the x-intercepts.

y-intercept:
$f(0) = 2(0 + 1)(0 + 6)$
$f(0) = 2(1)(6)$
$f(0) = 12$
The y-intercept is 12.

> I knew that the y-intercept is 12 from the standard form of the quadratic function. However, I decided to verify that my factoring was correct.
>
> I noticed that this value can be obtained by multiplying the values of a, r, and s from the factored form of the function:
> $f(x) = a(x - r)(x - s)$

Axis of symmetry:

$$x = \frac{-6 + (-1)}{2}$$

$$x = -3.5$$

> The axis of symmetry passes through the midpoint of the line segment that joins the x-intercepts. I calculated the mean of the two x-intercepts to determine the equation of the axis of symmetry.

$$f(x) = 2(x + 1)(x + 6)$$
$$f(-3.5) = 2(-3.5 + 1)(-3.5 + 6)$$
$$f(-3.5) = 2(-2.5)(2.5)$$
$$f(-3.5) = -12.5$$

The vertex of the parabola is $(-3.5, -12.5)$.

> The vertex lies on the axis of symmetry, so its x-coordinate is −3.5. I substituted −3.5 into the equation to determine the y-coordinate of the vertex.

$$f(x) = 2x^2 + 14x + 12$$

> I plotted the x-intercepts, y-intercept, and vertex and then joined these points with a smooth curve.

Domain and range:
$$\{(x, y) \mid x \in R, y \geq -12.5, y \in R\}$$

> The only restriction on the variables is that y must be greater than or equal to −12.5, the minimum value of the function.

Your Turn

Sketch the graph of the following function:
$$f(x) = -3x^2 + 6x - 3$$
a) How does the graph of this function differ from the graph in *Example 1*?
b) How are the x-intercepts related to the vertex? Explain.

EXAMPLE 2 **Using a partial factoring strategy to sketch the graph of a quadratic function**

Sketch the graph of the following quadratic function:
$$f(x) = -x^2 + 6x + 10$$
State the domain and range of the function.

Elliot's Solution

$f(x) = -x^2 + 6x + 10$

$f(x) = -x(x - 6) + 10$

I couldn't identify two integers with a product of 10 and a sum of 6, so I couldn't factor the expression. I decided to remove a partial factor of $-x$ from the first two terms. I did this so that I could determine the x-coordinates of the points that have 10 as their y-coordinate.

$-x = 0$	$x - 6 = 0$
$x = 0$	$x = 6$
$f(0) = 10$	$f(6) = 10$

The points (0, 10) and (6, 10) belong to the given quadratic function.

I determined two points in the function by setting each partial factor equal to zero.

When either factor is zero, the product of the factors is zero, so the value of the function is 10.

$x = \dfrac{0 + 6}{2}$

$x = 3$

Because (0, 10) and (6, 10) have the same y-coordinate, they are the same horizontal distance from the axis of symmetry. I determined the equation of the axis of symmetry by calculating the mean of the x-coordinates of these two points.

$f(3) = -(3)^2 + 6(3) + 10$

$f(3) = -9 + 18 + 10$

$f(3) = 19$

I determined the y-coordinate of the vertex.

The vertex is (3, 19).

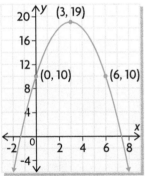

$f(x) = -x^2 + 6x + 10$

The coefficient of the x^2 term is negative, so the parabola opens downward.

I used the vertex, as well as (0, 10) and (6, 10), to sketch the parabola.

Domain: $\{x \mid x \in R\}$

Range: $\{y \mid y \leq 19, y \in R\}$

The only restriction on the variables is that y must be less than or equal to 19, the maximum value of the function.

Your Turn

a) **i)** Apply the partial factoring strategy to locate two points that have the same y-coordinate on the following function:
$$f(x) = -x^2 - 3x + 12$$

ii) Determine the axis of symmetry and the location of the vertex of the function from part i).

iii) Explain how the process you used in parts i) and ii) is different from factoring a quadratic function.

b) Explain whether you would use partial factoring to graph the function
$$g(x) = -x^2 - 4x + 12$$

EXAMPLE 3   Determining the equation of a quadratic function, given its graph

Determine the function that defines this parabola. Write the function in standard form.

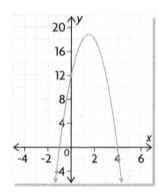

Indira's Solution

The x-intercepts are $x = -1$ and $x = 4$.
The zeros of the function occur when
x has values of -1 and 4.

$y = a(x - r)(x - s)$
$y = a[x - (-1)][x - (4)]$
$y = a(x + 1)(x - 4)$

> The graph is a parabola, so it is defined by a quadratic function.

> I located the x-intercepts and used them to determine the zeros of the function. I wrote the factored form of the quadratic function, substituting -1 and 4 for r and s.

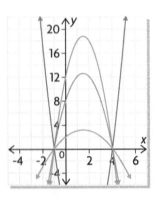

I knew that there are infinitely many quadratic functions that have these two zeros, depending on the value of a. I had to determine the value of a for the function that defines the blue graph.

The y-intercept is 12.

$y = a(x + 1)(x - 4)$

$(12) = a[(0) + 1][(0) - 4]$

$12 = a(1)(-4)$

$12 = -4a$

$-3 = a$

From the graph, I determined the coordinates of the y-intercept.

Because these coordinates are integers, I decided to use the y-intercept to solve for a.

In factored form, the quadratic function is

$y = -3(x + 1)(x - 4)$

I substituted the value of a into my equation.

In standard form, the quadratic function is

$y = -3(x^2 - 3x - 4)$

$y = -3x^2 + 9x + 12$

My equation seems reasonable, because it defines a graph with a y-intercept of 12 and a parabola that opens downward.

Your Turn

If a parabola has only one x-intercept, how could you determine the quadratic function that defines it, written in factored form? Explain using the given graph.

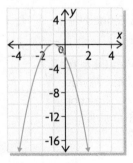

EXAMPLE **4** **Solving a problem modelled by a quadratic function in factored form**

The members of a Ukrainian church hold a fundraiser every Friday night in the summer. They usually charge $6 for a plate of perogies. They know, from previous Fridays, that 120 plates of perogies can be sold at the $6 price but, for each $1 price increase, 10 fewer plates will be sold. What should the members charge if they want to raise as much money as they can for the church?

Krystina's Solution: Using the properties of the function

Let y represent the total revenue.
$y = $ (Number of plates)(Price)
Let x represent the number of $1 price increases.
$y = (120 - 10x)(6 + x)$

> For each price increase, x, I knew that $10x$ fewer plates will be sold.
>
> If I expanded the factors in my function, I would create an x^2 term. This means that the function I have defined is quadratic and its graph is a parabola.

$0 = (120 - 10x)(6 + x)$
$120 - 10x = 0$ or $6 + x = 0$
     $-10x = -120$ $x = -6$
        $x = 12$
The x-intercepts are $x = -6$ and $x = 12$.

> To determine the zeros of the function, I substituted zero for y. A product is zero only when one or both of its factors are zero, so I set each factor equal to zero and solved each equation.

$x = \dfrac{12 + (-6)}{2}$

$x = 3$

$y = (120 - 10x)(6 + x)$
   $y = [120 - 10(3)][6 + (3)]$
   $y = (90)(9)$
   $y = 810$
The coordinates of the vertex are (3, 810).

> I determined the equation of the axis of symmetry for the parabola by calculating the mean distance between the x-intercepts.
>
> I determined the y-coordinate of the vertex by substituting into my initial equation.

To generate as much revenue as possible, the members of the church should charge $6 + $3 or $9 for a plate of perogies. This will provide revenue of $810.

> The vertex describes the maximum value of the function. Maximum sales of $810 occur when the price is raised by $3.

Jennifer's Solution: Using graphing technology

Revenue = (Number of plates)(Price)
$$y = (120 - 10x)(6 + x)$$

I let y represent Revenue and I let x represent the number of $1 price increases. For each $1 price increase, I knew that 10 fewer plates will be sold.

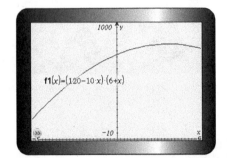

I graphed the equation on a calculator. Since a reduced price may result in maximum revenue, I set my domain to a minimum value of −5 and a maximum value of 5.

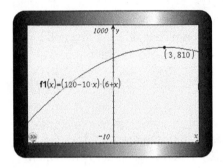

I used the calculator to locate the vertex of the parabola.

The members of the church should charge $3 more than the current price of $6 for a plate of perogies. If they charge $9, they will reach the maximum revenue of $810.

Your Turn

A career and technology class at a high school in Langley, British Columbia, operates a small T-shirt business out of the school. Over the last few years, the shop has had monthly sales of 300 T-shirts at a price of $15 per T-shirt. The students have learned that for every $2 increase in price, they will sell 20 fewer T-shirts each month. What should they charge for their T-shirts to maximize their monthly revenue?

In Summary

Key Ideas

- When a quadratic function is written in factored form
$$y = a(x - r)(x - s)$$
each factor can be used to determine a zero of the function by setting each factor equal to zero and solving.
- The zeros of a quadratic function correspond to the x-intercepts of the parabola that is defined by the function.
- If a parabola has one or two x-intercepts, the equation of the parabola can be written in factored form using the x-intercept(s) and the coordinates of one other point on the parabola.
- Quadratic functions without any zeros cannot be written in factored form.

Need to Know

- A quadratic function that is written in the form
$$f(x) = a(x - r)(x - s)$$
has the following characteristics:
  - The x-intercepts of the graph of the function are $x = r$ and $x = s$.
  - The linear equation of the axis of symmetry is $x = \dfrac{r + s}{2}$.
  - The y-intercept, c, is $c = a \cdot r \cdot s$.

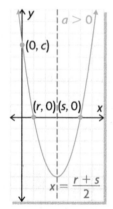
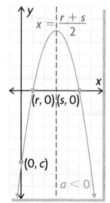

- If a quadratic function has only one x-intercept, the factored form can be written as follows:
$$f(x) = a(x - r)(x - r)$$
$$f(x) = a(x - r)^2$$

CHECK *Your Understanding*

1. Match each quadratic function with its corresponding parabola.

a) $f(x) = (x - 1)(x + 4)$ **d)** $f(x) = (x - 1)(x - 4)$

b) $f(x) = (x + 1)(x - 4)$ **e)** $f(x) = (1 - x)(x + 4)$

c) $f(x) = (x + 1)(x + 4)$ **f)** $f(x) = (x + 1)(4 - x)$

i)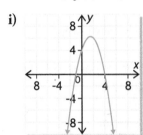

iii)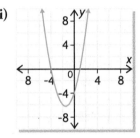

v)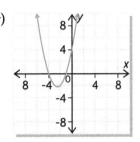

ii)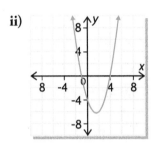

iv)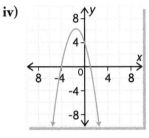

vi)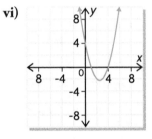

2. For each quadratic function below

  i) determine the x-intercepts of the graph

  ii) determine the y-intercept of the graph

  iii) determine the equation of the axis of symmetry

  iv) determine the coordinates of the vertex

  v) sketch the graph

  a) $f(x) = (x + 4)(x - 2)$ **c)** $h(x) = 2(x + 1)(x - 7)$

  b) $g(x) = -2x(x - 3)$

3. A quadratic function has an equation that can be written in the form $f(x) = a(x - r)(x - s)$. The graph of the function has x-intercepts $x = -2$ and $x = 4$ and passes through point $(5, 7)$. Write the equation of the quadratic function.

PRACTISING

4. For each quadratic function, determine the x-intercepts, the y-intercept, the equation of the axis of symmetry, and the coordinates of the vertex of the graph.

  a) $f(x) = (x - 1)(x + 1)$ **d)** $f(x) = -2(x - 2)(x + 1)$

  b) $f(x) = (x + 2)(x + 2)$ **e)** $f(x) = 3(x - 2)^2$

  c) $f(x) = (x - 3)(x - 3)$ **f)** $f(x) = 4(x - 1)^2$

5. Sketch the graph of each function in question 4, and state the domain and range of the function.

6. Sketch the graph of
$$y = a(x - 3)(x + 1)$$
for $a = 3$. Describe how the graph would be different from your sketch if the value of a were 2, 1, 0, -1, -2, and -3.

7. Sketch the graph of
$$y = (x - 3)(x + s)$$
for $s = 3$. Describe how the graph would be different from your sketch if the value of s were 2, 1, 0, -1, -2, and -3.8.

8. Byron is planning to build three attached rectangular enclosures for some of the animals on his farm. He bought 100 m of fencing. He wants to maximize the total area of the enclosures. He determined a function, $A(x)$, that models the total area in square metres, where x is the width of each rectangle:
$$A(x) = -2x^2 + 50x$$

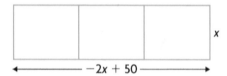

a) Determine the maximum total area.
b) State the domain and range of the variables in the function.

9. Paulette owns a store that sells used video games in Red Deer, Alberta. She charges $10 for each used game. At this price, she sells 70 games a week. Experience has taught her that a $1 increase in the price results in five fewer games being sold per week. At what price should Paulette sell her games to maximize her sales? What will be her maximum revenue?

10. For each quadratic function below
   i) use partial factoring to determine two points that are the same distance from the axis of symmetry
   ii) determine the coordinates of the vertex
   iii) sketch the graph

   a) $f(x) = x^2 + 4x - 6$ d) $f(x) = -x^2 - 8x - 5$

   b) $f(x) = x^2 - 8x + 13$ e) $f(x) = -\frac{1}{2}x^2 + 2x - 3$

   c) $f(x) = 2x^2 + 10x + 7$ f) $f(x) = -2x^2 + 10x - 9$

Math in Action

Paper Parabolas

On an 8.5 in. by 11 in. piece of lined paper, mark a point that is close to the centre, near the bottom edge. Label this point P.

- Fold the paper, at any angle, so that any point on the bottom edge of the paper touches point P. Crease the paper along the fold line, and then open the paper.
- Fold the paper again, but at a different angle, so that another point on the bottom edge of the paper touches point P. Crease the paper.
- Continue this process until you have many different creases in the paper on both sides of P.
  - What shape emerges?
  - Compare your shape with the shapes made by other students. How are the shapes the same? How are they different?
  - How does changing the location of point P affect the shape that is formed?
  - The creases intersect at several points. How could you determine whether a set of these points is on a parabola?

11. Determine the equation of the quadratic function that defines each parabola.

a)

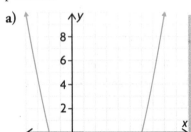

c)

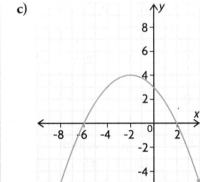

b)

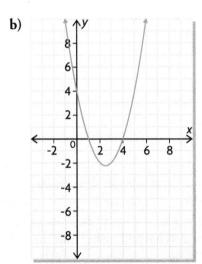

d)

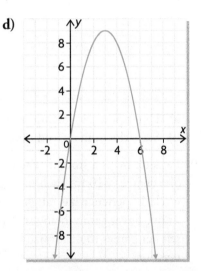

12. a) Use two different algebraic strategies to determine the equation of the axis of symmetry and the vertex of the parabola defined by the following function:

$$f(x) = -2x^2 + 16x - 24$$

b) Which strategy do you prefer? Explain.

13. Determine the quadratic function that defines a parabola with x-intercepts $x = -1$ and $x = 3$ and y-intercept $y = -6$. Provide a sketch to support your work.

14. How many zeros can a quadratic function have? Provide sketches to support your reasoning.

15. On the north side of Sir Winston Churchill Provincial Park, located near Lac La Biche, Alberta, people gather to witness the migration of American white pelicans. The pelicans dive underwater to catch fish. Someone observed that a pelican's depth underwater over time could be modelled by a parabola. One pelican was underwater for 4 s, and its maximum depth was 1 m.

    a) State the domain and range of the variables in this situation.
    b) Determine the quadratic function that defines the parabola.

16. Elizabeth wants to enclose the backyard of her house on three sides to form a rectangular play area for her children. She has decided to use one wall of the house and three sections of fence to create the enclosure. Elizabeth has budgeted $800 for the fence. The fencing material she has chosen costs $16/ft. Determine the dimensions that will provide Elizabeth with the largest play area.

17. A water rocket was launched from the ground, with an initial velocity of 32 m/s. The rocket achieved a height of 44 m after 2 s of flight. The rocket was in the air for 6 s.

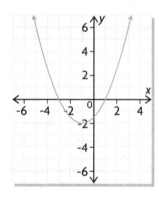

    a) Determine the quadratic function that models the height of the rocket over time.
    b) State the domain and range of the variables.

Closing

18. Identify the key characteristics you could use to determine the quadratic function that defines this graph. Explain how you would use these characteristics.

        6.3 Factored Form of a Quadratic Function   **349**

Extending

19. The Chicago Bean is a unique sculpture that was inspired by liquid mercury. It is 66 ft long and 33 ft high, with a 12 ft arch underneath. The top curved section that connects the three red dots in the photograph forms a parabola.

   a) Determine the quadratic function that connects the three red dots. Assume that the ground (the green line) represents the x-axis of the graph. Write the function in standard form.

   b) What are the domain and range of the variables?

   c) If the parabola extended to the ground, what would the x-intercepts be, rounded to the nearest tenth?

20. A local baseball team has raised money to put new grass on the field. The curve where the infield ends can be modelled by a parabola. The foreman has marked out the key locations on the field, as shown in the diagram.

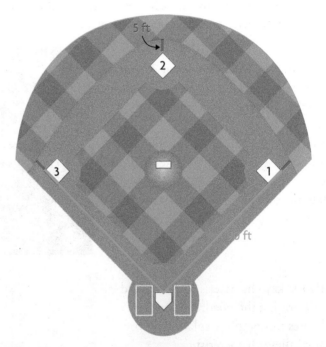

   a) Determine a quadratic function that models the curve where the infield ends.

   b) State the domain and range of the variables. Justify your decision.

   c) Graph the quadratic function.

21. The National Basketball Association (NBA) mandates that every court must have the same dimensions. The length of the court must be 6 ft less than twice the width. The area of the court must be 4700 ft^2. Use this information to determine the dimensions of a basketball court used by the NBA.

FREQUENTLY ASKED Questions

Q: **What are the characteristics of a quadratic function?**

A: The following are the key characteristics of a quadratic function:

- The equation is of degree 2.

- The graph is a parabola.

- The y-coordinate of the vertex of the parabola is a maximum if the parabola opens down and a minimum if the parabola opens up.

- The domain of the function is the set of real numbers. The range is restricted by the y-coordinate of the vertex. However, if the function is being used to model a situation, then the situation may restrict the domain and the range.

- The graph of the function contains a vertical axis of symmetry that passes through the vertex.

Q: **How can you use the information that is available from the standard or factored form of a quadratic function to sketch its graph?**

A: The standard form is

$$y = ax^2 + bx + c$$

From this form, you can determine that the y-intercept of the graph is $y = c$.

The factored form is

$$y = a(x - r)(x - s)$$

From this form, you can determine

- the zeros (r and s), which provide the x-intercepts $x = r$ and $x = s$

- the y-intercept, determined by multiplying a, r, and s

- the equation of the axis of symmetry, $x = \dfrac{r + s}{2}$

- the location of the vertex, determined by substituting the x-coordinate of the vertex, $\dfrac{r + s}{2}$, into the equation

From both forms, you can determine the direction in which the parabola opens: upward when $a > 0$ and downward when $a < 0$.

> **Study | Aid**
> - See Lesson 6.1.
> - Try Mid-Chapter Review Question 1.

> **Study | Aid**
> - See Lesson 6.2, Examples 2 and 3, and Lesson 6.3, Examples 1, 3, and 4.
> - Try Mid-Chapter Review Questions 2 to 8 and 10.

Study | *Aid*
- See Lesson 6.3, Example 2.
- Try Mid-Chapter Review Question 9.

Q: What is partial factoring, and how is it used to sketch a graph?

A: Starting with the standard form of a quadratic function, factor only the terms that contain the variable x. The two partial factors can be used to locate two points that have the same y-coordinate, and so are equidistant from the axis of symmetry. Partial factoring can be used when a function cannot be factored completely.

For example: Sketch the graph of the following quadratic function:

$$f(x) = 2x^2 - 4x + 9$$

$f(x) = 2x^2 - 4x + 9$ $f(x) = 2x(x - 2) + 9$	Factor the terms that include x.
$2x = 0 \qquad x - 2 = 0$ $x = 0 \qquad\qquad x = 2$ $(0, 9)$ and $(2, 9)$ are points on the parabola.	Set each partial factor equal to zero. This allows you to identify two points on the graph with a y-coordinate of 9.
$x = \dfrac{0 + 2}{2}$ $x = 1$	Determine the equation of the axis of symmetry, which is located midway between $(0, 9)$ and $(2, 9)$.
$f(1) = 2(1)^2 - 4(1) + 9$ $f(1) = 7$ The vertex of the parabola is at $(1, 7)$.	Locate the y-coordinate of the vertex by substituting into the quadratic function.
	From these three known points, you can sketch the graph.

PRACTISING

Lesson 6.1

1. Which of the following are quadratic functions?
   a) $y = 3x + 4$
   c) $y = x^2 + 2x - 9$
   b) $y = 2x(x - 5)$
   d) $y = 2x^3 + 4x^2 - 5$

Lesson 6.2

2. a) Determine the y-intercept of the following quadratic function:
$$y = -x^2 + 8x$$
   b) Graph the function.
   c) From your graph, determine the equation of the axis of symmetry, the location of the vertex, the x-intercepts, and the domain and range of the function.

3. Consider the standard form of a quadratic function:
$$y = ax^2 + bx + c$$
   a) Explain how the value of a affects the graph of the parabola.
   b) Provide supporting examples, with their graphs.

4. Match each graph to an equation below. Justify your decisions.

a)
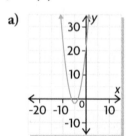

c)
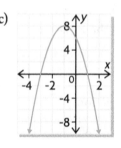

b)
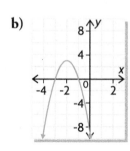

d)
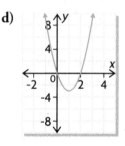

   i) $y = -2x^2 - 4x + 6$ **iii)** $y = -3x^2 - 12x - 9$
   ii) $y = 3x^2 - 6x$ **iv)** $y = x^2 + 10x + 23$

5. A flare is often used as a signal to attract rescue personnel in an emergency. When a flare is shot into the air, its height, $h(t)$, in metres, over time, t, in seconds can be modelled by
$$h(t) = -5t^2 + 120t$$
   a) Identify the x-intercepts of the parabola.
   b) When did the flare reach its maximum height, and what was this height?
   c) What was the height of the flare after 15 s?
   d) State the domain and range of the function.

Lesson 6.3

6. The points $(-4, 6)$ and $(2, 6)$ lie on a parabola. Determine the equation of the axis of symmetry of the parabola.

7. Determine the equation of this quadratic function.

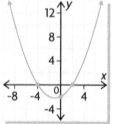

8. The zeros of a quadratic function are -6 and 12. The graph of the function intersects the y-axis at -36.
   a) Determine the equation of the quadratic function.
   b) Determine the coordinates of the vertex.
   c) State the domain and range of the function.

9. Sketch the graph of the following quadratic function:
$$y = 3x^2 + 6x - 18$$

10. Pedalworks rents bicycles to tourists who want to explore the local trails. Data from previous rentals show that the shop will rent 7 more bicycles per day for every $1.50 decrease in rental price. The shop currently rents 63 bicycles per day, at a rental price of $39. How much should the shop charge to maximize revenue?

Vertex Form of a Quadratic Function

GOAL

Graph a quadratic function in the form $y = a(x - h)^2 + k$, and relate the characteristics of the graph to its equation.

EXPLORE...

- Quadratic functions can be written in different forms. The basic quadratic function is $y = x^2$.
  Use a calculator to graph the following quadratic functions. Explain how the basic function is related to each function. Describe how the changes in the function affect the graph.
  a) $y = (x - 3)^2$
  b) $y = x^2 - 5$
  c) $y = (x + 1)^2 - 2$
  d) $y = (x + 4)^2 + 6$
  e) $y = -2(x + 1)^2 + 3$
  f) $y = 3(x - 2)^2 - 4$

INVESTIGATE the Math

A high-school basketball coach brought in Judy, a trainer from one of the local college teams, to talk to the players about shot analysis. Judy demonstrated, using stroboscopic photographs, how shots can be analyzed and represented by quadratic functions. She used the following function to model a shot:

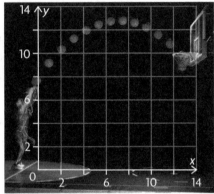

$$y = -0.1(x - 8)^2 + 13$$

In this function, x represents the horizontal distance, in feet, of the ball from the player and y represents the vertical height, in feet, of the ball above the floor.

Judy mentioned that once she had a quadratic equation in this form, she did not need the photographs. She could quickly sketch a graph of the path of the ball just by looking at the equation.

? How could Judy predict what the graph of the quadratic function would look like?

A. Graph the following function:

$$y = x^2$$

Change the graph by changing the coefficient of x^2. Try both positive and negative values. How do the parabolas change as you change this coefficient?

B. For each function you graphed in part A, determine the coordinates of the vertex and the equation of the axis of symmetry.

C. Graph this function:

$$y = x^2 + 1$$

Change the graph by changing the constant. Try both positive and negative values. How do the parabolas change as you change the constant? How do the coordinates of the vertex and the equation of the axis of symmetry change?

D. Graph this function:

$$y = (x - 1)^2$$

Change the graph by changing the constant. Try both positive and negative values. How do the parabolas change as you change the constant? How do the coordinates of the vertex and the equation of the axis of symmetry change?

E. The equation that Judy used was expressed in vertex form:

$$y = a(x - h)^2 + k$$

Make a conjecture about how the values of a, h, and k determine the characteristics of a parabola.

Communication | *Tip*

A quadratic function is in vertex form when it is written in the form $y = a(x - h)^2 + k$

F. Test your conjecture by predicting the characteristics of the graph of the following function:

$$y = -0.1(x - 8)^2 + 13$$

Use your predictions to sketch a graph of the function.

G. Using a graphing calculator, graph the function from part F:

$$y = -0.1(x - 8)^2 + 13$$

How does your sketch compare with this graph? Are your predictions supported? Explain.

Reflecting

H. Does the value of a in a quadratic function always represent the same characteristic of the parabola, whether the function is written in standard form, factored form, or vertex form? Explain.

I. Neil claims that when you are given the vertex form of a quadratic function, you can determine the domain and range without having to graph the function. Do you agree or disagree? Explain.

J. Which form of the quadratic function—standard, factored, or vertex—would you prefer to start with, if you wanted to sketch the graph of the function? Explain.

APPLY the Math

EXAMPLE 1   Sketching the graph of a quadratic function given in vertex form

Sketch the graph of the following function:
$$f(x) = 2(x - 3)^2 - 4$$
State the domain and range of the function.

Samuel's Solution

$f(x) = 2(x - 3)^2 - 4$
Since $a > 0$, the parabola opens upward.
The vertex is at $(3, -4)$.
The equation of the axis of symmetry is
$x = 3$.

> The function was given in vertex form. I listed the characteristics of the parabola that I could determine from the equation.

$f(0) = 2(0 - 3)^2 - 4$
$f(0) = 2(-3)^2 - 4$
$f(0) = 2(9) - 4$
$f(0) = 18 - 4$
$f(0) = 14$
Point $(0, 14)$ is on the parabola.

> To determine another point on the parabola, I substituted 0 for x.

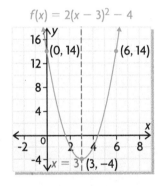

> I plotted the vertex and the point I had determined, $(0, 14)$. Then I drew the axis of symmetry. I used symmetry to determine the point that is the same horizontal distance from $(0, 14)$ to the axis of symmetry. This point is $(6, 14)$. I connected all three points with a smooth curve.

Domain and range:
$\{(x, y) \mid x \in R, y \geq -4, y \in R\}$

Your Turn

Sketch the graph of the following function:
$$f(x) = -\frac{1}{2}(x + 6)^2 + 1$$
State the domain and range of the function. Justify your decision.

| EXAMPLE 2 | Determining the equation of a parabola using its graph |

Liam measured the length of the shadow that was cast by a metre stick at 10 a.m. and at noon near his home in Saskatoon. Other students in his class also measured the shadow at different times during the day. They had read that, when graphed as shadow length versus time, the data should form a parabola with a minimum at noon, because the shadow is shortest at noon. Liam decided to try to predict the equation of the parabola, without the other students' data.

Determine the equation that represents the relationship between the time of day and the length of the shadow cast by a metre stick.

Liam's Solution

I have the points (10, 85.3) and (12, 47.5).

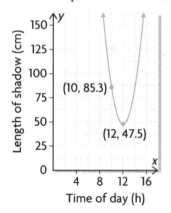

I measured the length of the shadow in centimetres. My measurements were 85.3 cm at 10 a.m. and 47.5 cm at noon.

I drew a sketch of a parabola using (12, 47.5) as the vertex, since the length of the shadow at noon should be the minimum value of the function.

$f(x) = a(x - h)^2 + k$
$f(x) = a(x - 12)^2 + 47.5$

I decided to use the vertex form of the quadratic function, since I already knew the values of h and k in this form.

Solving for a:
$85.3 = a(10 - 12)^2 + 47.5$
$85.3 = a(-2)^2 + 47.5$
$85.3 = 4a + 47.5$
$37.8 = 4a$
$9.45 = a$

I knew that (10, 85.3) is a point on the parabola. I substituted the coordinates of this point into the equation and then solved for a.

The function that represents the parabola is
$f(x) = 9.45(x - 12)^2 + 47.5$

The domain and range of this function depend on the hours of daylight, which depends on the time of year.

Your Turn

Donald, a classmate of Liam's, lives across the city. Donald measured the length of the shadow cast by a metre stick as 47.0 cm at noon and 198.2 cm at 4:00 p.m. Determine a quadratic function using Donald's data, and explain how his function is related to Liam's function.

| EXAMPLE **3** | Reasoning about the number of zeros that a quadratic function will have |

Randy claims that he can predict whether a quadratic function will have zero, one, or two zeros if the function is expressed in vertex form. How can you show that he is correct?

Eugene's Solution

$f(x) = 2(x - 2)^2 - 5$
Conjecture: two zeros

The vertex of the parabola that is defined by the function is at $(2, -5)$, so the vertex is below the x-axis. The parabola must open upward because a is positive. Therefore, I should observe two x-intercepts when I graph the function.

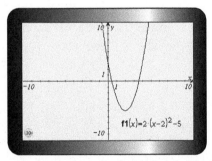

To test my conjecture, I graphed the function on a calculator. I can see two x-intercepts on my graph, so the function has two zeros.

The graph supports my conjecture.

$f(x) = x^2$
$f(x) = (x - 0)^2 + 0$
Conjecture: one zero

I decided to use the basic quadratic function, since this provided me with a convenient location for the vertex, $(0, 0)$.

Since the vertex is on the x-axis and the parabola opens up, this means that I should observe only one x-intercept when I graph the function.

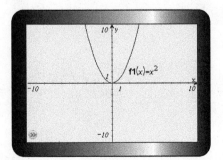

To test my conjecture, I graphed the function on a calculator. Based on my graph, I concluded that the function has only one zero.

The graph supports my conjecture.

$f(x) = 2(x + 3)^2 + 4$

Conjecture: no zeros

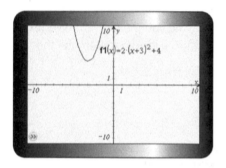

The vertex of the parabola that is defined by this function is at $(-3, 4)$, and the parabola opens upward. The vertex lies above the x-axis, so I should observe no x-intercepts when I graph the function.

To test my conjecture, I graphed the function on a calculator. I concluded that the function has no zeros.

The graph supports my conjecture.

Your Turn

a) Define three different quadratic functions, in vertex form, that open downward. One function should have two zeros, another should have one zero, and the third should have no zeros.

b) Explain how you were able to connect the number of zeros to each function.

EXAMPLE 4   Solving a problem that can be modelled by a quadratic function

A soccer ball is kicked from the ground. After 2 s, the ball reaches its maximum height of 20 m. It lands on the ground at 4 s.

a) Determine the quadratic function that models the height of the kick.

b) Determine any restrictions that must be placed on the domain and range of the function.

c) What was the height of the ball at 1 s? When was the ball at the same height on the way down?

Tia's Solution

a) Let x represent the elapsed time in seconds, and let y represent the height in metres.

$y = a(x - h)^2 + k$

> Since I knew the maximum height and when it occurred, I also knew the coordinates of the vertex. I decided to use the vertex form to determine the equation.

The maximum height is 20 m at the elapsed time of 2 s.

Vertex:

$(x, y) = (2, 20)$

$y = a(x - 2)^2 + 20$

> I substituted the known values.

Solving for a:

$f(x) = a(4 - 2)^2 + 20$
$0 = a(2)^2 + 20$
$0 = 4a + 20$
$-20 = 4a$
$-5 = a$

> To determine the value of a, I substituted the coordinates of the point that corresponds to the ball hitting the ground, $(4, 0)$.

The following quadratic function models the height of the kick:

$f(x) = -5(x - 2)^2 + 20$

b) Time at beginning of kick:

$x = 0$

Time when ball hits ground:

$x = 4$

> At the beginning of the kick, the time is 0 s. When the ball lands, the time is 4 s. I can only use x-values in this interval. Time in seconds is continuous, so the set is real numbers.

Domain: $\{x \mid 0 \leq x \leq 4, x \in R\}$

Vertex: $(2, 20)$
Height of ball at beginning of kick: 0 m
Height of ball at vertex: 20 m

Range: $\{y \mid 0 \leq y \leq 20, y \in R\}$

> The ball starts on the ground, at a height of 0 m, and rises to its greatest height, 20 m. The ball is not below the ground at any point. Height in metres is continuous, so the set is real numbers.

c) $f(x) = -5(x - 2)^2 + 20$

$f(1) = -5(1 - 2)^2 + 20$

$f(1) = -5(-1)^2 + 20$

$f(1) = -5 + 20$

$f(1) = 15$

> I used the vertex form of the quadratic function to determine the height of the ball at 1 s.

The ball was at a height of 15 m after 1 s.
This occurred as the ball was rising.

Equation of the axis of symmetry:

$x = 2$

Symmetry provides the point (3, 15).
The ball was also 15 m above the ground at 3 s.
This occurred as the ball was on its way down.

> I knew that point (1, 15) is 1 unit to the left of the axis of symmetry of the parabola. The other point on the parabola, with height 15 m, should be 1 unit to the right of the axis of symmetry. This means that the x-coordinate of the point must be 3.

Your Turn

The goalkeeper kicked the soccer ball from the ground. It reached its maximum height of 24.2 m after 2.2 s. The ball was in the air for 4.4 s.

a) Define the quadratic function that models the height of the ball above the ground.

b) How is the equation for this function similar to the equation that Tia determined? Explain.

c) After 4 s, how high was the ball above the ground?

In Summary

Key Idea

- The vertex form of the equation of a quadratic function is written as follows:
$$y = a(x - h)^2 + k$$
The graph of the function can be sketched more easily using this form.

Need to Know

- A quadratic function that is written in vertex form,
$$y = a(x - h)^2 + k$$
has the following characteristics:
  - The vertex of the parabola has the coordinates (h, k).
  - The equation of the axis of symmetry of the parabola is $x = h$.
  - The parabola opens upward when $a > 0$, and the function has a minimum value of k when $x = h$.
  - The parabola opens downward when $a < 0$, and the function has a maximum value of k when $x = h$.

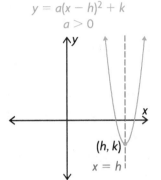

$y = a(x - h)^2 + k$
$a > 0$

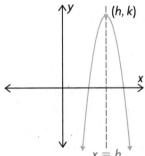

$y = a(x - h)^2 + k$
$a < 0$

- A parabola may have zero, one, or two x-intercepts, depending on the location of the vertex and the direction in which the parabola opens. By examining the vertex form of the quadratic function, it is possible to determine the number of zeros, and therefore the number of x-intercepts.

Two x-intercepts	One x-intercept	No x-intercepts

CHECK Your Understanding

1. For each quadratic function below, identify the following:

   i) the direction in which the parabola opens
   ii) the coordinates of the vertex
   iii) the equation of the axis of symmetry

   a) $f(x) = (x - 3)^2 + 7$
   b) $m(x) = -2(x + 7)^2 - 3$
   c) $g(x) = 7(x - 2)^2 - 9$
   d) $n(x) = \dfrac{1}{2}(x + 1)^2 + 10$
   e) $r(x) = -2x^2 + 5$

2. Predict which of the following functions have a maximum value and which have a minimum value. Also predict the number of x-intercepts that each function has. Test your predictions by sketching the graph of each function.

   a) $f(x) = -x^2 + 3$
   b) $q(x) = -(x + 2)^2 - 5$
   c) $m(x) = (x + 4)^2 + 2$
   d) $n(x) = (x - 3)^2 - 6$
   e) $r(x) = 2(x - 4)^2 + 2$

3. Determine the value of a, if point $(-1, 4)$ is on the quadratic function:

$$f(x) = a(x + 2)^2 + 7$$

PRACTISING

4. Which equation represents the graph? Justify your decision.

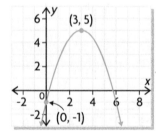

   A. $y = -\dfrac{2}{3}x^2 + 5$ **C.** $y = -\dfrac{2}{3}(x - 3)^2 + 5$

   B. $y = -(x - 3)^2 + 5$ **D.** $y = \dfrac{2}{3}(x - 3)^2 + 5$

5. Match each equation with its corresponding graph. Explain your reasoning.

a) $y = (x - 3)^2$ **c)** $y = -x^2 - 3$

b) $y = -(x + 4)^2 - 2$ **d)** $y = (x - 4)^2 + 2$

i)
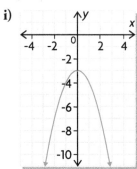

iii)
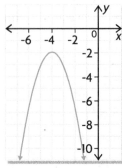

ii)
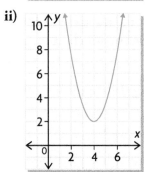

iv)
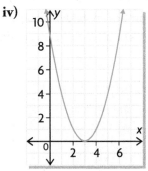

6. Explain how you would determine whether a parabola contains a minimum value or maximum value when the quadratic function that defines it is in vertex form:

$$y = a(x - h)^2 + k$$

Support your explanation with examples of functions and graphs.

7. State the equation of each function, if all the parabolas are congruent and if $a = 1$ or $a = -1$.

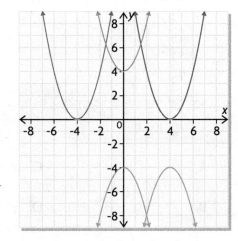

8. Marleen and Candice are both 6 ft tall, and they play on the same university volleyball team. In a game, Candice set up Marleen with an outside high ball for an attack hit. Using a video of the game, their coach determined that the height of the ball above the court, in feet, on its path from Candice to Marleen could be defined by the function

$$h(x) = -0.03(x - 9)^2 + 8$$

where x is the horizontal distance, measured in feet, from one edge of the court.

a) Determine the axis of symmetry of the parabola.
b) Marleen hit the ball at its highest point. How high above the court was the ball when she hit it?
c) How high was the ball when Candice set it, if she was 2 ft from the edge of the court?
d) State the range for the ball's path between Candice and Marleen. Justify your answer.

9. a) Write quadratic functions that define three different parabolas, all with their vertex at $(3, -1)$.
b) Predict how the graphs of the parabolas will be different from each other.
c) Graph each parabola on the same coordinate plane. How accurate were your predictions?

10. Without using a table of values or a graphing calculator, describe how you would graph the following function:

$$f(x) = 2(x - 1)^2 - 9$$

11. For each graph, determine the equation of the quadratic function in vertex form.

a)

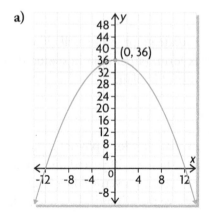

b)

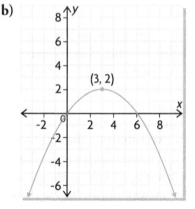

12. The vertex of a parabola is at $(4, -12)$.
  a) Write a function to define all the parabolas with this vertex.
  b) A parabola with this vertex passes through point $(13, 15)$. Determine the function for the parabola.
  c) State the domain and range of the function you determined in part b).
  d) Graph the quadratic function you determined in part b).

13. The height of the water, $h(t)$, in metres, that is sprayed from a sprinkler at a local golf course, can be modelled by the function

$$h(t) = -4.9(t - 1.5)^2 + 11.3$$

where time, t, is measured in seconds.
  a) Graph the function, and estimate the zeros of the function.
  b) What do the zeros represent in this situation?

14. A parabolic arch has x-intercepts $x = -6$ and $x = -1$. The parabola has a maximum height of 15 m.
  a) Determine the quadratic function that models the parabola.
  b) State the domain and range of the function.

15. Serge and a friend are throwing a paper airplane to each other. They stand 5 m apart from each other and catch the airplane at a height of 1 m above the ground. Serge throws the airplane on a parabolic flight path that achieves a minimum height of 0.5 m halfway to his friend.
  a) Determine a quadratic function that models the flight path for the height of the airplane.
  b) Determine the height of the plane when it is a horizontal distance of 1 m from Serge's friend.
  c) State the domain and range of the function.

Closing

16. Liz claims that she can sketch an accurate graph more easily if a quadratic function is given in vertex form, rather than in standard or factored form. Do you agree or disagree? Explain.

Extending

17. Peter is studying the flight path of an atlatl dart for a physics project. In a trial toss on the sports field, Peter threw his dart 80 yd and hit a platform that was 2 yd above the ground. The maximum vertical height of the atlatl was 10 yd. The dart was 2 yd above the ground when released.
  a) Sketch a graph that models the flight path of the dart thrown by Peter.
  b) How far from Peter, horizontally, was the atlatl dart when it reached a vertical height of 8 yd? Explain.

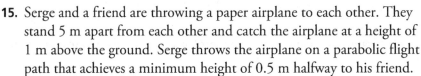

An atlatl is used to launch a dart. It has been used as a hunting tool by peoples all over the world for thousands of years.

18. When an airplane is accelerated downward by combining its engine power with gravity, the airplane is said to be in a power dive. At the Abbotsford International Air Show, one of the stunt planes began such a manoeuvre. Selected data from the plane's flight log is shown below.

t	0	4	8	16
h(t)	520	200	40	200

a) Define a function, $h(t)$, that models the height of the plane above the ground, in metres, over time, t, in seconds, after the manoeuvre began.
b) How low to the ground did the plane get on this manoeuvre?
c) How long did it take for the plane to return to its initial altitude?

19. A bridge is going to be constructed over a river, as shown below. The supporting arch of the bridge will form a parabola. At the point where the bridge is going to be constructed, the river is 20 m wide from bank to bank. The arch will be anchored on the ground, 4 m from the edge of the riverbank on each side. The maximum height of the arch can be between 18 m and 22 m above the surface of the water. Create two different quadratic functions that model the supporting arch. Include a labelled graph for each arch.

6.5 Solving Problems Using Quadratic Function Models

YOU WILL NEED

- graphing technology

GOAL

Solve problems involving situations that can be modelled by quadratic functions.

EXPLORE...

- Consider the three figures below.

Figure 1

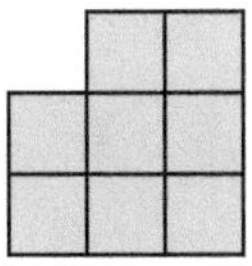

Figure 2

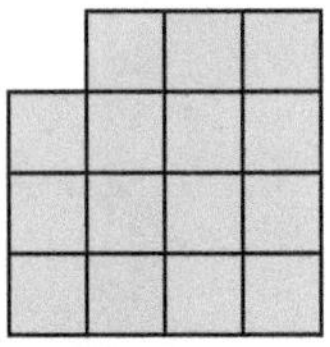

Figure 3

a) Create a table of values to compare the figure number, x, with the number of squares in each figure, y.

b) Graph the points. Then use your graph to predict the next three points in the pattern.

c) Determine a quadratic function that models the pattern.

d) Does the function you created enable you to state the domain and range for the context of the situation? Explain.

LEARN ABOUT the Math

The largest drop tower ride in the world is in an amusement park in Australia. Riders are lifted 119 m above the ground before being released. During the drop, the riders experience free fall for 3.8 s. The riders reach a speed of 37.5 m/s before magnetic brakes begin to slow down the platform. (This happens where the rail begins to move away from the supporting pillar in the photograph.)

A quadratic function can be used to model the height of the riders, H, in metres and the time, t, in seconds after the platform has been released.

The value of the constant a in the vertex form of $H(t)$ is:

$$a = -0.5g$$

where g is the acceleration due to gravity. On Earth, $g = 9.8 \text{ m/s}^2$.

? How high above the ground will the riders be when the brakes are applied?

EXAMPLE 1 **Applying quadratic models in problem solving**

Determine the height above the ground where the brakes are applied.

Georgia's Solution

$H(t) = a(t - h)^2 + k$

> I decided to use the vertex form of the quadratic function to model the height of the riders over time, since this problem contains information about the vertex.

The vertex is at (0, 119).
$h = 0$
$k = 119$
$H(t) = a(t - 0)^2 + 119$

> The vertex represents the height of the platform, 119 m, at time 0, when the platform is released.

Acceleration:
$a = -0.5(9.8)$
$H(t) = -0.5(9.8)(t - 0)^2 + 119$
$H(t) = -4.9t^2 + 119$

> The value of a is determined by gravity.

When $t = 3.8$ s:
$H(3.8) = -4.9(3.8)^2 + 119$
$H(3.8) = -4.9(14.44) + 119$
$H(3.8) = -70.756 + 119$
$H(3.8) = 48.244$

> I substituted $t = 3.8$ into my function and evaluated the expression.

The riders are approximately 48 m above the ground when the magnetic brakes are applied, 3.8 s after the ride begins.

> I decided to round my answer to the nearest whole number.

Reflecting

A. Explain why zero was used for the t-coordinate of the vertex.

B. Could the other forms of the quadratic function have been used in this situation? Explain.

APPLY the Math

EXAMPLE 2   Representing a situation with a quadratic model

Mary sells sugar-coated mini-doughnuts at a carnival for $6.00 a bag. Each day, she sells approximately 200 bags. Based on customer surveys, she knows that she will sell 20 more bags per day for each $0.30 decrease in the price. What is the maximum daily revenue that Mary can achieve from doughnut sales, and what is the price per bag for this maximum revenue?

Pablo's Solution: Modelling using properties of the function

Let x represent the number of $0.30 decreases in the price, where:

Revenue = (Price)(Number of bags sold)

Price = $6 - 0.30x$

Number of bags sold = $200 + 20x$

$R = (6 - 0.30x)(200 + 20x)$

> I defined a variable that connects the price per bag to the number of bags sold.

> If the price drops from $6 in $0.30 reductions x times, then the price per bag will be $(6 - 0.3x)$ and the number of bags sold will be $(200 + 20x)$.

$0 = (6 - 0.3x)(200 + 20x)$

$0 = (6 - 0.3x)$ or $0 = (200 + 20x)$

> The equation is in factored form. I determined the zeros of the function.

$0.3x = 6$ or $-20x = 200$

$x = \dfrac{6}{0.3}$ or $x = \dfrac{200}{-20}$

$x = 20$ or $x = -10$

Equation of axis of symmetry:

$x = \dfrac{20 + (-10)}{2}$

$x = 5$

> Because the axis of symmetry passes through the vertex, which is the point of maximum revenue, I knew that 5 is the number of $0.30 reductions that result in maximum revenue.

The price for a bag of doughnuts, P, that results in maximum revenue is

$P = 6 - 0.30(5)$

$P = 6 - 1.50$

$P = 4.50$

The price per bag that produces maximum revenue is $4.50.

$R = [6 - 0.3(5)]\,[200 + 20(5)]$

$R = [6 - 1.5]\,[200 + 100]$

$R = (4.5)(300)$

$R = 1350$

> The x-coordinate of the vertex is 5. I used this value to determine the y-coordinate of the vertex.

The maximum daily revenue for doughnut sales is $1350, when the price per bag is $4.50.

Monique's Solution: Modelling using graphing technology

Let x represent the number of $0.30 decreases in the price, where:

Revenue = (Price)(Number of bags sold)

Price = $6 - 0.30x$

Number of bags sold = $200 + 20x$

$y = (6 - 0.30x)(200 + 20x)$

I defined a variable that connects the price per bag to the number of bags sold.

I created an equation that models the situation in the problem.

If the price drops by $0.30 x times, then the price per bag will be ($6 - 0.3x$). The number of bags sold will be ($200 + 20x$).

I chose y to represent revenue.

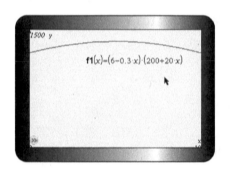

I graphed the function on my calculator.

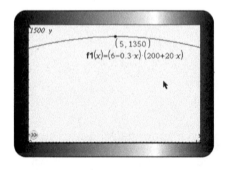

I used the calculator to determine the coordinates of the vertex.

The vertex is (5, 1350).

5 is the number of $0.30 price reductions and $1350 is the maximum daily revenue.

The price per bag of doughnuts, P, is

$P = 6 - 0.30(5)$

$P = 6 - 1.50$

$P = 4.50$

The price per bag that will produce the maximum daily revenue of $1350 is $4.50.

6.5 Solving Problems Using Quadratic Function Models

Your Turn

Javier's saltwater candy booth is beside Mary's mini-doughnut stand at the carnival. Javier has determined that if he raises the price of his candy by $0.25 per bag, he will sell 25 fewer bags each day. Javier currently sells 300 bags at $5.50 per bag.

a) How much should Javier charge to generate the maximum revenue per day?
b) Describe any similarities and differences between the two booths.
c) What assumptions is Javier making if he is only looking at generating maximum revenue? Explain.

EXAMPLE 3   ## Solving a maximum problem with a quadratic function in standard form

A large cosmetics company is developing a new advertising campaign. The company has obtained data from the 2006 Census of Canada about the population of females between 25 and 65 years of age, the company's potential customers. Analysis of the data has provided the company with this quadratic model for the percent of women, y, at any given age, x, in the Canadian population:

$$y = -0.007x^2 + 0.623x - 5.094$$

Determine the age group that the company should target to maximize the percent of the female population that uses its cosmetics.

Gina's Solution

Defined quadratic function:

$y = -0.007x^2 + 0.623x - 5.094$

I entered the function into my graphing calculator.

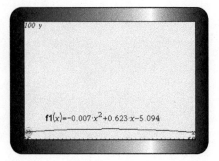

I used the information provided in the problem to set the domain as $25 \le x \le 65$.

I knew that the y-values in the question refer to a percent, so I set the range as $0 \le y \le 100$.

The result was a graph with a vertex that was difficult to see.

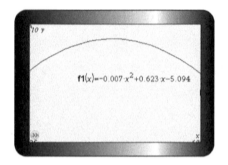

I adjusted the range so I could see the parabola more clearly.

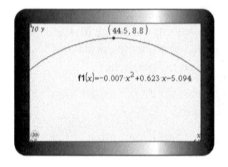

I used the calculator to locate the coordinates of the vertex.

The vertex is at (44.5, 8.8).

44.5 is the age of women in Canada that results in the largest percent of the Canadian female population, which is about 9%.

The cosmetics company should target women around the age of 45, since this group makes up about 9% of women in Canada between the ages of 25 and 65.

I decided to round my answer to the nearest whole number.

Your Turn

The same company has a line of men's fragrances. Based on many mall surveys, the marketing team has determined that the function

$$y = -0.015x^2 + 0.981x - 6.828$$

models the percent of male respondents, y, at any given age, x, in the Canadian population.

a) What age should the marketing team target in its advertisements?

b) How is this model different from the model for women's cosmetics? How is it the same?

EXAMPLE **4** **Determining a quadratic function that models a situation**

The underside of a concrete underpass forms a parabolic arch. The arch is 30.0 m wide at the base and 10.8 m high in the centre. What would be the headroom at the edge of a sidewalk that starts 1.8 m from the base of the underpass? Would this amount of headroom be safe?

Domonika's Solution

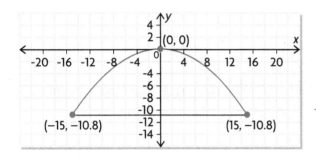

To model the underpass, I decided to sketch a parabola with its vertex at the origin, (0, 0). I knew that this would simplify my calculations to determine points on the parabola.

I knew that the parabola must open downward to model the underpass.

The arch is 10.8 m high and 30 m wide, so I plotted points $(-15, -10.8)$ and $(15, -10.8)$.

I connected the three points with a smooth curve.

Using the vertex form of the quadratic function to model the parabola:

$y = a(x - h)^2 + k$
$h = 0$
$k = 0$

$y = a(x - 0)^2 + 0$
$y = ax^2$

$-10.8 = a(15)^2$

$-\dfrac{10.8}{225} = a$

$-0.048 = a$

$y = -0.048x^2$

I substituted the x- and y-coordinates of one of the known points into the quadratic function to determine the value of a.

I wrote the quadratic function that models the arch.

The edge of the sidewalk is 1.8 m from the base of the parabola.

$$15.0 - 1.8 = 13.2$$

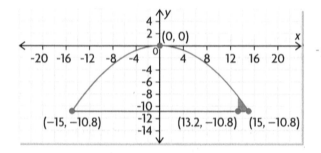

(−15, −10.8)   (13.2, −10.8)   (15, −10.8)

I assumed that the sidewalk would be on the following line:

$$y = -10.8$$

I plotted point (13.2, −10.8).

I coloured the space between the sidewalk and the parabola. The highest point of the coloured region is the headroom above the edge of the sidewalk.

$y = -0.048(13.2)^2$
$y = -8.363\ldots$

I knew that the x-coordinate of the point directly above the edge of the sidewalk is 13.2. I substituted 13.2 into the quadratic function to determine the y-coordinate of this point.

Therefore, (13.2, −8.4) is the approximate location of a point on the parabola that corresponds to the least headroom above the sidewalk.

Headroom above the sidewalk, H, is
$H = -8.363\ldots - (-10.8)$
$H = 2.436\ldots$ m

To determine the minimum headroom, I subtracted the y-coordinate of the base of the parabola from the y-coordinate of the point above the sidewalk.

On the edge of the sidewalk, the headroom will be about 2.4 m. This is higher than most people are tall, even when standing on a skateboard, so the plan for the sidewalk is safe.

Your Turn

Another concrete underpass, on the same stretch of road, is also 30.0 m wide at the base of its arch. However, this arch is 11.7 m high in the centre. The sidewalk under this arch will also be built so that it starts 1.8 m from the base of the underpass.

a) How much headroom will the sidewalk under this arch have?
b) What is the difference in headroom for the two sidewalks?

In Summary

Key Idea

- The form of the quadratic function that you use to model a given situation depends on what you know about the relationship:
  - Use the vertex form when you know the vertex and an additional point on the parabola.
  - Use the factored form when you know the *x*-intercepts and an additional point on the parabola.

Need to Know

- When a function is a quadratic function, the maximum/minimum value corresponds to the *y*-coordinate of the vertex. The algebraic strategy you use to locate the vertex depends on the form of the quadratic function.

Quadratic Function	Algebraic Strategy to Determine the Vertex
Standard form: $f(x) = ax^2 + bx + c$	Use partial factoring to determine two points on the parabola with the same *y*-coordinate, then the axis of symmetry, and then the *y*-coordinate of the vertex: $f(x) = x(ax + b) + c$
Factored form: $f(x) = a(x - r)(x - s)$	Set each factor equal to zero to determine the zeros. Use the zeros to determine the equation of the axis of symmetry, then determine the *y*-coordinate of the vertex.
Vertex form: $f(x) = a(x - h)^2 + k$	The vertex is (h, k).

- All maximum/minimum problems can be solved using graphing technology, if you know the quadratic function that models the situation.

CHECK Your Understanding

1. Use the given information to express a quadratic function in vertex form:

$$y = a(x - h)^2 + k$$

   a) $a = 3$, vertex at $(0, -5)$ **c)** $a = -3$, vertex at $(-1, 0)$

   b) $a = -1$, vertex at $(2, 3)$ **d)** $a = 0.25$, vertex at $(-1.2, 4.8)$

2. The vertex of a parabola is at $(-5, 2)$. The parabola also includes point $(-1, -4)$. Determine the quadratic function that defines the parabola.

PRACTISING

3. Determine the quadratic function, in vertex form, that defines each parabola.
   a) vertex at $(0, 3)$, passes through $(-2, 11)$
   b) vertex at $(3, 0)$, passes through $(-1, 8)$
   c) vertex at $(-1, 4)$, passes through $(3, -12)$
   d) vertex at $(2, -5)$, passes through $(4, -7)$

4. Determine the quadratic function that includes the factors $(x - 3)$ and $(x - 7)$ and the point $(6, 3)$. Write the equation for the function in vertex form.

5. For each quadratic function below
   i) sketch the graph of the function
   ii) state the maximum or minimum value
   iii) express the function in standard form

   a) $f(x) = -(x - 1)(x + 3)$
   b) $g(x) = 4(x - 3)(x - 2)$
   c) $m(x) = 3(x - 2)^2 - 4$
   d) $n(x) = -0.25(x + 4)^2 + 5$

6. Determine the quadratic function, in vertex form, that defines each parabola.

   a)
   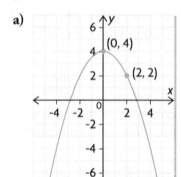

   c)
   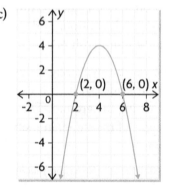

   b)
   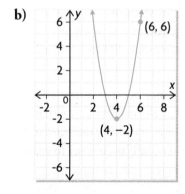

   d)
   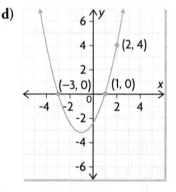

6.5 Solving Problems Using Quadratic Function Models

7. A stunt pilot performs a manoeuvre called the death spiral by flying the airplane straight up, cutting power to the engine, and then allowing the airplane to fall toward the ground before restarting the engine.
   a) The altimeter in the airplane reads 1375 m when the engine is turned off and reads 1000 m 15 s later. The airplane achieves its maximum height 5 s into the manoeuvre. Model the death spiral with a function, $h(t)$, that describes the height of the airplane, in metres, above the ground over the time, t, in seconds, after the engine is turned off.
   b) How high does the airplane get on this manoeuvre?

8. Bill and Ben are on a bridge, timing how long it takes stones they have dropped to hit the water below. A quadratic relation can be used to determine the distance, D, in metres, that a stone will fall in the time, t, in seconds after it is released. In this relation, $a = -0.5g$, where g is acceleration due to gravity, which is approximately 9.8 m/s^2 on Earth. Ben starts a timer when Bill releases a stone, and he stops the timer when the stone hits the water below. The mean time of several trials is 3 s.
   a) Determine a quadratic function that models the falling stones.
   b) How high above the water are Bill and Ben? Explain your answer.
   c) On Saturn's moon, Titan, the value of g is 1.35 m/s^2. Suppose that Bill and Ben are astronauts and they are standing at the top of a cliff on Titan. If they record the time for a stone to fall from their hands to the bottom of the cliff as 3 s, how high is the cliff, to the nearest hundredth of a metre?

9. A stone was thrown straight down from a high point on the Enderby Cliffs near Enderby, British Columbia. The stone travelled 180 m before hitting the ground. The stone took 5 s to reach the ground. The height of the stone, in metres, can be modelled by the quadratic function

$$h(t) = -5t^2 + V_0 t + h_0$$

where V_0 represents the initial velocity of the rock, h_0 represents the initial height, and t represents the time in seconds.
   a) Determine the initial velocity of the rock.
   b) Write the quadratic function from question 8a) in standard form. Provide your reasoning.

10. An ice cream shop sells 700 ice cream cones per day at a price of $4.50. Based on the previous year's sales, the owners know that they will sell another 100 ice cream cones for every $0.50 decrease in price.
    a) How should the owners price their cones if they want to maximize their daily revenue?
    b) How much extra revenue will be gained by the price change?

11. Police can use a quadratic function to model the relationship between the speed of a car and the length of the skid marks it makes on the pavement after the driver starts to brake. Based on this relationship, if a car is travelling at 100 km/h, the car will leave skid marks that are 70 m long under full braking.

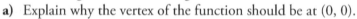

   a) Explain why the vertex of the function should be at (0, 0).

   b) Determine a quadratic function that relates the speed of a car, x, measured in kilometres per hour, to the stopping distance, D, measured in metres.

   c) How long would the skid marks be for a car that is travelling at 60 km/h, rounded to the nearest tenth?

   d) What factors, other than speed, might affect the length of the skid marks? Explain.

12. The Lions Gate Bridge in Vancouver is a suspension bridge. The main span, between the two towers, is 472 m long. Large cables are attached to the top of both towers, 50 m above the road. Each large cable forms a parabola. The road is suspended from the large cables by a series of shorter vertical cables. The shortest vertical cable measures about 2 m. Use this information to determine a quadratic function that models one of the large cables.

13. A parking lot is being constructed under a historic hotel. The entrance to the parking lot is through a parabolic arch that is 9 ft high at its centre and 13 ft wide at its base.

   a) Determine a quadratic function, $h(x)$, that relates the height of the arch, in feet, to its width, x, in feet. State the domain of this function.

   b) What is the widest vehicle, 6 ft high, that can enter the parking lot through the arch?

   c) What is the tallest vehicle, 6 ft wide, that can enter the parking lot through the arch?

   d) Suggest wording for a sign to warn drivers about the restrictions for vehicles about to enter the parking lot.

14. A large radio-telescope dish was built in a hollow at Arecibo in Puerto Rico. The parabolic surface contains 38 778 slightly curved aluminum panels, each measuring 1 m wide and 2 m long. If a cross-section of the dish were placed on a coordinate grid so that the maximum width, 305 m, was aligned along the x-axis, the vertex of the parabola would be 21.94 m below the origin. Determine a quadratic function that models the cross-section of the dish.

15. The owner of a small clothing company wants to create a mathematical model for the company's daily profit, p, in dollars, based on the selling price, d, in dollars, of the dresses made. The owner has noticed that the maximum daily profit the company has made is $1600. This occurred when the dresses were sold for $75 each. The owner also noticed that selling the dresses for $50 resulted in a profit of $1225. Use a quadratic function to model this company's daily profit.

Closing

16. A dinner theatre has 600 season ticket holders. The owners of the theatre have decided to raise the price of a season ticket from the current price of $400. According to a recent survey of season ticket holders, for every $50 increase in the price, 30 season ticket holders will not renew their seats.

   a) What should the owners charge for each season ticket in order to maximize their revenue?

   b) How many people will still buy season tickets if the owners decide to apply the new price?

   c) How might the size of the audience affect the dinner theatre? Explain.

Extending

17. An oval reflecting pool has water fountains along its sides. Looking from one end of the pool, streams from fountains on each side of the pool cross each other over the middle of the pool at a height of 3 m. The two fountains are 10 m apart. Each fountain sprays an identical parabolic-shaped stream of water a total horizontal distance of 8 m toward the opposite side.

   a) Determine an equation that models a stream of water from the left side and another equation that models a stream of water from the right side. Graph both equations on the same set of axes.

   b) Determine the maximum height of the water.

18. A straight bicycle path crosses two roads, forming a triangle as shown. A developer wants to create a rectangular section within the triangle and then subdivide the section into smaller rectangular lots. She wants the rectangle to be the maximum possible area.

The length of the rectangle can be defined as $(600 - x)$.

The width of the rectangle, y, can be defined as $\dfrac{2x}{3}$.

a) Write a quadratic function that defines the area of the rectangular section of land.

b) What is the maximum area for the rectangle?

c) Determine the dimensions of the rectangle that result in the maximum area.

d) The developer plans to mark out 20 m by 30 m lots. How many lots will be available?

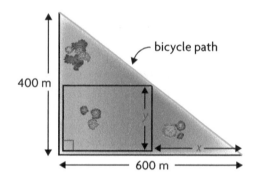

Trap Shooting

Trap shooting involves hitting clay discs using a shotgun. The sport was introduced to the Olympics in 1900, but the first Olympic competition using the current rules was in 1952. In this competition, there are five shooting stations, and the shooters rotate through the stations. Targets are launched from a single "house." Programmed machines randomly launch the targets from the house in the proportion 10 to the right, 10 to the left, and 5 straight on, so the targets are similar and fair for all the shooters.

The shooters must hit as many targets as they can. Each shooter has 10 s in which to signal the release of a target. Once a shooter has fired a shot, the next shooter calls for a target. Men must fire 125 shots, and women must fire 75 shots.

Canadians have won gold medals twice in this sport. Walter Ewing won in 1908, and George Généreux won in 1952.

Susan Nattress is one of Canada's most decorated trap shooters. She was born in Medicine Hat, Alberta, and has competed in six Olympic Games.

A. Is a quadratic function an appropriate model to represent a "shot" in this competition? Explain.

Curious Counting Puzzles

Consider the following puzzles:

How many handshakes
will there be if 8 people
must shake hands with each
other only once?

How many lines can be
drawn that connect each
pair of points if there are
8 points in total?

How many acute angles are
there in this diagram?

How are these three puzzles related to each other?

The Strategy

A. For each problem, use inductive reasoning to generate data. Begin
your reasoning process by examining the cases where the number of
people, points, and lines is 0. Then look at other cases by increasing
the number of people, points, and lines systematically by 1 each time.

B. Graph your data. What type of function can be used to model each
situation?

C. Determine the function that represents each relationship.

D. Explain how these problems are related to each other.

Creating a Variation of the Puzzle

E. Create a related problem that can be modelled by the function you
determined above.

F. Explain how the function can be used to solve your problem.

1. Sketch each of the following quadratic functions. Explain why you chose the method you used.
   a) $f(x) = x^2 - 8x + 12$
   b) $f(x) = -2(x + 1)(x - 5)$
   c) $f(x) = 0.5(x + 2)^2 - 7$
   d) $f(x) = -2x^2 - 8x$

2. Determine the y-intercept, x-intercepts, equation of the axis of symmetry, and vertex of the parabola that is defined by each quadratic function.
   a) $y = -1(x + 3)(x - 5)$
   b) $y = (2x - 3)(x + 4)$

3. Workers who were improving a section of highway near Rogers Pass, British Columbia, used dynamite to remove a rock obstruction. When the rock shattered, the height of one piece of rock, $h(t)$, in feet, could be modelled by the function
$$h(t) = -16t^2 + 160t$$
where t represents the time, in seconds, after the blast.
   a) How long was the piece of rock in the air?
   b) How high was the piece of rock after 2 s?
   c) What was the maximum height of the piece of rock?

4. A quadratic function has zeros of -1 and -3, and includes the point $(1, 24)$. Determine the quadratic function.

5. A parabola has a y-intercept of -4 and a vertex at $(3, -7)$. Determine the equation of the parabola in standard form.

6. Dimples the Clown has been charging $260 to perform at a children's party. Dimples is too busy to keep up with his bookings, and thinks that charging more for his performances will result in fewer bookings but more revenue. If he raises the charge by $80 per party, he expects to get one fewer booking per month. Dimples performs at 20 children's parties each month at his current price. How much should he charge to maximize his monthly revenue?

7. A builder wants to place a parabolic arch over the doorway of a home she is building. She wants the highest point in the arch to be over the middle of the doorway. The arch she wants to use is defined by the quadratic function
$$y = -\frac{5}{18}x^2 + 5x - \frac{25}{2}$$
where x is the horizontal distance from the left edge of the building, in feet, and y is the height of the arch, in feet, above the steps. The doorway is 8 ft wide. What will be the height of the arch above the top step? Is this headroom reasonable? Explain.

WHAT DO You Think Now? Revisit **What Do You Think?** on page 321. How have your answers and explanations changed?

FREQUENTLY ASKED Questions

Study | Aid
- See Lesson 6.4, Examples 1 and 2.
- Try Chapter Review Questions 10 and 11.

Q: **How can you graph a quadratic function in vertex form, $y = a(x - h)^2 + k$?**

A: Use the information provided by the form of the quadratic equation.

For example: Sketch the graph of the following quadratic function:

$$y = 7(x - 4)^2 + 10$$

The vertex is at (4, 10).	Determine the coordinates of the vertex, (h, k).
$y = 7[(5) - 4]^2 + 10$ $y = 7(1)^2 + 10$ $y = 17$ One other point on the graph is (5, 17).	Locate one other point on the function by substituting a value for x into the equation. In this example, substitute 5 for x because the calculation is easy to check.
Another point on the graph is (3, 17), because 3 is the same distance from 4 as 5 is. (Another way of looking at this is that $(x - 4)^2 = 1$ when x is 5 and when x is 3.)	Apply symmetry to the first located point. In this example, the vertical line of symmetry is $x = 4$.
	Connect the three points with a smooth curve.

Study | Aid
- See Lesson 6.4, Examples 2 and 4, and Lesson 6.5, Examples 1, 2, and 3.
- Try Chapter Review Questions 15 to 19.

Q: **Which form of the quadratic function should you use to solve contextual problems?**

A: If you want to know the maximum or minimum value, you should use the vertex form.

If you want to know the y-intercept, you should use the standard form.

If you want to know the x-intercepts, you should use the factored form.

Q: **How can you determine a quadratic function that models a situation described in a problem?**

A1: If you are given the vertex and one other point on the parabola, write the function in whatever form is easiest to determine. You can then rewrite the function in standard form.

For example: The vertex of a parabola is $(-2, -4)$, and $(2, 6)$ is another point on the parabola.

Study **Aid**

• See Lesson 6.4, Example 4, and Lesson 6.5, Examples 1 and 4.
• Try Chapter Review Questions 13 and 14.

$y = a(x - h)^2 + k$ $\quad y = a(x + 2)^2 - 4$	Substitute (h, k), the coordinates of the vertex, into the vertex form of the quadratic function.
$y = a(x + 2)^2 - 4$ $\quad (6) = a[(2) + 2]^2 - 4$ $\quad 6 = a[16] - 4$ $\quad 10 = 16a$ $\quad \dfrac{10}{16} = a$ $\quad \dfrac{5}{8} = a$	Using the coordinates of the other known point, (x, y), solve for a.
$y = \dfrac{5}{8}(x + 2)^2 - 4$	Substitute the value of a into your quadratic function.

A2: If you are given two x-intercepts and another point on the graph, substitute the coordinates of these points into the factored form of the quadratic function.

For example: The x-intercepts of a parabola are $x = -2$ and $x = 4$. Another point on the parabola is $(6, 64)$. Determine the quadratic function that defines the parabola.

$y = a(x - r)(x - s)$ $\quad y = a(x + 2)(x - 4)$	Substitute $(r, 0)$ and $(s, 0)$ into the factored form of the quadratic function.
$y = a(x + 2)(x - 4)$ $\quad (64) = a[(6) + 2][(6) - 4]$ $\quad 64 = a[16]$ $\quad 4 = a$	Substitute the coordinates, (x, y), of the other known point into your equation and solve for a.
$y = 4(x + 2)(x - 4)$	Substitute the value of a into your quadratic function.

PRACTISING

Lesson 6.1

1. Graph the following quadratic functions without using technology.
   a) $f(x) = x^2 - 6x + 8$
   b) $g(x) = -2(x + 1)(x - 3)$
   c) $h(x) = 0.5(x + 4)^2 - 2$

Lesson 6.2

2. Monish is taking a design course in high school. He wants to create a model of Winnipeg's River Arch digitally by placing one of the bases of this arch at the origin of a graph on a coordinate grid. He knows that the arch spans 23 m. Explain how to determine the equation of the axis of symmetry for his model.

3. The points $(-2, -41)$ and $(6, -41)$ are on the following quadratic function:
   $$f(x) = -3x^2 + 12x - 5$$
   Determine the vertex of the function.

4. Trap shooting is a sport in which a clay disk is launched into the air by a machine. Competitors are required to shoot the disk with a shotgun while the disk is in the air. The height, $h(t)$, in metres, of one clay disk after it is launched is modelled by the function
   $$h(t) = -5t^2 + 30t + 2$$
   where t represents time after launch, in seconds.
   a) Determine the maximum height of the disk.
   b) State the domain and range for this function.

5. In the photograph, the fisherman is holding his fishing rod 0.5 m above the water. The fishing rod reaches its maximum height 1.5 m above and 1 m to the left of his hand.

   a) Determine the quadratic function that describes the arc of the fishing rod. Assume that the y-axis passes through the fisherman's hand and the x-axis is at water level.
   b) State the domain and range for the function that models the fishing rod.

6. Determine, to the nearest hundredth, the coordinates of the vertex of the following quadratic function:
   $$q(x) = 0.4x^2 + 5x - 8$$

Lesson 6.3

7. a) Rewrite the following quadratic function in factored form:
   $$f(x) = 2x^2 - 12x + 10$$
   b) Identify the zeros of the function, and determine the equation of the axis of symmetry of the parabola it defines.
   c) State the domain and range of the function.
   d) Graph the function.

8. Determine the x-intercepts of the graph of this quadratic function:
   $$f(x) = 2x^2 - 5x - 12$$

9. Determine the vertex of the parabola that is defined by each quadratic function. Explain your process.
  a) $f(x) = 3x^2 - 6x + 5$
  b) $g(x) = -1(x + 2)(x + 3)$

Lesson 6.4

10. Determine the quadratic function, written in vertex form, that defines each of these parabolas.

a)

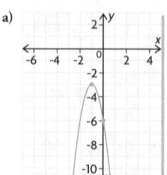

b)

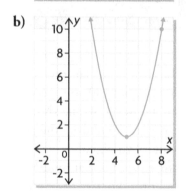

11. a) State the direction of opening of the parabola that is defined by the following quadratic function:

$$y = 2(x - 3)^2 - 7$$

  b) Provide the equation of the axis of symmetry and the coordinates of the vertex of the parabola.
  c) State the domain and range of the function.
  d) Sketch the parabola.

12. Determine the quadratic function that defines this parabola:

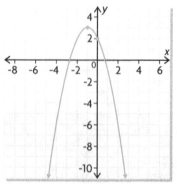

13. Determine the quadratic function with zeros of -4 and -2, if the point $(-1, -9)$ is also on the graph of this function.

14. Determine the quadratic function that defines the parabola that has a vertex at $(3, -5)$ and passes through $(-1, -9)$.

15. The High Level Bridge in Edmonton is the source of the Great Divide Waterfall, which is open to the public on holiday weekends in the summer. The water falls a vertical distance of 45 m from the bridge and reaches the North Saskatchewan River 10 m horizontally from the base of the bridge. Determine a quadratic function that models the path of the water.

16. The Ponte Juscelino Kubitschek in Brasilia, Brazil, has three identical parabolic arches as shown above. Each arch is 61 m high and spans 219 m at a height of 10 m above the water.

a) Determine a quadratic function that models one of the arches.

b) What other information would you need to determine the total span of the bridge?

17. A two-lane highway runs through a tunnel that is framed by a parabolic arch, which is 20 m wide. The roof of the tunnel, measured 4 m from its right base, is 4 m above the ground. Can a truck that is 4 m wide and 5 m tall pass through the tunnel?

18. Marcelle has ordered 80 m of stacking stones so that she can create a raised garden. She needs to place the stones on only three sides, since the garden will be built against her fence. Determine the dimensions that will enable Marcelle to maximize her planting area, and determine the maximum area of the garden.

19. On the 13th hole of a golf course, Saraya hits her tee shot to the right of the fairway. Saraya estimates that she now has 130 yd to reach the front of the green. However, she needs to clear some pine trees that are 40 yd from the green. The trees are about 10 yd high. Determine two different quadratic equations that model the flight of a golf ball over the trees and onto the green. Write one of your functions in factored form and the other in standard form.

Parabolas in Inuit Culture

Traditional Inuit homes include arched domes, called igloos, that are made of snow blocks. The internal design of an igloo makes use of the principle that hot air rises and cold air sinks. In a typical igloo, hot air from the qulliq (seal oil lamp) and from human bodies rises and is trapped in the dome. Cold air sinks and is pooled at the entrance, which is lower than the living area. There are ventilation holes for the release of carbon dioxide.

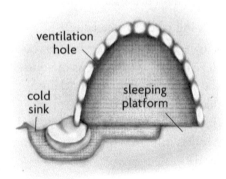

? How can quadratic functions be used to model the cross-section of an igloo?

A. From the Internet or another source, obtain a picture of an igloo that appears to have a parabolic cross-section that you can use to estimate the size of an igloo.

B. Draw and label cross-sectional models of the interior of an igloo. Assume that each snow block is 1 ft thick. Also assume that the entrance to the igloo is 2 ft below the snow line.

C. Model the cross-sections of the arches on the exterior and interior of the igloo using quadratic functions, assuming that both arches are parabolic. State the domain and range of each function.

D. Based on your quadratic models, how close to the entrance of the igloo can a person who is 5 ft 6 in. tall stand, without ducking or bending?

> **Task | Checklist**
>
> ✔ Is your model neatly drawn and labelled?
>
> ✔ Have you stated and justified all the assumptions that support your quadratic models?
>
> ✔ Have you used appropriate mathematical language?

Identifying Controversial Issues

While working on your research project you may uncover some issues on which people disagree. To decide on how to present an issue fairly, consider some questions you can ask yourself or others as you carry out your research.

1. What is the issue about?

Identify which type of controversy you have uncovered. Almost all controversy revolves around one or more of the following:

- Values—What should be? What is best?
- Information—What is the truth? What is a reasonable interpretation?
- Concepts—What does this mean? What are the implications?

2. What positions are being taken on the issue?

Determine what is being said and whether there is reasonable support for the claims being made. You can ask questions of yourself and of others as you research to test the acceptability of values claims:

- Would you like that done to you?
- Is the claim based on a value that is generally shared?

If the controversy involves information, ask questions about the information being used:

- Is there adequate information?
- Are the claims in the information accurate?

If the controversy surrounds concepts, look at the words being used:

- Are those taking various positions on the issue all using the same meanings of terms?

3. What is being assumed?

Faulty assumptions reduce legitimacy. You can ask:

- What are the assumptions behind an argument?
- Is the position based on prejudice or an attitude contrary to universally held human values, such as those set out in the United Nations Declaration of Human Rights?
- Is the person presenting a position or opinion an insider or an outsider?

Insiders may have information and understanding not available to outsiders; however, they may also have special interests. Outsiders may lack the information or depth of understanding available to insiders; however, they may also be more objective.

4. What are the interests of those taking positions?

Try to determine the motivations of those taking positions on the issue. What are their reasons for taking their positions? The degree to which the parties involved are acting in self-interest could affect the legitimacy of their positions.

Identifying a controversial issue

Sarah chose the changes in population of the Western provinces and the territories over the last century as her topic. Below, she describes how she identified and dealt with a controversial issue.

Sarah's Explanation

I found that population growth can involve controversial issues. One such issue is discrimination in immigration policy. When researching reasons for population growth in Canada, I discovered that our nation had some controversial immigration policies.

From 1880 to 1885 about 17 000 Chinese labourers helped build the British Columbia section of the trans-Canada railway. They were paid only half the wage of union workers. When the railway was finished, these workers were no longer welcome. The federal government passed the *Chinese Immigration Act* in 1885, putting a head tax of $50 on Chinese immigrants to discourage them from staying in or entering Canada. In 1903, the head tax was raised to $500, which was about two years' pay at the time. In 1923, Canada passed the *Chinese Exclusion Act*, which stopped Chinese immigration to Canada for nearly a quarter of a century. In 2006, Prime Minister Stephen Harper made a speech in the House of Commons apologizing for these policies.

I decided to do some more research on Canada's immigration policies, looking at historical viewpoints and the impact of the policies on population growth in the West and North. I will include a discussion about the effects of these policies in my presentation and report.

Your Turn

A. Identify the most controversial issue, if any, you have uncovered during your research.

B. Determine the different positions people have on this issue and the supporting arguments they present. If possible, include any supporting data for these different positions.

C. If applicable, include a discussion of this issue in your presentation and report.

Quadratic Equations

▶ **LEARNING GOALS**

You will be able to develop your algebraic and graphical reasoning by

- Solving quadratic equations by graphing, by factoring, and by using the quadratic formula
- Solving problems that involve quadratic equations

? A dolphin's height, $h(t)$, in metres, when jumping in the ocean can be modelled by the equation

$$h(t) = -5t^2 + 10t$$

where t is the number of seconds from the beginning of the jump.

What could you find out about the dolphin's jump by substituting different values into this equation?

Factoring Design

Jasmine labelled points around a circle with quadratic expressions and their factors, as shown below. Then she made a design by drawing lines to connect each expression to its factors.

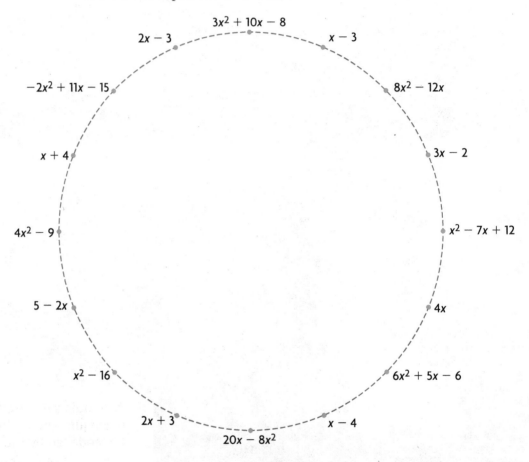

? How can you factor each quadratic expression to find out what Jasmine's design looks like?

A. Draw and label a circle to match Jasmine's circle. Factor each quadratic expression, and record your factors in a table like the one below.

Quadratic Expression	Factor	Factor

B. Join each quadratic expression to its two factors. Use different colours if you want.

C. Compare your design with a classmate's design. Do your designs look the same?

D. Create a design of your own, using at least six quadratic expressions. Exchange designs with a classmate. Was your classmate able to complete your design?

WHAT DO You Think?

Decide whether you agree or disagree with each statement. Explain your decision.

1. A graph is a useful tool to use to solve an equation.

2. The x-intercepts or zeros of a function are also solutions to its equation.

3. Since a quadratic function can be written in factored form as a product of two factors, quadratic equations will have two solutions.

Solving Quadratic Equations by Graphing

GOAL

Solve quadratic equations by graphing the corresponding function.

INVESTIGATE the Math

EXPLORE...

- Graph the quadratic function $y = x^2 + 5$. How could you use your graph to solve the equation $21 = x^2 + 5$? What are some other equations you could solve with your graph?

Bonnie launches a model rocket from the ground with an initial velocity of 68 m/s. The following function, $h(t)$, can be used to model the height of the rocket, in metres, over time, t, in seconds:

$$h(t) = -4.9t^2 + 68t$$

Bonnie's friend Sasha is watching from a lookout point at a safe distance. Sasha's eye level is 72 m above the ground.

? How can you determine the times during the flight when the rocket will be at Sasha's eye level?

A. What is the value of $h(t)$ when the rocket is at Sasha's eye level?

B. Substitute the value of $h(t)$ that you calculated in part A into the function

$$h(t) = -4.9t^2 + 68t$$

quadratic equation

A polynomial equation of the second degree; the standard form of a quadratic equation is
$ax^2 + bx + c = 0$
For example:
$2x^2 + 4x - 3 = 0$

to create a **quadratic equation**. You can solve this quadratic equation to determine when the rocket is at Sasha's eye level. Rewrite the quadratic equation in standard form.

C. Graph the function that corresponds to your equation. Use the zeros feature on your calculator to determine the t-intercepts.

D. Graph $h(t) = -4.9t^2 + 68t$. On the same axes, graph the horizontal line that represents Sasha's eye level. Determine the t-coordinates of the points where the two graphs intersect.

E. What do you notice about the t-coordinates of these points?

F. When will the rocket be at Sasha's eye level?

Reflecting

G. How were your two graphs similar? How were they different?

H. Describe the two different strategies you used to solve the problem. What are the advantages of each?

APPLY the Math

EXAMPLE 1 Verifying solutions to a quadratic equation

The flight time for a long-distance water ski jumper depends on the initial velocity of the jump and the angle of the ramp. For one particular jump, the ramp has a vertical height of 5.0 m above water level. The height of the ski jumper in flight, $h(t)$, in metres, over time, t, in seconds, can be modelled by the following function:

$$h(t) = 5.0 + 24.46t - 4.9t^2$$

How long does this water ski jumper hold his flight pose?

The skier holds his flight pose until he is 4.0 m above the water.

Olana's Solution

$h(t) = 5.0 + 24.46t - 4.9t^2$
$4.0 = 5.0 + 24.46t - 4.9t^2$

> I substituted 4.0 for $h(t)$ to get a quadratic equation I can use to determine the time when the skier's height above the water is 4.0 m.

$0 = 1.0 + 24.46t - 4.9t^2$

> I subtracted 4.0 from both sides to put the equation in standard form.
>
> In standard form, $h(t) = 0$. Therefore, the solutions to the equation are the t-intercepts of the graph of this function.

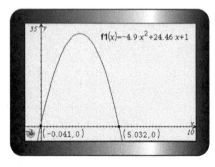

The graph shows $f1(x) = -4.9x^2 + 24.46x + 1$ with points $(-0.041, 0)$ and $(5.032, 0)$.

I graphed the function on a calculator. I adjusted the window to show the vertex and the x-intercepts. I used the calculator to determine the x-intercepts.

The *t*-intercepts are 5.032 and −0.041.

I reread the problem to make sure each solution made sense. Time can't be negative in this situation, so the jumper did not come out of his pose at −0.041 s. Although (−0.041, 0) is a point on the graph, it doesn't make sense in the context of this problem.

Verify:
$$4.0 = 5.0 + 24.46t − 4.9t^2$$
$$t = 5.032$$

LS	RS
4.0	$5.0 + 24.46(5.032) − 4.9(5.032)^2$
	$5.0 + 123.082 \ldots − 124.073 \ldots$
	$4.009 \ldots$

$$LS \doteq RS$$

I verified the other solution by substituting it into the original equation. The left side was not quite equal to the right side, but I knew that this was because the calculator is set to show values to three decimal places. The solution is not exact, but it is correct.

The ski jumper holds his flight pose for about 5 s.

Your Turn

Curtis rearranged the equation $4.0 = 5.0 + 24.46t − 4.9t^2$ a different way and got the following equation:

$$4.9t^2 − 24.46t − 1.0 = 0$$

a) Graph the function that is represented by Curtis's equation. How does this graph compare with Olana's graph?

b) Will Curtis get the same solution that Olana did? Explain.

EXAMPLE **2**   Graphing to determine the number of roots

Lamont runs a boarding kennel for dogs.
He wants to construct a rectangular play space
for the dogs, using 40 m of fencing and an
existing fence as one side of the play space.

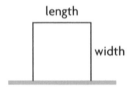
length

width

a) Write a function that describes the area, A, in
square metres, of the play space for any width,
w, in metres.

b) Write equations you could use to determine
the widths for areas of 250 m², 200 m²,
and 150 m².

c) Determine the number of possible widths
for each equation using a graph.

Lamont's Solution

Let A represent the area of the play space
in square metres.
Let l and w represent the dimensions of
the play space in metres.

a) $l + 2w = 40$

$\quad\quad l = 40 - 2w$

> From the diagram, I could see that the total length
> of fencing can be expressed as two widths plus one
> length. I needed a function that just used variables
> for area and width, so I rewrote my equation to
> isolate l.

$\quad\quad\quad lw = A$

$(40 - 2w)w = A$

$40w - 2w^2 = A$

> I wrote the formula for the area of the play space
> and substituted $40 - 2w$ for l. Then I simplified the
> equation.

b) $\quad\quad 40w - 2w^2 = 250$

$-2w^2 + 40w - 250 = 0$

$\quad\quad 40w - 2w^2 = 200$

$-2w^2 + 40w - 200 = 0$

$\quad\quad 40w - 2w^2 = 150$

$-2w^2 + 40w - 150 = 0$

> To determine the equation for each area, I
> substituted the area for A. Then I rewrote each
> quadratic equation in standard form.

c)

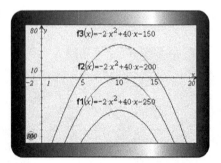

I graphed the corresponding function for each equation.

I can't make a play space with an area of 250 m² using 40 m of fencing.

The graph of the first function,

$f_1(w) = -2w^2 + 40w - 250,$

did not cross the w-axis. There are no w-intercepts, so there are no solutions, or **roots**, to the equation.

If I make the play space 10 m wide, the area will be 200 m².

The graph of the next function,

$f_2(w) = -2w^2 + 40w - 200,$

intersected the w-axis at its vertex. There is one w-intercept, $w = 10$, so there is one root.

If I make the play space 5 m wide or 15 m wide, the area will be 150 m².

The graph of the third function,

$f_3(w) = -2w^2 + 40w - 150,$

has two w-intercepts, $w = 5$ and $w = 15$. This equation has two roots.

roots

The values of the variable that make an equation in standard form equal to zero. These are also called solutions to the equation. These values are also the zeros of the corresponding function and the x-intercepts of its graph.

Your Turn

Is it possible for a quadratic equation to have more than two roots? Use a graph to explain.

EXAMPLE **3**   Solving a quadratic equation in non-standard form

Determine the roots of this quadratic equation. Verify your answers.
$$3x^2 - 6x + 5 = 2x(4 - x)$$

Marwa's Solution

$f(x) = 3x^2 - 6x + 5$

$g(x) = 2x(4 - x)$

I wrote corresponding functions, $f(x)$ and $g(x)$, for each side of the equation to determine the roots.

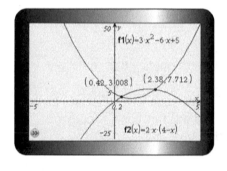

I graphed each function on a calculator. Then I used the calculator to determine the points of intersection.

The solutions are $x = 0.420$ and $x = 2.380$.

I knew that the solutions of the quadratic equation are the x-coordinates of the points of intersection.

Verify:

$3x^2 - 6x + 5 = 2x(4 - x)$

$x = 0.420$

I verified the roots by substituting them into the original equation. Both solutions are valid.

LS	RS
$3(0.420)^2 - 6(0.420) + 5$	$2(0.420)(4 - 0.420)$
$3.009\,...$	$3.007\,...$
LS $\doteq$ RS	

Verify:

$3x^2 - 6x + 5 = 2x(4 - x)$

$x = 2.380$

LS	RS
$3(2.380)^2 - 6(2.380) + 5$	$2(2.380)(4 - 2.380)$
$7.713\,...$	$7.711\,...$
LS $\doteq$ RS	

The roots are $x = 0.420$ and $x = 2.380$.

Your Turn

Rewrite $3x^2 - 6x + 5 = 2x(4 - x)$ in standard form. If you graphed the function that corresponds to your equation in standard form, what x-intercepts would you expect to see? Why?

In Summary

Key Ideas

- A quadratic equation can be solved by graphing the corresponding quadratic function.
- The standard form of a quadratic equation is

$$ax^2 + bx + c = 0$$

- The roots of a quadratic equation are the x-intercepts of the graph of the corresponding quadratic function. They are also the zeros of the corresponding quadratic function.

Need to Know

- A quadratic equation is any second-degree equation that contains a polynomial in one variable.
- If a quadratic equation is in standard form
  - you can graph the corresponding quadratic function and determine the zeros of the function to solve the equation
- If the quadratic function is not in standard form
  - you can graph the expression on the left side and the expression on the right side as functions on the same axes
  - the x-coordinates of the points of intersection of the two graphs are the roots of the equation
- For any quadratic equation, there can be zero, one, or two real roots. This is because a parabola can intersect the x-axis in zero, one, or two places.

CHECK Your Understanding

1. Solve each equation by graphing the corresponding function and determining the zeros.
   a) $2x^2 - 5x - 3 = 0$ b) $9x - 4x^2 = 0$

2. Solve each equation by graphing the expressions on both sides of the equation.
   a) $x^2 + 5x = 24$ b) $0.5x^2 = -2x + 3$

3. Rewrite each equation in standard form. Then solve the equation in standard form by graphing.
   a) $6a^2 = 11a + 35$ b) $2p^2 + 3p = 1 - 2p$

4. For each graph, determine the roots of the corresponding quadratic equation.

a)

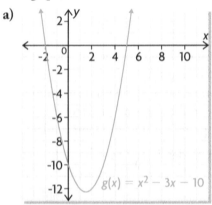

$g(x) = x^2 - 3x - 10$

b)

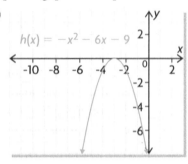

$h(x) = -x^2 - 6x - 9$

PRACTISING

5. Solve each equation by graphing the corresponding function and determining the zeros.

a) $3x^2 - 6x - 7 = 0$ **c)** $3b^2 + 8b + 7 = 0$

b) $0.5z^2 + 3z - 2 = 0$ **d)** $0.09x^2 + 0.30x + 0.25 = 0$

6. Solve each equation by graphing the expressions on both sides of the equation.

a) $3a^2 = 18a - 21$ **c)** $4x(x + 3) = 3(4x + 3)$

b) $5p = 3 - 2p^2$ **d)** $x^2 - 3x - 8 = -2x^2 + 8x + 1$

7. A ball is thrown into the air from a bridge that is 14 m above a river. The function that models the height, $h(t)$, in metres, of the ball over time, t, in seconds is

$$h(t) = -4.9t^2 + 8t + 14$$

a) When is the ball 16 m above the water?

b) When is the ball 12 m above the water? Explain.

c) Is the ball ever 18 m above the water? Explain how you know.

d) When does the ball hit the water?

8. Solve each quadratic equation by graphing.

a) $5x^2 - 2x = 4x + 3$

b) $-2x^2 + x - 1 = x^2 - 3x - 7$

c) $3x^2 - 12x + 17 = -4(x - 2)^2 + 5$

d) $5x^2 + 4x + 3 = -x^2 - 2x$

9. The stopping distance, d, of a car, in metres, depends on the speed of the car, s, in kilometres per hour. For a certain car on a dry road, the equation for stopping distance is

$$d = 0.0059s^2 + 0.187s$$

The driver of the car slammed on his brakes to avoid an accident, creating skid marks that were 120 m long. He told the police that he was driving at the speed limit of 100 km/h. Do you think he was speeding? Explain.

10. Solve the following quadratic equation using the two methods described below.

$$4x^2 + 3x - 2 = -2x^2 + 5x + 1$$

a) Graph the expressions on both sides of the equation, and determine the points of intersection.

b) Rewrite the quadratic equation in standard form, graph the corresponding function, and determine the zeros.

c) Which method do you prefer for this problem? Explain.

11. The length of a rectangular garden is 4 m more than its width. Determine the dimensions of the garden if the area is 117 m².

12. Kevin solved the following quadratic equation by graphing the expressions on both sides on the same axes.

$$x(7 - 2x) = x^2 + 1$$

His solutions were $x = 0$ and $x = 3.5$. When he verified his solutions, the left side did not equal the right side.

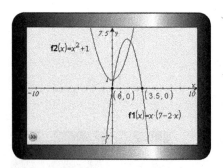

Verify:

$$x(7 - 2x) = x^2 + 1$$

$x = 0$

LS	RS
$x(7 - 2x)$	$x^2 + 1$
$(0)(7 - 2(0))$	$(0)^2 + 1$
$(0)(7)$	$0 + 1$
0	1
LS ≠ RS	

$x = 3.5$

LS	RS
$x(7 - 2x)$	$x^2 + 1$
$(3.5)(7 - 2(3.5))$	$(3.5)^2 + 1$
$(3.5)(7 - 7)$	$12.25 + 1$
0	13.25
LS ≠ RS	

a) Identify Kevin's error.

b) Determine the correct solution.

13. Solve each equation.

a) $0.25x^2 - 1.48x - 178 = 0$

b) $4.9x(6 - x) + 36 = 2(x + 9) - x^2$

Closing

14. Explain how you could use a graph to determine the number of roots for an equation in the form $ax^2 + bx = c$.

Extending

15. On the same axes, graph these quadratic functions:

$$y = -2x^2 + 20x - 42$$
$$y = x^2 - 10x + 21$$

Write three different equations whose roots are the points of intersection of these graphs.

Solving Quadratic Equations by Factoring

GOAL

Solve quadratic equations by factoring.

LEARN ABOUT the Math

The entry to the main exhibit hall in an art gallery is a parabolic arch. The arch can be modelled by the function

$$h(w) = -0.625w^2 + 5w$$

where the height, $h(w)$, and width, w, are measured in feet. Several sculptures are going to be delivered to the exhibit hall in crates. Each crate is a square-based rectangular prism that is 7.5 ft high, including the wheels. The crates must be handled as shown, to avoid damaging the fragile contents.

EXPLORE...

• What values could you substitute for n and x to make this equation true?
$(3x + n)(7x - 7) = 0$

7.5 ft

? What is the maximum width of a 7.5 ft high crate that can enter the exhibit hall through the arch?

EXAMPLE **1**   Solving a quadratic equation by factoring

Determine the distance between the two points on the arch that are
7.5 ft high.

Brooke's Solution

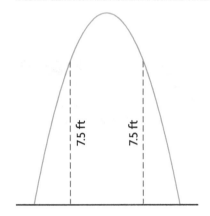

7.5 ft   7.5 ft

I sketched the situation.

The crate can only fit through the part of the arch that is at least 7.5 ft high. The arch is exactly 7.5 ft high at two points.

The following function describes the arch:
$h(w) = -0.625w^2 + 5w$

The height of the crate is 7.5 ft.
$$7.5 = -0.625w^2 + 5w$$

I wrote an equation, substituting 7.5 for $h(w)$.

$$0.625w^2 - 5w + 7.5 = 0$$

I rewrote the equation in standard form.

I decided to subtract $-0.625w^2 + 5w$ from both sides so the coefficient of w^2 would be positive.

$$\frac{0.625w^2}{0.625} - \frac{5w}{0.625} + \frac{7.5}{0.625} = \frac{0}{0.625}$$

I divided by 0.625 to simplify the equation.

$$w^2 - 8w + 12 = 0$$
$$(w - 2)(w - 6) = 0$$

I factored the equation.

$$w - 2 = 0 \quad \text{or} \quad w - 6 = 0$$
$$w = 2 \qquad\qquad w = 6$$

If the product of two factors is 0, then at least one factor must equal 0.

The parabola reaches a height of exactly
7.5 ft at widths of 2 ft and 6 ft.

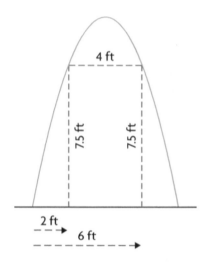

4 ft

7.5 ft

7.5 ft

2 ft

6 ft

I determined the difference between the widths to determine the maximum width of the crate.

To fit through the archway, the crate cannot be more than 4 ft wide.

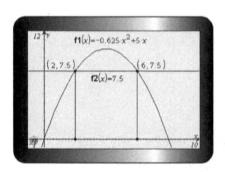

$f1(x) = -0.625 \cdot x^2 + 5 \cdot x$

$(2, 7.5)$

$(6, 7.5)$

$f2(x) = 7.5$

I checked my solution by graphing $y = -0.625x^2 + 5x$ and $y = 7.5$.

The x-coordinates of the points of intersection are 2 and 6, so my solution is correct.

Reflecting

A. How did rewriting the equation in standard form and then factoring it help Brooke determine the roots?

B. Was Brooke's decision to divide both sides of the equation by 0.625 (the coefficient of w^2) reasonable? Explain.

C. Describe another way that Brooke could verify the solutions to her equation.

D. Tim says that if you know the roots of an equation, you can use factors to determine the equation. How could Tim use the roots 2 and 6 to determine the equation that Brooke solved?

E. Can you always use factoring to solve a quadratic equation? Explain.

APPLY the Math

EXAMPLE 2   Solving a quadratic equation using a difference of squares

Determine the roots of the following equation:

$$75p^2 - 192 = 0$$

Verify your solution.

Alberto's Solution

$$75p^2 - 192 = 0$$

$$\frac{75p^2}{3} - \frac{192}{3} = \frac{0}{3}$$

                I noticed that 3 is a factor of both 75 and 192.

$$25p^2 - 64 = 0$$

$$(5p - 8)(5p + 8) = 0$$

             I noticed that $25p^2$ and 64 are both perfect squares, so $25p^2 - 64$ is a difference of squares.

$$5p - 8 = 0 \quad \text{or} \quad 5p + 8 = 0$$

$$5p = 8 \qquad\qquad 5p = -8$$

$$p = \frac{8}{5} \qquad\qquad p = -\frac{8}{5}$$

             I determined the roots.

The roots are $\dfrac{8}{5}$ and $-\dfrac{8}{5}$.

$$75p^2 - 192 = 0$$

$$75p^2 = 192$$

$$p^2 = \frac{192}{75}$$

$$p^2 = \frac{64}{25}$$

$$p = \pm\sqrt{\frac{64}{25}}$$

$$p = \pm\frac{8}{5}$$

             I decided to verify my solutions by solving the equation using a different method.

I isolated p^2 and then took the square root of each side. I knew that p^2 has two possible square roots, one positive and the other negative.

My solution matched the solution I obtained by factoring.

Your Turn

How can you tell that any equation with a difference of squares is factorable?
What can you predict about the roots?

EXAMPLE **3**   Solving a quadratic equation with only one root

Solve and verify the following equation:

$$4x^2 + 28x + 49 = 0$$

Arya's Solution

$4x^2 + 28x + 49 = 0$

$(2x + 7)(2x + 7) = 0$

I factored the trinomial. I noticed that both factors are the same, so there is only one root.

$2x + 7 = 0$

$x = -3.5$

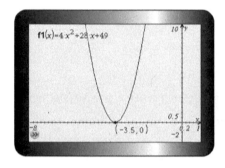

I decided to verify my solution by graphing the corresponding quadratic function.

I noticed that the vertex of the function is on the x-axis at −3.5, so my solution makes sense.

Your Turn

How can factoring an equation help you determine whether the equation has two roots or one root?

EXAMPLE **4**   Using reasoning to write an equation from its roots

Tori says she solved a quadratic equation by graphing. She says the roots were −5 and 7. How can you determine an equation that she might have solved?

Philip's Solution

$x = -5$ or $x = 7$

The x-intercepts of the quadratic function are the roots of the equation.

$x + 5 = 0$ $x - 7 = 0$

One factor is $x + 5$.

The other factor is $x - 7$.

I decided to use the roots to help me write the factors of the equation.

$(x + 5)(x - 7) = 0$

$x^2 + 5x - 7x - 35 = 0$

$x^2 - 2x - 35 = 0$

I wrote the factors as a product. Since each root is equal to 0, their product is also equal to 0.

I simplified to write the equation in standard form.

Your Turn

The x-intercepts of the graph of a quadratic function are 3 and -2.5.
Write a quadratic equation that has these roots.

EXAMPLE **5**   Describing errors in a solution

Matthew solved a quadratic equation as shown.
Identify and correct the error in Matthew's solution.

$$4x^2 = 9x$$
$$\frac{4x^2}{x} = \frac{9x}{x}$$
$$4x = 9$$
$$x = 2.25$$

Raj's Solution

Matthew made an error in the second line
of his solution. When he divided both sides
by x, he eliminated a possible factor, $x = 0$.

$\frac{4x^2}{x}$ and $\frac{9x}{x}$ are not defined when $x = 0$, so Matthew cannot divide by x.

Correctly solving the equation:

$$4x^2 - 9x = 0$$
$$x(4x - 9) = 0$$

To solve the equation, I rewrote it in standard form and then factored the left side.

$$x = 0 \quad \text{or} \quad 4x - 9 = 0$$
$$x = 0 \quad \text{or} \qquad 4x = 9$$
$$x = 2.25$$

For my equation to be true, either x or $4x - 9$ must equal 0.

Verify:
$$4x^2 - 9x = 0$$
$$x = 0 \qquad\qquad\qquad x = 2.25$$

I verified each solution by substituting it into the original equation. For both solutions, the left side is equal to the right side. Therefore, both solutions are correct.

LS	RS	LS	RS
$4x^2 - 9x$	0	$4x^2 - 9x$	0
$4(0)^2 - 9(0)$		$4(2.25)^2 - 9(2.25)$	
$0 - 0$		$20.25 - 20.25$	
0		0	
LS = RS		LS = RS	

Your Turn

What number will always be a root of an equation that can be written
in standard form as $ax^2 + bx = 0$? Explain how you know.

CHECK Your Understanding

1. Solve by factoring. Verify each solution.
   a) $x^2 - 11x + 28 = 0$ **c)** $2y^2 + 11y + 5 = 0$
   b) $x^2 - 7x - 30 = 0$ **d)** $4t^2 + 7t - 15 = 0$

2. Solve by factoring.
   a) $x^2 - 121 = 0$ **e)** $s^2 - 12s + 36 = 0$
   b) $9r^2 - 100 = 0$ **f)** $16p^2 + 8p + 1 = 0$
   c) $x^2 - 15x = 0$ **g)** $-14z^2 + 35z = 0$
   d) $3y^2 + 48y = 0$ **h)** $5q^2 - 9q = 0$

PRACTISING

3. Solve by factoring. Verify each solution.
   a) $x^2 - 9x - 70 = 0$ **c)** $3a^2 + 11a - 4 = 0$
   b) $x^2 + 19x + 48 = 0$ **d)** $6t^2 - 7t - 20 = 0$

4. Solve each equation.
   a) $12 - 5x = 2x^2$ **c)** $49d^2 + 9 = -42d$
   b) $4x^2 = 9 - 9x$ **d)** $169 = 81g^2$

5. Geeta solved this equation:
$$20x^2 - 21x - 27 = 0$$
   Her solutions were $x = 0.75$ and $x = -1.8$.
   a) Factor and solve the equation.
   b) What error do you think Geeta made?

6. Determine the roots of each equation.
   a) $5u^2 - 10u - 315 = 0$ **c)** $1.4y^2 + 5.6y - 16.8 = 0$

   b) $0.25x^2 + 1.5x + 2 = 0$ **d)** $\frac{1}{2}k^2 + 5k + 12.5 = 0$

7. The graph of a quadratic function has x-intercepts -5 and -12.
Write a quadratic equation that has these roots.

8. A bus company charges $2 per ticket but wants to raise the price. The
daily revenue that could be generated is modelled by the function

$$R(x) = -40(x - 5)^2 + 25\ 000$$

where x is the number of 10¢ price increases and $R(x)$ is the revenue in
dollars. What should the price per ticket be if the bus company wants
to collect daily revenue of $21 000?

9. Solve and verify the following equation:

$$5x - 8 = 20x^2 - 32x$$

10. Identify and correct any errors in the following solution:

$$5a^2 - 100 = 0$$
$$5a^2 = 100$$
$$a^2 = 25$$
$$\sqrt{a^2} = \sqrt{25}$$
$$a = 5$$

11. Identify and correct the errors in this solution:

$$4r^2 - 9r = 0$$
$$(2r - 3)(2r + 3) = 0$$
$$2r - 3 = 0 \quad \text{or} \quad 2r + 3 = 0$$
$$2r = 3 \qquad\qquad 2r = -3$$
$$r = 1.5 \quad \text{or} \qquad r = -1.5$$

12. **a)** Write a quadratic function with zeros at 0.5 and -0.75.
   b) Compare your function with a classmate's function. Did you get
   the same function?
   c) Working with a classmate, determine two other possible functions
   with the same zeros.

13. Sanela sells posters to stores. The profit function for her business is

$$P(n) = -0.25n^2 + 6n - 27$$

where n is the number of posters sold per month, in hundreds, and $P(n)$ is the profit, in thousands of dollars.

a) How many posters must Sanela sell per month to break even?

b) If Sanela wants to earn a profit of $5000 ($P(n) = 5$), how many posters must she sell?

c) If Sanela wants to earn a profit of $9000, how many posters must she sell?

d) What are the domain and range of the profit function? Explain your answer.

14. Samuel is hiking along the top of First Canyon on the South Nahanni River in the Northwest Territories. When he knocks a rock over the edge, it falls into the river, 1260 m below. The height of the rock, $h(t)$, at t seconds, can be modelled by the following function:

$$h(t) = -25t^2 - 5t + 1260$$

a) How long will it take the rock to reach the water?

b) What is the domain of the function? Explain your answer.

The Nahanni River in the Northwest Territories is a popular area for wilderness tours and whitewater rafting.

15. a) Create a quadratic equation that can be solved by factoring. Exchange equations with a classmate, and solve each other's equations.

b) Modify the equation you created so that it cannot be factored. Explain how you modified it. Then exchange equations with a classmate again, and solve each other's equations a different way.

Closing

16. a) Explain the steps you would follow to solve a quadratic equation by factoring.

b) When does it make sense to solve a quadratic equation by factoring? When does it make sense to use graphing?

Extending

17. One root of an equation in the form $ax^2 + c = 0$ is 6.

a) What can you predict about the factors if there is no bx term in the equation?

b) Determine the other root.

c) Write the equation in factored form.

d) Write the equation in standard form.

18. The perimeter of this right triangle is 60 cm. Determine the lengths of all three sides.

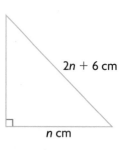

$2n + 6$ cm

n cm

Solving Quadratic Equations Using the Quadratic Formula

- graphing technology

GOAL

Use the quadratic formula to determine the roots of a quadratic equation.

EXPLORE...

- Kyle was given the following function:

  $y = 2x^2 + 12x - 14$

  He wrote it in vertex form:

  $y = 2(x + 3)^2 - 32$

  How can you use the vertex form to solve this equation?

  $2x^2 + 12x - 14 = 0$

LEARN ABOUT the Math

Ian has been hired to lay a path of uniform width around a rectangular play area, using crushed rock. He has enough crushed rock to cover 145 m².

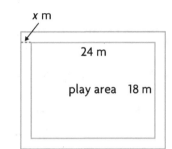

x m

24 m

play area 18 m

? **If Ian uses all the crushed rock, how wide will the path be?**

EXAMPLE **1**	Using the quadratic formula to solve a quadratic equation

Determine the width of the path that will result in an area of 145 m².

Alima's Solution

Area of border = Total area − Play area
The play area is a constant, (length)(width)
or (24 m)(18 m) or 432 m².

The total area of the playground, *P*,
can be represented as

$P = \text{(length)(width)}$
$P = (2x + 24)(2x + 18)$

> I wrote a function that describes how the area of the path, *A* square metres, changes as the width of the path, *x* metres, changes.

The area of the path, $A(x)$, can be represented as

$A(x) = (2x + 24)(2x + 18) - 432$
$A(x) = 4x^2 + 84x + 432 - 432$
$A(x) = 4x^2 + 84x$

$$145 = 4x^2 + 84x$$

I substituted the area of 145 m² for $A(x)$.

$$4x^2 + 84x - 145 = 0$$
$$a = 4, b = 84, \text{ and } c = -145$$

I rewrote the equation in standard form:

$$ax^2 + bx + c = 0$$

Then I determined the values of the coefficients a, b, and c.

Quadratic formula:

$$x = \frac{-b \pm \sqrt{b^2 - 4ac}}{2a}$$

$$x = \frac{-84 \pm \sqrt{84^2 - 4(4)(-145)}}{2(4)}$$

$$x = \frac{-84 \pm \sqrt{9376}}{8}$$

$$x = \frac{-84 + \sqrt{9376}}{8} \quad \text{or}$$

$$x = \frac{-84 - \sqrt{9376}}{8}$$

$$x = 1.603 \dots \text{ or } x = -22.603 \dots$$

The **quadratic formula** can be used to solve any quadratic equation. I wrote the quadratic formula and then substituted the values of a, b, and c from my equation into the formula.

I simplified the right side.

I separated the quadratic expression into two solutions.

quadratic formula
A formula for determining the roots of a quadratic equation in the form $ax^2 + bx + c = 0$, where $a \neq 0$; the quadratic formula is written using the coefficients of the variables and the constant in the quadratic equation that is being solved:

$$x = \frac{-b \pm \sqrt{b^2 - 4ac}}{2a}$$

This formula is derived from $ax^2 + bx + c = 0$ by isolating x.

The solution -22.603 is inadmissible.

I knew that the width of the path couldn't be negative, so $-22.603 \dots$ is an **inadmissible solution**.

inadmissible solution
A root of a quadratic equation that does not lead to a solution that satisfies the original problem.

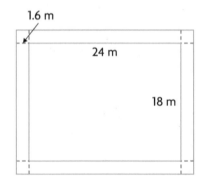

1.6 m

24 m

18 m

I sketched the path and verified my solution by determining the area of the path. To do this, I added the areas of all the rectangles that make up the path.

$$18(1.603 \dots) = 28.866 \dots \text{ m}^2$$
$$24(1.603 \dots) = 38.489 \dots \text{ m}^2$$
$$(1.603 \dots)(1.603 \dots) = 2.571 \dots \text{ m}^2$$

Area of path $= 2(28.866 \dots) + 2(38.489 \dots) + 4(2.571 \dots)$
Area of path $= 144.999 \dots \text{ m}^2$

The total area is very close to 145 m².
The path should be about 1.6 m wide.

Reflecting

A. Why did Alima need to write her equation in standard form?

B. Which part of the quadratic formula shows that there are two possible solutions?

C. Why did Alima decide not to use the negative solution?

D. In this chapter, you have learned three methods for solving quadratic equations: graphing, factoring, and using the quadratic formula. What are some advantages and disadvantages of each method?

APPLY the Math

EXAMPLE 2   Connecting the quadratic formula to factoring

Solve the following equation:
$$6x^2 - 3 = 7x$$

Adrianne's Solution

$$6x^2 - 3 = 7x$$
$$6x^2 - 7x - 3 = 0$$
$$a = 6, \; b = -7, \text{ and } c = -3$$

First, I rewrote the equation in standard form to determine the values of a, b, and c.

$$x = \frac{-b \pm \sqrt{b^2 - 4ac}}{2a}$$

$$x = \frac{-(-7) \pm \sqrt{(-7)^2 - 4(6)(-3)}}{2(6)}$$

I wrote the quadratic formula and substituted the values of a, b, and c.

$$x = \frac{7 \pm \sqrt{121}}{12}$$

I simplified the right side. I realized that 121 is a perfect square.

$$x = \frac{7 \pm 11}{12}$$

$$x = \frac{18}{12} \quad \text{or} \quad x = \frac{-4}{12}$$

$$x = \frac{3}{2} \quad \text{or} \quad x = \frac{-1}{3}$$

I determined the two solutions.

Verify:
$$6x^2 - 7x - 3 = 0$$
$$(3x + 1)(2x - 3) = 0$$

$$3x + 1 = 0 \quad \text{or} \quad 2x - 3 = 0$$
$$3x = -1 \qquad\qquad 2x = 3$$
$$x = \frac{-1}{3} \qquad\qquad x = \frac{3}{2}$$

If the radicand in the quadratic formula is a perfect square, then the original equation can be factored. I decided to verify my solution by factoring the original equation.

The solutions match those I got using the quadratic formula.

Your Turn

Sandy was given the following equation:
$$12x^2 - 47x + 45 = 0$$

She used the quadratic formula to solve it.

Could Sandy use factoring to verify her solutions? Explain how you know.

$$x = \frac{-(-47) \pm \sqrt{(-47)^2 - 4(12)(45)}}{2(12)}$$

$$x = \frac{47 \pm \sqrt{49}}{24}$$

$$x = 2\frac{1}{4} \quad \text{or} \quad x = \frac{5}{3}$$

EXAMPLE 3   Determining the exact solution to a quadratic equation

Solve this quadratic equation:
$$2x^2 + 8x - 5 = 0$$
State your answer as an exact value.

Quyen's Solution

$$2x^2 + 8x - 5 = 0$$
$$a = 2, b = 8, \text{ and } c = -5$$

> The equation was in standard form. I determined the values of a, b, and c.

$$x = \frac{-b \pm \sqrt{b^2 - 4ac}}{2a}$$

$$x = \frac{-(8) \pm \sqrt{8^2 - 4(2)(-5)}}{2(2)}$$

> I wrote the quadratic formula and substituted the values of a, b, and c.

$$x = \frac{-8 \pm \sqrt{104}}{4}$$

$$x = \frac{-8 \pm \sqrt{4}\sqrt{26}}{4}$$

> I simplified the expression.
>
> I noticed that one factor of 104 is 4, which is a perfect square. I simplified the radical.

$$x = \frac{-8 \pm 2\sqrt{26}}{4}$$

> I simplified the fraction.

$$x = \frac{-4 \pm \sqrt{26}}{2}$$

$$x = \frac{-4 + \sqrt{26}}{2} \quad \text{or} \quad x = \frac{-4 - \sqrt{26}}{2}$$

> Another way to write my solution is to show two separate values.

Your Turn

Solve the following quadratic equation:
$$5x^2 - 10x + 3 = 0$$
State your answer as an exact value.

EXAMPLE **4** Solving a pricing problem

A store rents an average of 750 video games each month at the current rate of $4.50. The owners of the store want to raise the rental rate to increase the revenue to $7000 per month. However, for every $1 increase, they know that they will rent 30 fewer games each month. The following function relates the price increase, p, to the revenue, r:

$$(4.5 + p)(750 - 30p) = r$$

Can the owners increase the rental rate enough to generate revenue of $7000 per month?

Christa's Solution

$$(4.5 + p)(750 - 30p) = r$$

$$3375 + 615p - 30p^2 = r$$

I simplified the function.

$$3375 + 615p - 30p^2 = 7000$$

$$-30p^2 + 615p + 3375 = 7000$$

I substituted the revenue of $7000 for r and wrote the equation in standard form.

$$-30p^2 + 615p - 3625 = 0$$

$$\frac{-30p^2}{-5} + \frac{615p}{-5} - \frac{3625}{-5} = \frac{0}{-5}$$

I divided each term by -5 to simplify the equation.

$$6p^2 - 123p + 725 = 0$$

$$p = \frac{-b \pm \sqrt{b^2 - 4ac}}{2a}$$

I didn't try to factor the equation since the numbers were large. I decided to use the quadratic formula.

I substituted the values of a, b, and c into the quadratic formula.

$$p = \frac{-(-123) \pm \sqrt{(-123)^2 - 4(6)(725)}}{2(6)}$$

$$p = \frac{123 \pm \sqrt{-2271}}{12}$$

I simplified the right side.

$\sqrt{-2271}$ is not a real number, so there are no real solutions to this equation. It is not possible for the store to generate revenue of $7000 per month by increasing the rental rate.

I noticed that the radicand is negative.

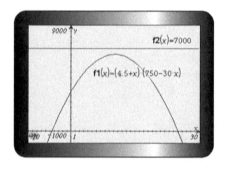

To verify my answer, I graphed

$y = (4.5 + x)(750 - 30x)$ and $y = 7000$

There is no point of intersection.

Your Turn

Is it possible for the store to generate revenue of $6500 per month by increasing the rental rate? Explain.

In Summary

Key Idea

- The roots of a quadratic equation in the form $ax^2 + bx + c = 0$, where $a \neq 0$, can be determined by using the quadratic formula:

$$x = \frac{-b \pm \sqrt{b^2 - 4ac}}{2a}$$

Need to Know

- The quadratic formula can be used to solve any quadratic equation, even if the equation is not factorable.
- If the radicand in the quadratic formula simplifies to a perfect square, then the equation can be solved by factoring.
- If the radicand in the quadratic formula simplifies to a negative number, then there is no real solution for the quadratic equation.

CHECK Your Understanding

1. Solve each equation using the quadratic formula. Verify by graphing.
   a) $x^2 + 7x - 5 = 0$
   c) $2a^2 - 5a + 1 = 0$
   b) $8x^2 + 35x + 12 = 0$
   d) $-20p^2 + 7p + 3 = 0$

2. Solve each equation using the quadratic formula.
   a) $x^2 + 5x - 6 = 0$
   c) $25x^2 - 121 = 0$
   b) $4x + 9x^2 = 0$
   d) $12x^2 - 17x - 40 = 0$

3. Solve each equation in question 2 by factoring. Which method did you prefer for each equation? Explain.

PRACTISING

4. Solve each quadratic equation.

  a) $3x^2 + 5x = 9$ **c)** $6x - 3 = 2x^2$

  b) $1.4x - 3.9x^2 = -2.7$ **d)** $x^2 + 1 = x$

5. The roots for the quadratic equation

$$1.44a^2 + 2.88a - 21.6 = 0$$

are $a = 3$ and $a = -5$. Verify these roots.

6. Solve each equation. State the solutions as exact values.

  a) $3x^2 - 6x - 1 = 0$ **c)** $8x^2 + 8x - 1 = 0$

  b) $x^2 + 8x + 3 = 0$ **d)** $9x^2 - 12x - 1 = 0$

7. A student council is holding a raffle to raise money for a charity fund drive. The profit function for the raffle is

$$p(c) = -25c^2 + 500c - 350$$

where $p(c)$ is the profit and c is the price of each ticket, both in dollars.

  a) What ticket price will result in the student council breaking even on the raffle?

  b) What ticket price will raise the most money for the school's donation to charity?

8. Akpatok Island in Nunavut is surrounded by steep cliffs along the coast. The cliffs range in height from about 125 m to about 250 m.

  a) Suppose that someone accidentally dislodged a stone from a 125 m cliff. The height of the stone, $h(t)$, in metres, after t seconds can be represented by the following function:

$$h(t) = -4.9t^2 + 4t + 125$$

  How long would it take the stone dislodged from this height to reach the water below?

  b) Predict how much longer it would take for the stone to reach the water if it fell from a height of 250 m. Discuss this with a partner.

  c) The height of a stone, $h(t)$, in metres, falling from a 250 m cliff over time, t, in seconds, can be modelled by this function:

$$h(t) = -4.9t^2 + 4t + 250$$

  Determine how long it would take the stone to reach the water.

  d) How close was your prediction to your solution?

9. Keisha and Savannah used different methods to solve this equation:

$$116.64z^2 + 174.96z + 65.61 = 0$$

  a) Could one of these students have used factoring? Explain.

  b) Solve the equation using the method of your choice.

  c) Which method did you use? Why?

Akpatok Island gets its name from the word *Akpat*, the Innu name for the birds that live on the cliffs.

10. The Moon's gravity affects the way that objects travel when they are thrown on the Moon. Suppose that you threw a ball upward from the top of a lunar module, 5.5 m high. The height of the ball, $h(t)$, in metres, over time, t, in seconds could be modelled by this function:

$$h(t) = -0.81t^2 + 5t + 6.5$$

a) How long would it take for the ball to hit the surface of the Moon?

b) If you threw the same ball from a model of the lunar module on Earth, the height of the ball could be modelled by this function:

$$h(t) = -4.9t^2 + 5t + 6.5$$

Compare the time that the ball would be in flight on Earth with the time that the ball would be in flight on the Moon.

Six lunar modules landed on the Moon from 1969 to 1972.

11. A landscaper is designing a rectangular garden, which will be 5.00 m wide by 6.25 m long. She has enough crushed rock to cover an area of 6.0 m² and wants to make a uniform border around the garden. How wide should the border be, if she wants to use all the crushed rock?

Closing

12. Discuss the quadratic formula with a partner. Make a list of everything you have both learned, from your work in this lesson, about using the quadratic formula to solve quadratic equations.

Extending

13. The two roots of any quadratic equation are

$$x = \frac{-b + \sqrt{b^2 - 4ac}}{2a} \quad \text{and} \quad x = \frac{-b - \sqrt{b^2 - 4ac}}{2a}$$

a) Determine the sum of the roots of any quadratic equation.

b) Determine the product of the roots of any quadratic equation.

c) Solve the following quadratic equation:

$$10x^2 - 13x + 4 = 0$$

Determine the sum and the product of its roots.

d) Determine the sum and the product of the roots of the quadratic equation in part c), using your formulas from parts a) and b). Do your answers match your answers from part c)?

e) Determine the sum and the product of the solutions to questions 1 d), 2 a), 5, and 7.

f) How could you use your formulas from parts a) and b) to check your solutions to any quadratic equation?

The Golden Ratio

The golden ratio has been discovered and rediscovered by many civilizations. Its uses in architecture include the Great Pyramids in Egypt and the Parthenon in Greece. The golden ratio is the ratio of length to width in a rectangle with special properties, called the golden rectangle. This rectangle appears often in art, architecture, and photography.

The Manitoba Legislative Building

If you section off a square inside a golden rectangle so that the side length of the square equals the width of the golden rectangle, you will create a smaller rectangle with the same length : width ratio. Mathematicians sometimes use the Greek letter *phi*, φ, to represent this ratio.

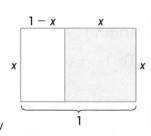

To determine the golden ratio, you need to know that the ratio of length to width in the original rectangle, $\dfrac{1}{x}$, is equal to the ratio of length to width in the smaller rectangle, $\dfrac{x}{1 - x}$.

A. Solve the following equation for x to determine the width of a rectangle with length 1. Then determine $\dfrac{1}{x}$ to get the golden ratio, φ.

$$\frac{1}{x} = \frac{x}{1 - x}$$

B. Work with a partner or group to find golden rectangles in the photograph of the Manitoba Legislative Building.

C. Find more golden rectangles in architecture, art, and nature. Present your findings to the class.

FREQUENTLY ASKED Questions

Q: **How can I solve a quadratic equation by graphing?**

A1: If the quadratic equation is in standard form, enter the corresponding function on a graphing calculator. Determine the x-intercepts of the parabola. These are the solutions to the equation.

A2: If the quadratic equation is not in standard form, you can graph the expressions on the left and right sides separately. The solutions to the equation are the x-coordinates of the points of intersection of the two functions.

Q: **How can I solve a quadratic equation algebraically?**

A: Write the equation in standard form:

$$ax^2 + bx + c = 0$$

Then determine the roots of the equation by factoring or by using the quadratic formula.

> **Study | Aid**
> * See Lesson 7.1, Examples 1 to 3.
> * Try Mid-Chapter Review Questions 1 and 2.

> **Study | Aid**
> * See Lessons 7.2, Examples 1, 4, and 5, and 7.3, Examples 1, 3, and 4.
> * Try Mid-Chapter Review Questions 5, 6, and 8.

Factoring	Using the quadratic formula
If the expression $ax^2 + bx + c$ is factorable, then the equation $ax^2 + bx + c = 0$ is true when either of the factors is equal to 0.	$x = \dfrac{-b \pm \sqrt{b^2 - 4ac}}{2a}$
For example: $$2x^2 + 2x = 5x + 20$$ $$2x^2 - 3x - 20 = 0$$ $$(2x + 5)(x - 4) = 0$$ $2x + 5 = 0 \quad$ or $\quad x - 4 = 0$ $\quad 2x = -5 \qquad\qquad x = 4$ $\qquad x = -\dfrac{5}{2}$	For example: $$3x^2 - 4x - 5 = 0$$ $a = 3, b = -4,$ and $c = -5$ Substitute these values into the quadratic formula. $x = \dfrac{-(-4) \pm \sqrt{(-4)^2 - 4(3)(-5)}}{2(3)}$ $x = \dfrac{4 \pm \sqrt{76}}{6}$
The roots are $-\dfrac{5}{2} \quad$ and $\quad 4$	The radicand is positive, so the equation has a solution. $x = \dfrac{4 + \sqrt{76}}{6} \quad$ or $\quad x = \dfrac{4 - \sqrt{76}}{6}$ The roots are $\dfrac{2 + \sqrt{19}}{3} \quad$ and $\quad \dfrac{2 - \sqrt{19}}{3}$

PRACTISING

Lesson 7.1

1. Solve by graphing and determining the x-intercepts.
   a) $0.5x^2 + 3x - 3.5 = 0$
   b) $-3x^2 + 18x - 17 = 0$

2. Solve by graphing the expressions on both sides of the equation and determining the x-coordinates of the points of intersection.
   a) $2x^2 - 6x = 5$
   b) $-3x^2 + 4x = x^2 - 7$
   c) $x(5 - 2x) = 3(x - 1)$
   d) $5x - 0.25x^2 = 2(0.1x^2 - 3)$

3. If a skydiver jumps from an airplane and free falls for 828 m before he safely deploys his parachute, his free fall could be modelled by the function
   $$h(t) = -4.9t^2 + 10t + 828$$
   where $h(t)$ is the height in metres and t is the time in seconds (ignoring air resistance). How long did this skydiver free fall?

Lesson 7.2

4. Rewrite each equation in standard form, and solve it by factoring. Verify each solution.
   a) $x(x + 3) = 4$
   b) $2z(z - 3) = -5(z - 9)$

5. Solve by factoring. Verify each solution.
   a) $2x^2 + 5x - 3 = 0$
   b) $36a^2 + 60a + 25 = 0$
   c) $8c^2 - 26c + 15 = 0$
   d) $1 - 8p + 16p^2 = 0$
   e) $4t^2 - 81 = 0$
   f) $9x^2 = 256$
   g) $5w - 3w^2 = 0$
   h) $7x = 3x^2$

6. Write a quadratic equation, in standard form, that has the roots $\dfrac{1}{2}$ and -6.

Lesson 7.3

7. Solve each equation by using the quadratic formula.
   a) $3k^2 + 5k - 1 = 0$
   b) $8n^2 + 15n + 6 = 0$
   c) $35x^2 - 98x + 56 = 0$
   d) $8y^2 + 90y + 187 = 0$

8. Solve each equation by graphing, by factoring, or by using the quadratic formula. Explain how you chose the method that you used.
   a) $2p^2 + 11p + 12 = 0$
   b) $3x(x - 4) = 2(5 - x^2)$
   c) $12a^2 + 23a + 7 = 0$

9. An electronics company sells personal video recorders (PVRs) for $189. At this price, the company sells 500 PVRs per day. The company wants to raise the price of the PVRs to increase its revenue. The revenue function is
   $$r(d) = -300d^2 + 7165d + 94\,500$$
   where $r(d)$ is the revenue, in dollars, and d is the number of $20 price increases.
   a) If the company wants to generate revenue of $125\,000 per day, how much will the price have to increase?
   b) Is it possible for the company to earn revenue of $140\,000 per day by selling PVRs? Explain your reasoning.

Solving Problems Using Quadratic Equations

GOAL

Analyze and solve problems that involve quadratic equations.

LEARN ABOUT the Math

The engineers who designed the Coal River Bridge on the Alaska Highway in British Columbia used a supporting arch with twin metal arcs.

The function that describes the arch is

$$h(x) = -0.005\ 061x^2 + 0.499\ 015x$$

where $h(x)$ is the height, in metres, of the arch above the ice at any distance, x, in metres, from one end of the bridge.

EXPLORE...

- A right triangle has sides of length x, $2x + 4$, and $3x - 4$. Write a quadratic equation to determine the value of x. Is there more than one solution?

? How can you use the width of the arch to determine the height of the bridge?

EXAMPLE 1   Solving a problem by factoring a quadratic equation

Determine the distance between the bases of the arch. Then determine the maximum height of the arch, to the nearest tenth of a metre.

Morgan's Solution

The coordinates of the maximum are (x, y), where x is halfway between the two bases of the arch and y is the height of the arch.

> I reasoned that the bridge is symmetrical and resting on the vertex of the arch.

$$h(x) = -0.005\ 061x^2 + 0.499\ 015x$$
$$0 = -0.005\ 061x^2 + 0.499\ 015x$$

> I wrote an equation to determine the x-coordinates of the bases of the arch. The height at each base is 0 m, so the value of $h(x)$ at these points is 0.

$$0 = -5.061x^2 + 499.015x$$
$$0 = x(-5.061x + 499.015)$$

------- I multiplied both sides by 1000 and factored the equation.

$$x = 0 \quad \text{or} \quad -5.061x + 499.015 = 0$$
$$-5.061x = -499.015$$
$$x = 98.600\ldots$$

------- I solved the equation.

One base is at 0 m, and the other is at 98.600… m. The width of the arch is 98.600… m.

------- The width of the arch is the distance between the two bases.

Equation of axis of symmetry:
$$x = \frac{0 + 98.600\ldots}{2}$$
$$x = 49.300\ldots$$
The x-coordinate of the vertex is 49.300 …

------- The function is quadratic, so the arch is a parabola with an axis of symmetry that passes through the vertex.

$$h(x) = -0.005\,061x^2 + 0.499\,015x$$
For $x = 49.300\ldots$,
$$y = -0.005\,061\,(49.300\ldots)^2 + 0.499\,015\,(49.300\ldots)$$
$$y = -12.300\ldots + 24.601\ldots$$
$$y = 12.300\ldots \text{ m}$$

------- The height of the arch is the y-coordinate of the vertex of the parabola.

The distance between the bases of the bridge is 98.6 m.
The height of the arch above the ice is 12.3 m.

Reflecting

A. How did determining the x-coordinates of the bases of the arch help Morgan determine the height of the arch?

B. What reasoning might have led Morgan to multiply both sides of the equation by 1000?

C. How did Morgan know that the equation $0 = -5.061x^2 + 499.015x$ could be factored?

D. How else could Morgan have solved her quadratic equation?

APPLY the Math

EXAMPLE 2   Solving a number problem by graphing

Determine three consecutive odd integers, if the square of the largest
integer is 33 less than the sum of the squares of the two smaller integers.

Hailey's Solution

Let the three integers be $2x - 1$, $2x + 1$, and $2x + 3$.

$$(2x + 3)^2 + 33 = (2x - 1)^2 + (2x + 1)^2$$

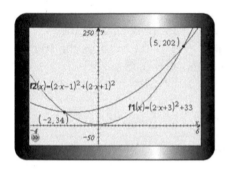

The points of intersection are $(-2, 34)$ and
$(5, 202)$. The two possible values of x are -2 and 5.

If $x = -2$,

$2x - 1$	$2x + 1$	$2x + 3$
$2(-2) - 1$	$2(-2) + 1$	$2(-2) + 3$
-5	-3	-1

The integers are -5, -3, and -1.

If $x = 5$,

$2x - 1$	$2x + 1$	$2x + 3$
$2(5) - 1$	$2(5) + 1$	$2(5) + 3$
9	11	13

The integers are 9, 11, and 13.
The consecutive odd integers could be -5, -3,
and -1, or they could be 9, 11, and 13.

> Odd numbers are not divisible by 2. According to
> the problem, if I add 33 to the square of the largest
> number, my result will equal the sum of the squares
> of the two smaller numbers.

> I graphed both sides of my equation and
> determined the points of intersection.

> I determined three consecutive odd integers for
> each value of x.

> My answers seem reasonable. $13^2 = 169$ and this is
> 33 less than $9^2 + 11^2$, which is 202. $(-1)^2 = 1$ and
> this is 33 less than $(-5)^2 + (-3)^3$, which is 34.

Your Turn

Why was Hailey's method better for solving the problem than simply
guessing and testing numbers?

EXAMPLE **3**   Solving a problem by creating a quadratic model

Synchronized divers perform matching dives from opposite sides
of a platform that is 10 m high. If two divers reached their maximum
height of 0.6 m above the platform after 0.35 s, how long did it take
them to reach the water?

Canadians Émilie Heymans
and Blythe Hartley won
bronze medals at the
2004 Olympic Games.

Oliver's Solution

Let t represent the time in seconds.
Let $h(t)$ represent the height in metres over time.

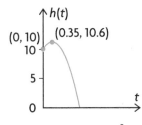

> I sketched a graph to show how the divers' height
> changed as time passed. I knew that the vertex
> of the parabola was (0.35, 10.6) because the
> maximum height of 10.6 m (0.6 m above the 10 m
> platform) was attained after 0.35 s.

$$h(t) = a(t - 0.35)^2 + 10.6$$

> I wrote a quadratic function in vertex form.

$$10 = a(0 - 0.35)^2 + 10.6$$
$$10 = a(-0.35)^2 + 10.6$$
$$10 = 0.1225a + 10.6$$
$$-0.6 = 0.1225a$$
$$-4.897... = a$$

> The platform is 10 m high. Therefore, when $t = 0$,
> $h(t) = 10$. I substituted these values into my equation
> and solved for a.

$$f(x) = -4.897... (x - 0.35)^2 + 10.6$$

> I wrote a function to represent the dive. I knew that
> the height would be 0 when the divers hit the water.

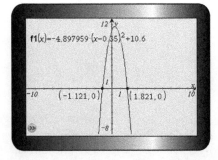

> I graphed my function and determined the
> x-intercepts.

The zeros of my function are -1.121 and 1.821.
The solution -1.121 s is inadmissible.

> Time cannot be negative in this situation.

The divers reached the water after about 1.821 s.

Your Turn

How does Oliver's first graph show that there is only one solution
to the problem?

EXAMPLE **4**   Visualizing a quadratic relationship

At noon, a sailboat leaves a harbour on Vancouver Island and travels due west at 10 km/h. Three hours later, another sailboat leaves the same harbour and travels due south at 15 km/h. At what time, to the nearest minute, will the sailboats be 40 km apart?

Nikki's Solution

Let t be the number of hours it will take for the sailboats to be 40 km apart.

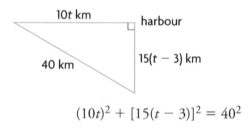

10t km

harbour

40 km

15(t − 3) km

I drew a diagram to show the paths of the two sailboats. They are sailing at right angles to each other.

The first boat travels t hours at 10 km/h.

The second boat leaves 3 h later, so it travels for $t - 3$ h at 15 km/h.

$$(10t)^2 + [15(t - 3)]^2 = 40^2$$

I used the Pythagorean theorem to write an equation that relates the distances travelled to the 40 km distance between them.

$$(10t)^2 + (15t - 45)^2 = 40^2$$
$$100t^2 + 225t^2 - 1350t + 2025 = 1600$$
$$325t^2 - 1350t + 425 = 0$$
$$13t^2 - 54t + 17 = 0$$

I simplified my quadratic equation and wrote it in standard form. Then I divided both sides by 25.

$$t = \frac{-b \pm \sqrt{b^2 - 4ac}}{2a}$$

$$t = \frac{-(-54) \pm \sqrt{(-54)^2 - 4(13)(17)}}{2(13)}$$

$$t = \frac{54 \pm \sqrt{2032}}{26}$$

$$t = 0.343\ldots \quad \text{or} \quad t = 3.810\ldots$$

I used the quadratic formula to solve for t, the number of hours that it will take for the boats to be 40 km apart.

The solution 0.343... h is inadmissible.
(0.81 ... h)(60 min/1 h) = 48.6 min
The boats will be 40 km apart at 3:49 p.m.

The boats could not be 40 km apart after 0.343... h, because the second boat has not yet left the harbour and the first boat is less than 10 km out.

Your Turn

a) Tomas solved the same problem. However, he used t to represent the time for the second boat's journey. How would the labels on Tomas's diagram be different from the labels on Nikki's diagram?

b) Use Tomas's method to solve the problem.

In Summary

Key Ideas

- A function, a graph, or a table of values can represent a relation. Use the form that is most helpful for the context of the problem.
- Depending on the information that is given in a problem, you can use a quadratic function in vertex form or in standard form to model the situation.

Need to Know

- A problem may have only one admissible solution, even though the quadratic equation that is used to represent the problem has two real solutions. When you solve a quadratic equation, verify that your solutions make sense in the context of the problem.

CHECK Your Understanding

1. The engineers who built the Coal River Bridge on the Alaska Highway in British Columbia used scaffolding during construction. At one point, scaffolding that was 9 m tall was placed under the arch. The arch is modelled by the function

$$h(x) = -0.005\,061x^2 + 0.499\,015x$$

   a) Describe a strategy you could use to determine the minimum distance of this scaffolding from each base of the arch.
   b) Use your strategy from part a) to solve the problem.
   c) Compare your strategy and solutions with a classmate's strategy and solutions. What other strategies could you have used?

PRACTISING

> **Communication | Tip**
>
> The formula $V = \pi r^2 h$ can also be written as a quadratic function:
>
> $f(r) = \pi r^2 h - V$

2. A company manufactures aluminum cans. One customer places an order for cans that must be 18 cm high, with a volume of 1150 cm³.
   a) Use the formula $V = \pi r^2 h$ to determine the radius that the company should use to manufacture these cans.
   b) Graph the function that corresponds to $0 = \pi r^2 h - V$ to determine the radius.
   c) Which method do you prefer? Explain why.

3. The sum of two numbers is 11. Their product is -152. What are the numbers?

4. A doughnut store sells doughnuts with jam centres. The baker wants the area of the jam to be about equal to the area of the cake part of the doughnut, as seen from the top. The outer radius of a whole doughnut is 6 cm. Determine the radius of the jam centre.

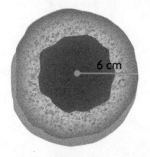

6 cm

5. Duncan dives with a junior swim club. In a dive off a 7.5 m platform, he reaches a maximum height of 7.94 m after 0.30 s. How long does it take him to reach the water?

6. A jet skier leaves a dock at 8 a.m. and travels due west at 36 km/h. A second jet skier leaves the same dock 10 min later and travels due south at 44 km/h. At what time of day, to the nearest minute, will the two jet skis be 20 km apart?

7. Alexis sells chocolate mousse tortes for $25. At this price, she can sell 200 tortes every week. She wants to increase her earnings, but, from her research, she knows that she will sell 5 fewer tortes per week for each price increase of $1.
   a) What function, $E(x)$, can be used to model Alexis's earnings, if x represents the price increase in dollars?
   b) What higher price would let Alexis earn the same amount of money she earns now?
   c) What should Alexis charge for her tortes if she wants to earn the maximum amount of money?

8. Two consecutive integers are squared. The sum of these squares is 365. What are the integers?

9. Brianne is a photographer in southern Alberta. She is assembling a display of photographs of endangered local wildlife. She wants each photograph in her display to be square, and she wants the matte surrounding each photograph to be 6 cm wide. She also wants the area of the matte to be equal to the area of the photograph itself. What should the dimensions of each photograph be, to the nearest tenth of a centimetre?

Closing

10. Quadratic equations that describe problem situations are sometimes complicated. What are some methods you can use to simplify these equations and make them easier to solve?

Extending

11. Aldrin and Jan are standing at the edge of a huge field. At 2:00 p.m., Aldrin begins to walk along a straight path at a speed of 3 km/h. Two hours later, Jan takes a straight path at a 60° angle to Aldrin's path, walking at 5 km/h. At what time will the two friends be 13 km apart?

12. Frances is an artist. She wants the area of the matte around her new painting to be twice the area of the painting itself. The matte that she wants to use is available in only one width. The outside dimensions of the same matte around another painting are 80 cm by 60 cm. What is the width of the matte?

Determining Quadratic Patterns

Many geometric patterns have connections to algebra. Examining a pattern can help you develop a formula that describes the general rule for the pattern.

The Puzzle

This pattern grows as a new row of tiles is added to each figure.

How many tiles would you need to construct a figure with 12 rows?

The Strategy

A. Copy this table.

Number of Rows	0	1	2	3	4			
Number of Tiles in Bottom Row	0	1	2	3				
Total Number of Tiles	0	1	3	6				

B. Complete your table for the next three figures in the pattern above.

C. Explain how you would determine the total number of tiles in figures with 8, 9, and 10 rows.

D. Write a quadratic equation that gives the total number of tiles in a figure with any number of rows.

E. Test your equation by using it to determine the total number of tiles in a figure with 12 rows. Check your answer by extending your table.

F. When you developed your equation for the pattern, did you use inductive or deductive reasoning? Explain.

1. The acceleration due to gravity on Mars is 3.8 m/s^2. Suppose that a rocket is launched on Mars, with an initial velocity of 64 m/s^2. The height of the rocket, $h(t)$, in metres, after t seconds can be modelled by the following function:

$$h(t) = -\frac{1}{2}(3.8)t^2 + 64t$$

   a) Graph the function. How long will the flight last?
   b) At what time will the rocket reach a height of 400 m?
   c) Will the rocket reach a height of 550 m? Explain.

2. Solve the following equation by graphing the expressions on both sides of the equation:

$$(2x - 7)(x + 2) = (3 - x)(1 + 4x)$$

3. Solve by factoring. Verify each solution.
   a) $81y^2 - 625 = 0$ c) $3c^2 - 48 = 0$
   b) $12z - 6z^2 = 0$ d) $5h^2 = 4h$

4. Solve by factoring. Verify each solution.
   a) $x^2 + 11x + 24 = 0$ c) $5c = c^2 - 6$
   b) $8a^2 + 31a - 4 = 0$ d) $25x^2 + 10x + 5 = 5x^2 - 3x + 3$

5. Solve by using the quadratic formula.
   a) $x^2 + 5x - 8 = 0$ c) $0.25x^2 - 0.3x + 0.09 = 0$
   b) $4x^2 - 12x - 3 = 0$ d) $5x^2 + 6x + 7 = 0$

6. Determine three consecutive even integers, if the square of the largest integer less the square of the middle integer is 20 less than the square of the smallest integer.

7. The Yukon Bridge is a suspension bridge with a parabolic shape. Its height, $h(w)$, in metres, can be represented by the equation

$$h(w) = 0.005\,066w^2 - 0.284\,698w$$

   where the height is 0 m at the endpoints and w is the length of a straight line from one endpoint to the other.
   a) Determine the length of line w.
   b) What is the maximum drop in height from line w to the bridge?

The Yukon Bridge spans the Tutshi River in northern British Columbia. To build the Yukon Bridge, engineers had to rig a temporary skyline. This skyline was used to transfer drilling equipment and to anchor rods to the far side of the river. A helicopter was used to install the support towers on the far side of the river.

8. A rectangle is 5 cm longer than it is wide. The length of the diagonal of the rectangle is 18 cm. Determine the dimensions of the rectangle, to the nearest centimetre.

WHAT DO You Think Now? Revisit **What Do You Think?** on page 395. How have your answers and explanations changed?

FREQUENTLY ASKED Questions

Study | Aid
- See Lesson 7.4, Examples 1 to 4.
- Try Chapter Review Questions 5 to 10.

Q. **What strategies can you use to solve contextual problems that involve quadratic equations?**

A: Problems that involve quadratic equations can be solved with or without graphing technology.

If you don't have access to graphing technology, you can use these strategies:

- Express the equation in standard form:

$$ax^2 + bx + c = 0, a \neq 0$$

  Try to factor the expression $ax^2 + bx + c$. If it is factorable, set each factor equal to zero and solve the resulting linear equations.

- For equations that are not factorable, use the quadratic formula:

$$x = \frac{-b \pm \sqrt{b^2 - 4ac}}{2a}$$

  The quadratic formula can always be used to solve quadratic equations that have solutions.

If you have access to graphing technology, you can use these strategies:

- Express the equation in standard form:

$$ax^2 + bx + c = 0, a \neq 0$$

  Graph the corresponding function:

$$f(x) = ax^2 + bx + c$$

  Locate the zeros of the function. These are the x-intercepts of the graph of the function. The values of the x-intercepts are the solutions or roots of the quadratic equation.

- If the equation is not expressed in standard form, you can graph the left and right sides of the equation by treating each side as a function. The solutions to the equation are the x-coordinates of the points of intersection of the two functions.

Q. When solving contextual problems that involve quadratic equations, will the solution(s) to the equation always be solutions to the problem?

Study **Aid**
- See Lesson 7.4, Examples 1 to 4.
- Try Chapter Review Questions 5 to 10.

A: No. Often the context of the problem requires that restrictions be placed on the independent variable in the function modelling the situation. If a solution does not lie within the restricted domain of the function, then it is not a solution to the problem. Such solutions are called inadmissible.

For example, consider this problem:

Sylvia dives from a tower whose platform is 10 m above the surface of the water. Her dive can be modelled by the function

$$h(t) = -4.9t^2 + 1.5t + 10$$

where $h(t)$ represents her height above the water, in metres, and t represents time from the start of her dive, in seconds. How long does it take for Sylvia to enter the water, to the nearest tenth of a second?

$0 = -4.9t^2 + 1.5t + 10$	The diver's height is 0 m when she enters the water.
$t = \dfrac{-b \pm \sqrt{b^2 - 4ac}}{2a}$ $t = \dfrac{-1.5 \pm \sqrt{(1.5)^2 - 4(-4.9)(10)}}{2(-4.9)}$ $t = \dfrac{-1.5 \pm \sqrt{198.25}}{-9.8}$ $t = \dfrac{-1.5 \pm 14.080...}{-9.8}$	Solve the quadratic equation using the quadratic formula.
$t = -1.283...$ or $t = 1.589...$ In this case, $t = -1.283...$ is an inadmissible solution. Sylvia takes 1.6 s to enter the water.	The domain of $h(t)$ is $t \geq 0$, where $t \in R$, since time must be positive in the context.

PRACTISING

Lesson 7.1

1. Solve by graphing.
   a) $6x^2 - 13x + 6 = 0$
   b) $64x^2 + 112x + 49 = 0$
   c) $-5x^2 - 8x + 3 = 0$
   d) $-0.25x^2 + 2x + 5 = 0$

2. Solve by graphing.
   a) $3t - t^2 = -6$
   b) $4n^2 + 1 = n + 3$
   c) $b(9 - 3b) + 7 = 2(b - 5) + (0.5)b^2$
   d) $c^2 - 38c + 340 = 3c^2 - 96c + 740$

Lesson 7.2

3. Solve by factoring. Verify each solution.
   a) $s^2 - 7s - 60 = 0$
   b) $10x^2 + 17x - 20 = 0$
   c) $2a^2 + 10a + 12 = 0$
   d) $-3x^2 - 5x + 2 = 0$
   e) $16d^2 - 169 = 0$
   f) $8r - 3r^2 = 0$
   g) $3x^2 - 2x = 81 - 2x - x^2$
   h) $4(m^2 - 4m + 6) = 3(2m^2 + 8)$

Lesson 7.3

4. Solve by using the quadratic formula.
   a) $117x^2 - 307x + 176 = 0$
   b) $f^2 + 2f - 2 = 0$
   c) $7h^2 + 6h = 5$
   d) $6x^2 + 8x + 4 = 0$

Lesson 7.4

5. Determine three consecutive positive odd integers, if the sum of the squares of the first two integers is 15 less than the square of the third integer.

6. A right triangle has a perimeter of 120 cm. One side of the triangle is 24 cm long. Determine the length of the other side and the length of the hypotenuse.

7. A fishing boat leaves a dock at noon and travels due west at 40 km/h. A second boat leaves the same dock 20 min later and travels due south at 51 km/h. At what time, to the nearest minute, will the two boats be 116 km apart?

8. A skydiver jumps out of an airplane at an altitude of 3.5 km. The altitude of the skydiver, $H(t)$, in metres, over time, t, in seconds, can be modelled by the function

$$H(t) = 3500 - 5t^2$$

   a) How far has the skydiver fallen after 10 s?
   b) The skydiver opens her parachute at an altitude of 1000 m. How long did she free fall?

9. Two integers differ by 12. The sum of the squares of the integers is 1040. Determine the integers.

10. Tickets to a school dance cost $5. The projected attendance is 300 people. The dance committee projects that for every $0.50 increase in the ticket price, attendance will decrease by 20. What ticket price will generate $1562.50 in revenue?

A Teaching Tool

Have you ever heard the following saying?
"To teach is to learn twice."
For this task, you will illustrate and explain what you have learned about quadratic equations, using a format of your choice.

? How do you solve a quadratic equation?

A. Choose a format for your presentation. Here are some possibilities:
- short story
- song
- poem or rap
- multimedia presentation
- mobile
- flow chart
- T-shirt design

B. In your presentation, explain the three methods that can be used to solve a quadratic equation. Determine the important concepts to explain for each method.

C. Write a quadratic equation, and show how to solve it using the method you think is best. Explain your solution, including why you chose the method you did.

> Task | **Checklist**
> ✔ Are your explanations clear?
> ✔ Did you use appropriate mathematical language?

The Final Product and Presentation

Your final presentation should be more than just a factual written report of the information you have found. To make the most of your hard work, select a format for your final presentation that will suit your strengths, as well as your topic.

Presentation Styles

To make your presentation interesting, use a format that suits your own style. Here are some ideas:

- a report on an experiment or an investigation
- a summary of a newspaper article or a case study
- a short story, musical performance, or play
- a web page
- a slide show, multimedia presentation, or video
- a debate
- an advertising campaign or pamphlet
- a demonstration or the teaching of a lesson

Here are some decisions that other students have made about the format for their presentation:

Project 1: Weather Predictions
Muhamud has researched the mathematics of weather predictions. He has decided to make his presentation a demonstration of how a weather report is prepared, including the mathematics used, followed by an actual television weather report. He plans to submit a written report on his research and conclusions, as well.

Project 2: Gender Differences
Ming has studied the differences between the responses of females and males on cognitive aptitude tests. To illustrate her findings, she will have the class complete one of the assessment tasks during her presentation and then compare the results with standardized norms. In her report, Ming plans to include testing she has done on randomly selected students at her school.

Executive Summary

Sometimes, it is effective to give your audience an executive summary of your presentation. This is a one-page summary of your presentation, which includes your research question and the conclusions you have made. Ask your teacher about making copies of your summary for the class.

PROJECT EXAMPLE   Creating Your Presentation

Sarah chose the changes in population of the Western provinces and the territories over the last century as her topic. Below, she describes how she determined which format to use for her presentation.

Sarah's Presentation

Because most of my supporting information is graphical, I am going to use a multimedia slide show. I will include some tables and graphs to show that the population of British Columbia and Alberta grew faster than the population of the rest of the Western and Northern provinces and territories. I will give all of the audience members an executive summary of my research, which will include my research question, my data (with the necessary supporting visuals), and my conclusions. I will give my teacher the full report.

Evaluating Your Own Presentation

Before giving your presentation, you can use these questions to decide if your presentation will be effective:
- Did I define my topic well? What is the best way to define my topic?
- Is my presentation focused? Will my classmates find it focused?
- Did I organize my information effectively? Is it obvious that I am following a plan in my presentation?
- Am I satisfied with my presentation? What might make it more effective?
- What unanswered questions might my audience have?

Your Turn

A. Does your topic suit some presentation formats better than others? Explain why.

B. From which presentation format do you think your audience will gain the greatest understanding? Why?

C. Choose a format for your presentation, and create your presentation.

D. Use the questions provided in Evaluating Your Own Presentation to assess your presentation. Make any changes that you think are needed, as a result of your evaluation.

NEL

Proportional Reasoning

▸ LEARNING GOALS

You will be able to develop your spatial sense and proportional reasoning by

- Solving problems that involve rates
- Solving problems that involve scale diagrams
- Determining the relationships among scale factors, surface areas, and volumes of similar objects, and using these relationships to solve problems

? The diameter of the Moon is about one-quarter the diameter of Earth. How could this information be used to estimate the relationships between the surface areas and volumes of the Moon and Earth?

Interpreting the Cold Lake Region

YOU WILL NEED
- calculator
- measuring tape or ruler

Cold Lake is a city in Alberta's Lakelands, near its border with Saskatchewan. The following map shows information you could get from an Internet search. If you did not know the scale of the map, however, you would have difficulty judging distances and the sizes of specific locations.

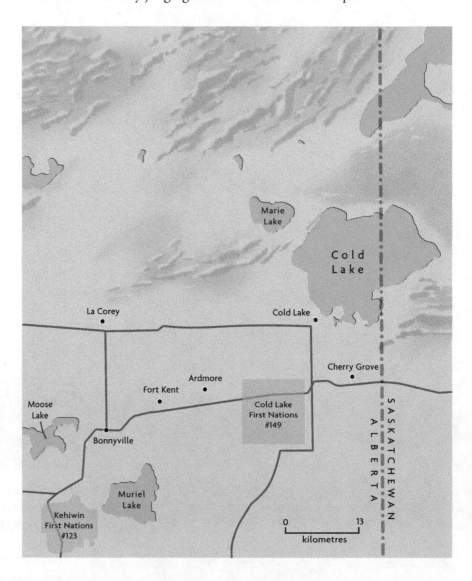

The scale of this map is 2 cm equals 13 km.

❓ What more can you learn about the Cold Lake region from this map?

A. French exchange students are taking a field trip to visit some points of interest in the Cold Lake region. They are starting their trip in Bonnyville. While waiting for the bus Marie and some of her classmates go into the District Historical Museum to see the Poitras Collection of French folk art. While she is in the museum, the bus arrives. The bus is parked 300 m from the museum, and it is going to leave in 5 min. Can Marie catch the bus if she walks? Explain.

B. The first stop on the field trip is a horse farm and equestrian centre in La Corey. Estimate the distance that the bus must travel by road.

C. From La Corey, the students are going to the Alex Janvier Art Gallery in Cold Lake. Estimate the distance that the bus must travel by road.

D. In Alex Janvier's *Morning Star*, there are four distinct areas of colour in the outside ring. Each area of colour represents a period in First Nations history. The total area of the painting is about 418 m².
   i) What is the area of one quadrant of the painting?
   ii) Describe an area in your school or community that is about the same size as one quadrant of the painting.

E. On the way back to Bonnyville, the students will visit Cold Lake First Nations Reserve #149. Estimate the area of the reserve.

F. The graph to the right shows the distance travelled over time on the last two legs of the students' field trip.
   i) On which leg was the bus travelling faster? Explain how you know.
   ii) Estimate the difference in the speeds of the bus on these two legs of the trip.

WHAT DO You Think?

Decide whether you agree or disagree with each statement. Explain your decision.

1. Joe walked 5 km in 2 h, and Steff walked 3 km in 1.25 h. The only way to compare these rates is to express each rate numerically, as a unit rate.

2. Natalie needs to buy ground beef so that she can make lasagna for a party. There are two supermarkets and a butcher in her town. Price is the only factor that she needs to consider when deciding where to buy the ground beef.

3. When a 2-D shape or a 3-D object is enlarged or reduced, all of its measurements are affected by the scale factor in the same way.

Among the prominent citizens of Cold Lake is Alex Janvier, a Dene artist born on Le Goff Reserve, Cold Lake First Nations. *Morning Star*, one of his most celebrated works, is displayed in the Canadian Museum of Civilization in Gatineau, Québec.

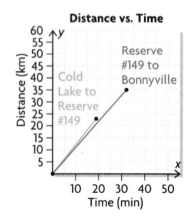

Distance vs. Time

Comparing and Interpreting Rates

EXPLORE...

- World-class sprinters can run 100 m in about 9.8 s. If they could run at this rate for a longer period of time, estimate how far they could run in a minute, in an hour, and in a day.

Communication | Tip

The time 01:20:34.7, or 80:34.7, can also be written as 1 h 20 min 34.7 s or as 80 min 34.7 s.

GOAL

Represent, interpret, and compare rates.

INVESTIGATE the Math

A triathlon consists of three different races: a 1.5 km swim, a 40 km bike ride, and a 10 km run. The time it takes to "transition" from one race to the next is given as "Trans" in the official records. The setup for the transition area is different in different triathlons.

Simon Whitfield of Victoria, British Columbia, participated in the triathlon in both the 2000 and 2008 Olympic Games. His results for both Olympics are shown below.

2000 Sydney Olympic Games Triathlon: Men

			Swimming		Cycling		Running	
Rank	Athlete	Country	Time	Trans	Time	Trans	Time	Total Time
1	Whitfield	Canada	17:57	0:22	58:54	0:18	30:54	1:48:24.02

2008 Beijing Olympic Games Triathlon: Men

			Swimming		Cycling		Running	
Rank	Athlete	Country	Time	Trans	Time	Trans	Time	Total Time
2	Whitfield	Canada	18:18	0:27	58:56	0:29	30:48	1:48:58.47

? How can you compare Simon's speeds in his two Olympic medal-winning triathlons?

A. Compare Simon's times for each race segment in the two triathlons, ignoring the transition times. Which race segment had the greatest difference in Simon's times?

B. Speed, the ratio of distance to time, is an example of a **rate**. Create a distance versus time graph to compare Simon's swimming speeds in these triathlons. Express time in hours and distance in kilometres.

C. Carmen claims that Simon swam faster in the 2000 Sydney Olympic Games Triathlon than in Beijing in 2008. Explain how the data in the table and in the graph you created in part B support her claim.

D. Determine the slope of each line segment on your distance versus time graph. What do these slopes represent?

E. Do the slopes you determined in part D support Carmen's claim? Explain.

rate

A comparison of two amounts that are measured in different units; for example, keying 240 words/8 min

Communication | Tip

The word "per" means "to each" or "for each." It is written in units using a slash (/).

Reflecting

F. Can the slopes of line segments on a graph be used to compare rates? Explain.

G. Are the slopes of the line segments on your distance versus time graph **unit rates**? Explain.

H. Can the swimming speeds in each triathlon be calculated directly from the information given? Explain.

APPLY the Math

> ### EXAMPLE 1   Comparing two rates expressed in different units

Natasha can buy a 12 kg turkey from her local butcher for $42.89. The local supermarket has turkeys advertised in its weekly flyer for $1.49/lb. There are about 2.2 lb in 1 kg. Which store has the lower price?

Natasha's Solution: Comparing using estimation

Butcher:

A 12 kg turkey from the butcher costs about $43.

Supermarket:

The price of a turkey from the supermarket, T, is

$$T = \left(\frac{\$1.50}{1 \text{ lb}}\right)\left(\frac{2 \text{ lb}}{1 \text{ kg}}\right)(12 \text{ kg})$$

$T = \$36$

A 12 kg turkey from the supermarket costs about $36.

A turkey from the butcher costs $\dfrac{\$43}{12 \text{ kg}}$, and a turkey from the supermarket costs $\dfrac{\$36}{12 \text{ kg}}$. So, the price of a 12 kg turkey is about $7 less at the supermarket.

> To make a comparison, I needed to estimate the prices of two turkeys that are the same size, measured in the same units.

> I multiplied the price per pound by the conversion rate for pounds to kilograms, which is approximately 2 lb/1 kg, and then I multiplied by 12 kg, the mass of the turkey. This gave me an estimate of the price of a similar turkey from the supermarket.

Dimitri's Solution: Comparing using unit rates

Butcher:

The price per kilogram for a turkey from the butcher, B, is

$$B = \frac{\$42.89}{12 \text{ kg}}$$

$$B = \frac{\$3.574...}{1 \text{ kg}}$$

> To make a comparison, I expressed each price as a unit rate, using the same units.

> I divided the price of a 12 kg turkey from the butcher by the mass. This gave me the price per kilogram for a turkey from the butcher.

The price per kilogram for a turkey from the butcher is $3.57/kg.

Supermarket:

The price per kilogram for a turkey from the supermarket, S, is

$$S = \left(\frac{\$1.49}{1 \, \cancel{lb}}\right)\left(\frac{2.2 \, \cancel{lb}}{1 \, kg}\right)$$

$$S = \frac{\$3.278}{1 \, kg}$$

I multiplied the price per pound by the conversion rate for pounds to kilograms, which is approximately 2.2 lb/1 kg. This gave me the price per kilogram for a turkey from the supermarket.

The price per kilogram for a turkey from the supermarket is $3.28/kg.

The price of a turkey is 29¢/kg less at the supermarket.

Your Turn

Describe how you could use a graph to compare the price of a turkey from the butcher and from the supermarket.

EXAMPLE 2   Connecting the slope of a line segment to a rate

Describe a scenario that could be represented by this graph. Compare the rates shown, and discuss why the rates may have changed.

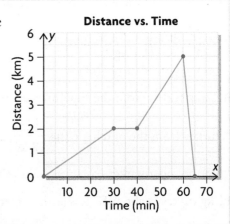

Gilles's Solution

$$\text{Slope} = \frac{\Delta y}{\Delta x}$$

$$\text{Slope} = \frac{y_2 - y_1}{x_2 - x_1}$$

$$\frac{\Delta d}{\Delta t} = \frac{d_2 - d_1}{t_2 - t_1}$$

To choose a reasonable scenario, I decided to calculate the slope of each line segment. This meant dividing the change in distance by the change in time.

The first line segment has endpoints (0, 0) and (30, 2).

$$\text{Slope}_1 = \frac{2 - 0}{30 - 0}$$

$$\text{Slope}_1 = \frac{2}{30} \text{ km/min}$$

$$\left(\frac{2 \text{ km}}{30 \text{ min}}\right)\left(\frac{60 \text{ min}}{1 \text{ h}}\right) = 4 \text{ km/h}$$

The second line segment is horizontal.

$$\text{Slope}_2 = 0 \text{ km/h}$$

The slope represents the rate of change of distance over time, in kilometres per minute, for each line segment. This speed is a unit rate, since the numerical value of the second term is equal to 1.

I converted each rate in kilometres per minute to kilometres per hour to help me describe the scenario. The speed represented by the first line segment is 4 km/h.

The third line segment has endpoints (40, 2) and (60, 5).

$$\text{Slope}_3 = \frac{5 - 2}{60 - 40}$$

$$\text{Slope}_3 = \frac{3}{20} \text{ km/min}$$

$$\left(\frac{3 \text{ km}}{20 \text{ min}}\right)\left(\frac{60 \text{ min}}{1 \text{ h}}\right) = 9 \text{ km/h}$$

The fourth line segment has endpoints (60, 5) and (65, 0).

$$\text{Slope}_4 = \frac{0 - 5}{65 - 60}$$

$$\text{Slope}_4 = \frac{-5}{5} \text{ or } -1 \text{ km/min}$$

$$\left(\frac{-1 \text{ km}}{1 \text{ min}}\right)\left(\frac{60 \text{ min}}{1 \text{ h}}\right) = -60 \text{ km/h}$$

The graph could represent the distance that a person travelled and the time for the trip. Each line segment on the graph could represent a different part of the trip.

I decided that the rates of change were close to the rates at which a person could walk, run, and drive. I made up a story to match the graph and the rates of change that I calculated

The first line segment represents a person walking at a rate of 4 km/h for 30 min to get from home to a variety store.

4 km/h is a reasonable rate at which a person could walk. The graph shows that the distance is increasing during this period.

The second line segment represents the person stopping at the store for 10 min to buy something or talk to someone.

This makes sense, since the distance travelled did not change between 30 min and 40 min.

The third line segment represents the person jogging at a rate of 9 km/h for 20 min to get to a friend's house.

It's difficult to walk at 9 km/h, so I decided that the person must be jogging. The distance was increasing faster during this period.

The fourth line segment represents the person travelling at the greatest rate, 60 km/h, for an additional 5 min. This is because the person received a phone call from home, to say that dinner is ready. The person gets a ride home from a friend.

> The rate of change is negative. This means that the person's distance, relative to the starting point, is decreasing. The person must be travelling back to the starting position. A person can't walk or run at 60 km/h, so I decided that the person must be travelling by car.

EXAMPLE 3   Solving a problem involving rates

When making a decision about buying a vehicle, fuel efficiency is often an important factor.

The gas tank of Mario's new car has a capacity of 55 L. The owner's manual claims that the fuel efficiency of Mario's car is 7.6 L/100 km on the highway. Before Mario's first big highway trip, he set his trip meter to 0 km so he could keep track of the total distance he drove. He started with the gas tank full. Each time he stopped to fill up the tank, he recorded the distance he had driven and the amount of gas he purchased.

Fill-up	Total Distance Driven (km)	Quantity of Gas Purchased (L)
1	645	48.0
2	1037	32.1

On which leg of Mario's trip was his fuel efficiency the best?

Katrina's Solution: Using a graph

Distance driven on leg 1 = 645 km

> First, I needed to determine how far Mario drove on each leg of the trip. Since the trip meter was initially set to 0 km, I knew that he drove 645 km on the first leg. I had to subtract the first trip meter reading from the second trip meter reading to determine the distance he drove on the second leg.

Distance driven on leg 2 = 1037 − 645
Distance driven on leg 2 = 392 km

Gas used on leg 1 = 48.0 L
Gas used on leg 2 = 32.1 L

> Since Mario began each leg with a full tank, the amount of gas he purchased at each fill-up tells me the amount of gas he used on each leg of the trip.

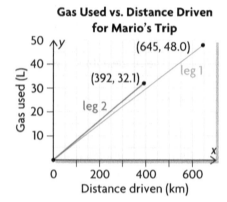

Gas Used vs. Distance Driven for Mario's Trip

I created a graph of Gas used versus Distance driven by plotting the ordered pairs (Distance driven, Gas used). I used distance driven on the horizontal axis, because I noticed that distance is the second term in the manufacturer's fuel efficiency. The slope of the line segment for each leg of the trip represents the change in fuel use over distance.

The blue line segment is less steep than the red line segment, so its slope is less. This means the fuel efficiency of the car was better on the first leg of the trip.

The fuel efficiency is better when you use less gas to drive the same distance, so I knew I was looking for the line segment that was less steep.

Grant's Solution: Using unit rates

Leg	Distance Driven (km)	Gas Used (L)
1	645 − 0 = 645	48.0
2	1037 − 645 = 392	32.1

I used a table to organize the information I needed to determine the fuel efficiency on each leg of the trip as a unit rate, in litres per kilometre. For each leg of the trip, I had to determine the distance that Mario drove and the amount of gas that was used.

First leg:

$$\text{Fuel efficiency} = \frac{\text{Gas used}}{\text{Distance driven}}$$

$$\text{Fuel efficiency} = \frac{48.0 \text{ L}}{645 \text{ km}}$$

$$\text{Fuel efficiency} = 0.074... \text{ L/km}$$

I calculated the car's fuel efficiency on each leg of the trip by dividing the gas used by the distance driven.

Second leg:

$$\text{Fuel efficiency} = \frac{\text{Gas used}}{\text{Distance driven}}$$

$$\text{Fuel efficiency} = \frac{32.1 \text{ L}}{392 \text{ km}}$$

$$\text{Fuel efficiency} = 0.081... \text{ L/km}$$

The fuel efficiency of the car was better on the first leg of the trip.

The fuel efficiency is better when you use less gas to drive the same distance.

Your Turn

Did the car achieve the manufacturer's fuel efficiency rating of $\frac{7.6 \text{ L}}{100 \text{ km}}$ on either leg of the trip? Explain.

CHECK Your Understanding

1. Compare the following situations, and determine the lower rate.
   a) At store A, 8 kg of cheddar cheese costs $68.
   At store B, 12 kg of cheddar cheese costs $88.20.
   b) At gas station A, 44 L of fuel costs $41.36.
   At gas station B, 32 L of fuel costs $31.36.

2. Compare the following situations, and determine the greater rate.
   a) It takes 4 h 15 min to drain tank A, which holds 300 L of water.
   It takes 2 h 10 min to drain tank B, which holds 150 L of water.
   b) Person A runs 400 m in 1 min 15 s.
   Person B runs 1 km in 5 min 20 s.

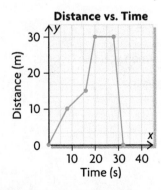

Distance vs. Time

3. The graph to the left shows how an all-terrain vehicle (ATV) travels over time.
   a) Over which interval of time is the ATV travelling the slowest? Over which interval is it travelling the fastest?
   b) When does the ATV start to return to its starting position? When does it get there?
   c) What does a zero slope mean in the context of this graph?

PRACTISING

4. Apple juice is sold in 1 L bottles and 200 mL boxes. A 1 L bottle sells for $1.75, and fifteen 200 mL boxes sell for $4.99.
  a) Determine the unit rate, in dollars per millilitre, for each size.
  b) Which size has the lower cost per millilitre?

5. The list price for a 925 mL container of paint is $20.09. A 3.54 L container of the same paint costs $52.99. Which container has the lower unit cost?

6. When Rupi goes to her aerobics class, she can burn 140 Cal in 20 min. When she plays hockey for 1.5 h, she can burn 720 Cal. Which activity burns Calories at a greater rate?

7. For each of the following, compare the two rates and determine the lower rate.
  a) whole chickens: $3.61/kg or 10 lb for $17.40
  b) jogging speeds: 6 mph or 2 km in 10 min
  c) fuel efficiency: 10.6 L/100 km or 35.1 L of fuel needed to travel 450 km
  d) driving speeds: 30 m/s or 100 km/h

> **Communication** | **Tip**
>
> 1 kg ≐ 2.2 lb
> 1 km ≐ 0.6 mi (miles)

8. Jay can buy a 25 lb bag of bird seed for $21.30 from the Farmers Co-op. The pet store in town sells an 18 kg bag for $24.69. At which store can Jay buy bird seed at a lower cost? Explain how you know.

9. Shelley has two choices for a long-distance telephone plan:
  • her telephone company, which charges 4¢/min
  • a device that plugs into her Internet modem, which costs $19.95 with an additional charge of 1.5¢/min
Shelley makes, on average, 50 min of long-distance calls per month. Which option would be cheaper on an annual basis? Justify your decision.

10. On Monday, a crew paved 10 km of road in 8 h. On Tuesday, the crew paved 15 km in 10 h. Draw a graph to compare the crew's daily paving rates.

11. Draw a graph that shows how, over one day, the outdoor temperature starts at 24 °C, decreases at a rate of 1.5 °C/h for 5 h, remains constant for 2 h, and then increases by 0.75 °C/h for 4 h.

12. A hotel shuttle bus takes David from the airport to his hotel. Use the distance versus time graph to the right to create a story that describes David's bus trip.

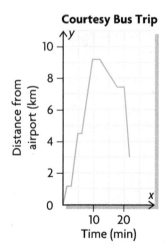

Courtesy Bus Trip

8.1 Comparing and Interpreting Rates   **451**

flask

beaker

graduated
cylinder

drinking
glass

13. Suppose that tap water, flowing from a faucet at a constant rate, is used to fill these containers. Match each of the following graphs with the appropriate container. Justify your choices.

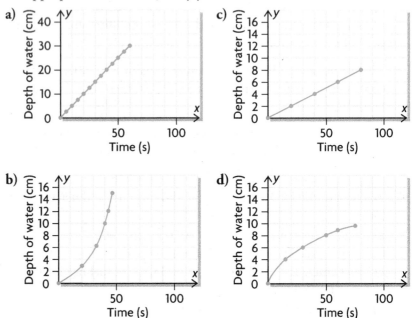

a)

Depth of water (cm) vs Time (s)

b)

Depth of water (cm) vs Time (s)

c)

Depth of water (cm) vs Time (s)

d)

Depth of water (cm) vs Time (s)

14. The following table shows the amount of greenhouse gases emitted by fossil fuel production in Canada from 1990 to 2006. During which period was the amount emitted increasing at the greatest rate? Justify your decision.

Year	Greenhouse Gases from Fossil Fuel Production (megatonnes)
1990	103
1995	127
2000	151
2003	161
2006	158

15. At the 2002 Olympics, speed skater Cindy Klassen of Winnipeg, Manitoba, finished out of the medals. Four years later, at the 2006 Olympics, she won five medals in women's speed skating, including gold in the 1500 m race. Compare her speeds in the 1500 m race in 2002 and 2006. In which portion of the race did her speed differ the most?

Games	Age	City	Rank	Time	300 m	700 m	1100 m
2002 Winter	22	Salt Lake	4	1:55.59	25.65	54.17	1:24.09
2006 Winter	26	Torino	1	1:55.27	25.42	53.83	1:23.50

Closing

16. a) When comparing rates, when is an estimate sufficient and when is a precise solution needed? Use specific examples to support your answer.

b) When comparing rates, when is a graphing strategy a good approach and when is a numerical strategy better? Use specific examples to support your answer.

Extending

17. Water is poured into a container like the one to the right at a constant rate. Sketch a graph of depth versus time to represent this situation.

18. Scientists estimate that the processing power of the human brain is equivalent to about 100 million MIPS (million computer instructions per second).

a) In 2005, a typical home computer could process about 7000 MIPS. About how many of these computers were equivalent to the processing power of the brain?

b) Determine the processing power of a computer you use. How many of these computers are equivalent to the processing power of the brain?

History | **Connection**

Ivy Granstrom

Ivy Granstrom was born in 1911 in Glace Bay, Nova Scotia, but lived most of her life in Vancouver, British Columbia. She was blind from birth. For 76 consecutive years, she participated in the annual English Bay Polar Bear swim and was affectionately known as the Queen of the Polar Bears. When she was 64 years old, she was struck by a car. Doctors told her that she would always need a wheelchair. However, she began her own rehab program, walking, jogging, and then running. Soon after, she participated in blind sports competitions for the visually impaired. She established herself as one of world's fastest runners in the Masters Division, setting 25 world records for athletes aged 60 years and older, competing against sighted athletes. She raced until 2001 with Paul Hoeberigs, who ran behind, tethered by a cord and calling out directions. Ivy was a Sports B.C. Athlete of the Year in 1982, inducted into the Terry Fox Hall of Fame in 2001, and made a Member of the Order of Canada in 1989. In 2009, she still held the world record in the 1500 m race for women aged 85 and over. Her time of 10:33.40 was established in 1997. She passed away in 2004.

A. If Granstrom ran the mile race at her world record rate for the 1500 m race, could she break the record, which was 11:03.11 in 2009? Justify your answer.

Solving Problems That Involve Rates

EXPLORE...

- A car travels at 80 km/h. What other rates, expressed using different units, could be used to describe the speed of the car? What would be some of the advantages of using these other rates?

GOAL

Analyze and solve problems that involve rates.

LEARN ABOUT the Math

Jeff lives in a town near the Canada–U.S. border. The gas tank of his truck holds about 90 L. He can either buy gas in his town at $1.06/L or travel across the border into the United States to fill up at $2.86 U.S./gal.

? **Which option makes the most sense economically?**

EXAMPLE 1 Solving a problem that involves multiple rates

Jeff's Solution

The cost to fill up at a gas station in Canada, D, is

$$D = (90 \text{ L})\left(\frac{\$1.06 \text{ Cdn}}{1 \text{ L}}\right)$$

$$D = \$95.40 \text{ Cdn}$$

It will cost $95.40 to fill up in Canada.

> First, I determined the cost to fill up at a gas station in Canada.

Converting 90.0 L into U.S. gallons, G, is

$$G = (90 \text{ L})\left(\frac{1 \text{ gal}}{3.79 \text{ L}}\right)$$

$$G = 23.746... \text{ gal}$$

> I needed to convert the volume that my gas tank holds in litres into U.S. gallons. I know that 1 U.S. gallon is equivalent to 3.79 L.

The cost in U.S. dollars, U, for about 23.7 U.S. gal is

$$U = (23.746... \text{ gal})\left(\frac{\$2.86 \text{ U.S.}}{1 \text{ gal}}\right)$$

$$U = \$67.915... \text{ U.S.}$$

The cost in Canadian dollars, C, for about 23.7 U.S. gal is

$$C = (\$67.915... \text{ U.S.})\left(\frac{\$1.02 \text{ Cdn}}{1 \text{ U.S.}}\right)$$

$$C = \$69.273... \text{ Cdn}$$

> I determined the cost to fill up in U.S. dollars. I needed to convert U.S. dollars into Canadian dollars. The exchange rate today is $1 U.S./$1.02 Cdn.

It will cost $69.27 Cdn to fill up in the United States.
Difference in cost = $95.40 − $69.273...
Difference in cost = $26.13...
Today, it is more economical for me to fill up in the United States. I will save about $26.

> How much I save depends on the price of gas at each station.

Reflecting

A. What other factors will affect Jeff's savings each time he considers where to fill up?

B. Jeff has only considered the cost to fill up his truck. What other factors should he consider when deciding where he will buy gas?

C. Jeff thinks that saving less than $10 is not worth his time. If he had half a tank of gas in his truck, would it be worthwhile for him to fill up in the United States today? Justify your answer.

APPLY the Math

EXAMPLE 2   Connecting rates to contextual situations

Describe a situation in which each unit rate might be used. Identify and explain factors that could influence the unit rate in this situation.

a) 0.05 mg/kg   **b)** 98.5¢/L   **c)** 7.2 MBps

Mangat's Solution

a) 0.05 mg/kg could be the rate at which a certain type of medicine must be administered. This rate means that 0.05 mg of medication is needed for each kilogram of a patient's mass. The type of medication used could influence the quantity administered per kilogram of body mass.

> I needed a situation in which a very small mass of a substance (milligrams) is related to a kilogram. I knew that medicine is prescribed according the mass of a patient, which can be measured in kilograms.

b) 98.5¢/L could represent the rate at which consumers pay for 1 L of gasoline.
This rate could be influenced by the type of gas chosen. It could also be influenced by the current cost of gasoline per barrel, which could be affected by war, weather, time of year, holidays, and supply and demand.

> I needed a situation in which a cost in cents is related to a volume in litres. Gasoline is sold in litres.

c) 7.2 MBps could be the rate at which information is transferred over a computer network.
This rate could be influenced by
- the type of network (wireless versus wired).
- the type/quality of the network card.
- the type of router used.

> I needed a situation in which megabytes (MB) are related to time in seconds. Data transfer can be measured this way.

Your Turn

Think of two other unit rates that you are familiar with. State one or two factors that could influence these rates.

EXAMPLE **3**   Reasoning to solve a rate problem

Paula is asked to order snacks for an office meeting of 180 people. She decides to order dessert squares, which come in boxes of 24. She estimates that she will need 2.5 squares/person. How many boxes should she buy?

Mila's Solution: Calculating using unit analysis

Formula to describe the snack order:

$$\text{Number of boxes} = \left(\frac{1 \text{ box}}{\text{Number of squares}}\right)\left(\frac{\text{Number of squares eaten}}{1 \text{ person}}\right)(\text{Number of people})$$

$$\text{Number of boxes} = \left(\frac{1 \text{ box}}{24 \text{ squares}}\right)\left(\frac{2.5 \text{ squares}}{1 \text{ person}}\right)(180 \text{ persons})$$

> Paula estimated that each person would eat about 2.5 squares.

Number of boxes = 18.75
Paula should buy 19 boxes.

> I rounded up my answer to the nearest number of boxes.

Joe's Solution: Estimating using proportional reasoning

There are about 25 squares in each box.
If each person eats 2.5 squares, then
Paula needs one box for every 10 people.
There are 18 groups of 10 in 180.

> I decided to estimate. I knew that each person will eat about 2.5 squares. Estimating 25 squares/box made the numbers easier to work with, using mental math.

Paula needs to buy at least 18 boxes.
She should order 19 boxes to be safe.

> I know that I underestimated, since I estimated 25 squares/box and there are only 24 squares/box.

Your Turn

If each person at the meeting eats about 1.5 squares on average, how many boxes of squares will be left over?

EXAMPLE **4**   Solving a problem that involves different rates

Amelia walks briskly, at 6 km/h. When she walks at this rate for 2 h, she burns 454 Cal. Bruce walks at a slower rate, 4 km/h, burning 62 Cal in 30 min. If Amelia walks for 3 h, how much longer will Bruce have to walk in order to burn the same amount of Calories?

April's Solution: Using a function

The amount of Calories that Amelia burns each hour when she walks at 6 km/h, A, is

$$A = \frac{454 \text{ Cal}}{2 \text{ h}}$$

$A = 227$ Cal/h

If $A(t)$ represents the amount of Calories that Amelia burns and t represents the time in hours, then
$A(t) = 227t$

> I assumed that Amelia walks at a constant rate, so I could use a linear function to represent the relation between Calories burned and time.

For 3 h,
$A(3) = 227(3)$
$A(3) = 681$ Cal
Amelia burns 681 Cal in 3 h.

The amount of Calories that Bruce burns each hour when he walks at 4 km/h, B, is
$$B = \frac{62 \text{ Cal}}{0.5 \text{ h}}$$
$B = 124$ Cal/h
If $B(t)$ represents the amount of Calories that Bruce burns and t represents the time in hours, then
$B(t) = 124t$

> I assumed that Bruce also walks at a constant rate.

For 681 Cal,
$B(t) = 681$ Cal
681 Cal $= (124$ Cal/h$)t$
$5.491... \text{ h} = t$

> I needed to know how long it takes Bruce to burn 681 Cal, so I substituted 681 Cal for $B(t)$.

Bruce will need to walk for about 5.5 h to burn the same amount of Calories that Amelia burns in 3 h. Bruce will need to walk for an additional 2.5 h.

> I rounded the time to the nearest tenth of an hour.

Joanna's Solution: Using equivalent ratios

The rate for Calories burned is Cal/h. When Amelia walks at 6 km/h for 2 h, she burns 454 Cal. When she walks for 3 h, she burns x Calories. These rates are equivalent.

> I assumed that Amelia walks at a constant rate, so the rate at which she burns calories will also be constant.

$$\frac{454 \text{ Cal}}{2 \text{ h}} = \frac{x}{3 \text{ h}}$$

$$3 \cancel{h}\left(\frac{454 \text{ Cal}}{2 \cancel{h}}\right) = x$$

$$681 \text{ Cal} = x$$

> I wrote an equation using equivalent rates to determine the amount, in Calories, that Amelia burns in 3 h. The units in the ratios are the same, so I am confident that my answer will be in the correct units, Calories.

Bruce burns 62 Cal in 0.5 h. He must burn 681 Cal in t hours.

$$\frac{62 \text{ Cal}}{0.5 \text{ h}} = \frac{681 \text{ Cal}}{t}$$
$$62t = 340.5 \text{ h}$$
$$t = 5.491... \text{ h}$$

> I wrote an equation using a pair of equivalent rates, where 681 Cal must be burned by Bruce to match Amelia. Then I solved for t.

Converting 0.491... h into minutes, M, is

$$M = (0.491... \text{ h})\left(\frac{60 \text{ min}}{1 \text{ h}}\right)$$

$M = 29.516... \text{ min}$

Bruce will need to walk for about 5 h 30 min
to burn the same amount of Calories that
Amelia burns in 3 h.

Bruce will need to walk for about 2 h 30 min longer
to burn the same amount of Calories.

Your Turn

If Bruce walks for 2 h, for how long does Amelia need to walk to burn
the same amount, in Calories, as Bruce? Round your answer to the
nearest minute.

In Summary

Key Idea

- When you are given a rate problem that involves an unknown, you can
  solve the problem using a variety of strategies.

Need to Know

- Often, a problem that involves rates can be solved by writing an
  equation that involves a pair of equivalent ratios. To be equivalent
  ratios, the units in the numerators of the two ratios must be the same,
  and the units in the denominators must be the same. Paying attention
  to the units in each term of the ratios will help you write the equation
  correctly.
- A multiplication strategy can be used to solve many rate problems, such
  as problems that require conversions between units. Including the units
  with each term in the product and using unit elimination helps you
  verify that your product is correct.
- When a rate of change is constant, writing a linear function to represent
  the situation may be useful when solving problems.

CHECK Your Understanding

1. **a)** 50 L of oil costs $163. How much oil, to the nearest litre, could
   you buy for $30?
   b) It takes 3 min 25 s to fill a 75 L gas tank. How long, to the nearest
   minute, will it take to fill a 55 L gas tank?

c) 8 kg of beef costs $68.00. How much will it cost, to the nearest cent, for 1.5 kg of beef?

d) The adult dosage of an antibiotic medicine is 25 mL/80 kg. How much medicine is needed for a person with a mass of 95 kg?

2. Two competing stores have 350 mL cans of pop on sale this week. Supersaver is selling a case of 24 cans for $5.99. Gord the Grocer is selling cans of the same pop in cases of 12, with three cases for $9.99.

a) Which store is selling soft drinks at the lower price per can?

b) Besides price, what other factors should be considered when determining which store offers the better buy for a consumer?

PRACTISING

3. A screw has 32 turns over a distance of 24 mm of thread.

24 mm

Another screw, with the same pattern, has 42 mm of thread. How many turns does it have?

4. The Wildcats won 12 of their first 20 games. At this rate, predict how many games they will win during the 30-game season.

5. Mario borrowed $1000 and paid $40 simple interest. If he borrowed the money for eight months, what interest rate was he charged?

6. Describe a situation in which each rate might be used. Identify any factors that could influence the rate in this situation.

a) $7.23/kg
b) 20 mL/90 kg
c) $1.08/100 g
d) −1.5 °C/km
e) 20 g/L
f) $4.99/ft²

7. Basic units of data are transferred by a particular computer at 12 MB (megabytes) every 2 s. How long will it take this computer to transfer 1.5 GB (gigabytes) of data? (1 GB is equivalent to 1024 MB.)

8. Melanie wants to defrost a frozen roast, which weighs 2.68 kg, in her microwave. To find out how much time she needs, she looks in a cookbook. She reads that 2 lb of meat takes 15 min to defrost. How long, to the nearest minute, should she set the timer for?

> **Communication | Tip**
> 1 kg ≐ 2.2 lb

9. A nurse administers a vaccine that comes in a 10 mL bottle. The adult dosage is 0.5 cc (1 cc = 1 mL). How many adults can the nurse vaccinate before the bottle is empty?

10. Tonya works 50 h every three weeks. At this rate, how many hours will she work in one year? Explain how you could solve this problem using two different strategies.

11. Chris and her friend Elena drove from Vancouver to Yellowknife for a reunion. They took turns driving, so they only needed to stop for gas or food. They drove the 2359 km distance in 36 h 12 min.
   a) Determine their average speed to the nearest tenth of a kilometre per hour.
   b) They used 231.2 L of fuel. Determine their average fuel consumption per 100 km.
   c) Chris and Elena spent $252.05 on fuel. What was the average cost of a litre of gas?

12. Manpret has taken a job as a nurse in the community health centre in Tuktoyaktuk, Northwest Territories. She plans to ship her car, furniture, and personal effects to Tuktoyaktuk by barge from Vancouver. She has found these shipping rates online:
   • light-duty vehicles: $0.2015/lb
   • furniture and personal effects: $0.2734/lb

   Manpret knows that her car has a mass of 1250 kg. She estimates that she has roughly 550 lb of furniture and personal effects. Calculate her cost to ship these items to her destination.

13. Emma runs a kennel near Wild Horse, Alberta. She has decided to purchase dog food from a U.S. supplier. The supplier sells 40 lb bags for $38.95 U.S. The exchange rate is $1 U.S. for $1.05 Cdn on the day that she orders the food.
   a) How much, in Canadian dollars, does Emma spend to buy 20 bags of dog food?
   b) Each dog eats about 4 kg/week and Emma boards an average of 12 dogs per day. Will the 20 bags of dog food last two months? Explain.
   c) What other factors should she have considered before she ordered from this supplier?

14. The map to the left shows Prince Albert National Park in Saskatchewan. The scale of the map is 1.3 cm to 20 km.
   a) Estimate the area of the park in hectares. One hectare (1 ha) is equivalent to 10 000 m^2.
   b) The annual cost to monitor and fight forest fires in this region is about $48/ha. Estimate the annual fire management expenditure for the park.

15. Paula wants to buy bottled water.
   • Store A, located 12 km from her home, is selling 500 mL bottles in a case of 24 for $4.99.
   • Store B, located 20 km from her home, is selling 330 mL bottles in a case of 24 for $3.49.
   • It costs Paula $0.14/km to run her car.

   Which store would you recommend for Paula to buy her water? Explain.

16. A cargo jet leaves an airport that is 2000 ft above sea level at 6:30 a.m. The jet climbs steadily to a cruising altitude of 37 000 ft, at a rate of 7000 ft/min. After cruising at this altitude for 40 min, the jet descends steadily at a rate of 3500 ft/min to an airport that is 5500 ft above sea level. What time does the jet land?

17. The low temperature for a certain day was recorded as $-5.3\ ^\circ$C at 3:30 a.m. The temperature then rose steadily until the high temperature was recorded as 11.8 $^\circ$C at 5:45 p.m. A weather forecaster predicted the same temperature increase rate for the next day, from a low of $-7\ ^\circ$C at 3 a.m. Estimate the temperature at 7 a.m. the next day.

Closing

18. A particular type of paint can be purchased at two local stores. Bren's Interior Design sells the 870 mL size for $7.99, while Home Suppliers sells the 3.7 L size for $27.99. This type of paint will cover an area of 10 m²/L. Suppose that you want to paint a room that is 2.4 m high and has the dimensions shown to the right. One wall has a door that measures 80 cm by 205 cm. Another wall has a window that measures 100 cm by 130 cm.
   a) Based on cost, at which store should you buy the paint?
   b) In addition to cost, what other factors should you consider when deciding where to buy the paint?

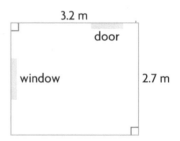

Extending

19. A pendulum is pulled to the left. When released, it swings from left to right, but never returns to its initial position. The time required for one complete oscillation is called the *period* of the pendulum. The time, T, in seconds, for one period of the pendulum is given by the equation

$$T = 2\pi\sqrt{\frac{L}{9.8}},$$

where L is the length of the pendulum in metres. How many periods will a 2 m pendulum complete over 1 h?

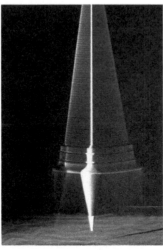

20. A new saltwater pool is being filled by four different pumps, which pump water from a nearby ocean into the pool. The first pump can fill the entire pool with water in two days. The second pump requires three days, and the third pump requires four days. The fourth pump needs only 6 h. How long will it take to fill the pool if all four pumps are used?

8.2 Solving Problems That Involve Rates **461**

Analyzing a Rate Puzzle

Filling irregular shaped containers with water at a constant rate can produce some interesting results.

The Puzzle

A container is constructed from a connected sequence of rectangular prisms as shown below.

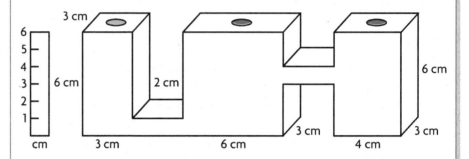

Each connecting piece has dimensions of 1 cm by 2 cm by 3 cm. Water is dripping into the hole on the left (marked in blue) at a constant rate of 1 cm³/min. The marks to the left of the container measure the height, in centimetres, of the water in the container as it fills.

A. Will one prism be filled before the others? Explain.

B. Determine the time needed for the water to reach each of the height marks indicated to the left of the container.

C. Use your times to plot a graph of water height versus time.

D. Between which two height markers did the water level rise at the slowest rate? Explain how you know.

The Strategy

E. Describe the strategy you used to determine the information needed to create your graph.

Modifying the Puzzle

F. There are other holes in the container, indicated in red. If the container were filled at the same rate through either of those holes, would the length of time needed to fill the container change? Explain.

G. Would your graph change if you filled the container through a different hole? Explain.

FREQUENTLY ASKED Questions

Q: **How do you compare rates? When is one strategy more effective than another?**

A: Here are three strategies you can use to compare rates:

- It is often effective to express the rates as unit rates using the same units.

  For example, organic cashews may be sold for $18.95/kg at one store and $9.49/lb at another store. To determine which rate, or price, is less expensive, you can convert the rate in kilograms to a rate in pounds and then calculate the equivalent unit rate to make a proper comparison. (Alternatively, you could convert the rate in pounds to a rate in kilograms. The choice of which rate to convert might be affected by other comparisons that you need to make to solve a problem.)

Study | Aid
- See Lesson 8.1.
- Try Mid-Chapter Review Questions 1 to 5.

$9.49/lb | $18.95/kg

1 kg : 2.2 lb

$$\frac{\$18.95}{1 \text{ kg}}\left(\frac{1 \text{ kg}}{2.2 \text{ lb}}\right) \doteq \$8.61/\text{lb}$$

$18.95/kg is less expensive.

This strategy is effective when you need to know and use the numerical value of each rate.

- On a graph of a relation, the slope of a line that joins two points is equivalent to the average rate of change.

  For example, car A travels 50 m in 4 s, and car B travels 40 m in 4 s. If these data are plotted on a graph, it is clear that car A is travelling at a greater rate than car B, because the blue line is steeper than the red line.

  This strategy is effective when you need to know which rate is greater or lesser, but you do not need to know the numerical values. However, the numerical values could be determined by calculating the slopes of the lines:

$$\text{Slope} = \frac{\Delta y}{\Delta x}$$

$$\text{Slope} = \frac{y_2 - y_1}{x_2 - x_1}$$

$$\text{Rate of change for car A} = \frac{50 - 0}{4 - 0} \text{ or } 12.5 \text{ m/s}$$

$$\text{Rate of change for car B} = \frac{40 - 0}{4 - 0} \text{ or } 10.0 \text{ m/s}$$

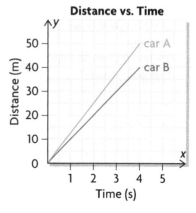

Distance vs. Time

- Rates can also be compared by writing them as equivalent rates, with the second terms numerically the same.

  For example, suppose that you burn 320 Cal in 20 min of spin class and 210 Cal in 15 min of jogging. You can compare these rates by determining the amount of Calories burned in an hour by doing each activity, using the fact that there are 60 min in an hour.

Spinning:	Jogging:
$\dfrac{320 \text{ Cal}}{20 \text{ min}}\left(\dfrac{60 \text{ min}}{1 \text{ h}}\right) = 960$ Cal/h	$\dfrac{210 \text{ Cal}}{15 \text{ min}}\left(\dfrac{60 \text{ min}}{1 \text{ h}}\right) = 840$ Cal/h

  Spinning burns Calories at a greater rate.

Study Aid

- See Lesson 8.2, Example 1.
- Try Mid-Chapter Review Question 6.

Q: **When you are comparison shopping, what factors, other than unit price, should you consider?**

A: The factors to consider will depend on the situation.

For example, if you want to buy a pair of jeans and you know the prices at two different stores, you might also consider
- the distance to each store and the time you will need to get there.
- the cost of fares you will pay or gas you will use to travel there and back.
- how busy each store will be.
- the exchange rate on the dollar, if one or both stores are located in the United States.

Study Aid

- See Lesson 8.2, Example 1, Example 3 (Mila's Solution), and Example 4 (Joanna's Solution).
- Try Mid-Chapter Review Questions 7 and 8.

Q: **Why is analyzing the units in a rate problem a useful strategy?**

A1: Often, a problem that involves rates can be solved by writing an equation. The equation you write will involve a pair of equivalent ratios. In this kind of equation, the units in the numerators of the two ratios must be the same and the units in the denominators must be the same. Paying attention to the units in each term of these ratios will help you write the equation correctly.

A2: Sometimes, a rate problem can be solved by using a multiplication strategy. When you use this strategy, including the units with each term in the product will help you verify that you have multiplied the quantities correctly. The units should cancel to leave you with the correct units for your answer.

PRACTISING

Lesson 8.1

1. Carol can key at the rate of 65 words/min. Jed can key 290 words in 5 min. Who is faster? Explain how you know.

2. Harry filled the 75 L gas tank of his pickup truck for $73.88. Stan paid 95¢/L to fill up his truck. Who paid less per litre for fuel?

3. For each of the following, compare the two rates and determine the lower rate.
   a) Calories burned: 300 Cal/h or 4 Cal/min
   b) water usage: 30 L/day or 245 L/week
   c) ground beef: $8.40/kg or $3.99/lb
   d) cycling speeds: 2 miles in 5 min or 5 km in 20 min

4. a) Draw a graph to show Lyn's body temperature, based on this description:
   • rising at a constant rate from 98.6 °F to 102 °F over a period of 3 h
   • remaining at 102 °F for 2 h
   • falling back to 98.6 °F over a period of 5 h
   b) During which interval of time was the rate of change in her body temperature the greatest?

5. The following graph shows elevation versus time for a skier who descended a mountain.

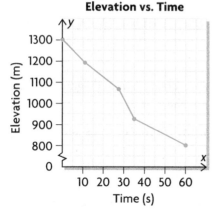

Elevation vs. Time

a) During which interval of time was the skier's speed the greatest? Explain.

b) During which interval of time was the skier's speed the least? Explain.

c) Estimate the skier's speeds for the intervals you identified in parts a) and b).

d) What was the skier's average speed over the entire run?

Lesson 8.2

6. Martin is shopping for a new MP3 player. The one he wants is on sale for $119.95 at Giant Electronics, located in his town. He has found the same MP3 player for $105.99 on the Internet, on the website for a U.S. store. Today's exchange rate is $1 U.S. = $1.08 Cdn.
   a) Determine which store has the lower price in Canadian dollars.
   b) What factors, besides the list price, should Martin consider before he makes the purchase?

7. An airplane travels 300 miles in 36 min. At this rate, how far will it travel in 2 h?

8. Sam bought a used fishing boat in the United States and brought it back to Canada. According to the literature that came with the boat, the gas tank holds 25 gal. The marina where Sam docks his boat sells gas for $1.08/L. Determine the cost to fill the gas tank at this marina. (The conversion rate is 1 U.S. gal/3.785 L.)

9. Hicham El Guerrouj of Morocco ran 1500 m in 00:03:26.00 in Rome, Italy, in July 1998. Just under a year later, he ran the mile in 00:03:43.13 on the same track.
   a) Determine his average speed in each race.
   b) Compare the distances run and his average speeds in both races.
   c) Discuss some factors that may have led to his average speeds being different in these two races.

Scale Diagrams

YOU WILL NEED

- calculator
- grid paper
- ruler
- protractor

EXPLORE...

- Construct a scale drawing that models an airplane flying N20°E at 160 km/h for 2.5 h. What factors must you keep in mind?

GOAL

Understand and use scale diagrams involving 2-D shapes.

INVESTIGATE the Math

Maxine is moving into a new apartment. Before moving day, she wants to decide where to place her furniture in her new living room. When she visited the apartment, she drew this rough sketch of the room's layout and recorded some measurements.

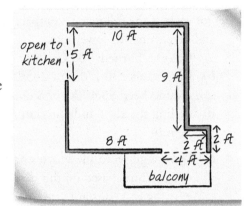

She has also measured her large furniture, which she wants placed by the movers. These measurements are shown in the table below.

Furniture	Dimensions (width by length)
couch	40 in. by 90 in.
loveseat	40 in. by 66 in.
wall unit	20 in. by 60 in.

scale diagram

A drawing in which measurements are proportionally reduced or enlarged from actual measurements; a scale diagram is similar to the original.

scale

The ratio of a measurement on a diagram to the corresponding distance measured on the shape or object represented by the diagram.

? How can you use a **scale diagram** of this room, on an 8.5 in. by 11 in. sheet of paper, to determine where to place these pieces of furniture?

A. Determine a **scale** you can use to create a scale diagram of the living room on an 8.5 in. by 11 in. sheet of paper.

B. Use your scale to determine what the lengths of walls and openings in your scale diagram should be.

C. Create your scale diagram of the living room.

D. Use your scale to determine the dimensions of each piece of furniture that needs to be placed.

E. Select a strategy to determine a good location for each piece of furniture. Add the three pieces of furniture to your scale diagram.

Reflecting

F. Compare your diagram with your classmates' diagrams. How are they the same, and how are they different?

G. Maxine used a **scale factor** of $\dfrac{1}{16}$ to create her diagram. Explain the advantages of using this scale factor.

H. Does it make sense that the scale factor you used for your diagram had to be less than 1? Explain.

scale factor

A number created from the ratio of any two corresponding measurements of two similar shapes or objects, written as a fraction, a decimal, or a percent.

Communication | *Tip*

A scale is a ratio or rate, so it always includes units. A scale factor is a number without units.

APPLY the Math

EXAMPLE 1   Drawing a 2-D scale diagram that requires a reduction

A builder plans to construct a house on a rectangular lot, as shown in this sketch.

Draw a scale diagram of the lot and house using a scale of 1 m : 500 m.

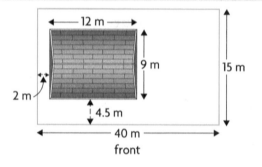

Eric's Solution

Lot dimensions:

Lot length $= 40$ m$\left(\dfrac{1}{500}\right)$

Lot length $= 0.08$ m

Lot width $= 15$ m$\left(\dfrac{1}{500}\right)$

Lot width $= 0.03$ m

House dimensions:

House length $= 12$ m$\left(\dfrac{1}{500}\right)$

House length $= 0.024$ m

House width $= 9$ m$\left(\dfrac{1}{500}\right)$

House width $= 0.018$ m

Since the scale is 1 m : 500 m, which is less than 1, I knew that my scale diagram would be a reduction of the actual house and lot. The scale factor is

$$\dfrac{1\ \text{m}}{500\ \text{m}} = \dfrac{1}{500}$$

I multiplied all of the measurements by the scale factor.

Insets from left and front of lot:

Front inset $= 4.5$ m$\left(\dfrac{1}{500}\right)$

Front inset $= 0.009$ m

Left inset $= 2$ m$\left(\dfrac{1}{500}\right)$

Left inset $= 0.004$ m

Lot dimensions:

Lot length $= 0.08 \cancel{m}\left(\dfrac{100 \text{ cm}}{1 \cancel{m}}\right)$

Lot length $= 8.0$ cm

Lot width $= 0.03 \cancel{m}\left(\dfrac{100 \text{ cm}}{1 \cancel{m}}\right)$

Lot width $= 3.0$ cm

House dimensions:

House length $= 0.024 \cancel{m}\left(\dfrac{100 \text{ cm}}{1 \cancel{m}}\right)$

House length $= 2.4$ cm

House width $= 0.018 \cancel{m}\left(\dfrac{100 \text{ cm}}{1 \cancel{m}}\right)$

House width $= 1.8$ cm

> All the measurements I calculated for my scale diagram are in metres, but my ruler is in centimetres. To draw the diagram accurately, I converted the measurements to centimetres.

Insets from left and front of lot:

Front inset $= 0.009 \cancel{m}\left(\dfrac{100 \text{ cm}}{1 \cancel{m}}\right)$

Front inset $= 0.9$ cm

Left inset $= 0.004 \cancel{m}\left(\dfrac{100 \text{ cm}}{1 \cancel{m}}\right)$

Left inset $= 0.4$ cm

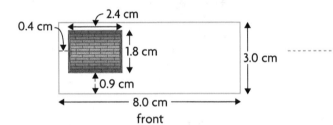

front

> I used the measurements I calculated to draw the lot and then the house. I noticed that I could draw the rectangle for the house only one way, since the house had to be inside the lot by a margin of 4.5 m on one side.

Your Turn

Joe decided to draw a scale diagram of the lot and house using a scale factor of 0.01. Explain how his diagram would differ from Eric's diagram.

EXAMPLE 2   Drawing a 2-D scale diagram that requires an enlargement

Jess designed the logo shown for an environment club. She wants to enlarge the logo so that it can be applied to the front of a baseball cap. The hat company has suggested a scale factor of $\dfrac{5}{3}$. Draw a scale diagram of the logo as it will appear on the baseball cap.

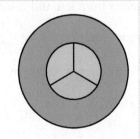

Jess's Solution

Diameter of outer circle = 3 cm
Diameter of inner circle = 1.5 cm
Length of each line segment = 0.75 cm
Measure of all sector angles = 120°

> I measured the diameters of the outer and inner circles on my logo design, and I recorded the measurements. I thought that the three line segments were radii of the inner circle, but I measured them just to be safe. I also measured the angle of each sector.

New outer diameter = $3 \text{ cm}\left(\dfrac{5}{3}\right)$ or 5 cm

New inner diameter = $1.5 \text{ cm}\left(\dfrac{5}{3}\right)$ or 2.5 cm

New line segments = $0.75 \text{ cm}\left(\dfrac{5}{3}\right)$ or 1.25 cm

Measure of all new sector angles = 120°

> I calculated the new measurements for the enlarged logo by multiplying each linear measurement by the scale factor of $\dfrac{5}{3}$. Since the original logo and the enlarged logo are similar, I knew the measure of all the sector angles would be 120°.

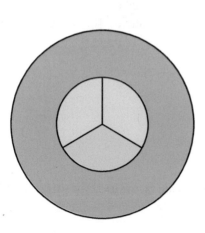

> I drew the larger circle by setting my compass radius to 5 cm. Then I drew the smaller circle by using the same centre and setting my compass radius to 2.5 cm. I drew the vertical radius of the inner circle and used a protractor to measure angles of 120° from this radius to draw the other two radii. Finally, I coloured in the enlarged logo using the same colours I used for my logo design.

Your Turn

Jess initially thought of using a scale factor of 400%.
a) Draw the logo using this scale factor.
b) Why do you think she decided to use the recommended scale factor?

EXAMPLE 3 | Determining scale factor

The diameter of the animal cell that is represented by this scale diagram is actually 0.25 mm. What scale factor was used to draw this scale diagram?

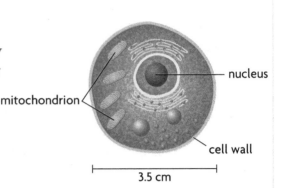

nucleus

mitochondrion

cell wall

3.5 cm

Hannah's Solution

Let *k* be the scale factor of the diagram.

$$k = \frac{\text{Diagram measurement}}{\text{Actual measurement}}$$

$$k = \frac{35 \ \text{mm}}{0.25 \ \text{mm}}$$

$$k = \frac{35}{0.25}$$

$$k = \frac{3500}{25}$$

$$k = \frac{140}{1}$$

The diameter of the cell in the diagram is 3.5 cm, and the actual diameter is 0.25 mm. I expressed both measurements in millimetres and then wrote a ratio.

To eliminate the decimal, I multiplied both terms in the ratio by 100 and then simplified.

The scale factor used for the scale diagram is 140.

Your Turn

Explain why it makes sense that the scale factor used for this scale diagram is greater than 1.

CHECK Your Understanding

1. Determine the scale factor that was used to transform diagram X into diagram Y. Express your scale factor as a fraction and as a percent.

a)

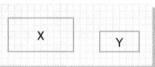

b)

(diagram with circles X and Y)

2. Determine if the original will be larger or smaller than the scale diagram after the given scale factor is applied.

   a) scale factor: 112%   **b)** scale factor: 0.75   **c)** scale factor: $\dfrac{4}{9}$

3. On a plan, an actual length of 6 ft is represented by 5 in.
   a) Determine the scale of the plan.
   b) Determine the scale factor used to make the plan.

4. The following two polygons are similar. Determine the lengths of sides g, h, x, and y to the nearest tenth of a unit.

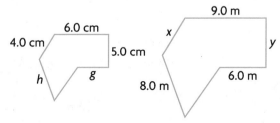

PRACTISING

5. The Garry oak is a tree that is found on Vancouver Island. The original acorn for these scale diagrams was 1.9 cm long. Determine the scale factor that was used for each diagram.

a)

b)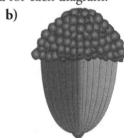

c)

6. The floor plan of an apartment is shown to the right, drawn using a scale factor of 0.005.

   a) What are the actual dimensions of each bedroom?

   b) What are the actual dimensions of the living room?

   c) Which room has the greatest area?

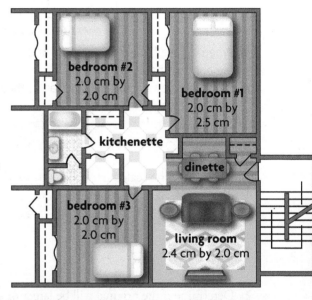

bedroom #2
2.0 cm by
2.0 cm

bedroom #1
2.0 cm by
2.5 cm

kitchenette

dinette

bedroom #3
2.0 cm by
2.0 cm

living room
2.4 cm by 2.0 cm

7. Yani wants to make a scale diagram of the floor plan of his school. He wants his diagram to fit on an 8.5 in. by 11 in. sheet of paper. The school is 650 ft long and 300 ft wide at its widest point.

   a) What would be a reasonable scale for Yani to use so that his diagram will fit on the sheet of paper?

   b) Assume that the school's floor plan is a rectangle. Draw a scale diagram using the scale you determined in part a).

8. Ken has made a sketch of the floor plan of his bedroom. Draw an accurate scale diagram of his bedroom on 1 cm grid paper, using a scale factor of $\frac{1}{50}$.

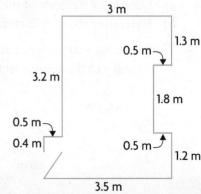

3 m

1.3 m

0.5 m

3.2 m

1.8 m

0.5 m

0.4 m

0.5 m

1.2 m

3.5 m

9. A computer chip on a circuit board has a rectangular shape, with a width of 6 mm and a length of 9 mm. Plans for the circuit board must be drawn using a scale factor of 15. Draw a scale diagram of the computer chip as it would appear on the plans.

10. This top view of a hex-nut must be enlarged by a scale factor of 250% for a display at a trade show.
    a) Measure the necessary distances on the diagram.
    b) Determine what the corresponding distances on the enlarged diagram should be.
    c) Draw the scale diagram of the hex-nut.

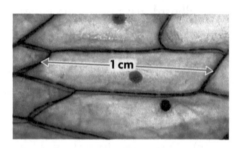

11. Sara has a microscope with a lens that magnifies by a factor of 40. She was able to capture the image of a slide containing onion cells, as shown. In the image, the cell was about 1 cm long. How long is the actual onion cell, to nearest hundredth of a millimetre?

12. a) Using the map scale, estimate the distance from
       i) Yellowknife to Fort Norman
       ii) Fort Providence to Fort Norman
    b) Of the three locations on the map, which two are closest to each other?

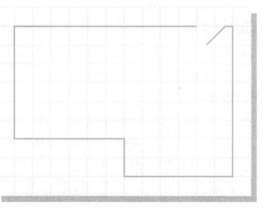

13. This scale diagram, drawn on 0.5 cm grid paper, shows the floor plan of a greenhouse, drawn using a scale ratio of 1:75.
    a) Determine the perimeter of the greenhouse.
    b) Determine the area of the floor of the greenhouse, to the nearest tenth of a square metre.

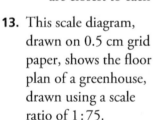

14. Determine the scale factor used in each situation.

    a) The actual diameter of a penny is 19 mm. In a scale diagram, the diameter of a penny is 5.7 cm.

    b) The actual width of a door is 30 in. In a scale diagram, the width of the door is $1\frac{1}{2}$ in.

    c) The diagonal of an actual stamp is 2.5 cm long. In a scale diagram, the diagonal is 1.0 m long.

    d) The height of an actual communications tower is 55 ft. In a scale diagram, the height of the tower is 6 in.

15. A billboard measures 4.5 m by 3.5 m. Draw a scale diagram of the billboard that fits in a space measuring 20 cm by 15 cm.

16. The floor plan for a garden shed is shown below. The area of the actual floor is 72 m².

    a) Determine the actual area that each square on the floor plan represents.

    b) Determine the actual distance that 5 mm on the floor plan represents.

    c) Determine the scale of the plan.

    d) Determine the scale factor that was used to draw the floor plan.

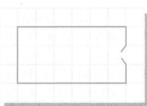

Communication | Tip

The given measurement for a television is the length of a diagonal across the viewing area.

17. The viewing areas of most LCD televisions are similar rectangles. Regardless of the size of a television, the length : width ratio is often 16 : 9. Rahj has built-in bookshelves that are 4 ft wide. There is a vertical distance of 26 in. between each shelf. Show that a 42 in. LCD television will fit on one of these shelves.

18. a) Use geometric shapes to create a logo that will fit in a space measuring 12 cm by 12 cm.

    b) Draw a scale diagram of your logo using a scale factor of 25%.

    c) Draw a scale diagram of your logo using a scale factor of 1.5.

Closing

19. When drawing a scale diagram on a sheet of paper, how do you decide what scale factor to use? What do you need to consider?

Extending

20. Sanjay has 34 in. of red oak moulding that is 1 in. wide. He would like to use this moulding to frame a photograph, as shown. The photograph measures 12 in. by 8 in., so the frame would require more moulding than he has.

    a) By what scale factor should he reduce the photograph so that he can use the wood he has to make the frame?

    b) What are the dimensions of the reduced photograph?

8.4 Scale Factors and Areas of 2-D Shapes

GOAL

Solve area problems that involve similar 2-D shapes.

INVESTIGATE the Math

Quilting is as old as ancient Egypt, if not older. For most of its history, however, quilting was used to make clothing. Pieced quilts, made by sewing pieces of fabric into blocks and then sewing together the blocks, are a more recent development.

Norma is making a quilt by sewing together congruent pieces of cloth. To create a larger quilt, she sews together more congruent shapes. She makes sure that the larger quilt is similar in shape to the original quilt.

? **How does the area of the larger quilt relate to the area of the original quilt?**

A. Suppose that Norma uses square pieces of fabric. Use square pattern blocks to represent these pieces of fabric.

Measure the dimensions of one square, and determine its area. Create a table like the one below, and record the dimensions and area.

Length (in.)	Width (in.)	Area (in.²)

B. Starting with one square, add enough squares to create a larger square that has double the original dimensions. Record its dimensions and area in your table.

C. Add more squares to create a larger square that has three times the original dimensions. Record the dimensions and area of the larger square in your table.

D. Predict the area of a square that has four times the original dimensions. Check your prediction, and record the dimensions and area of this square in your table.

E. As the square grows larger, how does its area relate to the scale factor k and the area of the original square?

YOU WILL NEED

- calculator
- ruler
- pattern blocks

EXPLORE...

1.2 cm
2.0 cm

- Determine the area of the shaded region. If both radii are doubled, does the area also double?

Area Formulas	
Shape	**Formula**
triangle h b	$A = \dfrac{1}{2}bh$
rectangle w l	$A = lw$
square s s	$A = s^2$
parallelogram h b	$A = bh$
trapezoid a h b	$A = \dfrac{1}{2}h(a + b)$
circle r	$A = \pi r^2$

F. Suppose that Norma uses congruent triangular pieces of fabric. Repeat parts A to E using triangular pattern blocks and a table like the one below.

Base (in.)	Height (in.)	Area (in.²)

G. Suppose that Norma uses congruent rectangular pieces of fabric. Repeat parts A to E using pieces of U.S. letter or U.S. legal paper and a table like the one shown in part A.

H. Make a **conjecture** about the relationship among the area of a shape, the scale factor, and the area of a larger similar shape.

Reflecting

I. Do you think your conjecture will hold when you decrease the dimensions of a shape by a specific scale factor? Explain.

J. Do you think your conjecture will hold for other similar shapes, such as parallelograms, trapezoids, or circles? Explain.

K. Do you think your conjecture will hold for any pair of similar 2-D shapes? Explain.

APPLY the Math

EXAMPLE **1**	Reasoning about scale factor and area

Jasmine is making a kite from a $2:25$ scale diagram. The area of the scale diagram is 20 cm². How much fabric will she need for her kite?

Jasmine's Solution: Reasoning about scale as an enlargement

Scale factor $= \dfrac{25}{2}$ or 12.5

> As the scale factor is greater than 1, the kite is an enlargement of the scale diagram.

$k = 12.5$

> k represents the scale factor for the enlargement.

Area of kite $= k^2$(Area of scale diagram)
Area of kite $= (12.5)^2(20 \text{ cm}^2)$
Area of kite $= 3125 \text{ cm}^2$

> I know that the scale diagram and the actual kite are similar shapes. This means that the area of the actual kite can be determined by multiplying the area of the scale diagram by the square of the scale factor.

I will need at least 3125 cm² of fabric for my kite.

> This amount of fabric will cover the frame exactly. I'll need more than this amount, since I'll have to sew the fabric to the frame.

Hank's Solution: Reasoning about scale as a reduction

Let k represent the scale factor.

$$k = \frac{2}{25}$$

> The scale diagram is a reduction of the kite since the scale factor is less than 1.

Area of scale diagram $= k^2$(Area of kite)

$$\frac{\text{Area of scale diagram}}{\text{Area of kite}} = k^2$$

> Since the scale diagram and the actual kite are similar shapes, the area of the scale diagram equals the product of the square of the scale factor k and the area of the actual kite.

Let x represent the area of the kite.

$$\frac{20 \text{ cm}^2}{x} = \left(\frac{2}{25}\right)^2$$

> I substituted the information I knew into the equation.

$$\frac{20 \text{ cm}^2}{x} = \frac{4}{625}$$

$$12\,500 \text{ cm}^2 = 4x$$

$$3125 \text{ cm}^2 = x$$

Jasmine will need at least 3125 cm² of fabric for her kite.

> This amount of fabric will cover the frame exactly. She will need a little more than this amount, so that she can sew the fabric to the frame.

Your Turn

If the scale diagram for the kite had been drawn using a scale ratio of $1:20$, and the area of the scale diagram had been 30 cm², how much fabric would Jasmine have needed for her kite?

EXAMPLE 2   **Reasoning about scale factor and area to determine dimensions**

Jim's laptop has a monitor with the dimensions 9 in. by 12 in. The image on his laptop is projected onto the screen of a whiteboard. According to the documentation for the whiteboard, its screen area is 2836.6875 in.².

a) The image on the whiteboard is similar to the image on the laptop. Determine the scale factor used to project the images on the laptop to the whiteboard.

b) Determine the dimensions of the whiteboard.

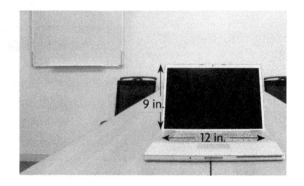

Rani's Solution

a) Area of monitor $= lw$
   Area of monitor $= (9 \text{ in.})(12 \text{ in.})$
   Area of monitor $= 108 \text{ in.}^2$
   Let k represent the scale factor.
   Area of whiteboard $= k^2(\text{Area of monitor})$
   $2836.6875 \text{ in.}^2 = k^2(108 \text{ in.}^2)$
   $\dfrac{2836.6875 \text{ in.}^2}{108 \text{ in.}^2} = k^2$
   $26.265... = k^2$
   $\sqrt{26.265...} = k$
   $5.125 = k$

> The laptop's monitor is a rectangle, so I determined its area by multiplying its length, l, and width, w.

> The image on the laptop and the image on the whiteboard are similar rectangles. This means that the area of the image on the whiteboard is equal to the square of the scale factor times the area of the image on the laptop.

> Since the image on the whiteboard is larger than the original, I know that $k > 1$. A scale factor of 5.125 makes sense.

The dimensions of the image on the whiteboard are an enlargement of the dimensions of the image on Jim's laptop by a factor of 5.125.

b) Let x represent the length of the whiteboard.
   $x = (12 \text{ in.})(5.125)$
   $x = 61.5 \text{ in.}$
   Let y represent the width of the whiteboard.
   $y = (9 \text{ in.})(5.125)$
   $y = 46.125 \text{ in.}$

> To determine the dimensions of the whiteboard, I multiplied the length and width of the laptop's monitor by the scale factor.

The whiteboard is about 61 in. long by 46 in. wide.

Your Turn

A circular icon on Jim's laptop has a diameter of 2 cm. Calculate the area of this icon on the whiteboard.

In Summary

Key Idea

- If two 2-D shapes are similar and their dimensions are related by a scale factor k, then the relationship between the area of the similar shape and the area of the original shape can be expressed as:

  Area of similar 2-D shape $= k^2(\text{Area of original shape})$

Need to Know

- If the area of a similar 2-D shape and the area of the original shape are known, then the scale factor, k, can be determined using the formula

  $$k^2 = \dfrac{\text{Area of similar 2-D shape}}{\text{Area of original shape}}$$

CHECK *Your Understanding*

1. Two similar rectangles, A and B, are shown to the right.
   a) Determine the scale factor that produced the enlargement from rectangle A to rectangle B.
   b) Determine the areas of rectangle A and rectangle B.
   c) How many rectangles congruent to rectangle A would fit in rectangle B?

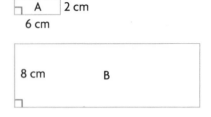

2. The table below gives data for enlargements and reductions of the triangle shown to the right. Complete the table.

Length of Base (cm)	Height of Triangle (cm)	Scale Factor	Area (cm²)	Area of scaled triangle / Area of original triangle
3.0	4.0	1	6.0	1
		3		
1.5				
			600.0	
		25%		

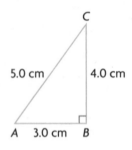

PRACTISING

3. The parallelogram shown to the right has an area of 42 cm². It is going to be enlarged by a scale factor of 5. Determine the area of the enlarged parallelogram.

4. Determine the area of each figure after it is enlarged by a scale factor of 2.

a)

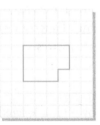

b)

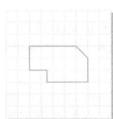

c)

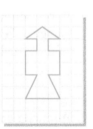

5. Determine the area of each figure, to the nearest tenth of a square unit, after it is reduced by a scale factor of $\frac{1}{3}$.

a)

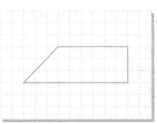

b)

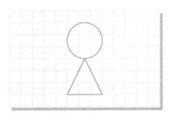

6. Tammy downloaded a photograph, which measured 4 in. by 6 in., from her camera to her laptop. Then Tammy used a software program to enlarge the dimensions of the photograph by 150% so that it would fit in a frame she already had.

   a) What are the inside dimensions of the frame she already had?

   b) By what percent was the area of the photograph increased in the enlarging process?

   c) Explain how you could determine the area of the enlarged photograph using two different strategies.

7. Stop signs on city, town, and rural roads are regular octagons. Describe how you would create a similar stop sign that is quadruple the area of a typical stop sign for increased visibility on a two-lane highway.

8. △ABC and △DEF are similar triangles. The sum of the lengths of AB and DE is 35 cm. The area of △DEF is 144 cm².

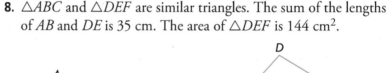

   a) Determine the scale factor that relates △ABC to △DEF.

   b) Determine the area of △ABC.

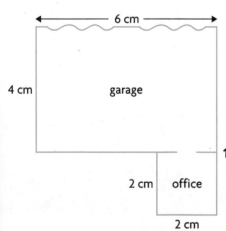

9. The sketch to the left of a service garage and an attached office was drawn using a scale ratio of 1 : 500. On this diagram, the area of the garage is 24 cm² and the area of the office is 4 cm². Determine the area of the actual garage and the actual office in square metres.

10. A rectangular display, with the dimensions 2 m by 3 m, is located in the lobby of city hall to show the citizens the layout for the new People's Park. The display was created using a scale ratio of 1 : 120.

   a) The parks department estimates that the city spends $0.75/m² to maintain a park from spring through fall. Estimate the cost to maintain People's Park.

   b) A rectangular model, with the same dimensions, was used to represent Meadow Park. The scale ratio used was 1 : 250. Estimate the cost to maintain Meadow Park.

11. A gymnasium wall is 20 ft high and 120 ft long. Peggy has been asked to paint a mural on the wall. The mural must be $\frac{1}{4}$ the area of the wall and the mural and wall must be similar. The mural must also be centred on the wall. Draw a scale diagram that shows the dimensions of the wall, the dimensions of the mural, and where the mural should be placed.

12. The scale ratio for two similar rectangles is $1:2$. The sum of their areas is 40 cm^2. Determine the area of each rectangle.

13. Determine the scale factor that relates each pair of similar shapes.

a)

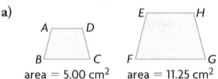

area = 5.00 cm^2 area = 11.25 cm^2

b)

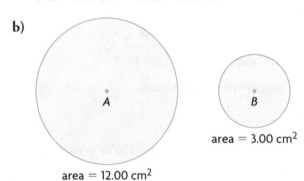

area = 3.00 cm^2

area = 12.00 cm^2

14. In the diagram to the right, the large triangle, outlined in black, is an enlargement of the small triangle, outlined in red. The small triangle is congruent to the other small triangles, which are equilateral and have side lengths of 1 unit.

a) Determine the value of the scale factor, k.

b) Explain how k relates the perimeters and areas of the large and small triangles.

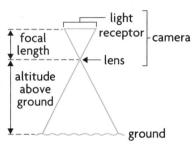

15. Aerial photographs are often used to show parcels of land that are for sale. The camera used to take the photograph below had a focal length of 0.152 m. The altitude of the airplane was 7600 m when the photograph was taken. The ratio of the camera's focal length to the airplane's altitude is the scale factor for the photograph.

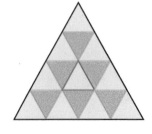

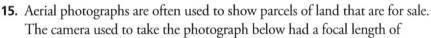

a) Determine the scale of the aerial photograph.

b) Determine the area of the parcel of land shown in the photograph in hectares. The conversion rate is 1 ha per 10 000 m^2.

c) Determine the value of the parcel of land, if it sells for \$375/ha.

8.4 Scale Factors and Areas of 2-D Shapes   **481**

16. You would like to renovate the kitchen in your home, and you need to create floor plans of the renovations for the contractor.
    a) Measure and record the dimensions of your kitchen. Include doors and measurements of any counters, appliances, or furniture that take up floor space.
    b) On one piece of paper, draw two scale diagrams: the first diagram showing the existing kitchen and the second diagram showing how you would like the kitchen to appear after the renovation.
    c) Compare the area of the open floor space in the two versions of the kitchen. Which version is more spacious?

Closing

17. Explain the difference between the following processes:

    A. Reduce a 2-D shape by a scale factor of $\frac{1}{2}$.

    B. Divide the area of the same 2-D shape by 2.

    Use examples to support your explanation.

Extending

18. A polygon has its dimensions increased by 180% to create a similar polygon. The dimensions of the new polygon are then reduced by 50% to create a third polygon. What percent of the area of the original polygon is the area of the third polygon?

19. A company that manufactures cardboard boxes currently makes boxes with dimensions of 12 in. by 16 in. by 12 in. The company plans to make a new, larger box by increasing the current dimensions by 150%. Cardboard costs $0.05/sq ft. How much more will it cost to make the larger box?

Similar Objects: Scale Models and Scale Diagrams

Understand and use scale models and scale diagrams that involve 3-D objects.

INVESTIGATE *the Math*

Sameer is an engineer for an electronics company. His company currently sells a popular mini-MP3 player. It comes packaged in a box with the dimensions shown.

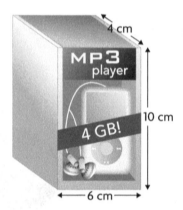

His team of engineers has designed a larger version of the mini-MP3 player, which has improved features and greater storage capacity. A new box must be created for this new MP3 player.

❓ How can you create a new box that is similar to the original box?

A. Make a net for the original box.

B. Choose a reasonable scale factor that you can apply to the net you made in part A in order to create a larger box.

C. Make the new net for the larger box.

D. Use your net to construct a model of the larger box.

E. How are the dimensions of the boxes related?

F. Are your boxes **similar objects** ? Explain.

YOU WILL NEED

- calculator
- ruler
- centimetre grid paper
- scissors
- tape

EXPLORE...

- How do the dimensions of each small cube relate to the overall dimensions of the Rubik's Cube®?

similar objects

Two or more 3-D objects that have proportional dimensions.

Reflecting

G Are the lengths of the diagonals of each pair of corresponding faces in both boxes proportional?

H. Compare the new box you created to the new boxes created by your classmates. Are all of these boxes similar? Explain.

I. Juan claims that other kinds of objects, such as triangular prisms, cylinders, pyramids, cones, and spheres, can be similar, provided that they have the same shape. Do you agree or disagree? Explain.

J. Is it possible for two irregular 3-D objects to be similar? Explain.

APPLY the Math

EXAMPLE 1   Determining if two objects are similar

Sandeep is a chef. In his restaurant, he uses frying pans of various sizes. Are his frying pans similar?

Sandeep's Solution

$$\frac{\text{Bottom diameter of large pan}}{\text{Bottom diameter of small pan}} = \frac{30 \text{ cm}}{20 \text{ cm}} \text{ or } \frac{3}{2}$$

> They look similar. To check, I measured corresponding parts of the pans and compared my measurements.

$$\frac{\text{Depth of large pan}}{\text{Depth of small pan}} = \frac{6 \text{ cm}}{4 \text{ cm}} \text{ or } \frac{3}{2}$$

$$\frac{\text{Handle length of large pan}}{\text{Handle length of small pan}} = \frac{24 \text{ cm}}{16 \text{ cm}} \text{ or } \frac{3}{2}$$

The two pans are similar objects. The large pan is an enlarged version of the small pan, by a factor of 1.5.

> The corresponding measurements of the pans are proportional.

Your Turn

The top diameter of the large pan is 33 cm. Determine the top diameter of the small pan.

EXAMPLE **2** Determining actual dimensions from a scale model

Esmerelda bought this toy tractor to give to her younger brother for his birthday. The dimensions of the toy are given in the diagram to the right. The scale ratio on the package is 1:16. She knows that her brother will want to know the size of the real tractor. How can she determine the dimensions of the real tractor?

12.7 cm

9.5 cm   19.1 cm

Esmerelda's Solution

The scale model is similar to the real tractor. ------------

> I know that all scale models are similar to the real objects. Their measurements are proportional to the corresponding measurements of the real objects.

The scale factor is $\dfrac{1}{16}$.

I need to multiply each of the dimensions ------------
of the model by 16.

> Since the model is a reduction of the real tractor, the real tractor is an enlargement of the model by a scale factor of 16.

Actual height $= 16(12.7 \text{ cm})$
Actual height $= 203.2 \text{ cm}$

Actual width $= 16(9.5 \text{ cm})$
Actual width $= 152.0 \text{ cm}$

Actual length $= 16(19.1 \text{ cm})$
Actual length $= 305.6 \text{ cm}$

Actual height $= 2.032 \text{ m}$ ------------
Actual width $= 1.520 \text{ m}$
Actual length $= 3.056 \text{ m}$

> I converted the measurements from centimetres to metres by multiplying by $\dfrac{1 \text{ m}}{100 \text{ cm}}$. This made the numbers more meaningful for my brother.

The actual height of the real tractor is about 2.0 m,
the actual width is about 1.5 m, and the actual length is about 3.1 m.

Your Turn

The diameter of the rear tires on the model is 6.0 cm. What is the diameter of the rear tires on the real tractor?

EXAMPLE **3** Enlarging from a scale diagram to determine actual dimensions

Nadia has found plans for a bookend in a woodworking magazine. The plans include a scale diagram, with a scale ratio of 1:5.

Determine the dimensions (length, width, height, and base thickness) of the actual bookend.

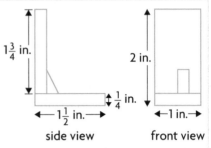

side view   front view

Nadia's Solution

3-D scale diagrams are similar to the real objects.

> I know that all 3-D scale diagrams are similar to the real objects. Their measurements are proportional to the corresponding measurements of the real objects.

The scale factor is

$$\text{Diagram : Actual} = 1:5 \text{ or } \frac{\text{Diagram}}{\text{Actual}} = \frac{1}{5}$$

> To determine the measurements of the actual bookend from the scale diagram, I need to determine the reciprocal of the scale factor given. Since $\frac{5}{1}$ is greater than 1, the actual bookend is an enlargement of the scale diagram.

$$\text{Base length} = \left(1\frac{1}{2} \text{ in.}\right)5$$

> I multiplied each dimension in the diagram by 5 to determine the actual dimensions of the bookend.

$$\text{Base length} = \frac{15}{2} \text{ in. or } 7\frac{1}{2} \text{ in.}$$

$$\text{Base thickness} = \left(\frac{1}{4} \text{ in.}\right)5$$

$$\text{Base thickness} = \frac{5}{4} \text{ in. or } 1\frac{1}{4} \text{ in.}$$

$$\text{Base width} = (1 \text{ in.})5$$
$$\text{Base width} = 5 \text{ in.}$$

$$\text{Overall height} = \left(1\frac{3}{4} \text{ in.} + \frac{1}{4} \text{ in.}\right)5$$

$$\text{Overall height} = (2 \text{ in.})5 \text{ or } 10 \text{ in.}$$

The dimensions of the actual bookend are $7\frac{1}{2}$ in. by 5 in. by 10 in., with a base thickness of $1\frac{1}{4}$ in.

Your Turn

What would the dimensions of the bookend have been if the scale ratio on the plans had been 2:9?

EXAMPLE **4**   Drawing a scale diagram of a 3-D object

Céline is an engineer. She is working on a city project, replacing old storm-sewer pipes with new concrete pipes. Each pipe has an inner diameter of 1.50 m, a wall thickness of 0.18 m, and a length of 2.5 m. How can she create a scale drawing of one of these pipes?

Céline's Solution

Drawing the entire pipe, as I see it, involves perspective. This will distort the actual measurements. Drawing a side view and a front view of the pipe will enable me to use proportional measurements.

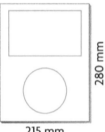

280 mm

215 mm

> I decided to split my piece of paper in half. I will use the top half to draw a scale diagram of the side view of the pipe, and the bottom half to draw a scale diagram of the front view.

Paper width:Actual length of pipe = 215 mm:2500 mm
The ideal scale ratio for the width of the paper is about 1:12.

> I compared the width of the paper to the length of the pipe, in millimetres.

Paper length:2(Actual diameter of pipe) = 280 mm:3500 mm
The ideal scale ratio for the length of the paper is also about 1:12.

> To check that the diagram would fit on the length of the paper, I compared the length of the paper to the diameter of two pipes, with allowance for a space between them. I estimated that this would be about 3.5 m before scaling.

Using a scale factor of $\dfrac{1}{20}$:

> I decided to round down to $\dfrac{1}{20}$. This scale factor is less than $\dfrac{1}{12}$, and 20 is a number that is easy to divide into the actual measurements, resulting in numbers I can draw line segments for accurately.

Scale diagram pipe length $= \dfrac{2.5 \text{ m}}{20}$ or 0.125 m

Scale diagram inner diameter $= \dfrac{1.5 \text{ m}}{20}$ or 0.075 m

> I divided each of the actual measurements by 20 to determine the corresponding measurements on the scale diagram.

Scale diagram wall thickness $= \dfrac{0.18 \text{ m}}{20}$ or 0.009 m

Scale diagram pipe length = 125 mm
Scale diagram inner diameter = 75 mm
Scale diagram wall thickness = 9 mm

> Since the smallest unit on my ruler is mm, I multiplied each measure by $\dfrac{1000 \text{ mm}}{1 \text{ m}}$ to convert the measurements to millimetres.

Side view:

Length = 125 mm

Width = 75 mm + 9 mm + 9 mm or 93 mm ---------------- The width of the pipe is the sum of the inner diameter and twice the thickness of its wall.

Front view:

Inner diameter = 75 mm

Outer diameter = 93 mm

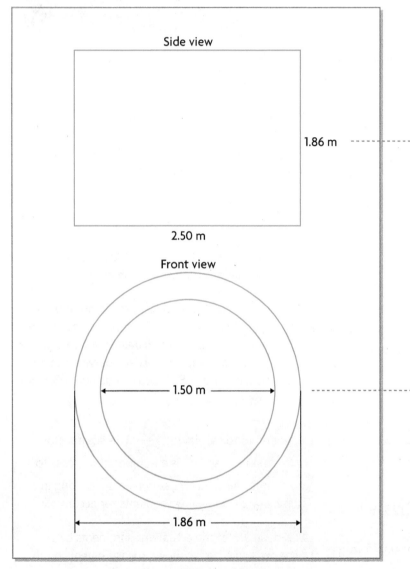

The side view of the pipe will look like a rectangle. I added the inner diameter to the wall thickness at the top and bottom of the pipe to determine the width of the pipe.

The front view looks like two circles. The outer diameter corresponds to the width of the rectangle.

Shown at 50% of actual size

Your Turn

Draw a scale drawing of the pipe using a scale factor of $\frac{1}{15}$.

In Summary

Key Ideas

- Two 3-D objects that are similar have dimensions that are proportional.
- The scale factor is the ratio of a linear measurement of an object to the corresponding linear measurement in a similar object, where both measurements are expressed using the same units.
- To create a scale model or diagram, determine an appropriate scale to use based on the dimensions of the original object and the size of the model or diagram that is required.

Need to Know

- You can multiply any linear measurement of an object by the scale factor to calculate the corresponding measurement of the similar object.
- You can determine the scale factor k, used to create a scale model of an object by using any corresponding linear measurements of the object and the scale model:

$$k = \frac{\text{Linear measurement of scale model}}{\text{Corresponding linear measurement of object}}$$

- When a scale factor is between 0 and 1, the new object is a reduction of the original object.
- When a scale factor is greater than 1, the new object is an enlargement of the original object.

CHECK Your Understanding

1. For each of the following, determine whether the two objects are similar and justify your decision.

a)

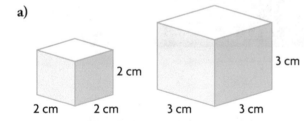

b)

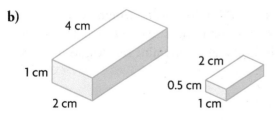

c)

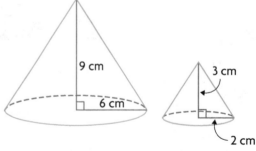

d)

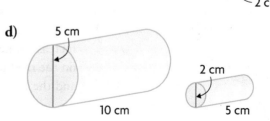

2. The National Basketball Association (NBA) uses a basketball with a diameter of 25 cm. The Women's National Basketball Association (WNBA) uses a basketball with a diameter of 22 cm.
   a) Are these balls similar? Explain.
   b) Determine the scale factor that relates
      i) the NBA ball to the WNBA ball
      ii) the WNBA ball to the NBA ball

3. One of the most famous ships in Canadian sailing history is the *Bluenose*. Launched in 1921 from Nova Scotia as a fishing vessel, the *Bluenose* operated in the rough waters off the coast of Newfoundland. The *Bluenose* became very famous for its speed, winning all the great classic sailing races on the American east coast. Mark has a 1:100 scale model of this ship. The model has a length of 52 cm, a beam (width) of 8.5 cm, and a height of 43 cm. Calculate the length, beam, and height of the actual ship.

PRACTISING

4. Toni works for a moving company. The company sells three different-sized boxes, as shown.
   a) Are the boxes similar? Explain.
   b) The letters on the boxes (S, M, L for small, medium, large) increase in height in proportion to the size of the box. The red M on the medium box is 24 cm tall. Determine the heights of the S and the L.

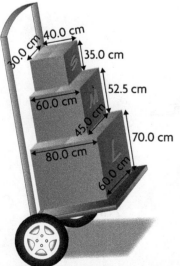

30.0 cm   40.0 cm   35.0 cm
60.0 cm   52.5 cm
45.0 cm   70.0 cm
80.0 cm
60.0 cm

5. Last summer, Ed visited the Royal Tyrrell Museum in Drumheller, Alberta, to see the fossil and dinosaur exhibits. While he was there, he purchased a 1:40 scale model of the *Albertosaurus libratus*, which was native to the area over 70 million years ago. The length of the model is 21.5 cm, and the height is 9.5 cm. Determine the length and height of this species of dinosaur.

6. A 1:18 scale model of a car has the dimensions shown. Determine the dimensions of the actual car.

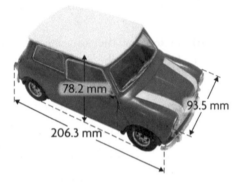

78.2 mm

93.5 mm

206.3 mm

7. The bald eagle is Canada's largest bird of prey. It has a body length of about 90 cm and, while perched, a height of about 75 cm. Hank is a woodcarver who wants to create a carving, to scale, of a bald eagle while perched. He has a block of wood that is 150 cm long, 150 cm wide, and 200 cm high.

  a) Suggest a scale factor that Hank could use for his carving.
  b) If he uses the scale factor you suggested in part a), determine the height and length of the eagle he will create.

8. A carving of Tecumseh, the Shawnee leader of a confederacy that fought in the war of 1812, is located in the Wood Carving Museum in Windsor, Ontario. The carving is $6\frac{1}{2}$ ft tall by $2\frac{1}{2}$ ft wide. The museum wants to sell replica models that are 26 in. tall in the gift shop.

  a) What scale factor must be used to produce these models?
  b) Determine the width of these models.

9. Umiaks are boats that are used in the Arctic for transportation and for traditional whale hunting. The frame of an umiak is built from spruce wood. Traditionally, the outer cover was made from animal skins, such as walrus and bearded-seal skins, but today it can be made from ballistic nylon. A typical umiak is 32 ft long, with a beam (width) of 48 in. Determine these dimensions on a scale model built using a scale ratio of 1:24.

10. Some model train enthusiasts enjoy building villages on their layouts. Two popular scale ratios for model trains are HO (1:87) and N (1:160). Nick has found a building that he would like to add to his N-scale layout, but its dimensions are for an HO-scale layout. The dimensions are 6 in. long by $8\frac{1}{2}$ in. tall by 4 in. wide.

   a) Estimate what the dimensions of the building would be in N scale.
   b) Determine the conversion ratio for HO:N.
   c) Determine the dimensions of the building in N scale, to the nearest eighth of an inch.

11. The measurements of a scale model of a passenger jet are shown. The model was made using a scale factor of $\frac{1}{200}$. The floor of Hangar 77 at the Calgary International Airport measures 46.6 m long by 71.9 m wide. How many of these passenger jets could fit in this hangar?

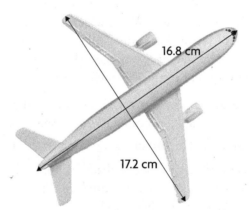

16.8 cm

17.2 cm

12. Take a photograph of a structure or building, as well as a referent—an object with a known height or length. For example, you could include a metre stick or another student in your photograph.
   a) Estimate the measurements of the structure or building using only your photograph.
   b) Describe how you used a scale factor to determine the measurements.

13. Draw a scale diagram that shows the top, front, and side views of this coffee table. Assume a uniform thickness of 5 cm for all the pieces of wood. Each leg is inset 10 cm from the edge of the tabletop, and the bottom shelf is 10 cm above the ground. Use a scale factor of $\frac{1}{10}$.

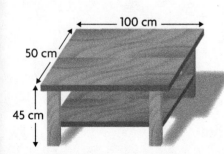

100 cm

50 cm

45 cm

14. The specifications for a steel washer are shown.

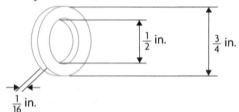

Draw a scale diagram of the top, side, and front views of the washer, using a scale ratio of 4:1.

15. This chest freezer has the dimensions indicated. Draw a scale diagram of the top, side, and front views of the freezer, so that all three views fit on a single page of standard paper.

16. Choose an object in your classroom, and measure its dimensions. Draw a scale diagram of the object that shows top, side, and front views.

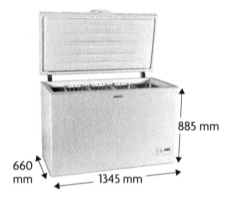

885 mm

660 mm

1345 mm

17. Suppose that you increase the dimensions of a box, which is the shape of a rectangular right prism, by 150%.
   a) Do you think the area of the base of the box will also increase by this scale factor? Justify your decision.
   b) Will the volume of the box also increase by this scale factor? Justify your decision.

Closing

18. How is the process for solving problems that involve similar objects the same as the process for solving problems that involve similar shapes? How is the process different?

Extending

19. A juice company plans to enlarge this can by a scale factor of 1.5.
   a) The new can will be made from the same metal, in the same thickness, as the smaller can. By what factor will the cost of the metal increase?
   b) The cost of the metal that is needed to make the larger can is $0.045. Determine the cost of the metal that is needed to make the smaller can.

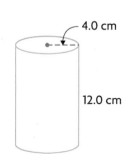

4.0 cm

12.0 cm

20. The surface area of a right cone is 100 cm². Its dimensions are reduced by 50% to produce a similar cone. Determine the surface area of the similar cone.

Scale Factors and 3-D Objects

EXPLORE...

- Suppose that you are trying to decide whether you should order an 8 in. pizza or a 16 in. pizza. How much more pizza will you have if you order the 16 in. pizza instead of the 8 in. pizza? What assumptions are you making?

GOAL

Solve problems that involve scale factor, surface area, and volume.

INVESTIGATE the Math

Rostrum blocks are used as props in drama productions. They are three-dimensional objects of various sizes, such as cubes, right rectangular prisms, right triangular prisms, and right cylinders. Many of these objects have a horizontal top surface to stand on, sit on, lean on, or rest other props on.

Kayley, a set carpenter, has been asked to create sets of similar rostrum blocks. She needs to know the surface areas of the blocks, so she can determine how much material she will require to build them. She also needs to know their volumes, so she can predict how much space they will take up in the storage area between shows.

? What is the relationship between the scale factor and the surface areas of two similar objects? What is the relationship between the scale factor and the volumes of two similar objects?

A. Suppose that Kayley wants to make a set of similar cubes. Use linking cubes to act as models.

Measure the dimensions of one linking cube, and determine its surface area and volume. Create a table like the one below, and record your findings.

Length (cm)	Width (cm)	Height (cm)	Surface Area (cm²)	Volume (cm³)

B. Starting with a single cube, add enough cubes to create a larger cube with dimensions that are double the dimensions of the single cube. Record the dimensions, surface area, and volume of the larger cube in your table.

C. Add more cubes to create a cube with dimensions that are three times greater than the dimensions of a single cube. Record the dimensions, surface area, and volume of the larger cube in your table.

D. Predict the surface area and volume of a cube with dimensions that are four times greater than those of a single cube. Check your predictions, and then record the dimensions, surface area, and volume in your table.

E. As the cube grows larger, how does its surface area relate to the scale factor k and the surface area of the original cube? How does its volume relate to the scale factor k and the volume of the original cube?

F. Suppose that Kayley wants to create a set of right triangular prisms. Repeat parts A to E using triangular pattern blocks and a table like the one below.

Side Length of Base (in.)	Height of Triangular Base (in.)	Height of Prism (in.)	Surface Area (in.²)	Volume (in.³)

G. Suppose that Kayley wants to create a set of right prisms with rectangular bases. Repeat parts A to E using rectangular blocks and a table like the one shown in part A.

H. **i)** Make a **conjecture** about the relationship among the surface area of the original object, the scale factor, and the surface area of a larger similar object.

ii) Make a conjecture about the relationship between the volume of the original object, the scale factor, and the volume of a larger similar object.

Reflecting

I. Do you think your conjectures will hold when you decrease the dimensions of an object by a specific scale factor? Explain.

J. Do you think your conjectures will hold for other similar objects, such as pyramids, cones, cylinders, or spheres? Explain.

K. Do you think your conjectures will hold for any pair of similar 3-D objects? Explain.

Formulas	
Object	**Surface Area and Volume**
rectangular prism 	$SA = 2(lw + lh + wh)$ $V = lwh$
right triangular prism 	$SA = bh + l(a + b + c)$ $V = \dfrac{1}{2} bhl$
right cylinder 	$SA = 2\pi r^2 + 2\pi rh$ $V = \pi r^2 h$
right pyramid 	$SA = l^2 + 2ls$ $V = \dfrac{1}{3} l^2 h$
right cone 	$SA = \pi r^2 + \pi rs$ $V = \dfrac{1}{3} \pi r^2 h$
sphere 	$SA = 4\pi r^2$ $V = \dfrac{4}{3} \pi r^3$

APPLY the Math

EXAMPLE 1 Reasoning about relationships among scale factor, surface area, and volume

Prove the scaling conjectures for the surface area and volume of a rectangular right prism with dimensions $l \times w \times h$.

Connor's Solution: Proving the conjecture for surface area

The surface area of the original rectangular right prism, $SA_{original}$, can be expressed as

$SA_{original} = 2(lw + lh + wh)$

Let k be the scale factor.
The surface area of a new scaled rectangular right prism, SA_{new}, can be expressed as

$SA_{new} = 2[(kl)(kw) + (kl)(kh) + (kw)(kh)]$

$SA_{new} = 2[k^2(lw) + k^2(lh) + k^2(wh)]$

$SA_{new} = 2k^2[(lw) + (lh) + (wh)]$

$SA_{new} = k^2(SA_{original})$

The conjecture is valid for the surface area of a rectangular right prism.

> I decided to prove the conjecture for surface area.

> The rectangular right prism will be scaled by a factor of k. To ensure that the scaled prism is similar to the original, each of the dimensions of the original prism must be multiplied by k.
> $l_{new} = k \cdot l_{original}$
> $w_{new} = k \cdot w_{original}$
> $h_{new} = k \cdot h_{original}$

> k^2 is a common factor.
>
> The expression inside the brackets is the same as the expression for the surface area of the original prism.

Isabelle's Solution: Proving the conjecture for volume

The volume of the original rectangular right prism, $V_{original}$ can be expressed as

$V_{original} = lwh$

Let k be the scale factor.
The volume of a new scaled rectangular right prism, V_{new}, can be expressed as

$V_{new} = (kl)(kw)(kh)$

$V_{new} = k^3 lwh$

> I decided to prove the conjecture for volume.

> The rectangular right prism will be scaled by a factor of k, so each of the dimensions will be multiplied by k.

$$V_{new} = k^3(lwh)$$
$$V_{new} = k^3(V_{original})$$

> The expression inside the brackets is the same as the expression for the volume of the original prism.

The conjecture is valid for the volume of a rectangular right prism.

Your Turn

Prove the scaling conjectures for the surface area and volume of a sphere.

EXAMPLE 2   Solving a surface area problem

The Great Pyramid of Giza in Egypt was built on a square base, with the dimensions shown.

An artist who works with plate glass wants to build a replica of the pyramid for an installation at an art gallery. The artist is restricted by the floor dimensions, which are 6.0 m by 6.0 m, and the ceiling height of 3.5 m. As well, the glass sculpture must have room for a 1.0 m walkway around its base.

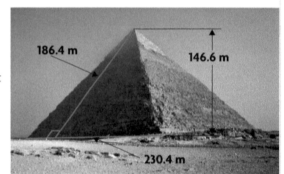
186.4 m   146.6 m
230.4 m

a) What scale factor might the artist use to build the sculpture?

b) How much glass will the artist need to build the sculpture?

Twila's Solution

a)

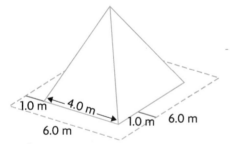
1.0 m   4.0 m
6.0 m   1.0 m   6.0 m

> I drew a diagram to show the situation. The artist's sculpture will be a pyramid that is similar to the actual pyramid in Giza. Since 1.0 m of clearance is needed on each side of the sculpture's base, the longest possible side length is 4.0 m.

$$k = \frac{\text{Side length for base of original pyramid}}{\text{Side length for base of sculpture}}$$

$$k = \frac{230.4 \text{ m}}{4.0 \text{ m}}$$

$$k = 57.6$$

$$k \doteq 60$$

> Since I knew the measures of the side lengths of both bases, I chose to determine a scale factor, k, that could be used to create the sculpture. Then I rounded up my answer to a convenient value. If I had rounded down, the sculpture would not have fit, as $\frac{1}{60}$ is less than $\frac{1}{57.6}$.

I'll test a scale factor of $\frac{1}{60}$ to determine the height of the sculpture from the height of the original pyramid.

The height of the sculpture must be less than 3.5 m.
Height of sculpture = (Scale factor)(Height of original pyramid)
Height of sculpture = $\left(\frac{1}{60}\right)$(146.6 m)

> I checked that the height of the sculpture would fit in the display area.

Height of sculpture = 2.443... m
2.4 m is less than 3.5 m, so the sculpture will fit.
The artist could use a scale factor of $\frac{1}{60}$.

b) $\dfrac{SA_{sculpture}}{SA_{original}} = k^2$

> I knew the dimensions of the original pyramid. I can determine the surface area of the sculpture, $SA_{sculpture}$, by calculating the surface area of the original, $SA_{original}$.

$SA_{sculpture} = k^2(SA_{original})$

$SA_{sculpture} = \left(\dfrac{1}{60}\right)^2 (SA_{original})$

> Since the base is a square, each of the triangular faces is congruent.
>
> The expression in square brackets is the formula for the surface area of a square-based pyramid.

$SA_{sculpture} = \left(\dfrac{1}{60}\right)^2 [\text{Area of base} + 4(\text{Area of each triangular face})]$

$SA_{sculpture} = \left(\dfrac{1}{60}\right)^2 \left[b^2 + 4\left(\dfrac{bs}{2}\right)\right]$

> In the original pyramid, b is the length of one of the sides of the square base, which is 230.4 m. In the original pyramid, s is the slant height (altitude) of each triangular face, which is 186.4 m.

$SA_{sculpture} = \left(\dfrac{1}{60}\right)^2 \left[(230.4 \text{ m})^2 + 4\left(\dfrac{(230.4 \text{ m})(186.4 \text{ m})}{2}\right)\right]$

$SA_{sculpture} = 38.604... \text{ m}^2$
The artist will need about 38.6 m² of glass to build the sculpture in the given space.

Your Turn

The gift shop at the art gallery would like to sell miniature replicas of the artist's sculpture. A scale ratio of 1 : 50 will be used to make the replicas.
  a) Determine the dimensions of the replicas.
  b) Determine the amount of glass that will be needed to make each replica.

EXAMPLE **3**   Solving a capacity problem

The smaller tank in the photograph has a capacity of 1400 m³, and the larger tank has a capacity of 4725 m³.

a) During the refining process, both tanks are filled with oil from a pumping station at the same rate. How many times longer will it take to fill the larger tank than it will take to fill the smaller tank?

b) How many times greater is the radius of the larger tank than the radius of the smaller tank?

Spherical tanks are often used to store oil and gas at refineries, since this shape is the most economical to build.

Esther's Solution

a) $\dfrac{V_{\text{large}}}{V_{\text{small}}} = \dfrac{4725 \ \text{m}^3}{1400 \ \text{m}^3}$

$\dfrac{V_{\text{large}}}{V_{\text{small}}} = 3.375$

> Since both tanks are being filled at the same rate, the factor that relates the capacities of the tanks will tell me the relationship between the times needed to fill the tanks. I decided to use V_{large} to represent the capacity (interior volume) of the large tank and V_{small} to represent the capacity of the small tank.

It will take a little more than three times longer to fill the larger tank than it will take to fill the smaller tank.

> The larger tank holds 3.375 times more oil than the smaller tank.

b)

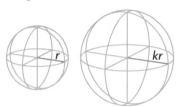

$V_{\text{large}} = k^3 \cdot V_{\text{small}}$

$\dfrac{V_{\text{large}}}{V_{\text{small}}} = k^3$

$3.375 = k^3$

$\sqrt[3]{3.375} = k$

$1.5 = k$

> The only dimension that varies in a sphere is the radius. Therefore, any two spheres are similar objects, with radii related by a scale factor of k.

> The capacities of the tanks are related by a factor of 3.375. Therefore, the scale factor that relates the radii of the tanks is the cube root of this number.

The inner radius of the larger tank is 1.5 times greater than the inner radius of the smaller tank.

Your Turn

The larger tank is going to be reduced by a scale factor of 0.6 to build another small tank. Determine the capacity of the new small tank.

CHECK *Your Understanding*

1. Each pair of objects is similar.
   i) By what factor is the surface area of the larger object greater than the surface area of the smaller object?
   ii) By what factor is the volume of the larger object greater than the volume of the smaller object?

a)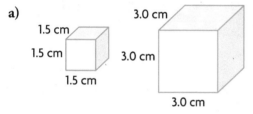

b)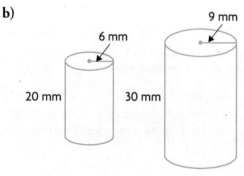

c)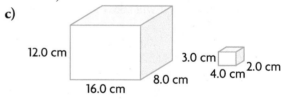

d)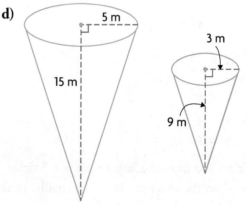

actual dice

2. A stage director needs a pair of large dice for a scene with children playing a board game. He estimates that the measure of each edge of each enlarged die must be 600 mm.
   a) What scale factor must he apply to create the enlarged dice?
   b) How many times greater will the surface area of each larger die be?
   c) How many times greater will the volume of each larger die be?

3. A model of a ship is built to a scale ratio of $1:30$. The model is 16 cm tall, and the area of one sail is 8.5 cm^2. What are the corresponding measurements of the actual ship?

PRACTISING

4. An oil tank has a capacity of 32 m^3. A similar oil tank has dimensions that are larger by a scale factor of 3. What is the capacity of the larger tank?

5. A soft-cover book will be modified so that it has large print for people who are visually impaired. To maintain the same number of pages, both the print size and page dimensions will be tripled.
   a) The area of each page in the original book is 500 cm^2. Determine the area of each page in the large-print book.
   b) The same type of paper will be used for the pages in the large-print book. By what factor will the volume of the paper change? Justify your answer.

6. Brenda is a potter. She is creating two similar vases, with their dimensions related by a scale factor of $\frac{3}{4}$. The larger vase has a volume of 9420 cm^3. Determine the volume of the smaller vase.

7. The dimensions of a right octagonal pyramid are enlarged by a scale factor of 1.5. Determine the value of each of the following ratios.
   a) $\dfrac{\text{Volume of large pyramid}}{\text{Volume of small pyramid}}$ **c)** $\dfrac{\text{Base perimeter of large pyramid}}{\text{Base perimeter of small pyramid}}$
   b) $\dfrac{\text{Surface area of large pyramid}}{\text{Surface area of small pyramid}}$

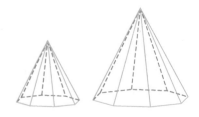

8. A jewellery box has a volume of 4500 cm^3. Its lid has a surface area of 375 cm^2. If each dimension of the jewellery box is tripled to create a prop for a theatre production, by what factors would the surface area of the lid and the volume of the box increase?

9. Celine's grandmother brought her a set of Russian dolls from St. Petersburg. The dolls stack inside each other and are similar to each other. The diameters of the two smallest dolls are 2.0 cm and 3.5 cm. The scale factor is the same from each doll to the next larger doll. Celine estimates the smallest doll has a volume of about 8 cm^3. Estimate the volume of the largest of the five dolls.

10. Mario made a scale model of an airplane using linking cubes.
   a) How many linking cubes would he need to make a model with dimensions five times as large?
   b) By what factor is the surface area of the new model greater than the surface area of the first model?

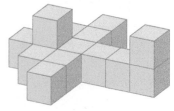

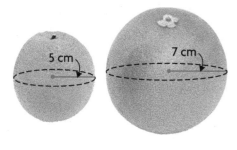

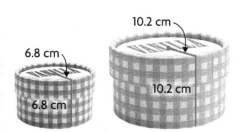

11. Adele wants to compare Earth and the Moon by creating spherical models. She has decided to represent Earth with a sphere that has a radius of 10.0 cm.
    a) What is the radius of the sphere she should use to represent the Moon? Round your answer to the nearest tenth of a centimetre.
    b) Determine the ratio that compares the circumference of the model of Earth to the circumference of the model of the Moon.
    c) Determine the ratio that compares the surface area of the model of Earth to the surface area of the model of the Moon.
    d) Determine the ratio that compares the volume of the model of Earth to the volume of the model of the Moon.

12. Markian likes both oranges and grapefruits. He wonders how much more fruit he gets in a grapefruit. Estimate how many times greater the volume of a grapefruit is, compared with the volume of an orange.

13. A baseball has a diameter of about 2.9 in. A softball has a diameter of about 3.8 in. By what percent is the amount of leather needed to cover the softball greater than the amount of leather needed to cover the baseball?

14. Josephine packages her ice cream in right cylindrical cardboard containers, in the two different sizes shown.
    a) Determine the factor by which the height of the letters in "VANILLA" differs on the two containers.
    b) Determine the factor by which the surface areas of the lids differ.
    c) Determine the factor by which the capacities of the two containers differ.
    d) How much ice cream does each container hold, to the nearest cubic centimetre?

15. Suppose that your class is sending shoeboxes filled with school supplies to schools in need after a devastating earthquake. A cardboard manufacturer has donated two sizes of shoeboxes. The small shoebox is 18.0 cm long, 11.5 cm wide, and 9 cm high. The large shoebox is 36.0 cm long, 23 cm wide, and 18 cm high.
    a) Matty claims that it will take about twice as much paper to wrap the large shoebox for shipping. Do you agree? Justify your decision.
    b) Is the volume of the small shoebox half the volume of the large shoebox? Explain how you know.

16. Show that when the dimensions of each given object are enlarged/reduced by a scale factor of k, the surface area of the resulting similar object has changed by a factor of k^2 and its volume has changed by a factor of k^3.
  a) right cylinder
  b) right cone

Closing

17. Two similar right rectangular prisms have the dimensions 3 m by 4 m by 2 m and 6 m by 8 m by 4 m. Explain how you can determine the number of smaller prisms that will fit in the larger prism.

Extending

18. A travelling circus holds performances under a large tent, as shown. A smaller version of this circus, which visits smaller communities, uses a similar tent with a volume of 580 m³. How many times greater is the floor area of the larger tent, compared with the floor area of the smaller tent?

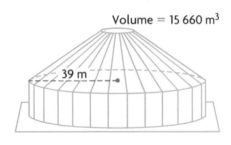

Volume = 15 660 m³

39 m

19. A manufacturer has created a spherical model of the Moon, using a scale ratio of 1 : 11 580 000. The model fits exactly into a cubic box with a volume of 27 000 cm³.
  a) Determine the surface area of the Moon.
  b) Determine the volume of the Moon.

20. A bakery sells two sizes of birthday cakes. The small cake has a diameter of 10 in., and the large cake has a diameter of 12 in. The small cake sells for $14.00. What should the price of the large cake be? Justify your answer, and state any assumptions you are making.

Rate of Employment between 1993 and 2009

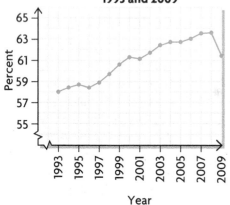

Source: Statistics Canada, Labour Force Survey

1. This graph shows the percent of Canadians who worked (the rate of employment) between 1993 and mid-2009.
   a) When was the rate of employment increasing? When was it decreasing?
   b) Identify when the employment rate did not change.
   c) When was the employment rate increasing the fastest? When was it increasing the slowest?
   d) Suggest some factors that may influence how this rate changes with time.

2. A model airplane has a scale ratio of 1:500. To paint the model, Michael used 5 mL of paint. Assuming the same kind of coverage for the paint, how many litres of paint would be needed to paint the actual airplane?

3. A company's logo has a rectangular shape, which measures 4 cm by 6 cm, on its letterhead. The company would like to advertise in the community and has decided to put an enlargement of the logo on the boards in the local hockey rink. The size of the logo is restricted to an area no larger than 1.5 m². Determine the greatest dimensions that the company could use.

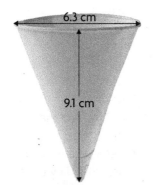

4. To save money, a company that makes drinking cups for dentists has decided to reduce the size of its cups by a scale factor of $\frac{3}{4}$.
   a) Determine the radius, r, and the height, h, of the new cup.
   b) Determine the slant height, s, of the new cup.
   c) How much material does the company save for each cup it makes?
   d) When filled, approximately how much less water does the new cup hold, compared with the original cup?

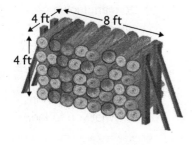

5. A cord of wood is stacked in a pile with a volume of 128 ft³. Three cords of wood will be stacked in a pile with dimensions that are similar to the dimensions of the first cord. Predict how much longer the second pile will be, compared with the original pile.

6. A pizza shop advertises cheese or pepperoni pizzas at the prices listed in the table.
   a) Is the scale factor used for price the same as the scale factor used for the diameter, area, or volume? Explain.
   b) Determine the "best buy"—the diameter that gives the most pizza for the least cost.

Diameter (in.)	Price ($)
10	6
12	8
14	10

WHAT DO You Think Now? Revisit **What Do You Think?** on page 443. How have your answers and explanations changed?

FREQUENTLY ASKED *Questions*

Q: What are scale diagrams and scale models, and what are they used for?

A: A scale diagram is a drawing that is a reduction or an enlargement of a 2-D shape or 3-D object. A scale model is a reduced or enlarged model of a 3-D object. A scale diagram or scale model is similar to the actual shape or object. To create a scale diagram or model, the same scale factor is applied to all the linear measurements.

For example, to create a model of a train using a scale ratio of $1:40$, multiply every linear measurement of the train by the scale factor of $\frac{1}{40}$ or 0.025. Scale factors less than 1 (such as $1:40$, $\frac{1}{40}$, 0.025, and 2.5%) indicate a reduction. Scale factors greater than 1 (such as $3:2$, $\frac{3}{2}$, 1.5, and 150%) indicate an enlargement.

Scale diagrams and scale models allow you to visualize or handle shapes or objects that might otherwise be too large or too small to see and manipulate.

Some objects, such as buildings, may be represented using multiple 2-D scale diagrams. For example, plans for a building allow you to compare the sizes of rooms, decide where doors should be placed, and so on, before spending money on construction.

> **Study | Aid**
> - See Lesson 8.3, Examples 1 to 3.
> - See Lesson 8.5, Examples 1 to 3.
> - Try Chapter Review Questions 5 to 7 and 11 to 13.

Q: How are the areas of two similar shapes related?

A: When two shapes are similar, their corresponding dimensions are proportional. The ratio of a pair of corresponding dimensions is a number called the scale factor. The scale factor is often represented by k. The areas of two similar shapes are related by the square of the scale factor.

Area of similar shape $= k^2$(Area of original shape)

For example, these two circles are similar.

The scale factor that relates the dimensions of the small circle to those of the large circle is 3. So,

Area of large circle $= 3^2$(Area of small circle)

Area of large circle $= 9$(Area of small circle)

> **Study | Aid**
> - See Lesson 8.4, Examples 1 and 2.
> - Try Chapter Review Questions 8 to 10.

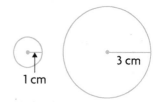

Study | Aid

- See Lesson 8.6, Examples 1 and 2.
- Try Chapter Review Questions 14 to 16.

Q: **How are the surface area and volume of similar objects related?**

A: Consider the Rubik's Cube shown. It consists of 27 individual cubes, each similar to the Rubik's Cube itself. The scale factor between the length of a side of an individual cube and the length of a side of the Rubik's Cube is $\frac{3}{1}$ or 3.

The Rubik's Cube has a surface area of (6)(9) or 54 square units. Each individual cube has a surface area of 6 square units. The ratio of the surface areas is $\frac{54}{6}$ or 9. This is the value of the scale factor squared.	The Rubik's Cube has a volume of (3)(3)(3) or 27 cubic units. Each individual cube has a volume of 1 cubic unit. The ratio of the volumes is $\frac{27}{1}$ or 27. This is the value of the scale factor cubed.
The surface area of the similar object, $SA_{similar}$, is related to the original object, $SA_{original}$, by the square of the scale factor. $SA_{similar} = k^2(SA_{original})$	The volume of the similar object, $V_{similar}$, is related to the original object, $V_{original}$, by the cube of the scale factor. $V_{similar} = k^3(V_{original})$

Study | Aid

- See Lesson 8.6, Example 3.
- Try Chapter Review Question 16.

Q: **If you know the surface areas or volumes of two similar objects, how can you determine the scale factor that relates their dimensions?**

A: Area increases/decreases by the square of the scale factor, k, that relates the original object to the similar object. Therefore, the scale factor is the square root of the ratio of the surface areas.	Volume increases/decreases by the cube of the scale factor, k, that relates the original object to the similar object. Therefore, the scale factor is the cube root of the ratio of the volumes.
For example, in the Rubik's Cube, $$k^2 = \frac{\text{Surface area of Rubik's Cube}}{\text{Surface area of small cube}}$$ $$k^2 = \frac{54}{6}$$ $$k = \sqrt{9}$$ $$k = 3$$	For example, in the Rubik's Cube, $$k^3 = \frac{\text{Volume of Rubik's Cube}}{\text{Volume of small cube}}$$ $$k^3 = \frac{27}{1}$$ $$k = \sqrt[3]{27}$$ $$k = 3$$

PRACTISING

Lesson 8.1

1. An athlete runs the first lap of a race slightly faster than the second lap, and then runs the final lap the fastest. Draw a distance versus time graph that compares the athlete's average speed on each lap.

2. For each of the following, compare the two rates and determine the lower rate.
   a) frozen hams: $2.58/kg or $0.226/100 g
   b) cycling speeds: 35 km/h or 15 min to travel 4.5 mi
   c) fuel efficiency: 6.5 L/100 km or 38 L of fuel needed to travel 560 km
   d) speed of a falling object: 10 m/s or 60 km/h

Lesson 8.2

3. Based on her best consistent pace in practice, Petra believes that she can run her next marathon at an average pace of 3.75 min/km. An official marathon course is 42.195 km long. To qualify for the Boston Marathon, she must run a marathon in 3 h 40 min or better. If she manages to maintain her target pace throughout her next marathon, will Petra qualify to run in the Boston Marathon?

4. Doris wants to buy new carpet for her living room, which has the dimensions shown. She plans to order about 10% extra, so that she has enough to allow for loss during cutting. She can buy the carpet locally for $36.95 per square yard, or she can buy it from a store in a nearby city for $33.99 per square yard. However, the store in the nearby city charges $100 for delivery.

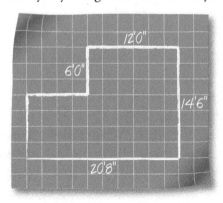

a) How much carpet should Doris buy?
b) Where should she buy the carpet? Explain.

Lesson 8.3

5. In Humboldt, Saskatchewan, there is a 2.4 m by 2.0 m reproduction of a stamp that honours John Diefenbaker, Canada's 13th prime minister. What scale factor was used to make the reproduction?

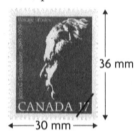

6. Find a 2-D shape in your classroom, and measure its dimensions.
   a) Determine a reasonable scale factor you can use to create a scale diagram on half of a sheet of standard paper.
   b) Draw a scale diagram of your shape.

7. An airplane starts at point A. It flies N30°E, at a speed of 125 mph, for 5 h to point B. Then it flies S20°E, at a speed of 100 mph, for 3 h to point C.
   a) Make a scale drawing of the airplane's flight path.
   b) Explain how you could estimate the distance from point C to point A without using trigonometry.

Lesson 8.4

8. The owners of a local pizzeria advertise their Gynormous pizza as being 40% bigger than their competitors' pizzas. They do not say, however, what they mean by "bigger."
   a) If they mean that the diameter is 40% greater, what is the percent increase in area?
   b) If they mean that the area is 40% greater, what is the percent increase in diameter?
   c) Which of these two meanings do you think was implied by the owners of the pizzeria? Explain.

9. The area of the larger regular octagon is exactly 2500 m².

8 m

a) Determine the area of the smaller octagon.
b) Determine the scale factor, to the nearest hundredth, that was used to enlarge the smaller regular octagon.

10. a) Suppose that you put a 5 in. by 7 in. picture in a copy machine and click "enlarge 110%." What will the dimensions of the copy be?
b) By what percent will the area of the picture increase?

Lesson 8.5

11. In a local store, Serena saw a toy pig with a scale ratio of 1 : 16. She estimated that the toy pig was about 10 cm long. She searched online and found a similar toy pig, with a scale ratio of 1 : 64. Estimate the length of the online toy.

12. At the Visitor Centre in 100 Mile House, British Columbia, there is a display of a giant pair of cross-country skis. An average person would use skis that are 200 cm long and poles that are 150 cm long. The giant skis are 12.0 m long.

a) Determine the scale factor that was used to create the display.
b) Determine the length of the poles in the display.

13. Jonas collects and builds model airplanes. He wants to build a 1 : 20 scale model of a floatplane. He searches the Internet for information about the real plane and learns that it has a wingspan of 36 ft, a length of 26 ft 2 in., and a height of 7 ft 6 in. Jonas wants to build a glass display case, in the form of a rectangular prism, for his scale model. He wants the dimensions of the display case to be 20% larger than each dimension of the model. Determine the dimensions of Jonas's display case.

Lesson 8.6

14. Cone A is a reduction of cone B, with a scale factor of 1 : 9. Cone A has a volume of 20 cm³. What is the volume of cone B?

15. A chocolate bar is sold in a package, as shown. The manufacturer doubles the volume of the chocolate to create a larger bar, similar in shape to the original bar. Determine the surface area, to the nearest square centimetre, of the package that is needed for the new bar.

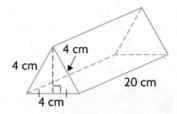

4 cm
4 cm
4 cm
20 cm

16. A cellphone company advertises that it has created a similar version of its most popular phone, reducing the volume and mass of the original phone by 48.8%. The original phone is a rectangular prism, 50 mm wide by 95 mm long by 10 mm high. Determine the dimensions of the new phone.

Mice To Be Here

A graphic artist is creating computer-generated images for an animated movie. She has to create a school used by mice for the movie. She needs to scale everything that would appear in a regular school down to a size that is appropriate for mice.

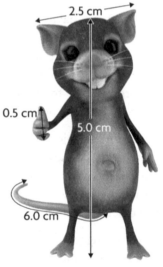

? What scale factor should she use?

A. Determine the scale factor she should use, based on the relative sizes of the cartoon mice and humans. Explain your thinking.

B. Pick a classroom in your school and some objects that are found in this room. Determine the dimensions of a similar room for the movie and the dimensions of similar objects. Then determine the volume of one similar object that the mice would use in their school, as well as the surface area of another similar object.

C. Based on the dimensions of the similar objects, and assuming that there will be 20 mice in the classroom, do you still believe that your scale factor is appropriate? Explain why or why not. If not, adjust the scale factor and repeat.

D. Normal "travelling" speed for a mouse is 200 cm/s. Determine whether students could walk from one end of a room to the other in the same time that a mouse would travel a similar distance in the room in their school.

E. If the scale factor for the movie were based on the speeds of mice and humans instead of their sizes, what would be the dimensions of the similar room and objects from part B?

Task | *Checklist*
- ✔ Did you include your scale factors?
- ✔ Did you show your work for all the calculations?
- ✔ Did you justify and explain your thinking clearly?

Peer Critiquing of Research Projects

Now that you have completed your research for your question/topic, prepared your report and presentation, and assessed your own work, you are ready to see and hear the research projects developed by your classmates. You will not be a passive observer, however. You will have an important role—to provide constructive feedback to your peers about their projects and their presentations.

Critiquing a project does *not* involve commenting on what might have been or should have been. It involves reacting to what you see and hear. For example, pay attention to
- strengths and weaknesses of the presentation.
- problems or concerns with the presentation.

Think of suggestions you could make to help your classmate improve future presentations.

While observing each presentation, consider the content, the organization, and the delivery. Take notes during the presentation, using the following rating scales as a guide. You can also use these scales to evaluate the presentation.

Content

Shows a clear sense of audience and purpose.	5	4	3	2	1
Demonstrates a thorough understanding of the topic.	5	4	3	2	1
Clearly and concisely explains ideas.	5	4	3	2	1
Applies mathematical knowledge and skills developed in this course.	5	4	3	2	1
Justifies conclusions with sound mathematical reasoning.	5	4	3	2	1
Uses mathematical terms and symbols correctly.	5	4	3	2	1

Organization

Presentation is clearly focused.	5	4	3	2	1
Engaging introduction includes the research question, clearly stated.	5	4	3	2	1
Key ideas and information are logically presented.	5	4	3	2	1
There are effective transitions between ideas and information.	5	4	3	2	1
Conclusion follows logically from the analysis and relates to the question.	5	4	3	2	1

Delivery

Speaking voice is clear, relaxed, and audible.	5	4	3	2	1
Pacing is appropriate and effective for the allotted time.	5	4	3	2	1
Technology is used effectively.	5	4	3	2	1
Visuals and handouts are easily understood.	5	4	3	2	1
Responses to audience's questions show a thorough understanding of the topic.	5	4	3	2	1

Keep these rating scales in mind as you prepare your own presentation.

Your Turn

A. Think of an excellent presentation you have observed. List five aspects of this presentation that made it effective.

B. What are some common difficulties that students encounter when giving presentations to their peers? Suggest how each of these difficulties could be avoided or dealt with.

C. When critiquing a presentation, it is essential that you do not allow your own opinions about the topic to influence your analysis. Explain why.

1. i) Express each quadratic function in factored form, and determine
   - the x-intercepts.
   - the equation of the axis of symmetry.
   - the coordinates of the vertex.
   - the y-intercept.
   ii) Sketch the graph of each function.
   iii) State the domain and range of each function.
   a) $f(x) = x^2 - 8x$ b) $y = x^2 + 2x - 15$

2. i) For each quadratic function, determine
   - the equation of the axis of symmetry.
   - the coordinates of the vertex.
   - the y-intercept.
   ii) Sketch the graph of each function.
   iii) State the domain and range of each function.
   a) $y = -2(x - 3)^2 + 8$ b) $g(x) = 0.5(x + 2)^2 - 1$

3. Determine the equation of the quadratic function shown to the left. Express the equation in factored form and standard form.

4. The parabola $f(x) = 4x^2 + 24x + 31$ has $x = -3$ as its axis of symmetry.
   a) Does the parabola open up or down? Explain.
   b) Determine the coordinates of the vertex of the parabola.
   c) Does the parabola have a maximum value or a minimum value? Explain how you know.

5. Ryan owns a small music store. He currently charges $10 for each CD. At this price, he sells about 80 CDs a week. Experience has taught him that a $1 increase in the price of a CD means a drop of about five CDs per week in sales. At what price should Ryan sell his CDs to maximize his revenue?

6. Determine the roots to the quadratic equation, where $y = 0$.
   a)
   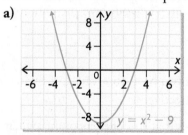
   b)
   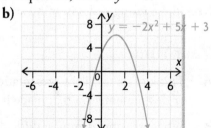

7. Solve each equation.
   a) $(x - 5)(2x + 1) = 0$
   b) $x^2 - 4x - 32 = 0$
   c) $3x^2 - 10x = 8$
   d) $x^2 - 6x - 10 = 0$
   e) $2(x - 3)^2 - 8 = 0$
   f) $1.5x^2 = 6.1x - 1.1$

8. Two skydivers jump out of an airplane at an altitude of 4.5 km. Their altitude, in metres, is modelled by the function $h(t) = 4500 - 5t^2$, where t is the time in seconds after jumping out of the airplane.
  a) Determine the altitude of the skydivers after 5 s.
  b) The skydivers opened their parachutes at an altitude of 1500 m. Determine how long they were in free fall.

9. A rapid-transit company currently has 5000 passengers daily, each paying a fare of $2.25. The company estimates that for each $0.50 increase in the fare, it will lose 150 passengers daily. The company must have $15 275 in revenue each day to stay in business. Determine the minimum fare that the company can charge to produce this revenue.

10. State the restrictions on the variable in each equation, and then solve the equation.
  a) $9 = \sqrt{x - 1} + 1$ **b)** $-3 = \sqrt{5y + 1}$

11. The time T, in seconds, for a pendulum to swing back and forth is called its period. The formula that is used to calculate the period of a pendulum is

$$T = 2\pi\sqrt{\frac{L}{g}},$$

where L is the length of the pendulum in metres

and g is the acceleration due to gravity, 9.81 m/s².

The pendulum on a grandfather clock has a period of 2 s. Calculate the length of the pendulum.

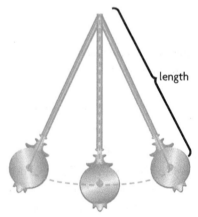
length

12. Carol can read at a rate of one page per minute. Joanna can read at a rate of one page every 40 s. Both girls need to read a 180-page story for English class. How much longer will Carol take to read the story?

13. In an aerial photograph, a rectangular plot of land measures 3 cm by 5 cm. The scale ratio used in the photograph is 1 : 50 000.
  a) Determine the dimensions of the plot of land.
  b) Determine the area of the plot of land in hectares.
     (The conversion rate is 1 ha/10 000 m².)

14. A new underground holding tank for storm runoff is going to be built as part of a town's waste-water management system. The new tank will be similar to the current tank. The interior dimensions of the current tank are shown here. Engineers estimate that the capacity of the new tank needs to be 10 times the capacity of the current tank. Estimate the interior dimensions of the new tank, to the nearest metre.

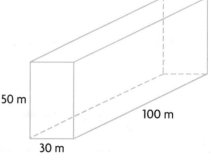
50 m
100 m
30 m

Glossary

A

absolute value: The distance of a number from 0 on a number line; the absolute value of x is denoted as

$$|x| = \begin{cases} x, & \text{If } x \geq 0 \\ -x, & \text{If } x < 0 \end{cases}$$

e.g., $|-5| = 5$

Both 5 and -5 are 5 units from 0.

alternate exterior angles: Two exterior angles formed between two lines and a transversal, on opposite sides of the transversal.

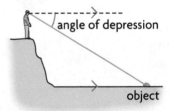

alternate interior angles: Two non-adjacent interior angles on opposite sides of a transversal.

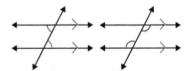

angle of depression: The angle between a horizontal line and the line of sight when looking down at an object.

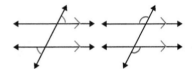

angle of elevation: The angle between a horizontal line and the line of sight when looking up at an object.

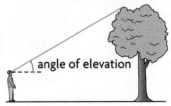

axis of symmetry: A line that separates a 2-D figure into two identical parts. For example, a parabola has a vertical axis of symmetry passing through its vertex.

B

bell curve: See **normal curve.**

C

circular reasoning: An argument that is incorrect because it makes use of the conclusion to be proved.

confidence interval: The interval in which the true value you're trying to determine is estimated to lie, with a stated degree of probability; the confidence interval may be expressed using $\pm$ notation, such as 54.0% $\pm$ 3.5%, or ranging from 50.5% to 57.5%.

confidence level: The likelihood that the result for the "true" population lies within the range of the confidence interval; surveys and other studies usually use a confidence level of 95%, although 90% or 99% is sometimes used.

conjecture: A testable expression that is based on available evidence but is not yet proved.

converse: A statement that is formed by switching the premise and the conclusion of another statement.

convex polygon: A polygon in which each interior angle measures less than 180°.

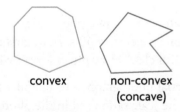

convex   non-convex
                (concave)

corresponding angles: One interior angle and one exterior angle that are non-adjacent and on the same side of a transversal.

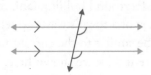

cosine law: In any acute triangle,

$$a^2 = b^2 + c^2 - 2bc \cos A$$
$$b^2 = a^2 + c^2 - 2ac \cos B$$
$$c^2 = a^2 + b^2 - 2ab \cos C$$

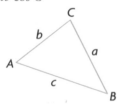

counterexample: An example that invalidates a conjecture.

D

deductive reasoning: Drawing a specific conclusion through logical reasoning by starting with general assumptions that are known to be valid.

deviation: The difference between a data value and the mean for the same set of data.

dispersion: A measure that varies by the spread among the data in a set; dispersion has a value of zero if all the data in a set is identical, and it increases in value as the data becomes more spread out.

E

entire radical: A radical with a coefficient of 1, for example $\sqrt{6}$.

exterior angle of a polygon: The angle that is formed by a side of a polygon and the extension of an adjacent side.

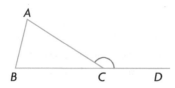

$\angle ACD$ is an exterior angle of $\triangle ABC$.

exterior angles: Any angles formed by a transversal and two parallel lines that lie outside the parallel lines.

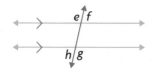

e, f, g, and h are exterior angles.

extraneous root: A root that does not satisfy the initial conditions that were introduced while solving an equation. Root is another word for solution.

F

frequency distribution: A set of intervals (table or graph), usually of equal width, into which raw data is organized; each interval is associated with a frequency that indicates the number of measurements in this interval.

frequency polygon: The graph of a frequency distribution, produced by joining the midpoints of the intervals using straight lines.

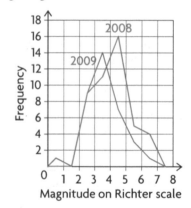

G

generalization: A principle, statement, or idea that has general application.

H

histogram: The graph of a frequency distribution, in which equal intervals of values are marked on a horizontal axis and the frequencies associated with these intervals are indicated by the areas of the rectangles drawn for these intervals.

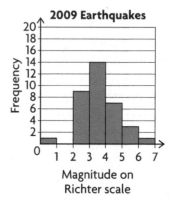

I

inadmissible solution: A root of a quadratic equation that does not lead to a solution that satisfies the original problem.

inductive reasoning: Drawing a general conclusion by observing patterns and identifying properties in specific examples.

interior angles: Any angles formed by a transversal and two parallel lines that lie inside the parallel lines.

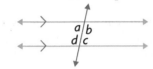

a, b, c, and *d* are interior angles.

invalid proof: A proof that contains an error in reasoning or that contains invalid assumptions.

L

line plot: A graph that records each data value in a data set as a point above a number line.

margin of error: The possible difference between the estimate of the value you're trying to determine, as determined from a random sample, and the true value for the population; the margin of error is generally expressed as a plus or minus percent, such as $\pm 5\%$.

maximum value: The greatest value of the dependent variable in a relation.

mean: A measure of central tendency determined by dividing the sum of all the values in a data set by the number of values in the set.

median: A measure of central tendency represented by the middle value of an ordered data set. For example, the median of 3, 3, 4, 5, 6 is 4. If the data set has more than one middle value, the median is the mean of the two. For example, the median of 3, 3, 5, 6 is also 4.

M

minimum value: The least value of the dependent variable in a relation.

mixed radical: A radical with a coefficient other than 1; for example, $3\sqrt{5}$.

mode: A measure of central tendency represented by the value that occurs most often in a data set. For example, the mode of 2, 2, 4, 5, 6 is 2.

N

non-adjacent interior angles: The two angles of a triangle that do not have the same vertex as an exterior angle.

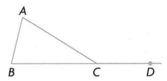

$\angle A$ and $\angle B$ are non-adjacent interior angles to exterior $\angle ACD$.

normal curve: A symmetrical curve that represents the normal distribution; also called a **bell curve.**

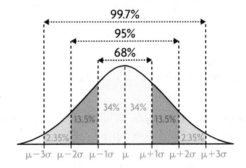

normal distribution: Data that, when graphed as a histogram or a frequency polygon, results in a unimodal symmetric distribution about the mean.

O

outlier: A value in a data set that is very different from other values in the set.

P

parabola: The shape of the graph of any quadratic relation.

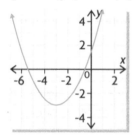

perfect square: A perfect square is a whole number that is the square of another number. For example, 64 is a perfect square.

premise: A statement assumed to be true.

principal square root: The positive square root of a real number, x, denoted as $\sqrt{x}$; for example, the principal square root of 16 is $\sqrt{16}$, or 4.

proof: A mathematical argument showing that a statement is valid in all cases, or that no counterexample exists.

Q

quadratic equation: A polynomial equation of the second degree; the standard form of a quadratic equation is

$$ax^2 + bx + c = 0$$

For example:

$$2x^2 + 4x - 3 = 0$$

quadratic formula: A formula for determining the roots of a quadratic equation in the form $ax^2 + bx + c = 0$, where $a \neq 0$; the quadratic formula is written using the coefficients of the variables and the constant in the quadratic equation that is being solved:

$$x = \frac{-b \pm \sqrt{b^2 - 4ac}}{2a}$$

This formula is derived from $ax^2 + bx + c = 0$ by isolating x.

quadratic relation: A relation that can be written in the standard form

$$y = ax^2 + bx + c, \text{ where } a \neq 0$$

For example:

$$y = 4x^2 + 2x + 1$$

R

range: The difference between the maximum value and the minimum value in a data set.

rate: A comparison of two amounts that are measured in different units; for example, keying 240 words/8 min.

rationalize the denominator: The process used to write a radical expression that contains a radical denominator into an equivalent expression with a rational denominator.

restrictions: The values of the variable in an expression that ensure it to be defined.

roots: The values of the variable that make an equation in standard form equal to zero. These are also called solutions to the equation. These values are also the zeros of the corresponding function and the x-intercepts of its graph.

S

scale: The ratio of a measurement on a diagram to the corresponding distance measured on the shape or object represented by the diagram.

scale diagram: A drawing in which measurements are proportionally reduced or enlarged from actual measurements; a scale diagram is similar to the original.

scale factor: A number created from the ratio of any two corresponding measurements of two similar shapes or objects, written as a fraction, a decimal, or a percent.

secondary square root: The negative square root of a real number, x, denoted as $-\sqrt{x}$; for example, the secondary square root of 16 is $-\sqrt{16}$, or -4.

similar objects: Two or more 3-D objects that have proportional dimensions.

sine law: In any acute triangle,

$$\frac{a}{\sin A} = \frac{b}{\sin B} = \frac{c}{\sin C}$$

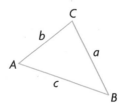

standard deviation: A measure of the dispersion or scatter of data values in relation to the mean; a low standard deviation indicates that most data values are close to the mean, and a high standard deviation indicates that most data values are scattered farther from the mean. The symbol used to represent standard deviation is the Greek letter σ (sigma).

standard normal distribution: A normal distribution that has a mean of zero and a standard deviation of one.

T

transitive property: If two quantities are equal to the same quantity, then they are equal to each other.

If $a = b$ and $b = c$, then $a = c$.

transversal: A line that intersects two or more other lines at distinct points.

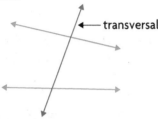
transversal

two-column proof: A presentation of a logical argument involving deductive reasoning in which the statements of the argument are written in one column and the justifications for the statements are written in the other column.

U

unit rate: A rate in which the numerical value of the second term is 1; for example, keying 240 words/8 min expressed as a unit rate is 30 words/min.

V

vertex: The point at which the quadratic function reaches its maximum or minimum value.

Z

z-score: A standardized value that indicates the number of standard deviations of a data value above or below the mean.

z-score table: A table that displays the fraction of data with a z-score that is less than any given data value in a standard normal distribution.

zero: In a function, a value of the variable that makes the value of the function equal to zero.

Answers

Chapter 1

Lesson 1.1, page 12

1. e.g., The manager made the conjecture that each type of ski would sell equally as well as the others.
2. Tomas's conjecture is not reasonable. $99(11) = 1089$
3. e.g., The sum of two even integers is always even. For example, $6 + 12 = 18$ $34 + 72 = 106$
4. e.g., The yellow symbolizes the wheat fields of Saskatchewan, the green symbolizes the northern forests, and the fleur de lys represents la Francophonie.
5. e.g., Mary made the conjecture that the sum of the angles in quadrilaterals is 360°.
6. e.g., The fewest number of triangles in a polygon is the number of sides subtracted by 2.

Polygon	heptagon	octagon	nonagon
Fewest Number of Triangles	 5	6	7

7. e.g., The result is always an even number ending with a decimal of .25.
8. **a)** e.g., The sums of the digits of multiples of 3 are always 3, 6, or 9.
9. e.g., The sum of one odd integer and one even integer is always odd.
   $3 + 4 = 7$
   $-11 + 44 = 33$
   $90 + 121 = 211$
10. e.g., The temperature on November 1 in Hay River never goes above 5 °C. My conjecture is supported by the data: none of the temperatures are above 5 °C.
11. e.g., Paula's conjecture is reasonable. When you multiply an odd digit with an odd digit, the result is odd:
    $1(1) = 1; 3(3) = 9; 5(5) = 25; 7(7) = 49; 9(9) = 81$
    Since the ones of a product are the result of a multiplication of two digits, squaring an odd integer will always result in an odd integer.
12. e.g., The diagonals of rectangles intersect each other at their midpoints. I used my ruler to check various rectangles.
13. e.g., Text messages are written using small keypads or keyboards, making text entry difficult. Abbreviations reduce the difficult typing that needs to be done, e.g., LOL is 3 characters, "laugh out loud" is 14.
14. e.g., Nick made the conjecture that the medians of a triangle always intersect at one point.

15. e.g., If March comes in like a lamb, it will go out like a lion. People may have noticed that when the weather was mild at the beginning of March, or near the end of winter, there would be bad weather at the end of March, or near the beginning of spring.
16. e.g., The town will be in the bottom right of the map near the mouth of the large river. People tend to live near bodies of fresh water, and this is one of the few flat areas on the map.
17. e.g., If social networking sites were the only way to pass information among people, it is reasonable that everyone would access such a site once per day to connect with people or obtain news. Because of various schedules (e.g., working or sleeping during the day, time zones), it is reasonable that it would take at least 12 h for the news to reach the whole Canadian population.
18. e.g., Thérèse's conjecture is possible. Cut the paper along the red lines. Unfold to form a hole larger than the original piece of paper.
19. e.g., A conjecture is a belief, and inferences and hypotheses are also beliefs. However, conjectures, inferences, and hypotheses are validated differently because they relate to different subjects: mathematics/logic, literature, and science.
20. e.g., The photograph is of a shadow of a statue holding a globe.
    The photograph is of a shadow of a soccer goalie, near the goal, holding the ball above her head.
    The picture is of a shadow of a child holding a ball above his head near a swing set.
21. e.g., The statement is not a conjecture. The company making the claim probably surveyed some dentists to get their opinion; however, these dentists' opinion may not represent that of all dentists.
22. e.g., Conjectures about sports may not be accurate because a player or a team's performance may change depending on the health of the player or the constitution of the team.

Lesson 1.2, page 17

1. e.g., The dimensions of the tabletops are the same. A ruler may be used to measure them.
2. e.g., The pattern will continue until 12345678987654321; after that, it will change. I can test my conjecture using a spreadsheet.
3. e.g., When two congruent regular polygons are positioned so that there is a common side, the polygon formed will have $2n - 2$ sides, where n is the number of sides in one original polygon. My conjecture is invalid. The resulting figure is 4-sided:

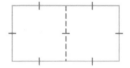

Lesson 1.3, page 22

1. e.g.,
   a) 0 is a number that is not negative, and is not positive.
   b) 2 is a prime number that is not odd.
   c) Muggsy Bogues was an NBA player who was 1.6 m (5 ft 3 in.) tall.

d) The height of a triangle can lie outside the triangle.

e) If a city's shape is roughly rectangular and it lies along a northeast-southwest axis, then the map will be set to accommodate the city's shape, and the north arrow would instead point toward a corner of the map.

f) $\sqrt{0.01} = 0.1$

g) $-10 + 5 = -5$

h) Travelling north in the southern hemisphere generally results in a warmer climate.

2. Disagree. e.g., The sides of a rhombus are equal, but its angles may not be 90°.

3. Disagree. e.g., $1(10) = 10$

4. Disagree. e.g., $9 + 12 = 21$

5. Disagree. e.g., $99.9 + 9 = 18.\ 18 \neq 9$

6. Disagree. e.g., a kite with angles of 90°, 45°, 90°, and 135°

7. e.g., Claire's conjecture seems reasonable because so many combinations are possible. I tried a few examples.

Number	Expression
6	$\dfrac{6}{\sqrt{4}}(7-5)$
10	$\dfrac{6(5)}{7-4}$
19	$4(5) - 7 + 6$

8. e.g., My evidence strengthens George's conjecture. For example,
$123456789 \cdot 4 + 9 = 493827165$
$1234567891011 \cdot 4 + 11 = 4938271564055$

9. e.g., The sum of digits in any multiple of 9 greater than zero will be divisible by 9.

10. e.g., Patrice's conjecture is reasonable. Integers separated by a value of 2 will both be odd or both be even, and their squares will both be odd or both be even. Adding two even numbers together and adding two odd numbers together result in an even number.

11. e.g., Geoff's conjecture is not valid. Kites and rhombuses have perpendicular diagonals.

12. e.g., Amy's conjecture could be changed to "When any number greater than 1 is multiplied by itself, it will be greater than the starting number."

13. e.g., Any real number is divisible by another real number.
$\dfrac{425.353}{1.35} = 315.076...\quad \dfrac{\pi}{\sqrt[3]{9}} = 1.510...$
Counterexample: 0 is a real number for which division is not defined.

14. Disagree. e.g., The number 2 cannot be written as the sum of consecutive numbers.

15. e.g., Blake's claim is not valid. The number 3 cannot be written as the sum of three primes.

16. e.g.,
a) $18 = 5 + 13$
$54 = 11 + 43$
$106 = 5 + 101$
b) A counterexample would be an even number that is not equal to the sum of two primes.

17. e.g.,
a) The number picked and the final result are the same.
b) I cannot find a counterexample. This does not imply that the conjecture is valid, but it does strengthen it.

18. e.g., Inductive reasoning can be used to make a conjecture; a conjecture is supported by evidence and can be invalidated by a counterexample.

19. Disagree. e.g., $4^2 - 3 = 13$

20. **a)** e.g.,

0%	There won't be rain, even if it's cloudy. Perfect for a day at the lake.
10%	Little chance of rain or snow. A good day for a hike.
20%	No rain is expected; good weather for soccer.
30%	There's a small chance of rain. I'll risk a game of ultimate at the local park.
40%	It might rain, but I might skateboard close to home.
50%	It's a good idea to bring an umbrella or rain jacket on the way to school.
60%	It's a very good idea to bring an umbrella or rain jacket on the way to school.
70%	The chance for no rain is 3 out of 10—I'll stay inside and watch a movie.
80%	Rain is likely. I'll read a book.
90%	It will almost certainly rain. I'll spend time surfing the Internet.
100%	It will definitely rain. I'll play a game of basketball indoors.

b) e.g., For probabilities of 30% or less, I'd definitely go outside because of the low chance of rain. For probabilities of 40%–50%, I would still go outdoors because it's about a 1 in 2 chance it will rain. For 60% or more, which is closer to a two-thirds chance that it will rain, I would definitely stay indoors.

21. Agree. e.g., If n is odd, its square will be odd. Two odd numbers and one even number added together result in an even number. If n is even, then three even numbers are added together, and that results in an even number.

Lesson 1.4, page 31

1. e.g., Let n be any number.
$(n-3) + (n-2) + (n-1) + n + (n+1)$
$+ (n+2) + (n+3) = 7n$
Since n is the median, Chuck's conjecture is true.

2. Austin got a good haircut.

3. e.g., The angles formed at the intersection of the diagonals are two pairs of opposite, equal angles.

4. e.g., Let $2n$ and $2m$ represent any two even numbers.
$2n + 2m = 2(n + m)$
Since 2 is a factor of the sum, the sum is even.

5. Let $2n + 1$ represent an odd number and $2m$ represent an even number.
$2m(2n + 1) = 4mn + 2m$
$2m(2n + 1) = 2(2mn + m)$
Since 2 is a factor of the product, the product is even.

6. e.g., Using the Pythagorean theorem, we can show that the first and third triangles have a right angle opposite the hypotenuse.
$4^2 + 3^2 = 16 + 9 \qquad 6^2 + 8^2 = 36 + 64$
$4^2 + 3^2 = 25 \qquad\quad\ 6^2 + 8^2 = 100$
$4^2 + 3^2 = 5^2 \qquad\quad 6^2 + 8^2 = 10^2$
So, angles a and c are 90°.
Angle b and the right angle are supplementary. Angle b is 90°.
Since angles a, b, and c are all 90°, they are equal to each other.

7. a) e.g.,

n	5	0	-11
$\times 4$	20	0	-44
$+ 10$	30	10	-34
$\div 2$	15	5	-17
$- 5$	10	0	-22
$\div 2$	5	0	-11
$+ 3$	8	3	-8

b)

n	n
$\times 4$	$4n$
$+ 10$	$4n + 10$
$\div 2$	$2n + 5$
$- 5$	$2n$
$\div 2$	n
$+ 3$	$n + 3$

8. e.g., The premises do not exclude other pants from being expensive.

9. e.g.,

n	n
$\times 2$	$2n$
$+ 6$	$2n + 6$
$\times 2$	$4n + 12$
$- 4$	$4n + 8$
$\div 4$	$n + 2$
$- 2$	n

10. e.g., Let $2n + 1$ represent any odd integer.
$(2n + 1)^2 = 4n^2 + 2n + 2n + 1$
The numbers $4n^2$ and $2n$ are even. The addition of 1 makes the result odd.

11. e.g.,
$4^2 - 6^2 = 16 - 36$ $\quad$ $5^2 - 7^2 = 25 - 49$
$4^2 - 6^2 = -20$ $\quad\quad$ $5^2 - 7^2 = -24$

Let n represent any number.
$n^2 - (n - 2)^2 = n^2 - (n^2 - 4n + 4)$
$n^2 - (n - 2)^2 = n^2 - n^2 + 4n - 4$
$n^2 - (n - 2)^2 = 4n - 4$
$n^2 - (n - 2)^2 = 4(n - 1)$
The difference is a multiple of 4.

12. e.g.,

Choose a number.	n
Add 5.	$n + 5$
Multiply by 3.	$3n + 15$
Add 3.	$3n + 18$
Divide by 3.	$n + 6$
Subtract the number you started with.	6

13. e.g., Let $abcd$ represent any four-digit number.
$abcd = 1000a + 100b + 10c + d$
$abcd = 2(500a + 50b + 5c) + d$
The number $abcd$ is divisible by 2 only when d is divisible by 2.

14. e.g., Let ab represent any two-digit number.
$ab = 10a + b$
$ab = 5(2a) + b$
The number ab is divisible by 5 only when b is divisible by 5.
Let abc represent any three-digit number.
$abc = 100a + 10b + c$
$abc = 5(20a + 2b) + c$
The number abc is divisible by 5 only when c is divisible by 5.

15. e.g., Let ab represent any two-digit number.
$ab = 10a + b$
$ab = 9a + (a + b)$
The number ab is divisible by 9 only when $(a + b)$ is divisible by 9.
Let abc represent any three-digit number.
$abc = 100a + 10b + c$
$abc = 99a + 9b + (a + b + c)$
The number abc is divisible by 9 only when $(a + b + c)$ is divisible by 9.

16. e.g.,
$$\frac{5^2}{4} = 6.25 \qquad \frac{11^2}{4} = 30.25 \qquad \frac{23^2}{4} = 132.25$$
When an odd number is squared and divided by four, it will always result in a decimal number ending with 0.25.
Let $2n + 1$ represent any odd number.
$$\frac{(2n + 1)^2}{4} = \frac{4n^2 + 4n + 1}{4}$$
$$\frac{(2n + 1)^2}{4} = \frac{4(n^2 + n) + 1}{4}$$
$$\frac{(2n + 1)^2}{4} = (n^2 + n) + \frac{1}{4}$$
$$\frac{(2n + 1)^2}{4} = (n^2 + n) + 0.25$$
An odd number squared, then divided by four, will always result in a decimal number ending with 0.25.

17. e.g., Joan and Garnet used inductive reasoning to provide more evidence for the conjecture, but their solutions aren't mathematical proofs. Jamie used deductive reasoning to develop a generalization that proves Simon's conjecture.

18. e.g., Let x represent the original number; let d represent the difference between x and its nearest lower multiple of 10.
Step 1: $x - d$
Step 2: $x + d$
Step 3: $(x + d)(x - d) = x^2 - d^2$
Step 4: $x^2 - d^2 + d^2 = x^2$

19. e.g., $n^2 + n + 2 = n(n + 1) + 2$
The expression $n(n + 1)$ represents the product of an odd integer and an even integer. The product of an odd integer and an even integer is always even (see question 5). Adding 2 to an even number results in an even number.

20. e.g., Conjecture: The product of two consecutive natural numbers is always even.
The product of two consecutive natural numbers is the product of an odd integer and an even integer.

Let $2n$ and $2n + 1$ represent any two consecutive natural numbers when the even number is less than the odd number.
$$2n(2n + 1) = 4n^2 + 2n$$
$$2n(2n + 1) = 2(2n^2 + n)$$
Let $2n$ and $2n - 1$ represent any two consecutive natural numbers when the odd number is less than the even number.
$$2n(2n - 1) = 4n^2 - 2n$$
$$2n(2n - 1) = 2(2n^2 - n)$$
In both cases, the product has a factor of 2. The product of two consecutive natural numbers is always even.

Mid-Chapter Review, page 35

1. e.g., The medicine wheel's spokes may have pointed toward celestial bodies at solstices and equinoxes.
2. e.g., The squares follow a pattern of $t + 1$ fours, t eights, and 1 nine, where t is the term number. For example, the second term, $t = 2$, is $667^2 = 444889$
   The 25th term in the pattern will be 25 sixes and 1 seven, squared, and the result will be 26 fours, 25 eights, and 1 nine.
3. e.g.,
   a) The sum of the numbers in the 10th row will be 512.
   b) The sum of any row is $2^{(r-1)}$, where r is the row number.
4. e.g., Glenda's conjecture seems reasonable. For the countries whose names begin with A, B, C, or S, there are 30 countries whose names end with a consonant and 42 whose names end with a vowel.
5. e.g., Igor Larionov is a Russian hockey player who was inducted into the Hockey Hall of Fame in 2008.
6. Disagree. e.g., The diagonals of parallelograms and rhombuses also bisect each other.
7. Disagree. e.g., For example, the conjecture "all prime numbers are odd" can be supported by 10 examples (3, 5, 7, 9, 11, 13, 17, 19, 23, 29), but the conjecture is not valid: 2 is an even prime number.
8. e.g.,
   a) If 5 is chosen, the result is 5. If 2 is chosen, the result is 5.
   Conjecture: The number trick always has a result of 5.

n	n
$+ 3$	$n + 3$
$\times 2$	$2n + 6$
$+ 4$	$2n + 10$
$\div 2$	$n + 5$
$- n$	5

   b) If 7 is chosen, the result is 7. If 4 is chosen, the result is 7.
   Conjecture: The number trick always has a result of 7.

n	n
$\times 2$	$2n$
$+ 9$	$2n + 9$
$+ n$	$3n + 9$
$\div 3$	$n + 3$
$+ 4$	$n + 7$
$- n$	7

9. e.g.,
   Let n, $n + 1$, $n + 2$, and $n + 3$ represent any four consecutive natural numbers.
   $$n + (n + 1) + (n + 2) + (n + 3) = 4n + 6$$
   $$n + (n + 1) + (n + 2) + (n + 3) = 2(2n + 3)$$
   Since 2 is a factor of the sum, the sum of four consecutive natural numbers is always even.
10. e.g.,
$(7 + 11)^2 = 324$	$(1 + 10)^2 = 121$	$(3 + 5)^2 = 64$
$7^2 + 11^2 = 170$	$1^2 + 10^2 = 101$	$3^2 + 5^2 = 34$
$(7 + 11)^2 > 7^2 + 11^2$	$(1 + 10)^2 > 1^2 + 10^2$	$(3 + 5)^2 > 3^2 + 5^2$

    Let n and m be any two positive integers.
    The square of the sum of two positive integers:
    $$(n + m)^2 = n^2 + 2mn + m^2$$
    The sum of the squares of two positive integers:
    $$n^2 + m^2$$
    Since $2mn > 0$ for all positive integers,
    $$n^2 + 2mn + m^2 > n^2 + m^2$$
    The square of the sum of two positive integers is greater than the sum of the squares of the same two integers.
11. e.g.,
    Let $2n + 1$ represent any odd integer.
    $$(2n + 1)^2 - (2n + 1) = (4n^2 + 4n + 1) - (2n + 1)$$
    $$(2n + 1)^2 - (2n + 1) = 4n^2 + 2n$$
    $$(2n + 1)^2 - (2n + 1) = 2(2n^2 + n)$$
    Since the difference has a factor of 2, the difference between the square of an odd integer and the integer itself is always even.

Lesson 1.5, page 42

1. e.g.,
   a) The statement "all runners train on a daily basis" is invalid.
   b) The reasoning leading to the conclusion is invalid. Rectangles also have four right angles.
2. e.g., The first line of the proof is invalid.
3. e.g., In line 5, Mickey divides by $(a - b)$, which is invalid because $a - b = 0$.
4. e.g., Noreen's proof is not valid. Neither figure is a triangle, as in each case what appears to be the hypotenuse is actually two segments not along the same line (determine the slope of the hypotenuse of each small triangle to verify). When no pieces overlap, the total area is the sum of the areas of the individual pieces. That total area is 32 square units.
5. Ali did not correctly divide by 2 in line 4.
6. a) e.g., With a street address of 630 and an age of 16:

630	630
$\times 2$	1 260
$+ 7$	1 267
$\times 50$	63 350
$+ 16$	63 366
$- 365$	63 001
$+ 15$	63 016

   b) Connie subtracted the wrong number for days of the year. There are 365 days in the year. Her final expression should be
   $$100n + 350 + a - 365 + 15 = 100n + a$$
   c) The number of the street address is multiplied by 100, making the tens and ones columns 0. The age can be added in without any values being carried.
7. e.g., In line 7, there is a division by 0. Since $a = b$, $a^2 - ab = 0$.

8. e.g., False proofs appear true because each mathematical step involved in the reasoning seems sound. In a false proof, there is one (or more) incorrect steps that are misinterpreted as being correct.

9. e.g., In general, strips of paper have two sides, a back and a front. A mark made on the front will not continue to the back unless the paper is turned over. When joined as described in the question, the piece of paper has only one side and is called a Mobius strip. A single, continuous mark can be made along the paper without turning it over.

10. e.g., The question is misleading. Each person initially paid $10 for the meal, but got $1 back. So, each person paid $9 for the meal. The meal cost $25. The waiter kept $2.
$$3(9) - 2 = 25$$

Lesson 1.6, page 48

1. **a)** inductive   **d)** deductive
   b) deductive   **e)** inductive
   c) inductive

2. e.g., Many solutions are possible. The middle triangle must add up to 15 (e.g., 1, 5, 9; 3, 4, 8) and the outer triangle must add up to 30 (e.g., 2, 3, 4, 6, 7, 8; 1, 2, 5, 6, 7, 9).

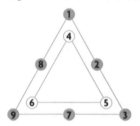

3.

4. **a)** e.g.,

1	2	3
333	666	999
333	666	999
333	666	999
+333	+666	+999
1333	2666	3999

   b) three

5. e.g.,

   a)
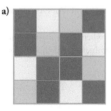

   b) Different approaches to the problem could include deductive reasoning or trial and error.

6. e.g., Let A represent one side of the river and B the other. Move goat to B; return to A. Move wolf to B; return with goat to A. Move hay to B; return. Move goat to B.

7. 28

8. The brother is a liar.

9. Bob is the quarterback, Kurt is the receiver, and Morty is the kicker.

10. e.g.,
    a) The pair 2, 6 cannot be in envelope 8 because the 6 is required for envelope 13 or 14.
    b) deductive

11. $abcd = 2178$

12. e.g.,
    a)
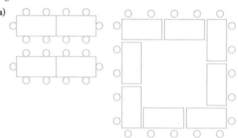

    b) The solution is simple and allows for everyone to be heard.

13. Tamara

14. 35

15. **a)** Suganthy
    b) deductive

16. Pour water from the second pail into the fifth one.

17. e.g., A problem can be solved using inductive reasoning if it has a pattern that can be continued. A problem can be solved using deductive reasoning if general rules can be applied to obtain the solution. It is not always possible to tell which kind of reasoning is needed to solve a problem.

18. 10 days

19. Arlene

20. Pick a fruit from the apples and oranges box. Because the label is incorrect, the fruit picked determines which label goes on this box: apple or orange. Say an orange was picked. Since the labels are incorrect on the two remaining boxes, the box with the apples label is the apples and oranges box, and the box that had the oranges label on it is the apple box.

Lesson 1.7, page 55

1. 120; the pattern is $n(n + 2)$

2. e.g., triple 20, double 3; double 20, double 10, double 3; triple 10, triple 10, double 3

3. e.g., To win, you must leave your opponent with 20, 16, 12, 8, and 4 toothpicks.

4.
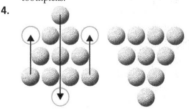

5. **a)** e.g.,
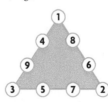

   b) e.g., I determined the possible combinations for 9, 8, and 7. I identified common addends and put those in the triangle's corners and completed the sides.

6. e.g.,
   a) Numbers in each column go up by 3. Numbers in each row go up by 4.

   b)

6	10	14
9	13	17
12	16	20

Selva's observation that the magic sum is three times the number in the middle square holds. My magic sum is 39.

   c) The numbers in any square follow the pattern below.

$n-7$	$n-3$	$n+1$
$n-4$	n	$n+4$
$n-1$	$n+3$	$n+7$

If $n-7$ is chosen, n and $n+7$ may be chosen, or $n+3$ and $n+4$ may be chosen. All possible choices are listed below.
$(n-7) + n + (n+7) = 3n$
$(n-7) + (n+3) + (n+4) = 3n$
$(n-4) + (n-3) + (n+7) = 3n$
$(n-4) + (n+3) + (n+1) = 3n$
$(n-1) + (n-3) + (n+4) = 3n$
$(n-1) + n + (n+1) = 3n$
All choices result in the magic sum, which is three times the number in the middle square.

7. e.g.,
   a) 3 (or 24 for all permutations)
   b) The number in the middle is always odd.
   c) Show that the number in the middle must be odd and that there are eight solutions for each odd number in the middle.

8. e.g., Put the two coins on the same diagonal.

9. Player O started the game.

10. **a)**

5	1	3	2	6	4
2	6	4	5	1	3
1	5	2	3	4	6
3	4	6	1	5	2
6	3	5	4	2	1
4	2	1	6	3	5

   b)

6	3	4	8	2	5	7	9	1
9	5	8	3	7	1	4	6	2
2	7	1	4	6	9	3	5	8
1	4	5	6	8	3	2	7	9
3	6	7	9	1	2	8	4	5
8	9	2	7	5	4	6	1	3
7	1	3	2	9	6	5	8	4
4	8	9	5	3	7	1	2	6
5	2	6	1	4	8	9	3	7

11. **a)**

2	7	6
9	5	1
4	3	8

   b)

2	9	4
7	5	3
6	1	8

12. 20

13.

30× **6**	**5**	36× **3**	2÷ **2**	**1**	18+ **4**
3+ **1**	**2**	**6**	7+ **4**	**3**	**5**
2	20× **4**	**5**	5− **1**	**6**	**3**
1− **5**	2− **3**	**1**	**6**	13+ **4**	**2**
4	7+ **1**	**2**	2− **3**	**5**	**6**
2÷ **3**	**6**	**4**	3− **5**	**2**	**1**

14. e.g., Using inductive reasoning, I can observe a pattern and use it to determine a solution. Using deductive reasoning, I can apply logical rules to help me solve a puzzle or determine a winning strategy for a game.

15. e.g.,
   a) I would play in a spot with the fewest possibilities for placing three of my markers in a row.
   b) Inductive reasoning helps me guess where my opponent will play; deductive reasoning helps me determine where I should play.

Chapter Self-Test, page 58

1. e.g.,
   a) Figure 4 would have one additional cube at the end of each arm, requiring 16 cubes in all. Figure 5 would have 5 cubes more than Figure 4, with one at the end of each arm, requiring 21 cubes in all.
   b) The nth structure would require $5n - 4$ cubes to build it.
   c) 121 cubes

2. His conjecture isn't reasonable: the chance of the coin coming up heads is 50%.

3. e.g., A pentagon with sides of length 2 has a perimeter of 10.

4. Let $2n + 1$ and $2n + 3$ represent two consecutive odd integers. Let P represent the product of these integers.
$P = (2n + 1)(2n + 3)$
$P = 4n^2 + 8n + 3$
$P = 2(2n^2 + 4n) + 3$
$2(2n^2 + 4n)$ is an even integer, 3 is an odd integer, and the sum of any even and odd integer is an odd integer, so the product of any two consecutive odd integers is an odd integer.

5. e.g.,

n	n
$\times 2$	$2n$
$+ 20$	$2n + 20$
$\div 2$	$n + 10$
$- n$	10

6. Darlene, Andy, Candice, Bonnie

7. The proof is valid; all the steps are correct.

Chapter Review, page 61

1. e.g., The diagonals of parallelograms always bisect each other. The diagrams in the question support my conjecture.

2. e.g.,
  a) The difference between consecutive triangular numbers increases by 1: 2, 3, 4, … The next four triangular numbers are 15, 21, 28, and 36.
  b) Each of the products is double the first, second, third, and fourth triangular numbers, respectively.
  c) The nth triangular number could be determined using the formula $\dfrac{n(n + 1)}{2}$.

3. e.g.,
  a) The sum of the cubes of the first n natural numbers is equal to the square of the nth triangular number.
  b) The next equation will be equal to 15^2, or 225.
  c) The sum of the first n cubes will be equal to $\left(\dfrac{n(n + 1)}{2}\right)^2$.

4. e.g.,
  a) $37 \times 15 = 555$
  b) The conjecture is correct.
  c) The breakdown occurs at $37 \times 30 = 1110$.

5. e.g.,
  a) A counterexample is an example that invalidates a conjecture.
  b) Counterexamples can help refine a conjecture to make it valid.

6. Disagree. e.g., Rhombuses and parallelograms have opposite sides of equal length.

7. Disagree. e.g., $5 - 5 = 0$

8. Six is an even number; therefore, its square is also even.

9. e.g.,
Let $2m + 1$ and $2n + 1$ represent any two odd integers.
$(2m + 1)(2n + 1) = 2mn + 2m + 2n + 1$
$(2m + 1)(2n + 1) = 2(mn + m + n) + 1$
The first term has a factor of 2, making it an even number. Adding 1 makes the product odd.

10. **a)** The result is the birth month number followed by the birthday, e.g., 415.

b)

m	m
$\times 5$	$5m$
$+ 7$	$5m + 7$
$\times 4$	$20m + 28$
$+ 13$	$20m + 41$
$\times 5$	$100m + 205$
$+ d$	$100m + 205 + d$
$- 205$	$100m + d$

The birth month is multiplied by 100, leaving enough space for a two-digit birthday.

11. **a)** e.g., Twice the sum of the squares of two numbers is equal to the sum of the squared difference of the numbers and the squared sum of the numbers.
  b) Let n and m represent any two numbers.
$2(n^2 + m^2) = 2n^2 + 2m^2$
$2(n^2 + m^2) = n^2 + n^2 + m^2 + m^2 + 2mn - 2mn$
$2(n^2 + m^2) = (n^2 - 2mn + m^2) + (n^2 + 2mn + m^2)$
$2(n^2 + m^2) = (n - m)^2 + (n + m)^2$
$2(n^2 + m^2) = a^2 + b^2$
Let a represent $n - m$ and b represent $n + m$.
A sum of two squares, doubled, is equal to the sum of two squares.

12. e.g., On the fourth line there is a division by zero, since $a = b$.

13. Julie did not multiply 10 by 5 in the third line.

n	Choose a number.
$n + 10$	Add 10.
$5n + 50$	Multiply the total by 5.
$5n$	Subtract 50.
5	Divide by the number you started with.

14. One of the women is both a mother and a daughter.

15.

Penny Pig	straw	small	Riverview
Peter Pig	sticks	large	Hillsdale
Patricia Pig	brick	medium	Pleasantville

16. e.g., Player X should choose the bottom left corner, then the top left corner, then the middle left or middle, depending on where Player X was blocked.

17. e.g.,
  a) yes
  b) There is no winning strategy in the game of 15. An experienced opponent will always succeed in blocking you.

Chapter 2

Lesson 2.1, page 72

1. e.g.,
   a) Horizontal beams are parallel.
      Vertical supports are parallel.
      Diagonal struts are transversals.
   b) No. The bridge is shown in perspective. Parallel lines on the bridge will not be parallel when they are traced, so corresponding angles will not be equal in the tracing.
2. $\angle EGB = \angle GHD$, $\angle AGE = \angle CHG$, $\angle AGH = \angle CHF$, $\angle BGH = \angle DHF$, $\angle EGA = \angle HGB$, $\angle EGB = \angle HGA$, $\angle GHD = \angle FHC$, $\angle GHC = \angle FHD$, $\angle EGA = \angle FHD$, $\angle EGB = \angle FHC$, $\angle GHD = \angle HGA$, $\angle GHC = \angle BGH$
   Yes, the measures are supplementary.
3. e.g., Draw a line and a transversal, then measure one of the angles between them. Use a protractor to create an equal corresponding angle elsewhere on the same side of the transversal. Use that angle to draw the parallel line.
4. e.g., The top edge of the wood is the transversal for the lines that are drawn. Keeping the angle of the T-bevel the same makes parallel lines because corresponding angles are equal.
5. a) No. Corresponding angles are not equal.
   b) Yes. Corresponding angles are equal.
   c) Yes. Corresponding angles are equal.
   d) No. Corresponding angles are not equal.
6. Disagree. The lines are equidistant from each other. It is an optical illusion.

Lesson 2.2, page 78

1. KP, LQ, MR, and NS are all transversals for the parallel lines WX and YZ.
   $\angle WYD = 90°$; $\angle WYD$ and $\angle AWY$ are interior angles on the same side of KP.
   $\angle YDA = 115°$; $\angle YDA$ and $\angle WAL$ are corresponding angles.
   $\angle DEB = 80°$; $\angle DEB$ and $\angle EBC$ are alternate interior angles.
   $\angle EFS = 45°$; $\angle EFS$ and $\angle NCX$ are alternate exterior angles.
2. a) Yes. Corresponding angles are equal.
   b) No. Interior angles on the same side of the transversal are not supplementary.
   c) Yes. Alternate exterior angles are equal.
   d) Yes. Alternate exterior angles are equal.
3. e.g.,
   a) Alternate interior angles are equal.
   b) Corresponding angles are equal.
   c) Alternate exterior angles are equal.
   d) Vertically opposite angles are equal.
   e) $\angle b$ and $\angle k$ and $\angle m$ are all equal in measure; $\angle b$ and $\angle k$ are corresponding angles, $\angle k$ and $\angle m$ are corresponding angles.
   f) $\angle e$ and $\angle n$ and $\angle p$ are all equal in measure; $\angle e$ and $\angle n$ are corresponding angles, $\angle n$ and $\angle p$ are corresponding angles.
   g) $\angle n$ and $\angle p$ and $\angle d$ are all equal in measure; $\angle n$ and $\angle p$ are corresponding angles, $\angle p$ and $\angle d$ are alternate exterior angles.
   h) $\angle f$ and $\angle k$ are interior angles on the same side of a transversal.
4. a) $\angle x = 60°$, $\angle y = 60°$, $\angle w = 120°$
   b) $\angle a = 112°$, $\angle e = 112°$, $\angle b = 55°$, $\angle d = 55°$, $\angle f = 55°$, $\angle c = 68°$
   c) $\angle a = 48°$, $\angle b = 48°$, $\angle c = 48°$, $\angle d = 48°$, $\angle e = 132°$, $\angle f = 132°$, $\angle g = 132°$

5. e.g.,
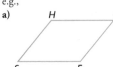
   I drew AB and used a protractor to create a 60° angle at A and at B. I drew BC and created a 120° angle at C, so that CD would be parallel to AB. Then I drew AD to intersect CD.
6. e.g.,
   a)
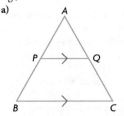
   b) $\angle S = 50°$
      $\angle H + \angle S = 180°$
      $\angle H = 130°$
      $\angle H + \angle O = 180°$
      $\angle O = 50°$
      $\angle S = \angle O$
7. a) e.g., The horizontal lines in the fabric are parallel and the diagonal lines are transversals. The diagonal lines falling to the right are parallel and the diagonal lines rising to the right are transversals.
   b) e.g., A pattern maker could ensure that lines in the pattern are parallel by making the corresponding, alternate exterior, or alternate interior angles equal, or by making the angles on the same side of a transversal supplementary.
8. a) The transitive property is true for parallel lines but not for perpendicular lines.
   b) If $AB \perp BC$ and $BC \perp CD$, then $AB \parallel CD$.
9. e.g., Theoretically, they could measure corresponding angles to see if they were equal.
10. e.g., errors: interior angles should be stated as supplementary, not equal. Since $\angle PQR + \angle QRS = 180°$, the statement that $QP \parallel RS$ is still valid.
11. e.g., The bottom edges of the windows are transversals for the vertical edges of the windows. The sloped roof also forms transversals for the vertical parts of the windows. The builders could ensure one window is vertical and then make all the corresponding angles equal so the rest of the windows are parallel.
12. e.g.,

$SR \parallel XO$	$\angle FOX$ and $\angle FRS$ are equal corresponding angles
$PQ \parallel XO$	$\angle FPQ$ and $\angle FXO$ are equal corresponding angles.
$PQ \parallel SR$	Transitive property

13. e.g.,
    a)
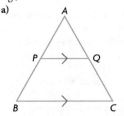
    b)

$\angle APQ = \angle ABC$	Corresponding angles
$\angle AQP = \angle ACB$	Corresponding angles
$\angle PAQ = \angle BAC$	Same angle
$\triangle APQ \sim \triangle ABC$	Corresponding angles in the two triangles are equal.

14. a) $\angle x = 120°$, $\angle y = 60°$, $\angle z = 60°$
b) e.g., Isosceles trapezoids have two pairs of congruent adjacent angles.

15. $\angle PTQ = 78°$, $\angle PQT = 48°$, $\angle RQT = 49°$, $\angle QTR = 102°$, $\angle SRT = 54°$, $\angle PTS = 102°$

16. $\angle ACD = \angle ACF + \angle FCD$
$\angle BAC = \angle ACF$
$\angle CDE = \angle FCD$
$\angle ACD = \angle BAC + \angle CDE$

17. a) Alternate straight paths will be parallel.
b)

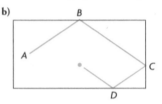

c) $AB \parallel CD$, $BC \parallel DE$
d) Yes, the pattern will continue until the ball comes to rest.

18. e.g.,

$\angle PQR = \angle QRS$	Alternate interior angles
$\frac{1}{2}\angle PQR = \frac{1}{2}\angle QRS$	Equality
$\angle TRQ = \frac{1}{2}\angle PQR$	Angle bisector
$\angle RQU = \frac{1}{2}\angle QRS$	Angle bisector
$\angle TRQ = \angle RQU$	Transitive property
$QU \parallel RT$	Alternate interior angles are equal.

19. e.g.,
a) Disagree; it is enough to show that any one of the statements is true.
b) Yes. Other ways are
$\angle MCD = \angle CDQ$, $\angle XCL = \angle CDQ$, $\angle LCD + \angle CDQ = 180°$, $\angle LCD = \angle QDY$, $\angle MCD = \angle RDY$, $\angle XCM = \angle QDY$, or $\angle XCL = \angle RDY$.

20. a) 8   **b)** 7
21. e.g.,
a) Measure the top angle of the rhombus at the left end of the bottom row; it will be the same size as the angle at the peak.
b) Opposite sides of a rhombus are parallel, so the top right sides of all the rhombuses form parallel lines. The top right side of the peak rhombus and the top right side of the bottom left rhombus are parallel. The left edge of the pyramid is a transversal, so the angle at the peak and the top angle of the bottom left rhombus are equal corresponding angles.

Mid-Chapter Review, page 85

1. a) Yes. Alternate interior angles are equal.
b) No. Interior angles on the same side of the transversal are not supplementary.
c) Yes. Alternate exterior angles are equal.
d) Yes. Vertically opposite angles are equal, and interior angles on the same side of the transversal are supplementary.

2. Quadrilateral $PQRS$ is a parallelogram because interior angles on the same side of the transversal are supplementary.

3. e.g., The red lines are parallel since any of the black lines can be used as a transversal to prove that corresponding angles are equal.
4. e.g.,

I drew $\angle ABC$. I measured it and drew $\angle BCD$ supplementary to it. Then I measured AB, made CD the same length, and connected A to D.

5. a) $\angle FEB = 69°$, $\angle EBD = 69°$, $\angle FBE = 36°$,
$\angle ABF = 75°$, $\angle CBD = 75°$, $\angle BDE = 75°$
b) Yes. e.g., $\angle FEB$ and $\angle EBD$ are equal alternate interior angles.

6. e.g.,
a)

$AC \parallel ED$	$\angle ABE$ and $\angle BED$ are equal alternate interior angles.

b)

$\angle BED = 55°$ and $\angle BFG = \angle BED$, therefore $\angle BFG = 55°$	$\angle BFG$ and $\angle BED$ are corresponding angles in $\triangle BFG \sim \triangle BED$.
$FG \parallel ED$	$\angle BFG$ and $\angle BED$ are equal corresponding angles for FG and ED.

c)

$AC \parallel FG$	$\angle ABF$ and $\angle BFG$ are equal alternate interior angles.

7. e.g., In each row of parking spots, the lines separating each spot are parallel. The line down the centre is the transversal to the two sets of parallel lines.
8. e.g., Yes, the sides are parallel. The interior angles are supplementary and so the lines are always the same distance apart.

Lesson 2.3, page 90

1. No. It only proves the sum is 180° in that one triangle.
2. Disagree. The sum of the three interior angles in a triangle is 180°.
3. a) $\angle YXZ = 79°$, $\angle Z = 37°$
b) $\angle DCE = 46°$, $\angle A = 85°$
4. $\angle R = \frac{1}{2}(180° - n°)$
5. e.g.,

$\angle CDB = 60°$	$\triangle BCD$ is equilateral.
$\angle CDB + \angle BDA = 180°$ $\angle BDA = 120°$	$\angle CDB$ and $\angle BDA$ are supplementary.
$\angle A = \frac{1}{2}(180° - 120°)$ $\angle A = 30°$	Since $\triangle BDA$ is an isosceles triangle, $\angle A$ and $\angle B$ are equal.

6. 120°
7. e.g.,

$\angle ASY = 53°$	Sum of angles in triangle is 180°.
$\angle SAD = 127°$	Given
$\angle ASY + \angle SAD = 180°$	Property of equality
$SY \parallel AD$	Interior angles on the same side of the transversal are supplementary.

8. e.g.,

a) The sum of $\angle a$, $\angle c$, and $\angle e$ is 360°.

b) Yes. $\angle b = \angle a$, $\angle d = \angle c$, $\angle f = \angle e$

c)

$\angle x + \angle a = 180°$ $\angle a = 180° - \angle x$	$\angle x$ and $\angle a$ are supplementary.
$\angle y + \angle c = 180°$ $\angle c = 180° - \angle y$	$\angle y$ and $\angle c$ are supplementary.
$\angle z + \angle e = 180°$ $\angle e = 180° - \angle z$	$\angle z$ and $\angle e$ are supplementary.
$\angle a + \angle c + \angle e$ $= (180° - \angle x) +$ $(180° - \angle y) + (180° - \angle z)$	I substituted the expressions for $\angle a$, $\angle c$, and $\angle e$.
$\angle a + \angle c + \angle e$ $= 540° - (\angle x + \angle y + \angle z)$	
$\angle a + \angle c + \angle e = 540° - 180°$ $\angle a + \angle c + \angle e = 360°$	$\angle x$, $\angle y$, and $\angle z$ are the angles of a triangle so their sum is 180°.

9. e.g.,

a) $\angle D \neq \angle C$

b)

$\angle DKU = \angle KUC$ $\angle DKU = 35°$	$\angle DKU$ and $\angle KUC$ are alternate interior angles.
$\angle DUK = 180° - (100° + 35°)$ $\angle DUK = 45°$	The sum of the angles of $\triangle DUK$ is 180°.
$\angle UKC = 45°$	$\angle DUK$ and $\angle UKC$ are alternate interior angles.
$\angle UCK = 100°$	Opposite angles in a parallelogram are equal.

10. e.g.,

$MA \parallel HT$	$\angle MTH$ and $\angle AMT$ are equal alternate interior angles.
$MH \parallel AT$	$\angle MHT = 70°$ and $\angle HTA = 45° + 65°$ are supplementary interior angles on the same side of transversal HT.

11. $\angle a = 30°$, $\angle b = 150°$, $\angle c = 85°$, $\angle d = 65°$

12. e.g.,

a) Disagree. $\angle FGH$ and $\angle IHJ$ are not corresponding angles, alternate interior angles, or alternate exterior angles.

b)

$\angle GFH = 180° - (55° + 75°)$ $\angle GFH = 50°$	The sum of the angles of $\triangle FGH$ is 180°.
$FG \parallel HI$	$\angle GFH$ and $\angle IHJ$ are equal corresponding angles.

13. $\angle J = 110°$, $\angle M = 110°$, $\angle JKO = 40°$, $\angle NOK = 40°$, $\angle KLN = 40°$, $\angle LNM = 40°$, $\angle MLN = 30°$, $\angle JOK = 30°$, $\angle LNO = 140°$, $\angle KLM = 70°$, $\angle JON = 70°$

14. $\angle UNF = 31°$, $\angle NFU = 65°$, $\angle FUN = 84°$

15. **a)** $\angle AXZ = 145°$, $\angle XYC = 85°$, $\angle EZY = 130°$

b) 360°

16. e.g.,

MO and NO are angle bisectors.	Given
$\angle LNP$ is an exterior angle for $\triangle LMN$.	
$\angle L + 2a = 2b$ $\angle L = 2b - 2a$ $\angle L = 2(b - a)$	An exterior angle is equal to the sum of the non-adjacent interior angles.
$\angle ONP$ is an exterior angle for $\triangle MNO$.	
$\angle O + a = b$ $\angle O = b - a$	An exterior angle is equal to the sum of the non-adjacent interior angles.

$\angle L = 2(b - a)$ $\angle O = b - a$ $\angle L = 2\angle O$	Substitution

17. e.g., Drawing a parallel line through one of the vertices and parallel to one of the sides creates three angles whose sum is 180°. The two outside angles are equal to the alternate interior angles in the triangle. The middle angle is the third angle in the triangle. Therefore, the three angles in the triangle add up to 180°.

$\angle PAB = \angle ABC$

$\angle QAC = \angle ACB$

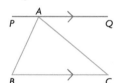

18. e.g.,

$\angle DAB + \angle ABD + \angle BDA = 180°$	The sum of the angles of $\triangle ABD$ is 180°.
$2\angle x + (90° + \angle y) + \angle y = 180°$ $2\angle x + 2\angle y = 90°$ $\angle x + \angle y = 45°$	
$\angle AEB = \angle x + \angle y$	$\angle AEB$ is an exterior angle for $\triangle AED$, so it is equal to the sum of the non-adjacent interior angles.
$\angle AEB = 45°$	Substitute $\angle x + \angle y = 45°$.

19. e.g.,

$\angle DLR = \angle LMN$	Corresponding angles
$\angle RLN = \angle LNM$	Alternate interior angles
$\angle LMN = \angle LNM$	Isosceles triangle
$\angle DLR = \angle RLN$	Transitive property

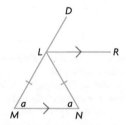

Lesson 2.4, page 99

1. **a)** 1800° **b)** 150°

2. 3240°

3. 19

4. e.g., The interior angles of a hexagon equal 120°. Three hexagons will fit together since the sum is 360°.

5. Yes. e.g., You can align parallel sides to create a tiling pattern; the angles that meet are the four angles of the parallelogram, so their sum is 360°.

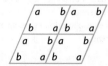

6. about 147°

7. e.g.,

a) $\dfrac{180°(n-2)}{n} = 140°$

$180°(n-2) = 140°n$

$180°n - 360° = 140°n$

$40°n = 360°$

$n = 9$

b) There are 9 exterior angles that measure
$180° - 140° = 40°$; $9(40°) = 360°$.

8. **a)** 45° **c)** 1080°
b) 135° **d)** 1080°

9. **a)** Agree
b) e.g., Opposite sides are parallel in a regular polygon that has an even number of sides.

10. **a)** 36° **b)** isosceles triangle

11. The numerator of the formula for $S(10)$ should be $180°(10-2)$; $S(10) = 144°$.

12. **a)** e.g., A single line drawn anywhere through the polygon. For convex polygons, it intersects two sides only. For non-convex polygons, it can intersect in more than two sides.
b) If any diagonal is exterior to the polygon, the polygon is non-convex.

13. **a)**

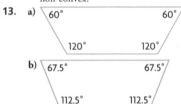

b)

14. 110°, 120°, 90°, 110°, 110°

15. 360°

16. **a)** $\angle a = 60°$, $\angle b = 60°$, $\angle d = 60°$, $\angle c = 120°$
b) $\angle a = 140°$, $\angle b = 20°$, $\angle c = 60°$, $\angle d = 60°$

17. 720°

18. e.g.,

$\triangle EOD \cong \triangle DOC$	$EO = DO$ and $DO = CO$ are given, and $ED = DC$ because the polygon is regular.
$\angle ODE = \angle ODC$ and $\angle ODE = \angle OED$	$\triangle EOD$ and $\triangle DOC$ are congruent and isosceles.
$\angle ODE + \angle ODC = 108°$	The interior angles of a regular pentagon are 108°.
$2\angle ODE = 108°$ $\angle ODE = 54°$ $\angle OED = 54°$	$\angle ODE = \angle ODC$ and $\angle ODE = \angle OED$
$\angle EAD = \angle EDA$	$\triangle ADE$ is isosceles because the polygon is regular.
$180° = \angle DEA + \angle EAD + \angle ADE$ $180° = 108° + 2\angle ADE$ $180° - 108° = 2\angle ADE$ $36° = \angle ADE$	
$180° = \angle FED + \angle EDF + \angle EFD$ $180° = 54° + 36° + \angle EFD$ $180° - 54° - 36° = \angle EFD$ $90° = \angle EFD$	$\angle EDF = \angle ADE$ and $\angle FED = \angle OED$

19. e.g., If a polygon is divided into triangles by joining one vertex to each of the other vertices, there are always two fewer triangles than the original number of sides. Every triangle has an angle sum of 180°.

20. Yes, e.g., A tiling pattern can be created by putting four 90° angles together or three 120° angles together.

21. regular dodecagon

Lesson 2.5, page 106

1. **a)** SSS
b) ASA, because you can determine the third angle.
c) SAS
d) SSS, because they are right triangles, you can use Pythagorean theorem to find the third side.

2. **a)** Yes, because you can determine the measure of the third angle, so the triangles are congruent by ASA.
b) No, because you don't know the length of any sides. These triangles will be similar, but there is no guarantee that they are congruent.

3. **a)** $AB = XY$; $\angle A = \angle X$; $AC = XZ$, so $\triangle ABC \cong \triangle XYZ$ by SAS
b) $FH = JK$; $\angle H = \angle K$; $HG = KL$, so $\triangle FHG \cong \triangle JKL$ by SAS
c) $CA = BU$; $AR = US$; $CR = BS$, so $\triangle CAR \cong \triangle BUS$ by SSS
d) $\angle O = \angle A$; $OG = AT$; $\angle G = \angle T$, so $\triangle DOG \cong \triangle CAT$ by ASA

4. Yes, e.g., If $XY < YZ$, then it is possible that two different triangles can be drawn. For example, in the diagram, two triangles are shown given that information: $\triangle XYZ$ and $\triangle SYZ$.

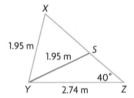

Lesson 2.6, page 112

1. **a)** $\triangle SLY \cong \triangle FOX$ (ASA)
b) Triangles cannot be proven congruent (SSA is not a congruence theorem).
c) $\triangle PET \cong \triangle DOG$ (SAS)
d) $\triangle RED \cong \triangle SUN$ (SSS)

2. **a)** $\angle CDB = \angle ABD$ (alternate interior angles); $DB = BD$ (common); $\angle CBD = \angle ADB$ (alternate interior angles); $\triangle CDB \cong \triangle ABD$ by ASA
b) $\angle POY = \angle NOY$ (given); $OY = OY$ (common); $\angle PYA = \angle NYA$, so $\angle PYO = \angle NYO$ (supplements of equal angles are also equal); $\triangle POY \cong \triangle NOY$ by ASA
c) $JL = NL$ (given); $\angle JLK = \angle NLM$ (vertically opposite angles); $KL = ML$ (given); $\triangle JLK \cong \triangle NLM$ by SAS

3. **a)** e.g., Yes, they appear to have the same size and shape.
b) e.g., Measure the length of the base of the triangle. Measure the angles next to the base, ASA.

4. e.g.,

$\angle T = \angle C$	Given
$TI = CA$	Given
$\angle I = \angle A$	Given
$\triangle TIN \cong \triangle CAN$	ASA
$IN = AN$	If two triangles are congruent, their corresponding parts are equal.

5. e.g.,

$TQ = PQ$	Given
$\angle TQR = \angle PQS$	Vertically opposite angles
$RQ = SQ$	Given
$\triangle TQR \cong \triangle PQS$	SAS
$TR = PS$	If two triangles are congruent, their corresponding parts are equal.

6. e.g.,

WY bisects $\angle XWZ$ and $\angle XYZ$	Given
$\angle XWY = \angle ZWY$	Each angle is $\frac{1}{2}$ of $\angle XWZ$.
$WY = WY$	Common side
$\angle XYW = \angle ZYW$	Each angle is $\frac{1}{2}$ of $\angle XYZ$.
$\triangle XWY \cong \triangle ZWY$	ASA
$XY = ZY$	If two triangles are congruent, their corresponding parts are equal.

7. e.g.,

$\angle PRQ = \angle PSQ$	Given
$\triangle PRS$ is isosceles.	Base angles are equal.
$PR = PS$	Two sides of an isosceles triangle are equal.
Q is the midpoint of RS.	Given
$RQ = SQ$	Midpoint cuts RS in half.
$QP = QP$	Common side
$\triangle PRQ \cong \triangle PSQ$	SSS
$\angle PQR = \angle PQS$	If two triangles are congruent, their corresponding parts are equal.
$\angle PQR + \angle PQS = 180°$	They form a straight line.
$\angle PQR = 90°$ and $\angle PQS = 90°$	Two angles that are equal and have a sum of $180°$ must each be $90°$.
$PQ \perp RS$	PQ and RS form $90°$ angles.

8. e.g.,

a)

$QP \perp PR; SR \perp RP$	Given
$\triangle QPR$ and $\triangle SRP$ are right triangles.	$QP \perp PR; SR \perp RP$
$PR = PR$	Common side
$QR = SP$	Given
In $\triangle QPR$: $QP^2 = QR^2 - PR^2$	Pythagorean theorem
In $\triangle SRP$: $SR^2 = SP^2 - PR^2$	Pythagorean theorem
$SR^2 = QR^2 - PR^2$	Substitution; $QR = SP$
$\therefore SR^2 = QP^2$ and $SR = QP$	Transitive property
$\therefore \triangle QPR \cong \triangle SRP$	SSS
$\angle PQR = \angle RSP$	If two triangles are congruent, then their corresponding angles are equal.

b)

$QP \perp PR; SR \perp RP$	Given
$\triangle QPR$ and $\triangle SRP$ are right triangles.	$QP \perp PR; SR \perp RP$
$PR = PR$	Common side
In $\triangle QPR$: $\sin \angle PQR = \frac{PR}{QR}$ In $\triangle SRP$: $\sin \angle RSP = \frac{PR}{PS}$ $QR = SP$	Given
$\frac{PR}{QR} = \frac{PR}{PS}$	$PR = PR$ and $QR = SP$, so the ratios are equal.
$\therefore \sin \angle PQR = \sin \angle RSP$	Transitive property
$\angle PQR$ and $\angle RSP$ are both acute angles.	Each angle is in a right triangle.
$\angle PQR = \angle RSP$	If the sines of two acute angles are equal, the angles must be equal.

9. e.g.,

$\angle ABC = \angle DEC$	Given
$\angle ACB = \angle DCE$	Vertically opposite angles
$\angle ABC + \angle ACB + \angle BAC = \angle DEC + \angle DCE + \angle EDC$	Sum of angles of a triangle is $180°$.
$\angle BAC = \angle EDC$	Since two pairs of angles of two triangles are equal, the third pair of angles must also be equal.
$AB = DE$	Given
$\triangle ABC \cong \triangle DEC$	ASA
$BC = EC$	If triangles are congruent, then their corresponding sides are equal.
$\triangle BCE$ is isosceles.	Two sides of the triangle are equal.

10. e.g.,

MT is the diameter of the circle.	Given
$\angle MAT = 90°$ and $\angle MHT = 90°$	An angle inscribed in a semicircle is $90°$.
$TA = TH$	Given
$MT = MT$	Common side
$AM = HM$	If two sides of two right triangles are equal, by using Pythagorean theorem, the third sides will be equal.
$\triangle MAT \cong \triangle MHT$	SSS
$\therefore \angle AMT = \angle HMT$	If two triangles are congruent, their corresponding angles are equal.

11. Duncan's proof contains two errors: $\angle ABF$ and $\angle DCE$ are not alternate interior angles. Also, he used AE and DF as sides of the two triangles. The sides are AF and DE.

Corrected Proof:

$AB \parallel CD$	Given
$\angle BAF = \angle CDE$	Alternate interior angles
$BF \parallel CE$	Given
$\angle BFA = \angle CED$	Alternate interior angles
$AE = DF$	Given
$EF = EF$	Common side
$\therefore AF = DE$	Segment addition
$\triangle BAF \cong \triangle CDE$	ASA

12. e.g.,

In △ACD, ∠ACD = ∠ADC	Given
△ACD is isosceles.	Base angles are equal.
AC = AD	Two sides of isosceles triangle are equal.
∠ACB + ∠ACD = 180°; ∠ADE + ∠ADC = 180°	The angles form a straight line.
∠ACB + ∠ACD = ∠ADE + ∠ADC	Transitive property
∠ACB = ∠ADE	Subtraction
CB = DE	Given
△ABC ≅ △AED	SAS

13. e.g.,

TA = ME	Given
∠MEA = ∠TAE	Given
AE = EA	Common side
△TEA ≅ △MAE	SAS
∠TEA = ∠MAE	Corresponding angles in congruent triangles are equal.
∠TEA − ∠MEA = ∠MAE − ∠TAE	Subtraction
∠TEM = ∠MAT	Substitution

14. e.g.,

GH⊥HL; ML⊥HL	Given
∠GHK = 90° and ∠MLJ = 90°	Perpendicular lines meet at right angles.
HJ = LK	Given
JK = KJ	Common side
HJ + JK = LK + KJ	Addition
HK = LJ	Substitution
GH = ML	Given
△GHK ≅ △MLJ	SAS
∠NKJ = ∠NJK	Corresponding angles in congruent triangles are equal.
△NJK is isosceles.	Base angles are equal.

15. e.g.,

PQ = PT	Given
△PQT is isosceles.	An isosceles triangle has two equal sides.
∠PQT = ∠PTQ	Base angles of isosceles triangle are equal.
QS = TR	Given
△PQS = △PTR	SAS
∠PSR ≅ ∠PRS	Corresponding angles in congruent triangles are equal.
△PRS is isosceles.	Base angles are equal.

16. e.g., Draw a diagram of a section of the crane's arm.

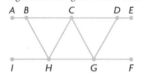

AE ∥ IF	Given
BH, HC, CG, and GD are all the same length.	Given
△HBC, △CHG and △GCD are isosceles.	Two sides are equal in each triangle.
∠CBH = ∠BCH ∠CHG = ∠CGH ∠DCG = ∠CDG	Base angles in an isosceles triangle are equal.
∠BCH = ∠CHG ∠CGH = ∠DCG	Alternate interior angles
∠CBH = ∠CHG ∠BCH = ∠CGH ∠CDG = ∠CGH ∠DCG = ∠CHG	Transitive property
∠BHC = ∠HCG ∠HCG = ∠CGD ∠BHC = ∠CGD	If two sets of angles in two triangles are equal, the third set is equal.
∴ △HBC ≅ △CHG, △HBC ≅ △GCD, △CHG ≅ △GCD	ASA
Since the crane is built so that all diagonal truss supports are equal, the rest of the triangles can be proven congruent in the same way.	

17. e.g.,

QA = QB	Given
∠Q = ∠Q	Common angle
AR = BS	Given
QA + AR = QB + BS	Addition
QR = QS	Substitution
△RQB ≅ △SQA	SAS
RB = SA	Corresponding sides of congruent triangles are equal.

18. Answers will vary.

19. e.g., Draw a parallelogram, *MILK*, with diagonals intersecting at *Y*.

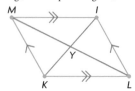

MI ‖ LK; MK ‖ IL	MILK is a parallelogram.
∠MIK = ∠LKI ∠LIK = ∠MKI	Alternate interior angles
IK = KI	Common side
△MIK ≅ △LKI	ASA
MI = LK	Corresponding sides of congruent triangles are equal.
∠IML = ∠KLM	Alternate interior angles
△MIY ≅ △LKY	ASA
MY = LY; IY = KY	Corresponding sides of congruent triangles are equal.
∴ Diagonals ML and IK bisect each other at Y.	MY = LY; IY = KY

20. e.g., Draw a rhombus, *ABCD*, with diagonals intersecting at *E*.

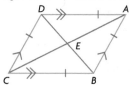

ABCD is a rhombus.	Given
DA ‖ BC; CD ‖ BA	Opposite sides of a rhombus are parallel.
AB = BC = CD = DA	All sides of a rhombus are equal.
∠ADE = ∠CBE; ∠DAE = ∠BCE	Alternate interior angles
△DAE ≅ △BCE	ASA
DE = BE; CE = AE	Corresponding parts of congruent triangles are equal.
∴ DB and CA bisect each other at E.	Definition of bisect
△DAE ≅ △BCE ≅ △BAE ≅ △DCE	SSS
∴ ∠AED = ∠CEB = ∠AEB = ∠CED	Corresponding parts of congruent triangles are equal.
∠AED + ∠CEB + ∠AEB + ∠CED = 360°	They form 2 pairs of supplementary angles.
∴ ∠AED = ∠CEB = ∠AEB = ∠CED = 90°	Algebra
∴ diagonals DB and CA are perpendicular to each other.	Definition of perpendicular

Chapter Self-Test, page 116

1. **a)** $a = 70°$, $b = 75°$, $c = 75°$
b) $a = 20°$, $b = 80°$, $c = 100°$
2. **a)** $x = 19°$ **b)** $x = 26°$

3. **a)** and **c)** e.g.,

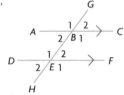

4. regular hexagons: six 120° angles; small triangles: three 60° angles; large triangles: one 120° angle and two 30° angles.
5. **a)**

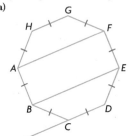

b) 45°
c) e.g.,

Extend BC to form exterior angles ∠ABI and ∠DCJ.	
∠ABI = 45° ∠DCJ = 45°	Exterior angles of a regular octagon
BE ‖ CD	Alternate exterior angles are equal.
∠CBE = 45°	Alternate interior angles
∠ABE = 90°	Supplementary angles
Similarly, by extending AH and following the process above, ∠FAB = 90°.	
∠ABE + ∠FAB = 180°	
AF ‖ BE	Interior angles on the same side of the transversal are supplementary.

6. e.g.,

OY = OZ	Radii of circle, centred at O
YX = ZX	Given
OX = OX	Common side
△OXY ≅ △OXZ	SSS
∠OXY = ∠OXZ	Corresponding angles of congruent triangles are equal.

7. e.g.,

LM = NO	Given
∠LMO = ∠NOM	Given
MO = OM	Common side
△LMO ≅ △NOM	SAS
∠LOM = ∠NMO	Corresponding angles of congruent triangles are equal.
LO ‖ MN	Alternate interior angles
LM ‖ ON	Alternate interior angles
LMNO is a parallelogram.	Opposite sides are parallel.

Chapter Review, page 119

1. e.g., The side bars coming up to the handle are parallel and the handle is a transversal.
2. **a)** ∠a, ∠e; ∠b, ∠g; ∠c, ∠f; ∠d, ∠h
b) No. e.g., The lines are not parallel, so corresponding pairs cannot be equal.

c) 8; e.g., $\angle a$, $\angle b$

d) Yes; $\angle a$, $\angle d$; $\angle b$, $\angle c$; $\angle e$, $\angle h$; $\angle f$, $\angle g$

3. $\angle a = 35°$, $\angle b = 145°$

4.

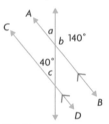

$\angle a + \angle b = 180°$	$\angle a$ and $\angle b$ form a straight angle.
$\angle a = 40°$	Substitution and subtraction
$\angle c = 40°$	Given
$\angle a = \angle c$	Corresponding angles are equal.
$AB \parallel CD$	

5. **a)** $a = 104°$, $b = 76°$, $c = 76°$

b) $a = 36°$, $b = 108°$, $c = 108°$

6. e.g.,

a)

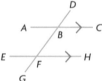

b) Measure $\angle ABF$ and $\angle BFH$. Measure $\angle DBA$ and $\angle BFE$. Both pairs should be equal.

7. e.g.,

$\angle QRS = \angle RST$	Alternate interior angles
$\angle QRS = \angle TRS$	Given
$\angle RST = \angle TRS$	Transitive property
$TS = TR$	Isosceles triangle

8. **a)** $x = 40°$, $y = 95°$, $z = 45°$

b) $x = 68°$, $y = 112°$, $z = 40°$

9. e.g.,

$\angle OPL = \angle POL$ $\angle OQN = \angle NOQ$	$\triangle OPL$ and $\triangle NOQ$ are isosceles.
$\angle PLO = 180° - (\angle POL + \angle OPL)$ $\angle QNO = 180° - (\angle NOQ + \angle OQN)$	The sum of the angles in each triangle is 180°.
$\angle PLO = 180° - 2\angle POL$ $\angle QNO = 180° - 2\angle NOQ$	Substitute $\angle OPL = \angle POL$ and $\angle OQN = \angle NOQ$.
$\angle PLO + \angle QNO = 180° - 90°$ $\angle PLO + \angle QNO = 90°$	$\angle PLO$ and $\angle QNO$ are the two acute angles in the right triangle LMN.
$(180° - 2\angle POL) +$ $(180° - 2\angle NOQ) = 90°$	Substitute the expressions for $\angle PLO$ and $\angle QNO$.
$\angle POL + \angle NOQ = 135°$	Isolate $\angle POL + \angle NOQ$ in the equation.
$\angle POQ = 45°$	$\angle POQ$, $\angle POL$, and $\angle NOQ$ are supplementary because they form a straight line.

10. **a)** 2340°

b) e.g., The sum of the 15 exterior angles is 360°, so each exterior angle is 360° ÷ 15 = 24°.

11. e.g.,

$\angle ABC = 108°$, $\angle BCD = 108°$, $\angle CDE = 108°$	The angles in a regular pentagon are 108°.
$\angle BCA + \angle BAC = 180° - 108°$	The sum of the angles of $\triangle ABC$ is 180°.
$2\angle BCA = 72°$ $\angle BCA = 36$	$\triangle ABC$ is isosceles with $\angle BCA = \angle BAC$.
$\angle ACD = \angle BCD - \angle BCA$ $\angle ACD = 108° - 36°$ $\angle ACD = 72°$	$\angle BCA + \angle ACD = \angle BCD$
$AC \parallel ED$	$\angle ACD = 72°$ and $\angle CDE = 108°$ are supplementary interior angles on the same side of the transversal CD.

12. $\triangle ABC \cong \triangle YXZ$ by ASA; $\triangle QRS \cong \triangle HJI$ by SAS; $\triangle DEF \cong \triangle MLN$ by SAS

13. **a)** $BC = XY$ or $\angle A = \angle Z$

b) $QR = GH$ or $\angle P = \angle F$

14. e.g.,

$XY = WZ$	Given
$YO = ZO$	Property of radii of a circle
$WO = XO$	Property of radii of a circle
$\triangle XYO \cong \triangle WZO$	SSS

15. e.g.,

$QT = SR$	Given
$\angle QTR = \angle SRT$	Given
$TR = TR$	Common side
$\triangle RTS \cong \triangle TRS$	SAS
$QR = ST$	$\triangle RTS \cong \triangle TRQ$

16. e.g.,

$\angle DAB = \angle CBA$	Right angles are equal.
$\angle DBA = \angle CAB$	Given
$AB = AB$	Common side
$\triangle DAB \cong \triangle CBA$	ASA
$\angle ADB = \angle BCA$	$\triangle DAB \cong \triangle CBA$

17. e.g.,

$LO = NM$	Given
$ON = ML$	Given
$LN = LN$	Common side
$\triangle LON \cong \triangle NML$	SSS $\cong$
$\angle OLN = \angle MNL$	$\triangle LON \cong \triangle NML$
$LO \parallel NM$	Alternate interior angles $\angle OLN = \angle MNL$

18. a) Step 3 is incorrect. $\triangle ADE$ is isosceles, but this cannot be used to show the equality of angles that are not part of the triangle.

b) e.g.,

$AB = AC$	·Given
$AD = AE$	Given
$\angle A = \angle A$	Common angle
$\triangle ABE \cong \triangle ACD$	SAS
$\angle DBF = \angle ECF$	$\triangle ABE \cong \triangle ACD$
$DB = EC$	Given
$\angle DFB = \angle EFC$	Vertically opposite angles
$\angle FDB = 180° - (\angle DBF + \angle DFB)$	Sum of angles in a triangle is 180°
$\angle FEC = 180° - (\angle ECF + \angle EFC)$	Sum of angles in a triangle is 180°
$\angle FEC = 180° - (\angle DBF + \angle DFB)$	Substitution
$\angle FDB = \angle FEC$	Transitive property
$\triangle DBF \cong \triangle ECF$	ASA
$BF = CF$	$\triangle DBF \cong \triangle ECF$

19. e.g.,

$DE = DG$	Given
$EF = GF$	Given
$DF = DF$	Common side
$\triangle DEF \cong \triangle DGF$	SSS
$EF = GF$	Given
$\angle EFH = \angle GFH$	$\triangle DEF \cong \triangle DGF$
$FH = FH$	Common side
$\triangle EFH \cong \triangle GFH$	SAS
$EH = GH$	$\triangle EFH \cong \triangle GFH$

Cumulative Review, Chapters 1–2, page 124

1. e.g.,
a) A conjecture is a testable expression that is based on available evidence but is not yet proven.
b) Inductive reasoning involves looking at examples, and by finding patterns and observing properties, a conjecture may be made.
c) The first few examples may have the same property, but that does not mean that all other cases will have the same property. e.g., Conjecture: The difference of consecutive perfect cubes is always a prime number.
$2^3 - 1^3 = 7$ $5^3 - 4^3 = 61$
$3^3 - 2^3 = 19$ $6^3 - 5^3 = 91$,
$4^3 - 3^3 = 37$ 91 is not a prime number.

2. Yes, her conjecture is reasonable.

3. One. e.g., Conjecture: All prime numbers are odd numbers. 2 is a prime number but is not odd.

4. Agree. e.g., The triangles across from each other at the point where the diagonals intersect are congruent. This makes the alternate interior angles equal, so the opposite sides are parallel.

5. a) Conjecture: The sum of two odd numbers is always an even number.
b) e.g., Let $2n + 1$ and $2k + 1$ represent any two odd numbers.
$(2n + 1) + (2k + 1) = 2n + 2k + 2 = 2(n + k + 1)$
$2(n + k + 1)$ is an even number.

6. e.g.,

Instruction	Result
Choose a number.	x
Double it.	$2x$
Add 9.	$2x + 9$
Add the number you started with.	$2x + 9 + x = 3x + 9$
Divide by 3.	$\dfrac{(3x + 9)}{3} = x + 3$
Add 5.	$x + 3 + 5 = x + 8$
Subtract the number you started with.	$(x + 8) - x = 8$

7. a) The number of circles in the nth figure is $1 + 5(n - 1) = 5n - 4$; there are 71 circles in the 15th figure.
b) Inductive. A pattern in the first few cases was used to come up with a formula for the general case.

8. Let $ab0$ represent the three digit number. Then, $ab0 = 100a + 10b = 10(10a + b)$, which is divisible by 10.

9. e.g., Turn one of the switches on for a short period of time and then turn it off. Turn on another of the switches and leave it on. Enter the room. Check which of the two light bulbs that is off is still warm. This light belongs to the switch that was turned on and then off. The light bulb that is on belongs to the switch that was left on. The last light bulb belongs to the last switch.

10. a) $\angle a = 75°$, $\angle b = 105°$, $\angle c = 105°$, $\angle d = 105°$
b) $\angle a = 50°$, $\angle f = 50°$, $\angle b = 55°$, $\angle e = 55°$, $\angle c = 75°$, $\angle d = 75°$
c) $\angle x = 50°$, $\angle y = 60°$
d) $\angle a \doteq 128.6°$, $\angle b \doteq 51.4°$

11. e.g., equal alternate interior angles, $\angle AEF = \angle DFE$.

12. a) 540°
b) 108°
c) 360°

13. e.g.,

$LO = MN$	Given
$\angle OLN = \angle MNL$	Alternate interior angles
$\angle LOM = \angle NMO$	Alternate interior angles
$\triangle LOP \cong \triangle NMP$	ASA

14. e.g.,

$\angle ADC = \angle CEA$	Right angles are equal.
$AC = AC$	Common side
$\angle CAB = \angle ACB$	$\triangle ABC$ is isosceles.
$\angle EAC = 180° - (\angle CEA + \angle ECA)$	Sum of angles in a triangle is 180°
$\angle DCA = 180° - (\angle ADC + \angle DAC)$	Sum of angles in a triangle is 180°
$\angle DCA = 180° - (\angle CEA + \angle ECA)$	Substitution
$\angle EAC = \angle DCA$	Transitive property
$\triangle ADC \cong \triangle CEA$	ASA
$AE = CD$	$\triangle ADC \cong \triangle CEA$

Chapter 3

Lesson 3.1, page 131

1. **a) i)**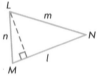

ii) $h = m \sin N$, $h = n \sin M$
$$\frac{m}{\sin M} = \frac{n}{\sin N}$$

b) i)

ii) $h = z \sin X$, $h = x \sin Z$
$$\frac{x}{\sin X} = \frac{z}{\sin Z}$$

2. **a) i)**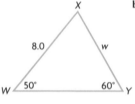

ii) $w = 7.1$

b) i)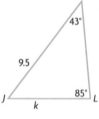

ii) $k = 6.5$

c) i)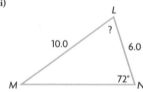

ii) $\angle M = 34.8°$

d) i)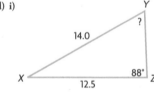

ii) $\angle Y = 63.2°$

3. Agree. $\sin X = \dfrac{h}{y}$ $\sin Y = \dfrac{h}{x}$
$h = y \sin X$ $h = x \sin Y$
$\therefore y \sin X = x \sin Y$

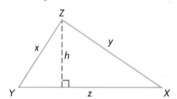

4. e.g., You need two sides and the angle opposite one of the sides or two angles and any side.

5. e.g., Yes, the ratios are equivalent.

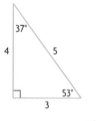

$$\frac{3}{\sin 37°} = 5$$
$$\frac{4}{\sin 53°} = 5$$
$$\frac{5}{\sin 90°} = 5$$

$$\frac{5}{\sin 23°} = 13$$
$$\frac{12}{\sin 67°} = 13$$
$$\frac{13}{\sin 90°} = 13$$

Lesson 3.2, page 138

1. $\dfrac{q}{\sin Q} = \dfrac{r}{\sin R} = \dfrac{s}{\sin S}$

2. **a)** $b = 37.9$ cm   **b)** $\theta = 61°$

3. **a)** $d = 21.0$ cm   **d)** $\theta = 64°$
b) $a = 26.1$ cm, $b = 35.2$ cm   **e)** $\theta = 45°$, $\alpha = 85°$
c) $y = 6.5$ cm   **f)** $\theta = 25°$, $\alpha = 75°$, $j = 6.6$ m

4. **a)** e.g., The lake's length is opposite the largest angle of the triangle and must also be the longest side. A length of 36 km would not make it the longest side.
b) 48.7 km

5. 32 ft 5 in.

6. **a)**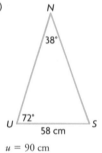

$u = 90$ cm

b)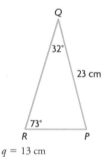

$q = 13$ cm

c)

$\angle M = 43°$

d)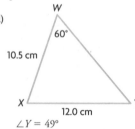

$\angle Y = 49°$

7. $a = 41.9$ m, $t = 44.9$ m, $\angle A = 67°$

8. **a) i)** $\sin 36.9 = \dfrac{n}{10}$, $n = 6.0$ cm

ii) $\dfrac{10}{\sin 90°} = \dfrac{n}{\sin 36.9°}$, $n = 6.0$ cm

b) e.g., Since $\sin 90° = 1$, you can rearrange the sine law formula to give the expression for the sine ratio.

9. a) Gimli

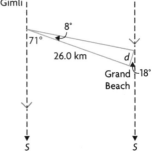

b) 3.6 km

10. a) e.g.,

b) The wires are 12.2 m and 16.7 m long, and the pole is 11.8 m high.

11. e.g., Use the Pythagorean theorem to determine the value of q, then use a primary trigonometric ratio to determine $\angle P$. $\sin P = \dfrac{8}{q} = \dfrac{8}{10}$

Use the Pythagorean theorem to determine the value of q, then use the sine law to determine $\angle P$. $\dfrac{8}{\sin P} = \dfrac{10}{\sin 90°}$

12. 11.4 km

13. 24.8 m

14. e.g.,

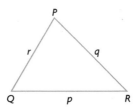

a) $\angle P, \angle R, q$

b) $\angle P, q, r$

15. Agree. Jim needs to know an angle and its opposite side.

16. e.g., You can determine $\angle R$ since the sum of the three angles of a triangle is 180°; you can use the sine law to determine q and r.

17. 19.7 square units

18. 10.2 cm

19. e.g.,

a) $\dfrac{a}{b}$ **b)** $\dfrac{\sin A}{\sin C}$ **c)** 1

Mid-Chapter Review, page 143

1. $\dfrac{x}{\sin X} = \dfrac{y}{\sin Y} = \dfrac{z}{\sin Z}$ or $\dfrac{\sin X}{x} = \dfrac{\sin Y}{y} = \dfrac{\sin Z}{z}$

2. a) e.g.,   **b)** $x = 8.8$

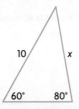

3. e.g., Disagree; you can't rearrange Nazir's expression so that f and $\sin F$ are in one ratio and d and $\sin D$ are in the other.

4. a) $x = 5.9$ cm, $\theta = 42.9°$

b) $x = 10.6$ cm, $y = 9.7$ cm, $\theta = 62.0°$

5. a) $\angle C = 60°$, $b = 12.2$ cm, $c = 13.8$ cm

b) $\angle L = 85°$, $l = 32.9$ cm, $m = 32.7$ cm

6. e.g., The value of either $\angle X$ or $\angle Z$ is needed to solve the triangle.

7. a) The tower at B is closer. e.g., The distance from tower B to the fire is length a, which is across from the smaller angle.

b) 3.1 km

8. 631 m

9. a) 84.2 cm   **b)** 82.3 cm

Lesson 3.3, page 150

1. a) No   **b)** Yes

2. 13 cm

3. $\angle P = 72°$

4. a) 6.9 cm   **b)** 14.7 cm

5. a) 34°   **b)** 74°

6. e.g.,

a)   **b)**

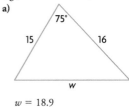   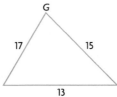

$w = 18.9$ $k = 28.4$

c)   **d)**

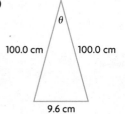   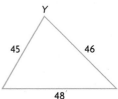

$\angle Y = 63.7°$ $\angle G = 47.4°$

7. a) $f = 6.3$ cm, $\angle D = 45.9°$, $\angle E = 69.1°$

b) $r = 10.1$ m, $\angle P = 38.6°$, $\angle Q = 61.4°$

c) $\angle L = 86.6°$, $\angle M = 56.6°$, $\angle N = 36.8°$

d) $\angle X = 75.2°$, $\angle Y = 48.0°$, $\angle Z = 56.8°$

8. a)   **b)** 5.5°

9. 53.0 cm

10. e.g., You can use the cosine law; the 70° angle is one of the acute angles across from the shorter diagonal. It is contained between an 8 cm side and a 15 cm side.

11. a) i) about 17 cm

ii) about 17 cm

b) e.g., The hour and minute hands are the same distance apart at 2:00 and 10:00, and the triangles formed are congruent.

12. No. e.g., When you put the side lengths into the cosine law expression, you do not get $-1 \le \cos \theta \le 1$.

13. 34.4 km

14. e.g., Kathryn wants to determine the length of a pond. From where she is standing, one end of the pond is 35 m away. If she turns 35° to the left, the distance to the other end of the pond is 30 m. How long is the pond? Use the cosine law to determine the unknown side length.

15. 423 cm²

16. area ≐ 8.2 cm²; perimeter ≐ 10.9 cm

17. e.g., The vertex angle at the handle of the knife is about 110°. Each of the sides of the knife is about 8.5 cm in length.

Lesson 3.4, page 161

1. a) sine law
b) tangent ratio or sine law
c) cosine law

2. a) part a: $\theta = 83.9°$, part b: $c = 1.9$ cm, part c: $\theta = 39.6°$
b) e.g., Using a trigonometric ratio is more efficient because you have fewer calculations to do.

3. a) Using the cosine law. **b)** 2.5 km

4. 29' 2", 31' 3"

5. a) 43.2 m **b)** about 13.3 m

6. a) e.g., Use the properties of parallel lines to determine the angle from the shadow up to the horizontal. Subtract that angle from 57° to determine the angle from the horizontal up to the sun. Both of these are angles of right triangles with one side along the tree. Subtract each angle from 90° to determine the third angle in each right triangle. Use the sine law to determine the height of the tree.

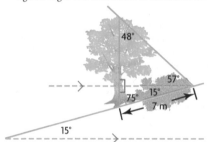

b) 8 m

7. 241.2 m

8. 293.9 m

9. a) 11.1 m **b)** 18.8 m

10. a) e.g., Connect the centre to the vertices to create congruent isosceles triangles and determine the angles at the centre. In one triangle, use the cosine law to determine the pentagon side length and multiply that answer by five.
b) 58.8 cm

11. a) 879.3 m **b)** about 40 s

12. a) 157.0 km
b) The airplane that is 100 km away will arrive first.

13. 85°, 95°, 85°, 95°

14. 520.2 m; e.g.,
Step 1 – Determine $\angle BDC$ in $\triangle BDC$.
Step 2 – Use the sine law to determine CD.
Step 3 – In $\triangle ADC$, use the tangent ratio to determine h.

15. e.g., Starr and David leave school from the same spot. Starr walks N65°E at 3 km/h while David walks S30°E at 4 km/h. How far apart are they after 20 min? The problem can be solved using the cosine law.

16. a) 63° **b)** 52°
17. 50.0 cm²

Chapter Self-Test, page 166

1. a) $\theta = 42.6°$ **b)** $c = 2.4$ cm
2. $\angle R = 52°$, $p = 25.0$ cm, $q = 18.9$ cm
3. 117.0 km
4. 11.6 cm
5. 130.5 m
6. 28.3 m²
7. e.g., If the angle is the contained angle, then use the cosine law. If it is one of the other angles, use the sine law to determine the other non-contained angle, calculate the contained angle by subtracting the two angles you know from 180°, then use the cosine law.
8. e.g., When two angles and a side are given, the sine law must be used to determine side lengths. When two sides and the contained angle are given, the cosine law must be used to determine the third side.

Chapter Review, page 168

1. No. e.g., $\angle C = 90°$, so this will be a right triangle.
2. Part d) is incorrect.
3. a) $x = 23.7$ m **b)** $\theta = 61.9°$
4. $\angle C = 55°$, $a = 9.4$ cm, $b = 7.5$ cm
5. 295.4 m
6. Part a) is not a form of the cosine law.
7. a) $x = 7.6$ m **b)** $\theta = 68.2°$
8. $a = 12.2$ cm, $\angle B = 44.3°$, $\angle C = 77.7°$
9. 58°
10. 11.1 m
11. 584 km
12. 5.5 km, N34.9°W

Chapter 4

Lesson 4.1, page 182

1. a) false c) false e) true
   b) false d) false f) false
2. a) iv b) i c) iii d) ii
3. a) $\sqrt{432}$ is an entire radical; $5\sqrt[3]{2}$ is a mixed radical
   b) $\sqrt{432} = 12\sqrt{3}$; $5\sqrt[3]{2} = \sqrt[3]{250}$
4. a) $6\sqrt{2}$ c) $2\sqrt[3]{5}$
   b) $10\sqrt{6}$ d) $5\sqrt[3]{2}$
5. a) $20\sqrt{10}$ c) $-2\sqrt[3]{9}$
   b) $-9\sqrt{35}$ d) $6\sqrt[3]{3}$
6. a) $\sqrt{2^4 \cdot 3^5}$ c) $\sqrt{2^7 \cdot 5^3}$
   b) $\sqrt{2^5 \cdot 5^5}$ d) $\sqrt{5^4 \cdot 3^3}$
7. e.g.,
   a) $\sqrt{14} \cdot \sqrt{14}$ c) $\sqrt[3]{8} \cdot \sqrt[3]{8}$
   b) $\sqrt{60} \cdot \sqrt{60}$ d) $\sqrt[3]{125} \cdot \sqrt[3]{27}$
8. a) $\sqrt{2^4 \cdot 2^2} = 8$ c) $\sqrt[3]{2^6 \cdot 5^3} = 20$
   b) $\sqrt{2^4 \cdot 3^2 \cdot 5^2} = 60$
9. Kenny's mistake was in thinking that $\sqrt{16} = -4$. $\sqrt{16} = 4$, the principal root.
10. a) e.g., 6.8; 6.86 c) e.g., 28; 28.11
    b) e.g., 201; 202.48 d) e.g., 9.7; 9.65
11. a) $\sqrt{180}$ c) $\sqrt[3]{896}$
    b) $\sqrt{1008}$ d) $\sqrt[3]{-108}$
12. a) $\sqrt{16}, \sqrt{48}, \sqrt{14}, \sqrt{18}, \sqrt{80}$
    b) $\sqrt{14}, 4, 3\sqrt{2}, 4\sqrt{3}, 4\sqrt{5}$
13. Disagree. The mixed radicals cannot be added because the indices of the radicals are different.
14. e.g., 64, 729
15. $20\sqrt{2}, 10\sqrt{8}, 5\sqrt{32}, 4\sqrt{50}, 2\sqrt{200}$; $20\sqrt{2}$ is in lowest form
16. a) 90 m/s b) 324 km/h
17. 67 km/h
18. a) $\sqrt{2^4 \cdot 5^3 \cdot 7} = 20\sqrt{35}$
    b) Yes, it could be a square, but the side lengths would not be a whole number of metres and the area would only be approximately equal to $\sqrt{14\,000}$ m².
19. e.g., 5, 12, 13 or 7, 24, 25; I looked for perfect squares that had perfect square sums.
20. a) true b) true

Lesson 4.2, page 188

1. a) like c) like
   b) unlike d) like, when simplified
2. a) $9\sqrt{6}$ c) $6\sqrt{2}$
   b) $4\sqrt{3}$ d) $-2\sqrt{10}$
3. $8\sqrt{3}$

4. a) $14\sqrt{2}$ b) 0
5. a) $11\sqrt{2}$ c) $20 + 9\sqrt{2}$
   b) $13\sqrt{3} + 6\sqrt{5}$ d) $11\sqrt{5} + 8\sqrt{15}$
6. a) $-4\sqrt{10}$ c) $13\sqrt{2} - 22$
   b) $-3\sqrt{3}$ d) $9\sqrt{2} - 18\sqrt{5} - 30\sqrt{3}$
7. a) $(11\sqrt{2} + 3\sqrt{7})$ cm b) 23.5 cm
8. e.g., Yes, the sum of any two sides is greater than the third side.
9. a) $8\sqrt{2} + 9\sqrt{3}$ b) $8\sqrt{3} + 10\sqrt{7}$
10. $(68\sqrt{2} + 80)$ cm
11. $8\sqrt{5}$ m
12. $5\sqrt{10}$ m
13. $3\sqrt{5}$ m
14. $17\sqrt{2}$
15. $3\sqrt{5} + 7\sqrt{6}$
16. e.g., His error is in going from the second last line to the last line, where he should not have added unlike radicals. The correct answer is $24\sqrt{6} + 12\sqrt{3}$.
17. e.g., The number of terms will be equal to the number of unlike radicals. For example,
    $\sqrt{108} + \sqrt{50} + \sqrt{16} - \sqrt{8} = 6\sqrt{3} + 5\sqrt{2} + 4 - 2\sqrt{2}$
    There are three unlike radicals when expressed in lowest form, so there are three terms in the final answer:
    $6\sqrt{3} + 3\sqrt{2} + 4$
18. $6\sqrt{6}$
19. a) $-\sqrt{2}$ b) $5\sqrt{3}$ c) $17\sqrt{5}$
20. e.g., They are the same in that radicals can be added and subtracted. This is done by adding and subtracting the number that precedes the radical, just as the coefficient of the variable in algebraic expressions are added and subtracted. They are different in that radical expressions may be written as mixed radicals or entire radicals and thus expressed in different forms.
21. 2 times longer

Lesson 4.3, page 198

1. a) $\sqrt{30}$ c) $12\sqrt{2}$
   b) $4\sqrt{15}$ d) $224\sqrt{6}$
2. a) $\dfrac{\sqrt{5}}{5}$
   b) e.g., It is the same as multiplying the radical by 1.
3. $\sqrt{16}; \dfrac{8}{2}; \dfrac{\sqrt{16}\sqrt{4}}{\sqrt{4}}$
4. a) $\sqrt{288}; 12\sqrt{2}$ c) $-\sqrt{1620}; -18\sqrt{5}$
   b) $\sqrt{5400}; 30\sqrt{6}$ d) $\sqrt{1176}; 14\sqrt{6}$
5. a) $14\sqrt{3} + 21$ d) $16\sqrt{6}$
   b) $4\sqrt{5} - 5\sqrt{2}$ e) $30 + 6\sqrt{10} + 5\sqrt{6} + 2\sqrt{15}$
   c) $2\sqrt{15} - 24\sqrt{2}$ f) $212 - 40\sqrt{6}$
6. a) e.g., $10\sqrt{1296} = 360$; $4(3) \cdot 3(2) \cdot 5 = 360$
   b) associative, commutative

7. a) e.g., $\sqrt{192} = \sqrt{64}\sqrt{3}$; $\sqrt{4800} = \sqrt{1600}\sqrt{3}$

b) $\sqrt{192} = 8\sqrt{3}$; $\sqrt{4800} = 40\sqrt{3}$; e.g., It helped to see the perfect squares.

8. Figure A

9. a) Figure A

b) e.g., No, I expressed both areas as entire radicals so that I could compare them:

$\sqrt{2592} > \sqrt{2500}$

10. e.g., The second line is incorrect:

$\sqrt{8} \neq \sqrt{2} + \sqrt{2} + \sqrt{2} + \sqrt{2}$

The correct solution is

$\sqrt{8} = \sqrt{2} \cdot \sqrt{2} \cdot \sqrt{2}$

$\sqrt{8} = 2\sqrt{2}$

11. a) Steve is incorrect.

b) $2 - 2\sqrt{2} + 1 = 3 - 2\sqrt{2}$

12. a) $T = 2\pi\sqrt{2}$ **b)** 8.89 s

13. a) $\dfrac{\sqrt{14}}{2}$ **c)** $-2\sqrt{3}$

b) $\dfrac{-\sqrt{5}}{20}$ **d)** $\dfrac{3}{2}$

14. a) 2   **c)** $-3\sqrt{5}$

b) $-4\sqrt{3}$ **d)** -7

15. Agree, $\sqrt{0.16}$ can be written as $\sqrt{\dfrac{16}{100}}$.

16. a) $\dfrac{5\sqrt{30}}{3}$ **c)** $\dfrac{3 + \sqrt{3}}{3}$

b) $\dfrac{2\sqrt{10} - 5}{5}$ **d)** $\dfrac{20 + 2\sqrt{15}}{15}$

17. a) $40\sqrt{10}$ m/s   **b)** 40 m/s

18. $\dfrac{\sqrt{42}}{7}$

19. a) $3\sqrt{2}$ **b)** $7\sqrt{5}$

20. B

21. a) e.g., You should keep numbers as radicals because your answer remains exact. For example,

$\sqrt{3} \doteq 1.73$

but

$1.73^2 = 2.9929$

$1.73^2 \neq 3$

whereas

$(\sqrt{3})^2 = 3$

b) 12

22. e.g., The rules that apply to multiplying and dividing algebraic expressions are similar to the ones for radicals. When simplifying these expressions, we multiply/divide variables and multiply/divide coefficients. For example,

$3\sqrt{2} \cdot 6\sqrt{5} = 18\sqrt{10}$

23. $\dfrac{1}{\sqrt[3]{3}} \cdot \dfrac{\sqrt[3]{3}}{\sqrt[3]{3}} \cdot \dfrac{\sqrt[3]{3}}{\sqrt[3]{3}} = \dfrac{\sqrt[3]{9}}{3}$

Mid-Chapter Review, page 203

1. a) 9   **c)** -4 **e)** 3

b) 15.8   **d)** -10.1 **f)** -5

2. a) $4\sqrt{2}$ **b)** $8\sqrt{2}$

c) cannot be expressed as a mixed radical

d) $-3\sqrt{6}$

e) $3\sqrt[3]{4}$

f) $-8\sqrt[3]{2}$

3. a) $\sqrt{75}$ **d)** $-\sqrt{32}$

b) $\sqrt{484}$ **e)** $\sqrt[3]{648}$

c) $\sqrt[3]{-13824}$ **f)** $\sqrt[3]{-1728}$

4. $4\sqrt[3]{-27}, -\sqrt{121}, -\sqrt{101}, -2\sqrt{25}, -2\sqrt[3]{8}$

5. The design with side lengths of 140 cm will use more stained glass.

6. a) $7\sqrt{3}$ **d)** $7\sqrt{7}$

b) $18\sqrt{2}$ **e)** $24\sqrt{2}$

c) $8\sqrt{5}$

7. a) $-2\sqrt{6}$ **d)** $-8\sqrt{10}$

b) -18 **e)** $-14\sqrt{3}$

c) $-11\sqrt{3}$

8. a) $5\sqrt{3} + 5\sqrt{6}$ **d)** $9\sqrt{2}$

b) $2 + 3\sqrt{3}$ **e)** $8\sqrt{3} - 5\sqrt{2}$

c) $\sqrt{7}$

9. $20\sqrt{6}$ cm by $10\sqrt{6}$ cm

10. a) $2\sqrt{14}$ **d)** $-2\sqrt{182}$

b) $2\sqrt{30}$ **e)** $-30\sqrt{30}$

c) $15\sqrt{3}$

11. a) $2\sqrt{2}$ **d)** $14\sqrt{5}$

b) -6 **e)** $-3\sqrt{5}$

c) $-\dfrac{\sqrt{2}}{2}$

12. a) $4\sqrt{2} + 5\sqrt{6}$ **c)** $5\sqrt{3} + 8\sqrt{30} + 5\sqrt{7} + 8\sqrt{70}$

b) $-168\sqrt{3} + 14\sqrt{6}$ **d)** -33

13. $\sqrt{58}$ m by $\sqrt{58}$ m

Lesson 4.4, page 211

1. a) $x \in R$ **c)** $x \geq -3, x \in R$

b) $x \geq 0, x \in R$ **d)** $x > 0, x \in R$

2. a) $x \in R$; $6x^2\sqrt{5}$

b) $x \in R$; $3x$

c) $x \geq 0, x \in R$; $4x\sqrt{3x}$

d) $x \geq 0, x \in R$; $-6x^3\sqrt{2x}$

3. a) $x \geq 0, x \in R$; $7\sqrt{2x}$

b) $x \geq 0, x \in R$; $54x\sqrt{3x}$

c) $x \geq 0, x \in R$; $10x$

d) $x > 0, x \in R$; $-3x^2$

4. a) $x \geq 0, x \in R$; $5x^2\sqrt{2}$

b) $x \geq 0, x \in R$; $-20x^2\sqrt{2}$

c) $x > 0, x \in R$; $-3x$

d) $x > 0, x \in R$; 2

5. a) Step 1: x^2

Step 2: x

Step 3: $7x + 3x$

b) e.g., Step 1: Express $\sqrt{x^3}$ as $\sqrt{x^2}\sqrt{x}$.
Step 2: Simplify $\sqrt{x^2}$.
Step 3: Simplify by taking a common factor.

6. a) $x \geq 0, x \in$ R; 0
b) $x \geq 0, x \in$ R; $2x^2 + 8x^4$
c) $x > 0, x \in$ R; $\dfrac{3\sqrt{x} - x\sqrt{x}}{x}$
d) $x > 0, x \in$ R; $x\sqrt{2}$

7. e.g., Dividing radicals and rationalizing radical expressions are similar in that they both use the rules of radicals. They are different in that rationalizing the denominator uses multiplication of a radical in the form of "1."

8. a) $x \geq 0, x \in$ R; $10x\sqrt{2}$
b) $x \geq 0, x \in$ R; $2x + 4x\sqrt{2x}$
c) $x \geq 0, x \in$ R; $-3x^2 + 12x\sqrt{x}$
d) $x \geq 0, x \in$ R; $x + 7\sqrt{x} + 10$

9. a) $x \geq 0, x \in$ R; $10\sqrt{x}$
b) $x \in$ R; $2x^2$
c) $y \geq 0, y \in$ R; $-6y^2 + 12\sqrt{y}$
d) $y \geq 0, y \in$ R; $25 - 10\sqrt{y} + y$

10. a) $x > 0, x \in$ R; x^3
b) $x > 0, x \in$ R; $2x$
c) $x \neq 0, x \in$ R; $5x$
d) $x \neq 0, x \in$ R; 2

11. a) $x \geq 9, x \in$ R
b) $x \geq -4, x \in$ R
c) $x \geq -2, x \in$ R
d) $x \geq \dfrac{2}{3}, x \in$ R

12. a) $\dfrac{\sqrt{5}}{\sqrt{5}}$ **b)** $\dfrac{\sqrt{x}}{\sqrt{x}}$ **c)** $\dfrac{\sqrt{7x}}{\sqrt{7x}}$ **d)** $\dfrac{\sqrt{x}}{\sqrt{x}}$

13. e.g., Multiply the numerator and denominator by $\sqrt{x}$.

14. a) He is incorrect. e.g., Only factors can be eliminated.
b) e.g., Expand and then try to factor and/or simplify.
c) $s > 26, s \in$ R

15. $x > 0, x \in$ R; $\dfrac{(9 - 2x^2)\sqrt{x}}{x}$

16. e.g., They are similar because in algebraic expressions you multiply coefficients and multiply variables. The same applies to radicals. Multiply the values preceding the radicals and multiply the terms inside the radicals. For example,
$3x \cdot 2x = 6x^2$ and
$3\sqrt{x} \cdot 2\sqrt{x} = 6\sqrt{x^2}$

17. She is incorrect. e.g., According to the order of operations, she must apply the exponents, and then add. So, she cannot simplify as she did.

Lesson 4.5, page 215

1. a) $x = 49$ **b)** $x = 29$ **c)** $x = 10$ **d)** $x = 28$
2. $A = 2.3$ m^2
3. $d = 0.08$ km
4. $V = 3.82$ m^3
5. a) Let x represent the number.
$\sqrt{2x + 5} = 7$
b) $x = 22$
c) $\sqrt[3]{2x + 5} = 7; x = 169$

Lesson 4.6, page 222

1. a) $x \geq 0, x \in$ R; $x = 16$ **c)** $x \geq -1, x \in$ R; $x = 3$
b) $x \geq 0, x \in$ R; $x = 36$ **d)** $x \geq -3, x \in$ R; $x = 13$
2. a) $x \in$ R; $x = -27$ **c)** $x \in$ R; $x = -12$
b) $x \geq 0, x \in$ R; $x = 12.5$ **d)** $x \geq -2, x \in$ R; $x = 16$
3. She is correct. e.g., I solved the original equation, verified my result, and found that the only root, 8, is an extraneous root.
4. a) $x \geq 0, x \in$ R; $x = 4$ **b)** $x \in$ R; $x = 1$
5. a) Square both sides of the equation.
b) Square both sides of the equation.
c) Cube both sides of the equation.
d) Add 1 to both sides of the equation.
6. a) $x \geq 3, x \in$ R; $x = 28$ **c)** $x \geq -\dfrac{3}{5}, x \in$ R; $x = \dfrac{109}{20}$
b) $x \in$ R; $x = 5$ **d)** $x \geq \dfrac{2}{3}, x \in$ R; $x = 22$
7. 7200 W
8. a) $x \geq -\dfrac{17}{2}, x \in$ R; $x = 4$
b) $x \in$ R; $x = 7$
c) $x \geq -\dfrac{3}{5}, x \in$ R; no solution; 1 is an extraneous root
d) $x \leq \dfrac{11}{2}, x \in$ R; $x = -8$
9. $\sqrt{x - 1} = -2$; no solution; 5 is an extraneous root
10. Agree. e.g., The first two equations have the same solution, but the third equation has no solution (the left side is greater than or equal to zero and the right side is negative).
11. 19.91 m
12. $818
13. 1 158 105.6 W
14. 1.41 m
15. $x \geq -\dfrac{5}{2}, x \in$ R; $x = \dfrac{7}{10}$
16. e.g., $\sqrt{x + 1} = 5$
Isolate the radical if necessary, then square both sides.
$x + 1 = 25$
Solve for x.
$x = 24$
17. $x \geq -5, x \in$ R; $x = 76$

Chapter Self-Test, page 225

1. a) $14\sqrt{6}$ **c)** $6\sqrt[3]{6}$
b) $-8\sqrt{14}$ **d)** $8\sqrt[3]{-5}$
2. least to greatest: $4\sqrt{5}, \sqrt[3]{1000}, 3\sqrt{12}, \sqrt{121}, 12\sqrt{2}$
3. a) $4\sqrt{3} + 2\sqrt{2}$ **b)** $\sqrt{11} - 8\sqrt{3}$
4. a) $-30\sqrt{2}$
b) $-18\sqrt{3} + 6\sqrt{30}$
c) $x \geq 0, x \in$ R; $9x + 12\sqrt{x} + 4$

5. a) $3\sqrt{5}$ **b)** $\dfrac{3\sqrt{35}}{5}$ **c)** $x > 0, x \in R; 3x^2$

6. a) $x \in R; 6x^3\sqrt{2}$

  b) $x \geq 0, x \in R; -6x^4\sqrt{x}$

7. 1.4 m^2

8. e.g., To ensure the radical has meaning, it is important to state restrictions (i.e., it is not possible to find the square root of a negative number). To do this, ensure that the radicand is greater than or equal to zero. For example,

  i) $\sqrt{x}$ **ii)** $\sqrt{x + 3}$

  The restrictions for these are:

  i) $x \geq 0$ **ii)** $x + 3 \geq 0$, so $x \geq -3$

9. a) $x \geq -\dfrac{5}{4}, x \in R; x = -1$

  b) No; e.g., I verified the root in the original equation.

Chapter Review, page 228

1. a) $6\sqrt{2}$ **c)** $2\sqrt{10}$

  b) $10\sqrt{6}$ **d)** $5\sqrt[3]{2}$

2. a) $\sqrt{180}$ **c)** $\sqrt{224}$

  b) $\sqrt{1008}$ **d)** $\sqrt[3]{-108}$

3. a) $6 + \sqrt{42}$ **c)** $8\sqrt{26} - 17\sqrt{2}$

  b) $6\sqrt{2} + 12\sqrt{3} + 4\sqrt{6}$ **d)** $36 - 24\sqrt{3} - 30\sqrt{6}$

4. a) $12\sqrt{7}$ **c)** $-80\sqrt{3}$

  b) $75\sqrt{10}$ **d)** $56\sqrt{3}$

5. a) $24 + 12\sqrt{3}$ **c)** $2\sqrt{30} - 48$

  b) $2\sqrt{5} - 5\sqrt{3}$ **d)** $18\sqrt{6} + 8$

6. The error occurred in going from the first line to the second line. Square roots of sums cannot be simplified by taking the square root of each term separately. The correct result is $2\sqrt{3}$.

7. a) $x \geq 0, x \in R; 4x^5\sqrt{2}$

  b) $x > 0, x \in R; -4x$

  c) $x > 0, x \in R; -\dfrac{64x}{3}$

  d) $x > 0, x \in R; \dfrac{\sqrt{30}}{9}$

8. 33.4 m

9. a) $x \geq 0, x \in R; x = 121$ **c)** $x \geq 0, x \in R; x = \dfrac{9}{7}$

  b) $x \geq -3, x \in R; x = 193$ **d)** $x \geq \dfrac{2}{5}, x \in R; x = \dfrac{578}{5}$

10. a) $x \geq -\dfrac{16}{3}, x \in R;$ no solution; 3 is an extraneous root

  b) $x \in R; x = \dfrac{71}{2}$

  c) $x \geq -4, x \in R; x = -1$

  d) $x \leq \dfrac{11}{3}, x \in R;$ no solution; 3 is an extraneous root

11. a) $x \geq 4, x \in R$

  b) Jenny made her mistake in step 1 when she subtracted from the right side instead of adding to it.

Chapter 5

Lesson 5.1, page 239

1. a)

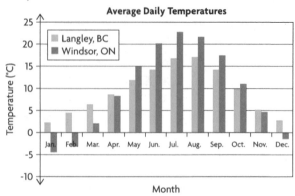

b)

	Langley, BC (°C)	Windsor, ON (°C)
Range	14.8	27.2
Mean	9.4	9.4
Median	9.2	9.6

c) e.g., The mean temperature for each city is the same, and the medians are close; however, the temperature in Windsor has a much greater range: it gets colder in winter and warmer in summer.

d) e.g., if you were living in one of the locations and moving to the other location

2. a)

	Unit 1 Test (%)	Unit 2 Test (%)
Range	24	61
Mean	71.2	71.2
Median	73	73
Mode	73	73

b) e.g., The class performed better on the Unit 1 test because the range of scores was smaller, with the mean, median, and mode being equal.

c) e.g., The modes were not very useful to compare in this context because they only tell me which mark occurred most often, not on which test the class performed better.

3. a) e.g.,

	1996 ($)	1998 ($)	2000 ($)
Range	95 567	127 616	98 952
Mean	163 440	176 937	187 434
Median	157 677	167 396	172 503

The data distribution is scattered fairly widely during each year; some cities are much lower or much higher than the mean.

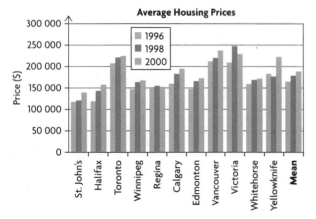

Average Housing Prices

The range between the maximum and minimum average prices in the 11 cities is the greatest in 1998, so that year some prices were much lower than average and some were much higher. Both the mean and the median of the average price in the 11 cities has steadily increased over the 5-year period. In all the cities except for Regina and Victoria, there has been an increase in price over the 5-year period. Also, Yellowknife has had the greatest increase in average price over the 5-year period.

b) e.g., if you were comparing housing costs in cities you are contemplating moving to

Lesson 5.2, page 249

1. a)

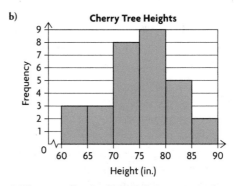

Frequency of Earthquakes by Magnitude

b) e.g., From 2005 to 2009, there were more earthquakes than from 2000 to 2004. The earthquakes in 2005–2009 tended to be of greater magnitude than those in 2000–2004. 2000–2004 had many more earthquakes that rated less than 3.0, although both periods had roughly the same number of earthquakes that rated more than 7.0.

2. a) 10–15 min interval

b) e.g., Most of the data is distributed in the 20–25 min interval and 30–35 min interval.

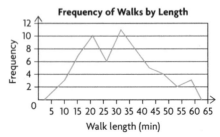

Frequency of Walks by Length

3. e.g.,

a)

Tree Height (in.)	Frequency
60–65	3
65–70	3
70–75	8
75–80	9
80–85	5
85–90	2

b)

Cherry Tree Heights

c) The range of heights 75–80 inches occurs most frequently. The range of heights 85–90 inches occurs least frequently.

4. e.g.,

a) Most withdrawals are multiples of 20. An interval width of 20 would give a good representation of the distribution of the data.

b)

Withdrawal ($)	Frequency
0–20	4
20–40	5
40–60	8
60–80	9
80–100	6
100–120	4
120–140	6
140–160	4
160–180	2
180–200	2

c)

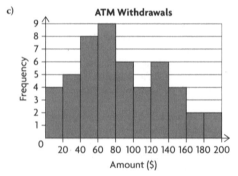

ATM Withdrawals

d) There are a lot more withdrawals under $100 than there are over $100. Withdrawals between $40 and $80 are the most frequent. Not many people made withdrawals over $160.

5. e.g,

a)

Final Scores	Frequency
30–40	1
40–50	8
50–60	10
60–70	8
70–80	3

b)

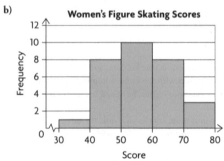

Women's Figure Skating Scores

c) No. It shows that three women scored between 70 and 80, but it does not show the range of scores for a top-five placement.

6. **a)**

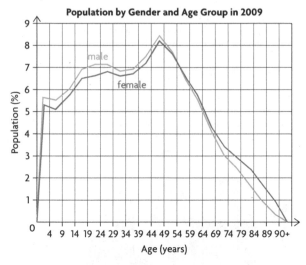

Population by Gender and Age Group in 2009

b) e.g., There are more males than females for all age groups up to 54 years. Starting at age 55, there are more women than men.

7. **a)**

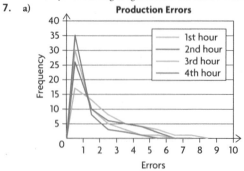

Production Errors

b) e.g., As the day progresses, the number of errors on a vehicle decreases. Fewer vehicles have large numbers of errors.

8. e.g.,

a) I chose interval sizes that created five interval spaces that worked for both tables.

Holly's Program	
Kilometres	Frequency
0–8	33
8–17	34
17–26	3
26–35	0
35–44	0

Jason's Program	
Kilometres	Frequency
0–8	39
8–17	29
17–26	9
26–35	6
35–44	1

b)

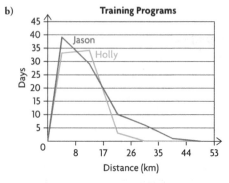

Training Programs

c) Holly's program involves more short distance running, while Jason's program involves more long distance running.

9.

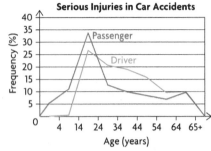

Serious Injuries in Car Accidents

Frequency (%) vs Age (years), with Passenger and Driver curves.

e.g., Younger drivers are involved in more accidents where there are serious injuries. Also, the greatest number of serious injuries for passengers is in the 15 to 24 age group; perhaps these passengers were in the same accidents as the young drivers who were seriously injured (i.e., out driving with friends).

10. e.g., Using intervals of equal width enables you to see the distribution more easily and to compare the data more effectively.

11. e.g.,
  a) Grouping raw data into intervals makes it easier to interpret the data accurately and to see the distribution. It also makes the data more manageable.
  b) Histograms compare data intervals side by side using bars, while frequency polygons compare data intervals using lines. Frequency polygons are useful when comparing two or more sets of data, because you can easily combine them on the same graph, making it easier to see differences or similarities in the data sets.

12. e.g.,
  a) 5116. I eliminated all rows in the table with a frequency of 0. Then I determined the midpoint for each remaining interval. Next, I multiplied the frequency of each row by the midpoint to estimate the total population for each row. I determined the mean of the products.
  b) 3115. The city with the median population is the 76th one, which occurs in the first row of the table. The 76th city out of 122 might have a population of
  $$\frac{76}{122} \cdot 5000 = 3114.754\ldots \text{ or } 3115.$$
  c) I assumed that 61 cities would be below 2500 and 61 cities would be between 2500 and 5000. Since 75 cities have a population of less than 1700, the estimates for both the mean and the median are higher than they should be.

Lesson 5.3, page 261

1. **a), b)** class A: 14.27; class B: 3.61
  c) Class B has the most consistent marks over the first five tests since it has the lowest standard deviation.
2. mean: 130.42 points; standard deviation: 11.51 points
3. **a)** mean: 130.36 points; standard deviation: 12.05 points
  b) e.g., Ali's mean and standard deviation are close to his team's. He is an average player on his team.
4. e.g.,
  a) The mean number of beads in company B's packages is much less consistent than the mean number of beads in company A's packages.
  b) company A
5. Group 1: mean: 71.9 bpm; standard deviation: 6.0 bpm
  Group 2: mean: 71.0 bpm; standard deviation: 4.0 bpm
  Group 3: mean: 70.4 bpm; standard deviation: 5.7 bpm
  Group 4: mean: 76.9 bpm; standard deviation: 1.9 bpm
  Group 3 has the lowest mean pulse rate. Group 4 has the most consistent pulse rate.

6. **a)** Diko   **b)** Nazra
7. **a)** mean: 10.5 TDs; standard deviation: 5.6 TDs
  b) e.g., He probably played fewer games in his rookie year (his first year) and his last year.
  c) mean: 11.7 TDs; standard deviation: 5.2 TDs
  d) The mean is higher and the standard deviation is lower.
8. **a)** mean: 1082 yards gained; standard deviation: 428.8 yards gained
  b) Allen Pitts
9. **a)** Fitness Express: mean: 18.3 h; standard deviation: 4.9 h
  Fit For Life: mean: 19.1 h; standard deviation: 5.3 h
  b) Fitness Express
10. Jaime's mean travel time is about 21.2 minutes and her standard deviation is 3.5 minutes. Since her mean time is more than 20 minutes, Jaime will lose her job.
11. yes; mean: 45.0 calls; standard deviation: 7.1 calls
12. **a)**

	Games Played	Goals	Assists	Points
Mean	57.5	12.5	16.1	28.6
Standard Deviation	11.4	11.6	13.1	24.5

  b) e.g., The standard deviation should decrease for games played and should increase for goals, assists, and points.
  c)

	Games Played	Goals	Assists	Points
Mean	60.1	13.4	17.2	30.7
Standard Deviation	8.7	11.8	13.3	24.9

  d) e.g., The means and standard deviations increased and decreased as I predicted.
  e) e.g., The statement is true for data, and for means because we can add fractions with the same denominator together. However, standard deviations cannot be added because of how they are calculated.
13. e.g., One twin is more consistent, while the other is less consistent, resulting in the same mean (85.0%) with different standard deviations (2.6%, 12.0%).
  Jane's scores: 80%, 85%, 82%, 87%, 86%, 84%, 87%, 85%, 85%, 89%
  Jordana's scores: 78%, 92%, 99%, 64%, 72%, 82%, 77%, 95%, 98%, 93%
14. **a)** group A: mean: 8.56 s; standard deviation: 7.99 s
  group B: mean: 5.55 s; standard deviation: 4.73 s
  b) yes; group B (the group given visual information)

Mid-Chapter Review, page 267

1. Paris: 15.6 °C; Sydney: 17.8 °C
2. e.g., Wayne Gretzky tended to score between 0 and 60 goals per season. He infrequently scored more than that.

Goals per Season

Number of seasons vs Goals

3. e.g.,
a) 5

b)

Text Messages	Jackson	Jillian
0–4	5	4
5–9	10	7
10–14	6	9
15–19	3	7
20–24	3	3
25–29	3	0

c)

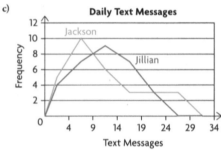

4. Jackson: mean: 11.6 messages; standard deviation: 7.4 messages
Jillian: mean: 11.7 messages; standard deviation: 6.0 messages
e.g., Jillian and Jackson send about the same number of text messages, but Jillian is more consistent with her daily amount.

5. a) range: $42.00; mean: $21.95; standard deviation: $8.24
b) range: $15.00; mean: $21.35; standard deviation: $4.54
c) Removing the greatest and least amounts reduces the standard deviation.

6. females: mean: $27 391.30; standard deviation: $7241.12
males: mean: $41 614.79; standard deviation: $19 542.92
e.g., Males tend to have larger salaries, but their salaries are less consistently close to the mean, suggesting a greater range.

Lesson 5.4, page 279

1. a) 47.5%   b) 15.85%   c) 0.15%

2. a)

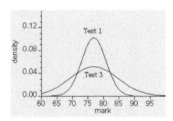

b) e.g., Test 1 and test 2 have different means, but the same standard deviation. Test 1 and test 3 have the same mean, but different standard deviations.
c) test 1: 84.8%; test 2: 79.1%; test 3: 99.2%

3. e.g.,
a) Yes. A graph of the data has a rough bell shape.

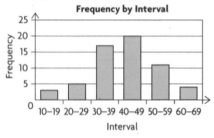

b) No. A graph of the data does not have a bell shape.

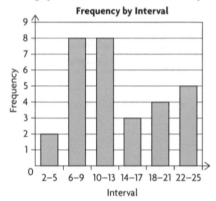

c) Yes. A graph of the data has a rough bell shape.

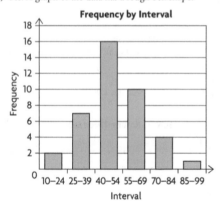

4. a) mean: 104.5 min; standard deviation: 22.3 min
b) e.g.,

Movie Length (min)	Frequency
59.5–82.0	3
82.0–104.5	33
104.5–127.0	7
127.0–149.5	3
149.5–172.0	3
172.0–194.5	1

c) e.g., No. 80% of the data is within 1 standard deviation of the mean.

5. **a)** **i)** mean: 45.2 °C; median: 45.5 °C; standard deviation: 1.7 °C

ii) e.g.,

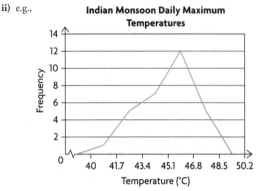

Indian Monsoon Daily Maximum Temperatures

iii) e.g., The median is close to the mean, but the frequency polygon is not symmetric around the mean, so the data is not normally distributed.

b) **i)** mean: 8.6; median: 8; standard deviation: 2.8

ii) e.g.,

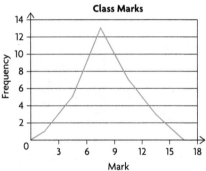

Class Marks

iii) e.g., The shape of the graph is roughly symmetrical with one peak in the middle tapering off to either side. The mean and median are fairly close to each other. The distribution is approximately normal.

6. about 3 years

7. **a)** mean: 10.5; standard deviation: 2.96

b) e.g.,

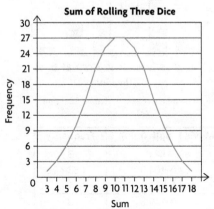

Sum of Rolling Three Dice

c) e.g., Yes, when you determine the percent of data in the various sections of the graph, they match the percent of data in a normal distribution.

8. **a)**

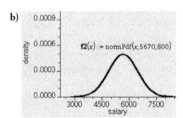

$f1(x) := \text{normPdf}(x, 5400, 800)$

b)

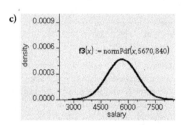

$f2(x) := \text{normPdf}(x, 5670, 800)$

c)

$f3(x) := \text{normPdf}(x, 5670, 840)$

9. e.g.,
a) Yes, when I determine the percent of the data within 1, 2, 3, and 4 standard deviations of the mean, they agree with the percents for a normal distribution.
b) The mean is 72.25, the median is 72, and the mode 73. The values are close together, so the golf scores appear to be normally distributed.

10. 2.5%, or about 3 dolphins

11. **a)** 44.6 kg–99.0 kg
b) 31.0 kg–112.6 kg
c) e.g., Julie assumed that the masses of North American men and women is normally distributed about the mean. However, men and women have different mean masses.

12. a) Yes

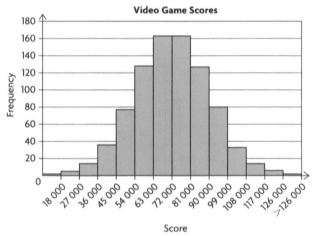

Video Game Scores

b) Yes; mean: 72 010 points; standard deviation: 18 394 points. The percent of scores within 1, 2, and 3 standard deviations are very close to the expected values for a normal distribution:
$\mu \pm 1\sigma = 68.35\%$
$\mu \pm 2\sigma = 94.94\%$
$\mu \pm 3\sigma = 99.53\%$

13. a) 68%, or about 41 dogs   **c)** 99.7%, or about 60 dogs
     b) 95%, or about 57 dogs   **d)** 50%, or about 30 dogs

14. mean: 482 kg; standard deviation: 17 kg

15. e.g., The 10 students could all have the highest marks in the class, so they would not be normally distributed.

16. e.g., No. The male dog would have been over 10 standard deviations heavier than average, and the female dog would have been over 13 standard deviations lighter than average. These masses are improbable.

Lesson 5.5, page 292

1. a) 4   **c)** -1.92
   b) -0.75 **d)** 2.455...

2. a) 89.25%   **c)** 98.50%
   b) 0.94%   **d)** 26.11%

3. a) 6.88%   **b)** 75.18%

4. a) -1.28 **c)** 0.25
   b) 1.28   **d)** -0.25

5. a) 1.892...   **c)** 0.505...
   b) -2.6875 **d)** 1.666...

6. a) 71.23%   **c)** 0.14%
   b) 3.92%   **d)** 99.16%

7. a) 91.15%   **c)** 24.83%
   b) 0.43%   **d)** 99.92%

8. a) 39.95%   **b)** 89.90%

9. a) $-0.439...$ **b)** 0.841...

10. a) English: 2.352... Math: 3.148...
    b) Math
    c) e.g., the job market, her preferences, whether absolute or relative marks are more important for university applications

11. 92.70%

12. water walking

13. a) 90.60% or 91.24%, depending on method used
    b) 3.11% or 3.14%, depending on method used

c) 0.88%; e.g., Someone might want to see if the percentage of high-school age mothers with young children is decreasing or increasing. Someone might use this data to justify funding for social programs targeting this group.

14. mean: 180 cm; standard deviation: 15.6 cm

15. a) 0.38%   **b)** 37.81%   **c)** 5.29

16. a) about 2   **b)** 10.56%

17. 50 months, or round down to 4 years

18. 76%

19. e.g., For the high-priced car, the z-score is 0.5, which means that about 69% of the repairs will be less than $3000; thus, 31% of the repairs will be more than $3000. For the mid-priced car, the z-score is 1.25, which means that about 89% of the repairs will be less than $3000; thus, 11% of the repairs will be more than $3000.

20. a) 131   **b)** 140   **c)** at least 108

21. A z-score is a value that indicates the number of standard deviations of a data value above or below the mean. It is calculated by subtracting the mean from the data value, and then dividing by the standard deviation. Knowing the z-score of two or more pieces of data in different data sets allows you to compare them, which is useful for making decisions.

22. a) 5.02 kg
    b) 62.1%; e.g., No; too many bags will have more than 5 kg of sugar.

23. a) mean: 150; standard deviation: about 9.6
    b) 1.1%

24. e.g., If the ABC Company wants its process to meet 6-Sigma standards, that is, to reject fewer than 1 bungee cord per 300 produced, what standard deviation does the company need to have in its manufacturing process? Answer: The ABC Company needs to reduce its standard deviation to 1.0 cm if it wants to reject only 0.33% of bungee cords.

Lesson 5.6, page 302

1. a) 95%
   b) 77.9%–84.1%
   c) 26.1 million to 28.2 million

2. a) 540.1 g to 543.9 g
   b) 50: 3.9 g; 100: 2.7 g; 500: 1.2 g

3. a) 90%
   b) 60.6%–67.4%
   c) about 19–22 students

4. a) With 95% confidence, it can be said that 78.8% to 83.2% of Canadians support bilingualism in Canada and that they want Canada to remain a bilingual country.
   b) e.g., I disagree with Mark. Without having more information about how the poll was conducted, it is impossible to tell if the poll was flawed.

5. a) 54.9%–61.1%
   b) e.g., Swift Current, Saskatchewan, has a population of 16 000 residents. Between 8784 and 9776 people would have answered the question correctly.

6. a) 99%; 84.7% to 93.3%
   b) 19 904 500 to 21 925 500

7. e.g.,
   a) The Canadian Press Harris-Decima surveyed Canadians in early 2010 to find out how people felt about a proposed rewording of "O Canada." The poll found that 74% of Canadians opposed the rewording, with a margin of error of 2.2 percentage points, 19 times out of 20.
   b) 71.8%–76.2%

c) With such a high percent of Canadians polled opposing the rewording, and the relatively tight confidence interval, I agree with the conclusion of the poll.

8. a) confidence interval: 174.8 g to 175.2 g
   margin of error: ± 0.2 g
   b) 135
   c) 55
   d) 78

9. a) With 90% confidence, it can be said that 49.5% to 58.5% of post-secondary graduates can be expected to earn at least $100 000/year by the time they retire.
   b) With 99% confidence, it can be said that 60.9% to 65.1% of online shoppers search for coupons or deals when shopping on the Internet.
   c) With 95% confidence, it can be said that Canadians spend an average of 17.5 h to 18.7 h online, compared to 16.3 h to 17.5 h watching television per week.
   d) With 95% confidence, it can be said that 36% to 42% of decided voters will not vote for the political party in the next election.

10. a) As the sample size increases, a larger proportion of the population is sampled, making the results more representative of the population, therefore reducing the margin of error.
    b) For the confidence level to increase, the size of the confidence interval must increase; therefore, the more confident you are that a value falls within the range, the more the margin of error increases.

11. a)

Sample Size	Pattern	Margin of Error
100		9.80%
400	$\sqrt{\dfrac{100}{400}} = \dfrac{1}{2}$	$9.80\% \cdot \dfrac{1}{2} = 4.90\%$
900	$\sqrt{\dfrac{400}{900}} = \dfrac{2}{3}$	$4.90\% \cdot \dfrac{2}{3} = 3.27\%$
1600	$\sqrt{\dfrac{900}{1600}} = \dfrac{3}{4}$	$3.27\% \cdot \dfrac{3}{4} = 2.45\%$
2500	$\sqrt{\dfrac{1600}{2500}} = \dfrac{4}{5}$	$2.45\% \cdot \dfrac{4}{5} = 1.96\%$
3600	$\sqrt{\dfrac{2500}{3600}} = \dfrac{5}{6}$	$1.96\% \cdot \dfrac{5}{6} = 1.63\%$

   b) i) 1.40%   ii) 2.19%
   c) e.g., The margin of error gets smaller at a much faster rate than the sample size grows. Therefore, a relatively small sample is needed to get a small margin of error.

Chapter Self-Test, page 305

1. a) 1999: mean: 43.4 in.; standard deviation: 3.0 in.
      2011: mean: 67.8 in.; standard deviation: 5.6 in.
   b) The heights for 2011 have a greater standard deviation. Children are much closer in height than teenagers, which is why there is greater deviation in the teenagers' heights.

2. a) e.g., The graph of the data shows a normal distribution.

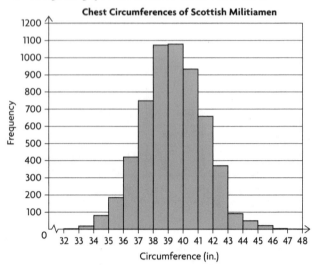

Chest Circumferences of Scottish Militiamen

   b) 1.06

3. e.g., Edmonton's temperature is lower on average, but less consistently close to the mean.

4. a) If the poll was conducted with a random sample of 1009 Canadians 100 times, you can be confident that 95 times the results would be that
   • 84.9% to 91.1% of people would say that the flag makes them proud of Canada
   • 76.9% to 83.1% of people would say that hockey makes them proud of Canada
   • 40.9% to 47.1% of people would say that our justice system makes them proud of Canada
   b) 26 160 611 to 28 269 789 people
   c) The margin of error would increase since the confidence level that would be used in the new poll increased to 99% from 95%.

Chapter Review, page 308

1. Twila: mean: 46.5 min; range: 25 min
   Amber: mean: 45.5 min; range 75 min
   e.g., Each girl spent about the same amount of time on homework every day, but Amber spends a greater range of times on homework than Twila.

2. e.g., More people aged 25 to 34 years old have higher levels of education.

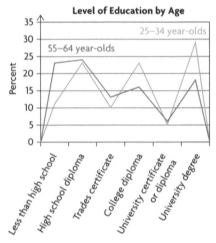

Level of Education by Age

3. a) e.g., Twila's data will have the lowest standard deviation. The numbers are closer to the mean.
b) Twila: 7.8 min; Amber: 26.9 min; yes

4. a)

Level of Education	Mean ($1000)	Standard Deviation ($1000)
No Diploma	18.8	2.6
High School	23.8	4.1
Post-Secondary	36.8	5.5

b) post-secondary
c) post-secondary
5. bag of sunflower seeds
6. female bear
7. a)

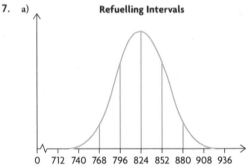

Refuelling Intervals

$\mu-3\sigma$ $\mu-2\sigma$ $\mu-1\sigma$ μ $\mu+1\sigma$ $\mu+2\sigma$ $\mu+3\sigma$

Kilometres per tank

b) 68%
c) 16%
d) 768 km and 880 km

8. a) mean: 36.9 °C; standard deviation: 0.4 °C
b) e.g., Yes. About 69% of the data is within one standard deviation of the mean, about 94% of the data is within two standard deviations of the mean, and about 99% of the data is within three standard deviations of the mean, which is close to the percents expected for a normal distribution.
9. 10.6%
10. Computers For All
11. a) Internet: 60.5% to 63.3%
Friends/family: 67.5% to 70.3%
Health line: 16.5% to 19.3%
b) Internet: 208 725 to 218 385 people
Friends/family: 232 875 to 242 535 people
Health line: 56 925 to 66 585 people
12. a) The margin of error of company A is larger than the margin of error of company B.
b) Company A's sample was larger than company B's sample.

Cumulative Review, Chapters 3–5, page 315

1. a) $x = 12.6$ cm **b)** $p = 7.6$ m
2. a) $40°$ **b)** $43°$
3. $d = 12.2$ cm, $\angle E = 44.3°$, $\angle F = 77.7°$
4. 3.5 km, N39.0°W
5. 92.9 m, 80.7 m
6. $48.2°, 73.4°, 58.4°$
7. a)

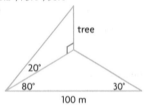

tree
$20°$
$80°$ $30°$
100 m

b) 19.4 m
8. a) i) $-\sqrt{320}$ **ii)** $\sqrt{12x^5}$
b) $x \geq 0, x \in \mathbb{R}$
9. a) $18\sqrt{2}$ **c)** $-3\sqrt{2}$
b) $43 + \sqrt{2}$ **d)** $\dfrac{1 - \sqrt{2}}{2}$
10. a) $7a\sqrt{3}$ **c)** $a \geq 0, a \in \mathbb{R}; 12\sqrt{a} - 15a$
b) $3x - 2x^2$ **d)** $x \geq 0, x \in \mathbb{R}; 32x - 24\sqrt{2x} + 9$
11. a) 13 **b)** 36
12. 256 ft

13. e.g.,

a)

Lifespan (years)	Frequency
9.5–10.0	1
10.0–10.5	1
10.5–11.0	0
11.0–11.5	1
11.5–12.0	1
12.0–12.5	0
12.5–13.0	7
13.0–13.5	9
13.5–14.0	5
14.0–14.5	3
14.5–15.0	2

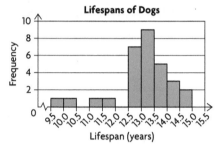

b) No

c) range: 5.2 years; standard deviation: 1.12 years. e.g., The data does not deviate very much from the mean.

14. e.g., Winnipeg and Whitehorse have approximately the same temperature in January, but the temperature varies more in Whitehorse.

15. a) 97.7%   **b)** 2.3%

16. a) 2.3%   **b)** 15.7%

17. a) margin of error: 3.1%, confidence level: 95%
   b) i) 20.0%–26.2%   **ii)** 9.5%–15.7%

18. e.g.,
   a) The confidence level decreases as the margin of error decreases because we can be less certain that the true mean is in the range specified.
   b) The confidence level decreases as the sample size decreases because there is more chance that the mean of a particular sample will fall outside the confidence interval.

Chapter 6

Lesson 6.1, page 324

1. a) not a quadratic relation   **d)** quadratic relation
   b) not a quadratic relation   **e)** quadratic relation
   c) not a quadratic relation   **f)** not a quadratic relation

2. a) not a quadratic relation   **d)** quadratic relation
   b) quadratic relation   **e)** not a quadratic relation
   c) quadratic relation   **f)** not a quadratic relation

3. b) 0   **c)** 17   **d)** -6

4. e.g., If $a = 0$, then $y = bx + c$, which is a linear relation, not a quadratic relation.

5. a) up, $a > 0$ **c)** up, $a > 0$
   b) down, $a < 0$ **d)** down, $a < 0$

6. a) up   **c)** up
   b) down   **d)** down

Lesson 6.2, page 332

1. a) $x = 4$ **b)** $(4, -16)$ **c)** $\{(x, y) \mid x \in R, y \geq -16, y \in R\}$

2. a) $(0, 8)$; e.g., $(1, 18)$, $(-1, 2)$ **b)** $(0, 0)$; e.g., $(1, 3)$, $(-1, -5)$

3. a) $(0, 0)$, $(2, 0)$; $(0, 0)$; $x = 1$; $(1, -2)$; $\{(x, y) \mid x \in R, y \geq -2, y \in R\}$
   b) $(-1, 0)$, $(6, 0)$; $(0, 4.5)$; $x = 2.5$; $(2.5, 9.2)$; $\{(x, y) \mid x \in R, y \leq 9.2, y \in R\}$

4. a) $x = 2$; $(2, -1)$; $\{(x, y) \mid x \in R, y \geq -1, y \in R\}$
   b) $x = 4$; $(4, 28)$; $\{(x, y) \mid x \in R, y \leq 28, y \in R\}$
   c) $x = 3$; $(3, -1)$; $\{(x, y) \mid x \in R, y \leq -1, y \in R\}$
   d) $x = 2.5$; $(2.5, -12.25)$; $\{(x, y) \mid x \in R, y \geq -12.25, y \in R\}$

5. a) graph d; $(2.5, -12.25)$ **c)** graph c; $(3, -1)$
   b) graph b; $(4, 28)$ **d)** graph a; $(2, -1)$

6. a) maximum of 4   **b)** minimum of -3 **c)** maximum of 2

7. a) i)

x	−4	−2	0	2	4
y	−3	3	5	3	−3

   ii)

x	−4	−2	0	2	4
y	22	4	−2	4	22

b) i)

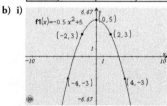

   ii)

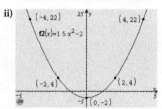

c) i) $\{(x, y) \mid x \in R, y \leq 5, y \in R\}$
   ii) $\{(x, y) \mid x \in R, y \geq -2, y \in R\}$

8. a)

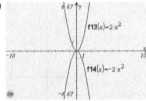

b) e.g., same vertex, axis of symmetry, and shape. One opens up, the other opens down.

c) e.g., vertex for both is (0, 4), original vertex moves up 4 units for each

9. a) $x = 3$ **c)** $x = -2$
b) $x = 5$ **d)** $x = -1$

10. $x = -3$

11. a) i)

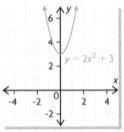

ii)

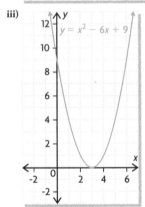

iii)

iv)

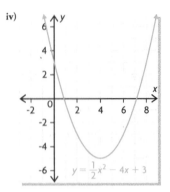

b) i) $x = 0$; (0, 3)   **iii)** $x = 3$; (3, 0)
ii) $x = -3.5$; (-3.5, 16.25)   **iv)** $x = 4$; (4, -5)

c) i) $\{(x, y) \mid x \in R, y \geq 3, y \in R\}$
ii) $\{(x, y) \mid x \in R, y \leq 16.25, y \in R\}$
iii) $\{(x, y) \mid x \in R, y \geq 0, y \in R\}$
iv) $\{(x, y) \mid x \in R, y \geq -5, y \in R\}$

12. 1.56 seconds

13. a) 31.9 m
b) $\{(x, y) \mid 0 \leq x \leq 5.1, x \in R, 0 \leq y \leq 31.9, y \in R\}$
c) 5.1 seconds

14. $\{(t, h) \mid 0 \leq t \leq 16.3, t \in R, 0 \leq h \leq 326.5, h \in R\}$

15. $\{(x, f(x)) \mid 0 \leq x \leq 2, x \in R, 4 \leq f(x) \leq 13.8, f(x) \in R\}$

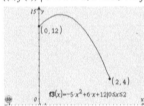

16. a) minimum since $a > 0$
b) Method 1: Determine the equation of the axis of symmetry.
$$x = \frac{-1 + 5}{2}$$
$$x = 2$$

Determine the y-coordinate of the vertex.
$y = 4(2)^2 - 16(2) + 21$
$y = 16 - 32 + 21$
$y = 5$
The vertex is (2, 5).

Method 2: Create a table of values.

x	−2	−1	0	1	2	3
y	69	41	21	9	5	9

The vertex is halfway between (1, 9) and (3, 9), which have the same y-value, so the vertex is (2, 5).

17. a) The y-coordinates are equal.
b) e.g., Substitute the x-coordinate from the axis of symmetry into the quadratic equation.

18. e.g., Yes, Gamez Inc.'s profit increased, unless the number of games sold was 900 000; then the profit is the same. For all points except $x = 9$, the second profit function yields a greater profit.

19. $y = -\frac{1}{2}x^2 - 3x + 10$

Lesson 6.3, page 346

1. a) iii d) vi
b) ii e) iv
c) v f) i

2. a) i) $x = -4, x = 2$ ii) $y = -8$ iii) $x = -1$ iv) $(-1, -9)$
v) $y = (x + 4)(x - 2)$

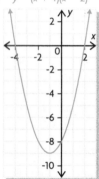

b) i) $x = 0, x = 3$ ii) $y = 0$ iii) $x = 1.5$ iv) $(1.5, 4.5)$
v) $y = -2x(x - 3)$

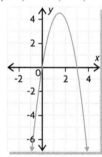

c) i) $x = -1, x = 7$ ii) $y = -14$ iii) $x = 3$ iv) $(3, -32)$
v)

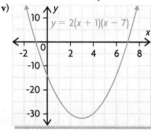

$y = 2(x + 1)(x - 7)$

3. $y = (x + 2)(x - 4)$

4. a) x-intercepts: -1, 1; y-intercept: -1; vertex: $(0, -1)$
equation of the axis of symmetry: $x = 0$
b) x-intercept: -2; y-intercept: 4; vertex: $(-2, 0)$
equation of the axis of symmetry: $x = -2$
c) x-intercept: 3; y-intercept: 9; vertex: $(3, 0)$
equation of the axis of symmetry: $x = 3$
d) x-intercepts: -1, 2; y-intercept: 4; vertex: $(0.5, 4.5)$
equation of the axis of symmetry: $x = 0.5$
e) x-intercept: 2; y-intercept: 12; vertex: $(2, 0)$
equation of the axis of symmetry: $x = 2$
f) x-intercept: 1; y-intercept: 4; vertex: $(1, 0)$
equation of the axis of symmetry: $x = 1$

5. a) $y = (x - 1)(x + 1)$

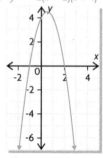

$\{(x, y) \mid x \in R, y \geq -1, y \in R\}$

b) $y = (x + 2)(x + 2)$

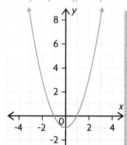

$\{(x, y) \mid x \in R, y \geq 0, y \in R\}$

c) $y = (x - 3)(x - 3)$

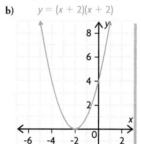

$\{(x, y) \mid x \in R, y \geq 0, y \in R\}$

d) $y = -2(x - 2)(x + 1)$

$\{(x, y) \mid x \in R, y \leq 4.5, y \in R\}$

e) $y = 3(x - 2)^2$

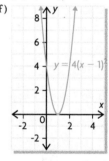

$\{(x, y) \mid x \in R, y \geq 0, y \in R\}$

f) $y = 4(x - 1)^2$

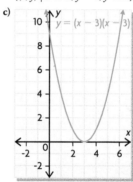

$\{(x, y) \mid x \in R, y \geq 0, y \in R\}$

6. $y = 3(x - 3)(x + 1)$

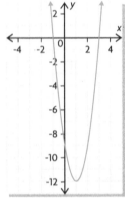

e.g., If $a = 1$ or $a = 2$, the graph would be stretched vertically. If $a = 0$, the graph would be linear. If $a = -1$ or $a = -2$, the graph would be stretched vertically and reflected in the x–axis. If $a = -3$, the graph would be reflected in the x–axis.

7. $y = (x - 3)(x + 3)$

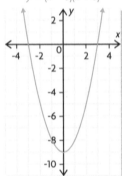

e.g.,
If $s = 2$, zeros at $x = 3$ and $x = -2$, the vertex moves to $(0.5, -6.25)$.
If $s = 1$, zeros at $x = 3$ and $x = -1$, the vertex moves to $(1, -4)$.
If $s = 0$, zeros at $x = 3$ and $x = 0$, the vertex moves to $(1.5, -2.25)$.
If $s = -1$, zeros at $x = 3$ and $x = 1$, the vertex moves to $(2, -1)$.
If $s = -2$, zeros at $x = 3$ and $x = 2$, the vertex moves to $(2.5, -0.25)$.
If $s = -3.8$, zeros at $x = 3$ and $x = 3.8$, the vertex moves to $(3.4, -0.16)$.

8. a) 312.5 m^2 **b)** $\{(x, y) \mid 0 \le x \le 25, x \in R, 0 \le y \le 312.5, y \in R\}$

9. $12, 720

10. a) i) e.g., $(0, -6), (-4, -6)$ **ii)** $(-2, -10)$
iii) $y = x^2 + 4x - 6$

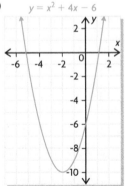

b) i) e.g., $(0, 13), (8, 13)$ **ii)** $(4, -3)$
iii)

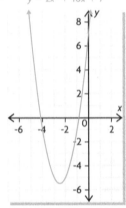
$y = x^2 - 8x + 13$

c) i) e.g., $(-5, 7), (0, 7)$ **ii)** $(-2.5, -5.5)$
iii) $y = 2x^2 + 10x + 7$

d) i) e.g., $(0, -5), (-8, -5)$ **ii)** $(-4, 11)$
iii) $y = -x^2 - 8x - 5$

e) i) e.g., $(0, -3), (4, -3)$ **ii)** $(2, -1)$
iii)

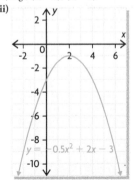
$y = -0.5x^2 + 2x - 3$

f) i) e.g., $(0, -9)$, $(5, -9)$ **ii)** $(2.5, 3.5)$

iii)

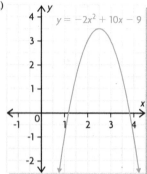

11. a) $y = \frac{1}{2}x^2 - 2x - 6$ **c)** $y = -\frac{1}{4}x^2 - x + 3$

b) $y = x^2 - 5x + 4$ **d)** $y = -x^2 + 6x$

12. a) e.g., Method 1: Use partial factoring.

$f(x) = -2x^2 + 16x - 24$

$f(x) = -2x(x - 8) - 24$

$-2x = 0$ $x - 8 = 0$

$x = 0$ $x = 8$

$f(0) = -24$ $f(8) = -24$

The points $(0, -24)$ and $(8, -24)$ are the same distance from the axis of symmetry.

$x = \frac{0 + 8}{2}$

$x = 4$

The equation of the axis of symmetry is $x = 4$.

$f(4) = -2(4)^2 + 16(4) - 24$

$f(4) = 8$

The vertex is $(4, 8)$.

Method 2: Factor the equation to determine the x-intercepts.

$f(x) = -2x^2 + 16x - 24$

$f(x) = -2(x^2 - 8x + 12)$

$f(x) = -2(x - 6)(x - 2)$

$x - 6 = 0$ $x - 2 = 0$

$x = 6$ $x = 2$

The x-intercepts are $x = 2$ and $x = 6$.

$x = \frac{2 + 6}{2}$

$x = 4$

The equation of the axis of symmetry is $x = 4$.

$f(4) = -2(4)^2 + 16(4) - 24$

$f(4) = 8$

The vertex is $(4, 8)$.

b) e.g., I prefer partial factoring because it is easier to determine the factors.

13. $y = 2x^2 - 4x - 6$

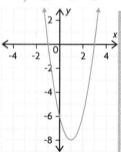

14. A quadratic function can have no zeros, one zero, or two zeros.

e.g.,

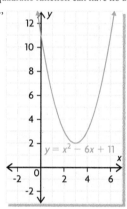

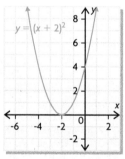

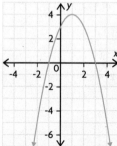

15. a) $\{(x, y) \mid 0 \le x \le 4, x \in R, -1 \le y \le 0, y \in R\}$ **b)** $y = \frac{1}{4}x^2 - x$

16. 12.5 feet by 25 feet

17. a) $h = -5.5t^2 + 33t$

b) $\{(t, h) \mid 0 \le t \le 6, t \in R, 0 \le h \le 49.5, h \in R\}$

18. e.g., The *x*-intercepts are $x = -3$ and $x = 1$. Therefore, $y = a(x - 1)(x + 3)$. Substitute a point on the graph, say $(3, 6)$, into the equation to obtain $a = \dfrac{1}{2}$.

19. **a)** $y = -0.019x^2 + 33$
b) $\{(x, y) \mid -33 \le x \le 33, x \in R, 12 \le y \le 33, y \in R\}$
c) $(-41.7, 0), (41.7, 0)$

20. **a)** $y = -0.0144x^2 + 132.279$
b) $\{(x, y) \mid -67.175 \le x \le 67.175, x \in R, 0 \le y \le 132.279, y \in R\}$
The grass closest to first and third base is the largest distance to the left or right. The grass closest to second base is the largest vertical distance.
c)

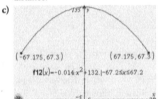

21. 50 feet by 94 feet

Mid-Chapter Review, page 353

1. **a)** not a quadratic function
b) quadratic function
c) quadratic function
d) not a quadratic function

2. **a)** $y = 0$
b)

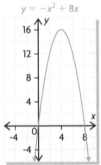

c) $x = 4$; $(4, 16)$; $x = 0$, $x = 8$; $\{(x, y) \mid x \in R, y \le 16, y \in R\}$

3. **a)** e.g., If $a > 0$, then the parabola opens up; if $a < 0$, then the parabola opens down.
b) $a > 0$

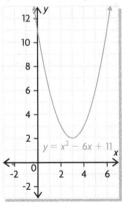

$a < 0$

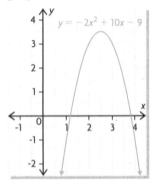

4. **a)** iv   **c)** i
b) iii   **d)** ii

5. **a)** $t = 0, t = 24$
b) 12 seconds, 720 metres
c) 675 metres
d) $\{(t, h) \mid 0 \le t \le 24, t \in R, 0 \le h \le 720, h \in R\}$

6. $x = -1$

7. $y = \dfrac{1}{4}x^2 + \dfrac{1}{2}x - 2$

8. **a)** $y = \dfrac{1}{2}x^2 - 3x - 36$
b) $(3, -40.5)$
c) $\{(x, y) \mid x \in R, y \ge -40.5, y \in R\}$

9.

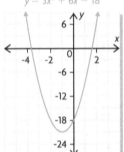

10. $26.25

Lesson 6.4, page 363

1. **a)** **i)** upward   **ii)** $(3, 7)$ **iii)** $x = 3$
b) **i)** downward   **ii)** $(-7, -3)$ **iii)** $x = -7$
c) **i)** upward   **ii)** $(2, -9)$ **iii)** $x = 2$
d) **i)** upward   **ii)** $(-1, 10)$ **iii)** $x = -1$
e) **i)** downward   **ii)** $(0, 5)$ **iii)** $x = 0$

2. a) maximum, 2 x-intercepts

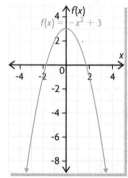

b) maximum, 0 x-intercepts

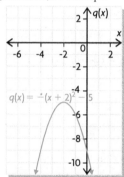

c) minimum, 0 x-intercepts

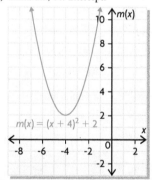

d) minimum, 2 x-intercepts

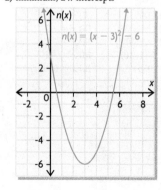

e) minimum, 0 x-intercepts

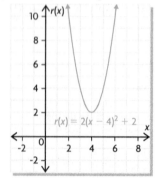

3. -3

4. C. The vertex is $(3, 5)$ and passes through the point $(0, -1)$.

5. a) iv; The vertex is $(3, 0)$.   **c)** i; The vertex is $(0, -3)$.
   b) iii; The vertex is $(-4, -2)$.   **d)** ii; The vertex is $(4, 2)$.

6. If $a > 0$, the parabola contains a minimum value. If $a < 0$, the parabola contains a maximum value.
   $a > 0, y = 2(x - 1)^2 - 7$

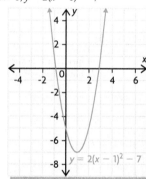

   $a < 0, y = -2(x - 2.5)^2 + 3.5$

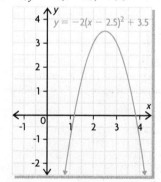

7. red, $y = (x + 4)^2$; $a = 1$ orange, $y = x^2 + 4$; $a = 1$
   purple, $y = (x - 4)^2$; $a = 1$ green, $y = -x^2 - 4$; $a = -1$
   blue, $y = -(x - 4)^2 - 4$; $a = -1$
   The parabolas are congruent.

8. a) $x = 9$ **c)** 6.5 ft
   b) 8 ft   **d)** $\{h(x) \mid 6.5 \le h \le 8, h \in R\}$

9. a) e.g., $y = (x - 3)^2 - 1$, $y = 2(x - 3)^2 - 1$, $y = -3(x - 3)^2 - 1$
   b) The second graph is narrower than the first graph, and the third graph opens downward instead of upward.

c)

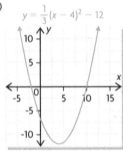

e.g., My predictions were accurate.

10. e.g., The vertex is $(1, -9)$, the graph opens upward, the equation of the axis of symmetry is $x = 1$, and the y-intercept is $(0, -7)$. I would draw a parabola that has all of these features.

11. a) $y = -\dfrac{1}{4}x^2 + 36$ **b)** $y = -\dfrac{2}{9}(x - 3)^2 + 2$

12. a) $y = a(x - 4)^2 - 12, a \neq 0, a \in R$

   b) $y = \dfrac{1}{3}(x - 4)^2 - 12$

   c) $\{(x, y) \mid x \in R, y \geq -12, y \in R\}$

   d)

$y = \dfrac{1}{3}(x - 4)^2 - 12$

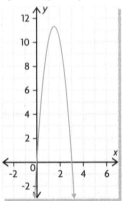

13. a) zeros: 0, 3

$y = -4.9(x - 1.5)^2 + 11.3$

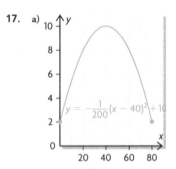

   b) e.g., One zero represents the location of the sprinkler and the other zero represents where the water lands on the grass.

14. a) $y = -2.4(x + 3.5)^2 + 15$

   b) $\{(x, y) \mid x \in R, y \leq 15, y \in R\}$

15. a) $y = 0.08(x - 2.5)^2 + 0.5$

   b) 0.68 m

   c) $\{(x, y) \mid 0 \leq x \leq 5, x \in R, 0.5 \leq y \leq 1, y \in R\}$

16. e.g., Agree. It is easier to graph the quadratic function when it is in vertex form because you can determine the vertex, the y-intercept, and direction of the graph without doing any calculations.

17. a)

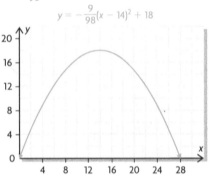

   b) The atlatl dart was 20 yd from Peter as it rose in the air, then 60 yd as it came down.

18. a) $h(t) = 5(t - 10)^2 + 20$ **b)** 20 m   **c)** 20 s

19. e.g., $-\dfrac{9}{98}(x - 14)^2 + 18$

$y = -\dfrac{9}{98}(x - 14)^2 + 18$

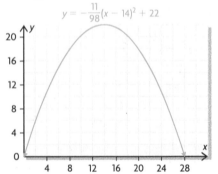

e.g., $-\dfrac{11}{98}(x - 14)^2 + 22$

$y = -\dfrac{11}{98}(x - 14)^2 + 22$

Lesson 6.5, page 376

1. a) $y = 3x^2 - 5$ **c)** $y = -3(x + 1)^2$

   b) $y = -(x - 2)^2 + 3$ **d)** $y = 0.25(x + 1.2)^2 + 4.8$

2. $y = -\dfrac{3}{8}(x + 5)^2 + 2$

3. a) $y = 2x^2 + 3$ **c)** $y = -(x + 1)^2 + 4$

   b) $y = \dfrac{1}{2}(x - 3)^2$ **d)** $y = -\dfrac{1}{2}(x - 2)^2 - 5$

4. $y = -(x - 5)^2 + 4$

5. a) i)

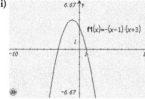

ii) maximum of 4
iii) $f(x) = -x^2 - 2x + 3$

b) i) $g(x) = 4x^2 - 20x + 24$

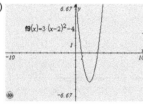

ii) minimum of -1
iii) $g(x) = 4x^2 - 20x + 24$

c) i)

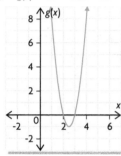

ii) minimum of -4
iii) $m(x) = 3x^2 - 12x + 8$

d) i)

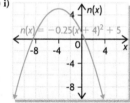

ii) maximum of 5
iii) $n(x) = -0.25x^2 - 2x + 1$

6. a) $y = -0.5x^2 + 4$
b) $y = 2(x - 4)^2 - 2$
c) $y = -(x - 4)^2 + 4$
d) $y = 0.8(x + 1)^2 - 3.2$

7. a) $h(t) = -5(t - 5)^2 + 1500$ **b)** 1500 m

8. a) $h(t) = -4.9t^2 + 44.1$ **b)** 44.1 m **c)** 60.75 m

9. a) -11 m/s
b) $h(t) = -5t^2 - 11t + 180$, as -11 is the initial velocity and 180 is the initial height when $t = 0$

10. a) \$4 **b)** \$50

11. a) At 0 km/h, the car would be stationary, so the length of the skid marks would be 0 m.
b) $D(x) = 0.007x^2$
c) 25.2 m
d) e.g., type of car, tires, road conditions

12. e.g., $y = \dfrac{3}{3481}x^2 + 2$

13. a) $h(x) = -\dfrac{36}{169}(x - 6.5)^2 + 9$; $\{x \mid 0 \leq x \leq 13, x \in R\}$
b) about 7.5 ft
c) about 7.1 ft
d) e.g., Drive through the centre of the road.
Maximum height = 7 ft. Maximum width = 7 ft.

14. $y = 0.00094x^2 - 21.94$

15. $p = -\dfrac{3}{5}(d - 75)^2 + 1600$

16. a) \$700 **b)** 420
c) e.g., With fewer people in the audience, it may be less enjoyable.

17. a)

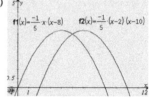

b) 3.2 m

18. a) $A = \dfrac{2}{3}x(600 - x)$ **c)** 300 m by 200 m
b) 60 000 m² **d)** 100 lots

Chapter Self-Test, page 383

1. a)

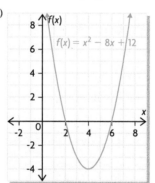

e.g., I used partial factoring to determine two points on the parabola with the same y-coordinate, then the axis of symmetry, and then the y-coordinate of the vertex.

b) $f(x) = -2(x + 1)(x - 5)$

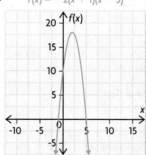

e.g., I plotted the x-intercepts and the y-intercept.

c)

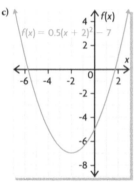

$f(x) = 0.5(x + 2)^2 - 7$

e.g., I plotted the vertex and the y-intercept.

d)

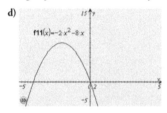

f11(x)=-2·x²-8·x

e.g., I factored the equation to determine the vertex and x-intercepts.

2. a) x-intercepts: -3, 5; y-intercept: 15; vertex: $(1, 16)$
equation of the axis of symmetry: $x = 1$
b) x-intercepts: 1.5, -4; y-intercept: -12; vertex: $(-1.25, -15.125)$
equation of the axis of symmetry: $x = -1.25$

3. a) 10 s   **b)** 256 ft   **c)** 400 ft

4. $f(x) = 3x^2 + 12x + 9$

5. $y = \dfrac{1}{3}x^2 - 2x - 4$

6. $900

7. The top of the arch is 10 feet high. The door will be 5.6 feet tall, which won't give enough headroom.

Chapter Review, page 386

1. a)

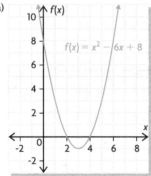

$f(x) = x^2 - 6x + 8$

b)

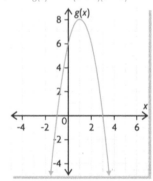

$g(x) = -2(x + 1)(x - 3)$

c)

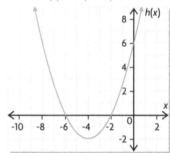

$h(x) = 0.5(x + 4)^2 - 2$

2. e.g., The zeros are $x = 0$ and $x = 23$; the equation of the axis of symmetry is $x = 11.5$.

3. $(2, 7)$

4. a) 47 m
b) $\{(t, h(t)) \mid 0 \le t \le 6.07, t \in R, 0 \le h(t) \le 47, h(t) \in R\}$

5. a) $y = -\dfrac{3}{2}(x+1)^2 + 2$
b) $\{(x, y) \mid -1 \le x \le 0, x \in R, 0.5 \le y \le 2, y \in R\}$

6. $(-6.25, -23.63)$

7. a) $f(x) = 2(x - 1)(x - 5)$
b) zeros: $x = 1$, $x = 5$
equation of the axis of symmetry: $x = 3$
c) $\{(x, y) \mid x \in R, y \ge -8, y \in R\}$
d)

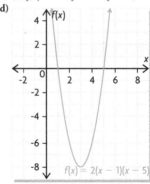

$f(x) = 2(x - 1)(x - 5)$

8. $x = -1.5, 4$
9. a) $(1, 2)$
   b) $(-2.5, 0.25)$
10. a) $y = -3(x + 1)^2 - 3$ b) $y = (x - 5)^2 + 1$
11. a) upward
    b) $x = 3, (3, -7)$
    c) $\{(x, y) \mid x \in R, y \geq -7, y \in R\}$
    d)

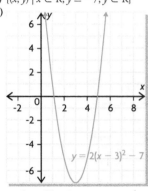

12. $y = -(x + 1)^2 + 3$
13. $y = -3(x + 4)(x + 2)$
14. $y = -\dfrac{1}{4}(x - 3)^2 - 5$
15. $y = -0.45x^2 + 45$
16. a) e.g., $-0.00425x^2 + 61$
    b) e.g., the positions of the arches
17. Yes
18. 20 m by 40 m, 800 m²
19. e.g., $y = -\dfrac{1}{360}(x - 65)(x + 65), y = -\dfrac{1}{360}x^2 + \dfrac{13}{36}x$

Chapter 7

Lesson 7.1, page 402

1. a)

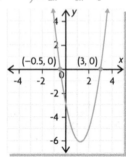

$x = -0.5, 3$

b)

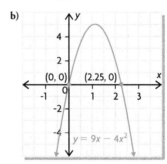

$x = 0, 2.25$

2. a)

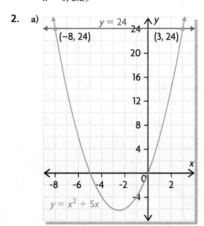

$x = -8, 3$

b)

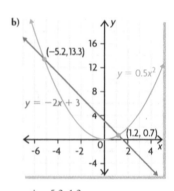

$x \doteq -5.2, 1.2$

3. a) $6a^2 - 11a - 35 = 0$

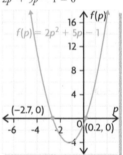

$a \doteq -1.7, 3.5$

b) $2p^2 + 5p - 1 = 0$

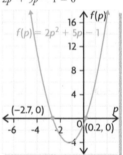

$p \doteq -2.7, 0.2$

4. a) $x = -2, 5$ **b)** $x = -3$

5. a)

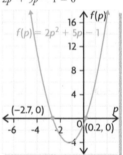

$x \doteq -0.8, 2.8$

b)

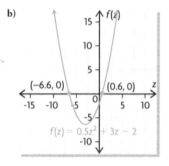

$z \doteq -6.6, 0.6$

c)

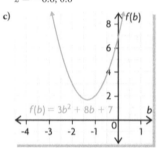

no real roots

d)

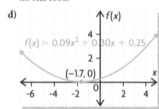

$x \doteq -1.7$

6. a)

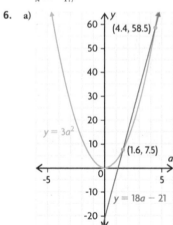

$a \doteq 1.6, 4.4$

b)

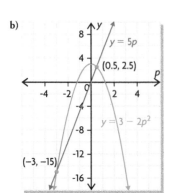

$p = -3, 0.5$

c)

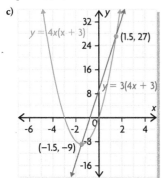

$x = 1.5, -1.5$

d)

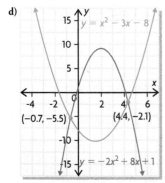

$x \doteq -0.7, 4.4$

7. a) $16 = -4.9t^2 + 8t + 14$

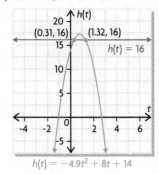

$t = 0.31$ s and $t = 1.32$ s

b) $12 = -4.9t^2 + 8t + 14$

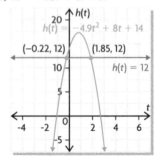

$t \doteq -0.22, 1.85$

$t \geq 0, t = 1.85$ s

c) No; the maximum height is less than 18.

d) $t \doteq 2.69$ s

8. a)

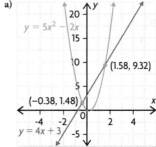

$x \doteq -0.38, 1.58$

b)

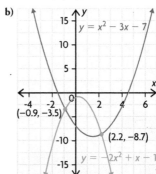

$x \doteq -0.9, 2.2$

c)

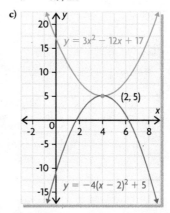

$x = 2$

d) $y = 5x^2 + 4x + 3$

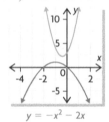

$y = -x^2 - 2x$

no solution

9. Yes, solving $120 = 0.0059s^2 + 0.187s$ indicates that the driver was travelling 127.65 km/h.

10. a) $y = 4x^2 + 3x - 2$

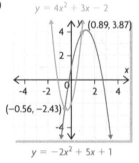

$y = -2x^2 + 5x + 1$

$(-0.56, -2.43), (0.89, 3.87)$

b) $6x^2 - 2x - 3 = 0$

$y = 6x^2 - 2x - 3$

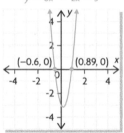

$x \doteq -0.6, 0.89$

c) e.g., I prefer using the method in part b) because there is only one function to graph.

11. 9 m by 13 m

12. a) Kevin did not determine the values at the point of intersection, but determined the zeros for the LS function.

b) $x = 0.153, 2.181$

13. a) $x = -23.887, 29.807$

b) $x = -0.605, 7.631$

14. e.g., If the function crosses the x-axis at more than one place, there are two roots; if the function touches the x-axis at one place, there are two equal roots; if the function does not cross the x-axis, there are no real roots.

15.

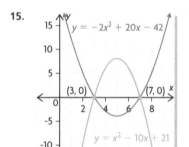

e.g., $3x^2 - 30x + 63 = 0$, $3x^2 - 30x = -63$, $x^2 - 10x + 21 = 0$

Lesson 7.2, page 411

1. a) $x = 4, 7$ **c)** $y = -5, -0.5$
b) $x = -3, 10$ **d)** $t = -3, 1.25$

2. a) $x = 11, -11$ **e)** $s = 6$
b) $r = \dfrac{10}{3}, -\dfrac{10}{3}$ **f)** $p = -0.25$
c) $x = 0, 15$ **g)** $z = 0, 2.5$
d) $y = -16, 0$ **h)** $q = 0, \dfrac{9}{5}$

3. a) $x = -5, 14$ **c)** $a = -4, \dfrac{1}{3}$
b) $x = -16, -3$ **d)** $t = -\dfrac{4}{3}, \dfrac{5}{2}$

4. a) $x = -4, \dfrac{3}{2}$ **c)** $d = -\dfrac{3}{7}$
b) $x = -3, \dfrac{3}{4}$ **d)** $g = \dfrac{13}{9}, -\dfrac{13}{9}$

5. a) $x = -0.75, 1.8$
b) e.g., Geeta may have had the wrong signs between the terms within each factor.

6. a) $u = -7, 9$ **c)** $y = -6, 2$
b) $x = -4, -2$ **d)** $k = -5$

7. e.g., $x^2 + 17x + 60 = 0$

8. The price of the ticket should be either $1.50 or $3.50. (That is, $x = -5$ or $x = 15$.)

9. $x = \dfrac{1}{4}, \dfrac{8}{5}$

10. Going from the second line to the third line, 100 divided by 5 is 20, not 25. Also, in the final step, it is possible that the final result could be positive or negative. Therefore, the two solutions are $a = -\sqrt{20}$ or $a = \sqrt{20}$.

11. The first line was incorrectly factored:
$4r^2 - 9r = 0$
$r(4r - 9) = 0$
$r = 0$ or $4r - 9 = 0$
$4r = 9$
$r = \dfrac{9}{4}$

$r = 0$ or $r = \dfrac{9}{4}$

12. a) e.g., $y = 8x^2 + 2x - 3$
   b) e.g., No, we had different functions.
   c) e.g., $y = 16x^2 + 4x - 6$, $y = -24x^2 - 6x + 9$
13. a) She must sell either 600 or 1800 posters to break even.
   b) She must sell either 800 or 1600 posters to earn a profit of $5000.
   c) She must sell 1200 posters to earn $9000.
   d) D: $n \geq 0$; R: $-27 \leq P \leq 9$
   If Sanela sells 0 posters, she will incur a loss of $27\,000$; her maximum profit is $9000.
14. a) 7 s
   b) D: $0 \leq t \leq 7$, where t is the time in seconds, since the rock begins to fall at 0 s and hits the water at 7 s
15. a) e.g., $x^2 - 2x - 8 = 0$
   b) e.g., $x^2 - 2x + 9 = 0$; I changed the "c" term.
16. a) i) Write the equation in standard form.
   ii) Factor fully.
   iii) Set each factor with a variable equal to zero (since the product is zero, one factor must be equal to zero).
   iv) Solve.
   b) When the quadratic equation is factorable, solve by factoring; otherwise, solve by graphing.
17. a) Since the equation is factorable, I can predict that it is a difference of squares.
   b) $x = -6$
   c) $\left(\sqrt{ax} + \sqrt{c}\right)\left(\sqrt{ax} - \sqrt{c}\right) = 0$, where $\dfrac{\sqrt{c}}{\sqrt{a}} = 6$
   d) $ax^2 - c = 0$
18. 10 cm, 24 cm, and 26 cm

Lesson 7.3, page 419

1. a) $x = \dfrac{-7 - \sqrt{69}}{2}, \dfrac{-7 + \sqrt{69}}{2}$

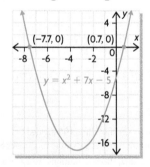

   b) $x = -4, -0.375$

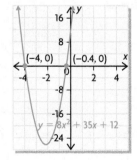

c) $a = \dfrac{5 - \sqrt{17}}{4}, \dfrac{5 + \sqrt{17}}{4}$

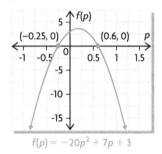

   d) $p = -0.25, 0.6$

2. a) $x = -6, 1$
   b) $x = -\dfrac{4}{9}, 0$
   c) $x = 2.2, -2.2$
   d) $x = -\dfrac{5}{4}, \dfrac{8}{3}$
3. e.g., I preferred factoring because it takes less time and there is less room for errors.
4. a) $x = \dfrac{-5 - \sqrt{133}}{6}, \dfrac{-5 + \sqrt{133}}{6}$
   b) $x = \dfrac{7 - \sqrt{1102}}{39}, \dfrac{7 + \sqrt{1102}}{39}$
   c) $x = \dfrac{3 - \sqrt{3}}{2}, \dfrac{3 + \sqrt{3}}{2}$
   d) no solution
5. The roots are correct.
6. a) $x = \dfrac{3 - 2\sqrt{3}}{3}, \dfrac{3 + 2\sqrt{3}}{3}$
   b) $x = -4 - \sqrt{13}, -4 + \sqrt{13}$
   c) $x = \dfrac{-2 - \sqrt{6}}{4}, \dfrac{-2 + \sqrt{6}}{4}$
   d) $x = \dfrac{2 - \sqrt{5}}{3}, \dfrac{2 + \sqrt{5}}{3}$
7. a) $0.73, $19.27
   b) $10
8. a) 5.5 s
   b) e.g., about 10 s as 250 m is twice 125 m
   c) 7.6 s
   d) e.g., My prediction was not close.
9. a) It may be possible, but the factors would not be whole numbers.
   b) $z = -0.75$
   c) e.g., I used the formula because I find it most efficient.

10. a) 7.28 s

b) 1.77 s; The ball would be in flight 5.51 s longer on the Moon.

11. 0.25 m

12. e.g.,

- The quadratic formula can be used to solve any quadratic equation.
- You can use it to solve a factorable equation if you find it too difficult to factor.
- The radicand can be used to tell you about the solution.
  - If it is a perfect square, then the equation is factorable. Both roots are rational numbers.
  - If it is not a perfect square, then the roots can be given as a decimal approximation, or you can choose to leave the radical in the solution and give the exact values.
  - If it is negative, then there is no solution.

13. a) $-\dfrac{b}{a}$

b) $\dfrac{c}{a}$

c) $x = 0.5, 0.8$; sum $= 1.3$; product $= 0.4$

d) Yes, the answers match.

e) 1. d) sum: $\dfrac{7}{20}$; product: $-\dfrac{3}{20}$

2. a) sum: -5; product: -6

5. sum: -2; product: -15

7. sum: 20; product: 14

f) e.g., Determine the sum and product of your proposed solutions, then check to see if they match the results obtained from the formulas in parts a) and b).

Mid-Chapter Review, page 424

1. a)

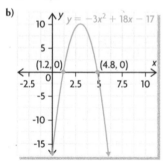

$$x \doteq -7, 1$$

b)

$$x \doteq 1.2, 4.8$$

2. a)

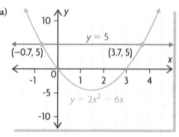

$$x \doteq -0.7, 3.7$$

b)

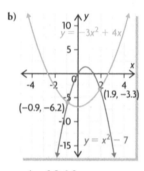

$$x \doteq -0.9, 1.9$$

c)

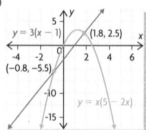

$$x \doteq -0.8, 1.8$$

d)

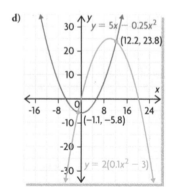

$$x \doteq -1.1, 12.2$$

3. 14 s

4. **a)** $x = -4, 1$
   b) $z = -4.5, 5$

5. **a)** $x = -3, \dfrac{1}{2}$ **e)** $t = -\dfrac{9}{2}, \dfrac{9}{2}$

   b) $a = -\dfrac{5}{6}$ **f)** $x = -\dfrac{16}{3}, \dfrac{16}{3}$

   c) $c = \dfrac{3}{4}, \dfrac{5}{2}$ **g)** $w = 0, \dfrac{5}{3}$

   d) $p = \dfrac{1}{4}$ **h)** $x = 0, \dfrac{7}{3}$

6. e.g., $0 = 2x^2 + 11x - 6$

7. **a)** $k = \dfrac{-5 - \sqrt{37}}{6}, \dfrac{-5 + \sqrt{37}}{6}$

   b) $n = \dfrac{-15 - \sqrt{33}}{16}, \dfrac{-15 + \sqrt{33}}{16}$

   c) $x = \dfrac{4}{5}, 2$

   d) $y = -\dfrac{17}{2}, -\dfrac{11}{4}$

8. **a)** $p = -4, -\dfrac{3}{2}$

   b) $x = \dfrac{12 - \sqrt{344}}{10}, \dfrac{12 + \sqrt{344}}{10}$

   c) $a = \dfrac{-23 - \sqrt{193}}{24}, \dfrac{-23 + \sqrt{193}}{24}$

9. **a)** The price will have to increase by $110.87 or $336.80.
   b) It is not possible as the maximum value according to the function is less than $140 000.

Lesson 7.4, page 430

1. **a)** e.g., Graph the equations and determine the intersection.
   b) 23.76 m
   c) e.g., Factor the equation to find the x-intercepts.

2. **a)** 4.51 cm
   b)

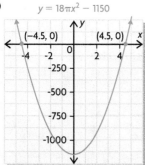

   $y = 18\pi x^2 - 1150$

   c) e.g., I prefer the method in part a) because it takes less time.

3. $-8, 19$
4. 4.24 cm
5. about 1.57 s
6. 8:27 a.m.
7. **a)** $E(x) = -5x^2 + 75x + 5000$
   b) $40
   c) $32.50
8. -14 and -13, or 13 and 14
9. about 29.0 cm

10. e.g., Underline key words, write what is given, write what you need to figure out, draw a picture, use a strategy previously used, and ask yourself if the answer is probable.
11. 6:30 pm
12. 14.4 cm

Chapter Self-Test, page 433

1. **a)**

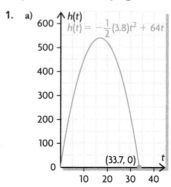

   $h(t) = -\dfrac{1}{2}(3.8)t^2 + 64t$

   33.7 s
   b) 8 s, 25 s
   c) No, the maximum height reached is less than 550 m.

2.

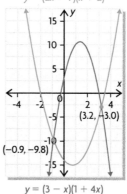

   $y = (2x - 7)(x + 2)$

   $y = (3 - x)(1 + 4x)$

   $x \doteq -0.9, 3.2$

3. **a)** $y = \dfrac{25}{9}, \dfrac{-25}{9}$ **c)** $c = 4, -4$

   b) $z = 0, 2$ **d)** $h = 0, \dfrac{4}{5}$

4. **a)** $x = -8, -3$

   b) $a = -4, \dfrac{1}{8}$

   c) $c = -1, 6$

   d) $x = -\dfrac{2}{5}, -\dfrac{1}{4}$

5. a) $x \doteq -6.27, 1.27$

b) $x \doteq -0.23, 3.23$

c) $x = \dfrac{3}{5}$

d) no solution

6. The numbers are 8, 10, and 12 or -4, -2, and 0.

7. a) 56.2 m

b) about 4 m

8. about 10 cm by 15 cm

Chapter Review, page 436

1. a)

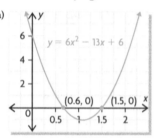

$x \doteq 0.6, 1.5$

b)

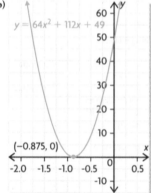

$x = -0.875$

c)

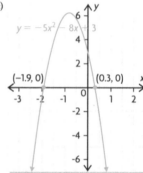

$x \doteq -1.9, 0.3$

d) $y = -0.25x^2 + 2x + 5$

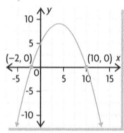

$x = -2, 10$

2. a)

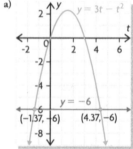

$t \doteq -1.37, 4.37$

b)

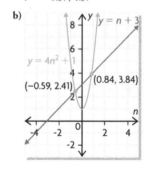

$n \doteq -0.59, 0.84$

c) $y = 2(b - 5) + 0.5b^2$

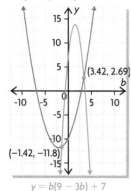

$y = b(9 - 3b) + 7$

$b \doteq -1.42, 3.42$

d) $y = c^2 - 38c + 340$

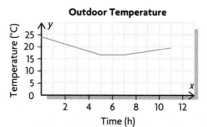

(11.3, 38.3)

(17.7, −19.3)

$y = 3c^2 - 96c + 740$

$c \doteq 11.3, 17.7$

3. a) $s = -5, 12$

b) $x = -2.5, 0.8$

c) $a = -3, -2$

d) $x = -2, \dfrac{1}{3}$

e) $d = 3.25, -3.25$

f) $r = 0, \dfrac{8}{3}$

g) $x = 4.5, -4.5$

h) $m = -8, 0$

4. a) $x = \dfrac{11}{13}, \dfrac{16}{9}$

b) $f \doteq 0.73, -2.73$

c) $h \doteq 0.52, -1.38$

d) no solution

5. The numbers are 1, 3, 5 or 3, 5, 7.

6. The other side is 45 cm; the hypotenuse is 51 cm.

7. 1:59 p.m.

8. a) 500 m

b) 22.4 s

9. ±16 and ±28

10. $6.25

Chapter 8

Lesson 8.1, page 450

1. a) store A: $8.50/kg; store B: $7.35/kg; store B has the lower rate

b) station A: $0.94/L; station B: $0.98/L; station A has the lower rate

2. a) tank A: 71 L/h; tank B: 69 L/h; tank A has the greater rate

b) person A: 5 m/s; person B: 3 m/s; person A has the greater rate

3. a) 20 s to 28 s; 28 s to 32 s

b) 28 s; 32 s

c) distance does not change; speed is zero

4. a) bottles: $0.001 75/mL; boxes: $0.001 66/mL

b) Boxes have the lower unit cost.

5. 925 mL container: $0.022/mL; 3.54 L container: $0.015/mL; The larger container has the lower unit cost.

6. aerobics: 7 cal/min; hockey: 8 cal/min; She burns calories at a greater rate playing hockey.

7. a) 10 lb for $17.40 is the same as $3.83/kg; $3.61/kg is the lower rate.

b) 6 mph is the same as 10 km/h; 2 km in 10 min is the same as 12 km/h; the first rate is lower.

c) 35.1 L for 450 km is the same as 7.8 L/100 km; this is the lower rate

d) 30 m/s is the same as 108 km/h; 100 km/h is the lower rate.

8. Farmer's Co-op: $0.852/lb; pet store: $0.623/lb; pet store has the lower rate

9. telephone company: $24/year; Internet: $28.95/year

10.

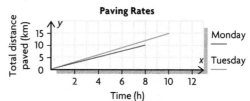

11.

Outdoor Temperature

12. e.g., In the first 10 min, the shuttle was driven away from the airport to pick up and drop off passengers at three different hotels; the farthest hotel was about 9 km away. Then the shuttle was driven toward the airport for one more pick-up/drop-off about 7.5 km from the airport. It continued toward the airport and stopped at one more hotel, where David disembarked. The whole trip took about 22 min.

13. a) graduated cylinder   **b)** flask   **c)** beaker   **d)** drinking glass

14. The rates for 1990–1995 and 1995–2000 are both 4.8 megatonnes/year.

15. The greatest speed difference is in the 700 m to 1100 m segment, by 0.113 m/s.

16. e.g.,
    a) An estimate is sufficient when you only need to know which rate is better, such as which car uses less fuel per kilometre. A precise answer is needed if you want to know how much fuel you will save for a particular trip.
    b) A graphing strategy is a good approach for comparing rates because you can visually compare the slopes. For example, a steeper slope for one lap of a car race on a graph of distance versus time means a faster speed. A numerical strategy is better if you want to know exactly how much faster one lap was compared to another.

17.

Depth of Water in a Flask

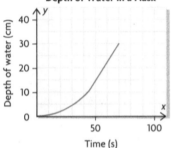

Time (s)

18. **a)** about 14 300
    b) e.g., 27 079 MIPS; about 3693

Lesson 8.2, page 458

1. **a)** 9 L   **c)** $12.75
    b) 3 min   **d)** about 30 mL
2. **a)** Supersaver: $0.25/can; Gord: $0.28/can; Supersaver has the lower unit price.
    b) e.g., size of container, amount that must be bought
3. 56 turns
4. 18 games
5. 6% per year
6. e.g.,
    a) cost for meat in a grocery store
    b) amount of medicine per body mass
    c) cost for cold cuts at the deli counter
    d) change in temperature as altitude changes when climbing a mountain
    e) density of a substance
    f) cost of flooring at a hardware store
7. 4 min 16 s
8. 44 min
9. 20

10. 867 h
Strategy 1: She works 50 h every 3 weeks; therefore, she works approximately 16.667 h in 1 week (50 h/3 weeks). Since there are 52 weeks in a year, she works approximately 866.7 h in a year (16.667 h/week × 52 weeks/year)
Strategy 2:
$$\frac{50 \text{ h}}{3 \text{ weeks}} = \frac{x}{52 \text{ weeks}}$$
Solve for x to get approximately 866.7 h.

11. **a)** 65.2 km/h   **b)** 9.8 L/100 km   **c)** $1.09/L
12. $704.50
13. **a)** $817.95
    b) no, for 8 weeks she would need 844.8 pounds
    c) e.g., What is the food's shelf-life? How much space will be needed to store the food? What are the shipping charges?
14. e.g.,
    a) about 400 000 ha
    b) about $19.2 million
15. store A: $0.416/L; store B: $0.441/L
Store A, because it is closer and the water is less expensive per litre.
16. 7:24 a.m.
17. −2.2 °C
18. **a)** Bren's Interior Design
    b) e.g., The distance to the store or whether a second coat will be needed.
19. 1268
20. 4.7 h

Mid-Chapter Review, page 465

1. Carol is faster because Jed's keying rate is 58 words/min.
2. Stan paid less per litre, because Harry paid $0.985/L.
3. **a)** 4 Cal/min   **b)** 30 L/day   **c)** $8.40/kg   **d)** 5 km in 20 min
4. **a)**

Temperature vs. Time

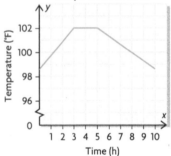

Time (h)

    b) interval 0 h to 3 h
5. **a)** The interval about 28 s to 35 s; the slope is steepest over this interval.
    b) The interval about 35 s to 60 s; the slope is least steep over this interval.
    c) about 19 m/s; about 5 m/s
    d) 8.3 m/s
6. **a)** U.S. store, $114.47
    b) e.g., return/exchange/repair policies, service, custom duties, delivery time, shipping costs
7. 1000 mi
8. $102.20
9. **a)** 7.28 m/s, 7.17 m/s
    b) The average speed is slightly less for the race that is slightly longer.
    c) e.g., Longer races typically have lower average speeds.

Lesson 8.3, page 471

1. **a)** $\frac{3}{5} = 60\%$ **b)** $\frac{3}{2} = 150\%$

2. **a)** original smaller **b)** original larger **c)** original larger

3. **a)** 5 in. : 6 ft or 5 in. : 72 in. **b)** $\frac{5}{72}$

4. $g = 4.0$ cm, $h \doteq 5.3$ cm, $x = 6.0$ m, $y = 7.5$ m

5. e.g.,
   a) 1.2 **b)** 1.8 **c)** 0.9

6. **a)** 1, 4.0 m by 5.0 m; 2, 4.0 m by 4.0 m; 3, 4.0 m by 4.0 m
   b) 4.8 m by 4.0 m
   c) bedroom 1, 20.0 m²

7. **a)** e.g., 1 in. : 100 ft
   b) e.g.,

6.5 in.

3 in.

8.

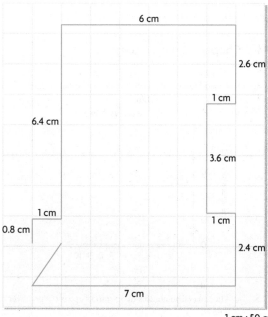

6 cm
2.6 cm
1 cm
6.4 cm
3.6 cm
1 cm
0.8 cm
1 cm
2.4 cm
7 cm
1 cm : 50 cm

9. The diagram should measure 13.5 cm by 9 cm.

10. e.g.,
    a) diameters: 1.6 cm, 2.5 cm, 3.4 cm; hexagon side: 2.0 cm
    b), c)

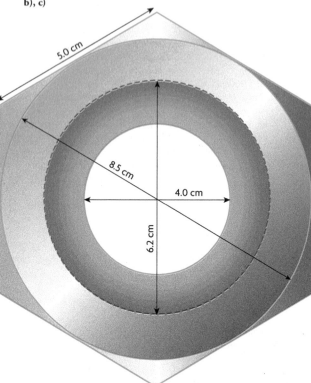

5.0 cm
8.5 cm
4.0 cm
6.2 cm

11. 0.25 mm

12. **a) i)** about 629 km
    ii) about 557 km
    b) Yellowknife and Fort Providence

13. **a)** 15 m **b)** 11.8 m²

14. **a)** 3 **b)** $\frac{1}{20}$ **c)** 40 **d)** $\frac{1}{110}$

15. e.g., The diagram could be a rectangle measuring 18 cm by 14 cm.

16. **a)** 4 m² **b)** 2 m **c)** 5 mm : 2 m **d)** $\frac{1}{400}$

17. width = 36.6 in., height = 20.6 in.

18. e.g.
    a) **b)** **c)**

19. e.g., The dimensions of the space you actually have for your scale diagram; how large you want the scale diagram to be in that space; and a comparison of the ratio of the dimensions of the available space to the ratio of the dimensions of the original.

20. a) 0.65   **b)** 7.8 in. by 5.2 in.

Lesson 8.4, page 479

1. a) 4   **b)** 12 cm², 192 cm²   **c)** 16

2.

Length of Base (cm)	Height of Triangle (cm)	Scale Factor	Area (cm²)	Area of scaled triangle / Area of original triangle
3.0	4.0	1	6.0	1
9.0	12.0	3	54.0	9
1.5	2.0	0.5	1.5	0.25
30.0	40.0	10	600.0	100
0.75	1.0	25%	0.375	0.0625

3. 1050 cm²

4. a) 44 units²   **b)** 52 units²   **c)** 50 units²

5. a) 2.5 units²   **b)** 1.3 units²

6. a) 6 in. by 9 in.
     b) 225%
     c) e.g., Enlarge each side by 150%, then multiply the new side lengths, or calculate the area of the smaller photo, then multiply by 2.25.

7. Enlarge each side length using a scale factor of 2.

8. a) $\frac{2}{3}$ **b)** 64 cm²

9. garage: 600 m², office: 100 m²

10. a) $65 000   **b)** $280 000

11.

120 ft; 5 ft; 10 ft; 20 ft; 5 ft; 30 ft; 60 ft; 30 ft

12. 8 cm² and 32 cm²

13. a) 1.5   **b)** 0.5

14. a) 4
     b) The perimeter of the large triangle is 4 times the perimeter of the small triangle; the area of the large triangle is 4² times the area of the small triangle.

15. a) 0.152 m : 7600 m = 1 m : 50 000 m
     b) 49 ha
     c) $18 300

16. a), b), e.g., If kitchen is about 10 ft by 20 ft and scale diagrams are drawn on 8.5 in. by 11 in. paper, scale factor could be $\frac{1}{48}$.
     c) e.g., Estimate or measure the open floor space areas in each diagram and compare.

17. e.g., The area is divided by 4 in process A.

18. 81%

19. about 46¢ more

Lesson 8.5, page 489

1. a) similar
     b) similar
     c) similar
     d) not similar

2. a) Yes, all spheres are similar.
     b) i) $\frac{25}{22}$ **ii)** $\frac{22}{25}$

3. length: 52 m; beam: 8.5 m; height 43 m

4. a) Yes, all dimensions are proportional.
     b) S: 16 cm; L: 32 cm

5. length: 8.6 m; height: 3.8 m

6. 1.41 m by 1.68 m by 3.71 m

7. a) 2   **b)** length: 180 cm; height: 150 cm

8. a) $\frac{1}{3}$ **b)** 10 in.

9. 16 in. by 2 in.

10. a) about 3 in. by 5 in. by 2 in.
     b) $\frac{87}{160}$
     c) $3\frac{1}{4}$ in. long, $4\frac{5}{8}$ in. high, $2\frac{1}{8}$ in. wide

11. 2

12. e.g.,
     a) 6 m tall, 5 m wide
     b) Measure the metre stick in the photo to determine the scale factor. Then multiply the building measurements by the scale factor to determine the building dimensions in metres.

13.

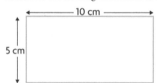

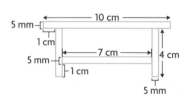

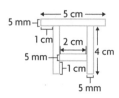

14.

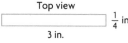

Top view

3 in. — $\frac{1}{4}$ in.

Side view

3 in.

$\frac{1}{4}$ in.

Front view

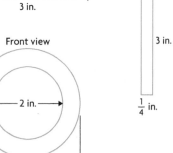

— 2 in. —

— 3 in. —

15. e.g., Using a scale factor of $\frac{1}{20}$, the views would have the following dimensions:

Top view rectangle: 6.7 cm by 3.3 cm
Side view rectangle: 3.3 cm by 4.4 cm
Front view rectangle: 6.7 cm by 4.4 cm

16. e.g., for an eraser measuring 7.0 cm by 2.0 cm by 0.5 cm, using a scale factor of $\frac{1}{2}$:

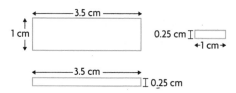

— 3.5 cm —

1 cm

0.25 cm ⊥

←1 cm→

— 3.5 cm —

⊥ 0.25 cm

17. **a)** no; The area of the base increases by the square of the scale factor.
b) no; The volume increases by the cube of the scale factor.
18. e.g., Both involve multiplying each dimension by a scale factor; shapes have two dimensions while objects have three dimensions.
19. **a)** 2.25
b) $0.02
20. 25 cm²

Lesson 8.6, page 500

1. **a) i)** 4 **ii)** 8
b) i) $\frac{9}{4}$ **ii)** $\frac{27}{8}$
c) i) 16 **ii)** 64
d) i) $\frac{25}{9}$ **ii)** $\frac{125}{27}$
2. **a)** 50 **b)** 2500 **c)** 125 000
3. 480 cm, 7650 cm²
4. 864 m³
5. **a)** 4500 cm²
b) 9; The thickness of the paper will not change.
6. 3974 cm³
7. **a)** 3.375 **b)** 2.25 **c)** 1.5
8. 9 and 27
9. 6600 cm³

10. **a)** 1750 **b)** 25
11. **a)** 2.7 cm **c)** 13.5
b) 3.7 **d)** 49.5
12. 2.7
13. 72%
14. **a)** 1.5 **c)** 3.375
b) 2.25 **d)** 988 cm³, 3334 cm³
15. **a)** No, it will take about four times as much ($k = 2$; $k^2 = 4$).
b) No, it is $\frac{1}{8}$ the volume of the large shoebox $\left(k = \frac{1}{2}; k^3 = \frac{1}{8} \right)$.
16. **a)** Surface area of scaled cylinder = $k^2(2\pi r^2 + 2\pi rh)$
Volume of scaled cylinder = $k^3(\pi r^2 h)$
b) Surface area of scaled cone = $k^2(\pi r^2 + \pi rs)$
Volume of scaled cone = $k^3\left(\frac{1}{3}\pi r^2 h \right)$
17. e.g., Consider the relationship between the volumes. The scale factor is 2, so the larger prism has a volume that is 8 times the volume of the smaller prism. Eight of the smaller prisms will fit inside the larger prism.
18. 9
19. **a)** 37 914 864 km² **b)** 21 952 700 000 km³
20. e.g., $20.16, assuming the heights are the same and that frosting costs the same as the interior of the cake.

Chapter Self-Test, page 504

1. **a)** increasing: 1993–1995, 1996–2000, 2001–2004, 2005–2008; decreasing: 1995–1996, 2000–2001, 2008–mid-2009
b) 2004–2005
c) 1998–1999; 2007–2008
d) e.g., general economic conditions
2. 1250 L
3. 1 m by 1.5 m
4. **a)** 2.4 cm, 6.8 cm **c)** 41.7 cm²
b) 7.2 cm **d)** 54.7 cm³
5. 3.5 ft
6. **a)** no
b) The largest pizza is the best buy.

Chapter Review, page 507

1.

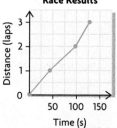

Race Results

Distance (laps)

Time (s)

2. **a)** The second rate ($2.26/kg) is lower.
b) The second rate (29 km/h) is lower.
c) The first rate is lower (the second is 6.8 L/100 km).
d) The first rate (36 km/h) is lower.
3. Yes, her projected time is under 2 h 39 min.
4. **a)** about 30 sq yards
b) locally (she will save about $10)
5. $\frac{3}{200}$

6. e.g.,

a) $\dfrac{1}{2}$

b) for a book cover, a rectangle 10.5 cm by 13.2 cm

7. a)

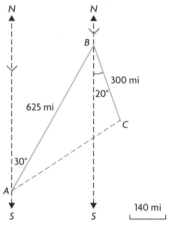

b) Use a ruler to measure the distance from C to A on the scale drawing in part (a); then use the scale to calculate the actual distance.

8. a) 96%

b) 18%

c) e.g., Many marketers stretch the truth to make themselves look as good as possible, and if the pizzeria owners are like this, then they probably mean (b).

9. a) about 309 m²   **b)** 2.84

10. a) 5.5 in. by 7.7 in.   **b)** 21%

11. 2.5 cm

12. a) 6   **b)** 9 m

13. 2 ft 2 in., 1 ft 7 in., 5.4 in.

14. 14 580 cm³

15. 403 cm²

16. 40 mm by 76 mm by 8 mm

Cumulative Review, Chapters 6–8, page 512

1. a) i) $f(x) = x(x - 8)$
  x-intercepts: $(0, 0)$, $(8, 0)$
  axis of symmetry: $x = 4$
  vertex: $(4, -16)$
  y-intercept: $(0, 0)$

ii)

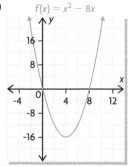

iii) domain: $x \in \mathrm{R}$
  range: $y \geq -16, y \in \mathrm{R}$

b) i) $y = (x + 5)(x - 3)$
  x-intercepts: $(-5, 0)$, $(3, 0)$
  axis of symmetry: $x = -1$
  vertex: $(-1, -16)$
  y-intercept: $(0, -15)$

ii)

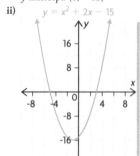

iii) domain: $x \in \mathrm{R}$
  range: $y \geq -16, y \in \mathrm{R}$

2. a) i) axis of symmetry: $x = 3$
  vertex: $(3, 8)$
  y-intercept: $(0, -10)$

ii)

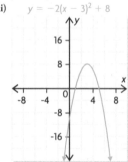

iii) domain: $x \in \mathrm{R}$
  range: $y \leq 8, y \in \mathrm{R}$

b) i) axis of symmetry: $x = -2$
  vertex: $(-2, -1)$
  y-intercept: $(0, 1)$

ii)

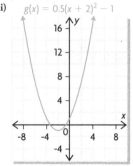

iii) domain: $x \in \mathrm{R}$
  range: $y \geq -1, y \in \mathrm{R}$

3. $y = -\dfrac{1}{4}(x + 4)(x - 8)$; $y = -\dfrac{1}{4}x^2 + x + 8$

4. **a)** up, because the coefficient of x^2 is positive
   b) $(-3, -5)$
   c) a minimum value, because it opens up

5. $13

6. **a)** $-3, 3$ **b)** $-\dfrac{1}{2}, 3$

7. **a)** $-\dfrac{1}{2}, 5$ **d)** $3 \pm \sqrt{19}$

    b) $-4, 8$ **e)** $1, 5$

    c) $-\dfrac{2}{3}, 4$ **f)** $\dfrac{61 \pm \sqrt{3061}}{30}$

8. **a)** 4375 m   **b)** 24.5 s

9. $3.25

10. **a)** $x \geq 1; x = 65$

     b) $y \geq -\dfrac{1}{5}$; no solution

11. 1 m

12. 60 min

13. **a)** 1500 m by 2500 m   **b)** 375 ha

14. 65 m by 108 m by 215 m

Index

Z-Score Table

To determine the percent of data with a z-score equal to or less than a specific value, locate the z-score on the left side of the table and match it with the appropriate second decimal place at the top of the table.

For example, when

$z = -1.15$

the percent of data that is 1.15 standard deviations below the mean is 0.1251, or 12.51%.

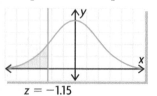

$z = -1.15$

z	0.09	0.08	0.07	0.06	0.05	0.04	0.03	0.02	0.01	0.00
−2.9	0.0014	0.0014	0.0015	0.0015	0.0016	0.0016	0.0017	0.0018	0.0018	0.0019
−2.8	0.0019	0.0020	0.0021	0.0021	0.0022	0.0023	0.0023	0.0024	0.0025	0.0026
−2.7	0.0026	0.0027	0.0028	0.0029	0.0030	0.0031	0.0032	0.0033	0.0034	0.0035
−2.6	0.0036	0.0037	0.0038	0.0039	0.0040	0.0041	0.0043	0.0044	0.0045	0.0047
−2.5	0.0048	0.0049	0.0051	0.0052	0.0054	0.0055	0.0057	0.0059	0.0060	0.0062
−2.4	0.0064	0.0066	0.0068	0.0069	0.0071	0.0073	0.0075	0.0078	0.0080	0.0082
−2.3	0.0084	0.0087	0.0089	0.0091	0.0094	0.0096	0.0099	0.0102	0.0104	0.0107
−2.2	0.0110	0.0113	0.0116	0.0119	0.0122	0.0125	0.0129	0.0132	0.0136	0.0139
−2.1	0.0143	0.0146	0.0150	0.0154	0.0158	0.0162	0.0166	0.0170	0.0174	0.0179
−2.0	0.0183	0.0188	0.0192	0.0197	0.0202	0.0207	0.0212	0.0217	0.0222	0.0228
−1.9	0.0233	0.0239	0.0244	0.0250	0.0256	0.0262	0.0268	0.0274	0.0281	0.0287
−1.8	0.0294	0.0301	0.0307	0.0314	0.0322	0.0329	0.0336	0.0344	0.0351	0.0359
−1.7	0.0367	0.0375	0.0384	0.0392	0.0401	0.0409	0.0418	0.0427	0.0436	0.0446
−1.6	0.0455	0.0465	0.0475	0.0485	0.0495	0.0505	0.0516	0.0526	0.0537	0.0548
−1.5	0.0559	0.0571	0.0582	0.0594	0.0606	0.0618	0.0630	0.0643	0.0655	0.0668
−1.4	0.0681	0.0694	0.0708	0.0721	0.0735	0.0749	0.0764	0.0778	0.0793	0.0808
−1.3	0.0823	0.0838	0.0853	0.0869	0.0885	0.0901	0.0918	0.0934	0.0951	0.0968
−1.2	0.0985	0.1003	0.1020	0.1038	0.1056	0.1075	0.1093	0.1112	0.1131	0.1151
−1.1	0.1170	0.1190	0.1210	0.1230	0.1251	0.1271	0.1292	0.1314	0.1335	0.1357
−1.0	0.1379	0.1401	0.1423	0.1446	0.1469	0.1492	0.1515	0.1539	0.1562	0.1587
−0.9	0.1611	0.1635	0.1660	0.1685	0.1711	0.1736	0.1762	0.1788	0.1814	0.1841
−0.8	0.1867	0.1894	0.1922	0.1949	0.1977	0.2005	0.2033	0.2061	0.2090	0.2119
−0.7	0.2148	0.2177	0.2206	0.2236	0.2266	0.2296	0.2327	0.2358	0.2389	0.2420
−0.6	0.2451	0.2483	0.2514	0.2546	0.2578	0.2611	0.2643	0.2676	0.2709	0.2743
−0.5	0.2776	0.2810	0.2843	0.2877	0.2912	0.2946	0.2981	0.3015	0.3050	0.3085
−0.4	0.3121	0.3156	0.3192	0.3228	0.3264	0.3300	0.3336	0.3372	0.3409	0.3446
−0.3	0.3483	0.3520	0.3557	0.3594	0.3632	0.3669	0.3707	0.3745	0.3783	0.3821
−0.2	0.3859	0.3897	0.3936	0.3974	0.4013	0.4052	0.4090	0.4129	0.4168	0.4207
−0.1	0.4247	0.4286	0.4325	0.4364	0.4404	0.4443	0.4483	0.4522	0.4562	0.4602
−0.0	0.4641	0.4681	0.4721	0.4761	0.4801	0.4840	0.4880	0.4920	0.4960	0.5000

z	0.00	0.01	0.02	0.03	0.04	0.05	0.06	0.07	0.08	0.09
0.0	0.5000	0.5040	0.5080	0.5120	0.5160	0.5199	0.5239	0.5279	0.5319	0.5359
0.1	0.5398	0.5438	0.5478	0.5517	0.5557	0.5596	0.5636	0.5675	0.5714	0.5753
0.2	0.5793	0.5832	0.5871	0.5910	0.5948	0.5987	0.6026	0.6064	0.6103	0.6141
0.3	0.6179	0.6217	0.6255	0.6293	0.6331	0.6368	0.6406	0.6443	0.6480	0.6517
0.4	0.6554	0.6591	0.6628	0.6664	0.6700	0.6736	0.6772	0.6808	0.6844	0.6879
0.5	0.6915	0.6950	0.6985	0.7019	0.7054	0.7088	0.7123	0.7157	0.7190	0.7224
0.6	0.7257	0.7291	0.7324	0.7357	0.7389	0.7422	0.7454	0.7486	0.7517	0.7549
0.7	0.7580	0.7611	0.7642	0.7673	0.7704	0.7734	0.7764	0.7794	0.7823	0.7852
0.8	0.7881	0.7910	0.7939	0.7967	0.7995	0.8023	0.8051	0.8078	0.8106	0.8133
0.9	0.8159	0.8186	0.8212	0.8238	0.8264	0.8289	0.8315	0.8340	0.8365	0.8389
1.0	0.8413	0.8438	0.8461	0.8485	0.8508	0.8531	0.8554	0.8577	0.8599	0.8621
1.1	0.8643	0.8665	0.8686	0.8708	0.8729	0.8749	0.8770	0.8790	0.8810	0.8830
1.2	0.8849	0.8869	0.8888	0.8907	0.8925	0.8944	0.8962	0.8980	0.8997	0.9015
1.3	0.9032	0.9049	0.9066	0.9082	0.9099	0.9115	0.9131	0.9147	0.9162	0.9177
1.4	0.9192	0.9207	0.9222	0.9236	0.9251	0.9265	0.9279	0.9292	0.9306	0.9319
1.5	0.9332	0.9345	0.9357	0.9370	0.9382	0.9394	0.9406	0.9418	0.9429	0.9441
1.6	0.9452	0.9463	0.9474	0.9484	0.9495	0.9505	0.9515	0.9525	0.9535	0.9545
1.7	0.9554	0.9564	0.9573	0.9582	0.9591	0.9599	0.9608	0.9616	0.9625	0.9633
1.8	0.9641	0.9649	0.9656	0.9664	0.9671	0.9678	0.9686	0.9693	0.9699	0.9706
1.9	0.9713	0.9719	0.9726	0.9732	0.9738	0.9744	0.9750	0.9756	0.9761	0.9767
2.0	0.9772	0.9778	0.9783	0.9788	0.9793	0.9798	0.9803	0.9808	0.9812	0.9817
2.1	0.9821	0.9826	0.9830	0.9834	0.9838	0.9842	0.9846	0.9850	0.9854	0.9857
2.2	0.9861	0.9864	0.9868	0.9871	0.9875	0.9878	0.9881	0.9884	0.9887	0.9890
2.3	0.9893	0.9896	0.9898	0.9901	0.9904	0.9906	0.9909	0.9911	0.9913	0.9916
2.4	0.9918	0.9920	0.9922	0.9925	0.9927	0.9929	0.9931	0.9932	0.9934	0.9936
2.5	0.9938	0.9940	0.9941	0.9943	0.9945	0.9946	0.9948	0.9949	0.9951	0.9952
2.6	0.9953	0.9955	0.9956	0.9957	0.9959	0.9960	0.9961	0.9962	0.9963	0.9964
2.7	0.9965	0.9966	0.9967	0.9968	0.9969	0.9970	0.9971	0.9972	0.9973	0.9974
2.8	0.9974	0.9975	0.9976	0.9977	0.9977	0.9978	0.9979	0.9979	0.9980	0.9981
2.9	0.9981	0.9982	0.9982	0.9983	0.9984	0.9984	0.9985	0.9985	0.9986	0.9986

Z-Score Table

Photo Credits

This page constitutes an extension of the copyright page. We have made every effort to trace the ownership of all copyrighted material and to secure permission from copyright holders. In the event of any question arising as to the use of any material, we will be pleased to make the necessary corrections in future printings. Thanks are due to the following authors, publishers, and agents for permission to use the material indicated. All material is copyright © of its respective copyright owners.

Chapter 1: Opener, pp. 2–3: David Cooper/GetStock; p. 5: Dan Thornberg/iStockphoto; p. 12: (top) Jon Faulknor/iStockphoto; p. 14: (left) Leighton Photography & Imaging/Shutterstock; p. 15: (top) Michael Wong/Allsport Concepts/Getty; p. 24: (bottom) NASA GPN-2000-001138; p. 25: joyfull/Shutterstock; p. 29: Minden Pictures/Masterfile; p. 35: Georg Gerster/Photo Researchers, Inc.; p. 37: The Canadian Press(Jeff McIntosh); p. 41: photointrigue/BigStock; p. 42: Pamplemousse/Getty; p. 43: Electrinity/Shutterstock; p. 44: (bottom) Vladimir Sazonov/Shutterstock; (top) Mrgreen/Dreamstime; p. 45: Wave RF/Photolibrary; p. 48: (bottom) Anthony Blake/Fresh Food Images/Photolibrary; p. 49: GJS/iStockphoto; p. 50: Kevin T. Gilbert/CORBIS; p. 53: (dartboards) Boris Yankov/iStockphoto; (darts) Galushko Sergey/Shutterstock; p. 54: stanfair/iStockphoto; p. 63: mammamaart/iStockphoto; p. 64: Rana Faure/Riser/Getty; p. 65: Monkey Business Images/Shutterstock.

Chapter 2: Opener, pp. 66–67: Terry Whittaker/Alamy; p. 72: (top) Brad Salomons/Shutterstock; p. 73: (bottom) Image Source/Jupiterimages Corporation; (top) Linda Webb/Shutterstock; p. 79: (bottom) Masyanya/Dreamstime; p. 80: (bottom) 2009fotofriends/Shutterstock; (top) travellinglight/iStockphoto; p. 81: (bottom) Alexander A.Trofimov/Shutterstock; (top) digitalreflections/BigStockPhoto; p. 82: Holger Mette/GetStock; p. 85: (car park) Hüseyin HIDIR/iStockphoto; p. 97: Iofoto/Dreamstime; p. 99: Irina Tischenko/iStockphoto; p.100: (bottom) E&E Image Library/Photolibrary; (top) Vladimir Sazonov/Shutterstock; p. 103: (ball) Kokhanchikov/Shutterstock; (left) Bettmann/CORBIS; p. 104: Galleria/Dreamstime; p. 107: 1000 Words/Shutterstock; p. 110: Florin Cirstoc/Shutterstock; p. 113: Arpad Benedek/iStockphoto; p. 115: Sergey Lavrentev/Shutterstock; p. 119: Pete Ryan/National Geographic/Getty; p. 121: © UNICEF. Please visit the UNICEF home page <http://www.unicef.org/>; p. 125: Frontpage/Shutterstock. **Chapter 3:** Opener, pp. 126–127: PLANETARY VISIONS LTD/SCIENCE PHOTO LIBRARY; p. 128: (left) James M Phelps, Jr/Shutterstock; p. 129: (bottom) Photo courtesy Pellerins Photography; (top) McCord Museum, Montreal, Canada, 2007; p. 130: Courtesy of InterMedia Outdoors; p. 137: (right) Dave Logan/iStockphoto; p. 139: (right) 2009 Jupiterimages Corporation; p. 140: Leif Norman/iStockphoto; p. 149: Brian Stablyk/Photographer's Choice RF/Getty; p. 152: (bottom) Festival du Bois; (top) arbit/Shutterstock; p. 153: Lowell Georgia/CORBIS; p. 154: Juan Carlos Munoz/age fotostock/Photolibrary; p. 157: Peter Oshkai/Alamy; p. 159: Miles Ertman/Masterfile; p. 162: (left) EML/Shutterstock; p. 164: Charles P. White; p. 169: (left) Todd Korol/Aurora Photos/GetStock; (right) Courtesy Head-Smashed-In Buffalo Jump; p. 171: (top) Image G-01561 Royal BC Museum, BC Archives; (bottom) Nantela/Dreamstime. **Chapter 4:** Opener, pp. 172–173: NASA KSC-06PD-0100; p. 174: (left) Nacivet/Photographer's Choice/Getty; (right) Photosindia/Photolibrary; p. 176: Pierre-Yves Babelon/Shutterstock; p. 183: (bottom) MACIEJ NOSKOWSKI/iStockphoto; (top) Wojciech Beczynski/Shutterstock; p. 184: Brand X Pictures/Jupiterimages Corporation; p. 189: RICHARD GLOVER/View Pictures/Photolibrary; p. 190: Universitätsbibliothek Kiel; p. 200: MistikaS/iStockphoto; p. 214: technotr/iStockphoto; p. 215: (bottom) CuboImages srl/Alamy; (top) Pedro Nogueira/iStockphoto; p. 219: Radius Images/Jupiterimages Corporation; p. 223: (left) Danomyte/Shutterstock; (right) Collin Orthner/iStockphoto; p. 224: (bottom) Arvind Balaraman/Shutterstock; (top) Hatonthestove/GetStock; p. 229: Christopher Futcher/iStockphoto. **Chapter 5:** Opener, pp. 234–235: Pauline S Mills/iStockphoto; p. 238: futureimage/iStockphoto; p. 241: Winnipeg Free Press/The Canadian Press(Ken Gigliotti); p. 249: Getty/Jupiterimages Corporation; p. 250: (bottom) Steve Russell/GetStock; (top) Alexandar Iotzov/Shutterstock; p. 252: Kurhan/Shutterstock; p. 253: (bottom) Permission to reproduce this map is provided by the Queen's Printer for Manitoba. The Queen's Printer does not warrant the accuracy or currency of the reproduction of this information; p. 254: Brand X Pictures/Jupiterimages Corporation; p. 257: Tim Pannell/Corbis; p. 259: Graphing calculator screen captures used throughout this book are from TI-nspire Computer Link; p. 261: Canadian Museum of Civilization, catalogue no. E-111, photographer Steven Darby; p. 262: The Canadian Press(Nathan Denette); p. 264: John Russell/National Hockey League/Getty; p. 265: ©2010 Magic Eye Inc.; p. 269: Duncan Walker/iStockphoto; p. 270: Ipatov/Shutterstock; p. 273: John Poirier/GetStock; p. 279: Vespasian/GetStock; p. 280: Eye Ubiquitous/Photolibrary; p. 281: (top) Brett Mulcahy/Shutterstock; (bottom) Zuzule/Shutterstock; p. 282: cynoclub/iStockphoto; p. 287: Maridav/Shutterstock; p. 288: nito/Shutterstock; p. 293: Vinicius Tupinamba/Shutterstock; p. 294: OJO Images/Chris Ryan/Getty; p. 295: Chris Lamphear/iStockphoto; p. 298: CLM/Shutterstock; p. 303: Nancy Brammer/iStockphoto; p. 309: Corbis/Photolibrary; p. 310: J & C Sohns/Picture Press/Photolibrary; p. 311: Iain Sarjeant/iStockphoto; p. 314: Image Source/Photolibrary.

Chapter 6: Opener, pp. 318–319: Brand X Pictures/Photolibrary; p. 322: 2011 Jupiterimages Corporation; p. 325: (bottom) Thomas Northcut/Photodisc/Jupiterimages Corporation (top) David Davis/Shutterstock; p. 327: MANDY GODBEHEAR/Shutterstock; p. 330: Gerard Vandystadt/Tips Italia/Photolibrary; p. 335: (bottom) Photodisc/White/Photolibrary; (top) Juice Images/Photolibrary; p. 336: Monkey Business Images/Shutterstock; p. 337: Alistair Scott/Shutterstock; p. 343: William Berry/Shutterstock; p. 349: (bottom) Ted Kinsman/Photo Researchers, Inc.; (top) iliuta goean/Shutterstock; p. 350: Mario Savoia/Shutterstock; p. 354: Heinz Kluetmeier/Sports Illustrated/Getty; p. 357: Ingram Publishing/Photolibrary; p. 359: Fuse/Jupiterimages Corporation; p. 365: Fredericton Daily Gleaner/The Canadian Press(James West); p. 366: (bottom) Toronto Star/GetStock; (top) Kurt De Bruyn/Shutterstock; p. 367: (bottom) 2011 Jupiterimages Corporation; (top) David Smith/iStockphoto; p. 368: Lonely Planet Images/Alamy; p. 370: Steve Skjold/GetStock; p. 378: Nikola Bilic/Shutterstock; p. 379: (bottom) StockTrek/Jupiterimages Corporation; (middle) 2011 Jupiterimages Corporation; (top) gopixgo/Shutterstock; p. 380: (bottom) Kristina Postnikova/Shutterstock; (top) get4net/Shutterstock; p. 381: The Canadian Press(Adrian Wyld); p. 386: (left) Andrew Park/Shutterstock; (right) Gunter Marx/GetStock; p. 387: The Canadian Press(Tim Smith); p. 388: (bottom) david kahn/iStockphoto; (top) Ron Giling/Lineair/Photolibrary; p. 389: White Fox/Tips Italia/Photolibrary. **Chapter 7:** Opener, pp. 392–393: jspix/imagebroker.net/Photolibrary; p. 396: Peter Barrett/Shutterstock; p. 397: Neale Cousland/Shutterstock; p. 399: Linda Lantzy/GetStock; p. 403: gaspr13/iStockphoto; p. 412: Krivosheev Vitaly/Shutterstock; p. 413: Robert Postma/First Light/Getty; p. 414: Rossario/Shutterstock; p. 418: Tanya Constantine/Blend/GetStock; p. 420: Olivier Goujon/SuperStock; p. 421: (bottom) Hugh Palmer/Red Cover/Photolibrary; (top) NASA GPN-2000-001144; p. 422: Dennis MacDonald/GetStock; p. 424: 2happy/Shutterstock; p. 428: ARIS MESSINIS/AFP/Getty; p. 431: (bottom) Corbis/Photolibrary; (top) Yanlev/Shutterstock; p. 433: First Light/Alamy; p. 436: Chris Cheadle/All Canada Photos/Photolibrary; p. 437: Hill Street Studios/Jupiterimages Corporation. **Chapter 8:** Opener, pp. 440–441: William Attard McCarthy/Shutterstock; p. 443: Marshall Ikonography/GetStock; p. 453: Newscom; p. 461: (left) Leonard Lessin/Peter Arnold Images/Photolibrary; (right) EyesWideOpen/Getty; p. 473: Karl Dolenc/iStockphoto; p. 475: Gerald Brack/iStockphoto; p. 477: Sean Nel/Shutterstock; p. 480: Mark Aplet/Shutterstock; p. 481: DariuszPa/Shutterstock; p. 483, 506: Photo: Icefields/Dreamstime. Rubik's Cube * used by permission of Seven Towns Ltd. www.rubiks.com; p. 484: mates/Shutterstock; p. 485: oriontrail/Shutterstock; p. 487: Paul65516/Dreamstime; p. 490: 2010 Photos.com, a division of Getty; p. 491: (bottom) Doug Allan/Getty; (top) Ronnie Wu/Shutterstock; p. 492: (top) Yuri Shirokov/Shutterstock; p. 493: ilian studio/GetStock; p. 494: (top) Hulton Archive/Getty; p. 497: Luciano Mortula/Shutterstock; p. 499: Eastimages/Shutterstock; p. 500: Gjermund Alsos/Shutterstock; p. 501: BrunoSINNAH/Shutterstock; p. 502: (boxes) design56/Shutterstock; (earth) NASA GPN-2000-001138; (grapefruit) Mustafa Ozdag/Shutterstock; (moon) robdigphot/Shutterstock; (orange) Steyno&Stitch/Shutterstock; p. 503: Denise Kappa/Shutterstock; p. 504: (paper cup) design56/Shutterstock; p. 507: Library and Archives Canada POS-000845/Canada Post Corporation 1980. Reproduced with Permission; p. 508: (bottom) Emily Riddell/First Light Associated Photographers/Photolibrary; (right) Igor Kovalenko/iStockphoto; p. 509: Julien Tromeur/Shutterstock; p. 510: Michael Newman/PhotoEdit

Text Credits

Chapter 1: p. 7: (Precipitation data) Environment Canada, National Climate Data and Information Archive, 2011; p. 57: (question 13) KenKen Puzzle LLC. Reproduced with permission. **Chapter 4:** pp. 232–233: "Table A2-14: Population of Canada, by province, census dates, 1851 to 1976." From the Statistics Canada Website, Section A: Population and Migration, http://www.statcan.gc.ca/pub/11-516-x/sectiona/4147436-eng.htm. **Chapter 5:** p. 239: *Canadian Climate Normals 1971-2000.* http://climate.weatheroffice.gc.ca/climate_normals Environment Canada 2011. Reproduced with the permission of the Minister of Public Works and Government Services Canada; p. 240: Housing prices chart adapted from Table 9: "Average Fair Market Value by Selected CMAs/CAs and Year – All Types," adapted from Statistics Canada publication Average Fair Market Value/Purchase Price for New Homes in Canada – Data from GST Administrative Records 1996 to 2000, Catalogue 64-507-XIE2002001, http://www.statcan.gc.ca/pub/64-507-x/64-507-x2002001-eng.pdf; p. 241: Flood frequency analysis for the Red River at Winnipeg, p. 357. http://article.pubs.nrc-cnrc.gc.ca/ppv/RPViewDoc?issn=1208-6029&volume=28&issue=3&startPage=355. Environment Canada 2011. Reproduced with the permission of Public Works and Government Services Canada; p. 246: (bottom) Based on "Magnitude/Intensity Comparison." Earthquake Hazards Program, United States Geological Survey, 2010. http://earthquake.usgs.gov/learn/topics/mag_vs_int.php; (top 5 graphs) *Earthquake Reports for 2005 to 2009* http://earthquakescanada.nrcan.gc.ca/index-eng.php. Reproduced with the permission of Natural Resources Canada, 2011; p. 251: Source: Population by sex and age group, adapted from Statistics Canada website, Summary Tables, http://www40.statcan.gc.ca/l01/cst01/demo10a-eng.htm (25 November 2010); p. 252: (accident statistics) Source: TP 3322 Canadian Motor Vehicle Traffic Collision Statistics: 2003, http://www.tc.gc.ca/eng/roadsafety/tp-tp3322-2003-menu-630.htm; (schedule) Canada Running Series 253: (demographics) Source: "Aboriginal Identity population by age groups, median age and sex, 2006 counts …, Where do Aboriginals live? … ," adapted from Statistics Canada publication Aboriginal Peoples, 2006 Census, 97-558-XWE2006002, http://www.statcan.gc.ca/bsolc/olc-cel/olc-cel?catno=97-558-XWE2006002&lang=eng&lang=eng; p. 265: (chart) From Zimmer. *Nelson Data Management 12,* 1E. 2003 Nelson Education Ltd. Reproduced by permission.www.cengage.com/permissions; p. 293: (heart rate) Statistics reprinted from Whitley, Schoene. "Comparison of Heart Rate Responses: Water Walking Versus Treadmill Walking." *PT Journal,* [Volume 67/Number 10, October 1987 p. 1502], with permission of the American Physical Therapy Association. This material is copyrighted, and any further reproduction or distribution requires written permission from APTA. www.apta.org; p. 293: (question 19) Copyright 2010 by the Society of Actuaries, Schaumburg, Illinois. Reprinted with permission; p. 293: (parenting statistics) Source: Table 3: "Distribution by age groups and census family status of mothers of children aged 4 years and under, Canada, 2001 and 2006", adapted from Statistics Canada publication *Families and Households,* 2006 Census, Catalogue 97-553, http://www.statcan.gc.ca/bsolc/olc-cel/olc-cel?catno=97-553-XWE&lang=eng; p. 294: (question 23) Source: 2001-2002 LSAT Percentile Table. Powerscore Test Preparation. http://www.powerscore.com/lsat/help/scale.cfm (August 21, 2010); p. 297: Adapted from the website of Andrew Heard, Political Science Department, SFU, http://www.sfu.ca/~aheard/elections/polls.html; p. 305: (question 4) Adapted from Angus Reid Public Opinion, A Vision Critical Practice https://www.angusreidforum.com/mediaserver/3/documents/20100630_CanadaDay_EN.pdf. **Chapter 8:** p. 504: (question 1) Based on Statistics Canada data Labour Force Historical Review, Catalogue 71F0004XCB, 2008, http://www.statcan.gc.ca/bsolc/olc-cel/olc-cel?lang=eng&catno=71F0004X and Statistics Canada CANSIM Database http://cansim2.statcan.gc.ca, CANSIM Table 051-0001.